MW01194399

AVID

READER

PRESS

Zbig

THE LIFE OF ZBIGNIEW BRZEZINSKI, AMERICA'S GREAT POWER PROPHET

Edward Luce

Avid Reader Press

NEW YORK   AMSTERDAM/ANTWERP   LONDON
TORONTO   SYDNEY/MELBOURNE   NEW DELHI

AVID READER PRESS
An Imprint of Simon & Schuster, LLC
1230 Avenue of the Americas
New York, NY 10020

First Avid Reader Press hardcover edition May 2025

AVID READER PRESS and colophon are trademarks of Simon & Schuster, LLC

Interior design by Ruth Lee-Mui

Manufactured in the United States of America

1   3   5   7   9   10   8   6   4   2

Library of Congress Cataloging-in-Publication Data
Names: Luce, Edward, [date] author.
Title: Zbig : the life of Zbigniew Brzezinski, America's great power prophet / Edward Luce.
Other titles: Life of Zbigniew Brzezinski, America's great power prophet
Description: First Avid Reader Press hardcover edition. | New York : Avid Reader Press, 2025. | Includes bibliographical references and index.
Identifiers: LCCN 2024059010 (print) | LCCN 2024059011 (ebook) | ISBN 9781982173647 (hardcover) | ISBN 9781982173654 (paperback) | ISBN 9781982173661 (ebook)
Subjects: LCSH: Brzezinski, Zbigniew, 1928–2017. | National Security Council (U.S.)—Biography. | Cabinet officers—United States—Biography. | Statesmen—United States—Biography. | United States—Foreign relations—20th century. | United States—Politics and government—20th century. | National security— United States—History—20th century. | Polish Americans—Biography. | Carter, Jimmy, 1924–2024.
Classification: LCC E840.8.B79 L84 2025 (print) | LCC E840.8.B79 (ebook) |
DDC 355/.033073092 [B]—dc23/eng/20250207
LC record available at https://lccn.loc.gov/2024059010
LC ebook record available at https://lccn.loc.gov/2024059011

ISBN 978-1-9821-7364-7
ISBN 978-1-9821-7366-1 (ebook)

Insert photographs courtesy of the Brzezinski family private collection, except as noted: (7) Newman House School, Ontario, Canada; (11) Council on Foreign Relations; (12) Weatherhead Center for International Affairs, Harvard University; (21) US National Archives and Records Administration; (46) Tom Williams; (48) The Norwegian Nobel Institute/Ken Opprann; (49) Official White House photo by Pete Souza; (50) *Morning Joe*.

For Niamh

Contents

Prologue

Hitler was dead. As news spread of the dictator's suicide, people on both sides of the Atlantic converged on downtowns and city squares to celebrate the end of the most pitiless war in history. Montreal, the capital of Quebec, Canada's francophone province, was no exception. Among those who abandoned their classrooms to join the throngs outside was seventeen-year-old Zbigniew Brzezinski, the second of four sons of the Polish consul general in Montreal. "Germany has capitulated!" he wrote in his diary on May 8, 1945.[1] "I heard the electrifying news this morning when I was at school. The city is full of flags, flowers, people, and joy. Only us, the Poles, are not partaking in this satisfaction from victory." Amid the blur of Union Jacks, Canadian Red Ensigns, and Stars and Stripes, Brzezinski spotted the occasional hammer and sickle. Sight of the dreaded Soviet flag dampened the joy of the soon-to-be-stateless young Pole. "We walked down the streets cheering," he recalled towards the end of his life. "But I remember at the same time feeling there was something wrong because I was aware that half of Europe was in the hands of another menacing dictatorship just as brutal as Hitlerism."[2]

Canadians could be forgiven for welcoming the Soviet red flag. In the titanic battle with Nazism, the Soviet Union had lost many times more soldiers and civilians than the United States and the British Empire combined. So critical had Josef Stalin, the Soviet dictator, been to the battle against Nazism that many Westerners, seemingly oblivious to his record, knew him by the moniker "Uncle Joe." Ten months later, in Fulton, Missouri, Winston Churchill, Great Britain's wartime leader, would jolt people to attention with his warning of an "iron curtain" descending across Europe. On that euphoric day in May, however, it took a Pole to express victory's bitter taste. The previous year, an anguished Brzezinski had recorded the suppression of the 1944 Warsaw Uprising, in which the German Army had razed the Polish city to the ground, leaving it the most ruined capital in Europe. The Red Army had sat passively for months on the left bank of the Vistula River, watching the Germans methodically level the city of Brzezinski's birth. The US president, Franklin D. Roosevelt, and Churchill had sporadically tried to aid the Polish resistance. But Allied airdrops had been blocked by Stalin until it was too late. Uncle Joe, who described the Polish fighters as "a handful of criminals," wanted the Germans to do his sordid work for him: to rob the Poles of any chance of self-liberation by liquidating their Home Army. A quarter of a million Varsovians died in that bloodbath. Barely any landmarks were left standing. When the Germans were finally ejected, the young Brzezinski was clear eyed: "The Soviet army overran Warsaw," he wrote in January 1945. "All the Poles understand that this is not a liberation but simply a change in the form of terror."[3]

Brzezinski's quest to hold the USSR to account was still burning three decades later in 1977, when President Jimmy Carter picked him to be his national security advisor at a waning stage of East-West détente. Brzezinski became the first person of Polish origin—and so far the last—to occupy that role. In between, he had learned to speak Russian fluently, become a Harvard and Columbia scholar, emerged as one of America's foremost Sovietologists, advised President John F. Kennedy, worked for President Lyndon Baines Johnson, served as chief foreign policy advisor to the ill-fated 1968 presidential candidacy of Hubert Humphrey, and gained a reputation as Henry Kissinger's most dogged rival. Brzezinski's detractors never stopped dismissing him as a "Pole" with the implication of dual loyalty. Like many immigrants, however, he said he was "insanely" proud of being an American. He saw no tension in his hyphenation. When he was naturalized as a citizen in Boston in 1958, the judge asked whether he would like to anglicize his difficult-to-pronounce name. Brzezinski declined. "America is the only country where someone called 'Zbigniew Brzezinski' can make a name for himself without changing his name," he would often say.[4] That was true. But his tongue twister of a name—"pronounced 'ZbigNieff BreshinSki,'" as Carter would instruct his first White House staff meeting in 1977[5]—offered a clue to his greatest strength and weakness.

The strength he manifested so early turned into a lifelong sense of mission. In 1953, the young Harvard student visited the recently opened Radio Free Europe (RFE) offices in Munich—Brzezinski's first trip across the Atlantic since he had left Poland on a boat fifteen years earlier. There he met Jan Nowak-Jeziorański, the head of the Polish section of RFE and legendary Warsaw "courier" who had maintained contact during the war between Warsaw and the Polish government in exile in London and provided accounts of the war to the British and Americans, including widely disbelieved reports of the Holocaust. The twenty-five-year-old Polish student's encyclopedic knowledge of the Polish underground and the exploits of the Home Army struck Nowak as uncanny.[6] Brzezinski's father later told Nowak that his son's life ambition was to liberate Poland from the Soviets. Nowak did not record his reaction, which we can only imagine was incredulous. Just as a rocket requires a launch vehicle, a significant life often begins with a motivating boost. Wounded Polishness—and a sense of amputated history—was Brzezinski's.

That clarity of purpose spurred Brzezinski to become one of America's leading Cold War scholars. Moreover, his fluency in Polish and Russian and his closeness to numerous Eastern European émigrés, of whom his Czech-speaking wife, Emilie Benes, was foremost, gave him an edge that many Sovietologists lacked. Many of his peers did not speak Russian well. Some did not speak it at all. Brzezinski's cultural marination gave his scholarship an incisive dimension. In his 1950 master's thesis at Montreal's McGill University, Brzezinski identified the "nationalities problem" as the Soviet Union's "Achilles' heel."[7] Non-Russian peoples inside the Soviet Union, as well as among its Warsaw Pact satellites in Eastern Europe, had retained their national feeling, he argued. They would not indefinitely tolerate what was widely felt as Russian imperialism, irrespective of the internationalism in which Marxism garbed itself. The Soviet Union was not a monolith; resentment of Russian colonialism could be enlisted to hasten the East Bloc's demise. It was an insight that eluded many, including Kissinger and most of Brzezinski's colleagues in the Carter administration. To many, Brzezinski's self-confidence came across as arrogant and sometimes reckless. Not only was he contesting the US government's wisdom in pursuing détente; he also insisted that what others saw as the lasting presence of the Soviet Union—a superpower that in a nuclear age must for everyone's sake be treated as America's equal—was in fact a shell of itself that was in the process of degenerating. All it needed was a helpful push. Churchill's "iron curtain" had turned out not to have been made of hard metal, Brzezinski argued; it was more like a "semi-permeable membrane."[8]

As a born-again Baptist farmer from Georgia, Carter was an unlikely patron. Against almost everyone's advice, from Kissinger on the right to the "wise men" of the increasingly dovish WASP establishment, Carter not only hired "Zbig," as he was generally known, but ignored the clamor to fire him when the political going got rough. Even in the depths of the Iran hostage crisis, which Brzezinski had helped trigger by insisting that the US should admit Iran's deposed shah for medical treatment, Carter stood by his controversial advisor. In addition to their friendship, Carter said that Brzezinski was alone among his officials in providing a strategic framework on how to outplay the USSR. The Cold War ended under President George H. W. Bush, nine years after Carter left office. But Soviet self-belief had been badly dented in the Carter years. The Carter administration "waged ideological war on the Soviets with a determination and an intensity that was very different from its predecessors," wrote Robert Gates, a former CIA director who had gotten his career break as a White House aide to Brzezinski.[9] The "fragile seeds" that Brzezinski planted—using human rights as a weapon against Moscow and stoking Eastern Europe's hopes of independence—would bear "lethal fruit" years later, said Gates.[10] Among its harvest was Poland's Solidarity movement. History records the Iron Curtain as having parted on November 9, 1989, when the Berlin Wall fell. But it had cracked on June 4, when Solidarity swept the Polish elections. Two months later, Moscow permitted Solidarity to form a government, thus ending the Communist monopoly on power. Berlin came three months later. Poland was the breach that opened the floodgates. Brzezinski played a significant role in protecting Lech Wałęsa's worker-intellectual alliance, then in nurturing it to victory. A few months later, *Time* magazine ran an interview with Brzezinski under the headline "Zbigniew Brzezinski: Vindication of a Hard-Liner." It was written by Strobe Talbott, who had been one of Brzezinski's most trenchant critics during the Carter years. Many factors contributed to the demise of the USSR. Jan Nowak, who had indulged the cocky young Brzezinski in Munich so many years before, thought that America's weaponization of human rights was the most important. Many people in Eastern Europe agreed.

In Washington, Brzezinski's disputatious character was something of his own Achilles' heel. In one former Soviet republic, now the central Asian nation of Kyrgyzstan, Brzezinski was welcomed on a visit in the 1990s as a modern "Nostradamus"[11] for his lonely predictions of the system's impending collapse. His role in helping bring about the USSR's disintegration is treated as critical in Russia, where he is still depicted as an archenemy. In 2014, Nikolai Patrushev, the ex-head of the former KGB (now called the FSB), who was national security advisor to Russian president Vladimir Putin, said that the USSR had been destroyed by a "plot hatched by Zbigniew Brzezinski and the CIA to weaken its economy."[12] Such overwrought judgments are hard to separate from Brzezinski's Polish origins, which Soviet leaders always viewed as a source of implacable bias. That was one point on which Moscow and much of Washington were in agreement. Brzezinski's Cold War impact is as underappreciated in today's US as it is overstated in Russia.

Suspicion of Brzezinski's allegedly overriding loyalty to Poland came from many quarters. W. Averell Harriman, perhaps the grandest postwar figure of the foreign policy establishment, spoke for many in his Anglophile world when he said that Brzezinski lacked the "American ethos" and would be "perfectly willing to get the United States into a conflict with Russia for the sake of Poland."[13] Robert Lovett, a secretary of defense in the early 1950s, who, like Harriman, had belonged to Yale's exclusive Skull and Bones society and was the epitome of the WASP establishment, said, "We shouldn't have a National Security Adviser like that who's not really an American. I can't imagine anyone negotiating with the Russians with [Brzezinski's] loathing and suspicion."[14] Brzezinski also had to contend with persistent accusations of anti-Israeli bias—and occasionally worse. He was part of Carter's team at the marathon 1978 Israel-Egypt peace talks at Camp David that resulted in the first recognition of Israel by an Arab country. Israel's parallel undertaking to open talks with the Palestinians, aimed at an eventual two-state solution, came to naught in spite of Carter and Brzezinski's efforts. Detractors used Brzezinski's Polishness against him. That he never lost his Polish accent, combined with Poland's reputation for anti-Semitism, made Brzezinski an obvious target. His willingness to call out the "Israel lobby" was one reason why Barack Obama, during his 2008 primary battle with Hillary Clinton, felt obliged to distance himself from Brzezinski in spite of having received a well-timed boost from his endorsement.

There is no basis to the allegations that Brzezinski was anti-Semitic. In 1977, Menachem Begin, Israel's hard-line prime minister and a fellow Polish speaker, presented Brzezinski with documents lauding Brzezinski's father's role in issuing exit visas to German Jews when he was the Polish consul in

Leipzig in the 1930s. Hitler's regime insisted that Warsaw recall Brzeziński senior. "The Jewish people, Dear Mr. Brzezinski, never forget a friend," Begin wrote in a letter to Brzezinski's father a few weeks later.[15] Begin's gesture, which took place in front of cameras, moved Brzezinski. But he was, for the most part, too proud to take notice of the whispering campaign against him.

A third group with whom Brzezinski fell out was the Democratic foreign policy doves. Brzezinski called them "McGovernites" after the disastrous 1972 presidential candidacy of George McGovern, who led the party leftward after the debacle in Vietnam. Brzezinski, who had dutifully backed the war, said they suffered from "Vietnam syndrome." In that category, he included Cyrus Vance, Carter's gentlemanly secretary of state and one of the last of the grand WASPs. Vance proved no match for Brzezinski's political skills. Brzezinski ultimately won most of the big policy battles with Vance, including normalizing relations with China; holding Moscow to account for its treatment of dissidents, including Jewish refuseniks; arming the Afghan resistance to Soviet invaders, and modernizing America's nuclear arsenal—a momentous strategic upgrade that is routinely misattributed to Ronald Reagan, Carter's successor and nemesis.

Why did Brzezinski not receive his full due? Washington is a town of factions and groups in which loyalty to your side and conformity to its line is overriding. Brzezinski had no tribe but his own. He belonged to no recognizable school of foreign policy; neither consistently a hawk nor a dove. He had little time for labels such as "realist" and "idealist." Nor was he an unswerving Democrat. In 1972, he voted for Richard Nixon against McGovern, and in 1988, he endorsed George H. W. Bush over Michael Dukakis. In glaring contrast to Kissinger, who was a master of seduction, Brzezinski had limited patience with the media. His unwillingness to play the Washington game took a toll on his influence. Though Reagan twice thought of hiring him as his national security advisor, both times he ran into opposition and dropped the idea. Over time, Brzezinski acquired more enemies on the right than on the left. That was most apparent in 2003, when he came out early and trenchantly against the Iraq War—a lonely stand that cut against how the Washington game is played. That he was proved right is secondary; the important thing is to keep within the bounds of political fashion. Kissinger, who supported the Iraq War, knew how to do that. Brzezinski did not care.

One of the reasons I decided to write this biography is because a life such as Brzezinski's offers a window on how the world works and what happens in history. Though I had no idea while Brzezinski was alive that I would become his biographer, I spoke to him a lot—often over lunch at his favorite haunts, Teatro Goldoni on K Street and later the Jefferson Hotel on 16th Street—during the last decade of his life. He was an acute observer of global events. His insights and deep fund of historical memory rarely failed to be of benefit to an inquiring journalist. This biography was a race against the actuarial clock. I interviewed more than a hundred of Brzezinski's contemporaries. Sadly, a few—notably, Walter Mondale, Carter's vice president; Ardeshir Zahedi, the shah of Iran's legendary ambassador to Washington; and Mikhail Gorbachev, the USSR's last leader, who had become friendly with Brzezinski after the Cold War—passed away before I could interview them. Others, such as Madeleine Albright, the former secretary of state who was one of Brzezinski's many protégés, died midway through this project after having been of great help to me. Though in the fading twilight of his life, Carter was also generous. Most of Brzezinski's Chinese and Soviet contemporaries were already old when Brzezinski became their counterpart. As a scholar he emphasized that the USSR had become an ossified "gerontocracy." I made use of Politburo minutes, Soviet memoirs, those of other foreign and American figures, and US national security and diplomatic archives. The Jimmy Carter Presidential Library in Atlanta was also a great resource. The files that Poland's secret police had kept on Brzezinski were also a rich source and often unintentionally comical. I was also given Brzezinski's lengthy and mostly unseen correspondence with Pope John Paul II, a prelate from Poland who became the first non-Italian pope in more than four hundred years and whose elevation was thought by the KGB to have been a "Brzezinski plot."

With no conditions—this is not an authorized biography—Brzezinski's children, Ian, Mark, and Mika, gave me unrestricted access to their father's extensive personal diaries, letters, and papers and his voluminous collection of documents housed in the Library of Congress. His recordkeeping was meticulous. Without the family's trust and generosity, this project would have been an uphill struggle. No life is a neat morality tale with a cinematic ending. That would be dull and almost certainly fictional. Brzezinski's story had me gripped from the moment I began to research it. Given the significance of what he did and the character of his times, it could not have been otherwise. He died in May 2017, just a few months into Donald Trump's presidency. He had been born into a privileged Warsaw family in 1928, the year Stalin consolidated power. That is where this book begins.

1

Interbellum Warsaw

Poland owes a corner of its soul to America, and vice versa. Woodrow Wilson, the United States' twenty-eighth president, elevated Poland's hopes with the famous Fourteen Points that he announced to Congress in 1918. They were the US president's list of reforms in the aftermath of the First World War that were designed to ensure that such mass slaughter could never repeat itself. Wilson's French counterpart, Georges Clemenceau, quipped, "God gave us the ten commandments and we broke them. Wilson gave us the Fourteen Points. We shall see." Wilson's idealism was lampooned in most European chancelleries. The Poles, at least, saw the virtue in Wilson's lengthy agenda. Poland's independence was the US president's thirteenth point. Wilson achieved most of his wish list, including the victorious powers' blessing for the newly proclaimed Second Polish Republic in the 1919 Treaty of Versailles.

But it was Józef Piłsudski, the founder of Poland's Second Republic, a figure who towered like a Colossus over the lives of the Brzezinskis and most people in their world, who took up arms and made it a reality. "When the war of the giants is over," Churchill predicted, "the war of the pygmies will begin."[1] Piłsudski led Poland's White Eagle army to an improbable victory over the Soviets in 1920. His feat of arms was dubbed the "Miracle on the Vistula." The Battle of Warsaw changed history. It closed off the "Red bridge" across which the USSR's Vladimir Lenin and Leon Trotsky had planned to spread their 1917 Bolshevik Revolution to Europe. Without Piłsudski, Poland would not have been reborn. Without the new Poland, Germany and countries beyond would have lain prostrate in the Red Army's path. Modern history might have been radically different. This event is burned into the memory of Poles yet largely forgotten by everyone else. The senior British observer in Poland, Edgar Vincent, Viscount D'Abernon, would later classify the Battle of Warsaw as "the eighteenth decisive battle of the world."[2]

It would be hard to overstate the pull of history on the Polish imagination. Zbigniew Brzezinski was born on an early-spring day in 1928 in his parents' elegant Warsaw apartment. No child of those circumstances and that time could hope to be free of history's entanglements for long. His entry into the world occurred at a rare moment when Poland existed as a self-ruled nation. He arrived at the midway point between the proclamation of Poland's Second Republic in 1918 and its extinction in 1939, when Brzezinski was eleven. At the start of the Second World War, Poland was split between the Soviets and the Germans under a sordid vivisection that they had delineated a few weeks earlier. Poland's extinction was settled in a secret protocol in the Molotov-Ribbentrop Pact (more widely remembered as the Nazi-Soviet Pact), in which Hitler and Stalin pledged mutual nonaggression in the coming war against the democracies. On October 31, 1939, barely two months after devising their plan, Vyacheslav Molotov, the Soviet foreign minister, could proclaim, "One swift blow to Poland, first by the German Army and then by the Red Army, and nothing was left of this ugly bastard of the Versailles Treaty." It was to that orphan of history that Brzezinski was born; he emerged into the eye of the storm—Poland's fleeting moment of interbellum serenity.

Brzezinski's upbringing was both cosmopolitan and fiercely Polish. Zbigniew was the first child of Tadeusz Brzeziński, a rising Polish diplomat, who had won recognition as a young officer at the "Miracle on the Vistula" fighting under Piłsudski's White Eagle flag.[3] Though he emerged unscathed, Tadeusz had seen action and won medals. He did not take part in the last great cavalry charge of European history. But his role in that historic battle was a source of deep family pride. Zbigniew was the second son of Leonia Brzezińska, who had already had one child, Jurek (later known as George), from a brief first marriage to another Pole of high birth. Her divorce, a rarity in devoutly Catholic Poland, was uncontroversial within her Warsaw milieu. Proof of that is that her ex-husband, Jerzy Żyliński, acted as an official witness at her second wedding. Even in the context of her relatively bohemian social life, an amicable divorce in that manner was remarkable. With her dark, flowing hair and fierce sense of self, Leonia was a catch in any context. Both of Zbigniew's parents came from a *szlachta* background, a type of Polish nobility. Leonia's further education was also a rarity for her gender in that time. Though a graduate of Warsaw's School of Political Science and its Conservatory of Music, she was also a belle of the town, rarely spotted without her furs and frequently surrounded by admirers. She was even known to the ballrooms of Vienna, where Tadeusz had studied law. More befitting of her time, Leonia was also an accomplished pianist and a regular at Catholic Mass.

Brzezinski's parents grew up in a late Habsburg–Romanov world that ceased to exist several years before they married. Their lives bridged two eras. It is as though each had one foot in a Tolstoy novel and the other in the twentieth century. Tadeusz's father, Kazimierz Brzeziński, born in 1866, was a judge in various provincial capitals in the Austro-Habsburg-ruled province of Eastern Galicia.[4] Unlike the Russian-ruled parts of Poland, where the use of Polish as a medium of instruction was forbidden and in some cases resulted in severe penalties, courts, schools, and other public institutions in the Habsburg-ruled part of Poland were permitted to use Polish. Because of the hopelessness of Poland's situation, the loci of most nationalist sentiment during its 123 years of partition were language, poetry, theater, and other arts. Lacking a nation-state, Poland existed in a so-called *rząd dusz*, or "government of souls." Within the poetry of Adam Mickiewicz, the Alexander Pushkin of Poland, and in the chords of Frédéric Chopin could be found "guns hidden under flowers." Though nourished by an earlier history of grand battles and the possession of vast territories, modern Polish national sentiment was intellectual in its essence. Kazimierz gained his doctorate of law from the University of Lvov (now Lviv), the chief metropolis of Eastern Galicia. He was a frenetic sponsor of Polish-language theaters, primary schools, and libraries in Przemysl, which became the seat of the Brzeziński family. Today the town sits just on the Polish side of the Ukrainian-Polish border. (Lviv is well inside Ukraine.) Kazimierz's calm impartiality led to quick preferment in Imperial Royal District Courts. Because of his judicious temperament and impeccable sense of dress, he was widely known as *arbiter elegantiarum* (the elegant judge). Zbigniew never met his paternal grandfather, who died of a heart attack in 1924. But he would spend many halcyon summer months with his widowed grandmother, Zofia, in the family's large home in Przemysl.

As the eldest of two sons, Tadeusz was on track to follow in his father's footsteps. Noted likewise for his sartorial exactness, Tadeusz also gained his doctorate in law from the University of Lvov.[5] He seemed destined to become a notable legal official in Habsburg-ruled Poland, as his father was. But war and the rebirth of his nation dramatically altered his life. In 1919, the recently graduated Tadeusz joined the newly formed Polish Army as a noncommissioned officer in the 2nd Rifle Regiment of Lvov. He fought in both the victorious 1919 Battle of Lvov against Ukrainian nationalists and in the more consequential Battle of Warsaw in 1920. After the war, he joined the newly formed Polish diplomatic service in Warsaw and in the early 1920s had brief postings to German Westphalia and the Rhineland. His role was to look after the interests of Polish minorities abroad, who numbered in the millions in Europe's largest coalfields, particularly in northwest Germany and northern France. Between 1924 and 1927, he headed the cultural section of Poland's consular service in Warsaw. It was there that he met Leonia.

Leonia Roman's family was also from a noble background.[6] The designation *szlachta* confuses foreigners and sometimes even Poles. Members of that class are often misleadingly described as belonging to the aristocracy. Yet they accounted for more than a tenth of Poland's population, roughly ten times the share of nobility in most other European societies. Nor does the category of burgher, which implies commercial wealth, fit their status. A better analogy might be to the caste of Rajputs in northern India—warriors by birth and inheritance but without necessarily possessing land or wealth. But even that comparison is misleading. The *szlachtas* were Poland's original citizens from the creation of the Polish-Lithuanian Commonwealth in the sixteenth century. They made up Poland's military officers, political class, and arbiters of nationhood. They elected the king of the grand hybrid kingdom from their ranks. Nobles in medieval England and France were powerful landowners who nevertheless owed total fealty to their hereditary sovereign. They also owned the labor of the peasants who worked their land. Most *szlachtas*, by contrast, were not significant landowners. Yet they were the social equals of their elected sovereign. They possessed full political rights and legal equality with the king generations before the idea of citizenship emerged in revolutionary France and America. Both sides of Brzezinski's family were *szlachta*.

In contrast to Brzezinski's paternal line, which grew up in the relatively free air of Habsburg Poland, Leonia's family, the Romans, came from the overtly Polonophobic Russian-ruled part of their partitioned nation. Their most celebrated ancestor was Wiktor Roman, who fought in the Polish cavalry with Napoleon's army in the Peninsular War in Spain. Roman earned a legendary reputation in the cavalry charge that won the 1808 Battle of Somosierra. The Poles' gallantry overwhelmed the Spanish forces and opened Madrid to Napoleon's occupation. The Corsican general attributed the victory to the valiant Poles. As a people recently deprived of a nation (Poland's final partition among Russia, Austria, and Prussia had occurred in 1795), the Polish cavalry had defected to Napoleon's cause as their best hope of reclaiming their homeland. That dream foundered at Waterloo in 1815. But the Roman family nevertheless flourished in czarist-ruled Poland. Both Brzezinski's maternal great-grandfather and grandfather, Antoni and Leon Roman, joined the Golden Hussars of Saint Petersburg, an elite Polish cavalry unit that had been co-opted into Romanov Russia. Future czars would often cut their teeth in the Golden Hussars. To qualify, a Pole had to prove he was a scion of at least seven generations of *szlachta* and pay 2,000 rubles, a significant sum. Both qualifications came easily to the Romans.

Unlike the Brzezińskis, who had fled to Habsburg Poland from the Russian part in the 1830s after an ancestor had participated in one of the failed uprisings against the czars, the Roman family owned two significant estates near Warsaw. Those were forfeited in the late 1890s after Leonia's grandfather pledged them as collateral for a neighbor's debts. The neighbor's bankruptcy threw the Romans into relative penury. In spite of the court's foreclosure, the Romans retained their social status. Leonia's father, Leon Roman, graduated as a lawyer from the University of Saint Petersburg and served in the Golden Hussars. He spent most of his career as a senior administrator in Russian Poland before switching to more senior jobs in independent Poland after 1920. Like many Poles in late-Romanov Russia, Leon encountered political suspicions in Saint Petersburg and moved to the less claustrophobic setting of Warsaw. There he managed the Warsaw-Vienna railway line before the outbreak of the First World War. Leonia spent her childhood in Warsaw. After the war, her father served as a senior administrator in various parts of Poland, including the city of Poznań.

From each of his parents' families, Brzezinski inherited a deep and ancient sense of Polish nationhood. But it was from the Brzeziński side, which had been active in Polish uprisings and more recent cultural endeavors to sustain the idea of Poland, that Brzezinski gained his spirit of activism. Poles of Brzezinski's class were in no doubt that their country had been occupied and dominated by inferior cultures—the Russians and the Prussians in particular. The

Austro-Habsburgs were viewed through a more benign lens. Tadeusz would often refer to Poland as "the Christ among nations," a phrase common in Polish literary circles.[7] The country would accordingly rise from the dead after three generations. Tadeusz imbued in the young Brzezinski a conviction that Poland was an advanced European civilization that had been brought low by the avaricious brutality of its less refined neighbors, Russia foremost among them. "We were Westerners in the East," Tadeusz felt. Poland had died—and it would come back to life—in the cause of Western civilization.[8]

By the time Leonia and Tadeusz met, the imperial setting of their early years had vanished. But their manners and style retained many of its trappings. In their faded photo albums of the 1920s, Leonia's glamour was undimmed. Later in life, Tadeusz said that his favorite city had always been Vienna: "It doesn't have the heaviness of so many German cities."[9] Warsaw came in a close second. Though born in Warsaw, Zbigniew lived until he was three in the northern French industrial city of Lille, where Tadeusz was consul general for Poland's young republic. Zbigniew spent only three years of his life in Poland, all of them in his first decade. From 1931 to 1935, the family was based in Leipzig, the largest city in Germany's Saxony region, where Tadeusz was also Poland's consul general. Those were formative years for Zbigniew. Only between 1935 and 1938 did he live for an unbroken period in his homeland. Yet he spent his first ten summers in Poland, often at his ancestral Brzeziński home.

Zbigniew grew up amid French and then German speakers. But his household was always Polish. Leonia made sure that the cook, the housekeeper, the driver, and other domestic staff came from home. The three children, including the youngest, Adam, who was born a year after Zbigniew, picked up French only after they moved to Montreal. In Leipzig they were tutored in German. Most of the Brzezińskis' interwar world, including their family papers and their various Warsaw residences, was buried in the rubble of wartime Poland. Leonia's private diaries and a modest collection of official documents traveled with them to the New World. They provide a lyrical and emotionally vivid account of the circumstances in which Zbigniew grew up. From an early age his older half brother, Jurek, was at boarding school in Warsaw. He joined them for the holidays in Germany or in Poland's Carpathian Mountains, where they would often spend their summers amid the region's peaks, cascading waterfalls, eagle's nest churches, and spa towns. It was Poland's Riviera. Leonia's children were radically unalike. She fretted that Jurek was a mediocre and easily distractable student. He would also stutter. The coddled baby of the family, Adam, Zbigniew's younger brother, was prone to ill health. He also had a tendency to put on weight. From time to time, Adam's parents worried that he was a slow learner. Adam would never be able to shake off either of those traits: his worrisome physical condition and his trouble with focusing. Zbigniew, on the other hand, was headstrong, independent, risk taking, and academically gifted.

Leonia loved to show off her children. In their family albums, whether on the Baltic seaside, in a Polish mountain spa town, or waving goodbye from various European train stations, the children are always dressed for the occasion: in full-bodied boy's bathing suits, wrapped in tiny fur coats with matching berets, or in the summer garb of miniature Polish gentlemen. As young as age six, Zbigniew's famed mental sharpness, distinct high-cheeked facial structure, and striking blond hair are recognizable. He stood out from the Brzezinski brood as emotionally detached and hard to please. "Zbysio, my son, why must you be so mean, so prickly?" Leonia confided to her diary during a Christmas in Leipzig in 1934. "You fancy yourself a man, a knight, who has no need for his mother, nor her caresses—you have to change, because my heart yearns towards you. It does hurt at times, oh my brave, edgy little boy!"[10]

Later in life, Leonia would tell the story of how the young Zbigniew had taken to sleeping on hard floors without pillows so that he could taste the discomfort that others less fortunate were forced to endure.[11] One time, though parched after an afternoon of hiking in mountains, he refused to drink water until the following morning so that he could feel what it was like to go without. There was something about Zbigniew, with his appetite for risk and pranks, that made him Leonia's golden child. "After his fourth lesson Zbysio is already skating by himself," she wrote in an entry from Leipzig. "Adaś, as he claims, is a bit too fat and not doing as well; he gets scared and clings to Mrs. Marysia [the nanny]."[12]

Hitler came to power when Zbigniew was five, midway through the family's time in Leipzig. One of his starkest recollections was of the frequent Nazi torchlight parades, which struck terror into the children. His parents imparted to the children an unequivocal fear of and contempt for the Nazis. In September 1933, Leonia accompanied her husband to the Leipzig trial of Marinus van der Lubbe, an unemployed Dutch Communist, and three apparently random Bulgarian Communists, who were accused of burning the Reichstag, Germany's parliament building—an incident, probably Nazi orchestrated, that Hitler exploited to impose emergency powers. It was the death knell of German parliamentary democracy. From the gallery, Leonia and Tadeusz saw the opening proceedings, which led to the Dutchman's conviction and the acquittal of the hapless Bulgarians, for the show trial that it was. "Police in front of the court. Ticket checked at the entrance. I was very concerned, afraid even—an unpleasant pat down (thorough, nasty)," she wrote. "It's just a political charade, a stage for comedy, to show the world how Hitler saved the world from the Communists—and every stage needs its actors. . . . It was a very unpleasant time. We left after the first intermission."[13]

A few days later, the Brzezińskis were invited to a farewell party for Leipzig's Jewish colony, which was thinning out in the wake of Hitler's initial flurry of Aryanization laws and the boycott of Jewish businesses. Many Polish Jews had fled Poland for Germany during the First World War and were now stateless. Tadeusz issued hundreds of *laisser-passer* documents and some Polish passports to enable their exit. His unofficial philanthropy caused him difficulties in both Berlin and Warsaw. Poland was discouraging Jewish immigration and putting growing pressure on Polish Jews—tragically to little effect, given what lay in store—to emigrate to Palestine. Leonia wrote, "There was a farewell party for the Jewish colony, very tender, very elegant, with tailcoats, evening gowns, speeches, flowers. Then there was a concert with wine, pastries, and cake. Father got a beautiful portrait of himself . . . his name was entered into the golden book—the diploma was presented; in a word they honored Father very much, extolling his contributions."[14]

For most Poles, the "Jewish question" was unrelated to the Polish one even though Jews made up more than a tenth of the country's population. To Tadeusz, whose job was to look after the interests of the Polish diaspora, the questions were the same for Polish Jews regardless of their legal status. "What caught us off guard was how quickly events moved: first with discrimination, then boycotting, then signs of 'Jude' scrawled across shop fronts, and Nazis in brown uniforms watching everyone who walked in," Tadeusz told a Canadian newspaper decades later.[15] In reply to one of several letters of complaint Tadeusz sent in protest at the mistreatment of Polish Jews, Saxony's Ministry of the Interior told him it was acting in response to the threat of "interlaced international Jewry." Tadeusz's stance went against the changing winds in Poland. Piłsudski's multiethnic sense of Polish nationhood was giving way to the darker nationalist ideology of Roman Dmowski, who had created the overtly anti-Semitic National Democracy movement. "Thank you for all you did to help my brethren in those dark days when so few stood with them in their indescribable plight," Israel's prime minister, Menachem Begin, wrote to Tadeusz more than forty years later.[16]

Zbigniew would often tell the story of how Leonia had refused to shake Hitler's hand at a grand reception. Her diary makes no mention of that courageous gesture. The Brzeziński parents did attend a concert in Dresden's city hall hosted by Joseph Goebbels, Hitler's chief propagandist, in which the *Führer* was the guest of honor. Few in the audience seemed much taken by Richard Wagner's *Tristan and Isolde*. The three-part opera went on for six hours. Most eyes were on the Austrian corporal. "A few minutes pass, and he walks in slowly, shouting erupts in the hall, and he bows and sits down. His face looks swollen, aged," she wrote. "We were both incredibly tired. The atmosphere is very formal—people are more interested in Hitler than in Tristan." Her ordeal nevertheless turned out to have been worth it. At a dinner afterwards, which went on to 5:00 a.m., they were seated with the mayor of Dresden, an Italian attaché, and Saxony's minister-president. "I was very adored," Leonia wrote. "They singled us out at the table and honored us."[17] The Brzezińskis somehow avoided contact with the German dictator.

Beyond the Nazis—"louts," as she often called them—the ostentatiously Catholic Leonia had little affinity for German culture. "It's so strange here, so cold," she wrote one Christmas. "As if God, the Church, and the festive spirit were all missing—a different unfamiliar world you could never get attached to and would gladly flee from."[18] The children's lives in Germany followed a schedule of home tutoring, regular attendance at Mass, sometimes daily, and a lot of outdoor activity: soccer, skating, hiking, and visits to the park. At Christmas and on their birthdays, their gifts often had a martial theme: a sheathed knife, toy soldiers, and books about famous battles, always Polish. There was barely a significant European clash of arms in which the Poles had not been present. Zbigniew was boastful of the Poles' critical role in keeping the Ottomans from the gates of Vienna in 1683.

On weekends they would take chauffeured road trips to Saxon castles, medieval churches, and mountain retreats. One time the family visited Martin Luther's hometown of Eisleben, which was also where the Protestant revolutionary had died. They toured his final residence. "There is an air of rigidness, a harsh way of life, devoid of warmth, sustained by a bare minimum. A spartan environment that feels more like a grave than a home," Leonia wrote.[19] She often described German women as drab and dowdy. It was different back home. For a time in the 1920s and the early 1930s, Warsaw was a growing international city. It boasted sixty cinemas, a revolving dance floor, and art deco buildings to rival Berlin's.[20] "We returned from Warsaw. There was a lot of joy and clamor, admiration for my appearance."[21] On another visit: "It was so nice in Warsaw, so giddy. Time flew by so quickly, each day held so many pleasures. . . . Good plays, great artists, a cheerful atmosphere, crowded cafés, pretty, well-dressed women, beautiful furs, music playing."[22] The sparkling urbanity and optimism of interwar Warsaw are a forgotten moment in modern European history. To the young Zbigniew and his mother, Warsaw was the epitome of metropolitan glamour.

But Leonia's mood and her judgments about time and place could also be fickle. Shortly before they returned to Warsaw, Tadeusz was the guest of honor at the unveiling of a statue of Chopin. As an emissary for Poland, Tadeusz was also a champion of Polish culture. He had been alerted to a trove of hitherto unknown Chopin scores in a private collector's basement that he reclaimed for his country. "One must appreciate the lengths to which the Germans went to accommodate and honor us," she wrote. "I thank Our Lady for all these bright days, months, and years that we spent here. Farewell, Leipzig, maybe I'll come and see you again one day, head your way with joy, because I had it very good here."[23] Leonia's mood swings could be dramatic. Zbigniew's relationship with his magnetic, often drama-prone, mother was never placid. Many children love to be smothered. Not Zbigniew, who saw himself as his father's son. Tadeusz was outshone at home by Leonia. His manners were courtly and self-effacing; Leonia's vivacity brooked no competition. Long after he moved to Canada, people spoke of Tadeusz as though he were a refugee from a different century: he would still kiss women's hands. He always seemed primed with the right word or gentle witticism. His thirst for history was deep, his memory encyclopedic.

As a public figure, Brzeziński senior set the tone for Zbigniew's ambitions. He also passed on a deep sensitivity about Poland's place in the world. The Brzeziński family's lodestar was Marshal Piłsudski. More distant Polish figures also loomed large. Of them Tadeusz Kościuszko, a Polish general who had fought with the American rebels against the British in the Revolutionary War and whose statue faces the White House from Lafayette Park, was prominent. The celebrity among Europeans in the revolutionary army was the Marquis de Lafayette. But Lafayette's potency was bolstered by the arrival of a French fleet. Kościuszko, who had fortified the encampment at West

Point and befriended Thomas Jefferson, came unaccompanied. Some military historians believe that his individual contribution to the war was greater than Lafayette's. Kościuszko disapproved as much of slavery on one side of the Atlantic as he did serfdom and anti-Jewish discrimination on the other. "He is as pure a son of liberty as I have ever known," said Jefferson.[24] Brzezinski grew up hearing stories of Kościuszko. Another Polish revolutionary was Casimir Pulaski, who became a general in the Continental Army and helped save George Washington from capture by the British. Those were the heroes of Brzezinski's childhood. After returning home from America's revolutionary wars, Kościuszko took up arms against Empress Catherine the Great's Imperial Russian Army. His return coincided with Poland's last brief flourish as a nation. Following Poland's promulgation of a modern constitution in 1791—only the second written constitution in history, just four years after America's—the country was partitioned between czarist Russia, the kingdom of Prussia, and the Austrian Empire. By 1795, Poland had been extinguished. In another secret protocol, Poland's three new imperial rulers agreed to stamp out the Polish nation for good. Prussia's Frederick the Great described the Poles as "slovenly trash" and likened what he saw as their deserved cultural fate to that of America's Iroquois. It would be hard to grow up hearing such stories and not be keen on national liberty.

Cavalry charges and triumphant battles populated Zbigniew's childhood imagination. As he grew older, he developed a historical sense of Polish civilization. Many of the storied Poles of his upbringing had made their name elsewhere: Chopin in France; the novelist Joseph Conrad in Great Britain; the renowned scientist Marie Curie in France; the great astronomer Nicolaus Copernicus in Prussia; the Polish revolutionaries fighting for America and in Napoleon's armies; and the flower of Poland's intelligentsia in every European capital. His nationalist inclinations were molded by the more inclusive idea of Poland popularized by Piłsudski and supported by Tadeusz. In the 1930s, Piłsudski's vision was increasingly supplanted in Poland by a more nativist politics that made second-class citizens of Jews and other minorities within its borders, notably Ukrainians and Belorussians. Piłsudski's so-called Promethean League envisioned Poland as the largest player in a multinational group of smaller Eastern European nations that together would be large enough to resist the squeeze of Germany to their west and Russia to their east—the country's eternal vulnerability. It would include all the former peoples ruled by czarist Russia from the Baltic Sea in the north to the Caspian and Black Seas in the south. During the Second World War, Tadeusz hosted talks in Montreal between Czechoslovak and Polish leaders to form a Polish-Czech union after the war. His initiative collapsed in 1941 when Czechoslovakia joined cause with the Soviets after Hitler ended the Nazi-Soviet Pact. Tadeusz's Prometheism lived on through Zbigniew.

The family's return to Warsaw in 1935 was not the joyous homecoming for which Leonia had yearned. Warsaw seemed less prosperous and carefree. Its politics were curdling. The economic situation was deteriorating. There were periodic air raid drills in a reminder of the darkening clouds around Poland. Leonia's father, Leon, died alone in his apartment when the family was on a brief sojourn in Italy. Her only sister, Marylka, left Poland for good with her family by boat to New York in 1936. Perhaps worst in terms of emotional shock was the death of Piłsudski. Zbigniew was among the crowds who watched the procession of the marshal's coffin through the streets of Warsaw before it was taken by train to the ancient royal seat of Kraków. Brzezinski never forgot that moment. "Józef Piłsudski died the day before yesterday!"[25] Leonia wrote in April 1935. "Tears stream down the face. The heart breaks at the thought of you no longer being there in Belvedere [the presidential palace]. Dead silence enshrouds Poland, eyes look on in trepidation about what comes next. . . . I did not know you, Marshal, but I felt your presence; wherever our home was, you were there. Thanks to you I was able to live through the most beautiful chapter in Poland's history. . . . I will teach and raise my sons to be yours forever."

To compound the gloom, Tadeusz would be leaving Warsaw soon. The following year, he took up his new role in the Soviet Ukrainian city of Kharkiv. Given the peril of the USSR's turmoil and his family's Polishness, Tadeusz deemed his third major posting unsuitable for the family. His stint in Kharkiv came three years after Stalin had engineered the tragedy of Ukraine's Holodomor, the great famine of the early 1930s caused by the brutal collectivization of Soviet agriculture. It had taken 3 million lives. Tadeusz's posting also coincided with Stalin's pitiless Moscow show trials. Though only eight hundred miles apart, Kharkiv was a world removed from interbellum Warsaw, where Tadeusz had left his family. While Leonia was raising their sons in *haut-bourgeois* Varsovian comfort, Tadeusz's tense circumstances in Kharkiv shifted arbitrarily from one day to the next. Without warning, the Polish diplomat's Soviet acquaintances would vanish following a midnight knock from the secret police. The Polish diplomat learned to restrict his interactions for fear of endangering those with whom he came into contact. The only light note was that Leonia, on her sole visit to Kharkiv, adopted a stray purebred Polish shepherd dog that she noticed wandering around the Polish compound. The children had stayed behind with their grandmother in Przemysl.

Tadeusz's posting lasted just eighteen months. But he would experience his leaves of absence in Warsaw as almost literal decompressions. On his visits home, he would tell Zbigniew dark tales of what he believed was Stalin's deliberate destruction of Ukraine. Both father and son adhered to Piłsudski's view that without an independent Ukraine, Poland could not survive for long. The linked fate of Poland and Ukraine was both an axiom of faith and an astute historical observation. Tadeusz's spell in Kharkiv came during a rare point in history when the stories of Poland and the then Soviet republic of Ukraine sharply diverged. Never fixed for long, the line between Poland and Ukraine would shift a couple of hundred miles west or a couple of degrees east every few decades—never more so than during in the twentieth century. During the interwar years, the previously Habsburg-ruled city of Lviv, which the Poles call Lwów and which was the metropolis of Tadeusz's youth, was in Poland. About a hundred miles to Lviv's east, millions of Soviet Ukrainians were entombed in a merciless new world that Tadeusz was trying to comprehend.

Interwar Poland, by contrast, was a vibrant young nation that for the majority of its short existence could claim to be a democracy of sorts. Yet the Poland of the mid- to late 1930s was noticeably less tolerant and its democracy less stable than the one in which Leonia and Tadeusz had come of age. Though still young, Poland was increasingly insecure. To one side lay the increasingly militaristic Nazi Germany; to the other a revolutionary Soviet Union, which was itching to strangle Poland's alleged reactionary imperialism in its cradle. The young country's supposed friends in London and Paris seemed too distracted and half-hearted to act as an effective counterbalance. Poland felt increasingly alone and ignored. During Poland's battle against the Red Army, trade unions in Britain had boycotted shipments to Warsaw with their Bolshevik-inspired "hands off Russia" campaign. With the exception of Churchill, the British Right did not take Poland seriously. In the early 1930s, Poland signed nonaggression pacts with both the USSR and Germany.

From 1934, Poland started to treat visiting Nazi dignitaries like royalty. Hermann Göring, the Third Reich's air minister, would go on annual hunts of wolves and bears in Poland, accompanied by senior Polish generals. In 1936, the Polish government received Goebbels with full state honors—an event that would have been inconceivable when Piłsudski was alive. Demonstrations by the Polish National Democracy (ND), the anti-Semitic nationalist party, were becoming more frequent. It was not the Poland of Tadeusz's hopes. When he saw a group of ND street thugs harassing Jews, he charged at them with his walking cane.[26] They were chanting: "Warsaw and Krakow to the Poles! Let the Jewish pigs go live in Palestine." Zbigniew, who was by Tadeusz's side, never forgot his father's rage at those youths. Though the Brzezińskis had no close Jewish friends, their idea of Poland was the same as Piłsudski's. Piłsudski had dreamed of a multiethnic federation in which Polish Jews played a full part. A 1928 political cartoon entitled "How the Right Sees the Government of Marshal Piłsudski" depicted the country's leader as an Orthodox Jew enjoying challah and gefilte fish while reading a Yiddish newspaper by the light of a menorah.[27] When Piłsudski died, Polish Jews mourned. They also felt dread.

The country's waning prospects echoed in strange ways the growing misfortunes of the Brzeziński family. Though the boys had adjusted comfortably to school in Warsaw, each fitted out in blazer and badged cap, both Zbigniew and Adam were struck with polio at the start of their second academic year. They spent touch-and-go weeks in intensive care. For a terrifying few weeks, during which Leonia never left their hospital room, their lives were in question. They pulled through. Adam was hit far more severely than his older brother. He caught meningitis and was nearly paralyzed. For months after Zbigniew had recovered, Leonia kept vigil day and night by Adam's bed. The disease was frequently lethal. "I no longer know a world outside my poor sons' room," she wrote after they had been discharged from the hospital. "We did all we could for the boys, got the best doctors—but I believe from the bottom of my heart that it was Our Lady who saved them."[28]

For most of the Brzezińskis' last two years in Warsaw, their lives revolved around the boys' convalescence. After six months, Adam still could not walk. Zbigniew was shaky but mobile. Leonia took them to Polish spa towns for mud and salt treatments. Life was one medical consultation after another. From orthotic fittings to galvanization and therapeutic massages, with long spells in military hospitals, their routines were grimly medical. Zbigniew still wore braces when he crossed the Atlantic. Adam never fully recovered. As Zbigniew regained his mobility, his mother's attention was monopolized by Adam. Zbigniew's days were increasingly unsupervised. He joined the neighborhood Boy Scouts, a key plank in any young Polish boy's patriotic education. Most of his peers would play an important role in the Polish Home Army's resistance during the Second World War. Many of them died. Zbigniew adored the uniform, the parades, and the camaraderie.

With his father in the USSR and his mother at Adam's side in various hospitals and sanatoria, Zbigniew tasted independence young. He was free to roam the streets of Warsaw. He knew the back alleys. Decades later, he would show first-time visitors around Warsaw as if he had never been away. He also buried himself in books. He loved to watch Warsaw's grand military parades, notably those on May 3, which commemorated the day the 1791 constitution had been adopted, and November 11, when the Second Republic was launched in 1918. "Like many people of my generation I had great confidence in its [the Polish Army's] military capabilities,"[29] Brzezinski said towards the end of this life. He was also becoming aware of the world outside his corner of Europe.

Zbigniew's first cousin Andrzej Roman, who would become his closest lifelong friend (and after the war Zbigniew's "eyes and ears" in Poland), recalled an eight-year-old Zbigniew who bore the clear imprint of his adult persona.[30] "The war in Spain had just broken out," he said. "We were supposed to play at war in Krucza Street [not far from the Warsaw castle in the ancient part of the capital], where his parents lived. So I said, 'Fine, let's play at war in Spain, and I'll play General Franco—pronounced the Polish way with a *tz* that sounded like *Franzo*.' Zbigniew answered with a grin. 'That's fine by me. I'll be General Franco (pronounced correctly with a hard *c*).' The conversation stuck in my memory. I had the impression that he had an advantage over me. He knew how to pronounce the name of the nationalist leader in Spain." Zbigniew still needed frequent therapy for his polio. He regained comfortable use of his legs only later in Canada, though never enough to play ice hockey, its national sport. In Warsaw, he channeled his energy into his studies. Reading became a passion. The gap between Zbigniew and Adam would only grow.

Leonia increasingly craved a new life. It is unclear whether Tadeusz lobbied his superiors for his next posting in Canada and, if so, whether it was on medical grounds or because he wished to take his family out of harm's way. Both motivations pointed across the Atlantic. Since at least 1936, when Hitler had reoccupied the Rhineland, the sense of impending war had been tangible to any sentient European—still more so to a Pole with as keen a political antenna as Tadeusz. But Leonia was agitating for her family to move. "Life in Warsaw is drab, the people are worn out, they're complaining, pessimism pervades the city," she wrote. "Poor material conditions make life dull, devoid of ambition, people live their lives with no tomorrow, aimless and empty. . . . I'm sick of this life. I'm suffocating in these rooms."[31]

By late 1937, the Brzeziński family's luck had begun to turn. Tadeusz had returned from Kharkiv with the dog, who in Canada became known as "Johnny." Leonia was also pregnant with a fourth child, it seems unexpectedly. She gave thanks to the Virgin Mary for her good fortune. Leszek was born in a Warsaw hospital in March 1938. "He's big, wonderful, adorable!" she wrote. "The birth went well, with God's help no complications."[32] Leonia hired a jolly nursemaid named Lidia. The biggest development, however, was news of their impending departure for Canada. At a critical moment in Poland's story, Leonia's prayers were starting to be answered. Among the benefits of moving to Montreal would be access to the availability of the newest medical treatments for Adam's polio.

The European storm of which Churchill had warned was gathering. Yet the Brzezińskis could not have known that they were leaving Poland for good. They set sail on October 12 on MS *Batory*, one of two ships of the Gdynia America Line that embarked from Poland's Baltic coast. The recently built port of Gdynia was considered an infrastructural jewel of Poland's Second Republic. Though less than twenty miles from the larger Polish harbor of Gdańsk, the new port gave Poland insurance against Germany's revanchist claims on the older port, which they called Danzig and which had been declared an "open city" in the Treaty of Versailles.

The Brzezińskis embarked on their Atlantic crossing just two weeks after Britain's prime minister, Neville Chamberlain, and his French counterpart, Édouard Daladier, ceded Czechoslovakia's German-speaking province of the Sudetenland to Hitler at their infamous last-ditch conference in Munich. Hitler's Panzer divisions completed the Sudetenland occupation two days before the Brzezińskis sailed for the United States. Shortly before Munich, Churchill said, "We seem to be very near the bleak choice between War and Shame. My feeling is that we shall choose Shame, and then have War thrown in a little later on even more adverse terms than at present."[33] The following March, Hitler broke his Munich pledge and annexed the rest of Czechoslovakia. Poland was evidently next on his list, which finally prompted Great Britain to guarantee Poland's security (France had already done so). By that time, the Brzezińskis had safely relocated to Montreal.

A few weeks before they left Poland, Leonia wrote, "Change is coming to our lives; I'm entering the second epoch of my life. I'm writing this down for posterity so that my sons may read it one day. . . . My dear sons, do you comprehend how far away we are going—to a new hemisphere!" Their Atlantic journey was a memorable one of raging storms, grand dinners at the captain's table, games of lotto, ballroom dances, and long spells on deck staring at the ocean. None of them had ever taken a journey by sea. The Brzeziński party amounted to ten: two parents, four boys, a nursemaid, a tutor, a nanny, and a dog. Along with MS *Piłsudski*, which they passed mid-Atlantic, the *Batory* was the pride of Poland's civilian maritime fleet. The boys were assigned cabins 2 and 4, which indicates the family's high social ranking. The 480-foot *Batory* had a capacity of 796 passengers. Of those, 46—the Brzezińskis among them—were in first class.

The *Batory* docked for a few hours in Copenhagen on the second day. Polish friends met the Brzezińskis at the port and gave them a brief motor tour of the city. Leonia also bought a modern stroller for Leszek. At a restaurant in Copenhagen in the mid-1970s—the first time he returned to Denmark's capital—Zbigniew Brzezinski related to his fellow diners with uncharacteristic emotion his memory of seeing Denmark's famous statue of the Little Mermaid. Seventy-four years later, the eighty-four-year-old Brzezinski returned to Gdynia for the first time since the family had set out in 1938. There were tears in his eyes. He remembered that as the ship set sail, he tried to extract a vow from his father that they would return to Poland the next summer. Though that paternal vow was not forthcoming, "I felt certain that I would go back to Poland soon."[34] His next visit to Warsaw took place in 1957. In 2015, he opened Poland's Emigration Museum in Gdynia. There is a plaque on its quayside commemorating the start of the family's 1938 journey across the ocean.

The Atlantic Ocean felt rough that autumn, though the ship's officers assured the Brzezińskis that it was behaving normally. The family spent much of the twelve-day crossing vomiting in their cabins. They were all maritime novices. Leonia's awe at the ocean's power was more than enough to bring out her faith: "You are too formidable, too vehement by nature; your frothing furious crests inspire fear, humility, draw words of prayer from the lips—oh, God, how great and unfathomable is your might."[35] One placid afternoon, Adam managed to go to the upper deck and stand on his own feet without falling, meriting additional gratitude to Our Lady—though he also spent much of the journey throwing up. Only Tadeusz was unaffected by the Atlantic surges.

Zbigniew could not stay below for long. He ran around deck with a pair of binoculars in hand, scanning the waters and classifying the maritime flags on the ships that he spotted.

The Brzezińskis' first sight of dry land in the Western Hemisphere was of Halifax, the capital of Canada's Nova Scotia province. It was bathed in autumn hues. They docked there for a few hours, toured the small city by taxi, and offered brief prayers in Halifax's cathedral. The last leg of their journey was to New York, where they would disembark and catch a night train to Montreal. In spite of Zbigniew's fond hopes, Leonia knew it was a decisive break in their lives; it would be no mere sojourn. Early into their passage, she had written, "We're off in pursuit of new joys, new graces from God, we're beginning what feels like another life. After all, our forefathers also dreamed of America."[36]

On October 24, their new existence began after MS *Batory* steamed into New York Harbor. Zbigniew was neither huddled nor hungry. Like his mother, he was impeccably dressed. Yet like countless masses before him—among them the fifteen-year-old Heinz Kissinger, a German Jewish refugee who had arrived in New York six weeks earlier—Zbigniew had his first glimpse of the Statue of Liberty. The ten-year-old spoke no English. He had no idea that his stint in the New World would be for life.

2

Between Two Worlds

In Newman House School's 1939–40 annual yearbook, the boys were asked to pick one subject on which they regarded themselves as an authority. The exercise was supposed to be lighthearted. John Graham said, "Arriving late"; Patrick Dunlop put down "Everything"; George Hemming said, "Movies"; Garrick Willcox said, "Grandmothers"; Adam Brzezinski went for "Romance"; and Collin Quinn simply entered his home address. Zbigniew Brzezinski put "European affairs."[1] He was not jesting. His personal diary, a habit he had started on his first day in Montreal and would continue intermittently for decades, soon turned into a chronicle of distressing events across the Atlantic. Happenings at the Brzezinski home merited the occasional entry. Canadian politics did not. The United States barely featured. The young Pole was obsessed with what was going on in Europe. In the following year's yearbook, next to the other entries—"Hollywood," "Eating," "Telling tales," and "Yawning"—Zbigniew wrote "Europe (foreign affairs)." Not speaking a word of English, the ten-year-old might have taken a while to acclimatize to the eccentric humor of the privileged classes in what then was often called British North America. In their first year, the Brzezinski brothers were the only non-Anglos in their Montreal prep school. But that explains little. Adam got the joke, and at the end of the year Zbigniew came in at the top of his class. He also won first prizes in religion (catechism) and Canadian history. At the end of his second academic year, he won the senior prize for

English and the schoolwide prize for literature. By the close of his third, during the course of which Japan attacked Pearl Harbor, the rest of the world suddenly became interesting to him.

Heading up Poland's consular mission in Montreal was both a career demotion for Tadeusz and a gift. Had he been in Warsaw a year later when the Germans occupied the country, he would almost certainly have been executed. If he had slipped through the German net, the Soviets would have seen him as a target. But his new role in Canada was not a trivial one, either. Polish arrivals had surged in the previous two decades, particularly after the US Immigration Act of 1924, which had virtually shut off the flow of Catholics and Jews to America. Many of Poland's recent arrivals were from Tadeusz's native Eastern Galicia, one of the poorest areas of the former Habsburg Empire, which in Vienna had been derisively known as "half Asia." A lot of Polish immigrants headed west to set up prairie farms in Alberta and Saskatchewan. Montreal also had an expanding Polish community. Since Poland had no ambassador in Ottawa, Tadeusz's visibility was higher than it might otherwise have been. When the Brzezinskis' train rolled in to Montreal's Gare Centrale, a large welcoming party awaited them. In addition to Polish officials—the consular staff, the rectors of local parishes, representatives of various Polish Canadian groups—the mayor of Montreal and the regional director of the Canadian National Railway were at the head of the reception committee. The Brzezinskis already felt like somebodies in Montreal. To Leonia, the bliss was instant. They were being welcomed to Elysium.

Their first impressions were of Canada's scale and beauty. "I admired its lovely landscape from the train window all morning," wrote Zbigniew.[2] "Forests and mountains can be seen in the distance." Like any other recent European arrivals in a big North American city, they were also struck by Montreal's wide avenues, the size of the houses, the public parks that stretched for miles, and the grand bridges straddling the great Saint Lawrence River that crosses the city. The Brzezinskis chose to live in Montreal's upholstered enclave of Westmount, the city's wealthiest anglophone neighborhood on one of the three peaks of Mount Royal (Mont Royal in French) from which the city derives its name. At about seven hundred feet above sea level, Westmount commands a sweeping view of the city below. Leonia felt reassured by the giant crucifix at its summit and the Catholic churches below them, including the celebrated Saint Joseph's Oratory. On alternating Sundays they went to a Polish church for Mass. Their temporary first house was much to her liking with its ash gray dining room in Louis XV style, the mahogany-fitted master bed-room, and a grand piano that she put to frequent use. Though she disapproved of their locally hired cook, Julia, who was "devoid of life and spirit," and their Polish Canadian housemaid, Sonia, who was "a simple woman, without any substance," their first ten months were a happy time.[3] The boys' Polish tutor, Józef Górzyński, kept the three older boys company and their Polish language up to scratch. They crammed separate English-language tutorials. Since they had arrived after the start of the 1938 academic year, their first few months were largely in Józef's hands. Meanwhile, the baby of the household, Lech, was attached to Lidia, his Polish nursemaid. In spring 1939, the Brzezinskis moved into their permanent residence at 60 Saint Sulpice Road, which was even higher up the mountain and much larger. It had twelve spacious rooms and a sweeping terrace that ran onto a fecund garden providing a "beyond lovely" view of the city. Their new life would begin among notable people in rarefied air; it was a perfect setting for the boys to take the dog on walks without worrying their parents. Zbigniew spent a lot of time on his bike spin-ning down the steep hill on Mount Pleasant Avenue, hoping a prospective girlfriend would catch a glimpse.[4] He and his younger brother also spent long afternoons washing and polishing the family's new black 107-horsepower Buick. On Zbigniew's eleventh birthday, his mother gave him a necktie and leather gloves. From his father he received a rifle.

The social highlight of Leonia's early months was the royal visit of King George VI and Queen Elizabeth, the first time a reigning British monarch had set foot on Canadian soil. George was also the first British sovereign to visit the United States. The royal tour began on May 16, 1939, in Montreal, the opening leg of their monthlong progress. The Brzezinski parents were invited to the state banquet at the Windsor Hotel, the city's finest, where the royal party was staying. Though Montreal was a French-speaking city with early hints of what would later become separatist inclinations, Montrealers turned out en masse for the spectacle and decorated its avenues with Union Jacks. Many collapsed from heat and exhaustion. Sixty-four children were separated from their parents during the parade. Canada's linguistic fault line was comi-cally highlighted by the royal toast of Montreal's mayor, Camillien Houde, who said, "I thank you from the bottom of my heart for coming. My wife here thanks you from her bottom too."[5] The Brzezinski boys watched the festivi-ties from the balcony of a Polish family's downtown apartment. Their par-ents overlooked no detail in their sartorial preparations. Tadeusz's tailcoat was bedecked with his Polish military medals. Leonia wore a white gown of silver lamé with a train and coral roses; pearls cascaded from her neck and ears. On her feet were dappled evening slippers. She also wore her cherished sable furs. She fell under the spell of Elizabeth, who radiated "warmth, femininity and some indescribable aura of kindness." Postwar Canadians would look back on that royal visit as the last sparkle of a closing era. Leonia did, too. "As I looked at you, Gracious King and Charming Queen, I wondered whether I would ever see you again. . . . It was a wonderful evening—one of the loveliest of my life!"[6] Leonia was in her element.

The only jolt to their almost dreamlike new life was the "electrifying" news in March 1939 that Hitler's army had occupied Prague, which Zbigniew recorded in his diary. Having been abandoned by Great Britain and France the previous year, the Czechs submitted to the Germans without a shot. Zbigniew's respect for the Czechs dropped. "Oh, Hitler!" wrote Leonia. "If not for you, it would be peaceful here on earth, but you poison everything."[7] Then in June, the boys' fondly regarded tutor had to take a boat back to Poland because he did not speak good enough English or French to qualify for a job. Leonia felt sorry for the young man, who wanted to stay. Fate had not been Józef's friend. For the most part, the family was so preoccupied with weekend trips to the lakes and peaks of Quebec's Laurentian Mountains, to the big tourist spots such as Niagara Falls in Ontario, where they crossed the bridge to the United States, and to other destinations (beaver farms, indigenous Canadian settlements, and so on) that they had little time to worry about the ominous rumblings from Europe. They regularly took train trips to New York, where Leonia's sister, Marylka, had settled. Leonia was titillated by a cabaret in the "negro district of Harlem" that "made the men blush."[8] The family was still in awe of the skyscrapers, the novelty of ice cream, the railroads that ran above the streets, and the American women, who "drink heavily and dance in a vulgar manner." Quebec's densely wooded mountains and plunging verdant ravines reminded them of Poland—with the important difference that Canada's natural splendor was reachable via smooth asphalt with convenient roadside stations. "I was thinking about you, my beloved parents, my father, my mother. Do you know how beautiful this place is, can you see it from up above? Can you see the comfortable lives people have here?"[9]

On September 1, the Brzezinskis' newfound serenity was shattered. Twelve days before the boys started at their new school, Newman House, Hitler invaded Poland. The Second World War had begun. From then on, no distraction—not sports, friendships, girls, or even family—could rival Zbigniew's obsession with the war. "Today at four o'clock [in the morning], the Germans entered Poland," he wrote in his diary.[10] "I hope we send the Krauts packing. Battles are under way in Gdańsk, Pomerania, and Silesia." Hitler announced that the invasion was retaliatory after an SS unit staged a false-flag Polish attack on a German radio station. Though the fighting was often intense and Polish forces killed up to twenty thousand German soldiers—the only heavy losses sustained by the Third Reich in the first year of war—they were no match for Hitler's combined air and ground motorized units, which included two thousand tanks supported by around eleven hundred German planes—the dreaded Luftwaffe and its Stuka dive-bombers. A new term, *Blitzkrieg*, entered the English language. Seventeen days after the Germans attacked, the Red Army swept into Poland from the east. By the end of September, Warsaw surrendered to German forces.

In those horrific few weeks, the world—and the Brzezinskis—was given a bloody foretaste of the new age of total war. Tadeusz had been able to tune in to Radio Warsaw. He and Zbigniew listened to it every evening. After Warsaw fell, the station managed to stay on the air for several days. Every thirty minutes during those first weeks of the war, the station would broadcast the first eleven notes of a Chopin polonaise followed by silence. Then one evening, Chopin was replaced by the opening chords of "Deutschland über Alles." The Brzezinskis felt Chopin's disappearance from the airwaves like the death of a close relative: it was as tangible a note of darkness as any other news. On October 15, Poland's Second Republic came to an end. There were more than 2 million German and Soviet troops on Polish soil—roughly one occupying soldier for every seventeen Poles. The Soviets rounded up as many members of the Polish intelligentsia as they could—mostly in the Polish reserve units—and sent them off to prison camps near Smolensk or on cattle trains to Kazakhstan and Siberia. Many of them were Tadeusz's peers. The family lost count of how many friends and acquaintances vanished or died. Millions more were to follow. Priests were deported. Whole echelons of the Polish nobility were executed. Though the Soviets sorted their victims by social rank rather than race, their methods were almost as brutal as the Nazis.

The Germans made no distinction between civilians and enemy soldiers. Piles of corpses littered the streets of Warsaw, which German planes bombarded day and night. In that brief hell of Soviet-Nazi partition, roughly two hundred thousand Polish civilians were killed in the fighting, in civilian-targeted bombing, and in the explicit program of ethnic cleansing. Hitler's goal was to create *Lebensraum*, or living space, for ethnic Germans. His roving Einsatzgruppen, the units whose job was to eliminate the Reich's racial enemies, set up hundreds of execution sites in German-occupied Poland. Both Slavs and Jews were classified by Hitler as *Untermenschen*—subhumans. The cramped Warsaw Ghetto, which at its peak housed 460,000 Jews, with an average of almost ten people per room, was created by the Nazis a year later. Though France and Britain declared war on Germany on September 3, they could do little to help the Poles. Canada joined the war a week later. Hitler intended his three-pronged pincer operation to awe the world with an exhibition of modern warfare. The psychological impact of Poland's lightning-fast partition was stunning.

All the Brzezinskis could do was sit there each night impotently digesting the crescendo of news about the infernos that were consuming their homeland. In the opening nightmare of Poland's occupation, they had no way of knowing whether their various siblings, cousins, aunts, and friends had survived the initial onslaught. They were benumbed by scarcely believable reports of Varsovians leaving their city by foot or on horse-drawn carts, only to be engulfed on the road "in viperous flame" by the diabolical Stukas.[11] There were daily fresh horrors of burned-out hospitals, massacred families, and villages put to the torch. "This morning Warsaw capitulated after a heroic two-week defense. Dreadful!" wrote Brzezinski.[12] His mother wrote, "Accursed Hitler, there are no words in the human language to describe you. You will be cursed not only by our people but by your own kin as well. . . . You will pay, monstrous deviant, for the suffering of our children, husbands, and brothers, with eternal torment."[13] Leonia also made some choice observations about Poland's fleeing government, a large chunk of which reached safety in France to set up a government in exile. News trickled through that the vehicle in which the wife of Józef Beck, Poland's foreign minister, made her escape was so laden with her infamous collections of hats and dogs that she had no room to pick up any children from Warsaw's swelling ranks of orphans. Reports of the flight of Poland's elite brought out Leonia's latent contempt for Poland's supine pre-war government. Poles had not forgotten the red carpet that had so often been laid out for Air Marshal Göring, Goebbels, and others, on their annual Polish hunting excursions. "You, Minister of Foreign Affairs, trusted the Germans. [You] welcomed all kinds of vermin into our midst so they could hunt and gorge themselves, bringing spies with them—you are to blame, too weak was your brain, too strong your hubris."[14]

Between September and Christmas 1939, Zbigniew's sole mention of his new school was "We were a bit scared at first, but not anymore." Most of his other entries were about the fate of what remained of Poland's army. Much of his information came from the Polska Agencja Telegraficzna, which produced a digest of Polish news that Tadeusz brought home from the consulate each night. He submitted himself to nightly cross-examinations by Zbigniew. The Brzezinski home also became the social headquarters of Polish émigrés living in Montreal and a stream of visiting Polish officials who had made it out in time. Any news, particularly about people they knew, was swapped and disseminated, however scrappy or secondhand. Their only topic was Poland.

Polish forces were supposed to retreat via Ukraine to the so-called Romanian bridgehead. But the general staff's exit plan had not accounted for the arrival of the Soviet army from the other direction—the Molotov-Ribbentrop protocol on Poland's partition having been kept secret. Roughly 120,000 Polish soldiers nevertheless made it to neutral Romania and Hungary and found their way first to France and then to Britain. In November, German U-boats torpedoed MS *Piłsudski*, which the Brzezinskis' liner, MS *Batory*, had passed on their way to New York a year earlier. "You were sailing so boldly, playing music, giving us heart—and now you lie on the bottom of the ocean floor," Leonia wrote.[15] The shock and heartbreak at what was happening to Poland never let up. Yet the Brzezinskis' lives went on. At Christmas, which they celebrated with several local Polish families, they treated guests to their first turkey dinner, though the occasion passed joylessly and "with quietly aching hearts."[16] Zbigniew went dressed in a white suit and cravat. At eleven, he was straining to be treated as a grown-up. He craved to be part of the grim adult discourse. The night before, the family had attended Christmas Mass, making it to bed only at 3:00 a.m.

Both Zbigniew and Adam were making rapid progress at school and conversing in English. Jurek was attending French night school and taking tutorials in English. Zbigniew had made an almost full recovery from polio and played center back on the school's soccer team. It is not hard to divine where Zbigniew's thoughts belonged. In the school's yearbook, he wrote two essays, one a nine-hundred-word breeze through Poland's history, starting with its conversion to Christianity in 966 and ending with its occupation by the Soviets and Germans the previous autumn. "As in the past, Poland believes in the final victory of justice and right and in the reconstruction of the State, even stronger and better than before," he concluded.[17] His other was a shorter work of fiction called "The Siege of Berlin, 19—?" In the story, Zbigniew is the commander of ten Polish divisions that encircle Berlin and carry out revenge for what the Germans did to Warsaw. "After ten days of constant gunfire, they wanted to speak with me. I refused because I wanted to make Berlin a pile of ruins," Zbigniew wrote. The Germans ran up a white flag and "our soldiers hanged Hitler and Göring." General Brzezinski nevertheless ordered that Berlin be reduced to rubble.

Still barely able to walk, Adam went under the surgeon's knife in June 1940 at the Sacré-Coeur Hospital in the Cartierville neighborhood of Montreal. He awoke from the operation yelling in agony and tearing at his leg plasters. The procedure turned out to be only a partial success. Adam would never regain full mobility. Zbigniew, meanwhile, was taking proverbial strides. Later that same month, with Adam still in the hospital, Zbigniew was packed off for five weeks at Camp Kinkora, a boys' summer resort seventy miles west of Montreal in the Laurentian foothills. Accompanied by his newly acquired friends from school, Wilson and Kevin, he was given the parental wave-off on his first stint away from home. For five weeks he almost forgot that the war existed. He learned how to swim and befriended four Polish refugees, three of whom would join Newman House the next year. Their father, Kazimierz Sosnkowski, was a senior Polish general who in 1943 would be appointed the commander of Poland's forces in exile. Prior to Zbigniew's summer spell of games, wholesome exercise, and new friendships, his diary and that of his mother had tracked the increasingly grim reports from the widening war in Europe: Hitler's lightning *Blitzkrieg* across the Low Countries, the shockingly rapid fall of France, the start of the Battle of Britain, and the bedraggled Polish Army's circuitous escape into the ever-shrinking bits of Europe not yet covered by Germany's Panzers.

Zbigniew's mind rarely strayed from the world war. Here is a typical diary entry: "Parents got into a car accident this morning. They are unharmed, but the car frame is broken. Also, the Italians took over Somalia."[18] In fact, Leonia's abrasions from the accident, which was caused by a tire blowing out on a slippery road, confined her to bed for a week. Tadeusz was heavily bruised in the ribs and chest. Adam had dressing applied to his head wounds. But Zbigniew's head belonged to Europe. He lived two lives. The first, which posed few obstacles, was his seemingly effortless enculturation into English-language schooling, and to Montreal's francophone rhythms. It was an almost placid existence surrounded by loved ones and family retainers in Montreal's sylvan upper reaches. The second, which resumed every evening and first thing in the morning, was when his mind inhabited Warsaw. He knew the names of the ruined buildings, the streets on which his friends had lived, the original whereabouts of aunts and cousins, yet little about their fates. Bits of news would drip in from the International Red Cross or from Poles fresh off the boat.

As the war progressed, Tadeusz's time was increasingly devoted to the training of a Polish army in Canada and to coping with the rising flood of Polish war refugees. In June 1940, the Polish government in exile had moved to London as France was succumbing to the *Blitzkrieg*. Polish fighter pilots were playing a critical role—second only to the British—in the skies above England. The Polish airmen dubbed Britain "the island of last hope." In Spitfires and Hurricanes, they engaged in dogfights with Messerschmitts as though they were defending their own homeland. "Had it not been for the magnificent material contributed by the Polish squadrons and their unsurpassed gallantry, I hesitate to say that the outcome of the Battle (of Britain) would have been the same,"[19] wrote Sir Hugh Dowding, Britain's air chief marshal, after the Battle of Britain had been won. Along with thousands of British women and children, the families of Polish leaders and soldiers were removed from harm's way on Atlantic convoys to Canada. One such passenger ship contained a large cache of Polish national treasures from Warsaw's royal castle. Its curators had the foresight to remove its most precious contents before the Germans could seize them. Tadeusz helped find safe storage for the treasures in Montreal and Ottawa.[20] He also chose the site—at Owen Sound, Ontario, on the Canada-US border—of the Polish Army's North American training camp. The support of the Polish war effort was being split between Britain and Canada. Among the early Polish military recruits to Owen Sound was Zbigniew's half brother, Jurek. Until his enlistment, Jurek had been somewhat directionless.

Tadeusz was playing an ever larger role in diasporic Poland's drive to regroup. He accompanied the big Polish names, including General Władysław Sikorski, who was both prime minister of the exiled Polish government and head of its army, on their visits to Canada. Sikorski was the face of Poland's defiance. On his frequent stops in Montreal, the commander of the Polish army in Canada, General Bolesław Duch, developed an attachment to Zbigniew. "He was incredibly nice to me maybe because he has a son my age, whose name is also Zbigniew, back in Warsaw," Zbigniew wrote.[21] Duch did not know what had happened to his son. The general was astonished by Zbigniew's grasp of military detail and his knowledge of what was happening in Poland. A visibly anxious Adam avoided eye contact with the general; he hated being quizzed by adults. He need not have worried; Zbigniew had commandeered the general's attention. Duch gave Zbigniew a Parker fountain pen, which he treated with a kind of talismanic reverence. At Duch's invitation, Zbigniew went alone for five days to Windsor as his guest. There he dined at the officer's mess and studied *Odsiecz*, the weekly military paper that aimed to recruit soldiers from North America's Polish diaspora. He also caught up with Jurek, who was getting ready to go to Scotland to complete his military training.

Leonia dreaded Jurek's impending deployment and was haunted by fear over the fate of the Brzeziński and Roman families in Poland. The household received its first good news from Poland via telegram in February 1940, almost six months after the country had been occupied. "God! They're alive!" she wrote.[22] Tadeusz's mother, and Leonia's brother, nephew, and aunt, among others, had somehow emerged unscathed from the first onslaught. Both the aunt and Tadeusz's mother passed away in the following months from natural causes. Leonia had tried to send money to her aunt via the Red Cross, but the man who had promised to carry out the transfer ran off with the cash. Leonia was also wracked with anxiety about the Brzezinskis' financial situation. The Polish government in exile had almost no revenue to pay salaries. Much of their dwindling budget was spent on entertaining Polish VIPs. Leonia created a small cosmetics laboratory at home to make traditional Polish beauty lotions to sell to Canadians. Her company was called Lady Beauty Products. With no means to pay the domestic staff, Leonia had to let them go. She was also forced to sell her beloved sable furs to the wife of the Dutch consul. "Zbys [Zbigniew] had tears in his eyes. He said he wanted me to wear them for his wedding. But what can you do . . . as much as it pains me, it was a necessary sacrifice to put bread on the table."[23] Every now and then a letter would somehow make its way through from Poland. "The poor things are eking out a living, I can feel their poverty and sorrow, but it's so hard for me to aid them. I have no money to send."[24]

The only significant development at home was the municipal authority's decision to destroy their pet dog, Johnny, whom Leonia had discovered years earlier in Kharkiv. Johnny had apparently been terrorizing the Westmount neighbors. "You are worse than jackals—curse Westmount, curse the police— the thug who dragged him away from me," wrote Leonia.[25] Zbigniew wrote, "The thrice damned police killed our Johnny. Our revenge will be terrible."[26]

• • •

On June 22, 1941, Zbigniew recorded matter-of-factly that "Russia was attacked by Germany, Finland, Hungary, and Romania." The Molotov-Ribbentrop Pact had ceased to exist. Operation Barbarossa—Hitler's reckless bid to subjugate and enslave most of the rest of the Slavic world with a *Blitzkrieg* on Moscow— had begun. Though the young Brzezinski did not yet know it, the war dynamic in Europe had shifted. Much to its distaste, the Polish government in exile found itself in the unnatural position of being formally allied to the Soviet Union. As an ally of the British and its guest in London, the exiled government had no choice but to follow Churchill's lead. On December 7, 1941, Zbigniew wrote with equal matter-of-factness, "Japan attacked the United States today." More than three thousand miles away, on hearing news of Japan's raid on Pearl Harbor, Churchill slept "the sleep of the saved" in the knowledge that the mighty United States would now be joining the war.[27] Four days after what Roosevelt called Japan's "dastardly act," Germany and Italy declared war on the United States.

A week after that, Zbigniew picked up a clutch of academic prizes at the school's Christmas awards. This time Adam was recognized, too. The accolades passed unremarked in Zbigniew's diaries, which were replete with accounts of naval encounters in the Pacific. Leonia, in contrast, had given up commenting on the world outside. Pearl Harbor went unnoticed. "Music began to play as the boys walked in a row—Adaś looked lovely, smiling and well groomed, Zbys had a serious air about him. 'Adam B 1st prize. Zbys B 1st prize'—both of them were called twice. I was very moved. Tears rolled down my face."[28] Though between them, they had swept the prizes, Zbigniew tersely noted that it had been a wonderful day. "I forgot to add that [Edward] Rydz-Śmigly [a Polish general] left Romania alongside a few officers."

Though temporarily excelling at school, Adam's physical woes had not abated. "Adaś has a waddling gait after all. My God, will he ever get to walk normally in his lifetime?"[29] Leonia wondered. He became moody and hypersensitive, always conscious of the eyes of others. Zbigniew, meanwhile, was now a mainstay in the school's soccer team. In the school yearbook's group portrait, Zbigniew stands in the center, hands defiantly on hips, with swept-back blond locks. Alone among the boys, he is wearing a white blazer amid the blue jackets of the rest. The eye is drawn to his hawklike nose and piercing gaze. There is a hauteur about him. In the yearbook, he authored seven essays, four more than any other student. One was a biographical sketch of Józef Piłsudski, the late founder of Poland's now-defunct Second Republic. There was a pen portrait of Bishop Lawrence Patrick Whelan, who had recently been installed as the auxiliary bishop of the Catholic diocese in Montreal; an essay on a visit to a fountain pen–making factory; a report entitled "Gentlemen in Battle Dress" about Canadian military deployments overseas; another exhorting Newman parents to invest in Victory Bonds, which would help speed the Allies to victory; a piece entitled "Polish Army Training in Canada"; and an update on "The Foreign Situation." In the last, he noted, "On December 7 1941, Japan attacked treacherously the United States and Great Britain [sic]. As to the Russian front, Hitler's objective to take Moscow before the coming of winter has not been achieved. . . . Whatever may happen, we remain patient and confident that the Germans will be defeated." A clue to his prolific output is there on its opening page; he appears as editor of the yearbook. "Last year did not bring us victory, but the new one will certainly bring us nearer to it," said the publication's unsigned editorial. Zbigniew's only personal disclosure amid his reams of bylined pieces was to mention his nineteen-year-old half brother, who had anglicized his name to George; he had arrived in Scotland and would soon be seeing combat. "I am very proud and at the same time jealous," he wrote of Jurek's recent deployment.[30]

Without having to move an inch, Zbigniew was getting a front-row seat on world events. In addition to the top brass and political leaders, the Brzezinskis hosted a stream of other notables for whom Montreal was often the first North American stop. Among them was Jan Karski, a stalwart of the Polish Underground who had been smuggled out of Poland in part to alert the allies to the Jewish Holocaust. As the home of Europe's largest Jewish population, Poland was the country with the most prolific Nazi killing machines, with death camps in Auschwitz-Birkenau, Treblinka, Chelmno, Belzec, Sobibór, and Majdanek. In July 1943, Karski told President Franklin D. Roosevelt about the vast crime unfolding. The president suggested that Karski repeat his story to Felix Frankfurter, a Supreme Court justice and only the second Jew in US history to serve on the country's highest court. Frankfurter refused to believe what Karski told him. "I didn't say I didn't believe him," Frankfurter told the accompanying Polish ambassador, Jan Ciechanowski, who, unusually for such a position, was Jewish and who could not suppress his indignation at Frankfurter's skepticism. "I said I *cannot* believe him."[31] Along with the US and British media, which had also been briefed, Washington seemed unable to comprehend the enormity of what Karski had laid out: the industrially processed industrial-grade murder of an entire population.

The Brzezinskis heard Karski's story before Washington did. En route to DC, Karski stopped in Montreal, where he spent his first night on North American soil. He had been flown to Canada by the Royal Air Force. On his first night, Karski dined at the Brzezinski residence. Zbigniew thus heard Karski's story before Roosevelt did. Decades later, Brzezinski said that his father had prompted the revelation by pressing Karski about the condition of Poland's Jews. "And [Karski] simply said, 'They are all being killed.' . . . 'What do you mean they're all being killed?' [Karski replied,] 'I've just said it. They're all being killed.' And my father said, 'You mean children? And women? And old people?' . . . [Karski firmly answered,] 'I've told you. They're all being killed.'"[32] At fifteen, Zbigniew could not be expected to process the scale of what he had just heard. Later, in Washington, he and Karski would become close friends. In a 2012 afterword to a posthumous book of Karski's writings on the Holocaust, Brzezinski wrote, "Someone had to pierce that veil of human incapacity to internalize a horror without limits. It's almost as much of a challenge to understand on an irrational level the notion of eternity. What does it really mean? No beginning? No end? Well, what does a crime without limits really mean? This is what Karski put before humanity."[33] It is hard to imagine that there were many people in North America—let alone adolescents—better briefed on the war than Zbigniew.

Through the Brzezinskis' eyes, the final two years of the war were a maelstrom of cognitive and emotional dissonance. The news from the front lines was both spectacularly good and awfully foreboding. The better the Allies did in Europe, the worse the situation became for Poland—including its government in exile. In 1943, the advancing Germans announced they had stumbled on a series of mass graves of Polish officers in the forest of Katyn near Smolensk. The estimated toll was twelve thousand. Subsequent investigations uncovered thousands more, putting the total murdered at around twenty-two thousand—shot in the back of the head and dumped into pits holding 250 corpses each. The Germans accused the Soviets of carrying out the murders before the Red Army had been driven out of Poland. Goebbels told Hitler that they could "dine out" on the propaganda for at least two weeks. Confident of their case, the Germans invited the International Red Cross to investigate the site. The London Poles echoed that demand. Stalin severed relations with the Polish government in exile and started to establish an alternative puppet government of Polish Bolsheviks, the Polish Committee of National Liberation, popularly known as the Lublin Committee. Fearful of alienating Stalin, whose help they desperately needed, Churchill and Roosevelt kept silent. The fifteen-year-old Zbigniew had no doubt that the Soviets had carried out the Katyn Massacre. Establishing Soviet guilt became one of his lifelong causes.

The identities of the Polish dead painted a stark picture. In a 1940 directive, Lavrentiy P. Beria, the head of the NKVD, the Soviet secret police, listed the victims as "the 14,700 former Polish officers, officials, landowners, police, intelligence agents, gendarmes, [military] settlers, and prison officers," as well as "the 11,000 members of various [counter-revolutionary] espionage and sabotage organisations, former landowners, manufacturers, Polish officers, officials and refugees."[34] The goal was to wipe out Poland's ruling classes. The death list included those who had fought with Piłsudski to defeat the Red Army in 1920—people whom Tadeusz knew and with whom he had fought. The Katyn Massacre was a window on Stalin's designs on Poland. To anyone paying attention, the Soviets had no intention of honoring their pledge to restore Poland's independence. They were hunting down and wiping out Poles with qualifications to govern.

At the conference of the Big Three in Tehran later in 1943, Roosevelt and Churchill half-heartedly pressed Stalin to commit to Poland's prewar borders. Stalin held firm on the so-called Curzon Line, which would mean returning much of Polish territory to the Soviet Union. He also fobbed them off with nebulous promises on Poland's right to self-determination. Few in the Polish diaspora, including the Brzezinskis, were fooled by his pledges. London and Washington's overriding priority was to defeat Germany, which meant keeping Stalin happy. That trade-off was bad news for Poland. As Churchill said after Hitler had turned on the Soviets in 1942, "If Hitler invaded Hell I would make at least a favourable reference to the Devil in the House of Commons." In practice, he and FDR were giving the Devil a lot more than compliments. Stalin would emerge from World War II with almost all the Polish territory that Russia had failed to capture in 1920. In Tehran, he also secured Churchill and Roosevelt's acquiescence to incorporate Lithuania, Latvia, and Estonia into the USSR. In the Brzezinskis' eyes, Poland's supposed benefactors were abandoning both her and her smaller neighbors to a merciless fate.

To Zbigniew, such concessions to Stalin could only stem from British and American ignorance rather than perfidy. A few weeks after the Tehran Conference, he mailed a prewar map of Poland to Winston Churchill. Number 10 Downing Street sent a polite acknowledgment of Zbigniew's letter assuring him that Britain's prime minister was grateful for the map.[35] But Poland's bad auguries were unmistakable. Such was Tadeusz's alarm that he started to test the boundaries of diplomatic protocol. "No matter what commitments Mr. Churchill has accepted at Tehran," he told the *Montreal Gazette*, "it appears extremely unfair to Poles that they should pay the price for any security or economic policy which in the end will only benefit one ally of the United Nations and which is detrimental to Poland."[36] Tadeusz's foreboding was well founded. Russia would take almost seventy thousand square miles of prewar Poland (roughly 42 percent of its Second Republic territory) from east of the infamous Curzon Line. Perhaps the only consolation was that Poland kept Gdańsk. Though Poland was partially compensated with the addition of former German territories on its side of the Oder-Neisse Line, the Poland that emerged from the war was almost a quarter smaller than before.

To add to Polish despair, General Sikorski, the face of independent Poland, was killed in a plane crash near Gibraltar in May 1943. "Terrible news!!" wrote Zbigniew. "His daughter Zofia, chief of staff General [Tadeusz] Klimecki, and a few other high-ranking officers all died with him. . . . General Sikorski was one of the greatest, if not the greatest, Polish living men."[37] Suspicions arose among Poles, and still linger, about the circumstances of Sikorski's death; his demise was convenient for the Soviets. At the time, Kim Philby, who was later exposed as a Soviet double agent, was the head of British intelligence for the Iberian Peninsula, which included Gibraltar. To Poles, the news was increasingly dark. The so-called Anders' Army, which took the name of its storied general Władysław Anders, suffered heavy losses at the Battle of Monte Cassino in May 1944 as the Allies advanced with painful slowness up the Italian peninsula. The morale of Polish troops had already taken a hit after the Big Three's conference in Tehran three months earlier, which confirmed their worst fears about Stalin's plans for Poland. After some prevarication caused by disaffection in his ranks, Anders agreed to keep his troops in the field. At the Big Three's Yalta Conference the following year, it became obvious that there was not much Churchill or Roosevelt could do to hold Stalin to his empty pledges. By then Poland was almost fully under Soviet control. Yalta would become a curse word in Brzezinski's vocabulary. "[Polish friends] are in low spirits and seem to think we have lost everything, down to our pride and honor," wrote Leonia in late 1944. "They are scared of the Bolsheviks—pitiable little people!"[38] Much later in life, Brzezinski wrote that Stalin's pledge to hold free and fair elections in Poland was a "transparent fig leaf for Soviet domination."[39] Stalin wagered that the British would be unable—and the Americans unwilling—to hold him to his word.

Leonia's firstborn, George, had already more than done his part. Having spent a year doing officer training in Scotland, where he had become his tank regiment's in-house cartoonist, George crossed the English Channel with his Polish mechanized division shortly after D-Day, June 6, 1944. A few days later, he was found unconscious facedown in the Normandy mud with a scar on his head and a missing clump of hair. He recovered quickly. Three months later, his entire unit was wiped out in a brutal engagement at Belgium's Leopold Canal. George was the only survivor. As the Germans were finishing off the wounded, he managed to make it across the waterway to safety. He was awarded Poland's Cross of Valor for bravery. He spent the next four months in casts at Wolverhampton's New Cross Hospital with broken bones and a bullet wound through the arch of his left foot. Given that George's stepfather was Poland's consul general, his story made it into the Canadian newspapers. "The poor boy went through so much, he was so brave," wrote Leonia. "He also sent me the most wonderful of presents—the Cross of Valor encased in a little box—I cried my eyes out and placed it in front of Our Lady, above our bed."[40] The following May, George came home. A cheering crowd met him and his comrades at the Montreal station. "Jurek returned to the bosom of his family," wrote Zbigniew. "The band was playing. Everyone was waiting with bated breath, and finally the soldiers entered with Jurek in the front."[41]

Though he was limping, with pus oozing out of his gaping foot, George's joyous homecoming gave Leonia respite from her Polish circle's mounting gloom about the war. The crushing failure of the 1944 Warsaw Uprising and Stalin's calculated indifference to the Polish Underground's fate offered further proof of Polish impotence. Moscow radio had exhorted the Polish resistance to rise up against the Nazis. The Soviet army had then stopped its advance and watched the Germans crush the resistance and destroy what remained of the city. Starting with the Warsaw royal castle, monuments and other significant buildings in Poland's capital had been dynamited by a Nazi unit whose sole purpose was to erase Polish culture. "There is no more Warsaw, only smoldering ruins," wrote Leonia. "Never again will I get to see my beloved city as I remember it."[42] Of Warsaw's prewar population of 1.2 million, only 400,000 remained. Many of the dead had been Zbigniew's fellow Boy Scouts in prewar Warsaw. Along with Brzezinski's cousin Andrzej Roman, they joined the partisans in the forests outside Warsaw. Andrzej survived the war, though he had bullet holes in his greatcoat. No other nation was treated as brutally by the Germans. As Churchill quipped, "Monday [Hitler] shoots Dutchmen,

Tuesday Norwegians, Wednesday French and Belgians stand against the wall, Thursday it is the Czechs who must suffer. . . . But always, all of the days, there are the Poles."

The more Poland fell into Stalin's lap, the more tenuous Tadeusz's prospects became. It was only a matter of time before a new Polish government would put him out of a job. Owing to the family's straitened circumstances, Zbigniew and Adam had to change school twice. The Brzezinskis could no longer afford Newman House's steep fees. Zbigniew's next two schools, Loyola High School and Académie Saint-Léon, both in Montreal, were also private. With the help of Church subsidies, they were more affordable. The change in environment made little difference to Zbigniew's performance. In his first year at Loyola, he came first in school with an exam score of 89 percent. He also earned five prizes—for Latin, English, history, algebra, and geometry. He then switched to Saint-Léon, from which he graduated as a "salutatorian" in 1945. He wore a tuxedo for the ceremony. He had already started classes at Montreal's McGill University, Canada's oldest and, by most accounts finest, university. At seventeen, he was on track to becoming a scholar. In his first year at McGill, his subjects were history, economics, politics, French, and German. "It is a great change in my life," he noted matter-of-factly. On his own initiative, he had started to learn Russian a year earlier. Tutored by an émigré Russian Tadeusz had found, he began his immersion by reading Pushkin's classic *The Captain's Daughter* in the original Russian.[43] Within a couple of years, he was leafing through back issues of *Pravda* and *Izvestia*, the leading Soviet newspapers. His mastery of Russian would prove indispensable to his academic rise. A knack for languages was one of his many intellectual strong points. Difficulty with introspection in any tongue would be a recurring deficiency.

Zbigniew's youthful pursuit of the opposite sex was indefatigable. At high school during the war, he gave his female targets secret code names such as "Estonia" and "Madagascar." His first recorded effort was with a "pretty girl" he met on New Year's Eve 1943 whom he wanted to take to the movies but changed his mind. More important, Berlin was repeatedly and heavily bombed and the Soviets claimed to be liberating Ukraine. His attention was still monopolized by the war. His first noted kiss was in June 1944 with a "Belgian girl I fancied . . . just to try it out!" He did not mention anything more, including her name. In the same entry he wrote, "Germany is under a very heavy bombardment, e.g., during only one raid the RAF dropped 5,040 tons of bombs." The same Belgian young lady featured again a few days later:

"I've already kissed her several times and she did not resist, quite the contrary! I have an impression, however, that I will get bored with her soon."[44] Shortly after Aachen and Strasbourg fell to the Allies, Zbigniew "scored" with another young woman, again unnamed. Generally it was hit and miss. Sometimes there was "necking," occasionally "heavy necking" and "caresses." At others, there was dancing "cheek to cheek" at one of Montreal's nightclubs, for which he was developing a taste. Sometimes his overtures fell flat. In a rare passage of self-reflection, he wrote, "Oh well, someday I will meet the right one, and I will know that is 'it.' At the moment, although I am lonely at times, I am managing O.K. and do not miss 'female companionship' much. The trouble with me is that very often, when I meet a nice girl, I put on a show of aloofness, conceit, and pride and that scares them away. That's what is meant by not having the right personality. . . . I can always think of some that like me, and would be happy if I went out with them. Unfortunately, they are usually not the ones I like."[45]

If the Yalta Conference had competition in Polish minds as the chief venue of Allied perfidy, it would be the Tehran Conference in 1943 or the Potsdam Conference in July 1945. The last took place two months after Germany's unconditional surrender. History records it as the first and last postwar meeting of the Allies that included the USSR. It was also the moment when Harry S. Truman, the new US president, told Stalin that the United States possessed an atom bomb. The main Allied powers, the US, the USSR, and Britain, agreed to divide Germany into four administrative zones, with France controlling the fourth. A few days after Potsdam, America dropped the "Little Boy" atom bomb on Hiroshima. Three days after that, "Fat Man" obliterated Nagasaki. "This is the way in which the Second World War ended," Zbigniew observed drily.[46] It was also at Potsdam that the victorious powers bowed to Stalin's facts on the ground and recognized the new Communist-led government of Poland. Canada followed suit, thus putting Tadeusz out of a job. That the Brzezinskis knew it was coming did not blunt their feelings of betrayal. Zbigniew called it a government of "Soviet agents and traitors." Amid the "paroxysms of joy" that Canadians expressed on Victory in Europe day a few weeks earlier, he had been overwhelmed "essentially by sadness—I knew that Poland was once again occupied." That was not how many Canadians felt—nor the Americans or the British. In one typical newspaper article, the Toronto Star reported that the Poles of Montreal had celebrated the anniversary of Poland's

"committee of liberation," the Moscow-assembled Lublin-based government
that had swept into Poland along with the Red Army. A response signed by
the Polish Club of McGill (of which Zbigniew was a member) took exception
to the article, which it said was "not only untrue but insulting" to Canada's
Poles. The letter, almost certainly composed by Zbigniew, went on, "Everyone knows that the committee of 'Liberation' originated in Moscow and was
composed of Communist agents. The fact that it was recognized by Britain
and the USA doesn't mean the Poles in Poland and abroad consider it as their
lawfully chosen government. This recognition, granted over the objections
of the Polish nation, constituted and still constitutes a flagrant violation of
international morality."[47]

Canada's declining sense of hospitality towards the exiled Poles was exacerbated by Tadeusz's refusal to vacate the Polish Consulate at 1410 Stanley
Street. After years of being on Montreal's A-list, he was having to get used
to the cold shoulder. Though his official function as a consul had ended, he
worked for another two years on the British-Polish Interim Treasury Committee, which London had created to wind down its wartime business with
Poland's now-moribund government in exile. When that work ended, Tadeusz's future in Canada came into question. He was unemployed. "The Canadian government does not now recognize the existence of the former Polish
government in London which you, at one time, represented in this country,"
Canada's foreign minister, Louis St. Laurent, wrote to Tadeusz in a letter that
triggered considerable angst. "[Your temporary new visa] will be subject to
reconsideration and renewal from year to year. During your stay in this country we would be grateful if you could refrain from any activities of a political
nature."[48] The tone of the letter came as a nasty shock to Tadeusz. As late as
1947, there were still lingering traces of the fraternal gratitude that Canadians
had poured out for the Soviets two years earlier.

As the reality of the Cold War began to sink in, however, Tadeusz found
that his legal status in Canada was more secure than he had feared. The Brzezinskis became Canadian citizens in 1951. Until then, they were halfway stateless. That did not inhibit Zbigniew from conducting the "activities of a [highly
conspicuous] political nature" (that Canada's foreign minister had warned his
father against) during his remaining five years in the country. At one point,
Zbigniew and a group of anti-Communist McGill friends overwrote the sign-
board outside the Polish Consulate, where Tadeusz had worked for almost a
decade. They scrawled: "Traitors to Poland. Future address Siberia."[49] On a

tip-off from Zbigniew, their graffiti was pictured in the local newspapers the next day. While excelling as a student, Zbigniew acquired a taste for political agitation and more lighthearted pranks. A noted victim of his exuberance was Hewlett Johnson, nicknamed "the Red Dean of Canterbury," a senior prelate in Britain's Anglican hierarchy, who was a world-famous apologist for Stalin. Later Hewlett was awarded the Stalin Peace Prize, Moscow's answer to the Nobel. Hewlett was also a regular guest of Poland's new government in Warsaw. Hewlett's speech to McGill students had to be called off shortly after it began. He was drowned out in jeering and catcalls. A future generation would call it "deplatforming." Zbigniew, who was foremost among the saboteurs, saw it as a necessary riposte to the equally noisy but far larger crowd of Soviet apologists on McGill's campus.[50]

Brzezinski made no effort to hide his disdain for the often privileged students who toed Moscow's line. As a professor at Columbia during New York's turbulent late 1960s, he would depict such firebrands as "spoiled children from the suburbs masquerading as actual revolutionaries."[51] From his early days at McGill, he felt most of the Communist students knew nothing about conditions behind the Iron Curtain and were soft-headed fodder for Russian propaganda. People such as Hewlett had gravitated towards Moscow in the 1930s as the only credible bulwark against the rise of European fascism. That was understandable given the situation at the time, when the democracies were weak and lacking conviction. Long after that context had faded, however, Moscow's apologists still clung on to a stubbornly romantic—and inexcusably mistaken—view of the USSR, he thought. In that respect, Brzezinski was of the same mind as George Orwell, whose early–Cold War novels, *Animal Farm* and *1984*, were dismissed by the Left as capitalist propaganda. Though Brzezinski admired Orwell, his bias was towards nonfiction.

His main political outlet at McGill was the student Progressive Conservative Party, also known as the Tory Club. McGill held regular "mock Parliaments," which staged debates and question times based on the Westminster parliamentary style. Brzezinski relished the thrust and parry. During one session at which he harangued the large Communist bloc, they periodically yelled "Nazi!" at him.[52] At another, he played the role of an opposition leader. The topic was the creation of the Atlantic Pact, as the recently created North Atlantic Treaty Organization (NATO) was commonly known. Brzezinski related in his diary that he "spoke, joked, shouted, interrupted etc. . . . then I asked the prime minister how he intends to fit his bill into provision 15 of the

Atlantic Pact. Following his answer, I pointed out to him that the Pact has only 14 articles. It was quite hilarious."[53] The Tories were heavily outnumbered on campus. Brzezinski joined what he saw as Communist-front student organizations to make life difficult for them. One such group was the Student Labour Club, whose executive he ousted in what they complained to the media was a "coup." Brzezinski turned up with a group of friends. They registered as members, then held an instant vote to elect a new committee. Their hostile takeover succeeded only because all but one of the club's executive committee members were in Yugoslavia helping to build a railway—a group that called itself the Beaver Brigade. Brzezinski's frequent accomplice was Andrew Bortnowski, a son of a former Polish general.

The controversy flared up again decades later when the *Montreal Gazette* published a vituperative attack on Brzezinski's role as Jimmy Carter's national security advisor, calling Brzezinski the "Darth Vader of U.S. politics."[54] His saturnine approach to politics had apparently been acquired at McGill. The piece included lengthy quotes by George Neuspiel, who had led the Beaver Brigade's Yugoslav trip and was the leader of the McGill Student Labour Club. "I always felt that the coup—any coup—the manipulation, the getting at the levers of power, was [Brzezinski's] understanding of what politics was all about," Neuspiel recalled. Brzezinski had also ousted the leadership of the Tory Club in another coup, he said. "Out of a relaxed, gentlemanly debating club, Zbig made a militant almost colored-shirt organization," said Neuspiel, who had gone on to become a "tweedy" professor in Ottawa.[55] Since the piece did not quote Brzezinski or any of his friends, it reads like a hit job. A few days later, the *Gazette* published a letter from Stanley Grossman, a former McGill student who strongly disputed the article's "anti-Brzezinski bias."[56] Grossman, who described his student politics as neither Tory nor Communist and who also sat on the Student Labour Committee, pointed out that Neuspiel and his friends were militants who had "only presented the views of the extreme left in labor matters, never permitting the viewpoints of experts with differing opinions." He added that the insinuation that Brzezinski was a fascist—Neuspiel's "colored-shirt" reference—was "utter nonsense, based on fantasy." That last observation was indisputable. Brzezinski not only despised fascism; he saw the "Red menace" as fascism's totalitarian sibling, a theme he would develop at Harvard. As for Neuspiel's other claims, Brzezinski was borrowing some of the Left's tactics against it, which were not very democratic and often puerile. He loved political theater. Which side's behavior was worse? That is hard to say. Brzezinski thought that his cause was righteous and that his opponents were privileged fools. They saw him as a reactionary troublemaker.

Zbigniew's escapades did not trouble his parents at all. "Zbys is a brilliant student, he's passing his exams with flying colors (he's ranked 1st in politics)," wrote Leonia. "He's very eager and spirited, he wages war on the Communists, organizes meetings and gives speeches."[57] The same could not be said of her two older children. Her youngest, Lech, was thriving in school and already showing the aptitude for science and engineering that would later become the basis of his successful vocation. The other two, George and Adam, were hopping from study to study and from job to job without any clear aim. Adam had become Leonia's part-time assistant at her Lady Beauty Products company, making face creams and a range of other products. His lack of a college degree and his lacking a spark for further education, however, were a source of concern. He could not hold down a paying job for long. "He's been very difficult to deal with, flying into a rage at the slightest remark; at times I am overcome with despair, at others pity, and end up forgiving him," Leonia wrote.[58] Zbigniew's closest sibling was grasping for something, she said, but he did not seem to know what it was.

Much the same applied to Zbigniew's older half brother. After being discharged from the army, George put his artistic talent to use by getting piece-rate jobs to decorate nightclubs and offices. He completed his studies in political science and commercial art in a Montreal night school. He, too, shifted from one short-term job to another. There were hints of posttraumatic stress disorder in his restlessness. He seemed to give up too easily. Even Zbigniew, who had hero-worshipped George when he was a soldier, found that frustrating. "Man should not be soft like butter," he wrote. "You can count on Jurek like rain in the Sahara."[59] A mutual female friend, Rhona, told Zbigniew that George was a "sweet fool."[60] About Zbigniew she said, "I am supposed to be inconsiderate of others, edgy, tense, but there is a great future in front of me." George eventually nailed down a vocation: he set up on his own as an independent commercial artist, chiefly as a creator of large murals for hotels, restaurants, and clubs. But he suffered from lifelong bipolar disorder and depression.

Leonia's biggest concern—and increasingly Zbigniew's, too—was Tadeusz's post-diplomatic future. His career decline had been vertiginous. That change in fortune engendered some bitterness in Leonia. Her husband had gone from being one of Montreal's wartime notables and a trusted confidant of successive leaders of Poland's government in exile to a string of stillborn careers, including advising a Quebecois financial institution on immigrant policy—a big trend in postwar Canada, which was seeing a surge in Polish arrivals; a period as a researcher of Eastern European history at the Quebec public library; pro bono work for the Canadian Polish Congress, which became his abiding passion and of which he later became president; and spells of being an insurance salesman, mostly over the telephone. A Habsburg gentleman at heart, Tadeusz never complained. His wife, who felt downwardly mobile, had no such compunction. "Tadús is working in the insurance industry. I feel horribly sorry for him; he deserves better, but the man never knew how to self-advertise. He's always been too gentle and couldn't elbow his way through the world." In Brzezinski family lore, Tadeusz's declining fortunes were mirrored by their periodic changes of residence. In 1950, the Brzezinskis had to vacate their beloved residence on Saint Sulpice Road and move to 421 Metcalfe Avenue, which was less expensive. Their new home was at a lower point on the Westmount elevation. They continued to lose residential altitude in the following years.[61]

But their direction was not all downhill. Indeed, their economizing in Montreal helped fund the consolation prize of their dreams. Their reward was a plot of land in the Laurentian Mountains, less than fifty miles northwest of Montreal, which they bought in 1945. They named it the Red and White Farm after the colors of the Polish flag. Their piece of land in Saint Morin allowed Tadeusz to become what one relative called a "gentleman farmer."[62] The house was situated on a three-acre plot with a small river running through it. Being close to the ski town of Saint Sauveur, it was also a draw for their sons in winter and a wooded retreat from Montreal in summer. Zbigniew went there often. The Brzezinskis kept pigs, a cow named Basia, chickens, and eventually horses. There was a smaller house on the property that they rented to tenants, the Roszkowskis, whom Leonia described as "amiable and polite Polish Jews."[63] They hired a former Polish soldier, Antoni Cichocki, to manage the farm full-time. It was the closest Tadeusz and Leonia could get to the Carpathian landscape of their past. The forests around their farm had an abundance of *rydze*, a reddish brown mushroom that features prominently in Polish cuisine. "It fulfilled our psychological need for having our own piece of land and reminded us of the Polish countryside," Tadeusz wrote years later.[64] It became an obligatory stop on the Polish-Canadian map. The Brzezinskis persuaded the diocese of Saint Sauveur, a few miles away, to set aside a portion of its cemetery for Poles. The graveyard turned into a posthumous hive of Polish émigrés, the final resting place of ministers from the government in exile, generals, and former diplomats.

The Red and White Farm was also a useful prop in Zbigniew's quest for romance. Towards the end of his time at McGill, he met a woman with whom the feelings were mutual. In a list of "women in my life"—a roster that started, a little surprisingly, in 1938—he listed twenty-two girls. Almost all of them were Anglo. Among them were Sally Pitfield, Cynthia Plant, and Brenda Turner. The only one for whom love was professed—repeatedly—was Ann Pitt, whom he met in late 1949. Though he did not know it, he was halfway through his final year in Canada. As a graduate, he had been assigned to teach politics and constitutionalism to a "conference group" of about fifty McGill undergraduates. The female participants had a better attendance rate than the males, which pleased Brzezinski. "Generally, the girls are more intelligent and manifest a greater interest in the course than the men," he wrote. Among them was Ann. "She's not only pretty but has brains too."[65] Their first encounter was at the annual Scottish Saint Andrew's Ball at Montreal's Windsor Hotel. Ann was one of the debutantes who caught his eye, though he had already noticed her sitting at the front of his class.

Ann blew hot and cold with Zbigniew. She would ignore him for days. Then they would go out for several consecutive nights to some club or other, often the Normandie Roof. They would "kiss awesomely." He broke his personal telephone record by talking to her for two and a half hours one night (mostly about Britain's general election, which Clement Attlee's Labour Party had just won narrowly). He would send Ann flowers, often red roses. They sometimes exchanged letters in the middle of the day. "Something beautiful" happened on the mountain one day when they were out walking, though he did not spell it out. He spoke to Ann about marriage, but they agreed that there might be "religious problems" since she was not a Roman Catholic. "Still I love her and she loves me and that is all that matters."[66] Unfortunately she had a rival suitor, a man named Barry, whose implied proposal she was weighing. The rivalry messed with Zbigniew's head. He referred to it as the "damn triangle." At some point, Ann evidently tired of Zbigniew's entreaties. He did not seem to register the change in her. She even wrote him a four-page letter saying that they should retain their "friendship for friendship's sake." Zbigniew read the opposite message to what Ann evidently intended. He told his diary that her letter was a roundabout declaration of love. They continued to meet at his urging. He told himself that she was still "playing games." Then one afternoon he walked into a café and saw Ann at another table. She pretended not to see him. From that point, his ardor began to cool. They still met for occasional lunches and afternoon strolls, and she kissed him good luck before his MA oral exam. But the passion was gone. "I think I am going to ignore her for a while," he declared. At a lunch several weeks after the breakup, they joked and laughed as they had so often done. "The atmosphere went a little sour when I started hitting on her, but it was OK in the end. It may be our last meeting until the beginning of the new academic year."[67] A few weeks later, Harvard offered him a place, which meant that it was indeed their last meeting. Zbigniew's first serious romance was over.

His path to Harvard was almost a straight one. But there were a couple of near derailments. Given the Brzezinski family's waning hopes of ever returning to Poland, where the situation was going from bad to worse, Zbigniew thought about seeking a career in Canada. He had a fleeting ambition to join Canada's Foreign Service. "I will be able to do more for Poland being Canadian, rather than Polish," he reasoned.[68] In 1949, McGill offered him a fellowship to study at Oxford University for a year. The British altered Brzezinski's life course by denying him a visa. Only Commonwealth citizens were eligible for the UK scholarship, and Zbigniew had not yet applied for a Canadian passport. Had he gone to Oxford, he might have become a distinguished Sovietologist, as well as promising material for All Soul's. Or he might have returned after his studies and risen up Canada's diplomatic ladder to become its first "ethnic" foreign minister, as he mused later in life.[69] But that option was now closed. His academic prowess at McGill was highly valued. Because the war had interrupted the studies of so many young Canadians, a large share of his cohort were in their late twenties or early thirties. Many had seen combat overseas in the Royal Canadian Air Force. The adolescent Brzezinski nevertheless outshone almost all of his peers. At nineteen, he ranked second in his class of 250 students in political science.[70]

Poland still accounted for a big share of Brzezinski's thoughts. But he felt increasingly frustrated at his inability to do anything to alter its bleak trajectory. Stalin had promised Churchill and Roosevelt at Yalta that he would permit "free and unfettered elections" in Poland. After seeing the poor election showing of Hungary's Communists in 1945, Moscow learned its lesson. The Polish elections of 1947 would be rigged. All those who had derived their power base from wartime resistance or exile in London had long since been jailed or shot, or had fled. A few weeks before the July 1945 Potsdam Conference, Beria's NKVD arrested sixteen members of the Polish Underground leadership and spirited them to Moscow. There they were put on trial for "collaboration with the Nazis," "planning a military alliance with Nazi Germany," and other fantastically contrived charges. These were the men who had led the doomed Warsaw Uprising against the Nazis while the Red Army drummed its fingers on the other side of the river. Twelve of them were sentenced to jail. Several did not make it out of prison alive. London and Washington chose to ignore the courtroom charade, an abdication that the leading scholar of Polish history, Norman Davis, would later describe as "obscene."[71] Zbigniew wrote, "[The Russians] will pay for this one day. Scoundrels!!"

The outcome of Poland's 1947 election was preordained: the Communist Democratic Bloc won 80 percent of the vote. With variations, the same had happened across Eastern Europe. In 1948, the last domino toppled when Czechoslovakia, the only remaining democratic holdout, fell to a Communist takeover. Moscow set the coup into motion after Czechoslovakia became the only Eastern European nation to accept America's offer of postwar reconstruction aid: the Marshall Plan, named after Secretary of State George C. Marshall, Jr. Though the USSR and its satellites had been eligible for the aid, Stalin sensed a trap and forbade their participation. Taking US money would involve opening up Moscow's books and ceding an implicit degree of sovereignty, as well as damaging Soviet pride. The Czechs ignored Stalin's memo. Stalin's ruthlessness was underlined by the fatal defenestration of Jan Masaryk, the ousted Czech foreign minister—though the Communists insisted that it was suicide. Either way, Masaryk's death was a shock. He was the son of Tomáš Masaryk, the first president of the Republic of Czechoslovakia and a friend of President Woodrow Wilson. Three months later, Edvard Beneš, the republic's long-standing leader who had led the wartime Czech government in exile in London and had returned to lead the country in 1945, died peacefully in bed at his family home in Bohemia. He had also been Czechoslovak leader in 1938 when his country was betrayed in Munich. With the passing of Beneš, any lingering hope of a Europe whole and free was gone. In an apt quirk of fate, the Beneš and Brzezinski families would later become entwined.

Though he remained obsessed with events in Poland, it was no longer the sum total of Brzezinski's worldview. The late 1940s was when he laid out the predicates for his future vocation as an Ivy League Sovietologist. His McGill

master's thesis, an eighty-thousand-word essay entitled "Russo-Soviet Nationalism," contained in embryo several of the books that he would write in
the 1950s and 1960s and was his first articulation of the worldview that he
took into government decades later. His thesis leaned heavily on the *Current
Digest of the Soviet Press*, a weekly bulletin that was as rich in information as
it was thick.[72] It was indispensable to any scholar in the rapidly growing field
of Soviet-area studies. He also put his new facility with Russian to good use,
immersing himself in the foundational tomes of the Soviet-Marxist creed, especially the writings of Lenin, Trotsky, and Stalin. At no point had he or his
family doubted that he would become a scholar of the Soviet Union. His career had chosen him in early adolescence.

The culmination was Brzezinski's audacious master's thesis, which laid
out a road map for defeating the Soviet Union. The gist of his argument was
that Soviet ideology should not be mistaken for internationalism; it was a new
variant of Russian chauvinism posing as champion of the world's proletariat.
After the Bolshevik Revolution of 1917, which Brzezinski would later argue
had been a coup, Lenin and Stalin had to grapple with the "problem of nationalities." As Marxists, they saw themselves as enemies of nationalism, including its Russian form. Just as the state would wither away after communism
triumphed worldwide, so, too, would primitive national loyalties. The Bolsheviks' problem was that they had inherited most of the czarist imperial map.
Russians accounted for just over half the population of the newly born Soviet
Union. Among the others were Ukrainians, Georgians, Azeris, Armenians,
Baltic peoples, and central Asians, notably the Kazakhs, Kyrgyz, Turkmans,
Uzbeks, and Tajiks.

Lenin's book *What Is to Be Done?* wrestled with how to achieve a socialist revolution. Brzezinski's view was that neither Lenin nor Stalin ever
resolved how to reconcile socialism with the diverse range of scripts, ethnic-
ities, languages, and religions of the vast Eurasian landmass they had seized.
The early Soviet state gave each nationality formal equality in a federation
of socialist republics. In practice, the USSR's encircled and backwards peas-
ant economy could only industrialize and survive in a hostile world through
the iron will of Russian central party control. That meant inculcating blind
obedience to the new Leviathan in Moscow while pretending that there
was equality among the nationalities. That Stalin was from Georgia—his
birth name was Besarion Jughashvili—proved helpful to the facade. The
establishment of cult of personality, first of Lenin, then more with the

omnipresence of Stalin, was how the Soviet peoples would become attached
to an abstract doctrine. Identification with a new kind of czar became necessary. "The Communist Party . . . cannot be photographed kissing small children," Brzezinski wrote.[73] Uncle Joe could. In Beria's words, Stalin was the
"greatest genius of mankind." To Brzezinski's mind, dictator worship made
a brutal kind of sense in a culture where "absolutism had held sway for centuries, where men have been taught to obey and not to think, to prostrate
themselves and not to assert themselves, to bow and not to shake hands."[74]

But Stalin could not easily dispense with the nationalities problem, which
was chiefly about non-Russians, Brzezinski argued. The last Soviet campaign
against the "White Russian chauvinists" had ended in 1930. That was when
Stalin's purges of other national leaderships began in earnest. Unlike the Russians, who suffered no deportations, Ukrainians, central Asians, Georgians,
and others were moved in their millions to other parts of the USSR. Their
leaders vanished into the maw of Siberia's expanding gulag. The more developed a Soviet republic's sense of national identity, the more brutal its uprooting. Russians settled on the vacated lands. Perhaps the worst victims were
Ukrainians. "The Ukrainians have a definite national tradition, customs, culture, literature, and history," he wrote.[75] Between 1926 and 1939, the population of native speakers in Ukraine had fallen from 23 million to 19.6 million.
During his consular spell in Kharkiv, Tadeusz had witnessed much of that
uprooting and passed it on to his oldest son. The Holodomor accounted for
a large chunk of Ukrainian depopulation. Over the same period, the number of Russians in Ukraine, notably in the Donbas, went from 5.8 million to
11.4 million. "It is noteworthy that mass deportations were never deployed
against the Russian population," he observed. "It is likewise noteworthy that
mass deportations were applied specifically against those populations which
have the most developed national consciousness (the Balts, the Ukrainians,
the Poles in the annexed territories, etc.)."[76] Native Russians took most of the
senior positions in each republic, even representing them in Moscow. Less
than a tenth of Kazakhstan's senior managerial positions, for example, were
held by Kazakhs, Brzezinski found. Russo-Soviet imperialism was leaving
European colonialism in the dust.

That was the premise of Brzezinski's thesis. The prognosis followed.
As the Second World War got under way, Stalin dropped the polite fiction
of equality between nationalities. His "Great Patriotic War" was a battle of
Russians against barbarians. He enlisted the symbols of traditional Russia,

including its great literature, unrivaled composers, world-historical czars, and even the recently persecuted Russian Orthodox Church, to the cause. The "peoples of the Soviet Union" made way for the "Soviet people." The USSR became the Motherland. Domestic enemies went from being "counterrevolutionaries" to "cosmopolitan anti-patriots." Trotsky, whose circle was heavily Jewish, was the original cosmopolitan enemy within. He was assassinated on Stalin's orders while in exile in Mexico in 1942. By contrast, Stalin's key henchmen were mostly non-Jewish. All of which, argued Brzezinski, was Stalin's dress rehearsal for how he would treat the Eastern European nations that had fallen under the USSR's sway at the end of the Second World War. Bringing Poland, Romania, Bulgaria, Hungary, Czechoslovakia, Albania, and Yugoslavia into the fold was Lenin's Soviet nationalities problem squared. Stalin had perfected his Russification playbook with the Soviet republics in the 1930s.

Brzezinski's academic debut was striking on three levels. First, it was bold. A twenty-one-year-old scholar was taking up cudgels against much of the prevailing Western scholarly wisdom, which accepted that the Soviets had forged a new national identity: *Homo sovieticus*. Brzezinski dismissed that alleged transformation as propaganda. Second, many of the big events that he addressed were happening in real time. His essay was not a detached evaluation of settled facts; new ones were being rapidly minted. Within the span of Brzezinski's time at McGill, the USSR went from being the West's brother in arms to its overriding existential threat—and a nuclear-armed rival after 1949. Nowhere were Soviet intentions clearer than in Eastern Europe. Third, his analysis offered a blueprint for how the West could win the Cold War. The West's strategy would require repudiation of Russia's claim to having a legitimate "sphere of interest" in Europe.

Brzezinski's recommendations followed from his analysis of the impact of Stalin's actions in Eastern Europe. He argued that the key to a possible Cold War strategy lay in Belgrade, where Josip Broz Tito's republic was refusing to submit to Stalin's dictates. The first sign of the Yugoslavia-Soviet split came in 1945 when Tito complained to Stalin of the thuggish behavior of Soviet troops in Belgrade. Rape of Serbian women by Russian soldiers was almost routine. Stalin protested that his tired soldiers should be permitted to have a little "fun." Moscow said that Tito's complaint was a slur on Soviet honor. But Tito had far greater scope to resist Stalin than most of his Eastern European counterparts. Unlike the other newly Communist states, Yugoslavia's revolution was not imposed on it by Moscow; its partisan revolution was homegrown. That Tito was from Croatia, not Serbia, which saw itself as a sister Orthodox culture to the Russians, may have sharpened the Yugoslav leader's sensitivity to Moscow's colonial overtones. Tito was especially resistant to Russification. In Poland and Czechoslovakia, the Russian language was being made compulsory in schools. Russian culture was given primacy. Tito insisted on sticking to the letter of the Soviet Union's original equality claim among socialist nations. For that, Yugoslavia was accused by Moscow of "bourgeois nationalism," which in Stalin's lexicon came a close second to fascism. In spite of the threat of Soviet invasion of Yugoslavia, Tito did not bend. "The belittling of the histories of other nations . . . the non-Marxist glorification of the whole of the pre-revolutionary Russian history . . . these are just a few of the revisionist deviations which you can find in the daily Soviet press," said Tito in a lengthy quote that Brzezinski included in his McGill monograph.[77]

Here was the Soviet Union's "Achilles' heel," Brzezinski argued. Yugoslavia's alienation was echoed on the streets of the Baltic states, Czechoslovakia, Hungary, and especially Poland. Each of those nations saw itself as culturally superior to its new (and in Poland's case, old) imperial master, which made for a shaky relationship between a backwards metropolis and its enlightened provinces. Though the road would be long and victory was nowhere in sight, Russia's "civilizing role" in Eastern Europe could be converted by the West into a boomerang against Moscow, Brzezinski argued. "Soviet 'patriotism' finds its historical foundation and its emotional basis in Russian tradition and character," he concluded. "Understanding the component elements of Russo-Soviet Nationalism may help a great deal the cause of Freedom." It would have been hard, perhaps impossible, for a student from a more typical Western background to have produced such an argument at Brzezinski's age. Some of his thesis's insights could only have come from his Polish experience. Running through his dissertation was an implied and powerful rebuke to the naiveté of Western scholarship.

Brzezinski's thesis more than passed muster with his McGill professors, although his chief mentor, Frederick Watkins, did have one or two stylistic criticisms. Brzezinski's prose, he said, was too wooden: "The sentences are apt to be too long and involved, and you should above all beware of overusing the dash (don't be afraid of commas)."[78] At the end of his penultimate academic year in Canada, McGill awarded Brzezinski the Andrew Mackenzie Fellowship in political science, which came with a stipend and some teaching duties. He received first-class honors in his undergraduate degree. A year later, and a day after he had celebrated his twenty-second birthday, Brzezinski was awarded an MA in economics and political science with the "highest distinction." At the start of his oral exam, one of the professors offered Brzezinski a cigarette and a glass of water. The panel then cross-examined him on English and Canadian government, theories of nationalism and Marxism, and the arguments behind his written submission on Russo-Soviet nationalism. The whole event went "swimmingly," according to Brzezinski. He was awarded a second consecutive $1,000 grant, ensuring his track to a tenured professorship at McGill.

He spent much of the summer of 1950 in a celebratory social whirl: dinners, parties, new romantic leads, and long weekends in Saint Morin. Though he had been offered postgraduate places at Berkeley and Duke in the United States, his heart was set on Harvard. "It seems like I will be at McGill next year," he wrote somewhat resignedly.[79] In mid-June, just when he had abandoned hope, Harvard offered Brzezinski a place to do his PhD. His elation gave way to despair when he realized he could not afford it. Whatever Polish family wealth had not been wiped out in the war was now locked in socialist Poland. Tadeusz was adjusting to relative penury in Montreal. At best, Leonia's cosmetics business brought in pocket money. In spite of his professors' strenuous entreaties, Brzezinski's McGill stipend could not be spent elsewhere. He would also forfeit another academic grant that he had just secured from the government of Quebec, which told him the money could be used to study only in Quebec. "What a terrible letdown! I wanted to go to Harvard so much."[80] Even then, he had anticipated problems getting a US visa. Being a Canadian-based Pole on a soon-to-be-useless diplomatic visa would create a bureaucratic nightmare with US immigration.

The rest of his summer was spent searching for a way through the thicket of financial and legal challenges blocking his path to Harvard. "I am literally going nuts," he wrote in August.[81] Finally, Harvard wrote to say that it could give him $500 to work as a research assistant at its recently established Russia Research Center. But that would not be enough on its own. Watkins, a kindly professor, who would undoubtedly have become Brzezinski's mentor had he stayed, managed to track down another McGill grant for $1,000 that could be used at Harvard. Doubtless Watkins, who was American and had taught at Harvard in the 1930s, had worked his contacts there, too. Between Watkins's connections and his own scrambling, Brzezinski secured the opening he craved. "Lots of running around after the visa. Going mad," he wrote in mid-September.[82] Owing, perhaps, to a little more string pulling, that, too, came through. At the end of the war, Watkins had been a senior research analyst at the Office of Strategic Services, the precursor of the CIA. But for the help of Watkins, Brzezinski would have had to settle for Canada.

He spent much of the summer cramming Russian in preparation for Harvard. But his final days in Montreal were dominated by Poland. Tadeusz, who was still the leading figure in the Polish Canadian world, hosted a big reception for Władysław Anders, the celebrated Polish general. Anders, like Tadeusz, had been stripped of his Polish citizenship by Warsaw's Communist government. He was one of Poland's Second World War heroes and a giant in Zbigniew's mind. In contrast to Anders's wartime renown, his visit to Montreal on that occasion was barely noticed by Canadians. But it was a big moment for Canadian "Polonia," which needed a morale boost. Tadeusz gave the keynote address in honor of Anders. The event was deemed a success. Zbigniew was among those toasting the general. Two days later, he left home. On September 19, 1950, he boarded a bus for Boston with a small suitcase and $20 in his pocket.[83] Having remained with his parents all through his McGill days, he would be living away from home for the first time. He would never reside in Canada again.

"My busy, brave, politicized, good son," Leonia wrote in her diary after he had left. "I'm so glad you are happy, that you have the opportunity to move up the ladder, that you are pursuing the goal that you set for yourself. My beloved, golden, little boy . . . how fervently I pray!"[84] The ebullient Zbigniew seemed to have little need of his mother's prayers, though he basked in her adoration. Harvard provided a higher rung on his ladder to academia. Yet in his mind Harvard was merely a step in a far greater mission, which, like his Sovietology, seems to have chosen him. He left a disparate family that had fallen on hard times: two of his siblings, Adam and George, were still trying to figure out their purpose in life and lapsing into and out of depression; the youngest Brzezinski offspring, Lech, was progressing at school, though in a rebellious early adolescence; his parents were reacting very differently to their gradual descent of the mountain—Tadeusz stoically, Leonia mostly in anguish. Alone in their clan, Zbigniew knew his direction and was unencumbered by doubt. The motto he chose for his final McGill yearbook entry was "When one is right, victory is only a matter of time."[85]

3

A Pole in Cambridge

At 3:00 a.m. on March 5, 1953, Merle Fainsod, Harvard University's leading Sovietologist, awoke irritably to a telephone call from his twenty-four-year-old research assistant. The excited Zbigniew Brzezinski was calling to let him know that the Soviet dictator, Josef Stalin, had died.[1] Fainsod said that Stalin would "be just as dead in the morning" and hung up.[2] The dictator passed away later that day. Brzezinski justified his intrusion by saying that the professor would want to be prepared for journalists to call him at dawn for comments on Stalin's death. Brzezinski's rude awakening offers an inimitable glimpse of how his mind worked: since Fainsod's sleep would in any case be interrupted, Brzezinski would save him the trouble by getting in first. Besides, what Cold War scholar would not want to know as soon as possible about the demise of one of history's greatest monsters?

By the time of Stalin's death, Brzezinski was an emerging figure in Soviet studies with more than one illustrious mentor behind him. Fainsod was his closest and most valuable. No amount of influential patronage, however, can substitute for drive. Brzezinski's ambition was relentless. Later in life, Brzezinski's critics would allege that Poland was his overriding motivation; his passion for freedom began and ended with his country of birth. That would confuse his formative years with the more complicated person he became. His fast-widening worldview was already manifest before he moved to America. A month after Harvard offered Brzezinski a place, he wrote to South Korea's ambassador in Washington to volunteer his services in the war against the Communist North. The Korean War, the first great conflict of the Cold War era, had begun just ten days after he had received his Harvard acceptance letter. Had Brzezinski's romantic and wholly impractical volunteer to arms been accepted, he would have had to quit the Harvard of his dreams before he began or awkwardly withdraw his offer to enlist in a war on the other side of the world. Thankfully for Harvard and possibly for South Korea, Brzezinski's offer was rebuffed. "Your willingness to serve is not only brave and generous, it shows an understanding of the menace of communism," wrote John M. Chang, South Korea's ambassador to the United States, in a personal reply to Brzezinski. "We have been advised that you must get in touch with your government, and in particular your local recruiting office. Nevertheless, you shall always have the gratitude of the free people of Korea."[3]

A year to the day (July 13, 1951) after South Korea had declined his military service, the CIA rejected Brzezinski's formal application. Though somewhat less romantic, his attempt to join America's still-youthful spy agency was hardly less impractical. As an alien student on a short-term US study visa, Brzezinski's bid was a long shot—although, unlike other federal agencies, the CIA was allowed to hire foreign nationals. It also posed the same dilemma of whether he would want to quit Harvard, having just completed his first year. In that case, however, the CIA might have missed a trick: Brzezinski's mix of languages, which included Russian, French, and German as well as Polish and English, was in short supply. "We regret very much that we have been unable to locate an opening in which your services could be fully utilized," wrote W. J. Harlan, head of the CIA's personnel department. "Your interest in our organization is greatly appreciated."[4]

A more accurate criticism of Brzezinski, which came mostly from former academic colleagues, was that he treated his studies as a stepping-stone to a larger arena. Since that was self-evidently true and since he saw no shame in it, he never wasted time on denials. In a letter to his parents early on at Harvard, he laid out his various options for his PhD thesis. The range of potential subject matters was wide. But his mind was already straying beyond the ivory tower. "I want to come up with something that would get me in touch with the government; that is very important," he told them.[5] Towards the end of his life he said, "I became a scholar because Harvard gave me the opportunity to be a scholar . . . but there was always something within me that drew me to action. . . . As I began to feel my oats, I began to crystallize my ambition, which was nothing less than formulating a coherent strategy for the United States so that we could eventually dismantle the Soviet bloc."[6] He had made an early stab at that strategy with his McGill thesis.

Almost as soon as Brzezinski arrived in Cambridge, Massachusetts, in late September 1950, he faced a momentous choice. Would he put himself under the tutelage of William Yandell Elliott in Harvard's Department of Government or that of Carl Friedrich, Elliott's chief rival? In addition to their contrasting intellectual styles, the professors' mutual dislike was legendary. Elliott was a storied son of Tennessee whose intellectually formative stage occurred when he was a Rhodes Scholar after serving in uniform in World War I. Although not a natural Democrat, he played a role as part of President Franklin D. Roosevelt's "Brain Trust" in 1930s Washington. Elliott's style was not to everyone's taste: he was an inveterate Anglophile (almost cartoonishly so), and there was a solipsistic flavor to his teaching, which paid as much heed to poetry as to ideology. Elliott and Friedrich overlapped in their passion for a muscular Atlanticism, in their enthusiasm for deepening Cold War collaboration between universities and government, and in their dread of the Soviets. In most respects, however, they were highly unalike. Friedrich was a German émigré who chose to remain in America and become a naturalized citizen after Hitler took power. In the late 1940s, as an advisor to General Lucius Clay, the military governor of the US-occupied zone of Germany, he had played a leading part in shaping West Germany's postwar Basic Law. The first line of West Germany's constitution read "Human dignity shall be inviolable." He had also helped set up the Free University of Berlin and advised postwar German universities on how to instill democratic values into their curricula. His most thoughtful academic work was about the need to check and disperse the awesome powers of the state. Whether in Nazi or Soviet form, Friedrich's priority was to understand totalitarianism—the better to defeat it.

The choice between Elliott and Friedrich was the kind that could change a student's future; it merited consultation and reflection. Brzezinski made his decision a few minutes into an introductory seminar by Elliott. The professor, who would later become an advisor to Richard Nixon, a future vice president and later president, apologized that he must cut short his talk because he was needed in Washington. His assistant would complete his introduction. "In walks this youngish, somewhat rotund . . . scholar, with a strong German accent, introduces himself and proceeds to tell us what to expect," recalled Brzezinski. "I listened to him carefully and the more I heard the more I sensed that [his] principal references were a variety of Germanic philosophers who influenced in their own way the evolution of history in Europe. And I concluded that this was not my meat. So I rather impolitely rose and left."[7] That was Brzezinski's first fleeting brush with Henry Kissinger. It was also the start of his collaboration with Friedrich.

Within a few weeks of arriving, Brzezinski had found the two key mentors, Friedrich and Fainsod, whom he would keep throughout his time at Harvard. His academic life toggled between the government department in the Littauer Center, on one side of Harvard Yard, and the Russian Research Center in Dudley Hall, on the other, close to the Charles River. Almost every resource he needed was within a few minutes' walk. The RRC was the epicenter of America's so-called Cold War university, in which large federal and philanthropic grants were feeding the mushrooming new world of Soviet studies. At that point, Harvard and Columbia dominated it. Since the exponentially growing field had been conjured from almost nothing, Brzezinski fitted in with remarkable speed. "Never before did so many know so little about so much," one wit observed in the mid-1940s about the hastily cobbled together teams of overnight Soviet specialists working at the Office of Strategic Services, the army and air force, and other federal agencies.[8] By 1950, the US government's knowledge deficiency about the Soviet Union was no longer a problem. In the words of one scholar, Soviet studies had gone "from laughing-stock to juggernaut."[9] The distinctly accented Brzezinski was at home among the congeries of refugees, émigrés, and recently naturalized Americans who populated the Cold War university. Other bright lights included Stanley Hoffmann, Adam Ulam, Richard Pipes, Alexander Gerschenkron, and Kissinger. Among Brzezinski's American-born colleagues were Samuel Huntington, McGeorge Bundy, Arthur Schlesinger, Arthur Schlesinger, Jr., and Barrington Moore, Jr. The US-born Fainsod was among the Cold War university's biggest luminaries.

Fainsod was more than just a mentor; he helped to fix Brzezinski's persistent financial worries. Within a few months of Brzezinski's enrolling at Harvard, he asked him to correct his undergraduates' essays on the Soviet Union.[10] A few months after that, Brzezinski became Fainsod's research assistant. From there, he morphed into his teaching assistant. He spent a lot of time at the RCC's Dudley Hall, a handsome specimen of late-nineteenth-century Boston civic architecture that would be inexcusably demolished in the 1960s. It was Brzezinski's chief intellectual home and where he did most of his writing. In addition to the prestige of being associated with the RRC, which had been set up by, among others, Fainsod and Friedrich, with seed money from the Carnegie Corporation, the center paid Brzezinski a stipend. That grew from $500 in 1950 to $1,500 the following year. Since that still proved insufficient, he had to find money elsewhere. That required torturous weeks of interviews with the National Committee for a Free Europe in New York City. The outfit, which had been set up on the famed US diplomat George Kennan's inspiration in 1949, was supposedly a private umbrella group. The fiercely anti-Communist owner of Time Inc., Henry Luce, and the filmmaker Cecil B. DeMille were on its board. One of its undertakings was Radio Free Europe. In reality, the CIA was its chief benefactor.

The committee's mission was to aid the cause of freedom, which included supporting the work of Eastern European émigrés. To qualify for a grant, Brzezinski had to convince them that he would not try to become a US citizen. He found that impossible to prove; his insistence that he would remain Polish was belied in their eyes by the fact that he had applied to join the CIA. He protested that aliens were eligible to work at the agency, which was why he had applied for a job there and not to the State Department. The skeptical grant officer, a man named Foster, turned him down. "What swine!" he told his parents. "They first sold our country. And now for $70 a month they are appointing themselves judges of our patriotism!"[11] Foster even demanded evidence that Brzezinski intended to return to Poland, which triggered further conniptions; Brzezinski had to explain what his likely fate would be if he went back. Foster added to Brzezinski's sourness by advising that he change his name to "Jack Burton or something like that" if he did apply for US citizenship.[12] Brzezinski was so outraged by that unpassable bureaucratic loyalty test that he enlisted every big name he could find to reverse the decision. After some wrangling, the committee agreed to revisit his application. His struggle worked. Foster even apologized to Brzezinski for the "misunderstanding" over where his loyalties lay. The money was deposited in his account, enabling Brzezinski to buy a Royal Arrow typewriter: $26 up front, the rest in $5 monthly installments.[13] He was overjoyed with his new machine, partly because he would not have to go to Dudley Hall every time he needed to write.

In his first academic year at Harvard, Brzezinski's results were unimprovable. He got straight A's in each of his four courses—which, he was informed, only 5 percent of graduates achieved.[14] As early as spring 1951, six months after he had enrolled, Brzezinski was told by Fainsod that he could become a leading Soviet scholar if that was his ambition. Brzezinski began helping with his most ambitious book, *How Russia Is Ruled* (1953), which would become a staple of Soviet studies for decades. In 1997, *Foreign Affairs* included the title on its list of its best one hundred books of the previous seventy-five years. Alongside Fainsod's tome was Brzezinski's 1960 book *The Soviet Bloc: Unity and Conflict.*

In spite of Fainsod's kindness, money was still a source of anxiety. In a letter to his parents, Brzezinski complained that he had to pay a dentist's charge of $4.75 after having been told that the consultation would be free.[15] In another he explained that the weekly bill for eating at his dining hall was $14, compared to paying $17 or $18 for much better food if he ate out. The difference was too much. "In other words, I will need to contract with this eatery of ours. The food in it remains unchanged, *mutatis mutandis,* in terms of its quality and volume." Several times Brzezinski asked his parents to remind his half brother, George, that he had promised to send him a cast-off suit. If the suit did not arrive soon, he would have to buy one himself as he could not continue to go around "constantly like a beggar in crumpled tropical trousers."[16]

Neither financial angst nor mounting research demands would keep him cloistered. Academic success came almost too easily. In 1952, he told his mother that his lowest grade at Harvard so far had been an A minus. His nearly unblemished record came at no expense to his burgeoning social life. For his first two years, Brzezinski stayed at Adams House, one of Harvard's twelve halls of residence and its oldest. Its venerable Colonial-style buildings were a short walk from Harvard Yard and roughly the same distance from Radcliffe College, the women's sister institution to Harvard. Radcliffe's residents were the object of much of Brzezinski's attention, as were those of Wellesley, the women's liberal arts college just outside Boston. Among his frequent hosts was the scholar Wiktor Weintraub, Harvard's professor emeritus of Polish language and literature, who would expound, pipe in hand, on all matters Polish. Another was Marian Dziewanowski, a mature doctoral student who had fought as a Polish cavalryman against the Germans in 1939. His later book on Polish communism was considered seminal. There was usually a group of Wellesley girls at both Weintraub and Dziewanowski's parties, which was an added incentive to show up.

In his first year, Brzezinski shared a room divided by a thin curtain with Richard Hatton, a fellow postgraduate, who was a naval veteran of the Pacific Theater in World War I. Hatton, who was a tireless student, often poring over his books until 2:00 a.m., was pained at the way Brzezinski got such good grades while working so little. He gave Brzezinski a "hypothetical example" of Student A, who is intelligent but works little and gets A grades, and Student B, who is intelligent, works very hard, but gets only B grades. "Am I that stupid that I won't guess what he's talking about?" Brzezinski asked himself.[17] He reassured his roommate that Student B's approach laid a far more solid basis for long-term success.

Hatton learned not to take his roommate on in an argument. Brzezinski's method was to prevail by force rather than seduction. He would bludgeon, set traps, ambush, and trip up. His manner, which did little to disguise that he thought he was cleverer than most people, left many of his interlocutors feeling bruised. Some of his fellow graduate students were already jealous of his rapid advancement. One asked if he really knew so much more about Russia or whether "I'm so gifted at pretending that everyone thinks I'm an expert and just gives me money."[18] But among his widening circle of friends, with whom he played tennis and chess and went on double dates and to graduate balls, Brzezinski's arrogance was outweighed by an infectious sense of humor. His taste was for pranks rather than jokes. He was also a loyal friend. Though Hatton was several years older, Brzezinski later went to great lengths to find him jobs when he was struggling.[19]

Being pressed for time was rarely Brzezinski's problem. He took buses back and forth to Montreal every month or two and wrote to his parents several times a week. They visited often. Brzezinski had little interest in American football, yet he hitchhiked with friends to the big Harvard games against Yale and Princeton. Those excursions took two or three days' round trip. He often went skiing in New Hampshire. Sometimes he and his friends borrowed a car and slept in it despite the subzero temperatures outside.

In Cambridge there was usually an invitation to a graduate ball or a debutante's party, many of which stretched until three or four in the morning. He consumed a lot of alcohol but rarely got visibly drunk. After one night of carousing with a large group of friends, he recorded that he had sunk several glasses of vodka "to uphold national honor." On another evening at Blinstrub's Village, a famous Boston nightclub owned by a Lithuanian immigrant and patronized by the likes of Jack Kennedy and Frank Sinatra, he lost interest in an otherwise attractive group of Polish women because they kept boasting about how often they got drunk. One of them, a girl named Marysia, said that in New York she and her Polish friends would get so "plastered they would get hiccups."[20] Brzezinski told them about his group of Polish friends in Montreal who also drank. Yet they had also formed a club for serious discussions and lectures. The girls looked pained. His lecture prompted "some consternation that a club needed to be organized etc." Brzezinski certainly knew how to put a damper on a bender. Even when he had been out most of the night, he would usually attend Mass on Sunday and often on weekdays. Boston had no shortage of Catholic churches; he was known at several.

In his second year at Harvard, Brzezinski got a new roommate, a Polish Jew from Vilnius, the capital of the Soviet republic of Lithuania, which had been part of the Polish-Lithuanian Commonwealth for centuries. Brzezinski greeted his new cohabitant, a student of architecture, as good news on two counts. First, he was rarely there, which gave Brzezinski the space he wanted. Second, he spoke fluent Russian, which gave Brzezinski the chance to practice. As he implied in a letter to his father, there was also a third benefit: their relationship opened his eyes to what it was like to be a Polish Jew. "He told me that as a boy he was an authentic Polish patriot and that Piłsudski meant everything to him in spite of the fact that throughout his childhood and his days at the Polish school, not a single Polish child would play ball with him. 'Can you understand [how it feels] to be a boy and seeing others play, and not wanting to play with you? Is it my fault that I was not born Mr. Brzezinski?' When he got to gymnasium, they would slap him in the face because he was a Jew. I don't blame him for not being especially sentimental about Poland; yet in our discussions (at least when I am there) he always praises Poles for their courage and the fact that some of them saved Jews during the war."

Another persistent—though mostly whispered—criticism of Brzezinski was that he was anti-Semitic. A key element of that charge was that he was from Poland, which had had a nasty pattern of turning on its ancient Jewish communities when scapegoats were needed. The word *pogrom*, which derives from the Russian Yiddish *pogromit*, meaning "devastation," gained currency in Poland during the nineteenth century. There is little in the private thoughts that Brzezinski disclosed to his diary, or in the volumes of letters he wrote to his family (all of which were in Polish), to support the allegation of anti-Semitism. Brzezinski's father, Tadeusz, mailed copies of *Kultura*, the Polish émigré journal published in Paris, to his son. After he had read one issue, Brzezinski complained to his father that it included "another idiotic article" by Felicjan Sławoj Składkowski, who had been Poland's prime minister in 1939 when the Germans and Soviets had invaded.[21] Prior to the war, Składkowski had launched an "economic struggle" against Poland's Jews. In that latest essay, Składkowski had boasted about having, as prime minister in the late 1930s, sent a Jewish city councilman to Bereza, Poland's notorious prewar internment camp for undesirables, for having taken a stand against Polish anti-Semitism. "In general our attitude toward the Jews was scandalous," wrote Brzezinski.

Brzezinski spent much of his first eighteen months in Cambridge trying to nail down the topic of his PhD thesis. The quest was less straightforward than he had hoped. A key criterion was that it should yield RRC travel funding so that he could go behind the Iron Curtain, preferably to the Soviet Union. Another was that it should be distinctive and useful enough to get him noticed in the wider world. During much of his first year, he thought he had solved that quandary after he began to research political control of the Soviet army. His first essay on the subject led to invitations to give talks about it, which, in turn, led to encouragement from both Fainsod and Friedrich to develop a thesis. Much of his material came from interviews that Fainsod had conducted with Soviet defectors from the Red Army. Brzezinski supplemented that material with wide reading of the Russian media and public speeches by Soviet defense chiefs. The result, which in 1952 yielded his first publication in an academic journal, the *Journal of Politics*, published by the Southern Political Science Association, was the most detailed breakdown to date of Soviet political control of its military.

The article, "Party Controls in the Soviet Army," traced how Moscow's paranoia about the risks of a coup d'état engendered a byzantine oversight system in which party commissars would shadow, and in many cases have seniority over, military commanders in the field. They would devise programs of political education for the troops, which would swallow up to six hours of their day. Unsurprisingly, the arrangement did not endear the commissars to the military rank and file, roughly 90 percent of whom, Brzezinski estimated, treated the propaganda sessions as endurance tests. Some even saw them as a chance to "catch up on sleep." Yet he cautioned against interpreting the Red Army as being prone to imminent unrest or mutiny. The source of much of his information about the Soviet military's missing esprit de corps came from Fainsod's defectors, who might be telling Americans what they wanted to hear. Moreover, the party was so omniscient that any hint of dissent could quickly be detected.[22]

Though heavily jargon ridden, Brzezinski's article won him recognition as a budding Sovietologist. Unfortunately, however, he discovered quite late into his research that it would be too risky to expand it into a PhD thesis. It turned out that a Washington-based postgraduate student's research on the same topic was further advanced. Brzezinski had no choice but to begin his search afresh. In his reaction to Brzezinski's essay, Fainsod said, "I wish all the other papers could be like yours."[23] To secure his doctorate, however, he would need a new source of inspiration. One possibility was to study party control over the agricultural sector—a suggestion of Fainsod, who said that that important topic had hitherto been inadequately addressed by economists. "Somehow that does not interest me," Brzezinski told his parents.[24] Other options that he explored, then rejected, included "The Impact of World War on the Organization of the CPSU" and "Soviet Prisoner of War Policy During World War II." The latter would have given him a reason to probe the 1940 Katyn Massacre in more detail. Neither fully satisfied him.

Friedrich opened Brzezinski's eyes to the possibility of tackling a bigger study on the nature of Soviet totalitarianism. Brzezinski hurriedly fashioned an argument about why purges were endemic to Bolshevik rule. It was eventually published as a book titled *The Permanent Purge: Politics in Soviet Totalitarianism*. This was Brzezinski's stab at diagnosing the psychological wellsprings of Soviet power. Regular bloodletting was its tool. "Totalitarianism has thus sought to give meaning to a life which for many had rapidly become mechanical, isolated, and frightening. And this desperate need of the individual to feel a sense of belonging and purpose provides the base for totalitarian violence," he wrote in the introduction.

His argument was that the purge was a normal tool of totalitarianism. Contrary to the prevailing view, purges were not "irrational" within the context of Stalin's system. In the absence of counterbalancing constitutional checks or any meaningful civil society, the purge functions as the regime's substitute for politics. Large-scale expungings of party members, show trials of disgraced Politburo leaders, and exemplary public cleansings filled the narrative vacuum of a society deprived of a sense of participation. Since the regime's control was total, it cut itself off from the void that it ruled; there was no feedback loop or means of gauging public opinion. The purges, which reached a frenzy in Stalin's show trials between 1936 and 1938 and continued in lesser form after the war ("the quiet purges"), were how the regime perpetuated its control. Stability was regarded as a threat. Total isolation bred total paranoia, which necessitated a constant reshuffling. The more arbitrary its pretext, the better. "The infallibility of the leader always means that those who are purged must have been exceedingly wrong—and implies that no sacrifice can be questioned, no elimination regretted, no bloodletting shirked."[25] Implicit in Brzezinski's thesis was that the Soviet system was incapable of reforming itself from within.

It took Brzezinski eighteen months to write his PhD thesis. In late May 1953, almost three months after the death of Stalin, his oral examiners, among them Friedrich and Fainsod, pronounced him "Dr. Brzezinski." "It looks wonderful," Brzezinski wrote of his bound thesis. "A red cover with gold lettering—the title and the name. What a sense of freedom!"[26] His choice of topic also came with a major supplemental benefit. Understanding the character of totalitarianism had become Friedrich's overriding purpose. His knowledge of the Nazi variant was detailed and personal. Before the war, Friedrich had fallen out with his brother, Otto, who had also moved to the US. Unlike Carl Friedrich, Otto returned to Germany and became a committed Nazi and profiting industrialist in the Third Reich. Though the brothers had since reconciled, Friedrich's obsession with what he saw as an entirely new form of autocracy—qualitatively different from the absolute monarchies and oriental despotisms of pre-twentieth-century history—continued to grow.

Friedrich's problem was that he knew comparatively little about the Soviet variety of totalitarianism. Brzezinski was his remedy. A few months after Brzezinski received his doctorate, Friedrich proposed that they coauthor a book on the subject. Not only would Brzezinski balance out their specialisms, he would do most of the drone work. "This is a major success for me," wrote Brzezinski.[27] Friedrich opened a door that would lead Brzezinski to scholarly fame far more quickly than he had dared to hope.

The year 1953 was when the future Brzezinski wanted began to take on distinct shape. Even before he finished his PhD, he became a Harvard instructor. For the previous two years, he had been teaching undergraduates every Wednesday and Friday under William Yandell Elliott's supervision in the Department of Government. His course on the history of political thought began with Solon and Lycurgus, the early Greek lawgivers of Sparta and Athens, and ended with Karl Marx and the modern liberal theorists. "It requires quite a bit of preparation," he told his parents in a rare admission that effort was sometimes required.[28] His new responsibilities involved a lot more work. They also meant more money. His yearly instructor salary was $4,500, which was more than double what he had been earning. The extra money enabled him to buy a brand-new Chevrolet Bel Air convertible for $2,500. It left him "absolutely penniless" yet reveling in the fact that his dream was "coming true." The purchase seems uncharacteristic, as he generally abhorred extravagance. In another sense, though, the car fit with his self-image of being a man on the move. He was beginning to tire of the endless Greyhound journeys up and down the East Coast. In newspaper profiles years later, Brzezinski was often depicted as loving his upward mobility. That had been true almost since he had arrived in the US. In 1952, he took his first plane flight, from Boston to Montreal. It was a near-religious experience. "If I have enough money, I will do nothing but fly," he vowed to himself.[29]

With the help of an RRC grant, Brzezinski's improving outlook meant that he could now afford to cross the Atlantic. It was his first time in Europe since 1938. He traveled tourist class (cabin 199) on SS *Ryndam* for the ten-day journey from Boston to Le Havre. The full Brzezinski contingent, which had converged on Harvard to witness him receive his doctorate a few days earlier, waved him off from Boston Harbor. Brzezinski spent July and August on a financially watchful version of a Victorian-style European grand tour. He crossed some of the continent by train with Fred Holborn, a Harvard classmate and the son of the distinguished German historian Hajo Holborn (another émigré from Hitler's Germany). Sometimes they hitchhiked. Brzezinski spent much of the rest of the trip with Nina Peterson, a student from Radcliffe whom he had bumped into in Paris. There was no romantic affinity—"she is far too cold." But he liked her companionship. They observed Europe's classical ruins and its postwar reconstruction. He was astonished by the low prices. In Paris, he could afford champagne and the best veal. In Rome and Florence, he lived even larger, although he was disappointed at how early Italian nightlife ended. He gawked at women in bikinis on the Venetian Lido and from the Promenade des Anglais in Nice. On his side trip to Belgrade, the capital of Yugoslavia, which had supplied his flimsy pretext for the academic travel grant, he had a meal of good-quality steak, salad, and melon for little more than 300 dinars (about a dollar). He was allowed to observe a meeting of the Yugoslavian Communist Party's Central Committee. He was struck by the ubiquity and intrusiveness of police surveillance of ordinary Yugoslavs.[30]

Another justification for his tour was to visit the office of Radio Free Europe in Munich. There he met Jan Nowak, the celebrated wartime resistance figure, who was heading RFE's Polish section. Nowak took Brzezinski out for drinks. He was so struck by the twenty-five-year-old student's knowledge that he invited him back the next day to record a radio interview. In addition to questions about Brzezinski's background, Nowak asked his views on what was likely to come after Stalin. Brzezinski was allowed to read letters from Polish workers, interview Russia researchers, and sit in on the RFE's board meeting. What most impressed him was the modernity of the broadcaster's offices and the lavish privileges available to its staff (chiefly access to American goods). It was, after all, a partly CIA-funded operation. He and Ms. Peterson also visited Hitler's "eagle's nest" at Berchtesgaden. They were admitted for free because he pretended to be a military officer traveling with his wife. In Vienna, he ventured from the British sector into the Russian one (the city was still divided, like Germany, among the victorious powers). He argued with a group of Soviet soldiers after they had reprimanded him for taking photographs. One soldier insisted on giving him a portrait of the recently deceased Stalin. Brzezinski asked instead for a picture of the new Soviet premier, Georgy Malenkov. His request elicited an apologetic shrug.

A clear subtext to his European grand tour was to reunite with Charlotte Graux, an aristocratic young Frenchwoman he had met in New York the previous year with whom he was instantly enchanted. Their brief dalliance had included passionate kissing. "I could fall in love this instant," he wrote.[31] Sadly for Brzezinski, Charlotte was now engaged to someone else. But she treated him as an honored guest, taking him to her family home in the Vosges and to her grandparental estate in the Ardennes. There Brzezinski got a whiff of how European aristocrats still lived. Two rings of a bell summoned guests to dinner, who were served an elaborate meal of haute cuisine by in-house waiters. Afterwards they moved to the drawing room for coffee and cultured repartee. In spite of the setting, or perhaps because of it, he could not get Charlotte's engagement out of his mind. "I only wish I had gotten here sooner," he wrote before he boarded the return boat to the US.

Brzezinski's pursuit of women at Harvard continued in the somewhat manic pattern he had set at McGill: a whirligig of dances, "caresses," "fondlings," and "neckings." None of his encounters lasted long. One or two intimacies were significant enough for the young women to introduce Brzezinski to their parents. At a champagne dinner at the Harvard Graduate Club, Brzezinski had wowed Babs Stoddard's parents with his display of French—the *maître de vin* being "a negro from Martinique."[32] Brzezinski and Babs then returned to his room, where they spent the rest of the evening "kissing each other ravenously and wrangling passionately."[33] Babs had "a wonderful body—like made of silk." Nothing came of their entanglement. Despite his erratic batting average, Brzezinski's schedule of blind dates and double dates did not flag. One evening in October 1953, he met Emilie Anna Benes, a Czech-origin art student four years his junior, who had recently graduated from Wellesley. Emilie was in fact there as the date of Brzezinski's Harvard colleague Samuel Huntington. Huntington and Brzezinski went on to become famous coauthors and collaborators. On that occasion, however, Brzezinski's collaborative side was conspicuously missing. His attraction was instant. Emilie was a twenty-one-year-old rising artist with a self-possession that set her apart from the debutante crowd. Perhaps fittingly, since her family was from Bohemia, though she was born in Switzerland, her style was also unorthodox. She had no taste for the contemporary outfit of poodle skirt, saddle shoes, and matching blouse and cardigan—or the bob that went with it. Her hair was not always perfectly in place. She was herself without making a statement about it.

As Eastern European castaways on American shores, Zbigniew and Emilie related to each other's stories, which had uncanny and multiple affinities. From that night on, no other love interest merits citation in Brzezinski's diary. Emilie Benes, whose nickname, Muska, was the one by which she was generally known, came from a distinguished Czechoslovakian family. Her great uncle, Edvard Beneš, had been Czechoslovakia's last democratically elected leader when the country fell to a Communist coup in 1948. Beneš was also the country's president in 1938 when British prime minister Chamberlain said he did not want to sacrifice British lives to a "quarrel in a faraway country, between people of whom we know nothing."[34] Muska had spent most of the Second World War in London, where her mother, Emilie Berta Zadna Benes, was a translator and interpreter for the Czech government in exile. In parallel with Tadeusz Brzezinski's wartime career, Muska's father, Bohus Benes, was appointed in 1941 to be the Czech government in exile's consul general in San Francisco. Prior to that, he had been the London press secretary to his uncle, the exiled Czech president.

The rest of the Benes family joined Bohus a year later. The eleven-year-old Muska's odyssey and that of her mother and two brothers, Václav and Bohus, nearly came to an end in the mid-Atlantic. German U-boats struck their convoy at night. Amid the ghastly *son-et-lumière* of drowning passengers and sinking vessels, the Benes family was evacuated from their passenger ship in rowboats.[35] When it became apparent that the torpedo that struck their ship had not exploded, they reboarded and continued unharmed to New York. The family's reuniting in California was not a happy one. Muska's mother later discovered that Bohus was concealing a second family in an act of de facto bigamy from which she never recovered. In 1951, she sued him for divorce on grounds of "extreme cruelty" in Superior Court of Alameda County. She won custody of their children, alimony payments, and possession of the family home in Berkeley. That bitter experience never left Muska, who by the time of her mother's divorce was on the East Coast studying at Wellesley. Barring a few grudging occasions, she refused to meet her father and did not get close to the half siblings he had fathered.

Within days of meeting, Zbigniew and Muska were inseparable. He drove her in his new Chevrolet to football games at Princeton and Yale. They took long walks together, attended the familiar circuit of balls and cocktail parties, and met almost every day. By letter from Montreal, where Brzezinski spent Christmas, he confessed that he had been on a couple of dates in Canada. Though they had known each other for less than three months, Muska's jealousy was rampant. "This made me quite mad," she wrote in her diary. "I didn't know how to react. Not only that but he had had a date just the night before [returning to Cambridge] and stayed up all night with her 'talking about Europe.' I bet! But he gave me such a lovely present (a scarf)."[36] Given Brzezinski's mischievous bent, his casual reference to those supposed dates, which he did not record in his diary, was likely tactical. He skipped his usual Yuletide sojourn at his parents' Saint Morin retreat and returned to Cambridge two days after Christmas. "We made mad love and I found out about all kinds of things that I did not know about before. OYOY!!" wrote Muska.[37] The next day, "We went to dinner. I was quite tired (I wonder why!)." Three weeks later, Brzezinski brought her a gift. "To my utmost horror I saw some dappled material and immediately knew what it was! Vanity Fair leopard spot panties."[38] On January 23, 1954, she pressed a flower into her diary. "Tonight for the first time, he told me he loves me. And I love him so, so much."

The first member of Brzezinski's family Muska met was Zbigniew's closest brother, Adam. He had moved to New York in 1952 to try to make a career as an advertising copywriter on Madison Avenue. Zbigniew would visit him in New York to take him to the movies or the theater and check on his situation. Adam's parents had never stopped worrying about him. He had failed to make his way in

Montreal and was hindered by lifelong physical scars from polio. What was left unsaid, because of Leonia's deep Catholic faith, was that Adam was gay. In the context of Adam's devout upbringing, a formal decision to come out—a phrase not then in usage—was never a realistic option. In 1950s America, even in New York, homosexuality was rarely open and necessitated continual vigilance. From Europe the year before, Brzezinski had written to tell his brother that he was traveling alone and how he much he valued solitude. Adam was single at the time and lonely. Zbigniew wanted to convey to his depressive brother that there was nothing wrong with that. At some point in the following months, Adam met someone. It did not last for long. In March 1954, Brzezinski wrote, "Adàs is in trouble. He is very upset, poor thing, because his friend left him."[39] Muska and Zbigniew drove down to New York and spent the weekend trying to cheer him up. That entailed forcing him out on the town to do things; they took him to lunch in Central Park, visited the Museum of Modern Art, then had dinner with Polish friends followed by a movie. The next day they attended Mass at Saint Patrick's Cathedral, then spent the afternoon on Staten Island. Then Muska and Zbigniew drove back to Boston.

Zbigniew and Muska's frenetic intervention was not enough. Probably nothing would have been. Two weeks later, on May 3, 1954, Adam took his life. He turned the oven gas on and stuck his head inside. Neighbors found him dead in his small apartment. Zbigniew was the first to find out. He was doing research at the RRC when one of Adam's colleagues telephoned to tell him. Zbigniew had to handle almost everything. He related the tragedy to his half brother, George, because his parents could not be reached. Then he headed to Boston's Logan Airport. There he waited for hours amid an intensifying thunderstorm only to learn that all flights had been canceled. He drove through the night in the lashing rain to New York. Late in the evening, he reached the police station, where he had to identify his brother's corpse. All he could bring himself to write was that he "went through some terrible moments" in the morgue and at his brother's apartment. His parents arrived there with George at 2:30 a.m.

Most of the logistics of handling the aftermath of Adam's death also fell to Zbigniew. Adam was buried a few days later in the Polish section of the cemetery in Saint Sauveur close to the Brzezinski retreat where the brothers had spent so much time. The challenge to Brzezinski of dealing with his parents' grief, which never receded, especially his mother's, was far greater. It changed the quality of their relationship. Shortly before he died, Adam wrote his mother a poem entitled "On Dreaming." Its final stanza was "To all these wondrous myths of blissful dreams, / there comes a date to part with paradise, / and then like lightning striking through the summer sky, / reality breaks the magic wand and casts you as a slave of time." After thirty years of keeping a diary, Leonia lost the habit soon after Adam's death. "And so my heart is broken in half, my world becomes smaller and lesser. Every morning I look at it through your eyes, and when I close them, you're all that I can see. My son, I am ending this diary, for I can no longer write now that you are gone."[40]

Always a filial son, Zbigniew turned into a morale booster and financial advisor to his parents. His letters increasingly omitted news that might worry them. His sense of parental care is illustrated by a letter he wrote more than four years after Adam's death. Leonia was still tormented by doubt about whether Adam would have entered Heaven given his unnamed transgressions—almost certainly the fact that he was gay, though the Church treated suicide as a mortal sin. Brzezinski was a social liberal. What is striking is the pains he took to soothe his mother's doubts with reasoning tailored to what was most likely to sway her distinctly illiberal moral code. "I'm confident that Adàs has God's grace where he is, because God wouldn't be what we understand by the notion of God if divine justice were to consist solely in adding and subtracting sins," he wrote. In reality, God would have taken into account Adam's polio, his suffering, his many disappointments and painful trials—and shown him heavenly compassion. That option was unavailable to the Church since it was a human institution that had to follow rules. God, however, was infinitely benevolent. "Therefore, I'm convinced that Mother's prayers, faith and trust, and Adam's whole life, open the door to the peace and happiness that he surely merited."[41]

Though Zbigniew drifted into a form of churchgoing agnosticism as he got older, he was deeply shaken by the manner of Adam's death. That Adam had taken his own life was never disclosed to Zbigniew's three children, who were born several years later. In the late 1990s, Zbigniew's nephew Matthew Brzezinski, an accomplished journalist and the son of Zbigniew's youngest brother, Lech, began writing a book in which he mentioned Adam's suicide. Zbigniew asked him to delete the account, which he did.[42] The subject remained taboo for the rest of his life. Adam's death almost certainly delayed Zbigniew's proposal of marriage to Muska. Two days before Adam died, Brzezinski wrote that he had "already had a more serious conversation" with her.[43] He eventually proposed on August 14, 1954, less than ten months after they had met. They were on the roof of Castle Hill, a Tudor Revival mansion forty miles north of Boston, on the night of a full moon at 1:00 a.m. The couple had a glittering night view of Massachusetts Bay. Muska wept and promised to make Zbigniew happy. Then they said a prayer. Muska wrote, "I answered now almost automatically because I had said it [in my head] so many times before."[44]

Though by no means as life changing, Carl Friedrich had asked Brzezinski to be his coauthor the same week in October 1953 that Brzezinski first met Muska. The project would prove to be a qualified success. On the positive side, Brzezinski was moving into the academic big leagues. Friedrich was a renowned scholar and institutional force on both sides of the Atlantic. Their focus—on the nature and future of totalitarianism—could hardly be more pertinent to the ominous Cold War atmosphere of the early to mid-1950s. The new Republican administration of Dwight D. Eisenhower, the Second World War US general and hero, was touting an aggressive doctrine of liberation that would "roll back" Soviet communism in Eastern Europe and elsewhere. "We shall never acquiesce in the enslavement of any people," Ike said in his inaugural address. His chief foreign policy spokesman was the austerely Christian and severely hawkish John Foster Dulles, the new secretary of state. Harvard and other Ivy League universities, particularly Yale, were a hive of recruitment drives for the CIA's new work in "psychological warfare," "covert operations," and other clandestine activities.

George Kennan's strategy of containment, which he had famously outlined in "The Sources of Soviet Conduct," his 1947 article for Foreign Affairs by-lined "X," was out of vogue. So, too, were musings about peaceful coexistence. China's intervention in the Korean War had reversed America's dramatic early advances up the peninsula and added to the lugubrious mood of Harry S. Truman's waning days in Washington. Kennan had not endeared himself to Dulles by contemptuously dismissing the frenzied debate about "Who lost China?" following the country's 1949 revolution. How could you lose a country you did not possess? he asked. Dulles, who grew to hate Kennan and was known to shout at him, forced his early retirement from the diplomatic service. But the loudest bullhorn in Washington, DC, was that of Joseph McCarthy, a senator from Wisconsin, whose "Red scare" was wrecking diplomatic, academic, and Hollywood careers across the country. Brzezinski's early Harvard years coincided with McCarthyism. Americans were also grappling with the ominous novelty of the nuclear shadow.

On the downside, however, and from the vantage point of internal Soviet developments, the Friedrich-Brzezinski project was becoming rapidly less timely. By strikingly unhelpful coincidence, the day after Stalin's death in March 1953—just six weeks after Eisenhower's inauguration—Friedrich hosted a big Harvard conference on totalitarianism.[45] From Friedrich's point of view, Stalin's death would have no impact on a regime incapable of changing from within. As the year went on, evidence to the contrary started to trickle out. In June, a few months before Friedrich invited Brzezinski to be his coauthor, Lavrentiy Beria, Stalin's dreaded henchman and head of the NKVD, was arrested in a Politburo coup led by Nikita Khrushchev and assisted by Georgy Zhukov, marshal of the Soviet Union. In December, two months after Brzezinski teamed up with Friedrich, Beria was executed. Though Moscow was carrying out another wide-ranging purge, its targets were mostly Beria's people.[46] That type of ideological cleansing would make the USSR a less terrifying place for most of its citizens. Brzezinski called it the "anti-purge purge."[47] The era of mass firing squads and wholesale population transfers was over.

The process of de-Stalinization was not yet acknowledged. Nor was it systematic; the gulags did not suddenly empty. As time went on, however, it became harder to ignore signs that the USSR was in transition from totalitarianism to authoritarianism. In February 1956, eight months before their book, *Totalitarian Dictatorship and Autocracy*, came out, Khrushchev delivered his (instantly famous) "secret speech" at the CPSU's Twentieth Party Congress. His address, which listed many of Stalin's "errors" and crimes and the terror that had stopped people from speaking out, was received as a bombshell by Communists everywhere. Marxist-Leninist orthodoxy was thrown into disarray. The myth of Stalin's infallibility was shattered. It was as though the Vatican had repudiated Saint Paul. Had either Brzezinski or Friedrich been a China expert, they could have pressed their case with greater resonance. Mao Zedong's "Great Leap Forward" was around the corner; China's Cultural Revolution was years in the future. By crude population count, totalitarianism was still arguably on the rise. But Friedrich and Brzezinski had placed their intellectual chips on Nazism and Stalinism, one of which had been demolished, the other of which was on the wane.

Brzezinski's phase of serial carousing and efficient cramming was also on the retreat. Not only was he writing or cowriting two books; his spare time was increasingly swallowed up by delicate negotiations over his upcoming wedding. Muska, who was mostly happy to go along with whatever made everyone else happy, created few headaches. But her idiosyncratic manners and Leonia's barely contained irritation with them were turning into a running sore. Leonia took great exception to being addressed in a letter from Muska as "Mrs. Brzezinski" rather than by the Polish endearment "Mamusia." That jibe came in spite of the fact that Muska was taking the trouble to learn Polish and write to her future parents-in-law in their language. Zbigniew angrily accused his mother of "nastiness" in addressing Muska as "Dear Miss Benes— I'm addressing you in this way as you obviously prefer it!"[48] He added, "She addresses you the way she feels at any given moment . . . it's not important, and there is no point in paying attention to such things."[49] Muska's habit of scrawling cartoonish pictures of talking kittens and other doodles alongside her words was regarded as inappropriate and immature. Brzezinski had to intercept his mother's reproaches. He lost all patience with Leonia's escalating inquiries about Muska's choice of wedding dress. "Mother, please take it up with Muska directly as I've had enough."[50]

The clash between absent-minded artist and highly strung Polish matron was barely lessened by Muska's agreement to convert to Catholicism. Brzezinski had already complained that Leonia was depriving Muska of "agency" by hijacking every detail of the wedding. Now Muska was entrusting her soul to the Brzezinskis. Though the Beneses' roots were Catholic, her upbringing had been secular. Her parents were married in a registry office. Her course of theological instruction was no small undertaking. Muska referred to her instructional monsignor as "ominous." By the time she was ready for her formal conversion, however, she knew the catechism far better than her fiancé. Her amused tolerance of the tough entry barriers to the Brzezinski family was expressed in doggerel that she exchanged with Zbigniew, a habit they kept up throughout their marriage: "Muska, a heart without wit, was in a Catholic fit, and when she learned from the holy priest that men and Gods were only beasts, she put on her Mummy's wig and ran off to call up Zbig."[51]

The wedding took place at Boston's Saint Ignatius of Loyola Church on Chestnut Hill on June 11, 1955. Brzezinski and his six ushers wore morning coats and top hats. The ushers were a mix of friends from Cambridge and Montreal, four of them Catholic. One of the others was Henry Rosovsky, a Jewish Russian refugee, who later became a Harvard economist. Brzezinski advised him to wear thick knee pads because he would be kneeling on cold marble for long spells.[52] Muska took her vows in a "chapel length gown of eggshell silk taffeta with a fitted bodice and bouffant skirt," according to a local newspaper report.[53] Since she had banned her father from attending, she was escorted up the aisle by Dr. Paul Dudley White, one of Harvard University's leading medical scholars, who had become an avuncular figure in Brzezinski's life. White's patronage was also a measure of Brzezinski's standing; he had treated Eisenhower earlier that year after the president had a cardiac arrest. The Whites also hosted a reception for three hundred people. Zbigniew and Muska were married by the same exacting Jesuit who had instructed Muska. Her mother, of whom Leonia did not approve (though it was the first time they had met), took pains to dress to the required standard. Keeping up appearances was not quite everything. But an exasperated Zbigniew came close to accusing Leonia of acting as though it was. In keeping with tradition, Zbigniew's half brother, George Zylinski, was his best man, a role that Zbigniew had played at his wedding in Montreal three and a half years earlier. Huguette Zylinski, George's French Canadian wife, was Muska's matron of honor.

In spite of the tension, the wedding was a success. Getting it out of the way was also an enormous relief. It had drained energy, generated friction, and robbed Brzezinski of time alone with the two things he most wanted: Muska and his work. "Muska is cooking lunch. I'm writing. I'm very happy!" he wrote a few days later.[54] Most of his efforts went towards creating a publishable version of his PhD thesis, "The Permanent Purge." Unlike his book on totalitarianism with Friedrich, which stuck mostly to Friedrich's intellectual framework, the work on purges was Brzezinski's own. His thesis, though linked to the theory of totalitarianism, was less vulnerable to Politburo coups. The reviews after it came out in early 1956 were respectful and modestly positive. One scholar called it a "dispassionate scholarly study."[55] Good feedback still trickled in for Brzezinski's aborted PhD research on the Soviet army, which he had turned into a published essay. Irrespective of de-Stalinization, the Soviets retained strict political control of the Red Army. The USSR's technological capabilities were also visibly advancing. The Soviet invasion of Hungary in October 1956 only reinforced America's thirst to learn more about the Soviet army's inner workings. Brzezinski was frequently asked to speak on Soviet-related topics by veterans' associations, churches, synagogues, military academies, including West Point, and libraries. He charged $50 plus travel expenses.

But the book on totalitarianism was starting to feel like an albatross. Friedrich, who was spending much of his time as a visiting professor at the University of Heidelberg in his native Germany, was slow to respond to Brzezinski's queries. Mailing corrected drafts across the Atlantic was cumbersome. At one point Friedrich reprimanded Brzezinski for failing to add footnotes to chapters that Friedrich had not yet written.[56] But he usually accepted Brzezinski's advice, even when it was unsound. Friedrich had set out five essential features of totalitarianism: a single mass party of true believers; a monopoly on violence; a monopoly on communications; terroristic police control; and a command economy. Brzezinski added a sixth: an official ideology. That addition was worthwhile, to say the least; any definition of totalitarianism that omitted a declared belief system would be incomplete. In the wake of Khrushchev's secret speech, Brzezinski showed less wisdom in brushing off Friedrich's suggestion that they delay the book's publication so that they could make revisions. In part, perhaps, because Brzezinski was getting tired of the project, he argued that they should not deviate from their schedule. "I think we are much safer sticking to our broad interpretation as you have developed it," he wrote.[57] Besides, Khrushchev's revelations about Stalin had bolstered their case that Stalin belonged in the same category as Hitler. Friedrich reluctantly concurred.

Publishers' timetables, particularly at the academic presses, are a source of anxiety for scholars in any field. When the book's topic is globally relevant and events are moving fast, they can turn relevant material into period pieces. Such was the fate of the Friedrich-Brzezinski collaboration. Between the time they submitted their final changes in summer of 1956 and the book's publication later in the year, Brzezinski made his first trip to the Soviet Union. It would be an exaggeration to say that his first direct exposure to the USSR—a monthlong trip that included Leningrad, Moscow, Kiev, Kharkiv, Odessa, Yalta, Tblisi, Sochi, and Moscow again—altered his perspective.[58] In some ways, his Soviet tour took him back to where he had left off with his bold McGill thesis. His views on the disruptive potential of the Soviet nationalities could be summed up by a soccer game he saw in Georgia. Barely half the crowd bothered to stand for the Soviet national anthem. His first sampling of the USSR, as well as several excursions to Eastern European satellite states in the mid- to late 1950s, only underlined in his mind the relevance of what he already knew: Moscow's Achilles' heel was its continuing failure to stamp out non-Russian nationalisms.

Though Brzezinski never put it quite so starkly, his USSR tour fueled doubts about the watertightness of his and Friedrich's totalitarian theory. As the philosopher Hannah Arendt had argued in her 1951 classic, *The Origins of Totalitarianism*, and Orwell in *1984*, what was unique and terrifying about totalitarianism was its obliteration of private space, whether in the arts, the

Church, or family life—and even the individual's confidence to indulge in private thoughts. That was what made it "total." Friedrich and Brzezinski's definition was less psychological than Arendt's. Set against the reality of long conversations with students in Russian restaurants, bored Intourist minders assigned to him by the state, and random encounters with people on the street, Soviet reality seemed to be a lot messier. On a seafront boulevard in Odessa, Brzezinski found himself surrounded by more than a hundred people wanting to hear what he thought of socialism. Some walked off in disgust after he summarized his criticisms. Others were happy to debate him. People seemed to be well informed about the injustices of the United States' Jim Crow South. When they asked him about "the Negro question," which was often, Brzezinski's stock answer was "Much like your anti-Semitism." That usually silenced them. Many expressed open contempt for Khrushchev. A Soviet lieutenant who had accompanied Brzezinski to the church where Stalin's mother was buried waxed lyrical about how Nikolai Bulganin, the Soviet premier who had supplanted Malenkov the previous year, was a cultured man. What about Khrushchev? Brzezinski asked. The soldier laughed contemptuously.

Quirky human encounters created the biggest impression on Brzezinski. At a restaurant in Yalta, a woman invited him to waltz with her. They danced a couple of times, to the evident discomfort of her soldier boyfriend. It turned out that both she and the soldier were married—just not to each other. In Kharkiv, the Ukrainian city where Brzezinski's father had been posted in the late 1930s, the guide kept telling him that America was the world's greatest country. Stalin, meanwhile, was "fine for Georgians but for no one else." Brzezinski spent an obligatory evening at the Bolshoi Theater in Moscow. More interesting was a play he saw in one of the capital's lesser theaters about an affair and a broken marriage. The ending was neither happy nor sad, just matter of fact. Brzezinski could not discern any ideological message: "No sharp antagonisms drawn—just a human problem." The audience was rapt. His minder in Moscow was a woman who worked for a Soviet textile trade union. When Brzezinski asked her why Americans had for so long been denied permission to visit the USSR, she said it was because the hotels had not been ready; it had had nothing to do with Stalin, who was generally blameless. Did that mean that she disagreed with the content of Khrushchev's secret speech? Brzezinski asked. She changed the subject.[59]

In a talk Brzezinski gave after going back to Harvard, he spoke of the overwhelming, oppressive drabness of life in the USSR. Although the terror had receded, the Soviet system stifled innovation. Brzezinski's tour contributed to a lasting shift in his thinking; in addition to the nationalities, authoritarian sterility—not Stalinist terror—was the USSR's long-term problem, he concluded. Brzezinski and Friedrich's totalitarianism book nevertheless sold well enough to merit a revised edition in 1965 and multiple translations. Though he no longer agreed with the book's thesis, Brzezinski basked in his newfound recognition. The reviews were all respectful. One or two were glowing. One criticism was that Italian Fascism should never have been bracketed with totalitarianism's Nazi and Soviet variants;[60] Mussolini's Italy had changed too much over its two decades and was consistently too incompetent to govern with anything like total control. Another was that their treatment of Communist China was too cursory. The most devastating critique was that the Soviet system was already showing itself capable of internal reform, which undercut their thesis.

Even their most trenchant critics, however, conceded that the book achieved its basic aim, which was to show that totalitarianism was a different beast from history's various species of dictatorship. Princeton's William Ebenstein was typical of many reviewers in observing that the book would be "immensely useful to all students of totalitarianism. . . . [It] is full of provocative ideas which force one to rethink the whole problem."[61] Though Eastern Europe was not a focus, Brzezinski helped popularize the phrase *captive nations* to describe the USSR's satellite states. In July 1959, Congress declared Captive Nations Week, which was commemorated during the rest of the Cold War.[62] The book also had staying power; in a 2003 essay for the *New Yorker*, Louis Menand bracketed Friedrich and Brzezinski's work with Hannah Arendt's as having for many years been a standard reference point on the subject. It had lost favor for a while in the 1960s. Left-wing critics saw it as a hypocritical way of sifting "good" authoritarian countries—those allied with the US and typically ruled by generals—from the "bad" ones—the Soviet Union and the rest of the Communist world. Friedrich retorted that totalitarianism and authoritarianism were opposites: "In a totalitarian society true authority is altogether destroyed."[63]

In spite of Friedrich's entreaties, Brzezinski had no desire to collaborate with him on the next edition. Friedrich was back at Harvard. By then Brzezinski had moved to Columbia University and the two were no longer in close touch. Brzezinski pleaded too many competing obligations. In truth, however, he had lost faith in their thesis. "I get the feeling that you have moved somewhat away from our joint position. Is that true?" asked Friedrich.[64] It was indeed, though Brzezinski let him down gently. Friedrich nevertheless kept his erstwhile protégé's name on the cover. By agreement he would take all new royalties and clarify for the reader that the revisions were solely his. Their exchanges remained friendly. Brzezinski had a big reason to be grateful to his former mentor; whatever the book's flaws and however much Brzezinski had evolved, Friedrich had given him his first taste of academic fame.

It was on a trip to Poland in 1957—Brzezinski's first visit to his homeland since he was a child—that he realized how American he now felt. Perhaps only Poland could have driven home that sentiment. There in Warsaw he saw the rubble of his childhood home.[65] Ironically, his grandmother's house was part of the new US Embassy complex. He had yearned to return to Poland from the moment he had left. It was only on his return that he realized how deeply North America had imprinted itself on his character in the nineteen years that had passed. His headstrong and often impatient ways clashed with the passivity, cynicism, and dead eyes of many of the Poles he encountered.

From then on, Brzezinski would visit Poland almost every year, usually at the Russia Research Center's expense—the first time on a tourist visa but more often as part of an official delegation. The UB (Urząd Bezpieczeństwa, or security office), generally known as the secret police, kept close tabs on his activities in both Poland and America. Later the UB, which had in the meantime been renamed the SB (Służba Bezpieczeństwa, or security service), opened a file on Tadeusz Brzezinski as well. They assigned him the code name "Ogiński" after Michał Kleofas Ogiński, a late-eighteenth-century Polish nationalist who had died an exiled, broken man after the partition of the Polish-Lithuanian Commonwealth.[66] "Ogiński" was by no means a disrespectful moniker. From the start, the Polish authorities treated Zbigniew Brzezinski as an agent of the imperialist West. His opening SB file read, "The subject is known as a so-called researcher of communism, in particular of the USSR. He specializes in issues related to political systems—he wrote a few papers in which he 'proves' that Hitler's totalitarianism is akin to Soviet totalitarianism. Definitely an enemy—ideologist, very active, gifted, and very clever." The case officer did not know who was funding the Poland trip, since it was well known that Brzezinski and his wife could "barely make ends meet."[67]

The SB went to some lengths to probe for a weakness on which they could blackmail Brzezinski. Family lore says that the effort included a failed sex trap, although there is no mention of that method in the SB files. The SB astutely concluded that a public intellectual humiliation that would expose Brzezinski's "gullibility and stupidity" could damage him the most. Brzezinski greatly prized his scholarly reputation and would pay a high price to avoid being ridiculed, thought the case officer. He was "a *Besserwisser* [know-it-all] driven by the internal need to show off." He was also a risk taker. "A well-doctored sensation could be leaked to the press in France, Italy, maybe Germany (though Germans express great interest in Brzezinski and adore him)."[68] In spite of setting up frequent encounters on both sides of the Atlantic—Brzezinski would happily agree to meetings in the US with Polish secret police posing as diplomats so that he could extract information from them—they never found their sensation. In one such meeting after Brzezinski had been denied a Polish visa because he had been branded an ideological enemy, his opening remark to the alleged Polish diplomat was "See, you don't need a visa to see me."[69]

They also kept a file on Andrzej Roman,[70] Brzezinski's first cousin and lifelong best friend, whom he would see every time he was in Warsaw. When still an adolescent, Roman had joined the Polish partisans late in the Second World War, an experience that Brzezinski envied and admired. Roman, who was a writer and intellectual, would pay a price for his ties to Brzezinski. Officials made sure that his writing career was confined to sports journalism, mostly at the *Kurier Polski*. He was often fired, then rehired in a more marginal role. He loved trying to outwit the censors by smuggling subversive views into his sports reporting. Brzezinski and later Muska, who accompanied him on many of his trips, would bring mink coats and other expensive items that Roman and his wife, Dagmara, could neither afford nor find in Polish stores. Sometimes they would give them dollars. Wherever Brzezinski went, he was scrutinized by easily spotted men "falling out of the trees," often in oversized raincoats.[71] In spite of the devastation the Nazis had wrought, he had no trouble retracing the missing landmarks of his childhood. He liked to take American colleagues to historical sites. On a 1958 visit sponsored by the Ford Foundation, Brzezinski took his hotel roommate, Eugene Rostow, the dean of Yale Law School, and other American colleagues to where the Warsaw Ghetto had been. All that remained was a monument to the vast number of Jews who had been killed and confined there. Brzezinski got their taxis to line up and shine their headlights on the scene. "It is night, and the monument with the surrounding destruction, makes an eerie impression . . . there isn't much that anyone can say," he wrote.[72]

On his first trip to Poland, it was clear to Brzezinski that his homeland was much less totalitarian than the USSR, in spite of pressure from Moscow. Even during the height of Stalinism in the late 1940s and early 1950s, Poland was too stubbornly Polish to acquiesce. By far the largest and most important of the Eastern European satellites, Poland was Moscow's least pliable student. Poland's Catholic Church was never shut down; agricultural collectivization covered barely a quarter of Poland's farms; and the country was largely spared the grisly show trials and executions that took place in Czechoslovakia, Hungary, and Bulgaria. Years earlier, Yugoslavia's Tito had insisted on different national "roads to socialism." Khrushchev was later to endorse Tito's formulation in a reconciliatory 1955 summit in Belgrade. The post-Stalin relaxation triggered outbursts of deep-simmering resentments in the satellites. The first spark was ignited in East Berlin three months after Stalin's death; it was harshly suppressed. In spite of Eisenhower's pledge to support enslaved peoples everywhere, Washington made only pro forma objections against the East German crackdown.

Far worse, in Brzezinski's view, was the Eisenhower administration's unwillingness to lift a finger when Soviet forces invaded Hungary in late 1956 to snuff out Premier Imre Nagy's short-lived liberal revolution. Brzezinski had initially been enthusiastic about John Foster Dulles's doctrine of rolling back Soviet communism. By 1956, he was no longer under any illusion that "rolling back" was a rhetorical substitute for a strategy. It sounded tough, much like the Eisenhower administration's nuclear doctrine of "massive retaliation." In the same way that nuclear war was unthinkable, rolling back was empty posturing, Brzezinski concluded. Dulles made it clear in advance of the Soviet invasion of Hungary that the US would not intervene—a statement that Brzezinski believed had convinced Moscow that it would pay no price for its invasion of Hungary.

What most enraged Brzezinski and others was that the Hungarian-language channels of Radio Free Europe and Radio Liberty, the US-funded broadcasters, had exhorted Hungarians to rise up. Washington had encouraged Hungarians to believe that America would come to their aid. As the Hungarian resistance was being crushed by Soviet tanks, Washington did nothing except provide relief and US visas to the few thousand fighters who made it across the border to Austria. Frank Wisner, deputy director of plans and management, the CIA's political warfare department, which had helped train and equip Hungarian agents, was so stricken by the death of so many of his Hungarian friends and so devastated by the US government's indifference that he had a nervous breakdown. Though he suffered from manic depression, Wisner's suicide a few years later could be read as a tragic comment on the macho face of a hollow stance.[73] In a trenchant essay for *Journal of International Affairs* the next year, Brzezinski dissected Dulles's shortcomings and declared "the bankruptcy of the liberation formula." The USSR had backed President Gamal Abdel Nasser's Egypt in its successful fight against Britain, France, and Israel's occupation of the Suez Canal, a crisis that unfolded at the same time as the invasion of Hungary. By contrast, America provided no support, moral or material, to its Hungarian friends. "For two fateful and bloody weeks the United States attitude was one of almost complete paralysis. . . . During these ten days the country [America] which four years before had proclaimed its official policy to be one of liberation limited itself to recommending in the United Nations on November 3 the studying of 'suitable moves.' No serious warning, as far as is known, was dispatched to Moscow." As Philip Mosley, a fellow Sovietologist whom Brzezinski cited, wrote, "Hope, divorced from power, is not a policy."[74]

Brzezinski's trips to Poland, which in 1956 had narrowly avoided Hungary's bloody fate in spite of having liberalized almost as radically, gave him inspiration for his evolving ideas about how to undermine the USSR. Within earshot of party officials in the foyer of Brzezinski's Warsaw hotel, a Polish professor asked whether he would be seeking asylum in Poland. Brzezinski took the query as a teasing acknowledgment of his visa problem. In an unsubtle jibe at Brzezinski, Poland's Ministry of Foreign Affairs had initially denied him a visa on the grounds that it could supply its own interpreters to the US delegation. The professor answered his own question about whether Brzezinski was planning to defect: "I guess not—one chooses exile in a socialist state only in a fit of absent-mindedness."[75] Signs of Poles' resentment of their Russian masters were not hard to find. One senior Communist Party figure boasted at length about how he had fought to keep Lublin's Catholic University open. When Brzezinski visited the university's rector, the Communist official insisted on leaving them alone for a private conversation. The church service that Brzezinski attended was full. At a Warsaw roundtable between Soviet, Polish, and US delegations, the Poles would often toe one line in public, then contradict it when the Russians were out of range. The fact that he could converse with Poles in Polish made a big difference. It was also helpful to his American colleagues. On the first night of his 1958 trip, he and his roommate, Rostow, were kept awake by two women shouting at each other outside their window. Rostow was tickled by Brzezinski's interpreting: "You have betrayed me and now you are living off my husband's money—you SOB I will kill you. I will kill you."

Perhaps Washington's most effective and thoughtful critic of Dulles's liberation doctrine was John F. Kennedy, the young senator from Massachusetts with whom Brzezinski was already acquainted. Brzezinski was an early member of the Kennedy fan club. That Brzezinski lived in Kennedy's home state might have helped. Like Brzezinski, Kennedy saw Poland as the Soviet Bloc's weakest link. In summer 1957, Fred Holborn, who had been Brzezinski's traveling companion in Europe years before, sent Brzezinski the draft of a big speech that JFK was planning. Holborn, who was now working on Kennedy's Senate staff, asked if Brzezinski could improve the text with "a little more ballast"[76] and suggestions on economic aid to Poland. Being well acquainted with Brzezinski's careful attitude to money, Holborn added that the Kennedy family estate could cover the cost of a long telephone call, if that was what he preferred. Kennedy's Senate speech would be a big element of his takedown of Eisenhower's Cold War strategy, which had not been going well. The speech's focus was Poland.

On the eve of ordering the invasion of Hungary the previous October, Khrushchev had flown to Warsaw with most of the Soviet leadership, including Bulganin and Molotov, to hold crisis talks with Władysław Gomułka, Poland's new leader. The nerve-wracking showdown took place against the backdrop of a near insurrection by Polish workers that had started in June with a strike in Poznań and had since spread. Gomułka, who had spent time in prison, having been accused of "right-wing nationalist deviation," had just been made Poland's leader. He was still a Communist, thus acceptable to the Polish party's dwindling Stalinist faction. But he was also a bold reformist, so welcomed by the rest of the party. Most significantly, he was a Polish nationalist.

To the Soviets, who amassed divisions on Poland's border, Gomułka posed a deep threat to the entire system. He managed to talk Khrushchev out of invading. In exchange for greater Polish autonomy, he pledged fealty to Soviet foreign policy. Khrushchev and his cohort flew back to Moscow. That dramatic turn became known as the "Polish October." Yet Gomułka's reprieve had come at a price: he agreed to contribute a Polish division to the Soviet invasion of Hungary. One reason Poland escaped Hungary's fate was that few Poles believed the US would come to their aid if the Soviets invaded. Such fatalism was ingrained: Churchill and Roosevelt's betrayal at Yalta was also fresh in

Poles' memories. Another difference was that Nowak's branch of Radio Free Europe did not exhort Poles to rise up with extravagant promises of Western help. Nowak's colleagues in the Hungarian-language service showed no such compunction.

Dulles responded to the events in Poland with the same passivity he had shown to Hungary. Hiding behind a nuclear bluff of massive retaliation was doing nothing to deter the Soviets. In his Senate speech Kennedy launched a frontal attack on Dulles: "This policy, if it can be called a policy, is easily stated and even more easily implemented. It requires practically no risk, no cost.... It is this attitude—of merely wanting and hoping—that caused us to be wholly unprepared for the events in Poland and Hungary last October."[77] Interestingly, he omitted the following remarkable passage from the draft that Holborn had sent to Brzezinski: "The Polish people—because of their religious convictions and strong patriotic spirit, because of their historic hatred of the Russians—are perhaps better equipped than any people on earth to withstand the present period of persecution, just as their forefathers withstood successive invasions and partitions from the Germans, and the Austrians and the Russians for centuries before them, and just as theirs was the only country occupied by Hitler that did not produce a 'quisling' [after Vidkun Quisling, Norway's wartime pro-Nazi leader, whose name became synonymous with collaboration]."

It is unclear if it was Brzezinski who recommended cutting that flight of Polonophilic oratory. But leaving it out aligned with Brzezinski's view that US assistance to Poland—mostly trade credits and debt relief—should be done in a way that would not fuel tensions between Warsaw and Moscow. Poland's autonomy was too precious to jeopardize with careless Cold War rhetoric. Brzezinski's imprint was nevertheless unmistakable in an equally hard-hitting address that Kennedy gave in May 1957 at the Overseas Press Club of America in New York City. "The so-called satellite nations constitute the *Achilles heel* [my italics] of the Soviet empire, the tender spot within its coat of iron armor, the potential source of an inflammation that could spread infectious independence throughout its system, accomplishing from within what the West could never accomplish from without."[78] In Kennedy, Brzezinski had found the US leader he had been craving: an intelligent rising star who knew the difference between strategy and posturing. Moreover, JFK needed no tutoring on the importance of Poland. He sent a note to Brzezinski thanking him for his suggestions, which had "served to sharpen the speech considerably."[79] Brzezinski's influence on JFK's foreign policy thinking would grow as his presidential campaign got under way.

Brzezinski's Harvard ascent got another boost when he was made assistant professor in 1956: his annual salary jumped by almost half, to $6,250.[80] Fainsod and Friedrich had pushed his case. His big goal was that rare prize, Harvard tenure. He continued to make extra cash by doing Russia research for Fainsod, and picking up speaking fees and modest payments for articles. But the new money did not go as far as he had hoped. Muska was having trouble finding a job. In the space of three weeks she received eleven rejections for various arts teaching positions. Brzezinski tried to keep her spirits up. Her sense of rejection took a further hit when Wellesley turned down her donation of outdoor sculptures that she had carved for her alma mater: on legal advice, the college regretted that the weather could damage the material.

Nor did Muska's relationship with Leonia improve. Their awkwardness could hardly be blamed on Muska, who spent considerable time in Boston tracking down and sending supplies for Leonia's beauty care company. She also made great efforts to conform with Leonia's idea of how a cultured young lady should look. "M. has been to the hairdresser and her hair is looking absolutely tidy," Brzezinski told his mother about a year after their wedding.[81] Another time he wrote, "Muszka has been dressing very smartly lately and is constantly combed and dressed up." Muska had also learned to address Leonia as "mother" in her letters, which she often signed "from *katecka* [kitten]" with a drawing to match. But the gulf between the disorganized artist, who often forgot to apply makeup, and her heavily perfumed mother-in-law, for whom formal displays of femininity were a sort of character test, could not be bridged. Leonia was prone to bouts of depression after Adam died. She refused social invitations and declared that there was no point in living. Zbigniew showed declining patience for his mother's self-pity. He exhorted her to "get off the sofa" and go out and meet people. "It is one thing to long and wait and believe that things are better over there [in Heaven], and quite another to give up completely and capitulate and drown in it."[82]

Tadeusz's financial woes further exacerbated Leonia's inertia. His efforts at selling insurance over the phone were destined to fail; the gentle ex-diplomat was a world apart from the always-be-closing salesman he needed to be. He tried his hand at various ventures, including setting up a travel agency, Terra Company, which arranged group tours to Poland. But his new business was vulnerable to changing political winds. His pro bono attempts to unite

Poland's highly fractious diaspora in Canada and beyond often fell under the jaundiced gaze of Poland's secret police. An SB report in 1960 noted that Tadeusz had begun to temper his criticisms of the Polish regime. The case officer speculated that he was moderating his views because he feared losing his license to take group tours to the country. In fact, as with many in the Polish of the diaspora, Tadeusz had dialed down his criticisms of Poland after its near miss of a Soviet invasion in 1956. He led several tours to the country. He also played a key role in brokering the repatriation of the royal treasures from the Wawel Royal Castle from Canada to their historical seat in Kraków—an encouraging sign that Warsaw was rehabilitating the symbols of Poland's decidedly un-Marxist and anti-Russian royal heritage.

Brzezinski could do only so much—a modest check here, a mailed plane ticket there—to ease his parents' financial woes. His business advice was specific, frequent, and mostly wasted on his father, whose heart was with the nonremunerating Polish diaspora. But Tadeusz, whom Muska adored (once describing him as "crazy cute" because of his kind and gentle manners[83]) was riveted by Zbigniew's academic life. At Harvard and beyond, Brzezinski was broadening his horizons. In the exchanges between him and his father, Poland was almost invariably the subject. They exchanged clippings and translated each other's Polish-language essays for émigré publications, notably *Kultura*, the Paris-based periodical that was read as far afield as Australia and Argentina. They swapped gossip about who was up and down in the Polish community and debated whether their parallel efforts would make any difference to Poland's future. Zbigniew insisted that they would. Tadeusz's optimism waxed and waned.

If Brzezinski's later detractors, notably Georgetown's WASP foreign policy elite, could have laid their hands on some of his letters to Montreal, they might have treated themselves to a celebratory glass of sherry. In one lengthy epistle to his father in which he was urging him to stick with his Polish diaspora work, Brzezinski insisted that his Harvard career was not as important as his father thought it was. "I've been bouncing from one immigration office to another for years, changing passports, working in the profession that is a welcome but vicarious occupation, in a country which is hospitable and free but not my own; and even if I did consider it my own, I wouldn't be considered a bona fide member by everyone."[84] What Tadeusz must keep reminding himself, Brzezinski told him, was that regaining a nation requires patience. "These things gain importance with time, as is evident from the Zionist movement." In the same letter Brzezinski offered to lend Tadeusz $75, admitting that it was a "drop in the ocean." But it could still come in handy. Some of Brzezinski's exhortations hit home. Tadeusz was elected president of the Canadian Polish Congress and led it for several years. Alas, the position came without a stipend. Brzezinski's amateurish business tips, on the other hand, did not take hold.

There was even less Brzezinski could do to assuage his mother's mourning for her loss of status and resentment at her straitened circumstances. The Brzezinski parents' money was so tight that Zbigniew once asked Leonia whether she had joined a recent Montreal street protest against a tram fare price hike. There was one step, however, that he and Muska could take to lift his parents' spirits: produce a grandchild. George and Huguette had already supplied them with two, Andrzej and Elise. As time went on, Leonia's inquiries about Muska's plans became increasingly unsubtle. Muska finally got pregnant in late 1957 after two and a half years of trying. They began to search for a family home. After their wedding, Brzezinski had moved out of the graduate student apartment at Kirkland House, where he had studied and hosted guests at all hours for the previous two years. That closed the chapter on Brzezinski's student days. The newly married couple's first residence was a rental apartment in downtown Cambridge. They had not meant to stay there for long, but were they were delayed by their difficulties in conceiving. The hunt for a house of their own could now get under way.

It did not take long. They fell in love with a roomy late-Victorian house at 16 Myrtle Street, Belmont, a wealthy suburb of Boston about seven minutes by car and fifteen minutes by bus to Harvard. It had three floors, a small backyard, and a garage. The property was in ugly condition, particularly its chipped brown exterior. But it held promise. The asking price was $19,500, which was beyond their reach. To Brzezinski's surprise, the sellers allowed themselves to be beaten down to $15,000. The clincher, it turned out, was a call that Mrs. White, the wife of Dr. White, Brzezinski's distinguished medical friend, placed to the head of the Belmont Savings Bank, who also happened to be the owner of the house. Mrs. White, whose husband had walked Muska down the aisle three years earlier, asked the banker whether the house was worth his asking price. Her call did the trick. The next day Brzezinski's offer was accepted. The stunned realtor told Brzezinski that he was very fortunate to get it so cheaply. "Clearly Mrs. White made a strong impression," he told his parents.[85] The same bank then provided him with a low-interest-rate mortgage of $13,000, a chunk of which they would use for extensive renovations.

Muska's outlook had brightened after she was hired to lecture on figurative art twice weekly at a local college. Her pregnancy was also going well. They planned to call the baby Marek if it was a boy and Barbara if it was a girl.[86] Her mother, who was still living in California, came in late June to help with the new baby. After doing a lot of the interior overhaul themselves, they had moved into 16 Myrtle Street a month before. Muska's water broke on June 26, 1958. In the hospital a few hours later, she delivered a stillborn girl. Their initial response was to grit their teeth and reassure themselves that she would quickly get pregnant again. After Muska returned home, she was hit by depression (though neither of them used that word). Muska's mother convinced her that a few weeks of recuperation in Berkeley would lift her spirits. Leonia, meanwhile, blamed Muska's stillbirth on overexertion from working on their new home. Zbigniew took the remark to imply that he was to blame and sent her an unusually vituperative reply. "I don't quite understand why Mother is insinuating that M. was overworking before delivery, and that it was not unrelated??? and that on the basis of the opinion of two acquaintances, and AGAINST THE OPINION OF OUR SPECIALIST and even M's mother. What ideas should this bring to mind?"[87]

It took a long time for Muska to get over the blow. Over the next few weeks, she sent Brzezinski a stream of thick letters from California, always signed "Kitten."[88] She worried about his "macaroni TV dinners" and the risk of his putting on weight. She complained when there was no answer in the evening when she tried to call. "I think of you often and long to be with you, talk to you, kiss you."[89] She advised him to quit his habit of taking stiff drinks after playing tennis. "And how is your temper? This is a very bad habit and it is something that I dislike very much." In another she wrote, "Each day a new experience, sorrowful or joyful, deep or superficial, brings us together. With a husband like you I'll get over our loss, and look forward with fist tightly clenched."[90] Judging by Muska's improving mood and her accounts of hikes in Yosemite, the recuperation did what it was meant to do. Conceiving again would be far more difficult.

On their return in September (Brzezinski had joined them for two weeks at the end of her stay) Muska's priority was to ensure that her husband completed his US citizenship application. He had submitted his paperwork more than a year earlier. One reason he had failed to follow up with the required in-person interview was that he had been approached by the CIA just after he filed his paperwork—shortly before his 1957 visit to Poland. Two CIA agents asked him to look out for a particular type of Soviet freight train while he was in Poland.[91] He was to report back to them whatever he found. In the same exchange, they somewhat creepily let it be known that they knew he had just filed his citizenship application. Brzezinski turned them down. He said it would be highly irregular for a visiting scholar to practice amateur espionage. Their crude hint also incited his pride and stubbornness. Muska nevertheless wore him down. His last mile to citizenship, which was complicated by his unusual consular history, was aided by his marriage to an American. Muska was already a citizen when they met. His case was assuredly boosted by Mrs. White's presence as a witness at his oral exam. Brzezinski became a US citizen on December 22, 1958. He was surprised at the elation he felt after the swearing-in. When they exited the court, he and his fellow new citizens were greeted by members of the Daughters of the American Revolution, who pinned Stars and Stripes buttons to their lapels. The woman who accosted Brzezinski misjudged the angle of the pin and grazed his chest. "See," he told her, "I am already shedding blood for America."[92]

Brzezinski, like Henry Kissinger, was on the way to becoming a leading figure among the rising breed of scholar-politician, all-knowing grand viziers to the sultans of their time. Each foreign-born scholar went as far as he could in the academy and in US foreign policy, using the first as a springboard to the second. In the process, they either enriched or contaminated both, depending on where you stood. In contrast to his German-origin rival, however, Brzezinski had a taste for political theater. On several occasions in the 1950s, he was invited to address students as a supposed guest Soviet lecturer by members of the faculty, Harvard's Sam Huntington and Henry Rosovsky among them. He would turn up with a fake mustache in a bemedaled Soviet uniform to make the pitch for communism. On one occasion he even added a Soviet baton to his act. The audience, which on a couple of occasions included officers in training at US military academies, among them West Point, would grow agitated by Brzezinski's Soviet propaganda. He once showed up at a Huntington lecture dressed like Stalin. "Well, you've read criticisms of it," he said. "Now I will defend it." He kept up the act for the full session.[93] The tension would evaporate after he revealed his true identity as a Polish-born Sovietologist. The pedagogical merits of Brzezinski's act are debatable. But it was memorable enough for colleagues to ask him back.[94] He could recite the USSR's worldview in his sleep. The idea, borne out by many students, was that he would take them out of their habits of thought to confront questions they might not otherwise have considered. It would take a heroic leap of imagination to picture Kissinger agreeing to such a ruse.

Brzezinski's most questionable political stunt was to disrupt the Soviet-hosted World Youth Festival in Vienna in 1959. It was the seventh Moscow-backed jamboree to spread the word that communism was about international peace and friendship. The previous one in Moscow in 1957 had landed the Soviets with a huge bill, which came to more than $100 million. It was the USSR's biggest international gathering since Stalin's funeral in 1953. Such was its propaganda value that the head of the KGB, Alexander Shelepin, was overseeing plans for the next one in Vienna, the first to take place outside the Soviet Bloc. The occasion presented the CIA with an irresistible sabotage opportunity. The agency's plan more or less succeeded. Its chief provocateurs were the rising American feminist Gloria Steinem and Brzezinski. On that occasion, he had no qualms about working with the CIA since it would involve no espionage and his activities would be taking place in neutral Austria. He and the intellectually fearless Steinem were enthusiastic about their roles as sowers of ideological confusion.

The US delegation was part of a CIA-front organization called the Independent Service for Information, which was headed by Steinem.[95] Most of its left-leaning student members had no idea who was funding their chartered plane and accommodation. Brzezinski, whose anticommunism was well known to the Soviets and to many American students, was omitted from the delegate list. He made his way to Vienna separately. There he pulled off the prank of his life. His and Steinem's aim was to puncture Moscow's "new look" image as a peace-loving friend of the world's oppressed. The festival churned out a *Pravda*-like newspaper every day. Brzezinski and Steinem published a rival news sheet in seven languages that painted the Soviets as reactionary imperialists. At the big meetings, they would pose awkward questions and find their microphones turned off. Small planes flew above the festival grounds towing signs that said REMEMBER TIBET, REMEMBER HUNGARY.

There was an element of bravado to their antics. Brzezinski and Walter Pincus, a Democratic Senate staffer who would later become a distinguished journalist, cut heart-shaped holes from the Algerian and Hungarian flags, which they unfurled above the festival grounds. They escaped the festival's security guards by crossing a roof plank to an adjacent building.[96] The Hungarian flag was meant to remind the seventeen thousand delegates about the

1956 Soviet invasion; the Algerian one to remind them that the US opposed both Soviet and European colonialism (in this case French). By the standards of the CIA's often comical bag of dirty tricks, the Vienna ploy was relatively tame and reasonably effective. The festival was a maelstrom of confusion. Fearing contamination, the Soviet authorities shunted the Hungarian delegation off to a barge on the Danube. The organizers wasted time and goodwill patting down the crowds to stop a tiny minority from handing out "Free Hungary" pins and pasting anti-Soviet posters anywhere. Whether those disruptions had any influence on the CIA's target audience—delegates from newly decolonized nations and youth from behind the Iron Curtain—is hard to tell. But the event was a disappointment for Moscow, which was good enough for the CIA headquarters at Langley.

Later in life, Brzezinski seemed mildly embarrassed by the episode, putting it down to youthful exuberance. Pincus described it as an exotic long weekend that offered college students the chance to meet Russians. One or two others, however, were outraged by the group's methods, which they saw as childish and manipulative. Inge Schneier, a Harvard student of psychology, who was studying techniques of brainwashing, was pressed by Brzezinski into going along. When she realized that the trip was a CIA-front operation, she confronted him; he was trying to get American "kids roughed up," she said, so he could generate headlines about their mistreatment. Brzezinski brushed Schneier's misgivings aside. Hurt by his response, she gave her side of the story to a *New York Times* reporter in Vienna. Schneier's version did not make it into print.[97] It was only years later, in 1967, that the CIA's role was exposed. By then, the Vietnam War was generating huge bitterness and cynicism about America's Cold War strategy and Langley's methods. In the late 1950s, however, the agency's reputation was still largely pristine. Schneier, who refused to speak to Brzezinski for years, later married Stanley Hoffmann, a Harvard colleague who would become a vitriolic critic of both Brzezinski and Kissinger. With hindsight, Vienna 1959 was Brzezinski's last display of agitprop. His motives were earnest. In that instance, his methods were not.

At the time, Brzezinski was consumed by two unquestionably serious endeavors: writing a book and getting tenure at Harvard. His book *The Soviet Bloc: Unity and Conflict*, published in 1960, was his crowning achievement as an academic. Critics instantly deemed it a major contribution to Cold War scholarship. It was a staple of university reading lists for the next three decades. In contrast to the seventeen books he wrote after that, *The Soviet Bloc* was almost entirely free of Cold War prescriptions. In retrospect, it is remarkable that it took until 1960 for an American scholar to tackle the Communist bloc as a whole. Until then, US Sovietology had treated communism as a monolith. The Eastern European satellites were seen as wards of a rising power. Moscow might encounter teething problems with their absorption; some, such as Poland, Hungary, and increasingly China, might be less pliant than others. Essentially, however, the world was settling into two mutually antagonistic poles. The job of scholars was to understand the USSR.

The idea that the Soviet Bloc was morphing into a coherent whole was both a misreading of its increasingly pluralistic character and a yawning oversight. After Brzezinski's book came out, "comparative communism" spread as a subject at universities, beginning with Brzezinski's own center in New York. As Brzezinski laid out in deep and richly sourced detail, Moscow was caught in a bind familiar to doctrinal empires throughout history, including Islam and the Catholic Church. To maintain credibility, Moscow had to uphold doctrinal purity. To keep the increasingly restive bloc in one piece, however, it had to allow some degree of national divergence. Who was to say when tolerated differences crossed the line into heresy? As the center's grip loosened, a rival one began to emerge in Beijing. Mao's China challenged Moscow's shift away from revolutionary orthodoxy.

Brzezinski sliced the Soviet Bloc's evolution into four phases. In the first, between 1945 and 1947, Moscow allowed Eastern European countries to move towards communism at varying paces and with some ideological latitude. In the second, between 1947 and 1953, the USSR imposed a rigidly Stalinist line. Moscow set up Cominform to ensure that no country strayed from the party line. In the third, after Stalin's death, from 1953 to 1956, Moscow disbanded Cominform and permitted separate roads to socialism. Countries such as Hungary, however, took the new license too far. In the fourth phase, after Khrushchev had consolidated his grip in 1956, Moscow tried to reassert control over its satellites. Faced with a choice between accommodating revisionism in the satellite countries and occupying them militarily, Moscow agonized between the two. The cost of invading every renegade satellite would be prohibitively high. More and more revisionism would have to be allowed. Over time, Soviet orthodoxy, like its historical forebears, would erode and meet the fate of all empires. "For the final consummation of this process, however, the ideology must first be denied both victories and enemies, a difficult and paradoxical task since denial of one can be construed as the manifestation of the other."[98] There, for the first time, but only in the book's final sentence, Brzezinski offered strategic advice. America's goal, he said, must be to hasten a peaceful unraveling of the Soviet Bloc. The project would require subtlety and skill.

The reviews were glowing. The following summary by the University of Notre Dame's Stephen D. Kertesz in the *American Slavic and East European Review*, was not untypical: "It is hardly possible in the space of a few paragraphs to do justice to the wide scope of Mr. Brzezinski's useful book. His chapters reflect mature scholarship and even Communist leaders might read them with some profit. They would learn a lot about themselves, their doctrines, their comrades and their late comrades."[99] The *New York Times* said that Brzezinski's volume was marked by "unusual insight, richness of information and stimulating thought."[100] Princeton University's Cyril Black said that Brzezinski's "persuasive analysis has added a new dimension to our understanding of this vital aspect of Soviet policy."[101] Hugh Seton-Watson, Britain's renowned scholar of central Europe, who had a reputation for being exacting, said that Brzezinski was "to be congratulated" for having produced "an excellent work." Perhaps the truest yardstick of the book's success was its shelf life. In *Foreign Affairs*' list of top books of the century, eight years after the Cold War had ended, Robert Legvold wrote, "Only once in the postwar period did someone tie together all dimensions of the Soviet world. . . . Brzezinski did this with an intellectual flair and clarity of argument and prose that set his book apart."[102] Brzezinski dedicated the book to Merle Fainsod.

Unfortunately for Brzezinski, his magnum opus was published a few months after he had been denied Harvard tenure, which came as a blow but not a shock. For the previous two years he had been setting up Plan Bs in the expectation that his Harvard hopes might be dashed. Among the university offers that he chose not to pursue or turned down were from Chicago, Cornell, Berkeley, and Duke. All of these were tenured positions. More than a year before Harvard disappointed Brzezinski, he had been musing about moving to Columbia University, which had also put out feelers to him. What Columbia lacked in relative prestige, it made up for in two respects. First, its campus was in metropolitan New York, not provincial Boston. "Here you live in Harvard, all friends are from Harvard, and the horizon is Harvard," he told his parents in 1958.[103] Second, it was halfway closer to Washington, DC. The term "Boswash" was coined in the 1960s to describe the increasingly busy traffic between America's most coveted Ivy League school and its federal capital. That was particularly true after 1961 when JFK filled his administration with fellow

Harvard alums, later labeled "the best and the brightest." Unlike Boston, however, New York was home to the big foundations, including Rockefeller and Ford, as well as to the Council on Foreign Relations, which at that point was still the foundry of US foreign policy consensus. Brzezinski had been itching for a while to make inroads in Washington.

In the 1970s and in currency ever since, a legend took hold that Brzezinski lost his Harvard professorship to Henry Kissinger. That account is so misleading as to be nearly false. The same applies to tales of their bitter rivalry at Harvard. Their spirit of competitiveness took hold years after both had moved elsewhere. In the 1950s, Kissinger and Brzezinski's academic circles intersected but did not closely overlap. Kissinger made his name as a diplomatic historian with his 1954 undergraduate thesis, "A World Restored: Metternich, Castlereagh and the Problems of Peace, 1812–1822." It was mellifluously written. His choice of topic was also remarkably bold given the topic's seeming irrelevance to the Cold War situation. The 383-page thesis was so long that it gave rise to the so-called Kissinger rule whereby undergraduate essays could not exceed 150 pages. It was also an unlikely commercial hit. Only in hindsight did the relevance of Kissinger's subject become apparent. His fascination with the success of the 1815 Congress of Vienna in creating a post-Napoleonic balance of power offered hints of his approach to Cold War strategy that he would later put into practice. One of his biographers, Walter Isaacson, found entertaining similarities between Kissinger's character portrait of Klemens von Metternich, the Habsburg cohero of his book, and what Kissinger himself would later become: "Napoleon said of him that he confused policy with intrigue"; "He was a Rococo figure, complex, finely carved, all surface"; "He excelled at manipulation, not construction."[104]

Kissinger was chiefly a student of European diplomatic history. He was never at any point considered to be a Sovietologist, in his own mind or that of any other scholar. As a protégé of William Yandell Elliott, he spent most of his time in the Harvard Department of Government. Brzezinski's main home was at the RRC. Kissinger's other big book at that point, *Nuclear Weapons and Foreign Policy* (1957), was a critique of the United States' doctrine of massive retaliation in which he controversially argued that limited nuclear war was winnable. In that respect his work was related to the USSR. But his focus was on deterrence and war-gaming in an era of potential mass annihilation, not on the USSR's internal character. Kissinger's promotion in 1958 did not come at Brzezinski's expense; they were not vying for the same professorship. What happened is easily recognizable to anyone familiar with academia's byzantine politics.

Kissinger had been made deputy head of the Center for International Affairs, a new outfit hosted by Harvard with seed money from the Ford Foundation.[105] His boss was Robert Bowie, who had recently become Brzezinski's newest Harvard mentor. Bowie had followed George Kennan and Paul Nitze as the third head of the State Department's policy and planning unit. Following a prolonged wooing, McGeorge Bundy, the dean of Harvard's Faculty of Arts and Sciences, convinced Bowie to head the new center. Bundy's plan was to make Kissinger his part-time number two with half of his salary paid by the Harvard Government Department and half by the Center for International Affairs (CFIA). The department, which had no regard for the upstart new center, did not like the arrangement. In a torturous compromise, the department voted to give Kissinger tenure in exchange for the CFIA's agreeing to fund an additional half chair that was filled by Stanley Hoffmann. The department also gave tenure to Hoffmann. The real rivalry had been between Hoffmann, another highly regarded European émigré, and Kissinger. As chance and bureaucratic compromise would have it, both of them emerged as winners. "The man who was my competitor when I was appointed was Stanley Hoffmann—and they solved it by appointing both of us."[106]

The department was now out of funds to promote Brzezinski. Almost as outraged as Brzezinski, Bowie and Fainsod launched a rearguard fight to keep him at Harvard. Bowie's solution was to give Brzezinski a full-time position at the CFIA that he would fund for the next five years. But that would require the department to vote unanimously for his tenure. Brzezinski got everyone's support minus one. Both Kissinger and Hoffmann voted yes. The dissenter was Adam Ulam, the department's only Polish-born professor. Ulam's veto sealed Brzezinski's fate. Since Ulam was Jewish, some supposed that he thought Brzezinski was anti-Semitic and had vetoed him accordingly. But that theory surfaced only years later. Ulam never explained his negative vote. He had also argued against Kissinger's promotion, but that did not require unanimity. A more plausible conjecture is that Ulam objected to scholars with political ambitions. Indeed, he shared that view frequently with colleagues. That fit his objections to both Kissinger and Brzezinski.

Either way, Brzezinski had an offer from Columbia in his pocket. A similar misfortune befell Brzezinski's old friend Samuel Huntington. Columbia also scooped him up. They went to New York together. "I am naturally a little disappointed but, I suppose, it was in the books," Brzezinski told a colleague.[107] He and Muska chose to smile at their fate. They called their June 1960 farewell bash "the shipwreck party." Everyone they knew, including Brzezinski's detractors, was invited to what turned into a famous gesture of defiance. People came in pirate costumes and consumed vodka and champagne in great volume. Brzezinski's overlabored message was that he did not care. "There was only one reason, to show that '*Je m'en fiche* [I don't give a damn],'" he recalled decades later.[108] When one door closes, another opens. After a decade at Harvard, Brzezinski would never go back. From Montreal to Boston and now New York, the thirty-two-year-old was heading down the East Coast with deliberate haste.

4

Falling Towards Washington

A Washington scholar was once asked what qualities it took to understand foreign policy. He quipped that you should be neither young nor
American.[1] At thirty-two, Brzezinski did not fit the first criterion. He could
be brash and wore his ambition on his sleeve, though his relentless drive was
bearing fruit. On the second, he was now an American, though he did not
typically think like one. A decade after moving to the US, he was part of arguably the most exciting presidential campaign the country had seen. That
was partly because it was America's first fully televised presidential contest.
Mostly, though, it was because of John F. Kennedy. His ability to channel the
hopes of a new generation—with vision and glamour—electrified millions.
Kennedy, who was only eleven years Brzezinski's senior, was also keen to portray himself as the choice of American intellectuals. The conservative writer
William F. Buckley, Jr., famously said, "I would rather be governed by the first
two thousand people in the Boston telephone directory than by the two thousand people on the faculty of Harvard University." The Republican nominee,
Richard Nixon, felt the same way. Kennedy, who treated his elite background
mostly as a selling point, was a strong advocate for bringing intellectual heavy-
weights into government.

Brzezinski's role in Kennedy's campaign should not be overstated—
though some did. A June 1960 front-page article in the *Wall Street Journal*
listed Brzezinski as the head of a Harvard "brain trust" that was advising

Kennedy.[2] Other members included John Kenneth Galbraith, America's most famous political economist, who had been a New Deal advisor to Franklin D. Roosevelt; William Langer, a history professor who had helped launch the Office of Strategic Services, the precursor of the CIA; and Wassily Leontief, a Soviet American economist who would later win the Nobel Memorial Prize in Economic Sciences. Each was old enough to be Brzezinski's father.

Ted Sorensen, a friend and advisor to Kennedy, invited the group to a lunch in Cambridge early in his presidential campaign. The gathering, and media reports about it, was the kind of stunt in which campaigns specialized: setting up crowded advisory boards that never met; the bigger the names, the better. In this case, however, Brzezinski's was neither well known nor easily pronounceable. A bewildered Brzezinski telephoned Sorensen to ask what was going on. The *Wall Street Journal* article said that the only useful advice provided during the lunch was "by a Harvard professor with the incredible name of Zbigniew Brzezinski who reads *Pravda* with his morning coffee and revels in the intrigues of the Kremlin."

Sorensen laughed off Brzezinski's inquiry. The newspapers had called him to ask about the group of senior professors advising Kennedy: "Don't take it too seriously. They had such a hard time with your name that I decided to name you as head of the group."[3] Though Brzezinski had advised Kennedy, he was not an intimate and did not lobby for a position in his administration; he wanted to influence it from the outside. He was on good terms with many in Kennedy's world, including McGeorge Bundy, the former dean of Harvard's Faculty of Arts and Sciences, who became Kennedy's national security advisor. From Harvard he also knew Arthur Schlesinger, Jr., who, like Sorensen, was part of the "Camelot" roundtable advising and writing speeches for the Massachusetts senator. Kennedy also read a lot of what Brzezinski wrote— both the campaign memos that he fired off and his increasingly prolific articles. "As usual I found your analysis both perceptive and stimulating," he wrote to Brzezinski in August 1960 in response to a memo on Khrushchev's political situation.[4]

The Cold War played a big part in the 1960 election. Kennedy's strategy was to present himself as more sophisticated than Nixon and to outhawk him. Kennedy's claim that the Soviets had achieved a growing "missile gap" over the United States was false. In reality, America's nuclear arsenal still dwarfed that of the Soviets. Sounding that alarm, however, proved to be effective politics. Rather than refute Kennedy's assertion, Nixon argued that he would be tougher on defense, which sounded less credible than it might have. He knew that the missile gap was mythical. Eisenhower had stopped him from publicly disclosing that fact because it would reveal the existence of the United States' U-2 spy plane program (which, among other benefits, had gathered proof of the USSR's paltry weapons stockpile). Another key strand of Kennedy's campaign was that he would replace the "empty oratory" of the Eisenhower-Nixon years with an approach that would improve conditions in the Soviet Union's captive nations. Extravagant promises of rollback had created dangerously false hopes. That position had the virtue of being true. In a speech JFK gave in Chicago five weeks before the 1960 election, he promised more economic engagement, cultural ties, and scientific exchanges with East Bloc countries. The aim would be to loosen the Soviet Union's grip on them. "Poland is a satellite government but the Poles are not a satellite people," he told the Polish American Congress to wild applause. "We have no right, unless we are prepared to meet our commitments, to incite them to national suicide. But neither can we abandon them, leaving them without hope for the future."[5]

Those lines were a condensed version of Brzezinski's Cold War strategy, which started to crystallize after he moved to Columbia. His and Muska's 215-mile move south from Boston to New York had been a pleasant one. They sold their house in Belmont for a lot more than they had paid for it. With a salary of $9,500, Brzezinski's earnings were again jumping by half. He was now tenured and valued by his grateful new colleagues at Columbia. Rather than live in Manhattan, the Brzezinskis bet on having a family, in spite of their anxiety over Muska's struggle to conceive since the stillbirth two years earlier. They bought a five-bedroom home in a quiet suburb of Englewood, New Jersey, for $27,000. The mortgage was only $9,000. In contrast to Harvard, which gave Brzezinski the feeling that he should show continuous gratitude for being there yet would never get a seat at the high table, Columbia went to considerable lengths to make his transition comfortable. "We shall make every effort to see that in the years to come you are satisfied with your choice," wrote David B. Truman, the head of Columbia's Public Law & Government department.[6] Among other welcome gestures, Truman found Brzezinski a convenient parking space on Columbia's Morningside Heights campus, a subsidy for the mortgage on his New Jersey home, and wide latitude for long leaves of absence to travel overseas.

To Truman and his colleagues, Brzezinski was a big part of the solution to Columbia's deficiencies. Though it had been the first US university to create a Russia center in 1946—two years before Harvard launched the RRC—its reputation was modest. Harvard supplied most of the ideas. Columbia's Russian Institute churned out the Russian-speaking graduates. But its research lacked intellectual heft. In a letter to his new colleague Alexander Dallin, a Russian émigré whose father had been on the losing Menshevik side of the Communist bloodletting in Russia's 1917 revolution, Brzezinski said that the Russian Institute "really needs a big kick in the pants."[7] The institute's scholars wrote inconsequential papers on abstruse corners of Soviet history that mostly sank without trace. People were happy there, he conceded, and the atmosphere was friendly. "But perhaps it ought to be just a touch less friendly and more productive. . . . If we want to make an impact and really shape the thinking of people, and not merely contribute material useful to others for footnoting, then we ought to bear this in mind."[8]

Brzezinski was the kick in the pants he was urging on Columbia. He was hired to bolster the university's Russia talent. The university quickly realized that it should let him run his own show if it wanted to keep him. A year after he moved to New York, he launched the Research Institute on Communist Affairs (RICA) with a $5.5 million gift from the Ford Foundation.[9] He would be its first director, with the freedom to hire big names who would attract notice by doing research of practical relevance to policy makers in Washington. Such largesse gave him a degree of patronage that could be put to good use in New York. Most important, RICA put Brzezinski's Cold War thinking onto the map. His new outfit would be dedicated to the study of "comparative communism," which Brzezinski had for years been trying to persuade Harvard to take seriously. It had a nearly instant effect. In 1962, a year after Brzezinski set up RICA, Harvard belatedly offered him the tenure he had craved for so long. It was a far more attractive offer than the one he had been denied two years before. He could effectively invent his own job description. He would take a full professorship and would have only light teaching duties, which would leave him plenty of time for travel and research. Harvard was wooing him with the kind of dream package that sets up a scholar for life.

But a lot had changed in the two years since Brzezinski had moved to New York. What had once been the pinnacle of his ambitions now seemed like the less exciting option. Running back to Harvard might be the sensible thing to do, but it would also close off paths that had started to open up—not least because of New York's closer proximity to Washington. In New York, he could shape his own life; Harvard would do that for him. After weeks of weighing the pros and cons, he turned Harvard down. One of the biggest cons was Muska's opposition. That Muska was happily settled in New Jersey weighed heavily on Brzezinski's decision. "I want to stay; they make me leave. Two years later should I just drop everything and run back?" Brzezinski wrote to Dallin. "I have made an honest woman of Columbia and what was a shot-gun wedding has now been legitimized by my decision."[10] It was a choice he never regretted. Neither did Columbia. Harvard tried again in 1965 to lure Brzezinski back. His rejection was swift: "Had I been given tenure at Harvard, I would have been delighted and I would have stayed. But then I was forced to think, what do I really want to be? I said to myself that I don't want to be crossing the Harvard Yard year after year carrying a folder, lecture number 7, 'joke used last year,' 'class reaction,' tweed jacket. I want to influence the world, shape American policy. And New York is better for that."[11]

Among New York's big plus points was that it was home to the Council on Foreign Relations (CFR), the crucible of American foreign policy think-ing. It was not obvious that someone like Brzezinski would be welcomed into the sanctum of a still WASP-dominated world. The council had been launched after the First World War to spread Woodrow Wilson's liberal in-ternationalism. The initial idea was to create a transatlantic body called the Institute of International Affairs with one branch in London and another in New York. That plan did not come to fruition. But it gives a clear sense of the council's Anglophilic origins; London's Chatham House (the Royal Institute of International Affairs) and New York's Council on Foreign Re-lations were its twin outcomes. CFR's mission was to secure America's rise as a global power, which meant taking on its deeply ingrained isolationist streak. By the 1930s, CFR's biggest donors were the Ford and Rockefeller Foundations. After World War II, it became the natural fount of ideas and people for the United States' Cold War struggle with the Soviet Union. In 1960, the chairman was John McCloy, who would later be widely cited as a leading face of the US establishment.[12] As the US high commissioner to Germany and advisor to FDR and almost every other president until Ronald Reagan, later president of the World Bank then chairman of Chase Manhat-tan, McCloy personified the American great and good. The recently built Pentagon, which he had overseen, was known as "McCloy's Folly."

McCloy was also one of the "wise men" portrayed in the eponymous book by Walter Isaacson and Evan Thomas. Each of them—McCloy, Robert Lovett, Averell Harriman, George Kennan, Dean Acheson, and Charles "Chip"

Bohlen—was a familiar sight at CFR's well-appointed Harold Pratt House on Park Avenue. Most came from families of largely British origin, in some cases recently. Acheson, who bore a clear resemblance to Anthony Eden, Great Britain's prime minister in the mid-1950s, who was also a close friend, was the son of an Anglican bishop who had emigrated to Connecticut. Harriman was a friend of Winston Churchill who would later marry Churchill's former daughter-in-law, Pamela. With the exception of the chiefly Scottish-origin Kennan, who came from a relatively penurious Ohio background, the wise men were scions of fortunes made largely during the "robber baron" era in the late nineteenth century or before. Bohlen's antecedents were German. But that was a distinction without much difference; he was also Episcopalian. Two of them went to Groton, the hallowed Massachusetts prep school that was a virtual facsimile of its English counterparts. Galbraith described the reigning ethos of nonpartisan service to country as the "Groton ethic." Almost all of them were on CFR's board. It was still rare to see a Jewish name on the council's roster. A Polish one had not yet featured.

Brzezinski arrived just in time to knock on the waning establishment's door. By the end of the 1960s, the old foreign policy consensus was as good as dead, its credibility pulverized in the jungles of Vietnam. Brzezinski would later describe the Vietnam War as the "Waterloo of the WASP elite."[13] The domino theory, which held that if one country fell to communism, its neighbor would be next—first Vietnam, then Thailand, and so on—was a product of CFR thinking. That theory, in turn, had been a natural outgrowth of the doctrine of containment, which Kennan had laid out in *Foreign Affairs*, CFR's flagship publication, in 1947. In 1960, the council was still the headquarters of the foreign policy elite. Kennedy was a Catholic in a largely Episcopalian world. Yet he was an unabashed admirer of the wise men. When it came to filling his cabinet, he offered Robert Lovett, a former defense secretary and storied CFR elder, his pick of jobs. Lovett was not interested in any, but suggested names for who might fill those roles. Kennedy unquestioningly took each of Lovett's recommendations.[14] Dean Rusk, the president of the Rockefeller Foundation, became his secretary of state; Douglas Dillon, a Wall Street banker, was appointed treasury secretary; and Robert McNamara, the chief executive officer of Ford Motor Company, became Kennedy's secretary of defense. McNamara was hailed in the media as one of the "whiz kids" of the new computer age.

Entry to the establishment was hard and turnover slow. Brzezinski nevertheless managed to gain admittance. Within months of moving to New York, he befriended Hamilton Fish Armstrong, the almost absurdly long-standing editor in chief of *Foreign Affairs*, who had been hired at its launch in 1922 and held the top job since 1928. Securing the patronage of the venerable Armstrong, which was happily bestowed since Brzezinski could be relied on to pitch cogent pieces and deliver on time, was indispensable. In 1962, he was given CFR membership. Among his sponsors was Harvard's Robert Bowie. Brzezinski was already churning out essays for *Foreign Affairs*. They were read by the people who mattered: at CFR, in the White House, on Capitol Hill, and in college and university faculties up and down the country. Brzezinski's networking was frenetic. The moment a big piece of his came out, he would mail copies of it to dozens of American foreign policy influencers, including his White House contacts, such as Bundy and Schlesinger; most of the wise men, especially Kennan and Harriman; leading senators, notably William Ful-bright and Hubert Humphrey, the chairman and leading figure on the Senate Foreign Relations Committee, respectively; and journalists such as George-town's Alsop brothers, Joseph and Stewart, Walter Lippmann, the dean of American columnists, and the *New York Times'* James "Scotty" Reston.

Decades later, Brzezinski and Fred Bergsten, a prolific Washington econ-omist, figured out that they held equal first place as the most published au-thors in *Foreign Affairs*.[15] By that stage of his career, Brzezinski's range was so broad that he was sometimes criticized, including by Kissinger, as a slave to intellectual fashion—a prisoner of the latest shiny trend. In his first few decades, however, the opposite was the case; the consistency of Brzezinski's focus was striking. His first cover essay for *Foreign Affairs* in July 1961 was en-titled "Peaceful Engagement in Eastern Europe," a clear descendent of the MA thesis he had written at McGill in the late 1940s, which in turn became the instantly recognizable strategy he took with him into government in the late 1960s and 1970s. The kernel of his academic and political career is laid out in that debut essay in *Foreign Affairs*.

In its first sentence, he stated that the United States had lacked a policy towards Eastern Europe since the start of the Cold War. The satellite states were treated as part of the USSR, which meant their only realistic path to free-dom lay through Moscow—either via internal Soviet reforms or because of Soviet collapse. Such passivity was a logical facet of Kennan's containment strategy, which was meant to stop further Soviet territorial advances. But Ken-nan had little to say about the Eastern European nations the USSR had already occupied. Frustrations over the limits of containment under Harry Truman had led to the fantasy of liberation under Dwight Eisenhower. That proved worse in practice than the fatalism it was trying to redress. The US needed a new strategy that would avoid both the passivity of containment and the hollow militancy of rollback. Brzezinski was proposing a pragmatic middle way that avoided both appeasement and the risk of nuclear war. Rather than interpreting all roads as leading to and from Moscow, the US should build bridges to Eastern Europe, he argued. That would include lifting travel restrictions, providing soft loans and export credits, and encouraging people-to-people exchanges, including sporting events and student scholarships. Such links would help stimulate further pluralism within the Soviet Bloc. The strategy could not be based on the threat of force or even the promise of eventual liberation. Saber rattling would only push the Soviet Bloc closer together. The tools should be economic, diplomatic, and above all peaceful. "Peaceful liberation would deny either that Eastern Europe is a satellite region or that we plot to make it a Western outpost," he concluded.[16] The region was Moscow's Achilles' heel, though the Soviets could not easily be tripped up.

The essay, which Brzezinski cowrote with MIT's William Griffith, whom he first met when Griffith was working in Munich for Radio Free Europe, did not land with a thud; it gathered force over time. "I think you will find that the basic strategy you recommended is being adopted," Kissinger wrote to Brzezinski in mid-1961.[17] That was not as dramatic as it sounded. President Kennedy embraced Brzezinski's language on bridge building but little more. What sounded good on the campaign trail, particularly when pitched at Polish American voters and others of Eastern European origin, had been displaced by rolling crises. Kennedy's humiliating first meeting with Khrushchev in Vienna, the 1961 showdown over Berlin and the Bay of Pigs fiasco later that year, followed by the Cuban Missile Crisis in 1962, had swallowed most of his "thousand days." Brzezinski's influence was nevertheless tangible.

"Forgive me for my delay in sending you a copy of your speech!" Arthur Schlesinger, Jr., wrote to Brzezinski in late July 1963 with an attached copy of an address that Kennedy had given in Berlin on June 26.[18] Earlier that day, Kennedy had thrilled crowds at the Rudolph-Wilde-Platz and irritated Khrushchev with his famous utterance "Ich bin ein Berliner [I'm a Berliner]." History has largely forgotten the formal speech that he delivered at the Free University of Berlin three hours later. Its theme and many of its words were Brzezinski's. "Justice requires us to do what we can do in this transition period to improve the lot and maintain the hopes of those on the other side," Kennedy told the assembled students and professors. "And when the possibilities of reconciliation appear, we in the West will make it clear that we are not hostile to any people or system providing they choose their own destiny without interfering with the free choice of others."[19] Though drowned out by the iconic images of Kennedy at the Brandenburg Gate, much of the substance that day was Brzezinski's.

Kennedy's assassination in Dallas four months later robbed the United States of its youngest president—and Brzezinski of his first American hero. JFK's death also deprived him of the only US leader to date, however distracted, to have at least nominally adopted his Cold War strategy. Along with colleagues, in a hushed Columbia common room, the catatonic Brzezinski watched CBS's Walter Cronkite deliver the news. Brzezinski rarely advertised his emotions. But the death of his first real American hero shook him deeply. Kennedy's murder was both a tragedy and a career setback. Brzezinski kept pushing his ideas with television appearances, books, public lectures, and op-eds. Though his manic schedule implied otherwise, this race was long distance. His debut piece two years earlier in *Foreign Affairs* had marked a shift from pure scholarship to usable strategy. It had also exposed him to the criticism that he was driven by his Polishness. That claim had barely surfaced at Harvard, where his background was seen as an attribute since he spoke both Russian and Polish. But in political circles, and particularly in Washington, Brzezinski's Polish roots evoked ambivalence—and sometimes hostility.

An early instance of that was a talk that Chip Bohlen, a "wise man" who had been Eisenhower's US ambassador in Moscow, gave at Chatham House in London in 1962. Bohlen was on the way to Paris as Kennedy's ambassador to France. In an account passed on to Brzezinski by his English friends, Bohlen had apparently dismissed Brzezinski's views on the grounds that he was a Pole "or that they [his scholarship] represent the Polish point of view," as he complained in a letter to Bohlen. "Leaving aside the fact that I was brought up on this side of the Atlantic and am one of many Americans of Polish origin, I am troubled by the thought that the views of, say, [Edward] Teller [a Hungarian-born nuclear physicist], Kissinger, or [George] Kistiakowsky [a Ukrainian American scientist who had been involved in the Manhattan Project], could also be easily dismissed on similarly irrelevant grounds."[20] Bohlen's reply was a model of courtesy. He praised Brzezinski as one of America's foremost Soviet scholars. But his attempt to clarify what he called Brzezinski's "garbled and

distorted version" unwittingly confirmed the basis of Brzezinski's complaint.
"I believe that I said during the discussion that your views on Polish matters,
particularly your advocacy of the recognition of the Oder-Neisse line, was affected by your particular interest in Polish matters, in which your background
played its part," he wrote. "There was certainly nothing in anything I said that
could be interpreted in the way that you received it."[21]

Since 1945, the Oder-Neisse Line had been Poland's border with Germany. Having lost almost half of its territory to what was now called the
"western Soviet Union," large chunks of which were incorporated into Be-
lorussia and Ukraine, Poland was partly compensated by Stalin with a slice
of what would become the German Democratic Republic (East Germany).
West Germany had refused to recognize Stalin's Polish border. Moreover, successive West German governments kindled hopes among Silesia's displaced
Germans—an influential voting bloc—that they would get their lands back.
To a lesser extent, Bonn nurtured similar hopes among German refugees from
Sudetenland, which had reverted to Czechoslovak sovereignty after the war. It
did not take a detailed knowledge of the region—let alone an Eastern European background—to know that any hint of German revanchism struck terror
into Polish and Czechoslovak hearts. Nazi Germany had been defeated less
than two decades before. No matter how imaginatively applied, peaceful engagement could not work while West Germany was perceived to hold a sword
of Damocles over Polish and Czech heads. That would only bind Poland and
Czechoslovakia closer to the USSR as the guarantor of their borders. Brzezinski had long argued that America should press West Germany to recognize
the Oder-Neisse Line. That step was in fact integral to his Cold War strategy.
Dismissing it as the product of Polish bias, as Bohlen and others were doing,
negated Brzezinski's entire approach. It would take several years for his logic
to break through in Lyndon Baines Johnson's Washington—and for Bonn to
grasp that its stance was backfiring. Bohlen had only been giving voice to a
widespread whispered suspicion: that Brzezinski's origins raised doubts about
his loyalty to America.

By contrast, Brzezinski's Polish background was an asset at Columbia,
where he set about hiring good émigré and American scholars of Eastern Europe and beyond; comparative communism expanded to include Vietnam,
North Korea, Mongolia, and, most important, China. Brzezinski's name was
also a growing draw for students. Among his doctoral students was Madeleine
Albright, the Czech-born daughter of Josef Korbel, a well-regarded scholar

and distinguished former diplomat. Albright's story was remarkably similar to Muska Brzezinski's. The two became instant friends. Albright was from a Czech background; her father was a diplomat; she had spent some of her childhood in wartime London; then she crossed the Atlantic and was eventually admitted to Wellesley a few years after Muska. Albright recalled Brzezinski giving guest lectures to Wellesley undergraduates in the late 1950s. "He would speak in complete paragraphs without notes," she said.[22]

His teaching style at Columbia could be merciless. If a student said something stupid, was late to class, or missed an essay deadline, verbal decapitation was assured. He would assign reading material in the original Russian. Unless a student was linguistically proficient, he or she would flounder. Brzezinski's marking was the inverse of grade inflation; he usually awarded one A per class. The upside to his economy of praise was that the students in question knew that they had earned it. When students got an A or A minus, they would receive a special congratulatory letter from Brzezinski. "You would be walking on air for days," said one of his postgraduate students.[23]

He was impatient with fools but had time for people with something interesting to say, regardless of whether he agreed with them. One of Albright's peers was editor of the *Daily Worker*, the weekly newspaper of the Communist Party of the United States of America. Brzezinski himself sometimes wrote for the *New Leader*, a magazine that had been founded by Mensheviks. "You wanted to impress him," Albright said. As his teaching style developed, he would conduct simulations of the White House Situation Room with students assigned roles on which they would be graded. It was the intellectual equivalent of gladiatorial combat. Creating foreign policy was about having "blood, guts, and personality," he told students. "It was also about efficiency of expression. "If you cannot express the essence of your approach in two pages, no policy maker is going to read it."[24]

Brzezinski believed that one of the best ways to test his ideas was through travel. He took every chance to do so. In 1960, he returned to the USSR and Yugoslavia—and visited Bulgaria, Mongolia, and Japan for the first time. The following summer, he visited several West African countries. Often Muska accompanied him. In late 1962 and early 1963, he and Sam Huntington embarked on a ten-week world tour. Huntington had returned to Harvard from Columbia after accepting an offer similar to the one Brzezinski had just refused. Their trip was funded by a grant from the Guggenheim Foundation to support a joint book they were researching that would compare the US and Soviet political systems.

Muska and Nancy Huntington went along. The group's itinerary included Japan, Hong Kong, Taiwan, Thailand, Vietnam, Laos, Burma, India, and Germany. In each country they met political leaders and scholars. They stayed for a week in New Delhi with John Kenneth Galbraith, whom Kennedy had sent there as ambassador. Galbraith set up a one-hour audience with Jawaharlal Nehru, India's aging and somewhat mournful prime minister. A few weeks earlier, India's military had been humiliated and Nehru's dreams of nonalignment shattered in a Himalayan border war with China.[25]

In Bonn, they had a meeting with Konrad Adenauer, who had been West Germany's chancellor since 1949 and would soon be stepping down. Brzezinski also caught up with Willy Brandt, the mayor of West Berlin and a rising star of the German Social Democrats. Brandt had given Brzezinski a tour of Germany's divided former capital two years before. At a seminar with political leaders, Brzezinski launched a withering attack on the Hallstein Doctrine, by which West Germany refused to have diplomatic relations with any country that recognized East Germany. That stance meant that Bonn had no embassy in any Eastern European capital. Brzezinski said that the Germans should waive Hallstein for captive nations. The policy, he felt, was "shrouded in clouds of legal fiction."[26] An outraged Christian Democrat leader shouted "*Das ist zu viel!* [That's too much!]" Brandt made a point afterwards of saying he agreed with what Brzezinski had said. Muska and Nancy partook of the more sumptuous side of the global tour. While Brzezinski and Huntington were quizzing Japan's military chief about the Soviet-occupied Kurile Islands, their wives were buying scrolls in Kyoto. "They're both in a shopping frenzy and need to be reined in, else they'll blow all our money," Brzezinski wrote. From Hong Kong, he reported, "Muska is fully recovered no doubt in small part due to the abundance of shops here."[27]

Even considering Brzezinski's peripatetic temper, his latest tour had a Jules Verne flavor to it. They spent Christmas among Cambodians near Angkor Wat, took a risky survey in a CIA plane of rebel Pathet Lao territory, dined on "Half-Chinese Half-Hindu [*sic*]" cuisine in Thailand, ate worms with chopsticks in Macau, and sampled the Ginza's risqué nightlife in Tokyo. The trip bolstered Brzezinski's Rolodex of rising politicians, many of whom would later lead their nations. His networking was expanding to half of the world. The tour also underlined what was turning into his lifelong affinity for Japan. Shortly after their return to America, Muska got pregnant again. After years of trying, the couple was fatalistic. Since the stillbirth, she had suffered a string of miscarriages. This time it worked. Shortly before Christmas, she delivered their first child, Ian. His father was ecstatic. In a letter to Arthur Ochs Sulzberger, publisher of the *New York Times*, with whom he was in the habit of making political bets for tiny sums of money, Brzezinski offered a new wager: "You might be interested to know that the first Polish-American President of the United States was born on 23rd December, 1963—or would you like to make a bet about that one too?"[28] Sixteen months after that, Muska gave birth to their second boy, Mark.

The trip also sped up the gestation of the 1964 Brzezinski and Huntington book *Political Power: USA/USSR*. Their purpose was to evaluate the increasingly fashionable claim that the rise of the industrial society was making the US and Soviet Union increasingly alike—the so-called convergence theory. That school of thought, which meant that the Cold War would resolve itself through peaceful sociological change, not ideological contest, had become popular in the 1950s with many of Brzezinski's Harvard colleagues. Chief of those was Barrington Moore, Jr., whose 1954 book *Terror and Progress USSR: Some Sources of Change and Stability in the Soviet Dictatorship* had argued that Soviet autocracy would be replaced by a system of "technical rationality," which would make the USSR and America increasingly similar over time. Two of Brzezinski's former supervisors at the RRC, Clyde Kluckhohn and Alex Inkeles, shared Moore's sociological bent. They, in turn, were buttressed by Talcott Parsons, a grand theorist of sociology who argued that social science, rather than "area studies" (in which scholars of various disciplines teamed up to study a country) held the key to what happens. In Parsons's view, "industrial man" was a universal type with overriding social qualities. Parsons's "structural functionalism" claimed to foresee the USSR's political future—in spite of the fact that he, like many of his sociological peers, spoke no Russian and had not yet visited the country.[29]

Such scholarship fueled Brzezinski's mounting disenchantment with academia. His skepticism had been piqued in the mid-1950s by publication of a study by Inkeles, Kluckhorn, and Raymond A. Bauer, *How the Soviet System Works: Cultural, Psychological, and Social Themes*, based on the Refugee Interview Project, in which the US Army had given Harvard scholars access to thousands of Soviet refugees in Germany. From their interviews, the authors concluded that nationality and language played almost no role in the self-perceptions of Soviet people. They wrote off ethnicity as an "ascriptive category,"[30] an arbitrary inheritance that no longer played much of a role in people's self-image. What animated ordinary Soviet people, they said, was their position within the social system.

The attraction of that school of thought was that it required no prior knowledge of a country's history, language, or people. One could decode the world without leaving campus. It also offered a reassuring take on the Cold War: ideology was dying; the West and East were destined to converge. In addition to being wrong, the downside to such bloodless abstraction, in Brzezinski's view, was that it made humanities increasingly irrelevant to the real world. Its preference for quantitative over qualitative and the conceptual over the empirical was pushing useful policy discussion away from universities and into the think tanks. "If you look at the [*American*] *Political Science Review*, it is very hard to see how you apply any of that to real life," Brzezinski thought.[31]

No reader of Brzezinski's academic work could miss that he was guilty of some of the stylistic traits he deplored. His weakness for highly Latinate jargon, particularly in his early writing, might partly be put down to the fact that English was his second language (and arguably his third, given his early facility with German). One of Muska's roles was to sift painstakingly through her husband's manuscripts to weed out any "semantic monstrosities,"[32] to which he confessed in one of his prefaces. Evidence of Muska's pruning and Brzezinski's involvement with nonacademic publications became more noticeable as the 1960s progressed. His book with Huntington provided a lucid, though contentious, rebuttal of convergence theory. Their goal was to rescue politics from sociology's encroachments. Industrial change, with all the rationalization, efficiency targets, and bureaucratic measures that come with it, may cause societies to seem alike, they conceded. In practice, politics and national traits persist.

Measured solely by industrial character, for example, there was little to distinguish West Germany's Essen under the Nazis from Detroit in wartime America. Such surface comparisons missed the point, which was that they served radically differently political machines. The same applied to contemporary America and the USSR. Far from converging, the two would continue to evolve along separate lines. It was notable, however, that the word *totalitarian* appears nowhere in their book. It had been partly in opposition to Brzezinski and Friedrich's 1956 tome that convergence theory was framed. Brzezinski had since abandoned that field. His fallback position, on the primacy of politics and Soviet party control, rested on firmer ground. "Brzezinski had solved 'the problem of power' analytically but doubted that Soviet leadership could solve it practically," wrote David Engerman, the leading historian of US Soviet studies.[33]

Freed from the burden of theory, Brzezinski's mind could dwell on the practical, which was where it was most lively. His relationship with Kissinger started to grow only after he left Harvard. Their correspondence in the 1950s was mostly about Brzezinski forwarding names, often Polish, for Kissinger's International Seminar, a Harvard summer program for foreign students that he had launched with his mentor, William Yandell Elliott. Kissinger would at times accept Brzezinski's names and at others politely turn him down. Shortly after Brzezinski's move to Columbia, the tone of their exchanges got friendlier. In a 1961 letter, Brzezinski enclosed a transcript of a Soviet domestic broadcast in which Kissinger's appearance was unflatteringly described. "I only hope that Ann [Kissinger's first wife] doesn't put you on Metrecal [a diet food] after this—but perhaps that is part of the Satanic Kremlin strategy: starve our chief expert to death!"[34]

A jocular tone crept into their exchanges. Occasionally it seemed forced. In one, Kissinger complained that Brzezinski had put his name forward for a television debate between the two with Kissinger playing the hard-liner. Protesting that he hated labels, he added, "How can I get a reputation for being wize [sic] if you will not let me pretend to be middle of the road?" Brzezinski replied, "Your reputation for being wize [at Columbia we spell it with an 'S' like in 'Soviet' or 'Stalin'] would not have been impaired." Kissinger responded, "What was that about Ztalin?"[35] Kissinger always insisted that the subsequent rivalry between the two was mostly one-sided and stemmed largely from the fact that Brzezinski was five years his junior. "Zbig was always one step behind me" was his retrospective explanation.[36] In 1963, he congratulated Brzezinski on being one of the United States' "Ten Outstanding Men of the Year" in *Look* magazine for the annual Junior Chamber of Commerce (Jaycee) award. Kissinger had won it in 1958. "I knew you were outstanding but I had never thought of you as that young," he wrote. "No wonder Muska prefers you to me." Brzezinski addressed his reply to "Dear Outstanding 1958."[37]

At that point, Kissinger and Brzezinski's worldviews did not so much clash as run on parallel tracks. In addition to his forensic attention to Eastern Europe, Brzezinski's focus was on internal Soviet politics, particularly after Khrushchev was ousted in a 1964 Politburo coup. Kissinger looked at the world from a higher altitude. Smaller nations rarely diverted him. His focus was superpower dynamics. He was, however, an open admirer of Charles de Gaulle, France's Olympian president, who was trying to sideline the US in Europe. In 1964, the Council on Foreign Relations commissioned Kissinger and Brzezinski to open its series on the transatlantic alliance with companion monographs. Kissinger's submission, *A Troubled Partnership*, was a paean to de Gaulle, whose grand diplomatic maneuvers he likened to the approach of Prussia's Otto von Bismarck. The late-nineteenth-century German chancellor ranked alongside the early nineteenth-century Austrian statesman Prince Klemens von Metternich in Kissinger's pantheon of great statesmen. To the annoyance of some, Kissinger admired de Gaulle's nose thumbing at the Anglo-Saxon powers—threatening to leave NATO and in 1963 vetoing the UK's application to join the European Common Market. Yet France's ambitions were too reliant on having a champion of de Gaulle's caliber. "A structure which can be preserved only if there is a great man in each generation is inherently fragile," Kissinger wrote. "This may be the nemesis of De Gaulle's success."

Brzezinski's book *Alternative to Partition: For a Broader Conception of America's Role in Europe* fleshed out his vision for ending Europe's Cold War division. The context was not auspicious. Washington's attention was being consumed mostly by the war in Vietnam. Indochina was supplanting the Iron Curtain as the Cold War's trip wire. President Johnson echoed Kennedy's sentiments on bridge building in Eastern Europe. But Johnson's mind—and at times it seemed his entire being—was consumed by the escalating struggle in Southeast Asia. To Brzezinski, Vietnam's domination of Washington's bandwidth spelled a missed opportunity. The USSR's grip over the East Bloc was looser than most people supposed. Backed by Mao's China, which had now split openly with Moscow, Romania and Albania were developing independent foreign policies—"a classic in graduated defiance."

At the same time, Poland, Czechoslovakia, Hungary, and other countries were clamoring for more trade credits and two-way trade with the West to ease their economic stagnation. The moment was ripe for a favorable Western response. Washington would first have to reverse decades of policy. The US had stuck to the line that détente in Europe could come only after German reunification. To Brzezinski that got the sequence back to front; détente would make German reunification possible. "The new American policy, regardless of its good beginnings and its basically right direction, still suffered from vagueness concerning the United States' goals in Eastern Europe and from contradictions with respect to the German question" he wrote of the previous two decades. That had to change. LBJ should use America's leverage to end Europe's dread of German militarism.

Brzezinski's book garnered strong accolades, including from Josef Korbel, Madeleine Albright's father, who said it offered the US a way out from "the dead-end policy of the status quo."[38] The University of California's David McClellan described his argument as "cogent and persuasive." He added that signs of growing nationalism across Eastern Europe created a paradox for LBJ: if Johnson wanted to encourage that trend, he must make sure not to undermine Eastern Europeans' sense of security—"a dilemma which Brzezinski discusses sensibly and realistically."[39] His book was also noticed in Washington, which was on the lookout for new Cold War thinking.

Since the start of the Vietnam War, the US media had acquired a taste for ornithological classification; diplomatic theorists were either hawks or doves, with the occasional owl thrown in. In foreign policy, there was little room for a crossbreed. Brzezinski's theories about peaceful engagement and pursuit of détente put him into the company of doves. Yet his support for the war in Vietnam made him a hawk, as it did of Kissinger. Both of them bought into the theory that Vietnam was a Cold War domino. The Sino-Soviet split, which was getting more splenetic all the time, also meant that Beijing (then referred to as "Peking" and occasionally as "Peiping") had replaced Moscow as the lead sponsor of global revolution. China was backing insurgencies in the farthest reaches of the "Afro-Asian" world. Beijing's best chance of landing a blow on the imperialist West, however, lay in next-door Vietnam. Stopping China, rather than the USSR, was Brzezinski's stated reason for backing the Vietnam War. It was a serious misjudgment. His ignorance of China was almost as deep as his knowledge of Russia. That Brzezinski and most of the rest of America's foreign policy world got Vietnam wrong is clear. That he missed Hanoi's deep-seated paranoia about China is also not in doubt, although he was in good company; Vietnam in the mid-1960s was only superficially comparable to Korea in 1950. Most thinkers in Washington saw it as a replay.

Another way of sorting out schools of foreign policy thought was to sift the realists from the idealists. Again, Brzezinski did not fit into either—and resisted attempts by others to brand him. Over Vietnam, however, he was more than willing to exchange blows with realists. One of the war's leading critics was Hans Morgenthau, founder of the American realist school. In 1965, the White House fired Morgenthau as a foreign policy consultant after he publicly criticized the war. Johnson's national security advisor, McGeorge Bundy, challenged Morgenthau to a televised debate. Bundy asked Brzezinski to be on his team. Though Bundy's theatrics infuriated Johnson, who distrusted intellectuals, especially from Harvard, Bundy's team was widely judged to have won the CBS encounter. That led to a follow-up encounter between Morgenthau and Brzezinski at the Chicago Council on Foreign Relations. The event degenerated into a personal clash. Morgenthau accused the absent Bundy of being a "shyster" and implied that Brzezinski was, too. The latter accused Morgenthau of nursing "injured dignity." On the substance, Morgenthau painted Brzezinski as a foot soldier of "doctrinaire globalism," which viewed every war, however far away, as a mortal threat to America's global standing. Brzezinski accused Morgenthau of underestimating the China threat; Vietnam, he said, was as important to Asia's future as Germany was to Europe's.[40]

At the time neither was deemed the obvious winner, though posterity would surely give that prize to Morgenthau. But Brzezinski's backing for LBJ's strategy did his career no harm. His stance was in line with the establishment, which still dutifully supported the war. One of Bundy's last acts before quitting was to arrange a meeting between LBJ and a group that he also labeled the "wise men," which included Acheson and Harriman. The august gathering gave its blessings to Johnson's Vietnam strategy. Brzezinski's TV performance had also brought him to Johnson's attention. Brzezinski, it turned out, was one of the few intellectuals LBJ could tolerate. After his clash with Morgenthau, Brzezinski told Bundy that the German-born professor had called him a shyster. "It takes one to know one," Bundy replied.[41] Bundy's next job was to head the Ford Foundation in New York, which would keep him and Brzezinski connected.

Making and sustaining such connections was critical to Brzezinski's rise. In that respect, he and Kissinger were in the same immigrant boat. Washington's archetypal foreign policy grandee was a product of the Ivy League, a legacy of old money, and a leading light of one of Wall Street's financial partnerships or one of New York's big law firms. Practicing diplomacy in Washington was a by-product of worldly success, not its manifestation. Good fortune paved the way for honorable public service, which was rarely sought and often declined. Neither Kissinger or Brzezinski could have followed that gilded path; they needed patrons. No family better fit that bill than the Rockefellers, the inheritors of the Standard Oil fortune and America's foremost philanthropists. In that instance, too, Kissinger was several years ahead of Brzezinski. He had been scooped up as a part-time advisor and strategic brain by Nelson Rockefeller in the 1950s. Rockefeller became governor of New York and had presidential ambitions. Kissinger supplied him with advice, memos, and the fairy dust of intellectual cachet. He played Michelangelo to Rockefeller's Lorenzo de' Medici. Kissinger was already a master of flattery. "The power of these people is unbelievable and their methods of operating extremely fascinating," Kissinger told a colleague. "On the other hand, they seem to me to come fairly close to performing the function of a good aristocracy."[42]

The relationship that Brzezinski struck up with David Rockefeller was not as intimate as Kissinger's with Nelson. Unlike his older brother, David had no wish to run for elective office; he took care of the family business. The jewel in the Rockefeller crown was Chase Manhattan Bank, which David ran. Yet he was a strong backer of CFR and became chairman of its board of directors for fifteen years. He was also a habitué of the Bilderberg Meeting, a yearly US-European confabulation of foreign policy minds at which Brzezinski was also becoming a regular. As was often true of the foreign policy "wise men," it was hard to disentangle Rockefeller's pro bono involvement in US foreign policy from his family's commercial interests. Critics alleged that the Rockefellers shrouded profit-making motives in philanthropic clothing. That claim was especially pertinent to an oil-rich country like Iran, which was both a major client of Chase and a focus of Rockefeller's public-spiritedness. David Rockefeller's friendship with Mohammad Reza Pahlavi, the shah of Iran, stretched back to the Second World War. Iran would become the downside of Brzezinski's relationship with Rockefeller.

In addition to Bilderberg, Brzezinski had often run across Rockefeller at Harold Pratt House and at New York social events. Their acquaintance drew closer in the late 1960s after the Brzezinskis stumbled on the hidden gem of Northeast Harbor in upstate Maine. The beauty of the small New England town and its Atlantic coastline had been an open secret for several decades among the East Coast's wealthiest families, including the Rockefellers. It was far more secluded than the New York Hamptons and more than three hundred miles north of Massachusetts' Nantucket Island. From Brzezinski's perspective, it was just a few hours' drive to Montreal, where his parents still lived.

William Burden, a New York financier who had been Eisenhower's ambassador to Belgium, introduced Muska and him to Maine. Brzezinski had been paid to speak to Burden's partners a couple of times. Burden's pedigree

was at least as impressive as the Rockefellers'. His great-grandfather was Cor-
nelius Vanderbilt, the wealthiest of America's nineteenth-century shipping
and railroad barons. Now, to one degree or another, Brzezinski had a Rockefeller and a Vanderbilt on his side. In the summer of 1965, Burden offered
the Brzezinskis use of one of the cottages on his palatial estate in Northeast
Harbor. A crewed boat was at their disposal. They accepted his hospitality for
the next two summers. The Burdens' main house, Sea Change, abutted the
water and contained a nuclear bunker, which was somewhat eccentric given
Maine's huge distance from any big city. It was built by one of the architects
who had designed Rockefeller Center and the Museum of Modern Art in New
York City. Burden, who was an avid art collector (he owned three Picassos, a
Mondrian, and a Monet) had succeeded Nelson Rockefeller as chairman of
MoMA in 1953. He told Brzezinski he could take the cottage for August. He
added, "We all thought your television performance was excellent and wished
it had just been a discussion between Hans Morgenthau and you."[43]

Rockefeller's secluded summer home was about a mile away at Seal
Harbor between the sea and Acadia National Park, a slice of New England
wilderness that had inspired the great American naturalists Ralph Waldo
Emerson and Henry David Thoreau. Its granite pool and circular rose garden was designed by Peggy Rockefeller, David's wife. The Brzezinskis would
often go sailing with the Rockefellers or meet them at the Harbor Club. It had
generation-long waiting lists and admission rules as steep as any in the country. Brzezinski did not have to wait; he was instantly admitted with Burden's
sponsorship.

With its craggy islands and verdant glades, Mount Desert Island was the
epitome of American Arcadia. For Brzezinski, it was an antidote to the New
York pressure cooker. It was also where he most exuberantly fulfilled his paternal role in the summer months they would spend there from now on. To
Muska, who had suspended most of her artist's work to be a full-time mother
in New Jersey, Northeast Harbor was an epiphany. She picked up the habit of
dragging large pieces of driftwood home to use as raw material for her sculptures. "Every time I look at the healthy faces of our children I think of you,"
Brzezinski told Burden.[44] In May 1967, the Brzezinskis had their third and
final child, a daughter they named Mika. Four months later, they bought a
property in Northeast Harbor for $16,000, which they somewhat unimagi-
natively called The Big Catch. It was a classic shingled Maine seafront house
with exposed beams, a *Gone with the Wind* staircase, a grand fireplace, fourteen

bedrooms, and a generous-sized porch. The only wrinkle was that the chimneys caught fire during their housewarming party. "It was some initiation," Brzezinski told Burden.

The previous summer, Brzezinski had taken his first full-time job in Washington; he had been appointed as an outside consultant to the State Department in 1964. In June 1966, he took a full-time job at the Policy Planning Council, which had been set up after the war as State's in-house generator of strategic thinking. The unit had drifted into relative abeyance since its heady "present at the creation" days when Dean Acheson was secretary of state and George Kennan had run the department. Kennan's office was next door to Acheson's on the seventh floor. Brzezinski's role was to come up with new ideas in an administration that was getting staler and more war obsessed by the day. The secretary of state, Dean Rusk, had been in that job since Kennedy appointed him in 1961. Johnson rarely took Rusk into his confidence. Loyal and dutiful, Rusk was no foreign policy entrepreneur.

State was a place, in Brzezinski's view, where ideas stayed unborn and initiatives went to die. His boss, Henry Owen, was a self-effacing international economist, Brzezinski's opposite in almost every respect. The two complemented each other well. Owen gave Brzezinski the space he needed to shine; Brzezinski seized it. Burden's letter of congratulation on his Washington appointment illustrated the cultural gulf between Brzezinski and his aristocratic benefactors. To Brzezinski, who took leave from Columbia, it was his next step on the ladder to power, which was his unwavering objective. To Burden, who had served in the War Department in the 1940s, a spell in public office was a mere rite of passage; it should never be an end in itself. "I am sure that you will find the experience most interesting," he wrote to Brzezinski. "As I have said before, I think it is a mistake to stay in government for too long a period, although it is of course necessary for one's experience."[45]

Within a few weeks Brzezinski figured out that to accomplish anything he must bend the rules. The Policy Planning Council had been designed for people of Brzezinski's description: academics with a desired expertise on temporary assignment. Buried in a corner of the State Department's sprawling Foggy Bottom building, the council had long since entered genteel decline. Brzezinski was not willing to settle for seminars. You could spend your days in decision-free planning meetings, writing memos that nobody read, then wake up one morning to realize you have accomplished nothing. He dubbed

Policy Planning the "Council of Bureau Studies." His solution was to smuggle ideas past the State Department and get them to the White House. That meant keeping close tabs on LBJ's sensibilities and choosing his moment. In an August 23 telegraphic note to himself, Brzezinski wrote, "Only way to get action: Pres needs something for domestic reasons; you feed it in. Foreign policy made on the run; function of domestic policy."[46] Two related neuralgias were gnawing at Johnson: the war in Vietnam and the likelihood that Robert F. Kennedy, the late president's brother, would challenge him for the 1968 Democratic nomination.

Brzezinski had been hired as a Soviet and Eastern European specialist. He had one imperative: to convert Johnson to "peaceful engagement." On paper it was not that hard a sell. Johnson was haunted by the fear that history would brand him a warmonger. The more deeply Vietnam sunk into quagmire, the keener his desire for East-West détente. The president had long been an enthusiast about "building bridges" to Eastern Europe. But he lacked a strategic framework. Brzezinski's new boss, Henry Owen, agreed that Brzezinski's peaceful engagement was the right strategy on its own merits. It was also a way for Johnson to regain the foreign policy initiative. They called it the "HO-ZB project." The plan was for LBJ to give a speech on it. Rusk showed little interest in the idea. Brzezinski needed sympathetic friends inside the White House. His allies were mostly to be found on the West Wing's domestic side, not among the National Security staff. Walt Rostow, Johnson's national security advisor, was devoting almost all of his time to the Vietnam War. Because they were more attuned to politics, LBJ's domestic staff, by contrast, were receptive to anything that could change the narrative. This White House was highly porous.

Brzezinski set about cultivating people close to the president. They included Bill Moyers, the White House press secretary; Hayes Redmon, who worked for Moyers; Harry McPherson, special counsel to the president; and John Roche, special consultant to the president. "The whole utility of this job lies in contacts. Otherwise hard to get things done," Brzezinski noted.[47] In his first few weeks, he met his new White House friends for lunch and dinner several times, together or singly. A favorite spot was the Metropolitan Club, two blocks from the White House. Sometimes he was invited to weekend tennis parties in Maryland or Virginia. His ferocious self-promotion also extended to foreign diplomats and journalists. Of the latter, Robert Novak, who had written the 1960 article on the Sorensen lunch, was a natural ally: "A really bright

go-getter, short, huge shoulders, brash."[48] Others included Joseph Kraft, a former speechwriter for JFK and now a syndicated columnist, and *Newsweek*'s
Leon Volkov, a Soviet air force pilot who had defected twenty years before
and was now the magazine's Russia specialist. Brzezinski's main target in the
Washington diplomatic corps was Berndt von Staden, West Germany's ambassador. They became friends. Another was Poland's ambassador, Edward
Droźniak.

It was one thing to write a speech for LBJ. Brzezinski finished the "HO-ZB"
draft on peaceful engagement in his first month. It was another to pin down
a date and venue where the president would deliver it. The White House was
awash with grandiose draft speeches that were never heard of again. Moreover,
Brzezinski had not met Johnson since he had become president (they had had
a desultory exchange during LBJ's unhappy days as Kennedy's vice president).
The plan was for Johnson to deliver the address before the late-September
visit of Ludwig Erhard, West Germany's chancellor. Brzezinski feared that if
Erhard heard about the speech, he would insist that it be watered down. Johnson would declare that Europe's postwar borders were inviolable, which would
bring an end to Washington's acquiescence in Bonn's refusal to recognize the
West German–Polish frontier. The speech would also make clear that German reunification could only follow détente, not the other way around—also
a reversal of long-standing Washington policy. The timing of Erhard's visit
was delicate. It was a precarious moment in West German postwar history.
The opposition Social Democrats, led by Willy Brandt, were pushing for an
overhaul of West Germany's Cold War maxims. Meanwhile, Erhard's coalition
partner, the Free Democrats, was threatening to bring Erhard's government
down in protest over its growing budget deficit. His chancellorship was hanging by a gossamer thread. Demonstrating his sway in Washington could help
save his job.

Johnson got along well with Erhard. He had entertained the rotund Bavar-
ian at his ranch in Texas in 1963, shortly after he became president. (Erhard
had asked whether Johnson was born in a log cabin. "That was Abe Lincoln,"
said Johnson. "I was born in a manger.") But Johnson had limits to what he
could do for his embattled West German counterpart. He had no intention of
backing off from Washington's demand that West Germany continue to pay for
the United States' huge military bases on its soil with "offsets." Erhard wanted
Johnson to lower that steep bill or at least to allow Bonn to divert some of its
offset spending from US arms to nonmilitary goods. But LBJ had his own

fiscal worries. The cost of the Great Society program and the war in Vietnam were draining the US of scarce dollars and threatening a balance-of-payments crisis. Should Erhard prove inflexible, Johnson's fallback threat would be to cut the number of US troops stationed in West Germany.[49]

Brzezinski did his best to get his speech onto Johnson's schedule before Erhard's visit. Foggy Bottom got the better of him; his plan was blocked by John Leddy, the State Department's Europe point man.[50] Brzezinski noted: "Middle-level appointees rigid, operational responses by instinct, little strategizing sense." The longer Brzezinski stayed in Washington, the greater his contempt for the State bureaucracy. A year later, he wrote: "HO [Henry Owen] says that Rusk really is head and shoulders over the rest of the 7th Floor. My reaction—but they are dwarfs!"[51] Erhard's two-day visit came and went. Though Johnson had received him warmly, Erhard flew back to Bonn in an even weaker position than when he had arrived. The window for Brzezinski's speech was closing. At that point he made the kind of move that would not have crossed the mind of a Foreign Service officer, let alone been considered professional: he fabricated a sense of urgency to get the White House's attention. Over lunch, Brzezinski told Harry McPherson, LBJ's special counsel, that he had learned from his Kennedy friends that Bobby was planning to give a big speech attacking Johnson's Cold War drift. It would be delivered on October 10, the third anniversary of the Nuclear Test Ban Treaty's entering into force, which JFK had wrapped up a few weeks before he was murdered. Brzezinski's alleged intelligence played into LBJ's neuralgia about the Kennedys. It was an open secret in Washington that Johnson and Bobby Kennedy loathed each other. A showdown in 1968 was expected. Without bothering to corroborate Brzezinski's story, the White House set up an LBJ speech in New York on October 7, three days before the expected RFK address. Though Brzezinski's original language was watered down, his message was not.

"Our task is to achieve a reconciliation with the East—a shift from the narrow concept of coexistence to the broader vision of peaceful engagement," Johnson told the National Conference of Editorial Writers in New York—to which he had invited himself. "Hand-in-hand with these steps to increase East-West ties must go measures to remove territorial and border disputes as a source of friction in Europe. The Atlantic nations oppose the use of force to change existing frontiers. . . . We respect the integrity of a nation's boundary lines."[52] The US media ignored Johnson's words; the West German government did not. Within a few weeks, the Free Democrats pulled out of Erhard's coalition.

The triggers of Erhard's downfall were complex. After nearly two decades of Christian Democrat rule, fatigue had been brewing. But the West German media and Brzezinski's State Department colleagues were in no doubt that Johnson had contributed, perhaps unwittingly, to Erhard's demise. Friends joked that Brzezinski had scalped the German leader. A West German diplomat told Brzezinski that he had a reputation for being dangerous. Robert Schaetzel, a State Department official, was overheard complaining about "ill-informed activists" inside the US government.[53] A few weeks after the speech, Erhard resigned. West Germany's SDP got its first taste of power when it went into coalition with the Christian Democrats under Kurt Kiesinger. Two years later, Willy Brandt became West German chancellor and launched a strategy called *Ostpolitik*, in which West Germany finally recognized Poland's borders.

To Brzezinski, LBJ's speech was a seminal lesson in the power of the federal government. Did he invent the Bobby Kennedy story? In the oral history interview he gave to the LBJ Presidential Library, he implied that he had. But he had taken care to inoculate it against contradiction. In his diary, he simply wrote, "I planted the idea with LBJ that RFK would give his speech if LBJ did not."[54] Were LBJ to go ahead with his speech, Bobby Kennedy would cancel his. Since Kennedy did not end up giving his, Brzezinski's friends had no reason to question his information. They jumped on the pretext Brzezinski supplied. If Johnson's stubborn faith in carpet-bombing North Vietnam to its senses could not be shaken, they could at least explore more promising initiatives on other fronts. The speech's impact on Erhard nevertheless surprised LBJ. One of Brzezinski's friends joked that before he came to Washington, the US had no European policy, but it had had allies. Now it had a policy but no allies. "I have the suspicion that he [Johnson] wasn't fully aware of the extent to which his speech actually involved a reversal of hitherto fundamental tenets of our policy towards Europe," Brzezinski said in his testimony for the LBJ library. Fourteen weeks after arriving in DC, Brzezinski had pulled off a minor policy coup. But his impact was fleeting.

The first time Brzezinski entered his State Department office on a Saturday was in late November, five months after his job began. Disclosure of that fact surprised Brzezinski's colleagues, who were used to working around the clock. He told them that he treated weekends as sacred except during national emergencies. Overwork did not boost efficiency; it dulled the mental senses. He need not have bothered. He was rushing to finish a memo on NATO reform for the secretary of state. In the end Rusk chose not to use his work, saying he preferred a more "nuts and bolts" approach. Brzezinski had been spending almost every weekend on the five-hour drive each way to New Jersey to see Muska and the kids. Halfway through his eighteen-month stint in Washington, the Brzezinski family expanded to five with Mika's arrival. He longed to spend an unbroken month with the "monsters." The tempo of his work made that impossible.

Muska's mother, Emilie Benes, who had never remarried, was doing her best to help her daughter out. After Ian was born in 1963, she left California and bought an isolated Hansel and Gretel cottage down a forest road near Englewood. She was a doting grandmother. Brzezinski was nevertheless bothered about motherhood's harrying impact on Muska. She was a "wonderful mother and a great housewife," but she was neglecting the romance necessary to sustain a happy marriage. "You hardly give a damn about your appearance," he wrote. "Your hair is atrocious . . . It really is a scandal." He urged her to make an appointment at a New York beauty salon. The letter ended with the instruction: "Destroy this,"[55] which Muska obviously ignored. Perhaps it was just a bad day for Brzezinski; he typed it out after a long drive back to DC. There was nothing before or since that compared with his unpleasant tone in that missive. "She is sweet, beautiful, sexy and good, in every respect be it bed or food," he wrote in one of the heroically amateurish love poems he composed. "She is a special kitten, and forever my heart she's smitten."[56]

Brzezinski's first exposure to government convinced him that the State Department could never be his natural home. The White House made foreign policy. Even when new policy came out of the president's mouth, State's instinct was to apply the brakes or work around it. LBJ's speech had set into motion a number of changes, including a bill that would extend most favored nation trading status to Eastern European countries and lift the ban on their membership of the Paris-based Organisation for Economic Co-operation and Development (OECD). State fought a rearguard action against both. Neither made it through Congress. Democrats were dutifully supportive but unexcited. Conservatives were suspicious. The conspiratorial John Birch Society claimed that Washington's plan was to force Americans to buy Communist goods. A few years earlier, the society had set up a "Committee to Warn of the Arrival of Communist Merchandise on the Local Business Scene."[57] LBJ's East Bloc outreach supplied more grist to its mill. Brzezinski spent a lot of his time trying to overcome the more routine blockages. By persuasion and occasional subterfuge, he inserted LBJ's language on peaceful engagement into statements and speeches by other officials. As a former outsider who would soon revert to that condition, he had greater latitude than his career colleagues to short-circuit bureaucratic lines of authority. He exploited that leeway. "I will be damned if I have to clear every piece of paper I write," he said.[58]

He gave speeches in his own name and wrote articles with almost the same freedom as he had at Columbia. He converted one piece, "Communism Is Dead," which first appeared in the *New Leader* in mid-1967, into a lecture at Washington's Overseas Press Club. Averell Harriman hated the title. Brzezinski confessed that his delivery came across as nervous and he spoke too rapidly. The heading was also misleading. Though he reiterated his now-familiar claim that communism had lost its appeal as a revolutionary force, the piece was an early defense of globalization. The Right wanted to create a Fortress America. The increasingly angry Left wanted to rebuild US society by disengaging from the world. Their endpoint was broadly the same and equally wrong. The only authentic world revolution was technological—and it was coming from the United States. America's dizzying pace of technological change was leaving the Communist bloc in the dust and rendering Marxist-Leninism a status quo ideology. The US should get ahead of the coming upheavals by forging a new community of developed nations, which would include Japan and, to an increasing extent, Eastern Europe.

Brzezinski's public freelancing elicited tut-tutting in the State Department. But LBJ's people liked his theme. Brzezinski was looking beyond the Cold War to trends that would shape a different future and trigger new forms of social upheaval. America's responsibility, he felt, was to take the lead. Johnson requested a memo on the subject. The fact that Brzezinski had written the memo rather than its message irritated Francis Bator, the deputy national security advisor, who remonstrated with him. Brzezinski pointed out that LBJ had personally asked for the memo and apparently liked it. He channeled it through Douglass Cater, an LBJ aide, whom he had recently befriended, and saw as "another pipeline to the White House."[59]

The memo paved the way for Brzezinski's first interaction with the president on May 21, 1967. The occasion was a meeting between LBJ and a group of the administration's in-house thinkers. Johnson was in a deepening funk about the anti–Vietnam War protests, which he blamed on "the intellectuals," whose approval he craved while also resenting them. That many of the offending intellectuals were from Kennedy's circle enraged him further. One or two,

such as Galbraith and Schlesinger, had been part of JFK's Camelot. Johnson
detested their disloyalty. It was Kennedy, after all, who had first entangled the
US in Vietnam. None of Kennedy's East Coast friends were complaining then.
"You know the difference between cannibals and liberals?" Johnson liked to
joke. "Cannibals eat only their enemies."[60] He enjoyed referring to William Ful-
bright, a leading Democratic critic of the war in the Senate, as "Senator Half-
bright."

The group comprised sixteen Johnson officials, including Brzezinski;
Bator, who had been a professor at Harvard; Arthur Okun, a Yale economist
on Johnson's Council of Economic Advisors; and Harold Brown, the secretary of the air force, who was also a physicist at Caltech. Bator wanted LBJ to
convene a meeting with intellectuals at Harvard, which could help bridge the
gulf over Vietnam. The idea was Bator's. The meeting lasted ninety minutes.
The first third was taken up by an LBJ rant against Anatoly Dobrynin, the
Soviet Union's silkily effective Washington ambassador. According to Johnson, Dobrynin had won over Defense Secretary Robert McNamara and Dean
Rusk to the idea of a bombing pause in Vietnam. It was eating away at the
president. Brzezinski wrote, "[Johnson] was very rambling, very emotional
and very set on continued bombing, no matter what."[61]

Brzezinski took a risk by telling Johnson that he agreed with those pushing for less bombing. At the time, he was working on a memo arguing for a reduction of fifty thousand in America's troop level in Vietnam. Johnson looked
surprised but said nothing. Brzezinski told the president why he thought a
meeting with Harvard intellectuals was a terrible idea: "They do not like you,
the more you try, the less they will like you." Johnson, he said, should not waste
his capital engaging with a small minority who would resent him no matter
what. Brzezinski was alone in stating that LBJ's style was the problem. The
other participants mostly echoed one another in saying that the Texan president was a victim of faculty snobbery. But Brzezinski's outspokenness, which
so unnerved the others that it caused sweaty palms, according to McPherson,
was not wasted.[62] The Harvard idea was dropped.

In spite, or perhaps because, of his contrarian style, Brzezinski had lodged
himself in Johnson's mind. "One thing is for sure—he will not forget what I
said," Brzezinski thought. That first encounter led to two one-on-one meetings with Johnson in the Oval Office—something that rarely took place and
almost never with an official from a forgotten corner of the State Department.
That day's gathering also led to a falling-out with Bator, who had done a lot

of preparatory work for the Harvard meeting. He accused Brzezinski of having done the president a "real disservice." Brzezinski responded that he would
"not compete with [Bator] in flattering LBJ."[63]

Brzezinski's first meeting with Johnson came a few weeks later. LBJ was
preparing for a much-awaited summit with Alexei Kosygin, the Soviet premier,
in Glassboro, New Jersey. The president had great hopes for the summit but
was getting conflicting advice. Rusk and Harriman, who was a State Department "ambassador at large," believed that Kosygin wanted to help Johnson out;
the Soviets would help extricate America from the war in Vietnam. But Johnson would have to ask the Soviets for their help, they said. Kosygin was ready
to use his leverage to get Hanoi to the negotiating table. Brzezinski dismissed
that advice as wishful thinking. He thought the Soviets wanted to appear to be
helpful to the Americans but were in fact taking active steps to prolong the war,
sending arms supplies, oil, and other war materials to Hanoi. Keeping America
bogged down in Vietnam was an easy way for Moscow to impose a mounting
toll on its ideological foe. America's Vietnam folly would also limit Washington's ability to exploit the Sino-Soviet split to Moscow's disadvantage.

LBJ's people requested another memo from Brzezinski, which led to his
appointment with Johnson. His first one-on-one Oval Office encounter with
a US president was brief. LBJ gave Brzezinski his trademark spiel about "grab-
bing commies by the balls and squeezing."[64] Brzezinski laid out his skepticism
about the USSR's supposed desire to be helpful. Johnson listened to Brzezinski. But his optimism about Soviet intentions was undimmed. As Brzezinski
predicted, LBJ extracted little from Kosygin at their June 1967 summit. Nothing tangible came of it, although the atmospherics were unusually friendly.
For a brief period, the phrase "spirit of Glassboro" came into vogue.

The administration's debate about Soviet intentions only sharpened in
the months following the Glassboro summit. As 1967 wore on, there was no
evidence of the USSR's restraining hand in Hanoi. The fighting in Vietnam
was only intensifying. Johnson was becoming ever more isolated within his
own administration. With the exception of the superhawkish and eternally
optimistic Walt Rostow, who thought the tide of war was always just about
to turn, few believed that more of the same would change anything on the
ground. Johnson listened only to Rostow; he screened out the growing chorus
calling for a bombing pause. The US Air Force's Operation Rolling Thunder
continued.

With the 1968 election looming, Harriman and others argued that there was an urgent need to get peace talks with the Vietnamese under way. In spite of evidence of Kosygin's double-dealing, they still believed that Moscow wanted to be helpful. The White House asked Brzezinski to write another memo analyzing Soviet intentions. LBJ was by now convinced of Kosygin's insincerity. He read aloud extracts of Brzezinski's memo to the National Security Council.[65] The recitation did Brzezinski no favors at State. Harriman, in particular, was enraged about Brzezinski's latest moonlighting. Both Kosygin and Tito had personally assured Harriman that the Soviets wanted peace in Vietnam. "What a jerk!" Brzezinski wrote. "What did he expect they would tell him?"[66] The clash between Brzezinski and Harriman was becoming personal. Since Brzezinski's advice was allegedly contaminated by Russophobia, it could hardly be otherwise. Harriman was developing an intense dislike for the outspoken, heavily accented upstart.

To his colleagues' surprise, Brzezinski announced that he would stick to his plan to return to Columbia in January 1968. Henry Owen told him that a better job would arise if he stayed on, particularly if LBJ won reelection. But Brzezinski had extracted everything from Washington that he could for the time being. He was also bored to distraction with the State Department's modus operandi. Early on he concluded that Rusk's daily staff meeting was a waste of time. Officials spent the first part of the meeting summarizing that day's news, as if people had not already read that morning's *New York Times*. Though Brzezinski had personally grown to like Rusk, who had displayed saintlike tolerance of his insubordinate tendencies, Foggy Bottom felt like a backwater. Rusk's team managed policy; they did not make it.

Over lunch in Washington, Brzezinski's old friend, Samuel Huntington, said he was right to go back to academia. If LBJ was reelected, Brzezinski could always pick up a more attractive government role in his second term. Huntington had risen quickly since his return to Harvard and was now head of the government department. He tried to convince Brzezinski to return to his alma mater. Brzezinski could tailor his job to whatever suited his ambitions. For the third and last time, Brzezinski turned down a Harvard professorship. He had contracted a severe dose of the Washington bug. New York was a far better base for his political ambitions. He requested and was granted a goodbye call on LBJ. Brzezinski told Johnson that his foreign policy record was far better than the "bugles and bungles" of his predecessors. The president liked that phrase. "Why are you leaving us when we need you?" LBJ asked. Brzezinski promised to help his reelection campaign.[67]

•   •   •

History rightly records 1968 as the year of American upheaval. It began and ended in turmoil. In late January, the Vietcong launched the Tet Offensive to coincide with the Vietnamese New Year. Though the insurgents suffered heavy losses, it helped end America's lingering faith in LBJ's ability to win the war. As Johnson had long dreaded, Bobby Kennedy launched his presidential bid in mid-March. Two weeks later, Johnson told a shocked nation that he would not be seeking reelection and would devote his remaining time in office to solving the situation in Vietnam. Five days after that, on April 4, Martin Luther King, Jr., was shot dead at a motel in Memphis. A few days later, Columbia University became the first of many US campuses to be stormed by student protestors. The uprising, which led to numerous clashes with New York City cops in tactical battle gear, was triggered by MLK's murder. On June 5, Bobby Kennedy fell to another assassin's bullet at the Ambassador Hotel in Los Angeles. He died a day later.

Each episode had a gut-wrenching impact on American society. The biggest jolt to Brzezinski's career was LBJ's abdication. In late May, Brzezinski agreed to become the foreign policy coordinator for Hubert Humphrey's campaign. The vice president had prevaricated for a month after LBJ's withdrawal before entering the race. Brzezinski was a natural choice. He had known Humphrey since he was a leading light on the Senate Foreign Relations Committee in the late 1950s. As vice president, Humphrey had been in regular correspondence with Brzezinski, who sent his own ideas and memos on request—about the Cold War, East-West relations, the Arab-Israeli conflict, and the war in Vietnam. Unusually for a vice president, Humphrey had even written a blurb for Brzezinski's 1965 book *Alternative to Partition*, saying that it "deserved the widest circulation." They had also met often during Brzezinski's recent spell in Washington.

Brzezinski's new role would be consumed by the Vietnam War. In mid-March 1968, two weeks before LBJ's announcement, he sent the secretary of defense, Clark Clifford, who had recently replaced McNamara, a memo laying out his bleak prognosis of America's prospects in Vietnam. Brzezinski had just returned from a flying visit to Saigon from which he concluded that even a million US troops (roughly double the existing deployment) would not be enough to win the war. Further escalation would only make matters worse. "Every additional soldier is politically counter-productive and militarily useless," he wrote. The United States should therefore redefine what it meant by victory. Equipping

South Vietnam to prevent a Communist takeover should be the goal. It was also long past time to be clear eyed about Moscow's support for North Vietnam, he argued. "The war has become a net asset politically for the Soviet Union."[68]

Brzezinski stopped short of echoing the call of Minnesota senator Eugene McCarthy for a full withdrawal. McCarthy was the Democratic challenger to LBJ (and then Humphrey). But his views were a world apart from the Johnson administration's grim determination to fight on. In his withdrawal address, LBJ had announced a sharp reduction of US bombing. But so far it had not induced much change in North Vietnam's military tactics. To Brzezinski's growing frustration, Humphrey was conflicted between his deep sense of vice presidential loyalty to LBJ and his campaign imperatives, which required that he call for a full bombing halt. Brzezinski developed a genuine affection for Humphrey during the course of the 1968 campaign. They remained friends for the rest of Humphrey's life. He was a widely respected Minnesota liberal who had risen to prominence in the late 1940s. He played a suitably effacing yet constructive role as vice-president to LBJ. Humphrey was a thoroughly decent man. That did not necessarily make him good presidential material. His dithering about whether he should run had been followed by even deeper paralysis about why he was running.

In early June, Brzezinski joined Humphrey's campaign on $85 per diem plus travel expenses.[69] He made a point, however, of insisting that for family reasons he could not be in Washington much and barely on the road at all. Humphrey's two closest aides, Ted Van Dyk and John Rielly, had both wanted the foreign policy job. As their second choice, both nominated Brzezinski. In a measure of how far Brzezinski's position had shifted, an article in the *New York Times* mentioned his name alongside George Ball, a long-standing Vietnam skeptic, as among those on Humphrey's team who were "critical of war."[70]

Brzezinski set up nine foreign policy task forces to advise the campaign. Most of them were led by his academic colleagues, a strikingly large share from Columbia—Samuel Huntington headed the "post-Vietnam" group, Marshall Shulman headed arms strategy and disarmament, Doak Barnett ran Asia policy, Richard Gardner led on Europe—and the East-West group was headed by Brzezinski's MIT friend William Griffith. Humphrey's Cold War policy was, unsurprisingly, identical to Brzezinski's.[71] Humphrey emphasized "reconciliation and peaceful engagement" with the Soviets in a statement in early July setting out foreign policy priorities. Understandably, the media paid most attention to what was glaringly absent from Humphrey's list: any mention of Vietnam.

A few days later—and after repeated prodding from his staff, including Brzezinski—Humphrey declared that his goal as president would be to "de-Americanize" the war. Yet he still felt unable to call for a bombing halt. Ironically, Humphrey's de-Americanization, which Nixon would call Vietnamization, would be the core of the "Nixon Doctrine" after he took office. Humphrey had at least permitted a crack of light to show between his campaign and the Johnson administration. To Brzezinski's frustration, Humphrey could not even bring himself to concede that he had done that. A UPI reporter asked him why he was distancing himself from LBJ. "That is a lot of nonsense," Humphrey replied. "The President would be the last man in the world to expect me to spend my time just applauding the yesterdays even though I think many good things have been done. I am a man ready for the future and intend to have something to say about it."[72] Just what that something would be, he had not yet figured out. Brzezinski wanted a Shakespearean Macduff; he was forced to make do with Hamlet.

The cost of Humphrey's indecision was mounting. Though he was on course to beat Eugene McCarthy for the Democratic nomination, his mandate would not be resounding. The risk that the Democratic National Convention, which would take place in Chicago in late August, would turn toxic was rising. Opinion polls showed that Americans were unconvinced that Humphrey was "his own man," as opposed to a cipher for LBJ. Johnson was not making Humphrey's life any easier. Years later, Robert Dallek, an LBJ biographer, revealed the extent of Johnson's ambivalence. LBJ had told aides that he would take Nelson Rockefeller, who was trailing Nixon in the Republican race, over Humphrey as the next president.[73] Even Nixon might be preferable. Johnson was showing no inclination to adjust his Vietnam policy for Humphrey's sake. There were also rumors that LBJ was planning to turn the Chicago convention into a eulogy to himself. That fear proved unfounded. What did happen in Chicago would be far worse.

Brzezinski redoubled his efforts to convince Humphrey that he needed to put blue water between himself and Johnson. "I am more and more convinced that every day's delay on making a fuller statement on Vietnam further diminishes the eventual impact of whatever you do say," he wrote to Humphrey on July 16. "There is a distinct danger that the public's negative feelings about the war will be transferred from Johnson to you."[74] Counterfactuals cannot be proved. Had the vice president delivered Brzezinski's attached speech in full, his fortunes would surely have improved. Brzezinski knew better than to include a call for a bombing cessation in his recommended draft; Humphrey would not do that without Johnson's approval. He feared that it could undermine the torturous four-way talks between the US and South Vietnam on one side and North Vietnam and the Vietcong on the other that Harriman was trying to get started in Paris. In addition, Johnson might retaliate by refusing to endorse him. Brzezinski's draft speech called for a cease-fire, military de-escalation, and a pledge that Humphrey would accept the results of free elections in South Vietnam—even if that meant including Communists in a new coalition. He would also set up a civilian construction corps to rebuild South Vietnam's economy.

Humphrey adopted most of Brzezinski's points, though Brzezinski was not the only one urging them (his day-to-day influence on the campaign was marginal). But they were dribbled out ineffectually over the coming weeks. Only the most alert of voters would have picked up a shift. After heavy arm-twisting from his staff, Humphrey plucked up the courage to request a meeting with LBJ to ask for a bombing halt in Vietnam. If Johnson turned him down, he would seek a green light to do so as a candidate, rather than as his vice president. Humphrey arrived clutching a statement that Brzezinski, Rielly, Van Dyk, and others had hammered out in a marathon session in the AFL-CIO's Washington headquarters the day before.[75] On July 25, the president and vice president met in the Oval Office for an hour and eleven minutes. Humphrey spent the first few minutes reading out his proposed statement. After he finished, Johnson exploded. If Humphrey said that in public, he said, he would be endangering the life of LBJ's son-in-law, who was in uniform in Vietnam. His fury rising, LBJ vowed to wreck Humphrey's campaign if he persisted with his disloyalty.

Humphrey was so shaken by Johnson's outburst that he abandoned the plan and spoke to barely anyone about what had happened. He nevertheless tried again two weeks later. They met for five hours at Johnson's Texas ranch on August 9, two weeks before the convention. Brzezinski was not invited down with Humphrey, and there is little record of what transpired between the flailing candidate and his brooding commander in chief. But it was obvious that the deflated Humphrey had again come back empty handed. The bombing would continue. Johnson's sole focus was on the peace talks in Paris—his last shot at solving the Vietnam War. LBJ would dial the bombing up or down depending how the North Vietnamese behaved in Paris. Brzezinski suspected that Humphrey had not even raised his request for a bombing halt again after LBJ's volcanic reaction the previous time. On ABC's *Issues and Answers* show two days later, he came up with a word salad when pressed on the specific conditions under which he would stop the bombing. It would be unwise to spell out "all of the facets of what I consider to be possible points of negotiation," he replied.[76]

With McCarthy refusing to concede defeat and unlikely to endorse Humphrey and the latter much too closely identified with the passionately reviled LBJ, the stage was set in Chicago for a disastrous Democratic National Convention. It did not disappoint. There was no role in Chicago for Brzezinski; at the best of times he did his best to avoid presidential conventions. He disliked the razzmatazz and superficiality. He spent half of August working from Maine, where he could spend time with Muska and the children, and then in Englewood. The ominous developments in Czechoslovakia, where a Hungary 1956–type liberal revolution had been gathering force—the so-called Prague Spring, led by Alexander Dubček—swallowed much of his time. He had somehow found space in mid-June to accept an invitation to address a conference in Prague. The mood he encountered among his Czech friends was euphoric. "Leninism has no relevance in an advanced modern society," Brzezinski told them.[77] He praised Dubček's "socialism with a human face" but warned the Czechs against provoking the Soviets by pulling out of the Warsaw Pact. It turned out that the Czechs had already crossed Moscow's red line. At a Warsaw Pact meeting in mid-July, Czechoslovakia was denounced as "counterrevolutionary," a reliable signal of an impending invasion.

Much as they had done with Hungary in 1956, the Soviets started to amass troops and armored divisions on Czechoslovakia's borders. The same reel was being replayed in LBJ's White House. Eisenhower had avoided any steps that he thought would give the Soviets a pretext to strike Hungary; Johnson did almost nothing to deter the Soviets from invading Czechoslovakia. In his memoirs, Johnson wrote, "We could only try to avoid any action that would further inflame the situation."[78] In truth, he was distracted by Vietnam. Richard Helms, the director of the CIA, said that efforts to alert the White House to the impending invasion were as futile as "peeing up a rope."[79] On July 14, a State Department spokesman said, "We have not involved ourselves in any way [in Prague]."[80] That was true to a fault. On August 20, Soviet tank divisions and 175,000 troops crossed the border into Czechoslovakia. Brzezinski wrote a statement for Humphrey that warned against the kind of US over-reaction that Nixon was urging. "It would be an error to conclude—indeed it would be playing into the hands of the worst elements in Soviet society—that the time has now come to reverse its policies of the last few years," it said. By their actions, the Soviets were themselves turning into the "gravediggers of communist totalitarianism."

Moscow could not have timed its invasion better. Had the Soviets shown signs of intervening a year before or after, Washington might have tried harder to deter them. In the midst of the worst phase of the Vietnam War—more than eighteen thousand US soldiers lost their lives in 1968, by far the bloodi-est year—the Soviet invasion caused barely a ripple. Americans were too con-sumed by the country's burning cities, student protests, and rising body count in Vietnam to do more than register the shocking events across the Atlantic. Humphrey waved through Brzezinski's Czechoslovakia statement. Hoping against hope, Brzezinski still had a few days before Chicago to inject some spine into his candidate on Vietnam. There is no evidence that Humphrey even read his advice. "I would urge you most strongly to release the statement on Vietnam this week," Brzezinski wrote on August 14.[81] But Humphrey would not be hurried. He also ignored a section about Vietnam that Brzezinski tried to insert into his acceptance speech. It called for a bombing halt, an imme-diate cease-fire, and military deescalation. The thirty-seven-minute address heralded the "end of an era and the beginning of a new day." But Humphrey did little to expand on why the current era deserved to end or what he would do to end the Vietnam War. The Soviet occupation of Czechoslovakia—the most disturbing Cold War development in years—merited only a brief ref-erence. Three weeks after the invasion, Humphrey said, "We hope—and we shall strive—to make this setback a very temporary one."[82]

Though vice presidential selection was well outside Brzezinski's remit, he tried to dissuade Humphrey from offering the slot to Senator Ted Ken-nedy, the last surviving brother. As with most of Brzezinski's 1968 campaign memos, they offer a revealing glimpse into how he was thinking, rather than any indication of what Humphrey was reading. Few candidates have time to absorb the barrage of papers that Brzezinski and his team churned out. If a Humphrey-Kennedy ticket won the November election, people would attri-bute their success to the Kennedy name, Brzezinski wrote in a memo entitled "Heads You Lose, Tails He Wins." Kennedy, he said, would always be getting in the way. If the ticket lost, Kennedy would inherit the party. "In either case, you will not be running as your own man."[83] Humphrey nevertheless sounded Kennedy out. To Brzezinski's relief, Kennedy was not interested. Prior to that, Humphrey had told Brzezinski absent-mindedly, "I tend to agree with your memorandum. . . . [Your advice] is well taken."[84] After an additional bout of hand-wringing over whether to approach Sargent Shriver, Kennedy's brother-in-law, or Fred Harris, a senator from Oklahoma, Humphrey finally settled on Ed Muskie, the Polish American senator from Maine. Muskie accepted the offer in Chicago. Walter Mondale, who had succeeded Humphrey in his Minnesota Senate seat, was named the campaign's cochair.

LBJ declined the invitation to speak in Chicago; he knew his presence would be provocative. American bombers were still raining munitions on Vietnam. Worse, LBJ was threatening to disown Humphrey if he adopted a unified convention plank on the war. His team had been trying to reconcile a party that was implacably split between a minority plank calling for rapid withdrawal and a more cautious majority one. The latter commanded barely more than half of the delegates. It was hard enough to unite Humphrey's and McCarthy's supporters behind one position. By the eve of the convention, Humphrey's team thought they had negotiated an acceptable compromise. On being told of the new formula, Johnson again lost his temper. He telephoned Humphrey and told him to revert to the majority plank. The unified one, he said, would endanger the lives of US troops in Vietnam and undercut his efforts to get peace talks going in Paris. A shaken Humphrey felt he had no choice but to comply. The campaign team was distraught. LBJ had threatened via surrogates to torpedo his candidacy if Humphrey stuck to his compromise with the minority peaceniks. Faced with a choice between the bullet of LBJ's hostility and the poison of a split party, Humphrey chose poison. Chicago had failed before it began.

Humphrey accepted the tarnished crown on August 28 at the International Amphitheatre in downtown Chicago. Throughout the four days of the convention, the hall was under constant siege. Signs proclaiming DUMP THE HUMP and HITLER, HUBERT AND HIROHITO could be seen though tear gas. Thousands of protestors, among them Allen Ginsberg, William S. Burroughs, Jean Genet, and Jerry Rubin, occupied nearby Grant Park; they were assaulted in uneven clashes with Mayor Richard Daley's Chicago police. Vietnam was not their sole cause. Among other demands, they called for full unemployment—"Let the machines do it"—and the abolition of money. The media were far more riveted by the events outside the hall than those within. Humphrey, who was interrupted by catcalls and boos, was easy to depict as a dinosaur from a smoke-filled past. His "show of unity" at the closing of the convention turned into an even bigger nightmare; his main rival, Eugene McCarthy, refused to appear on the podium. Chicago had turned into "a catastrophe," as Humphrey described it in his memoir.[85] Apart from Nixon, the winner of Chicago 1968 was Norman Mailer, whose essays in *Harper's Magazine* pierced the smoke to discern the meaning in the chaos. "The Democratic Party had here broken in two before the eyes of a nation like Melville's whale charging right out of the sea," he wrote. The Democratic leaders, he said, hovered "above a direction-less void, there to loose the fearful nauseas of the century."[86] Presidential candidates nearly always derive a poll bump from their conventions. Humphrey was history's most glaring exception.

Public fear of collapsing law and order probably did more than opposition to the Vietnam War to win the 1968 election for Nixon. It was the peak year of so-called white flight from the cities. Many in what Nixon dubbed the "silent majority" were no fans of the Vietnam War. But they were susceptible to Nixon's racial dog whistles—his so-called Southern Strategy—to wrest the desegregated South from Democratic hands. After the 1964 Voting Rights Act passed Congress, LBJ had turned to his aide Bill Moyers and said, "We just lost the South for a generation." That proved to be an understatement. The 1968 riots made it easier for Nixon to harvest the backlash. America's urban unrest was distinct from the Left's anti–Vietnam War and counterculture protests, although they sometimes overlapped. The Chicago riots were just one manifestation—albeit the most electorally significant—of educated youth's alienation. They picked up in the autumn where they had left off, Columbia at the forefront. Brzezinski was right in the middle.

The Columbia that Brzezinski had left for Washington in 1966 was still an orderly Cold War university. The campus to which he returned in early 1968 was a student war zone. He had no sympathy for counterculture politics. Senator McCarthy, who had dismissed the Soviet invasion of Czechoslovakia as unimportant, described Mayor Daley's Chicago police tactics as "worse than Prague."[87] Another Democratic senator likened the Chicago cops to the Gestapo. To Brzezinski such comments pointed to the ignorance of America's New Left. His jaundiced take was shared by most of his émigré colleagues from behind the Iron Curtain, Madeleine Albright included. In January, Brzezinski told George Kennan that he had outdone himself in a *New York Times* essay headlined "Rebels Without a Program," which criticized the

nihilistic self-indulgence of the campus rioters. "It was extraordinarily perceptive as well as courageous," he wrote.[88] In a *New Republic* article later that year,
he described the protests as "the death rattle of the historical irrelevants."[89]
That was his polite version of what he often said in private: the protestors
were spoiled brats from suburban homes risking nothing.

Columbia had been the first university to fall briefly to a hostile occupation in April. Grayson Kirk, the university president, was locked into his
office and held hostage. The student leader Mark Rudd had written Kirk a
letter stating the students' demands, which included total amnesty for their
occupation. The letter complained of "our own meaningless studies, our identity crises, and our revulsion with being cogs in your corporate machines." It
concluded with the Black Panther call "Up against the wall, motherfucker, this
is a stick-up."[90]

Brzezinski differentiated between the African American protestors from
Harlem, with whom he sympathized, and the mostly white campus protestors, whom he despised. The blacks were protesting against a Columbia University gymnasium being built on a piece of public land in Morningside Park.
It had one entrance from the campus into the upper level and another into its
lower level from the Harlem side of the park. To Harlem's residents it was yet
another example of racial gentrification (Columbia's expansion had already
displaced several thousand from their homes during the 1960s). It came with
the added indignity of segregated access to a de facto segregated gym. A few
days after Martin Luther King, Jr.'s, murder, Brzezinski wrote to the *Washington Post* calling for an annual Day of Reconciliation to commemorate what
King had stood for.[91] He felt very differently about the anti–Vietnam War protests. They were spearheaded by Students for a Democratic Society, an activist group that organized most of the marches. By the time the protests flared
up again in September, the two groups had split. The Harlem activists felt that
their specific demands were being hijacked by SDS's impractical utopianism.

At one angry protest in September, students converged on the School of
International Affairs (SIA) building, where Brzezinski's office was located.
They demanded that the faculty come outside to debate them. Brzezinski's
colleagues were "scared shitless," so he volunteered to go down and speak to
the students.[92] SDS had uncovered alleged long-standing SIA ties to the US
arms industry because of its relationship with the Institute for Defense Analyses, a think tank close to the Pentagon. Their inference was a big leap but not
absurd. Though Columbia obviously did not sell arms, its relationship to the

military-industrial complex had been cozy for decades. "Who rules Columbia?" the students chanted. Dressed in bandanas and motorbike helmets to
protect themselves from police batons, hundreds of students surrounded the
SIA building, which had a slogan-friendly consonance with "CIA." They demanded that it be closed down.

Brzezinski emerged to face the rabble. On the way down, he picked up
an apple as a prop to disguise his nervousness. He told the students they had
ten minutes to make their point. Their discussion was heated but did not turn
violent. His opponent was Michael Klare, an SDS activist and Columbia student. "I presented our reasons for closing down the SIA," Klare recollected.
"Brzezinski denied them and said what happened in this building was legitimate. Neither of us got the better of the other."[93] After the ten minutes elapsed,
Brzezinski said he must hurry back to his office "because I have to go back
and plan some more genocides." He was still holding his apple.[94] His lectures
would often be interrupted by fake bomb threats. "Under instructions not to
use elevators, we started down the stairs," recalled the Harvard scholar Adam
Ulam, who was a guest lecturer at one of Brzezinski's classes. "After three
floors, Zbig said, to hell with it, and we went back to complete the class, with
few defections among the students."[95]

Media profiles would often cite that episode to draw attention to Brzezinski's Vietnam hawkishness. The reality was less straightforward. Even before
the Humphrey campaign, Brzezinski had been churning out various plans to
pare down America's presence in Vietnam. His view of how much the Soviets
were benefiting from the war informed his growing skepticism. Many of those
who later accused him of being a hawk were themselves Vietnam hawks until
1966, which was roughly Brzezinski's arc.

In 1965, *New York Times* journalist David Halberstam, author of the subsequent best-selling book *The Best and the Brightest*, wrote, "Vietnam is a strategic country . . . perhaps one of only five or six nations that is truly vital to U.S.
interests."[96] Neil Sheehan, who would later break the Pentagon Papers scoop,
thought in 1964 that the "repercussions of an American defeat in Vietnam
would amount to a strategic disaster."[97] Averell Harriman would later criticize
"the old Cold War warriors who saw Vietnam as a Munich or a Berlin."[98] In
1965, however, Harriman was adamant that Vietnam's Communists must not
be appeased. "It would be like letting Hitler march into the Rhineland in the
1930s," he had said.[99] It is worth noting that Brzezinski never used the Munich analogy to advance whatever case he was arguing. His preferred historical

warning was Yalta. He did, however, often cite "Vietnam syndrome" during the 1970s. He was antagonized by those who claimed to have been doves all along.

The politics could hardly get worse for the Humphrey campaign after Chicago. Though the Republican National Convention in Miami could have posed problems for Nixon, it did not come under siege. The losing candidate, Nelson Rockefeller, was too much of a gentleman to withhold his endorsement, as McCarthy was still doing to Humphrey. Nixon also saw off a late challenge from Ronald Reagan, California's right-wing governor. Nixon emerged victorious from Miami with a unified party behind him. Rockefeller's exit was also a missed opportunity for Humphrey. As Walter Isaacson related in his biography of Kissinger, there had also been a Brzezinski angle to Rockefeller's campaign. At the first meeting of Rockefeller's policy team in April, Kissinger was asked how much time he could devote to the campaign. "Not as much as Nelson will want," he replied. Joseph Persico, the campaign speechwriter, suggested that they should bring in Brzezinski as a consultant. "Not at all the required depth," Kissinger replied.[100] From then on, Kissinger was at the Rockefeller campaign's disposal.

In July, Kissinger, who had since then been Brzezinski's opposite number for Rockefeller, met Samuel Huntington in Martha's Vineyard. Kissinger disclosed that he possessed a trove of Nixon opposition research that the Rockefeller campaign had compiled. Humphrey could put the Nixon "shit files" to good use. Over the phone, Kissinger told Brzezinski that he had hated Nixon for years. Casting around for ways to reboot Humphrey's flagging campaign, Brzezinski called Kissinger's office in September to remind him about his offer. Kissinger's assistant said, "You know, Dr. Brzezinski, that Kissinger is working for Nixon now?"[101] Kissinger's skill at keeping several balls in the air—juggling Rockefeller, Humphrey, and Nixon until one of them dropped—was a political virtuosity. In July, Humphrey's prospects were still good. By September, his numbers were in free fall.

Kissinger repeatedly denied the Nixon files story. "They could never show any letters or phone calls that supported it," he said.[102] That is true. But Huntington, Brzezinski, and Van Dyk all had similar recollections of Kissinger's offer. Huntington said he "was playing both sides. He had an office right next to mine at Harvard. He kept saying that he was going to cooperate . . . but he never did."[103] Years later, at a Senate ceremony honoring the dying Hubert Humphrey, Brzezinski said, "The greatest opportunity in my life was to serve in your campaign." Gesturing towards Kissinger in the audience, he added, "And I want to publicly thank Dr. Kissinger for the assistance that he offered."[104] Few people understood the dig. Generally, though, Brzezinski had no appetite to fan the story. But it was a significant moment. For the first time, Kissinger and Brzezinski, the two rising stars of US foreign policy, were on opposing teams. From then on, their disagreements would reverberate. That one was a Democrat and the other a Republican was partly an accident of sponsors.

Kissinger's alleged role in funneling timely nuggets of intelligence from the Paris peace talks to the Nixon campaign was more significant than his campaign hopping. A key piece of Kissinger's juggling act was his role as a consultant to the State Department. He was on good terms with people on Harriman's team in Paris, to whom he had easy access. They had no clue that he was working for Nixon. The Paris team included Cyrus Vance, Harriman's Paris lieutenant, who had been Johnson's deputy secretary of defense, and Richard Holbrooke, a junior State Department official. What happened in Paris could determine the fates of Johnson, Humphrey, and Nixon. To LBJ, the talks were his only shot at redemption. If he could deliver peace in Vietnam before leaving office, his place in history would be salvaged. To Humphrey, the faster the talks progressed, the better the chances that LBJ's actions would align with his campaign's dovish imperatives. Johnson needed North Vietnam to take "reciprocal" steps before he would halt the bombing. To Nixon, Paris was the potential October surprise that could sink his prospects. A successful outcome—or even the expectation that Paris might lead to an eventual settlement—could reverse his fortunes. His lead over Humphrey was in the double digits. But US public opinion was volatile.

Even before Kissinger offered his pro bono assistance, John Mitchell, Nixon's campaign manager, had set up a back channel to the South Vietnam government via Anna Chennault, a flamboyant Chinese American Washington socialite (dubbed "the steel butterfly") who was also chair of the "women for Nixon" campaign. Through Chennault, Nixon's campaign told the South Vietnamese delegation to stall progress at the Paris talks as they would get a better deal after he was elected. Via the FBI director, J. Edgar Hoover, who was wiretapping the South Vietnam Embassy and picking up its conversations with Chennault and other Nixon campaign staff, LBJ was kept fully aware of their subterfuge. He chose not to go to the media for fear that its publicization would push South Vietnam over the edge. This was in spite of the fact that a firestorm around Nixon's efforts to sabotage the Paris talks could have sunk his election chances.

Without Saigon's agreement, the talks could not go ahead. It was a three-way dance; Kissinger made it four. As Kissinger flew back and forth from the East Coast to France, his ear was attuned to the rapidly changing situation in Paris. Many observers suspected that Holbrooke was his chief source.[105] When the US delegation thought that North Vietnam was close to fulfilling Johnson's preconditions for a bombing halt, Kissinger alerted the Nixon campaign to the impending breakthrough. His main contact was Richard Allen, Nixon's deputy national security advisor and foreign policy man. Chennault then fed Kissinger's intelligence to the South Vietnam ambassador. The South Vietnamese delegation in Paris duly adjusted its demands by insisting on a longer interval between North Vietnam's compliance and the bombing halt, or that new conditions be imposed. That clandestine dialectic was repeated several times as the election approached. For Nixon, a bombing halt had to be prevented. Humphrey's imperative was the opposite.

Brzezinski's advice was single-minded. The two campaigns were fighting on uneven terms. He was working for a candidate whose fidelity to the rules and sense of honor were a mirror image of Nixon's methods. In a mid-September memo, Brzezinski pleaded with Humphrey to see the logic of presenting himself as a "new fresh leader." Humphrey, he said, needed to come across as his own man in the eyes of the American public: "This means deliberate distance from the recent past—and emphasis on your own policies." That might create an appearance of disloyalty to LBJ, he conceded. But he suggested a way around it: Humphrey would have to tell the American public that "your primary role is that of the candidate; it is a future-oriented political role. Your residual role is that of the Vice-President; it is a constitutional function that is necessarily passive. Hence you speak and act as the candidate and in that role you are not bound by the past."[106]

Brzezinski's frustration echoed that of Humphrey's entire team and his sympathizers in Paris. They included Harriman, who felt that Johnson was giving his vice president a raw deal. Through George Ball, Johnson's outgoing ambassador to the United Nations and a long-standing Vietnam dove, Harriman told Humphrey that he would do whatever he could in Paris to accelerate progress. Harriman and Vance read and suggested changes to a draft of a statement on Vietnam that Humphrey was to give in Salt Lake City on the last day of September. George Ball had in effect become Humphrey's back channel.

The "Salt Lake City Statement" almost reversed Humphrey's fortunes. After months of debating with himself, he finally came out for a bombing halt without telling LBJ in advance. He had just one condition: that North Vietnam respect the demilitarized zone dividing North from South. In addition to growing public doubts about Nixon, Humphrey's newfound boldness on Vietnam was enough to change the political weather. The disaffected Left began to drift back to Humphrey. McCarthy reluctantly endorsed him. He also managed to siphon off some "Rockefeller Republicans" who disliked Nixon and were unsettled by the surging third-party candidacy of George Wallace, the unreconstructed segregationist governor of Alabama and an inveterate Vietnam hard-liner. By mid-October, several polls showed Humphrey in a dead heat with Nixon. Brzezinski could only speculate what might have happened if Humphrey had taken the plunge a month before Chicago instead of a month after.

Yet Humphrey would travel only so far from LBJ's position. It is also worth speculating what might have happened had Humphrey disclosed Nixon's back-channel contacts to the South Vietnamese delegation, which managed to string out further delays until the end of October. Ever the loyal number two, Humphrey declined to go public about Nixon's sabotage. Aware of that lethal possibility, Nixon preemptively accused Johnson of allowing a parallel back channel between Harriman's Paris team and Humphrey's campaign via George Ball. That was enough to secure Johnson's and Humphrey's silence. On October 31, Johnson finally declared that Hanoi had met the conditions for a bombing halt. The Halloween announcement came less than a week before the election. Minus a day—and with Kissinger's help—Nixon had prevented the October surprise that he dreaded. He won the Electoral College comfortably. In terms of the popular vote, it was almost a photo finish: Nixon got 43.4 percent of the vote to Humphrey's 42.7 percent.

On the night of November 5, Brzezinski watched the results come in with Humphrey at his funereal headquarters in Minneapolis's Leamington Hotel. The outcome did not surprise him. His first inside experience of a presidential campaign had been a profoundly ambivalent one. He never said a bad word about Humphrey's character; Brzezinski admired his integrity and kindness. Yet he felt a guilty sense of relief at Humphrey's defeat. "By then I had concluded that Humphrey was a wonderful man but he would probably be a lousy president."[107] The indecisive way that Humphrey ran his campaign, his instinct to hedge, and most of all the ease with which Johnson had intimidated him, convinced Brzezinski that he did not have the guts to be a strong leader. Though Brzezinski was no admirer of Nixon, America's next president could rarely be accused of indecision.

Humphrey's painfully slow road to Damascus on Vietnam had shown what could have been accomplished. But it had come too late. Two weeks after the election, Brzezinski told Humphrey, "You were the only cheerful person on the plane. . . . It was your drive, your courage, your spirit that lit up the campaign and you single-handedly scared the hell out of your opponent on election night."[108] Humphrey replied with his "deep appreciation" for Brzezinski, who had supplied him with the tools to give Americans an "enlightened discussion of international issues." He added that he would present the Brzezinski team's copious stack of largely unread papers to President-Elect Nixon.

Brzezinski prepared to return to full-time academia in New York, though with a far bigger national profile than before. Had Humphrey won, Brzezinski thought that he might have been offered a serious job at the State Department, perhaps assistant secretary of state for Europe, or a White House role. Many on Humphrey's team assumed he would have become Humphrey's national security advisor. During the previous bruising and taxing five months, he had not had much time to gossip with colleagues about a Humphrey administration staffing chart. On November 30, something happened that revolutionized Brzezinski's outlook: Nixon asked Kissinger to be his national security advisor. Though Nixon and Kissinger had met only once—and it was a brief and awkward encounter—Nixon was offering Kissinger the plum foreign policy job in his administration. That Kissinger would be *primus inter pares*, Nixon left little doubt. Kissinger was not only the first person to whom Nixon offered a role; he made it clear that foreign policy would be run out of the White House. Kissinger, who had spent the previous months telling anyone in earshot that Nixon was a bad character who had to be stopped, claimed to be as shocked as anyone.

November 30 was the day that Brzezinski's rivalry with Kissinger was truly born. On hearing the news, Brzezinski went to a store in downtown Washington that sold stationery.[109] There he bought a small notebook in which he wrote down the names of his future national security team. Some of them, such as Robert Hunter, Bill Griffith, and Sam Huntington, had worked on the Humphrey campaign. Others, such as Bill Odom, a former PhD student, had not. Years later, he would offer White House jobs to most of the people in his notebook. To Brzezinski, Nixon's pick was a career-changing revelation: for the first time, it was clear that foreign-born Americans with difficult names could make it to the top. From then on, Brzezinski recalibrated his idea of what was possible. He wasted little time speculating on the reasons behind Nixon's choice. He had low tolerance for most conspiracy theories. Though he had recently had extensive exposure to Kissinger's acrobatic political skills, he remained an open admirer of his former Harvard colleague's intellectual talents.

Over time others would piece together plausible motives for Nixon's astonishing leap of faith. One obvious one was Kissinger's usefulness to the Nixon campaign in Paris. Though it is doubtful that Kissinger's intelligence on the Vietnam talks had been particularly valuable, he had shown qualities that Nixon prized above others: ruthlessness and a talent for subterfuge. Nixon later wrote, "One factor that had most convinced me of Kissinger's credibility was the length to which he went to protect his secrecy."[110] Given that they had met only once, there is a lot to unpack from that limpid sentence. The world, America, and Brzezinski were about to find out in spectacular fashion what that meant.

5

The Warrior Dove

In early December 1968, less than a month after Nixon's victory, prominent intellectuals assembled in Princeton for a bout of self-flagellation. Brzezinski was there, though he was beginning to look out of place in such company. It was a moment of peak cultural pessimism. Among other confessions, a gathering of America's best-known intellectuals pleaded guilty to collaborating with the CIA, enabling the Vietnam War, unwittingly helping to bring Nixon to power, and squandering society's trust. That was as far as the consensus went. Mostly they were at war with one another. American Sovietology was disintegrating into ideological factions, one of which—the "revisionist" school—had reappraised Stalin as a hero of Soviet industrialization; Stalin, they argued, had had to break eggs to make omelettes. The consensus was that the US was at least as much to blame for the Cold War as the Soviets, if not more. Much of the academy, including Harvard's Stanley Hoffmann, sympathized with the New Left. To Brzezinski's chagrin, Hoffmann had applauded the student occupations of university buildings. In Brzezinski's eyes and those of one or two older figures, notably George Kennan, the seminar epitomized the American Left at its navel-gazing worst. "If we gathered a group from Route 128 near Boston—engineers, scientists, programmers, social planners—and they went out on strike, there would be an immediate political effect," Brzezinski told the group of eighty scholars, activists, and writers. "However, if my colleagues and I all dropped dead today, there would be big obituaries tomorrow, but no social effect."[1]

According to the media, which treated the "Princeton Seminar" as a national event—the *New York Times* carried lengthy daily reports—it was a window on America's cultural disarray. The irony was that it was hosted by a group, the International Association for Cultural Freedom, that had originally been a CIA-front organization. Its original mission, under the name Congress for Cultural Freedom, had been to generate anti-Soviet propaganda in the democracies that were thought to be most vulnerable to Moscow's influence, notably West Germany, France, and Italy. In a spirit of "Physician, heal thyself," the health of US democracy was now the conference's urgent concern; this was the first time it was being hosted in the United States.

A lot had changed since its first meeting in West Berlin in June 1950. The Congress for Cultural Freedom's founding committee had boasted big names such as Arthur Koestler, the Hungarian author of *Darkness at Noon* (one of Brzezinski's favorite novels); the French anti-Communist scholar Raymond Aron; and Stephen Spender, the British-born writer who would later become US poet laureate. Many academics who had published articles in *Confluence*, *China Quarterly*, *Daedalus*, *Encounter*, and other CIA-backed publications had done so in ignorance of Langley's support, much as they attended the front's conferences without knowing who bought their plane tickets. That all changed in 1966 after the *New York Times* published an exposé of the CIA's backing of that group and other front organizations. Damaged by the revelations, the group renamed itself the International Association for Cultural Freedom. It dropped the CIA and found a new backer. Brzezinski helped arrange the funding through the Ford Foundation's president, McGeorge Bundy.

By the late sixties, however, the intellectual world could no longer agree on the West's common enemy. In the past couple of years, all that had once been solid seemed to have melted into air. The Vietnam War had destroyed America's faith in itself. Was the foe still Moscow, as everyone once thought? Or was it Washington, white America, WASPs, or some concealed structural force visible chiefly to French intellectuals? For most of the three days, Brzezinski watched in sardonic detachment as speaker after speaker targeted the US establishment, corporate America, the academy, or some other bugbear for this unsettling state of affairs. Kennan won few friends in a keynote speech that blamed America's worsening plight on "the angry, flamboyant demands of student mobs and black militants." Lillian Hellman, an aging left-wing playwright, rebuked Kennan for his lack of empathy with the young. "God knows many of them are fools, and most of them will be sellouts, but they're a better generation than we were," she said. "There's nothing to be despairing about except the American liberal."[2]

An enthused student leader, Sam Brown, jumped up to the microphone to confess that he now understood what it was like to fall for an older woman. But who could define the American liberal nowadays? Did America's crimes in Vietnam mean that LBJ, Hubert Humphrey, and even JFK now belonged in the same trash can as fascists? An SDS protestor outside the auditorium lost heart and went home after a college official insisted that he substitute "Down with" for "Fuck" on a banner that read "Fuck racism, imperialism, genocide, corporation capitalism, policy planners, etc.," a reminder of the counterculture's tendency to sweep all ailments, big or small, into one basket. Policy planning, moneymaking, genocide—what was the difference?

The only sane refuge was comedy. The speaker who came closest to winning everyone's affection was Edward Shils, a University of Chicago sociologist, who pronounced the death of everything. "The WASPs have abdicated. What has taken their place? Ants, fleas." His absurdist take was that whites, the police, WASPs, and the establishment had all been strangled by "the serpents of sociological terminology." When Jean-Jacques Servan-Schreiber, the French author of the best seller *The American Challenge*, asked Shils to talk more slowly because non-Americans could not follow his meaning, he shot back, "Many of the Americans don't either."[3] Shils's riposte caught the mood. To Brzezinski, the telling division was between the seminar's foreign participants and the younger Americans. Brzezinski's soul was with the foreigners. New Left radicals insisted that all the world's problems, not just the Vietnam folly, could be blamed on the US. The country, they said, should repent and disengage.

Coming at the moment it did and in the way that it was conducted, the seminar was a rite of passage for Brzezinski. His new rival, Kissinger, canceled his attendance after Nixon had tapped him on the shoulder forty-eight hours before it started. Kissinger did, however, make it to the closing dinner, where, according to one reporter, he gave his "inadvertent imitation of Peter Sellers doing Dr. Strangelove."[4] Brzezinski's bitterest clash was with a member of his own generation, Hoffmann, with whom he was rapidly falling out. That was not their first dispute. Hoffmann had published a rare negative review of Brzezinski's 1965 book, *Alternative to Partition*.[5] Building bridges was tilting at windmills, he argued; the Warsaw Pact would not be fooled by Brzezinski's transparent seduction. At Princeton, Brzezinski was a lonely American voice in favor of continued US engagement with the world, in spite of the continuing bloodshed in Vietnam. His viewpoint did not sit well with the New Left, which wanted the US to pull out from everywhere.

Brzezinski's stance provoked Hoffmann, who said America should give up trying to play the role of "cosmic Metternich." The nineteenth-century Austro-Hungarian statesman was Kissinger's hero, not Brzezinski's. But Hoffmann's dart was aimed at Brzezinski. "For me, you're only a modified version of Morgenthau [the arch-realist who thought in terms of spheres of interest]," Brzezinski said. Hoffmann retorted, "For me, you're only a modified version of Walt Rostow [LBJ's reviled outgoing national security advisor]." In Brzezinski's view, Hoffmann's purpose was to ingratiate himself with the students, a stance he had honed during the faculty lock-ins. Students on the other side of the Iron Curtain in Czechoslovakia, Poland, and elsewhere were being jailed, or worse, for the crime of wanting Western-style plural democracy. Here in America, meanwhile, students were denouncing that same system. Hatred of America was turning into the *Zeitgeist* of a generation ignorant of its own ignorance. "If we didn't know the rest of the world, we might conclude that America is the worst country in the world," said Eugen Loebl, a Czech dissident who had fled Prague a few months earlier.[6] Nineteen sixty-eight had been turbulent for everyone.

It was also the year that Brzezinski turned forty. He and Muska had three healthy young children, a rambunctious home life in New Jersey, and a beautiful vacation retreat in Maine. Their money problems were behind them. They had recently added a small skiing lodge in Vermont. "You should stop being such a miser," Brzezinski chided Muska in a letter urging her to spend more of their cash flow on herself.[7] The opposite was true of Brzezinski's parents, whose financial woes had continued to deteriorate. Now in their early seventies, they had sold their beloved farm in the Laurentian Mountains and once more been forced to downgrade their Montreal residence to something more affordable. They took in boarders to supplement their income. Tadeusz's life was lived with growing vicariousness through Zbigniew. He had tried and failed at a string of half-baked business ventures. He kept a meticulous book of newspaper clippings on his son's public appearances. The parent-son correspondence never flagged. Tadeusz and Leonia would sometimes join Zbigniew and Muska and their growing family in summer visits to Maine.

Muska's tense relations with Leonia persisted. Her judgmental mother-in-law would complain about the clutter and mess and rarely offer to help in the kitchen. She expected to be waited upon. Muska usually obliged. Tadeusz, on the other hand, was turning into even more of a gentle soul with age. He bore no trace of bitterness about his lost Polish world. Their youngest, Lech, had graduated from McGill in engineering and the University of Illinois in geo-engineering and taken a job at SNC-Lavalin, a Montreal-based engineering company. He had married a Polish medical student, Wanda Kotanski, whom he met on a visit to Warsaw in the early 1960s. Wanda set up her own medical practice in Montreal. George, Zbigniew's half brother and Leonia's first-born, was struggling to make ends meet and in the process of divorce. Cruel fate would soon add cancer to his woes, which included his bipolar condition. Zbigniew helped to fund the college fees of George's daughter, Elise, who would often stay for weeks at a time with the Brzezinskis in New Jersey and Maine. They provided her with a happy escape.[8]

The year of American social upheaval was also a turning point in Brzezinski's public life. Kissinger's elevation lifted his sights about what might be possible; the Democratic Party viciously turned in on itself; the WASP establishment was discredited by the war in Vietnam; and the Soviets crushed the Prague Spring. That last event was least noticed in the US. To Brzezinski it had been the year's most seminal event. He was with his family in Maine during Humphrey's campaign in mid-July 1968 when a *New York Times* reporter called to ask him about a piece just published in *Neues Deutschland*, East Germany's equivalent of *Pravda*. The editorial singled out Brzezinski as a starring instigator of Alexander Dubček's "counterrevolutionary" forces in Prague, where Brzezinski had addressed a conference a few days earlier.[9] Walter Ulbricht, East Germany's leader and the last of the inveterate Stalinists, personally requested the article. Ulbricht had been keeping a jaundiced eye on Brzezinski for years. The Western thinkers Ulbricht most feared were those who wanted to bridge the gulf between East and West. Ulbricht had taken the decision to erect the Berlin Wall in 1962 while Brzezinski's acquaintance Willy Brandt was still mayor of West Berlin. Brzezinski was amused by the exaggerated role Ulbricht had assigned him in the Prague Spring. Yet it was also a promising sign that he was hitting his target. "Only dogmatic Communists who desire continued cold war and are willing to run the risk of a nuclear confrontation would disagree with my views," Brzezinski told the *New York Times*. "It puts them in the same category as the extreme right wing in this country."[10]

Two days later, in mid-July, Ulbricht flew to Poland to attend a Warsaw

Pact summit that would spell Czechoslovakia's doom. The new Soviet first among equals, Leonid Brezhnev, who had sidelined Alexei Kosygin a few months before, presided over the meeting. The Soviets were leaning towards the military occupation of Czechoslovakia. The rest of the East Bloc leaders were split. Some, particularly Ulbricht, wanted to flatten the Czechs. Others, such as Poland's leader, Władysław Gomułka, thought they should turn ignore the ferment in Prague, which he predicted would peter out. But Ulbricht had a trump card to play on his Polish counterpart. At a bilateral lunch, he told Gomułka that he had a thick file of documents about Brzezinski's trouble-making visit to Prague in mid-June.[11] Gomułka's attitude suddenly altered: if Brzezinski was behind the Czechoslovak unrest, he would certainly recon-sider. According to Gomułka's interpreter, Erwin Weit, who would defect to the West a couple of years later, the Polish leader had long "detested" Brzez-inski. In his speeches, Gomułka frequently attacked Brzezinski by name and called him "an imperialist running dog."

The Polish leader made Ulbricht promise to send him the Brzezinski file after he returned to East Berlin. Ulbricht's goading, however, had already done the trick. In the postlunch plenary session with Brezhnev, Gomułka dropped his opposition. Polish troops joined the five-nation Soviet-led invasion of Czechoslovakia a month later. In an article several weeks after the invasion, *Neues Deutschland* quoted Ulbricht as holding Brzezinski partly to blame. Brzezinski's Prague lecture, which he had entitled "The End of Leninism," had shown a Western influence behind Czechoslovakia's betrayal, said Ulbricht. "In this lecture, Brzezinski proceeded from the assumption that Leninism can-not be applied to a modern developed society," he said. "Brzezinski did so very frankly, and he is one of the closest intimates of the US leadership."[12] Since Brzezinski had not yet held a senior US government position, the hobgoblin role that Ulbricht assigned him was overstated. Brzezinski had been annoying Ulbricht for years. Some of it sprang from the acuity of Brzezinski's observa-tions about shifting political sands in the Soviet world. In contrast to many of his fellow Sovietologists, Brzezinski's analyses delved beneath the surface of power struggles among well-known Soviet leaders such as Khrushchev, Kosy-gin, and Brezhnev. He explored lesser-known East Bloc figures, commissars, and ideologues and the power struggles beneath.

Since his work was most widely translated in Poland—albeit illegally—Brzezinski's writing irritated Gomułka even more than Ulbricht. In late 1967 and early 1968, the Polish leader had launched a nationwide anti-Zionist campaign to stamp out the student protests that had been spreading on Polish campuses. Blaming the unrest on Israel, with which Poland had severed relations in 1967 after its Six-Day War with Egypt, was easy. Gomułka was resorting to a time-honored anti-Semitic tactic to divert attention from his weakening hold on power. The effect on Polish Jews was brutal. Though only about thirty thousand Jews remained in Poland—out of the 3.6 million who had called Poland their home before the war, most of whom had been killed there—Gomułka's campaign drove out roughly two-thirds of those still left. Ironically, more of them chose to go to the US than to Israel. All Jewish adults leaving Poland were required to hand over most of their savings and possessions as an exit tax.

Outraged by Polish American silence, Brzezinski arm-twisted fellow board members of the Polish Institute of Arts and Sciences in America to join him in deploring Gomułka's campaign. After much cajoling, he eventually got them to comply. In an April 15 letter to the *New York Times*, the board condemned "the anti-intellectualism and anti-Semitic views and policies currently practiced by officials of the ruling communist party and government of Poland." The letter would not have escaped Gomułka's notice. Brzezinski later said, "There was a big flap on that board because some people felt that a lot of the Jews that were being expelled were senior communist officials and that this was not such a bad thing."[13]

The Polish leader could draw on twelve years' worth of SB (secret police) reports on Brzezinski. Having opened its file in 1957 with a crude character sketch, the SB had filled in a much more detailed portrait over the years. They not only knew which East Bloc countries he had visited and when—eight trips to Poland, five to the USSR, two apiece to Czechoslovakia and Yugoslavia, and one each to Romania, Bulgaria, and Hungary—but also a brief African tour in 1961, his round-the-world itinerary of 1962–1963, and visits to Western Europe. Brzezinski had an "average body structure [and] typical Slavic features."[14] In a June 1966 report, the agent said that Brzezinski "gives the impression of one of those Eastern European emigrants who must have lost a lot. Brzezinski's lectures reveal a fierce resentment against socialist Poland. They are half lectures and half political speeches."[15] It added that Brzezinski had just been appointed to "a US government body [State's Policy Planning Staff] that involved research aided by computers."[16]

Ahead of one of Brzezinski's visits, Poland's Ministry of the Interior trained a rotating group of "informed collaborators," mostly scholars, to extract information from him in cafés and over dinners in Warsaw. They were schooled with five questions on which they were to lure him into revealing intelligence: "Is *Ostpolitik* inspired by the United States? Does President Johnson share Brzezinski's views about the erosion of communism? How does Poland plan to settle its debts to the West? Where does Vietnam policy go now? What are the relations between Rusk and McNamara?" The Polish academics related back to the authorities that Brzezinski had spent much of the time pumping them for information about Poland. By 1967, the Polish government knew more than enough about Brzezinski to reach a conclusion: Washington had given him the role of "disseminating the camouflaged concept of the 'softening of socialist states' among Polish intellectuals." He presented himself as a scientist with a "legendary lack of bias." In truth, the report said, he was a "cunning careerist thirsty for political clout."[17] The Polish government put Brzezinski onto its list of disbarred persons. He was not allowed back into the country for several years. He continued to live rent free in Gomułka's head.

Brzezinski's infamy had also spread to other capitals, including Moscow. He surprised many on both sides of the Atlantic by describing Khrushchev's ouster in 1964 as a tepid-sounding "victory of the clerks."[18] Since then, he had relentlessly chronicled what he described as the ossification of an aging Soviet leadership that had lost all revolutionary appeal. Life in the USSR was stifling and gray. The Politburo leadership under Kosygin and now Brezhnev was inherently conservative. Their rise through the ranks had been sped up by Stalin's purges, which had eliminated anyone with a rival ideological credo.

The new generation of Soviet leaders reached exalted positions precisely because they were not revolutionary. The Soviet escalator worked on the basis of reverse natural selection,[19] which rewarded those with the least ability to adapt. After Stalin, totalitarianism had settled into something that was ultimately even more threatening to the job security of the Soviet apparatchiks: an orthodoxy in terminal decline. Brzezinski could not forecast when the Soviet system would end, or whether its ending would be peaceful or cataclysmic. Either way, America's job should be to hurry the inevitable along. Soviet leaders wanted to be taken seriously by Washington and treated as superpower equals. Brzezinski's writings kept puncturing their pretensions. Moscow projected an influence on him that he did not yet possess.

The Soviet elite consumed political theory with as much appetite as their American counterparts followed ball games (Kissinger excepted). Abstraction was their daily bread. They were creatures of a doctrinaire universe. It would be hard to imagine any political culture more removed from the instinctive pragmatism of the American tradition. It is no surprise, therefore, that Brzezinski's *Mitteleuropa* argumentative style made a bigger splash in the East Bloc than in the US. The Communist media's grand organs pored over Brzezinski's books as if they contained the elixir of US strategy. "He is a first-rate star in the ideological sky of the USA," a well-known Soviet ideologist wrote in Moscow's *Literaturnaya Gazeta* in March 1969.[20] Brzezinski's habit of couching his analysis in Marxist vocabulary was also tactical; he meant to harangue his targets in their liturgical tongue. East Germany's Ulbricht wrote, "Some people who call themselves Marxist but have forgotten or who have failed to grasp the laws of the class struggle should read this book very carefully. Very characteristically it is called *Alternative to Partition*."[21] According to Poland's *Nowe Drogi*, "Zbigniew Brzezinski [was the] first of the 'Sovietologists' to raise the question of diversity in the Soviet camp."[22]

Brzezinski spent 1969 conducting his normal teaching duties at Columbia. Apart from a brief side trip to Vietnam, he spent most of that hot, dry summer writing a book in Maine. Demand for his classes kept growing. "He was not so much virulently anti-Communist as virulently analytic," wrote Madeleine Albright.[23] The year 1969 was also the crest of American counterculture; the Woodstock music festival took place in mid-August. The agitation at Columbia had not died down. Among the protestors, Brzezinski's notoriety had continued to grow. Brzezinski felt disdain for what he saw as the university's spinelessness in the face of the students' unmeetable utopian demands backed by threats of violence. He continued to differentiate between black radicalism, for which he conveyed public sympathy, and its mostly white student bourgeois fellow travelers. In a letter to the *New York Times* in late 1969, he called for an inquiry into the shooting of Black Panther Fred Hampton, who had been killed while resisting arrest in Chicago. "One cannot suppress the suspicion that he was shot because he was both black and a Panther," Brzezinski wrote.[24]

By contrast, he was indifferent at best to the fate of campus protestors. At one such protest, students brought along a live pig which on which they had daubed "Zbig." They shouted, "A pig, a pig for Professor Zbig." In Brzezinski's words, "The deans were all scared shitless."[25] Several minutes later, two police cars pulled up. Brzezinski was about to revise his low opinion of Columbia's administrators when he learned that the emergency call had been placed by an animal protection society. Its employees were worried about the pig's safety, not Professor Zbig's.

On July 20, Neil Armstrong became the first human to set foot on the moon. After watching the historic moment on TV from Maine, the transfixed Brzezinskis renamed their vacation retreat Tranquility Base after the lunar camp. That it was the United States, not the USSR, that had pulled off the moon landing was a confirmation of Brzezinski's optimistic worldview. It was fitting that Zager and Evans's one-hit wonder, "In the Year 2525," was top of the charts. That year's biggest song was about a future in which babies are born in test tubes and machines take over humanity's tasks. The technological future was also a theme of Brzezinski's new book. There was a wide-eyed quality to his optimism. "An American does not share with his compatriots a common past but a common future," he said. Colleagues saw his sweeping book *Between Two Ages: America's Role in the Technetronic Era* (1970) as an eccentric deviation from his staple Cold War work—and a further step away from conventional scholarship. He named it after a line in the Hermann Hesse novel *Steppenwolf*, which said that humans were in greatest danger when caught in transition between two ages. He dedicated the book to his children, Ian, Mark, and Mika. In spite of his unwieldy portmanteau—a fusing of "technical" with "electronic"—there was nothing complicated about his argument. America, he said, was leading humanity's shift from the industrial to the technetronic.

Few things date quite as fast the past's idea of the future. Brzezinski's call that the US would drive the coming technological revolution was prophetic. Some of its specific forecasts—about manipulating the human brain through chemistry and biology, for instance—feel like a recycling of Aldous Huxley's *Brave New World*. Much of Brzezinski's book was an unabashed paean to US technologism. Yet he warned that the Information Age's expanded global reality was "simultaneously fragmenting and thrusting itself upon us." The technetronic impact would stoke the Third World's appetite for postindustrial America's success yet create an ever wider gulf between the West and the rest. The quest of the previous age had been for freedom. The spirit of the new one was about equality. Since material equality would move farther beyond reach, "equality of emotion" would be its substitute. As an "ambivalent disseminator" of global revolution, America was both the source of revolutionary disruption and its potential casualty. It would have to navigate the "acute tension between the kind of global stability and order that America subjectively seeks and the instability, impatience, and frustration that America unconsciously promotes." The US was becoming the focus of worldwide emulation, envy, admiration, and animosity. "The United States has emerged as the first global society in history," he wrote.[26]

That was the meretricious part of Brzezinski's book. He discussed it on television, gave interviews to the big newspapers, and was reviewed in the major publications. Most reviews contrasted his largely optimistic outlook to the dystopia of popular contemporary books, notably Alvin Toffler's *Future Shock*, William Braden's *The Age of Aquarius: Technology and the Cultural Revolution*, and Nigel Calder's *Technopolis: Social Control of the Uses of Science*. Brzezinski's was notable for its absence of gloom. "One of the most original books on political and social thought to appear in recent years," wrote Harvard historian John G. Stoessinger in *Foreign Affairs*. "This seminal work is bound to elicit major controversy and will be difficult to ignore."[27]

Others were less respectful: "A mishmash of Herman Kahn [a renowned American futurist] and Marshall McLuhan [the influential Canadian philosopher]," said one reviewer.[28] All of them ignored Brzezinski's core point. His book's real target was the Soviet Bloc. If America was the world's revolutionary force, the USSR was a conservative backwater. Soviet statistics made a mockery of Lenin's claim to be in the vanguard of history. The US had sixty-five thousand computers compared to the USSR's three thousand, almost all of which were for military use. American companies were producing dozens of different car brands. Fifty years after its revolution, the USSR's only car was produced in a joint venture with Fiat, the Italian auto company. The East Bloc had turned into a museum of the Industrial Age.[29] It was as though Brzezinski had written two separate works. The other one—a large section that appeared in the middle of his book—was what attracted Moscow's notice. He was aiming at the East Bloc's jugular.

Brzezinski's diagnosis did not just rob the USSR of its revolutionary élan; it went against the grain of American thought. Many people in the US government, notably the CIA, had accepted the popular "convergence theory" that the Soviet economy was fast catching up with America's. The USSR's edge had been boosted by the 1957 launch of the *Sputnik* satellite, which had triggered panic about its technological catch-up. Given how hard it was to find reliable Soviet data, American forecasters had little basis on which to dispute Khrushchev's prediction that the USSR would match America's economy by 1970. Shortly after Brzezinski's book came out, the CIA estimated that the Soviet economy was more than half the size of America's, and the gap was narrowing. That turned out to be a vast overestimate; its true size was revised years later to be about a sixth.[30]

Brzezinski was as little trained in economics as most economists are in geopolitics. Nor was he a technologist. But his take on what he called "the bureaucratization of boredom"[31] was much closer to the truth. He had ample opportunity to observe the Soviet Union firsthand and interact with its citizens in their own tongue. He lost few opportunities to comment on the drab, monotonous nature of Soviet society and the low morale of its people. His unflattering depiction of the USSR's stagnant living standards hit Moscow where it hurt.

The Soviet piece of Brzezinski's argument went almost unremarked at home. As Brzezinski had felt in Princeton, American pessimism was in vogue. Henry Kissinger's bleak forecast of declining US power was often described as "Spenglerian" after the early-twentieth-century German philosopher Oswald Spengler, who had written that the West was in civilizational decline. Kissinger's gloom fit better with America's mood in the late 1960s and early 1970s. For Kissinger, it was only a matter of time before the Soviets caught up with the United States. America, he said, should adjust its foreign policy accordingly. Détente and America's early-1970s embrace of Moscow's "peaceful coexistence" were in many respects the child of Kissinger's (and Nixon's) pessimism. "For a while longer we may be able to hold on to what we have and perhaps even extend our achievement by proceeding along familiar routes," Kissinger said.[32]

That was very different from Brzezinski's reading of America's improving prospects. To Kissinger, the Soviets were a permanent feature of the global landscape; US foreign policy must accommodate that reality. To Brzezinski, Kissinger's approach was based on a misguided fatalism. There was little doubt in his mind that the Soviets were in decline; Washington's goal should be to hurry them along.

As the 1970s progressed, Washington's take on Brzezinski was that his differences with Kissinger were opportunistic rather than principled. Brzezinski's ambition did increasingly feature in their rivalry. But their philosophical divide was evident long before Kissinger had been hired by Nixon. In the midst of the 1968 campaign, when Kissinger had been dexterously keeping several loyalties in play, he found time to send Brzezinski an essay he had written for *Daedalus* entitled "The White Revolutionary: Reflections on Bismarck." The "blood and iron" German leader was Europe's great nineteenth-century archrealist, wrote Kissinger. Through guile, force, manipulation, and deception, Bismarck had fashioned a great power from unpromising beginnings. In his reply to Kissinger, Brzezinski wrote, "On reading it (and I did enjoy it), I had the feeling of understanding better some of your current political involvements!"[33] They nevertheless kept up a close relationship throughout most of Kissinger's White House years.

A few weeks after taking office, Kissinger invited Brzezinski for lunch in Washington. He also asked Brzezinski to join a roundtable of outside thinkers who would advise the Nixon administration on its foreign policy agenda. Brzezinski was unable to make it. The following week they dined at Sans Souci, a block from the White House. The pricey French restaurant was where the two usually met. The interior was shaped like a theater to maximize dramatic entrances. Kissinger loved to be seen there on dates with celebrities, usually blond, from the media or Hollywood. Once or twice, he dated reporters who were covering him. The rotund intellectual had unexpectedly turned into the "playboy of the West Wing"—an image he loved to cultivate. "If no beautiful actress is available would you like to take me to dinner at Sans Souci?" Brzezinski wrote in July 1970.[34] Their tone was usually convivial. "You seemed to be in tip top shape," Brzezinski wrote a few months later. "Obviously your curricular, as well as extra-curricular, activities are good for your health!"[35]

Kissinger regularly solicited Brzezinski's input on policy; Brzezinski was always happy to oblige. Nixon's urgent priority, and thus Kissinger's, was to extricate the US from Vietnam. In his campaign, Nixon had promised Americans that he had a "secret plan" to end the Vietnam War. The only secret was that he had no plan. In spite of Nixon's 1968 shenanigans, the Paris peace talks were still going nowhere. Nixon replaced Harriman with Henry Cabot Lodge, a Republican and former US ambassador to Saigon. Lodge had no better luck than Harriman at finding a way through the process's frustratingly on-off character. Only Nixon could do that by seizing the initiative with a bold, decisive gesture.

In the buildup to Nixon's much-awaited address to the nation on Vietnam in late 1969, Brzezinski sent Nixon a two-page memo on what would be "the most important speech of your presidency."[36] Nixon should declare a ceasefire, he said, announce a limited US troop withdrawal, and set a date—say, two years hence—for full withdrawal.[37] Kissinger thanked Brzezinski for his thoughts, which had been inspired by another lightning visit to South Vietnam. Nixon's prime-time address on November 3, 1969, is best remembered for his appeal to the "great silent majority" of Americans who outnumbered the antiwar protestors. In the short term, the "Vietnamization" policy that Nixon unveiled turned into the opposite of the deescalation he had promised. To build up South Vietnam's forces so that Saigon could manage the war on its own, America must temporarily step up its military presence, he said.

"Peace with honor" had an appealing ring. In practice, it was an oxymoron. To achieve peace, the United States would have to get out of Vietnam. To do so with honor, it must stick around. Thus began an Alice in Wonderland phase in which America kept saying "Hello, I must be going" in a game that necessitated ever greater subterfuge. Its most egregious effect was Nixon's secret bombing of Cambodia. That tawdry chapter had begun six months earlier. In January 1970, Kissinger sent Brzezinski a letter congratulating him on "your new career as a part time (?) journalist." Brzezinski had just been given a column in *Newsweek* that was also carried in the *Washington Post*. In an alliterative splash, the magazine heralded its three new columnists: Ball, Bundy, and Brzezinski. It was Brzezinski's latest move into the limelight. "I hope you are prepared for the hazards as well as the rewards," said Kissinger.[38]

For the time being, Brzezinski kept the tone of his Nixon criticisms respectful. But he was privately shocked by Nixon's prime-time address on April 30, 1970, in which the president was forced to concede that he had expanded the war to neutral Cambodia (a year after having secretly ordered it). He had just announced the withdrawal of 150,000 US troops from Vietnam over the coming year. In his address he disclosed that the US drawdown was being put into jeopardy by Vietcong attacks from sanctuaries in neighboring Cambodia. "If, when the chips are down, the world's most powerful nation, the United States of America, acts like a pitiful, helpless giant, the forces of totalitarianism and anarchy will threaten free nations and free institutions throughout the world," Nixon told the nation. Even hawks thought he was exaggerating.

Brzezinski vented his dismay about Nixon's Cambodia speech to Kissinger in a May 23 conversation. Their talk went on for so long that Brzezinski typed its highlights in a two-page memcon (memorandum of conversation). Kissinger pleaded that he had had "very little to do with drafting" Nixon's address. He also agreed that the Vietcong's Cambodia headquarters to which Nixon had referred "does not in fact exist." That claim, he said, had been "inserted by the president himself."[39] Brzezinski did not record any doubts he might have had about Kissinger's protestations of innocence. It would later become clear that Kissinger had been intimately involved both in drafting Nixon's address and in developing his Cambodia policy.[40] Far from disputing the Vietcong's fictional Cambodian headquarters, Kissinger had been stoking the claim for months. Brzezinski's summary of their session is a striking example of the candor with which Kissinger shared apparent confidences that later turned out to have been misleading or false. Brzezinski was already a veteran of Kissinger's 1968 deceptions. It did not cause him to reappraise the utility of their exchanges.

Two days later Brzezinski wrote another memo for Nixon, politely disputing his claim that the Cambodian sideshow would validate itself. In addition to questions about his speech's impact on the war, he said, Nixon's words did not "provide an effective response to the widening and deepening sense of alienation among America's young."[41] Kissinger had requested Brzezinski's note. It is doubtful that he passed it on to Nixon.

One issue on which the two did agree was the hopeless state of mind of American intellectuals. Kissinger thought that Nixon's reelection in 1972 was already in the bag. Brzezinski needed no persuading. In his *Newsweek* column a few weeks earlier, he had written of "the alienated members of the American upper middle class whose craving for vicarious revolutionary virtue takes the form of wallowing in apocalyptic rhetoric at opulent penthouse cocktail parties."[42] That was a potentially self-harming commentary from a Polish American who wished to become the Democratic Party's version of Kissinger. Yet his scathing opinion was sincerely held. Kissinger was equally bitter about his former colleagues at Harvard. He ranted to Brzezinski about their willingness to lead the young down the path of extremism. When Kissinger left public office, which he told the skeptical Brzezinski would be before the end of Nixon's first term, he had no intention of returning to his alma mater, he said.

Kissinger's annoyance with the establishment had been reinforced by a recent meeting with David Rockefeller in his West Wing office. Nelson's younger brother and Brzezinski's sponsor was in a state of high anxiety about America's youth, who were continuing to tear up campuses, march in large numbers against the war, and occupy monumental Washington. "Look, you have to help us out with [our] young," Rockefeller had urged Kissinger. "You have to help us make an effective response."[43] Brzezinski noted that "Henry spoke contemptuously" about Rockefeller's request. Pandering to America's young was no way for a great nation to conduct itself, he said.

As a full-time professor, Brzezinski was in almost daily conversation with the young. His life was also increasingly tied up with David Rockefeller. Over the previous few years, his interests had spread to Japan, which happened to be one of Rockefeller's favorite countries. In the first half of 1971, Brzezinski took another sabbatical from Columbia to spend six months in Tokyo. Muska joined him for three months. Her mother looked after the children. The Brzezinskis had felt growing concern about the septuagenarian Emilie Benes's isolation in her remote forest cottage, although she was sprightly enough to hold down a full-time job managing an elderly care home. They helped her to buy a mock Tudor house next door to theirs. Her change of address served everyone's needs. It brought her closer to her grandchildren. They, their cherished dog, Dasha, and the family's two ducks, Napoleon and Josephine, could slip back and forth between the two houses through a gap in the fence.

She had more than enough vigor to help look after three unruly children while their parents were away. A former interpreter, she spoke no fewer than fourteen languages. The Brzezinski home was purely anglophone. The children grew up speaking neither Polish nor Czech. Brzezinski's mother-in-law tried, with little success, to teach them French. Brzezinski described Ian, the oldest, as a "whimsical, sensitive boy," Mark as "a real character, tough as bricks," and Mika as "a delightful and clever little girl."[44] In their soccer games in the family backyard, he gave Mika no leeway for being the youngest of the brood and a girl. In their occasionally nosebleed-inducing rough and tumble, she learned not to ask for quarter. Muska was in a pottery phase of her artistic journey. She sculpted statues that she then glazed and fired in the kitchen oven. Given the refinements of Japanese ceramics, the chance to spend more time in Tokyo was too tempting for her to pass up.

Brzezinski's interest in Japan was fueled by an urge to widen his aperture. To reach the top level of US foreign policy, he would need to be more than just a Sovietologist. Hastening the USSR's demise remained his chief obsession. But the arena in which the Cold War was being played out was increasingly global. A couple of years later, he changed the name of his Research Institute on Communist Affairs at Columbia to Research Institute on International Change. The Ford Foundation, assisted by Japan's Nomura Bank, funded Brzezinski's sojourn. Nomura gave him an office next to its chief executive officer at its headquarters in downtown Tokyo. The bank set up meetings with whomever he wanted to see from the prime minister downwards. From a foreign policy standpoint, Brzezinski's spell in Japan was fortuitously timed. It was the year of "Nixon shocks" to America's allies. In July 1971, Nixon stunned pretty much everyone in Washington, including his secretary of state, William Rogers, but not Kissinger (who had been working the back channels) with his bombshell declaration that he would soon be undertaking a historic trip to Mao's China.

Leaders in Europe and Japan felt bruised by Nixon's failure to consult them or even warn them of such a dramatic shift. Nixon had already generated deep insecurity with his so-called Nixon Doctrine, which would devolve security responsibilities onto America's allies. The idea that regional allies would shoulder a larger share of America's anti-Communist burden was partially an attempt to dress up Vietnamization as a coherent doctrine, South Vietnam being a formal ally. It nevertheless deepened angst that the US was planning to cut its overseas military presence. Nixon's drive for détente with the USSR was Europe's main source of paranoia. His overture to China would create similar neuralgia in Tokyo. In a second shock to both Japan and Europe in August 1971, Nixon said that the US would be exiting the gold standard and slapped a 10 percent surcharge on all imports. The US dollar would no longer be convertible into gold. At a stroke and without consulting his own Treasury Department, let alone the allies, Nixon pulled the plug on the postwar Bretton Woods system. Nixon was making America's allies poorer and more paranoid at the same time.

The Nixon shocks came a few weeks after Brzezinski and Muska had returned from Japan. During their stay in Tokyo, Brzezinski had picked up on Japan's deep insecurity about America's direction. Nixon made his two announcements while the Brzezinskis were in Maine. Brzezinski was writing a 150-page monograph about what he had learned from his time in Japan, which would be published the following spring as *The Fragile Blossom: Crisis and Change in Japan*. In the preface, he admitted that he was "not even remotely an expert" on the country. In a few impressionistic brushstrokes he then proceeded to make mincemeat of the increasingly fashionable view that Japan was the world's coming superpower. His short book did not explicitly mention a current US best seller, *The Emerging Japanese Superstate: Challenge and Response*. The book, written by the futurologist Herman Kahn, predicted that Japan would be the world's number one economy by the year 2000. In Brzezinski's view, Japan's economic miracle was already waning and its growth would decline sharply in the near future. He also disputed the widespread claim that Japan was on the cusp of becoming a nuclear power. Japan had the capability to go that route, he conceded. Given the choice, however, Tokyo would far prefer to remain under the US nuclear umbrella. Both of Brzezinski's insights were borne out. One reviewer complimented "the brilliance of [Brzezinski's] intuitive judgment" but added that he was naive about Tokyo's military ambitions.[45]

Brzezinski did not take issue with America's incipient "Japanic" (a short-lived neologism that surfaced many years after Brzezinski's book was published). With the huge and subsequent exception of Kissinger, he almost always avoided targeting by name those with whom he disagreed. He usually turned down offers to write book reviews because he did not want to turn intellectual disputes into personal feuds. "I hate reviewing books," he admitted to the editor of an academic journal in 1960. He found them "debilitating intellectually, demoralizing personally, and destructive collegiately."[46] Reviews barely feature in the gargantuan body of Brzezinski's life work. His real preoccupation with Japan was that it was being neglected by Nixon, whose careless treatment would have negative effects that could harm the United States. He gave a helpful précis of his forthcoming book in a September 1971 Newsweek column. "We are witnessing today not the take-off of Japan into the superpower phase of its history but the tail end of postwar Japanese economic recovery. . . . [Nixon's] China move hurt their pride; the economic move hit their pockets—and that's a pretty lethal combination," he wrote.[47] Brzezinski's intended audience was Nixon and Kissinger. They ignored his advice for Nixon to stop in Tokyo on his way to China. Brzezinski's personal and longer-term remedy for Japan's sense of isolation was to set up an institution comprising the United States, Europe, and Japan. David Rockefeller would be needed for the project.

Rockefeller and Brzezinski had been running into each other for more than a decade at the Council on Foreign Relations in New York, and at the annual Bilderberg Meetings that took place at invariably glittering venues in Europe. They had seen a lot of each other in Maine, where he and Muska would often be invited to join the Rockefellers for picnics or on one of their yachts. The couples were friendly, yet there was an invisible barrier that stopped them from becoming close; their backgrounds were too different and their disparity in wealth too vast to become intimates. Brzezinski had no personal financial ties to Rockefeller. But he needed Rockefeller's capital, convening power, and imprimatur for his next grand project, the Trilateral Commission. It took a while to convince Rockefeller of the idea's merit. Brzezinski, who had been contemplating Japan's geopolitical insecurity and the rich world's declining cohesion since the mid-1960s, tried to convince the Bilderberg's steering committee that its meetings should be expanded to include the Japanese. The consensus among Bilderberg's European members was consistently negative and occasionally hostile. They had no wish for a third party to bust in on their exclusive setup with the Americans.

Rockefeller, who was also something of a Japanophile, had no more success than Brzezinski in convincing the committee to expand its guest list. On their way back from the April 1972 Bilderberg Meeting in Belgium, the two hatched the idea of launching a new outfit. Their conversation took place on Rockefeller's private jet from Brussels to New York. In his autobiography, Rockefeller wrote that the Trilateral Commission idea had been his. He recounted how Bilderberg's steering committee in Brussels had again rejected his suggestion of adding Japan. On the way home, he had broached with Brzezinski the idea of setting up a rival conference. "Zbig considered this rebuff further proof that my idea was well founded and urged me to pursue it," he wrote. He added that he had already floated the concept in various meetings with Chase investment forums a month before the Brussels event.[48]

In reality the idea of the Trilateral Commission was Brzezinski's. He had been writing for several years about the need to set up a three-way community of developed nations that would include Japan, most recently in *Between Two Ages*, which had come out a year earlier. Six months before his conversation with Rockefeller over the Atlantic, Brzezinski coauthored a concept paper with Henry Owen, his former boss at the State Department, and Robert Bowie, his erstwhile Harvard mentor, which made the case for such a body.[49] In his diary, he noted that he raised the idea on the way to Brussels but Rockefeller was "suspicious."[50] By their return journey, Rockefeller had changed his mind. In history's grand tableau, the Trilateral Commission's precise origin is trivial. But it offers a glimpse of how money and ideas interact. Rockefeller wrote that after his rebuff in Brussels, "I arranged a follow-up meeting with Zbig, Robert Bowie of the Center for International Affairs at Harvard, Henry Owen of the Brookings Institution, and McGeorge Bundy of the Ford Foundation, who all heartily endorsed my proposal to form a trilateral commission."[51] Brzezinski never publicly disputed Rockefeller's recollection. In a private letter to Brzezinski many years later, Rockefeller referred to the plane journey in which "we both conceived the idea of the Trilateral Commission."[52]

Either way, it was on Rockefeller's plane in April 1972 that the plan was born. Three months later, Rockefeller hosted an exploratory weekend at Pocantico Hills, his family's sumptuous Hudson Valley estate. There were eighteen invitees, including four from Japan and five from Europe. In addition to Rockefeller and Brzezinski, the American group included Bowie, Owen, Bundy, and George Ball; Bayless Manning, a former dean of Stanford Law School; Fred Bergsten, a former Nixon administration economist; and George

Franklin, the Council on Foreign Relations' director of studies (and Rocke-feller's Harvard roommate). Among the Japanese were Kiichi Miyazawa, who would later become the country's prime minister, and Saburo Okita, a leading economist, a future foreign minister. The European group was dominated by figures who had been central to the rise of the European movement, mostly protégés of Jean Monnet, one of its chief architects. They included François Duchêne from France, Max Kohnstamm from the Netherlands, and Guido Colonna di Paliano from Italy.[53]

Both the Europeans and the Japanese were keen to pin down Rockefeller money for the commission's start-up costs, a financial anxiety that would become an institutional running sore. Rockefeller wanted the funding to be shared. The guests' long weekend was nevertheless a success. Rockefeller's palatial hospitality helped. At one point, with all of them gathered around the ornate swimming pool, they realized that its cooling system had failed. It was a sultry day, and the pool's water was unrefreshingly warm. Rockefeller got his estate's staff to ferry ice buckets back and forth from the main residence, which they emptied into the pool. Their antlike process eventually lowered the temperature. It was an unforgettable sight.[54]

Apart from launching the institution, the invitees needed to settle on a name, which they agreed on while sitting around the pool. Brzezinski dis-missed "Tripartite Commission" as being too redolent of the 1940 Tripartite Pact between the fascist Axis powers, Germany, Italy, and Japan. They settled on "Trilateral." The commission's real buzzword, which appeared in almost every early paper it published, was "interdependence," which roughly meant globalization—and contained an implied rebuke to Nixon's partial withdrawal from America's obligations to its allies. They could not have guessed that their earnest venture, which, in addition to the conferences, would churn out posi-tion papers on worthy topics such as foreign aid, trade barriers, floating curren-cies, and the future of democracy, would turn into an object of dark fascination on both right and left.

The Right saw it as the steering committee of "one-worldism" that wanted to rob the United States of its sovereignty. The evangelist Pat Robertson said the Trilateral Commission "sprang from the depths of something evil."[55] The Left saw it as a corporatist plot to impose a worldwide capitalist agenda. There were suf-ficient grains of truth in both conspiracy theories to give them life. The commis-sion was chaired and partly funded by one of America's most storied capitalists, and its bias was towards open borders and integration. It gathered a long roster of influential members. One of its early political recruits was the little-known governor of the state of Georgia. His name was Jimmy Carter.

As often happens, however, the conspiracists imputed a kind of B-movie glamour onto an institution that bore scant resemblance to the shadowy cabal they imagined it to be. As with Bilderberg, the commission's discussions took place under the Chatham House Rule, under which remarks could be quoted without disclosing who made them. Unlike Bilderberg, the commission's membership list was public, and its conference agendas were accessible. John Kenneth Galbraith famously resigned from the Council on Foreign Relations because he found it boring. At one or two points in the commission's early days, Brzezinski came close to doing the same. He had taken a year-and-a-half sabbatical from Columbia to work at the commission's office, which was, unsurprisingly, located in Rockefeller Plaza in midtown Manhattan. He had hoped its members would shake up conventional wisdom. In the first couple of years, he found it hard to get the three groups of participants to take clear stands on anything controversial, such as the 1973 Yom Kippur War, a response to the Organization of the Petroleum Exporting Countries (OPEC) oil embargo, or a new global monetary system. Even world fisheries proved divisive.

Eighteen months after its launch, Brzezinski gave his "brutal reflections" on an institution that in his view had so far had minimal public impact.[56] Moreover, the Europeans and Japanese had not been pulling their financial weight. Some of the bigger names, such as Italy's Giovanni Agnelli, had failed to show up for a meeting. Gradually, however, the commission became part of the landscape. The financial heft and cosmopolitan allure were Rockefeller's. As its first director, Brzezinski shouldered most of the real work. At the body's next meeting, the Canadian diplomat Peter Dobell said it should be renamed the Unilateral Commission because of Brzezinski's indefatigable contributions.[57] Though Dobell was joking, he was more right than wrong. The Trilateral Commission was where America's thirty-ninth president received his crash course in foreign policy. His chief instructor was Brzezinski.

Carter's improbable path to the Democratic nomination can, to a significant degree, be explained by the depth of the party's post-1972 despair. In Brzezinski's view, the party's doldrums were fully deserved. After Humphrey's 1968 defeat, the Democrats had been moving leftward, especially on foreign policy. The natural front-runner for the 1972 nomination was Ed Muskie, the senator from Maine who had been Humphrey's 1968 running mate. He was judged to have acquitted himself well on the campaign trail in inauspicious circumstances. In practice, the field was wide open. No fewer than fifteen candidates entered the 1972 Democratic primaries. The key omission was Ted Kennedy, who had done his reputation potentially irreparable harm on July 18, 1969, on the island of Chappaquiddick off the coast of Massachusetts. At around midnight, his car had careened off a bridge into the water where he had left his young female passenger, Mary Jo Kopechne, to drown. Though Kennedy claimed to have tried to save her, the Chappaquiddick disgrace clung to him.

The 1972 Democratic field was as ideologically diverse as the choice offered in many multiparty democracies, ranging from the repeat antiwar candidacy of Eugene McCarthy on the left to Henry "Scoop" Jackson, an uber-hawkish senator from Washington, on the right. In the middle were Humphrey (again) and Muskie. Having learned a trick or two from Kissinger in 1968, Brzezinski advised at least three candidates. Of them, Humphrey and Muskie demanded the most of him. Each was effusive about Brzezinski's efforts. "I wish I could find words to adequately thank you for our help and support during the campaign," wrote Muskie. "I shall always remember your contribution to our common effort."[58] Likewise from Humphrey: "It really was tremendously gratifying to me to know of your faithful support. . . . Well 'your candidate' put up a fight, and in retrospect I think it was a good fight, but lost."[59]

On request, Brzezinski also supplied advice and material to Jackson, though not to such a degree that the senator felt he was on his team. The eventual nominee, George McGovern, was the last person Brzezinski wanted to win. That did not stop McGovern's campaign from including Brzezinski on a list of foreign policy advisors that it published a few weeks after the 1972 Democratic National Convention in Miami. Abram Chayes, the Harvard Law professor who was coordinator of McGovern's brain trust, told the press that the names would not have agreed to advise the candidate if they had not shared his views.[60] Brzezinski took the highly unusual step of repudiating the McGovern campaign's claim in a letter to the *Washington Post*: "I find myself compelled to note that I am not in agreement with the Senator's views on foreign policy."[61]

For an ambitious Democratic operator, it was a sharp and personally risky public disavowal of the party's standard bearer. But Brzezinski could not bring himself to extend his campaign spread betting to a rank outsider whose neoisolationist views he reviled. In a reply to a congratulatory note from Cord Meyer, an old CIA hand who had known Brzezinski since he had orchestrated the saboteur delegation to the 1959 Communist youth festival in Vienna, Brzezinski was more brutal: "I think [McGovern] is a disaster in more ways than one, and he is setting back the political process in this country by many years. I hope he is soundly defeated."[62] Brzezinski got his wishes. McGovern's defeat was the most sweeping in modern history. He won just one state—Massachusetts—and the District of Columbia. His 37.5 percent share of the national vote was the most lopsided showing by a losing candidate since the nineteenth century. It was the nadir for a Democratic Party still at war with itself.

Brzezinski's opposition to McGovern was visceral and intellectual (in Brzezinski the two were rarely far apart). McGovern campaigned on a pledge to withdraw all US forces from Vietnam, impose sweeping cuts on the US defense budget, and disengage America from world affairs. He would cut US forces in Europe "to the bone." To Brzezinski, that was a reckless abdication from international reality and a misapplication of Vietnam's lessons. On that, he and Kissinger were in agreement. Kissinger later wrote that in the 1920s and 1930s, US isolationism had been based on the idea that America was too ethical to expose itself to the world. By contrast, Kissinger said, the country's latest isolationist phase, personified by McGovern, was motivated by the idea that America was too depraved for the world.

Brzezinski was also becoming increasingly critical of Nixon's foreign policy, notably his pursuit of a balance of power, which he saw as stemming from Kissinger's badly drawn analogy between the European peace that had followed the 1815 Congress of Vienna and the bipolar ideological contest of the late twentieth century. "A very traditional balance of power system could make sense in a very traditional age," he wrote to both Humphrey and Muskie.[63] But in a world of ideological contests and an era of "newly awakened peoples," the idea of a US-Soviet condominium was neither achievable nor desirable. The Cold War of the 1970s was too different from the situation in early-nineteenth-century Europe for Kissinger's idea of the balance of power to make practical sense.

Yet McGovern's remedies were worse than the disease. Much as foreign policy conservatives saw every international threat as a potential Munich, the Democratic Left was treating every overseas engagement as the next Vietnam. McGovern was an escapist isolationist who "simply pretends that if the problems of power are ignored they will somehow disappear," Brzezinski wrote.[64] His foreign policy rested on one issue: Vietnam. He had nothing to say about the Middle East, China, the Soviets, or any other foreign challenge. McGovern was also silent on the USSR's rapid catch-up in nuclear and conventional reach and "talked as if the US was the only power in the world spending money on arms."[65]

Much of Brzezinski's dislike of McGovern's platform stemmed from a cultural allergy to the radical chic intellectuals whom he saw as has having replaced the blue-collar unionist as the party's animating spirit. Brzezinski had been banging that drum since his participation in the chaotic Princeton seminar in late 1968. Mayor Richard Daley's Italian and Irish cops had given the counterculture demonstrators a beating in Chicago earlier that year. But it was the protestors who had won control of the party. Some of that had resulted from the rules changes McGovern himself had put into place after the Chicago convention. McGovern headed the DNC commission that did away with the role of bosses and smoke-filled rooms in favor of open primaries and quotas for women and minorities. The unions were the main losers.

The reforms left the Democrats exposed to the "more extreme and more noisy elements among the more well-to-do upper-middle-class liberals, who enjoy being vicarious radicals, and to the more frustrated and alienated college activists," Brzezinski wrote to Humphrey in 1970.[66] It also ceded the big American center ground to Nixon, much as Barry Goldwater's John Birch Society–fueled brand of conservatism had abandoned the middle to Johnson in 1964. Brzezinski's forebodings were well founded; McGovern's defeat was even worse than Goldwater's. McGovern had been smeared in a notorious newspaper column as the candidate of "acid, amnesty, and abortion."[67] Brzezinski did not disclose which way he voted in 1972. There were only two possibilities: either he abstained, or he went for Nixon. It was the first presidential election in which he had not endorsed a Democrat. McGovern's slogan "Come home America!" was the antithesis of everything Brzezinski believed.

In 1972 Nixon signed the Anti-Ballistic Missile Treaty (ABM Treaty) with the Soviets, a landmark of détente. The year yielded another ABM— "Anybody but McGovern"—that led to yet another chaotic Democratic convention. Because of wrangling over the party's changed delegate rules, McGovern gave his acceptance speech at 2:48 a.m., after the bulk of his TV audience had gone to bed. One of the leaders of the "Stop McGovern" rearguard action at the Miami Beach Convention Center was Jimmy Carter. On the day after McGovern's defeat to Nixon, Carter held a meeting of his closest Georgia advisors at the Governor's Mansion in Atlanta to discuss a possible presidential run.[68] He did not publicly declare for another two years. In the meantime, he would become one of the most studious politicians ever to campaign for the White House. Brzezinski provided his crash course in the world beyond the United States. The relationship between the naturalized American from Poland and the peanut farmer from Georgia was as improbable as that between the German Jewish refugee (Kissinger) and an anti-Semitic Quaker from southern California (Nixon). Among the numerous obstacles to Carter's presidential aspirations—being unknown, from the deep South, explicitly pious, an indifferent public speaker—ignorance of foreign policy was high on the list. Carter would rectify that shortcoming by becoming an "eager student"[69] of Brzezinski.

Their acquaintance was serendipitous. The Trilateral Commission decided it needed a Republican and a Democratic governor among its founding members. Brzezinski wanted a "forward looking Democratic governor who would be congenial to the Trilateral perspective."[70] The obvious choice was Florida's Reubin Askew. Then someone pointed out that Georgia's Jimmy Carter had opened state trade offices in Brussels and Tokyo. "Well, then he's obviously our man," Brzezinski said.[71] He also liked the fact that Carter belonged to a new generation of southern politicians who were progressive on civil rights. In a 1970 *Time* magazine cover story headlined "Dixie Whistles a Different Tune," Carter had been profiled as embodying a new force in southern politics. His gubernatorial campaign had in practice been replete with racial dog whistles. His skill at communicating to the white blue-collar worker in racial euphemisms that gave him room for plausible deniability was redolent of Nixon's 1968 tactics. Following his election, however, Carter had pivoted to a civil rights platform. He would later cause consternation among the state's good ol' boy crowd when he unveiled Martin Luther King, Jr.'s, portrait in the Georgia State Capitol. While Klansmen protested outside, Carter invited Coretta Scott King, MLK's widow, and other civil rights leaders inside to join him in singing "We Shall Overcome."[72]

Carter did almost all of his foreign policy homework at the Trilateral Commission. More than any other member, he would read every paper and attend every meeting starting with the opening one in London in spring 1973. It was at the commission meetings in Washington, Europe, and Japan that

Carter met and befriended leading lights of US foreign policy, as well as other rising world leaders. Almost no one counted him among the stars. In his campaign memoir, *Why Not the Best?*, Carter said he owed his knowledge of world affairs to the commission. At that point, Carter was the seeker and Brzezinski the sought after. Almost as soon as the 1972 election was over, jostling for the 1976 nomination began. Brzezinski had been called into meetings with almost every aspiring Democratic candidate, including Scoop Jackson (again), Ed Muskie (again), Ted Kennedy, Walter Mondale, and Morris Udall, a progressive congressman from Utah. Though the choice was broad, the contest felt stale before it got under way. One of the candidates' few common points was that they wanted Brzezinski's advice. Carter was especially solicitous.

In a *Washington Post* poll in November 1974, Carter was not even listed among the thirty-one possible contenders for the Democratic nomination. Gerald Rafshoon, one of Carter's Atlanta inner circle, had to correct that newspaper's recurring mistake of calling him "Governor Jimmy Collins."[73] On December 12, 1974, the serenely optimistic Carter was nevertheless only the second Democrat, after Udall, to declare his candidacy. The somewhat amused Brzezinski wrote Carter a letter, offering to help with foreign policy. He had no plans to be Carter's exclusive advisor. Carter replied, "The Trilateral Com experience has been a wonderful opportunity for me, and I have used it perhaps even more than you could know. Your friend, Jimmy."[74] In the following months, Carter decamped to Iowa. His bet was that a win in the first caucus, which was another product of McGovern's party reforms, would generate name recognition that would give him momentum going into New Hampshire, the first primary. That, in turn, would catapult him onto the national stage.

That strategy would become the standard route to the prize. Carter invented it. Until then, Iowa had not been on the primary map. At one of his early Iowa meetings, Carter's team had rented a conference room in a Des Moines hotel. There was enough food and Coca-Cola for two hundred people.[75] Only three showed up. On the advice of Jody Powell, Carter's young aide, Carter relocated to the street outside and accosted random pedestrians. Modestly introducing himself as "Jimmy" to unsuspecting locals turned into his unofficial campaign theme. Handshake by handshake, one diner drop-in at a time, he made himself known to Iowans. He would stay overnight at the homes of local supporters to save money. When he was forced to sleep at a hotel, it was usually a shared motel room. His roommate was often Powell, his most loyal aide and hard-partying Georgian. Powell would enter the bathroom in the morning to find Carter's washed undergarments hanging out to dry.

A few months after launching his campaign, Carter attended the Trilateral Commission's annual meeting in Kyoto. The forcefulness of his presentation on the Israel-Palestine dispute impressed Brzezinski. He was explicit in saying that Israel must accommodate Palestinian aspirations in a land-for-peace settlement. Brzezinski told himself, "This is a guy who's got chutzpah."[76] He complimented Carter on his speech. The grateful Carter asked Brzezinski to stand by his side at a session with the US press corps in Tokyo. He hoped that Brzezinski's presence would lend him credibility. The media had downgraded Carter's request to give a speech to the Foreign Correspondents' Club of Japan. They were so skeptical of Carter's prospects that they would grant him only a press conference. Brzezinski described the few reporters who turned up as "sardonic and even patronizing."[77] Their assumption was that Carter was auditioning to be a running mate of whoever won the nomination.

Never shedding his toothy smile, Carter took the humiliation with good humor. He patiently explained his strategic itinerary—Iowa to New Hampshire, then on to Florida and the national stage—to the point where "your headlines will say 'Carter frontrunner.'" None of the journalists seemed persuaded by the unorthodox path that Carter sketched out or by his vaunting ambitions. Although Carter had been campaigning for six months, he had only 2 percent national name recognition in the polls; "Jimmy who?" became his media nickname.[78] But his brassy performance made a believer of Brzezinski. He returned from Kyoto taken by Carter's decency, unflappable temperament, and "inner steel." Carter talked about power in the context of principle. Brzezinski felt that combination was sorely lacking in Washington.

Almost by accident, Brzezinski became Carter's key advisor. On his return to New Jersey, he extolled Carter's virtues to Muska, who urged him to follow up with a donation. He sent Carter a token $20 check and a note wishing him luck. Carter replied gratefully. A few weeks later, Brzezinski learned from the media that he was Carter's chief foreign policy advisor. This time he did nothing to contradict a surprise newspaper announcement. Though Carter was still an unknown quantity and was given no odds of winning the nomination, Brzezinski decided to gamble his future on a rank outsider who to everyone's surprise went on to win the Derby. But it was a calculated bet. Brzezinski did not have much time for Ted Kennedy and did not relish the prospect of Camelot returning to Washington. As it turned out, an agonized

Kennedy concluded it was still too early to risk his name. Brzezinski admired Scoop Jackson. He worked closely with the hawkish senator on his 1974 Jackson-Vanik amendment that denied trading benefits to countries that restricted Jewish emigration—a measure tailored solely for the USSR. But he thought him a bland campaigner and too much of a one-issue politician. Jackson was also too conservative for the rank and file. Udall, by contrast, was too liberal and threatened to become a replay of McGovern. Which left Carter. Both Muskie and Mondale had backed out. In a roundabout way, the Democratic Party was going through the same process of elimination as Brzezinski.

Carter's pitch was personal. He was an outsider to Washington at a time when the federal capital had rarely been held in lower esteem. His core promise and constant refrain—some would say the gauntlet he rashly threw down to a cynical media—was that he would never lie to the American people. He was liberal enough in his worldview to be acceptable to the Left. He called for nuclear disarmament, civil rights at home, human rights abroad, women's equality, and the restoration of American morality. Yet he was sufficiently Baptist and homespun to gain the trust of conservative Democrats and swing voters. Carter was "firmly astride the middle ground, a conservative to the conservatives, and a liberal to the liberals," wrote the *Financial Times'* Jurek Martin.[79] Though most liberals did not say grace before meals, let alone ask colleagues to kneel with them in prayer, Carter's brand of integrity suited the post-Watergate era. Nixon had insisted that he was not a crook. No one had taken him at his word. More than any other Democrat, particularly Kennedy, Carter could look people in the eye and make them believe that he was a truth teller. Gerald Ford brought his own presidential honeymoon to an abrupt end when he pardoned Nixon a month after he was sworn in. The long national nightmare might have ended, as Ford told the nation on August 9, 1974, when he took his oath of office; his own political ordeal was just starting.

As Carter's campaign took root, one of his rhetorical devices was to refer to the "Ford-Kissinger administration." It was in fact the Ford-Rockefeller administration, since the accidental president had appointed Kissinger's former patron Nelson Rockefeller as his vice president. Rockefeller's tenure was so unhappy that he declined to be Ford's running mate in 1976. The only remaining household name in Ford's administration was Kissinger. Brzezinski crafted Carter's attack on the "Nixon-Kissinger-Ford" foreign policy as amoral. The intention was to highlight the outsized role of Kissinger, whom Carter depicted as the "Lone Ranger" of US diplomacy and the "President of foreign policy." Since 1969, Kissinger had been bedazzling his global counterparts and the American media with his diplomatic enterprise and hyperactivity. During Nixon's first term, he had been the president's unusually empowered but never psychologically secure national security advisor. It was a complex relationship of near equals. Nixon drove détente, the opening to China, and the speed of the US military withdrawal from Vietnam. Kissinger helped shape and execute those initiatives, often covertly. Nixon's secretary of state, Bill Rogers, was rarely consulted and sometimes not even informed of what the White House was planning to do. So paranoid were Nixon and Kissinger about the State Department's tendency to leak that they relied solely on the Chinese interpreter for their historic 1971 meeting with Chairman Mao. The hapless State Department interpreter was left at the door. After his reelection, Nixon dispensed with Rogers and handed the job to Kissinger, who neverthe- less retained his role as national security advisor. That unique dual portfolio gave rise to the joke that the only time the US secretary of state and national security advisor got along was when Kissinger held both jobs.[80]

In one sense, the Watergate scandal suited Kissinger perfectly. Nixon's growing distraction over Watergate and his tendency to retreat inwards gave Kissinger increasing latitude to run foreign policy on his own. His near-pleni- potentiary moment reached its apogee in the months after the surprise 1973 Yom Kippur attack by Egypt on Israel. In the midst of Kissinger's shuttle di- plomacy, Nixon lost his vice president, Spiro Agnew, to corruption charges; fired Watergate special prosecutor Archibald Cox, as well as the attorney gen- eral and his deputy in the infamous "Saturday night massacre"; and retreated for long alcohol-fueled spells to his upstairs White House quarters. The battle between the Israeli and Egyptian armies in the Sinai Desert was no mere side- show: it was the most dangerous flash point in the US-Soviet relationship.

In that same period, Kissinger negotiated a cease-fire outline with Brezhnev, talking in the Kremlin until the small hours; returned to the United States the next day with a UN resolution that was passed that same night; and failed to persuade Saudi Arabia's King Faisal to hold off on an Arab oil embargo. Compared with the heavily lawyered protocols that more typically characterize US diplomacy, Kissinger's methods were swashbuckling. The moment of peak Kissinger drama was when he put US forces on DEFCON 3, the highest state of peacetime nuclear alert, when the Soviets had threatened to send ground forces to the Middle East after the cease-fire wobbled. Nixon was almost certainly not consulted before that late-evening escalation. He was upstairs and probably in his cups. In the midst of all that, Kissinger was controversially awarded the Nobel Peace Prize jointly with Le Duc Tho for the deal they had struck to end the Vietnam War. Most US secretaries of state would struggle with such a torrent of action over four years. All of that happened in the space of a few weeks.[81]

To Kissinger, "peace" meant absence of war. His goal was not to reach a dramatic breakthrough but to wear Israel's Arab neighbors down until they accepted its existence. That involved seemingly contradictory moves. At one point, he organized a massive airlift of US arms supplies to Israel; once the battle had turned, he did everything possible to prevent Israel from routing Egypt's Third Army. Humiliation of Egypt's president, Anwar Sadat, would make peace impossible. Balance was everything. Such versatility meant that Kissinger was inherently conniving. White House staffers saw him as an "exotic wunderkind."[82] Because of Nixon's anti-Semitism, Kissinger was obliged "to disguise his support for Israel because he was under suspicion from the very beginning." Kissinger even fooled the Israelis. At one point, demonstrators in Tel Aviv greeted him with banners saying "Hitler spared you to finish the job," "Jew boy," and "Kapo." When the situation dictated, he perfected the art of creating the illusion of action—"motion without movement," as he called it. He would cajole Israel's prime minister, Golda Meir, to acquiesce to one thing and Egypt's Sadat to something else, and present each as an authentic initiative to the other. "Policy may be based on knowledge," he wrote in his memoirs, "but its conduct is an art."[83]

To Brzezinski, Kissinger's nimble machinations were turning into the end itself, rather than the means by which an increasingly confused US foreign policy was shaped. In his view, there was far less to Kissinger's theatrics than met the eye. To his frustration, however, the media, which Kissinger fed with finely honed aperçus at virtuoso press conferences and on whose flattery he rarely stinted, rarely probed beyond the surface. Kissinger knew that most journalists preferred personalities to policy since they made foreign policy stories easier to digest. Reporters were also susceptible to praise. Brzezinski would treat anyone he thought a fool with disdain. Kissinger's style was to massage egos. Flattery worked as well on journalists as it did on politicians. Relations between the two remained friendly in spite of Brzezinski's growing doubts about Kissinger's stamp on détente.

For the most part, Brzezinski's public criticisms were tempered. He described the Nixon administration's escalatory response to the 1971 war in East

Pakistan, notably the decision to send an aircraft carrier to the Bay of Bengal, as "gratuitous."[84] Others saw Washington's role in the massacre-strewn birth of Bangladesh as callous and reckless. Ditto in terms of the secret bombing of Cambodia and Washington's role in encouraging the coup that ousted Chile's president, Salvador Allende. The tone of his correspondence with Kissinger remained cordial, and their lunch appointments, which took place every few weeks, did not flag. In response to Brzezinski's congratulations on becoming secretary of state, Kissinger encouraged his sparring partner to keep sending him ideas and point out where he was going wrong. "One always learns more from 'friendly critics' than from uncritical friends," he wrote to Brzezinski.[85]

Almost six years after Kissinger's move into government, however, Brzezinski removed his proverbial gloves. In a biting essay for the spring 1974 edition of *Foreign Policy*, a magazine he had helped launch with Sam Huntington three years earlier and on whose board he sat, he unloaded on Kissinger.[86] An eccentric aspect of Brzezinski's philippic was that he did not mention Kissinger by name. The essay was billed as a report card on the Nixon administration's foreign policy, which he awarded a C plus. In the same magazine two years earlier, he had given Nixon a B. But as Nixon's domestic position had deteriorated, his leverage over the increasingly one-sided détente with the Soviets had weakened. Brzezinski noted that America's "present Secretary of State" had recommended that Nixon read Oswald Spengler's *The Decline of the West*. Brzezinski could not fathom what in this "massive and generally turgid volume" would appeal to Nixon. The implication was that Nixon's declining fortunes at home were matched by his chief diplomat's pessimism about America's slipping global position.

The early phase of Nixon's administration had been relatively accomplished, Brzezinski wrote. Though the US withdrawal from Vietnam could have taken place more rapidly, it had nevertheless happened. The initial moves to encourage a US-Soviet thaw had been handled skillfully, as had the historic opening to China. Since then, however, Nixon's foreign policy had been mostly downhill. Central to its failures was the growing asymmetry of détente. The 1972 Moscow summit between Nixon and Brezhnev had produced a Strategic Arms Limitation Treaty (SALT) that allowed Soviets numerical superiority in missiles on the "spurious" basis that the US had a technological edge. To secure the deal before Nixon's reelection, America conceded the USSR's legal and symbolic sphere of influence in Eastern Europe. Nixon had also signed up to Moscow's language of "peaceful coexistence" and "noninterference" in each other's affairs. The US, in other words, had satisfied the Soviets' badly craved need to be treated as global equals while also conceding parity (at best) in nuclear firepower. The US had also agreed not to make a fuss about abuses inside the Soviet Bloc. Furthermore, Washington had approved almost $1 billion in highly preferential trade credits to the USSR that would not only help keep the ailing Soviet economy afloat but also buttress its political system. It included technical aid for the state-owned airline, Aeroflot, and technology transfer from NASA to the USSR's lagging space program. In case anyone misunderstood, America was also toning down Radio Free Europe's broadcasts and paring its budget for fear of offending the Soviets.

What was driving this increasingly one-sided détente? Brzezinski was clear that it was predicated on an expectation of American decline and an inherent bias towards a balance-of-power diplomacy in which the smaller actors were left out in the cold. Washington exhibited an "obvious fascination with enemies and an *ennui* with friends," he said, that was producing "bitterness and resentment" among America's allies. Their failure to be consulted was by now routine. A George Marshall or a Dean Acheson had never feared collaboration with "semiequals." Today's new foreign policy style, with its "unprecedented concentration of decision-making power," treated alliances as a chore. Evidence of that was the secretary of state's recent hasty Middle East summit with Brezhnev while failing to stop in any European capital for consultations on the way there or debriefings on the way back. Meanwhile, neglect of the rest of the world revealed an administration "largely devoid of moral concerns for the less fortunate majority that inhabit this planet."

What most stung Kissinger about Brzezinski's assault was his focus on the "secretive and personal style" of US foreign policy. Though the article was published two and a half years before the next presidential election, Brzezinski's conclusions would be repeated word for word ad nauseam by Carter on the campaign trail. Nixon and later Ford, Brzezinski said, was running a foreign policy that gave priority to the "personal over the political, the covert over the conceptual and the acrobatic over the architectural."[87] Nobody could be in any doubt that Kissinger was the sole target of Brzezinski's essay.

Kissinger's response, which came in a three-page personal letter a day after its publication, was hurt, irritated, remonstrative, and solicitous. His chief riposte was that Brzezinski was abandoning his long-held belief in peaceful engagement for a right-wing critique of détente. "I have just read with interest, if also amazement, your Foreign Policy article," Kissinger wrote. "Since I will be leaving for Moscow this evening to continue the pursuit of a détente which you either support or decry (depending on which Brzezinski you read) my thoughts will be necessarily both hasty and brief."[88]

His reply was in fact extensive. "I find it difficult to accept that the author of Peaceful Engagement in Europe's Future [Brzezinski's 1960 Foreign Affairs article] can now claim that we were too soft." Having offered a point-by-point rebuttal of Brzezinski's specific criticisms about SALT, preferential trade credits, failure to talk to allies, and the Middle East cease-fire talks, Kissinger turned to his chief concern, which was the "growing tendency on the part of some—which you now seem to echo—to adopt the same line of attack on détente that used to be the privileged property of the extreme right." Brzezinski had namelessly accused Kissinger of being an amoral opportunist. Kissinger now reciprocated Brzezinski's treatment in the third person.

"Those who have for so long argued from different premises leave one in awe at the rapidity with which they have been able to shift the philosophical ground for their attack. One can but wonder what has become of earlier claims that at least a part of the process of building a new relationship with the Soviets depends on expanded contacts between peoples, greater exchange of ideas, and the need to develop over time a vested interest in both countries in the maintenance of peace." He left an opening, however, for their conversation to continue. "Perhaps when I have returned from Moscow and we both have more time for reflection, we could sit down and go over in more detail some of our apparent areas of disagreement."[89] Kissinger's reply sidestepped Brzezinski's main criticism that the Soviets were exploiting détente for ideological mischief making—an observation that grew in force as the 1970s progressed. Brzezinski's far briefer reply was friendly, but he conceded nothing. He continued to support détente but not in that one-sided way. "The returns to us are not so clear cut," he reiterated.

In conversations with aides, Kissinger was apoplectic. "Brzezinski is a total whore. He's been on every side of every argument. He wrote a book on 'Peaceful Engagement' and now that we are doing most of what he said in the book, he charges us with weakness."[90] When those conversations were declassified several decades later, Brzezinski said, "Henry is a friend of mine—he must have meant 'bore.'"[91] They did remain "friends" in the Washington sense memorably defined by Harry S. Truman: "If you want a friend in Washington, get a dog." But Kissinger now vented often about Brzezinski in private.

Without the need for cajoling, Brzezinski had succeeded in getting Kissinger to host the Trilateral Commission's members at the State Department and signal his blessing for the group. Though Kissinger had little appetite for integrating US allies into an institutional arrangement—the so-called community of developed nations that Brzezinski had been extolling for years—he lost patience with the Brzezinski-Rockefeller road show. "We have all of these eunuchs from David Rockefeller's Trilateral Commission running around town saying that we are trying to confront the Arabs. . . . I don't know whatever possessed me to give those idiots my blessing," he said in a meeting in late 1974.[92] Yet the seeds of the eunuchs' idea were already planted in Kissinger's mind. A year later, the first G6 meeting was held in the Château de Rambouillet in France. It included the leaders of Japan, Great Britain, France, West Germany, Italy, and the United States.

Brzezinski never craved the campaign trail. When he went on the road for any length of time, it was almost always to somewhere overseas, not to the Midwest. At that stage of his children's lives, however, he tried to avoid superfluous travel. At one point in 1975, David Rockefeller invited him and Muska for a long weekend at his vacation home in the US Virgin Islands via his personal jet. Brzezinski said that he had already made plans with his kids.[93] During Carter's campaign, Brzezinski was physically absent most of the time. In addition to avoiding Iowa, he hardly ever made the trek down to the campaign headquarters in Atlanta. He orchestrated a large team of foreign policy advisors and channeled their prodigious output to Carter.

In contrast to Humphrey, Carter devoured every briefing paper they could supply; the more detailed, the better. But Brzezinski's input was mostly remote. If an aide handed Carter anything to do with foreign policy, his response was always "Has Brzezinski seen this?"[94] The governor would call the professor from time to time for long phone conversations. "Hiya, it's Jimmy here, how are you doing?" was his standard greeting.[95] They would discuss upcoming speeches, prep for media interviews, and swap observations about Ford and Kissinger's weaknesses. At first Brzezinski was gung ho for attacks on Kissinger. "Kissinger's foreign policy ought to be attacked directly, and his personal role in shaping it and giving it its somewhat dubious moral-political outlook," he wrote to Carter in late October 1975. "Given the fascination of the mass media with Kissinger, an attack directly on his foreign policy is likely to provoke a great deal of attention."[96]

Carter needed no further prodding. In the absence of Nixon, Kissinger was his optimal foil. The small-town lay preacher and former submarine officer wanted to remind voters that he was "untainted" by Washington. In his next letter in early November, Brzezinski somewhat parochially wrote, "I am delighted to see a key member of our Trilateral Commission doing so well."[97] In the intervening week, Carter had won a straw poll at the Jefferson-Jackson Dinner in Ames, Iowa, though he had come in second behind "uncommitted." Far better known figures, such as Birch Bayh, a senator from nearby Indiana, Scoop Jackson, Sargent Shriver, and Mo Udall, had trailed far behind him. With the exception of Jackson, the others were competing for the liberal mantle. That left the middle ground wide open for Carter. In contrast to his rivals, he seemed to have already met every Iowan at least once.

His victory led to a widely noticed article by the New York Times' celebrated political reporter R. W. "Johnny" Apple, who forecast that Carter would win the Iowa caucuses in early January. A prediction of that nature in the newspaper of record was worth a thousand TV advertisements that Carter could not yet afford. Brzezinski was as surprised as everyone else. Carter's serene confidence no longer seemed quite so otherworldly. Apple's piece sketched a self-effacing yet tenacious out-of-stater who relished discussing commodity prices, crop rotation, and agricultural machinery with Iowa's rural folk. Apple quoted one farmer, Fred McLain, who returned home one evening to find a handwritten note from Carter pinned to his front door. They had met only once before. Even Apple, however, seemed a little puzzled by Carter's success. The quiet-spoken governor's most popular line in the Ames dinner was, "Of all the speakers here tonight, I am the only one who is not a lawyer."[98]

Carter's foreign policy message was both beguilingly simple and wonkishly fleshed out. The simple part was that he could be trusted. America, he said, had mortgaged its prestige to a bunch of amoral characters who had besmirched the country's name by sponsoring foreign coups, carrying out covert CIA actions, bugging its own staff (a Kissinger innovation), making foreign policy in secret, and showering autocratic regimes with US arms. Washington had lost its integrity, which meant that America's foreign policy did not reflect the values of its people. At the Trilateral Commission, Carter had frequently used the word love, which was a first to its members. At that moment in a cynical decade—with US helicopters having in April 1975 evacuated the last stragglers from Saigon in the Vietnam War's humiliating postscript—Carter's folksy sentiments struck a rare chord. An electorate that had lost its trust in government was unusually primed to suspend its disbelief. "I want a government that is as good, and honest, and decent, and truthful, and fair, and competent, and compassionate, and as filled with love as are the American people," said Carter.[99] That simple idea came with straightforward goals. Carter wanted to reduce arms sales, aim for a world without nuclear weapons, withdraw US troops from South Korea, support black majority rule in southern Africa, including Rhodesia, and place human rights at the heart of US foreign policy. Government would be conducted in a spirit of transparency and collaboration. Carter would be its servant-leader.

As Carter started to amass delegates following his win in the Iowa caucuses (where again he came in second to "uncommitted"), the need for big foreign policy speeches grew. Conscious of his lack of credentials, Carter would emphasize the places he had visited as governor and as a member of the Trilateral Commission. He often did so by naming the country after the city: "Bonn, Germany," "Kyoto, Japan," "Rome, Italy," and so on. That made him sound like a wide-eyed tourist. Brzezinski tried to stamp that habit out. Carter's first big foreign policy speech in New York in February was not well reviewed. Carter was seen as naive and innocent in the ways of the world. His next speech, at the Chicago Council on Foreign Relations in March, was more honed. It was a little shorter on idealism and more explicit about the downsides to foreign policy cynicism. But it failed to impress. "Nobody even printed the text, which from his [Carter's] point of view was probably lucky," wrote James Reston.[100] Carter may have taken this to heart. His next speech in June at the Foreign Policy Association in New York was far more favorably received. It came across as hard-nosed but principled.

With each speech, Carter's references to Kissinger grew. His focus on Kissinger's "one-man diplomacy" had the benefit of creating news, highlighting Ford's perceived weakness as a commander in chief and exposing the duplicity with which US foreign policy was being conducted. He spoke with some relish of Washington's "secretive 'Lone Ranger' foreign policy—a one-man policy of international adventure."[101] By the time of his third big speech, the initial draft was so littered with jibes at Kissinger that Brzezinski felt he had to prune them. Kissinger was an ideal punching bag, he told Carter, but he should not become an obsession. Carter agreed to most of Brzezinski's cuts but insisted on retaining the phrase "Lone Ranger." After Brzezinski skimmed the US and international headlines the following day, he had to concede that Carter's instinct was good. "Lone Ranger" caught the mood. "I concede! You were absolutely right!" he scribbled next to a digest of positive headlines that he mailed to Carter.[102]

Ironically, Kissinger was by that stage well on the road to becoming a lame-duck secretary of state. In 1974, Ford had replaced him as national security advisor with Brent Scowcroft, a much lower-key figure who personified the role of honest broker. By 1976, however, Kissinger was turning into an electoral liability. An embattled Ford was trying to fend off a primary challenge from Ronald Reagan, the hard-line former governor of California, who attacked détente as a sellout to the Soviets. Rather than laying out the benefits of what Kissinger called "a generation of peace," a panicked Ford embraced "peace through strength," which was Reagan's rallying cry. "The word [détente] is a disaster," the grandee conservative writer Claire Booth Luce told Ford.[103] "We are going to forget the use of the word detente," said Ford in Peoria, Illinois, in early March.[104] It was a remarkable abandonment of the defining project of the past eight years. The following month, Kissinger told the *New York Times* that he would probably resign as secretary of state if Ford were reelected. Since people around the president had already been dropping hints to the media that Kissinger was on the way out, his hypothetical resignation was not taken seriously. That Carter was skewering Kissinger from the other side of the aisle only added to Kissinger's funk. "Hearing Brzezinski's snide words slung at him each day, not with a slightly embittered Polish accent but a smiling Georgia accent, drove Kissinger to near distraction," wrote Walter Isaacson.[105]

Carter's attack on détente was very different from Reagan's. The latter vowed to abandon détente as a "one-way street." Carter wanted to improve it. Brzezinski's mantra, which he drummed into Carter, was that détente should be "reciprocal and comprehensive." That was the more wonkish element of Carter's campaign. In Brzezinski's view it was also the meat of it. In essence, Carter was accusing Kissinger of false pessimism. Kissinger's management of US-Soviet relations was based on the bleak forecast that the USSR would probably overtake the US as a global force in the 1980s. Kissinger had allegedly said as much to a former chief of naval operations, Elmo R. Zumwalt, Jr., whose book *On Watch* came out in early 1976. "K. feels that U.S. has passed its historic highpoint like so many earlier civilizations," Zumwalt had written in a memo years earlier. "He believes U.S. is on downhill [*sic*] and cannot be roused by political challenge. He states that his job is to persuade the Russians to give us the best deal we can get. . . . The American people have only themselves to blame because they lack stamina to stay the course against the

Russians who are 'Sparta to our Athens.'"[106] Kissinger peevishly denied having said any such thing, not least because as a historian he knew that Athens had long outlived Sparta. But he had publicly shared similar mordancies on several occasions.

Kissinger's pessimism was Carter's case for optimism. Since the US was not in decline and held far more cards than Kissinger implied, Washington should insist that the Soviets meet far tougher standards, Carter argued. The previous year, Ford had provoked derision when he refused to meet Aleksandr Solzhenitsyn, the celebrated Soviet novelist and dissident, who had been thrown out of the Soviet Union the year before. Kissinger's advice was that Ford should not attend an AFL-CIO dinner in Washington in honor of Solzhenitsyn. His presence would offend the Soviets and threaten détente. That Solzhenitsyn was also a scathing critic of détente made the prospect all the more awkward.

America's moral abdication was bad enough, according to Carter (and even more to Reagan, who said that, "at Kissinger's insistence, Mr. Ford had snubbed Aleksandr Solzhenitsyn, one of the great moral heroes of our time"[107]). But Ford's meekness was also dangerous to national security. Far from ushering in a generation of peace, the Soviets had treated détente as a license to escalate support for revolutionary movements around the world—in Angola, Portugal, Syria, and elsewhere—without the risk of nuclear confrontation. "I support the objectives of détente," said Carter in March 1976, "but I cannot go along with the way it has been handled by Presidents Nixon and Ford. The Secretary of State has tied its success too closely to his personal reputation. As a result, he is giving up too much and asking for too little. He is trumpeting achievements on paper while failing to insist on them in practice."[108]

It had been apparent for most of the year that Carter would be the Democratic nominee. Whenever he insisted that US democracy was still vibrant, he cited his own meteoric rise as an example. Only a few months earlier, nobody had heard of the dogged born-again Christian who was doorstepping startled voters in Iowa, insisting that he would be their next president. Others, notably the Georgetown set, who recoiled from religious piety and mistrusted Brzezinski, were still disbelieving. "How can that be?" said an astonished Averell Harriman when he was informed that Carter would take the crown. "I don't even know Jimmy Carter, and as far as I know, none of my friends know him either."[109] But others, notably Joe Biden, the youthful senator from Delaware who became the first senator to endorse Carter, noticed his appeal: "Jimmy's not just a bright smile. He can win and he can appeal to more segments of the population than any other person," Biden said.[110]

As had been the case with other candidates in 1968 and 1972, however, Carter's path to the nomination was slowed by rearguard action. Having taken Iowa and New Hampshire, he had a moment of doubt in Massachusetts, where he came fourth behind Jackson, Udall, and, most worryingly, George Wallace, the segregationist Alabama governor, whose confinement to a wheelchair after an assassination attempt did not dent his ambition. But Massachusetts proved to be a blip. Carter went on to sweep Florida, Illinois, and the Carolinas. By then, his victory was numerically ensured. But he was still dogged by last-minute challenges from Jerry Brown, California's energetic young Democratic governor; Frank Church, an Idaho senator; and a brief-lived "ABC" movement: "Anyone But Carter." All of them fizzled out.

At the Democratic National Convention in mid-July, Carter ended the run of ill-tempered nightly wranglings that had bedeviled McGovern in 1972 and the chaos that had enveloped Humphrey's Chicago convention in 1968. Though it took place at Madison Square Garden in New York, an easy commute from Columbia, Brzezinski declined to attend. He was with the family in Maine. "It was too far away and I didn't like the circus atmosphere," he wrote in his diary.[111] But he was pleased to note that Carter had regurgitated his foreign policy suggestions almost word for word. A few days earlier, Carter had called for Brzezinski's advice on that piece of his address from his home in Plains, Georgia. With the sound of Amy, Carter's eight-year-old daughter, in the background yelling "It's time to eat!" Brzezinski dictated the paragraphs to Carter over the phone. Carter took them down by hand at his kitchen table, then inserted them into his speech.[112]

During the same call, Brzezinski urged Carter to refuse CIA briefings after he became the formal nominee since it would constrain his ability to speak freely as a candidate. Carter concurred. He also asked Brzezinski's advice about whom he should select as his running mate. Brzezinski said that Adlai Stevenson III, a son of the twice former Democratic presidential candidate and now an Illinois senator, was "not as bright as his father." Frank Church was a "phony." Scoop Jackson was "very decent, dedicated but one-dimensional on foreign affairs." Of John Glenn, the ex-astronaut and now Ohio senator, he asked, "Is there enough depth?" Ed Muskie, he said, was "irascible but experienced." Finally, Walter Mondale, the Minnesota senator, was "very bright but soft; always appointed to his office. Still very good." Carter said he agreed with those succinct appraisals. In the end he went for Mondale, who appealed to both the liberal and pro-union wings of the party.

The Democratic convention went off seamlessly. A party that had been at war with itself for the previous two cycles somehow pulled off a show in which Martin Luther King, Sr., George Wallace, and Richard Daley stood in unison behind one man. Carter's workmanlike forty-minute speech was delivered without a hitch. Brzezinski ensured that Carter made no mention of Kissinger, though there was a pointed reference to "the embarrassment of the C.I.A. revelations [that] could have been avoided if our Government had simply reflected . . . the high moral character of the American people." There was also an inventive sideswipe at Spenglerian pessimism. "I've never had more faith in America than I do today," said Carter. "We have an America that in Bob Dylan's phrase is busy being born, not busy dying."[113]

For the first time since 1964, it looked as though a Democrat was on course for the White House. Carter came out of New York with a thirty-three-point poll lead over Ford. A gap that thumping could never last. Some of it was narrowed at the Republican National Convention in Kansas City, where Reagan, after having conceded a close-run defeat to Ford, excited the party with a rousing concession speech. With traditional Republican discipline, the party united in condemnation of Carter as an ingénue who would easily be played by the Soviets. His name was cited from the podium no fewer than 113 times.[114] On Labor Day, his poll lead was still in the double digits. A comfortable win still looked possible.

In late July, Brzezinski and some of the team flew down to Plains, Georgia, to give Carter a briefing. It was Brzezinski's first visit to Pond House, Carter's modest family home, and his first meeting with Jimmy's wife, Rosalynn. They hit it off. After the sweaty two-and-a-half-hour drive from Atlanta, Brzezinski was struck by the sleepiness of Carter's hometown. It gave him a clearer sense of why Carter's modest origins were such a key part of his appeal. Brzezinski's job was to summarize East-West relations, followed by Henry Owen on the Middle East and Andrew Young, an African American congressman from Georgia and a former Martin Luther King, Jr., aide, whose topic was Africa. Rosalynn went out of her way to compliment Brzezinski's summation. He was surprised at how quiet Mondale was and how nervous he seemed.[115]

The campaign's spirits were upbeat. But Carter's fortunes were slowly starting to go downhill. Over the following weeks, Carter and Brzezinski spoke at length, for more than two hours one evening. During one call, after

Carter had attended a big fundraising reception at the Beverly Wilshire Hotel, he seemed to enjoy being teased by Brzezinski about hobnobbing with celebrities such as Warren Beatty. In a Q&A with the candidate, Carroll O'Connor, the actor who starred as the blue-collar racist Archie Bunker in the hit TV show *All in the Family*, pointed out that Carter had become the nominee without help from any of the stars in the room. "That's why I won the nomination," said Carter. It was a good riposte that captured a trace of bitterness about how the big donors and Democratic elites had placed their initial hopes on Kennedy, then run through everyone else, including Shriver and even Jackson, before having Carter thrust upon them. Like an old-fashioned populist, Carter owed his victory to the grass roots. He felt he owed the party nothing. With the chief exception of Brzezinski, Carter's long-serving coterie of Georgian advisors dominated the team.

Somewhere along the way, Carter lost his populist mojo. Thirty years later, people contrasted Barack Obama's brilliance at keeping vast audiences spellbound with his awkwardness in small gatherings. Carter was Obama's mirror image: he thrived on retail politics; the national stage obliterated that intimacy. Over the coming weeks, almost anything that could go wrong with his campaign did. Much of it was thanks to Carter's inexperience. In the first televised presidential debate, he seemed wooden and too caught up in detail. He also missed opportunities to target Ford's weakest spots, later admitting that he felt it would be impertinent to attack a sitting president. Though it was the first televised presidential debate since Nixon and Kennedy had squared off in 1960, the sound was lost for an agonizing thirty minutes. During that time the candidates clung stiffly to their lecterns, nervously sipping water, not exchanging a word. It might have been a good moment for Carter to crack jokes or mix with the audience. But his latent anxiety was showing. Ford was judged to have won the debate. On the eve of the second debate, which was on foreign policy, the two were level in the polls. The speed with which Ford had closed the canyon-wide gap was one of the most dramatic comebacks in modern presidential campaigns.

Pundits blamed Carter's decline on his fuzziness about the issues and a tendency to promise one thing to conservatives and another to liberals. One even joked that if Carter's likeness were carved into Mount Rushmore, it would need to have two faces. But his most egregious mistake was to give an interview to *Playboy* magazine in which he admitted to having "looked on many women with lust" and "committed adultery in my heart many times."

The goal of the interview had been to puncture his image as a sanctimonious Southern Baptist; the effect was to make him sound weirdly unpresidential. Religious types objected to his use of the words *screw* and *shack up*. Others just found his manner of speaking kooky. Even strong supporters, such as Marge Thurman, the chair of the Democratic Party of Georgia, were publicly critical. She described the take by ordinary voters as "bad, bad, bad . . . the reaction is uniformly negative."[116]

It was against that inauspicious backdrop that Carter asked Brzezinski to join him for the second debate in San Francisco in early October. His job was to prep Carter. There was just a month to go before polling day, and Ford had the momentum. Given the growing focus on Carter's inexperience, a lot was riding on his clarity in the foreign policy debate. Kissinger had been Ford's continuous briefer. In keeping with Carter's inexhaustible appetite, Brzezinski had supplied him with several hundred-page binders covering dozens of issues from South Africa's apartheid regime to the civil war in Angola and the scale of US conventional arms sales to right-wing client states.[117] But his goal was to persuade Carter to be more aggressive. He had less than three hours to get "JC to focus more sharply on the central issues."[118]

Key among those was Ford's weakness in dealing with the Soviet Union. The president had been pulverized on détente by Reagan in the Republican primaries and by Carter all along. A vital difference between the two schools of criticism was their view of the 1975 Helsinki Final Act. The treaty, in keeping with Brzezinski's long-held wish, recognized and legitimized the post–World War II borders in Eastern Europe. Brzezinski saw that as progress since it would allay Eastern Europe's fears of German revanchism and pave the way for East-West "peaceful engagement." It was also seen as a victory in Moscow. By contrast, conservatives saw Helsinki as American capitulation. The *New York Times* columnist William Safire compared the deal to Yalta.[119] Earlier in the year, Reagan had received airtime from NBC to say that Helsinki had given "our stamp of approval on Russia's enslavement of the captive nations."[120]

Carter's Helsinki critique was different from Reagan's. He urged its full implementation. As part of the Final Act, the Soviets had reluctantly agreed to a "third basket" of agreements, which enshrined freedom of movement and other human rights. That basket had been inserted by the Western Europeans against the wishes of Kissinger, who had feared that it would sink the agreement. Indeed, for most of the human rights part of the negotiations, the US did not even send a delegation. From the sidelines, Brzezinski had played a role in urging Western European governments to insist on adding that third basket. Essentially, the Soviets were being offered a trade-off. During most of the process, Kissinger wanted no part of that horse trade. The human rights provisions were presented to Moscow as the West's quid pro quo for recognizing the Soviet-drawn postwar boundaries.

Kissinger, whose team had no choice but to rejoin the closing phase of the negotiations, reassured Leonid Brezhnev and his foreign minister, Andrei Gromyko, that the language on human rights was just a formality. "Mr. Minister, why are we quibbling over these forms of words?" Kissinger asked Gromyko. "No matter what goes into that Final Act, I don't believe that the Soviet Union will ever do anything it doesn't want to do.[121] The Soviets reluctantly signed. Ford's decision not to attend the Solzhenitsyn dinner the previous year had coincided with the closing weeks of Helsinki. At the end of the year, Helmut Sonnenfeldt, a State Department official known as "Kissinger's Kissinger," made an apparent gaffe at a meeting of US ambassadors in London in which he asserted that the Soviets had an "organic relationship" with their satellite states. A somewhat distorted version of the so-called Sonnenfeldt Doctrine had been written up in the not always reliable syndicated column of Rowland Evans, Jr., and Robert D. Novak and then picked up by both Reagan and Carter. It provided more proof of Kissinger's addiction to spheres of interest; he was once again glossing over Eastern Europe's captivity.

It is a safe bet that few Americans knew about Helsinki and almost none about the quickly dubbed "Sonnenfeldt Doctrine" or its third basket. Yet that was the boulder on which Carter broke Ford's momentum. Brzezinski joined Carter the day before the debate at the Saint Francis Hotel in downtown San Francisco. "Ah, our barefoot candidate," said Brzezinski when Carter greeted him at his suite door shoeless.[122] Over sandwiches following an obligatory prayer next to Carter's bed, Brzezinski hammered into Carter the need for a direct attack. No more soft-pedaling. Together they wrote out Carter's opening statement and his critiques of détente and Helsinki. Much the same thing was happening a few blocks away at the Pacific Heights mansion of John A. Sutro, Jr., a Marin County judge with whom Ford was staying. Kissinger's aide William Hyland was Ford's main briefer. Ford's goal was to convince the TV audience that he had not conceded Soviet domination over Eastern Europe. But the president had overlearned his lines. Some of his mangling must have reflected his punch-drunkenness at having been attacked by Carter and

Reagan from both sides of the political spectrum on near-opposite grounds. Either way, he walked into a fateful trap set by Brzezinski.

In Carter's opening statement, he revived the Kissinger attack. Another taunting reference to Kissinger was meant to make Ford lose his cool—a trait for which he was known. "The Soviet Union knows what they want in detente, and they've been getting it. We have not known what we've wanted, and we've been out-traded in every instance," said Carter. "As far as foreign policy goes, Mr. Kissinger has been the President of this country. Mr. Ford has shown an absence of leadership and an absence of a grasp of what this country is and what it ought to be." Carter's insult duly rattled Ford, whose fatal gaffe came a few moments later in response to a question from the *New York Times'* Max Frankel on Helsinki. Frankel asked Ford whether Helsinki had sealed Moscow's control over Eastern Europe. "There is no Soviet domination of Eastern Europe, and there never will be under a Ford administration," said Ford. To check that he had heard Ford correctly, Frankel gave him a chance to clarify his answer. The president doubled down: "I don't believe . . . that the Yugoslavians consider themselves dominated by the Soviet Union. I don't believe that the Romanians consider themselves dominated by the Soviet Union. I don't believe the Poles consider themselves dominated by the Soviet Union. Each of those countries is independent."

As he watched just off the stage, Brent Scowcroft's face reportedly drained of color.[123] Hamilton Jordan, Carter's right-hand campaign man, let out a yelp of joy. Ford had just lost the election, in his view. The swing states were teeming with first- and second-generation Eastern Europeans. Brzezinski had schooled Carter on the "ethnic" voters' militant anti-Soviet worldview. The chuckling Carter knew a fish in a barrel when he saw one, though he took his time to shoot it. "In the case of the Helsinki agreement, it may have been a good agreement at the beginning, but we have failed to enforce the so-called Basket 3 part, which ensures the right of people to migrate, to join their families, to be free to speak out. The Soviet Union is still jamming Radio Free Europe," he said. "We've also seen a very serious problem with the so-called Sonnenfeldt document [*sic*], which, apparently, Mr. Ford has just endorsed, which said that there is an organic linkage between the Eastern European countries and the Soviet Union. And I would like to see Mr. Ford convince the Polish Americans and the Czech Americans and the Hungarian Americans in this country that those countries don't live under the domination and supervision of the Soviet Union behind the Iron Curtain."[124]

After the debate, Kissinger telephoned Ford to congratulate him on having done a wonderful job.[125] He made no mention of Eastern Europe. For everyone else, Ford's apparent ignorance, which he took a full week to correct, dominated the news. On the phone, Brzezinski and Carter agreed that the tide had turned. Brzezinski suggested ways in which Carter could exploit his newfound edge with the Eastern European voter. In a memo to the Carter campaign, Brzezinski advised the candidate to speak "more in sorrow than in anger." He added, "We regret that the President is either ignorant of an important problem in international affairs or indifferent (perhaps under Kissinger's and Sonnenfeldt's influence) to the fate of a large number of people who have kin in this country."[126] But the media was doing Brzezinski's job for him. On *Saturday Night Live*, Chevy Chase picked up on the gaffe to embellish an impersonation of Ford that depicted him as clueless. "Last year I visited the capital of Poland, and let me say from the outset that Milwaukee is a beautiful city," said Chase's Ford.[127]

A few weeks later, Ford lost the popular vote by just two percentage points. Had six thousand Ohio voters and eighteen thousand in Wisconsin chosen differently, Ford would have won the Electoral College. Carter won with fewer than three hundred Electoral College votes, which made 1976 one of the closest results of the twentieth century. Given the preponderance of "ethnics" in cities such as Cleveland and Milwaukee, it is hard to believe that Ford's screwup did not cost him the White House. The opinion pollster George Gallup called the second debate "the most decisive moment in the campaign."[128] Brzezinski and Kissinger both contributed heavily to that moment. From that point on, it was much harder for Ford to attack Carter's inexperience. Moreover, Carter's elevation of human rights hit home with both liberal and conservative voters. His message was a case study in appealing to both sides. To liberals, it highlighted America's hypocrisy in backing brutal regimes in countries such as Brazil, South Africa, and Chile; to conservatives, it showed that Carter was serious about undermining the Soviet Union.

The Brzezinskis spent election night around the TV at the Upper East Side apartment of Richard Gardner, a Columbia University colleague who had helped with the campaign. Cyrus and Gay Vance were also there.[129] Though Vance had rather quixotically backed Shriver in the primaries, Carter had also consulted him during the general election. A tense evening became progressively more cheerful, particularly after Pennsylvania was called for Carter. Brzezinski, who had spent the previous days cold-calling names from

the campaign's list of ethnic voters in Pennsylvania and Ohio, telephoned Rosalynn Carter in midevening to reassure her nervous husband that the New
York turnout had been heavy. There had been some doubt whether Carter
could win New York State. The nail-biting night was brought to an end only
at 3:30 a.m. Eastern Time when the networks declared it for Carter. Carter's
prayers had been answered, and Brzezinski's bet had paid off. His horse had
won the derby by a nose.

In his published memoir and private diaries, Brzezinski claimed that he had
not known what position Carter was planning to offer him. The president-
elect called Brzezinski several times after election day to consult on other
names. Their first call took place on November 29. Carter had left Brzezinski a
message at Columbia three days earlier that he had picked up only after he had
returned from spending a family Thanksgiving in Maine.[130] They spoke late at
night. Brzezinski had prepared a memo for Carter in which he recommended
Vance as a good secretary of state. "How do you see yourself fitting in?" Carter
asked.[131] Brzezinski said that his strengths were generalist: "My experience
is such that I can conceptualize, articulate, direct and cooperate—and that
therefore I can see myself as an Undersecretary of State or a Deputy Secretary
of State with a Secretary like Vance . . . or as the NSC man, the integrator and
energizer of policy for the president." The noncommittal Carter said, "That is
very helpful to me."

Carter called again a few days later to ask his opinion about more junior
appointments. Brzezinski had also drawn up a memo for that. His own role did
not arise. On December 7, Carter asked Brzezinski to fly down to Atlanta. The
weather was foul, and he endured a bumpy, storm-tossed flight. He pitched
up at the Georgia governor's mansion amid a biblical-scale downpour. The
gates to the mansion nevertheless teemed with photographers. Carter was in
an upstairs room with Mondale, Jordan, and Charles Kirbo, another longtime
aide from Atlanta. After greetings, Carter asked the others to clear the room.
Again he asked which position Brzezinski wanted. He repeated the same three
he had already mentioned, leaving that of national security advisor to last.
Carter said that Vance told him he had no objections to Brzezinski running
the NSC. "What would you do to overcome the Kissinger legacy?"[132] Carter
asked. Brzezinski said that it was all about having "an honorable personal relationship with the president." His purpose would be to enhance policy, not to
make it. Carter then called the others back into the room. But Carter's teasing

act still had not yet run its course. Carter's staff handed Brzezinski some FBI forms to fill out. He asked how long it would take for his name to be cleared. "Usually two or three days," joked Carter. "But in your case five to six weeks." Brzezinski flew back to DC that night in equally foul weather, still fuzzy about his future.

Unbeknownst to Brzezinski, a litany of people had been urging Carter not to appoint him to a big role. Kissinger, whom Carter had secretly consulted before the election, said that Brzezinski was "excessively emotional and not able to think impassively in the long term."[133] Richard Holbrooke, a campaign staffer and former Foreign Service officer who had since been the editor of *Foreign Policy*, was even blunter; he said that Vance and Brzezinski would not make a good team. "I think Brzezinski is too combative and has too strong a personal agenda for that job." Carter went silent for a while, then thanked him and abruptly hung up. "That was the end of any warmth between [Holbrooke and Carter]," wrote George Packer, Holbrooke's biographer.[134] Brzezinski's most heavyweight detractor was W. Averell Harriman, the grandest remaining figure of US-Soviet relations, who had befriended Stalin when he was ambassador to Moscow during the war. In fact, Carter had shown little interest in Harriman, who was keen to rectify the oversight of never having met the Democratic nominee.

A few weeks before the election, Harriman squeezed in a meeting with Carter while the nominee was on a brief visit to Washington, DC. Since Carter had not made the obligatory trek to Harriman's semihallowed Georgetown residence, Harriman went to the Carter campaign's town house on Capitol Hill. There he waited in line to meet the candidate. Their exchange was brief. Harriman mentioned that he was about to visit Brezhnev in Moscow and asked whether Carter had any message that he could deliver to the Soviet leader. Carter said he supported existing arms control agreements but would like to see deeper cuts in each side's nuclear arsenal. He said he backed the human rights provisions of the Helsinki Final Act and insisted that Jewish emigration from the USSR not be "put under the rug."[135]

Having relayed Carter's views to Brezhnev, Harriman was keen on his return to pass on the Soviet leader's somewhat anodyne and noncommittal response. But he could not get any time on Carter's calendar. Carter still had a campaign to wage. With the help of Holbrooke, who had been one of Harriman's aides at the Paris talks on Vietnam in 1968, Harriman inveigled an improvised moment on Carter's schedule. The venue was a midsized sedan taking Carter from a campaign stop in Bethesda on Washington's outskirts on a twenty-five-mile journey to Dulles International Airport in Virginia. Since there was a Secret Service man in front sitting next to the driver, Carter, Holbrooke, and the eighty-four-year-old Harriman had to squeeze into the back of the cramped and fogged-up car. Harriman spoke nonstop for the entire journey and continued his briefing in the pouring rain right up to the steps of Carter's plane. Carter later told Holbrooke that he was impressed by the octogenarian's tenacity. But his mind was on other things.

Harriman would not give up easily. He was an old man on a self-appointed mission. Following Carter's victory, Anatoly Dobrynin, the Soviet ambassador in Washington, contacted Harriman with a more specific message that Brezhnev had asked him to give to the president-elect. The Soviet leader wanted Carter to know that he would like to proceed in a "positive, constructive spirit" and put arms control at the center of their relationship.[136] During a call to relay that message to Carter, Harriman also volunteered his advice on presidential appointments. He urged Carter to appoint Vance as secretary of state. Vance had not only been Harriman's deputy in Paris but was also the epitome of what he believed a public servant should be. He had government experience as secretary of the army in LBJ's administration but had also excelled as a Wall Street lawyer. Vance was on the boards of IBM and the *New York Times* and a trustee of Yale, Harriman's alma mater. He was self-effacing, public spirited, and a consummate negotiator. Harriman also made sure to reiterate his long-held view—delivered for the first (and last) time to Carter—that Brzezinski was unsuited for any senior position. The Polish-born American was too rigidly anti-Soviet and would endanger détente, he volunteered.[137]

Harriman had been giving people a similar warning about Brzezinski's Polish bias for years. In 1974, a snippet of one such conversation was passed on to Brzezinski, who wrote Harriman a letter of complaint. "Since you are a blunt man, let me also say quite bluntly that I do not feel that Henry Kissinger's background disqualified him from dealing effectively with the Middle Eastern problem, nor do I think that your background as a millionaire capitalist prevents you from dealing intelligently with the Soviet communists," wrote Brzezinski.[138] In his reply, Harriman protested that his confidential remarks had been rendered inaccurately. He conceded that he had argued for Marshall Shulman, a Sovietologist peer of Brzezinski at Columbia, instead of Brzezinski for inclusion in a Democratic advisory group on the Soviet Union. From their first meeting in 1961, he had thought that Brzezinski's take on the USSR was "unrealistically hardline with a somewhat closed mind." But, he said, "I am quite ready to drop the past if you are." In that spirit he would be delighted to invite the Brzezinskis to a meal at his family's summer home in Connecticut. In a postscript he added, "I would be fascinated to hear about the Trilateral Commission."[139] A friendly correspondence ensued. But Harriman's reservations only calcified. In a dinner with Arthur Schlesinger, Jr., a couple of years later, he described Brzezinski as a "fool" and a "menace," somebody with "absolutely no understanding of the Russians."[140]

Brzezinski had plenty of other ill-wishers. Clark Clifford, the former defense secretary and a second-tier "wise man," advised Carter to make Brzezinski the first US ambassador to the Bermuda triangle.[141] Carter paid no heed. In mid-December, Carter called again. Brzezinski was with Muska at an event in New York's Automation House. "I want you to do me a favor," said Carter after Brzezinski had been tracked down. "I would like you to be my National Security Advisor." Brzezinski said that it would be an honor, not a favor. "Actually I knew as of some months ago that you were my choice, but I had to go through the process of selection," Carter said.[142] There had been some purpose behind Carter's game of hide-and-seek; his main concern was whether Vance and Brzezinski would be able to work together. Since each had commended the other to his respective job, that dilemma had resolved itself. Early in the campaign, Hamilton Jordan, the keeper of Carter's populist flame, vowed that if Carter won and went on to appoint Vance and Brzezinski to the two top jobs, he would conclude that he had failed and quit. Jordan now had to wriggle out of that pledge. The media gleefully obliged him to do so.[143]

Jordan's point had been that Carter was an authentic outsider. His pitch was that he would usher in new ways and new faces who could fix a corrupt and broken Washington. But by almost any measure, Carter's key appointments were the epitome of Beltway insiders. Not only that, but they were almost all members of the Trilateral Commission. Carter's top echelons included no fewer than eighteen commission members, among them himself; his vice president, Walter Mondale; his secretary of state, Cyrus Vance; his secretary of defense, Harold Brown; his secretary of the treasury, W. Michael Blumenthal; the deputy director of the CIA, Robert Bowie; and, of course, his national security advisor, Brzezinski, cofounder of the commission. That made Brzezinski the arch-Trilateralist and, to some, the one who controlled Carter puppet's strings. As outlandish conspiracy theories go, the one about the Trilateral Commission taking over the world was ready for prime time.

Three days after Carter had offered him the job, Brzezinski took a plane to Albany, Georgia, for the president-elect's unveiling of key appointments. He almost missed the flight.[144] Peter Bourne, the aide who was dropping Brzezinski off, got lost on the way to Andrews Air Force Base. He made the military plane with minutes to spare. Mondale traveled down with him. They were taken by motorcade—a first for Brzezinski—to an auditorium in Plains, Georgia. It was a rare occasion when Brzezinski felt jittery. In his introduction, Carter repeated the often used line that he had been an "eager student" of Brzezinski. There could be no mistaking the level of trust between America's thirty-ninth president and his national security advisor with the unpronounceable name. Brzezinski made some brief remarks about aiming for "reciprocal" détente with the USSR and for an Arab-Israeli peace process. His presentation was stiff. In his private thoughts, he was anything but intimidated. His moment had finally arrived. "I pray that 1) I will be able to do it well, and that 2) I can keep in touch with my family," he wrote. "It is however, a monumental opportunity to do some good, and on a historic scale."[145]

Just over a quarter century after arriving as a student in Boston, Brzezinski now stood on the threshold of American power. "Only now is it beginning to sink into me what an enormous responsibility this is," he wrote. Reached by the *Toronto Star* at home in Montreal, his father, Tadeusz, was a little more matter-of-fact. At school, he said, Zbigniew had not been good at mathematics or science. But "he was excellent in history, politics, and the social sciences."[146]

6

Zbig Heaven

Everything about Carter's inauguration signaled a new era. For the first time, a newly sworn-in US commander in chief dispensed with the presidential limousine. Alongside Amy, Rosalynn, and the Carters' three much older sons, Jack, Chip, and Jeff, the new president walked the mile and a half from Capitol Hill to the White House. The crowds along Pennsylvania Avenue reveled in their new president's down-to-earth style and the chance to glimpse and greet his family. Pomp and grandeur were out. Carter had announced that he would dispense with the US Marine band that played "Hail to the Chief" whenever he entered a room. Doormen were also out. A new economizing mindset was in. Carter ordered the White House thermostat to be set to 65°F. Brzezinski and his family shivered outside in the subzero wintry afternoon as they watched the parade from the presidential viewing stand, a giant peanut float capturing most of the attention. One of Brzezinski's former Trilateral Commission colleagues caught sight of him from behind a pedestrian barrier. "How are you feeling?" he yelled. "I'm in heaven!" Brzezinski shouted back.[1] From Brzezinski's boyish grin, it was clear that he meant it.

Brzezinski's induction into power had begun a few weeks earlier. Though operating from the president-elect's transition offices in the Old Executive Office Building, the team was already drafting executive orders. Before inauguration day, Brzezinski had selected most of his national security staff, many of them from the notebook he had kept since Kissinger's surprise appointment by Nixon eight years earlier. In late December, Carter invited his senior officials and their families to Georgia's Saint Simons Island for a "mini–cabinet meeting." The incoming first lady paired Mika, Brzezinski's daughter, with Amy and offered to look after her.[2] From that point on, the nine-year-old girls had regular playdates. Mrs. Carter even went out in search of Mika when she did not show up for lunch. Mark lounged in the pool with Walter Mondale and Hamilton Jordan. By the end of the long weekend, Brzezinski's high place in the pecking order—the second-best job in Washington, he thought—was set. He was the first national security advisor to be awarded cabinet rank.

Brzezinski used the away weekend to get Carter to sign off on his plan to streamline the National Security Council. No one else, including Vance, had input. A revised version of it would be published on the afternoon of January 20 as Carter's first two presidential directives (PD-1 and PD-2). During the Kissinger years, there had been seven NSC committees. Kissinger chaired them all. Under Brzezinski, there would be two types: the Policy Review Committee, which would deal with discrete policy areas and be chaired by the relevant department head, such as the secretary of state, defense, or the treasury, and the Special Coordination Committee, which would handle crosscutting issues, including arms control and crisis management, and be chaired by Brzezinski. Most of the thorniest decisions tended to be "crosscutting." In that sense, Brzezinski won the bureaucratic turf battle before Vance knew it was happening. "Coordination is predominance," Brzezinski often told his aides.[3] There was no Kissingerian subterfuge in Brzezinski's maneuver; it was a bank robbery in broad daylight. At the end of the cabinet meeting in Georgia, Carter read out the NSC reorganization plan. No one objected. Foreign policy would be made in the White House and implemented by the State Department. Brzezinski had Carter's acquiescence that his role would be to "integrate the total effort, to conceptualize it, to present it to the President, and to try to infuse the rest of the bureaucracy with it."[4]

It was only on the afternoon of January 20, after Brzezinski had for the first time entered his new West Wing office, having taken his fill of the inaugural parade, that Vance protested. Brzezinski barely had his feet under the desk before Vance telephoned from his State Department suite in agitation about the directives that had just been published. Brzezinski's deputy, David Aaron, had further soured the mood by apparently telling people that presidential directives would be issued without consultation, Vance had learned. Brzezinski reassured Vance that his authority would not be circumvented. But he stressed that the NSC final draft had been the president's.[5] That was technically true, but the blueprint was Brzezinski's. That evening, Vance and Brzezinski were placed next to each other at a celebration dinner hosted by Averell and Pamela Harriman at their Georgetown home. Vance had cooled off. He told Brzezinski that he had been whipped into high dudgeon that afternoon by his subordinates. The two could preempt such misunderstandings in future by discussing them in person. Brzezinski concurred. In that fashion and with the help of the finest Bordeaux, Vance and Brzezinski's opening clash ended amicably. In many administrations the internal fault lines can take months to reveal themselves. The Carter administration's chief one was visible before nightfall of inauguration day.

It is oddly fitting that their first day on the job concluded in Harriman's home. In spite of everything that had transpired between them, Harriman had invited Brzezinski to stay in one of the two guesthouses at the back of their garden until his family moved to Washington, which would happen after the end of the school year. Brzezinski unhesitatingly agreed to be Harriman's non-paying tenant for the next five months. Moreover, the entire Brzezinski clan stayed with the Harrimans during the inaugural festivities. Muska had driven the kids down from New Jersey, while Tadeusz and Leonia, Lech, Wanda, and their children had flown in from Montreal. Muska's mother was also there. The grandchildren were awestruck by the home's august decor and uniformed servants.[6] That Brzezinski felt comfortable accepting Harriman's hospitality is notable. The "wise man's" craving for daily White House gossip outweighed whatever disdain he felt for his upstart lodger. It was a quintessential Washington transaction. Richard Holbrooke, who was heading the State Department's Bureau of South and East Asian Affairs, took the other guesthouse.

The person who felt most at ease with the Harrimans was Vance. The fifty-nine-year-old Wall Street lawyer had been Harriman's protégé since the early 1960s and shared almost all of his mentor's sensibilities. Both were appalled by the Vietnam War. Each thought that the United States should strain every sinew to achieve lasting stability with the Soviet Union. Both saw government as a second career. Vance was the last of the old-fashioned WASPs. On hearing of Vance's appointment, Harriman said he felt safe with the Carter administration. As the most genial and experienced WASP of his generation, Vance had slotted naturally into Carter's purview. Other than attending a few Trilateral Commission events, they had no previous relationship. With the exception of Brzezinski, Harriman told anyone who would listen that the role of the national security advisor should be downgraded to that of a first-class White House clerk, "like a child at a formal dinner—seen but not heard." He was wasting his breath.[7]

Carter's first official appointment as president was with Brzezinski at 9:00 a.m. the next day in the Oval Office.[8] Except when Brzezinski was abroad, that one-to-one briefing would take place every day barring Sunday for the next four years. It was initially called the daily intelligence briefing. When Stansfield Turner, a former admiral, was confirmed as CIA director in February, he insisted that as intelligence chief, he should be the one to do the briefing. Carter did not like Turner's way of presenting, which consisted of reading out disparate pieces of intelligence without supplying a broader context. Brzezinski renamed it the national security briefing.[9] Turner was allowed to brief the president once a week with Brzezinski present. Later that would be downgraded to a twice-monthly appointment.

Brzezinski and Carter would usually meet at 7:30 a.m. for about half an hour without anyone else present. Each evening, Brzezinski would give Carter roughly a hundred pages of reading comprising intelligence reports, staff policy papers, and news items that he had winnowed down from the four hundred or so pages that he consumed each day. Carter would digest them without fail by the next morning. Often he would spot typos or spelling errors and scrawl corrections in the margins. That earned him the in-house nickname "grammarian in chief." The minutes and summaries of all NSC committee meetings were written by Brzezinski's staff. Vance and his peers did not get the chance to see or edit the reports before they were submitted to Carter. Brzezinski's control of the presidential paper flow was thus also sewn up before day one.

The two foreign policy challenges that would dominate Carter's first year and beyond had flared up in the days before he entered the White House. They were the parlous state of US-Soviet relations and Carter's ambitions for an Arab-Israeli peace agreement. Détente had in effect been in abeyance for two years. Ford's sidelining of Kissinger and Leonid Brezhnev's declining health had left bilateral relations to fester. Carter had made it plain that human rights would be the soul of his foreign policy, a pledge he reinforced in his otherwise unremarkable fifteen-minute inaugural speech. But the Soviets were unclear what Carter meant by that. Was he planning an ideological war on communism? If so, it would kill détente. Or was he just a naive preacher? In which case, he would soon learn. Anatoly Dobrynin, the Soviet Union's veteran ambassador to the United States who had been in the job since the Cuban Missile Crisis of 1962, was reassured by Harriman and Kissinger that most of the human rights talk had been campaign rhetoric. Carter was sincere but inexperienced. After a bumpy learning phase, détente would return to business as usual. Kissinger still warned Dobrynin that Brzezinski was "excessively emotional and not able to think impassively."[10]

Vance had gently raised human rights at his first meeting with Dobrynin: a breakfast at the State Department that was set up by Kissinger, who was in his final days on the job.[11] Brzezinski insisted that Carter was in earnest. The first time he met Dobrynin was at a dinner during the presidential campaign that was arranged by David Rockefeller. The circumstance left Dobrynin with the natural impression that the Rockefellers were "running a virtually no-risk political game."[12] The older brother, Nelson, had been Kissinger's sponsor, while David was Brzezinski's. Yet there were limits to David Rockefeller's sway over Brzezinski. When Dobrynin pressed for specifics on how Carter would differ from Ford, Rockefeller cut Brzezinski off. Pointing at Brzezinski, he said, "I have already told him that I don't see any particular differences."[13] Brzezinski could have delivered a semester of lectures on how Carter differed from Ford. In that instance, he chose to stay diplomatically silent. Either way, Dobrynin had strongly contrasting readings on the new president's intentions. He did not know which to believe. Events quickly resolved his confusion.

One of the items on Carter's first daily briefing with Brzezinski on January 21 was a public letter from Andrei Sakharov, the Soviet Union's leading physicist and best-known dissident. Sakharov had been awarded the 1975 Nobel Peace Prize for his courageous championing of human rights. The world now had a US president who saw the world the same way. Sakharov, who was blocked from leaving the USSR to accept the award, was a biting critic of détente. In the letter he appealed to Carter to embrace the Soviet dissidents' cause. In retrospect, his letter was the start of a new era. The United States was no longer losing lives in Indochina or anywhere else. For the first time in years, America was not on the ideological defensive.

On the first day of 1977, a group of Czech dissidents launched Charter 77, set up to monitor Prague's compliance with Helsinki's third basket on human rights. Similar watch groups had been proliferating in the USSR over the previous few months and in other satellite countries, especially Poland. The Soviets had launched a crackdown on Sakharov's group shortly after Carter's victory the previous November. Against Vance's advice but at

Brzezinski's urging, Carter sent Sakharov a public reply, implicitly endorsing his cause. Carter's letter both enraged and perplexed the Soviets. Nothing like it had happened while Kissinger was in office. Brezhnev could not fathom why Carter was poking the Moscow bear at the same time that he was seeking a nuclear arms control agreement. The Soviets made it clear that they would link progress on the nuclear talks—the Strategic Arms Limitation Treaty, or SALT II—to American restraint in other areas, most notably on human rights. Carter could not have both.

Vance instinctively sympathized with the Soviet disquiet. In his view, anything that got in the way of bringing SALT II to fruition would be a futile and potentially dangerous side game. For the sake of mankind, SALT II had to be the overriding priority. No cause, however just, could compete with the necessity of lessening the specter of nuclear war.[14]

Brzezinski, by contrast, thought that the Russians needed a nuclear treaty far more than the Americans. The Soviet economy was chronically stagnant. The country's rulers would soon be confronted with the stark choice between making deep cuts in military spending or risking their political grip by subjecting their people to even greater austerity. That Kissinger had allowed so much US technology to be transferred to the Soviet Union was only delaying Moscow's day of reckoning, Brzezinski thought. Knowingly or not, US companies were helping fuel the USSR's military expansion. Carter agonized between the two views. Thus began a dialogue of the deaf that was as much between Brzezinski and Vance as it was between Carter and Brezhnev. In his memoir, Dobrynin captured the incongruity of the Carter-Brzezinski-Vance team by citing the poem "Swan, Pike, and Crawfish" by the Russian Ivan Krylov. He described Vance as a "practical and balanced lawyer," while Brzezinski was a "vigorous and pushy academic."[15] The new president's character was a mystery.

Carter had campaigned on the promise of a nuclear-free world. His instinct was thus to propose deep cuts to US and Soviet nuclear arsenals. That would mean rejecting the unambitious interim deal that Ford and Kissinger had hammered out in Vladivostok in late 1974. The Vladivostok draft, along with many other decisions, had been languishing in the in tray for the past two years. Détente was in the balance. In Brezhnev's diplomatically worded first letter to Carter in early February, he proposed a straightforward ratification of what had been agreed with Ford at Vladivostok. But in his second letter in late February, which took Carter aback and which Brzezinski described as "cynical and sneering,"[16] Brezhnev hectored Carter for having corresponded with

Sakharov in the meantime. The Soviet leader warned Carter not to test his patience by opening talks with a "renegade" and "enemy of the Soviet state." Such an approach, he said, would endanger US-Soviet relations. "We do not intend to impose on your country or upon other countries our rules but neither shall we allow interference in our internal affairs, whatever pseudo-humanitarian slogans are used to present it," Brezhnev wrote. "We shall resolutely respond to any attempts of this kind."[17]

Brezhnev's letter hit Carter like a bucket of cold water. Brzezinski converted it into a teachable moment. The following week, against State Department advice, Carter met the Soviet dissident Vladimir Bukovsky, a human rights activist who had been granted asylum in Switzerland the previous year. The meeting further inflamed the Soviets. A few days later, Moscow arrested a group of dissidents, including Natan Sharansky, a prominent Jewish refusenik and colleague of Sakharov. They were charged with treason, which carried an automatic death sentence. This was aimed at Carter. For the first time, Carter responded positively to Brzezinski's idea of exploring openings to normalize relations with China. Such a move, in Vance's opinion, would endanger the SALT II talks by aiming a strategic dagger at Moscow's heart.

Much like the nuclear arms process, US-China talks had stagnated under Ford following the initial euphoria over Nixon's historic 1972 visit. The death of Mao Zedong in 1976 had also created uncertainty about China's direction. Many observers had speculated that a post-Mao China would repair its ideological breach with Moscow. Brzezinski's take was that the Sino-Soviet split was chiefly about clashing national interests, not doctrinal splits. The breach would therefore persist. Either way, the Soviets were desperate to avoid a two-front threat from both the West and the East. Moscow's goal was to neutralize the Western threat by securing another nuclear arms deal. That would enable it to shift more of its military firepower to the East. A US tilt towards China—in contrast to Kissinger's carefully balanced "equidistance"—would throw Soviet calculations into disarray.

Most immediately, Brezhnev's intemperate letter convinced Carter to go for a robust opening gambit in the SALT II talks. Vance argued that Carter should offer Vladivostok with only small modifications. Carter was increasingly inclined to go for something more sweeping. Brzezinski told Carter that it was his first big test as president. Would he allow himself to be cajoled by Brezhnev, much as a callow JFK had been bullied during his first meeting with Khrushchev in 1961? Or would he lay down a clear marker?[18]

Ironically, during the 1960 campaign, Kennedy had promised to bridge the mythical "missile gap" with the Soviets. At that point, America's nuclear arsenal was roughly four times the size of the Soviet one. By 1977, the Soviets had achieved rough parity depending on how you tallied each side's mind-bogglingly complex measures of range, size, precision, and throw weight. Many in Washington, including Senator Scoop Jackson and the recently formed Committee on the Present Danger, which included conservative arms control experts such as Paul Nitze, believed that by 1977, the Soviets were within spitting distance of strategic superiority. Carter could have exhumed Kennedy's 1960 slogan for his own campaign. Yet his dream had always been to close the nuclear gap by reducing both superpower arsenals, preferably to zero. The nuclear trends he inherited made that promise look naive.

Harold Brown, Carter's secretary of defense, thought that by the early 1980s the Soviets would be in a position to make a "cosmic roll of the dice."[19] By then the Soviet arsenal would have reached a scale that could overwhelm the United States with a first-strike attack. The Soviets' expanded arsenal would open a window of temptation before a new generation of US weapons had been deployed. The Pentagon called it the "vulnerability gap."

Brezhnev's letter was clarifying for Carter. After Dobrynin delivered it to Vance, the secretary of state read it a couple of times and then confided to the ambassador that he had warned Carter that he treated certain international problems, such as how difficult it was to negotiate arms deals, too lightly. "I hope Brezhnev's straightforward letter will make the president look at things somewhat differently," Vance concluded.[20] Carter's reply to Brezhnev, in which he conceded nothing on human rights or on his proposed steep nuclear arms cuts,[21] was delivered to Dobrynin by Brzezinski rather than Vance. That was meant to underline Carter's message: that Vance had lost the battle to frame a conciliatory response. After reading Vance's draft reply to Brezhnev, Carter said that it would "not have been worth the price of the stamp were we to mail it to Moscow."[22] Vance was also overruled on the nuclear proposal.

On March 10, Brzezinski chaired a meeting of the Security Coordination Committee (SCC), the entity that dealt with emergency and crosscutting issues, which he made sure included SALT II—to hammer out the options that Vance would take with him to Moscow later that month. They agreed on a package of sharp cuts and a nuclear freeze. They would slash the overall number of strategic nuclear launchers permitted to each side by the Vladivostok Agreement from 2,400 to between 1,800 and 2,000.[23] It would also reduce from 1,320 to 1,200 the number of multiple warhead launchers (multiple independently targetable reentry vehicles, or MIRVs) and limit to 550 the number of Soviet land-based MIRV-ed intercontinental ballistic missiles—the same as America's permitted ceiling. The new package would deprive the Soviets of the numerical ICBM advantage that they had negotiated with Kissinger in the SALT I treaty signed in Moscow in 1972. In simple terms, Carter was proposing a halt to the arms race that would start with cuts. His plan would also put the Ford-Brezhnev Vladivostok draft through the shredder. In that context, being in favor of steeper arms reductions was deemed to be the hawkish position. Sustaining high weapons stockpiles was dovish.

Brzezinski had few illusions that the Soviets would accept Carter's proposal. As a fallback in case of Soviet rejection, Vance was given a back-pocket "Vladivostok-minus" option. But the prospect of failure did not bother Brzezinski much. He saw the exercise as a "truth test." A clear *nyet* would "smoke the Russians out," which would rally an increasingly skeptical US public behind Carter's position.[24] There was broad agreement in Washington that the Soviets had exploited loose wording in SALT I to the point of cheating on the limits to which they had agreed. Kissinger's negotiators had not nailed down the meaning of "heavy," which allowed the Soviets to build only modestly less gargantuan missiles than their already vast SS-9s, which were in any case many times the size of America's Minutemen. Most nuclear experts did not believe that weight mattered since US missiles were more accurate. The US also had a triad of delivery options: land, submarine, and aircraft launchers. The Soviets could still only launch missiles from land. But the doomsday scale of Soviet ICBMs haunted America's imagination. It was as though the barbaric size of the siloed monsters betrayed Soviet intentions. As Stalin is said to have remarked, "Quantity has a quality all its own." A sign of the more hawkish mood on Capitol Hill was that Paul Warnke, Carter's dovish chief SALT negotiator and Vance's choice, was confirmed by 58 to 40 votes, which was well short of the two-thirds majority Carter desired from the Democratic-majority Senate.[25]

The mood in the run-up to Vance's ill-fated first visit to Moscow was increasingly skeptical. Carter and the first lady hosted Henry and Nancy Kissinger to dinner at the White House in late March, a week before Vance was due to go to Moscow. Cy and Gay Vance and Brzezinski were also there.[26] For most of the dinner they listened as Kissinger grandly held forth on the foreign policy landscape that Carter had inherited. He was nevertheless bullish that the administration's robust SALT II proposal stood a good chance of being accepted in Moscow. Carter's mood was buoyed by Kissinger's apparent vote of confidence. Nobody had more experience than he in negotiating with Brezhnev. To Dobrynin, however, Kissinger said the opposite several weeks later: "When I learned . . . what package Vance proposed in Moscow, I told Vance that he should not have entered negotiations with proposals like this in order to save his reputation in the eyes of the Soviet leadership."[27] The problem with Carter, he added, was that he was "trapped in his own propagandistic illusions." There was not a single "influential" person in his circle. Carter's weakness, in other words, was that he lacked a Kissinger.

At a press conference the day before Vance flew to Moscow, Carter made the rookie error of revealing his negotiating fallback option. "If we're disappointed, which is a possibility, then we'll try to modify our stance," he told the world. Brezhnev sharply rebuffed Vance in Moscow and gave him no chance to bring out his back-pocket proposal. Brezhnev opened proceedings by reading out a laborious statement about America's double standards on human rights, even citing his adversary's poor literacy statistics and juvenile delinquency to make his point. The ailing Soviet leader was so stung that he allowed his normally impassive foreign minister, Andrei Gromyko, to give a press conference lambasting the US nuclear offer as a "cheap and shady maneuver" that aimed for "unilateral advantage." He added that Carter's human rights focus had "poisoned the atmosphere." This was no mere rebuff. In the eyes of the media, Vance's trip to Moscow was Carter's first big failure as president. He had misunderstood the Soviets' negotiating boundaries and ruined Vance's prospects in advance by grandstanding on human rights. The fault, according to most US media accounts, lay in Washington, not Moscow.

The hapless Vance took almost all of the blame. Media coverage increasingly started to depict him as a victim of Brzezinski's bureaucratic skills. Brzezinski's press officer, Jerry Schecter, had to counter a stream of stories about Brzezinski's alleged contempt for Vance. The two had in fact been getting along reasonably well. In his diary, Brzezinski often described Vance as a gentleman. At Brzezinski's suggestion, Carter, Rosalynn, and he had taken the Marine One helicopter to Andrews Air Force Base to welcome Vance on his return from Moscow, a public gesture meant to convey unity and repair Vance's bruised morale.[28] Vance was visibly moved by the greeting party. But it did not quell the speculation. Schecter was asked by the *New York Times'* Charles Mohr to approve a quote in which Brzezinski had allegedly said, "I find it child's play to run circles around that clown Vance."[29] The newspaper killed the quote, which was made up. But Brzezinski felt awful. "Once they [the media] gang up on somebody, there is no escaping," he wrote. "It is grossly unfair to Vance, who is really quite able, very decent and energetic. . . . I can well imagine how he feels."[30]

Brzezinski was nevertheless feeling upbeat about his new job. While Vance was in Moscow, Brzezinski celebrated his forty-ninth birthday. He had just blown out the candles on the cake with which his staff had surprised him when Walter Mondale joined the office festivities. A few moments later, Carter slipped in. The vice president was midway through telling a story about how moving it was to play the cello. "I bet everyone weeps when you play the cello," the president interrupted.[31] By and large, it was still a relaxed White House. Brzezinski's nickname among the Georgians was "Woody Woodpecker," based on his resemblance to the cartoon character with his chiseled nose and crew-cut swept-forward hair. He disliked the moniker. In retaliation, Brzezinski called Hamilton Jordan, leader of the Georgia pack, and Carter's most trusted political advisor, "Porky Pig." To humor Brzezinski, Jordan changed his nickname to "Dr. Strangelove," which he cherished.[32] That night, the Harrimans toasted Brzezinski's birthday with champagne.[33]

In the previous three months, he had been able to make only two fleeting visits to Muska and the children in New Jersey. Carter, who was infamously censorious about nonmarital living arrangements among his younger Georgia staff, liked to tease Brzezinski about his bachelor existence. Office or media rumors of infidelity almost never dogged Brzezinski. He was an uxorious husband. He was nevertheless a prominent draw on the Georgetown social circuit. One morning as Brzezinski walked into the Oval Office, Carter asked, "Who was that long-legged blonde you were playing tennis with?"[34] The puzzled Brzezinski wondered how Carter could possibly know that he had played a set with the accurately described AP reporter on the White House tennis court—the "supreme court," as it was known. It turned out that there was a picture of them in action in that morning's *Washington Post*. "Well, I don't care, but you'd better have a damned good explanation for your wife," said Carter with the hint of a smile.[35] On another occasion, after Brzezinski was photographed with the actress Shirley MacLaine, Carter sent the picture to Muska with a note advising her to move to Washington as soon as possible.

From the start, Brzezinski was an object of media fascination. He did not have Kissinger's star power and lacked his predecessor's ability to hypnotize the press with intellectual pyrotechnics—"spectaculars," as Brzezinski called them. When Brzezinski talked to journalists, his instinct was to retreat behind highfalutin abstractions. Words such as *concomitant* and *preponderance* featured often. Nor did he have much taste for self-deprecation. Yet he was generally viewed as the primal force behind Carter's foreign policy. He was also seen as a sophisticate in a youthful and relatively provincial White House.

Moreover, Carter evidently respected and even admired Brzezinski in a way that had not been true of Nixon about Kissinger. Partly that was because of the narrower age difference. Carter was three and a half years older than Brzezinski; Nixon was more than a decade Kissinger's senior. Nixon had been vice president for two terms long before they met. Carter, by contrast, was a neophyte. A *Jerusalem Post* article neatly summarized how Washington differentiated Brzezinski from Kissinger: "Kissinger's trademark has been personal diplomacy. Brzezinski has a cold, analytical mind uninfluenced by emotional considerations. Kissinger is vain and sensitive to criticism. Brzezinski has a natural self-assurance and no great need for approval or admiration."[36] In one key respect, however, the two immigrant scholars were irresistibly comparable: each was seen as an overbearing national security advisor.

Brzezinski's reputation for being domineering quickly became a liability. Carter was not helping. Whenever the president wanted a group to be briefed on his foreign policy—whether a congressional gathering, the White House domestic staff, or a delegation from out of town—he would ask Brzezinski to take the stage. Carter would sit in the front row. Rosalynn would often take notes. Brzezinski could summarize and synthesize with overarching clarity. In a town of prolix bureaucrats and jargonized diffidence, that skill greatly appealed to the president. "I'd get in the car and say, 'Look, four things you need to know, the things you need to do, the things you need to say,'—like that, bang bang bang, that's it, finish, okay, bye," Brzezinski later said.[37] The president would publicly introduce Brzezinski in gushing terms as a preeminent scholar and his personal instructor in all matters foreign. He would attribute his election victory partly to Brzezinski. Much of this was true. But it was starting to get awkward. The phrase *eager student* kept resurfacing. In one memo, Brzezinski tried to persuade Carter not to use the word *learning* so often. Americans do not want a leader who presents himself as a "permanent student—not after the first 100 days anyhow," Brzezinski wrote in a private memo. Next to that line, Carter wrote, "OK." Brzezinski's point was that Americans want a president who knows his own mind. "Good ideas—I agree!!" wrote the president at the top.[38]

The problem was that Carter did not always seem to know his own mind. He seemed too busy trying to expand it. In addition to consuming every memo that came across his desk, he was learning Spanish, teaching Sunday school and, perhaps sensibly, taking a speed-reading course with the first lady. Each night he would read the Bible in Spanish for a set period of time. He tore through books. In the space of one weekend at Camp David, he read four.[39] That was four more than a couple of his successors could muster in a full presidential term. He did the same to a fault with briefing papers before taking decisions. No detail seemed too small. A few days into Carter's presidency, he asked Harold Brown and the defense chiefs to hash out the Pentagon budget in the Oval Office. Duplication and fiscal inefficiency drove him to distraction. Consumption of time did not. As ever, Brzezinski was in the room. The defense budget meeting started at 4:30 p.m. and went on to 11:30 p.m. Brzezinski wondered whether Carter was "doing this deliberately in order to impress us with his stamina."[40]

Each Monday morning, Carter held cabinet meetings that stretched for two or three hours. He had promised to restore openness and transparency after years of back-channel government. He had not appointed a chief of staff. There would be no scheming H. R. Haldeman–like figure in Carter's White House. Now he was inflicting that promise on his principals. Brzezinski, who used cabinet meetings as a chance to catch up on current affairs, with a copy of *Time* or *U.S. News & World Report* positioned surreptitiously on his lap, was not alone in questioning their utility. "Whenever there is a cabinet meeting, the rest of the day is shot," he complained.[41] On more than one occasion when one of their colleagues was giving an extended peroration, Vance and Brzezinski would exchange eye rolls. Carter liked it that way. He told Brzezinski that he felt comfortable making decisions only after he had mastered the details. The difficulties arose when Carter was given clashing interpretations of those details, particularly on anything concerning the Soviet Union. Indeed, when it came to the USSR, divergence was the norm.

The gulf in advice that Carter was getting from Vance and Brzezinski was accentuated by their temperaments: Vance, mild mannered, consensus seeking, always trying to split the difference, with a lawyer's eye for a negotiated outcome; Brzezinski, intellectual, sometimes dogmatic, impatient with obfuscation, and with a debater's relish for the clash of ideas. Their strikingly different personas were key to their incompatible worldviews. Brzezinski thought that Vance saw any kind of deal with the Soviets as a good thing in itself regardless of its content. SALT II, he felt, was a "fetishistic" preoccupation with Vance. He saw Vance's idea of foreign policy as episodic and case by case, much like a legal brief. Brzezinski, on the other hand, viewed the USSR as weak and degenerating yet prone to adventurism. Moscow was correspondingly desperate for a reboot of what Brzezinski saw as a one-sided relationship. With Kissinger-style détente, the USSR could sponsor Third World revolutions without the risk of starting a nuclear war. There was little chance Carter could reconcile the two men's approaches.

Before the election, Carter had consulted Stu Eizenstat, a long-standing *consigliere* from Atlanta, where he had practiced law, who had been the head of policy for the presidential campaign, on whether he should appoint both Vance and Brzezinski. Eizenstat, who went on to head Carter's domestic policy operation, demurred. Both were excellent choices, he said. But "like oil and water," they could never mix.[42] He advised Carter to choose one or the other. In 1861, Abraham Lincoln had appointed a "team of rivals" to his cabinet. Carter's picks catered to different organs in his body: Vance had Carter's heart; Brzezinski had Carter's brain. Their clashes were duly magnified by their respective staffs. Brzezinski had assembled what was widely judged to be a high-caliber team. He cut the size of Kissinger's (and latterly Scowcroft's) NSC staff in half to just thirty policy positions. Over time that grew back to around forty. There was no ideological pattern to Brzezinski's recruitment. He had an eye for analytical skills. His hiring philosophy was meritocratic.

Many of Brzezinski's picks came from the liberal wing of the Democratic Party. His deputy, David Aaron, had been a Senate aide to Mondale. Several staffers, including Robert Hunter, who ran the Europe desk, had worked for Ted Kennedy. He recruited Madeleine Albright from Ed Muskie's office to be his congressional liaison officer (she described her move as going "from Pole to Pole"[43]). Bill Odom, who became military affairs advisor, was a former PhD student of Brzezinski at Columbia. He had since become an army lieutenant colonel and had served as military attaché at the US Embassy in Moscow. Schecter, who was the NSC's first dedicated press secretary (as Albright was in her Capitol Hill role), was poached from *Time* magazine. Jessica Tuchman (later Matthews), who headed Brzezinski's "global issues" desk, was a young liberal with a doctorate in biochemistry. She had worked for Mo Udall. Robert Gates, who later became CIA director, had been poached by Scowcroft from Langley. Brzezinski retained Gates and developed a strong respect for his judgment. Rick Inderfurth, Brzezinski's special assistant, had been working for Frank Church's investigative Senate committee, which had done so much to rein in the CIA and expose the Nixon era's executive overreach. And Harvard's Samuel Huntington, dubbed "Zbig's Zbig," was persuaded to work for his old friend as the NSC's in-house strategic brain with the title "coordinator of security planning."

By any measure, Brzezinski had pulled together a strong team. Vance also assembled a highly regarded staff. Apart from the sheer scale of the State Department, with thousands of people working in its Foggy Bottom building, what distinguished their teams was that Vance's recruits were ideologically alike. Their worldview tended to conflate with Vance's. His best-known hires included Richard Holbrooke, a former Foreign Service officer, who was Brzezinski's fellow lodger at the Harrimans'. Holbrooke became assistant secretary of state for East Asian and Pacific Affairs. Tony Lake, also a former Foreign Service officer, had worked for Kissinger and Ed Muskie and was now Vance's head of policy and planning, George Kennan's old job. Lake had resigned from Kissinger's NSC over the secret bombing of Cambodia.

Les Gelb had worked in LBJ's Pentagon and had since then been the *New York Times*' diplomatic correspondent. He headed the State Department's Bureau of Political-Military Affairs. Marshall Shulman was a former colleague of Brzezinski at Columbia and a Sovietologist. He was Vance's USSR advisor. Once Holbrooke had found a place to live, Shulman replaced him as the Harrimans' lodger. Paul Warnke, a former Pentagon official, was Vance's chief SALT II negotiator. Hodding Carter III, a distant cousin of Jimmy, was the scion of a crusading family newspaper business in the South. He was the State Department spokesman. In 1978, he married Patricia Derian, a civil rights activist whom Jimmy Carter had picked for the new role of assistant secretary of state for human rights. Derian's view of human rights was almost the mirror image of Brzezinski's. She trained her sights on America's authoritarian allies; Brzezinski was preoccupied with the Soviet Bloc.

Though they came from diverse backgrounds, Brzezinski saw both Vance and his appointees as "McGovernites." That was misleading. Only Warnke had worked on McGovern's disastrous 1972 campaign. But all of Vance's hires had been marked in one way or another by the Vietnam tragedy. They were likewise dovish on the USSR and shared Vance's desire to reach a swift conclusion to SALT II. In the context of Carter's presidency, they would more accurately be described as Kissingerian. To a person, they wanted to preserve détente at whatever cost. Whenever Vance's staff sent over drafts of Carter speeches on the Soviet Union, the phrase "reciprocal and comprehensive" that preceded "détente" would be removed.[44] Brzezinski's NSC would reinstate the qualifiers.

State's anonymous leaks against Brzezinski, which became harsher and more frequent as Carter's presidency went on, were virtually indistinguishable in tone from Kissinger's. Carter would later express regret at his decision to give his cabinet principals the freedom to choose their own staff, which had deprived him of control.[45] He chiefly had Vance in mind. But in the war of the leaks, the NSC and State were mirror images. Brzezinski insisted that his staff did not leak. By that he meant that they did so only when authorized or when he himself was the source. Brzezinski's staff were disciplined and followed his lead. At times he sought and received Carter's permission to leak. At other times he did so of his own accord. Carter forgave him. When Brzezinski spoke on the record, State would immediately protest. "Almost without exception, Zbig had been speaking with my approval," Carter recalled. "The underlying State Department objection was that Brzezinski had spoken at all."[46]

Vance never leaked and strongly disapproved of the practice. His staff, notably Gelb, Carter, and Holbrooke, had no such compunction. They became serially anonymous briefers against Vance's wishes. One of Vance's predecessors, Henry Stimson, said, "Gentlemen do not read each other's mail." That was also Vance's approach. He put an end to Kissinger's practice of having an undeclared note taker listen in on every telephone call he made from Foggy Bottom. When he had notes taken, Vance informed his interlocutor. The disclosure inevitably changed the nature of the conversation. In that regard, he was profoundly un-Kissingerian. Brzezinski never tapped his own NSC staff, as Kissinger had routinely done, including Lake. But he was on the hunt for as much intelligence as he could find. At a particularly fraught moment in Carter's marathon 1978 Camp David peace talks, he asked whether he could read the transcripts of the calls made by Menachem Begin, Israel's leader, and Anwar Sadat, Egypt's leader. When Brzezinski discovered that the FBI was not tapping their cabins, he suggested that that should be rectified.[47] Both Vance and Carter were horrified at the thought of listening in on guests. His idea was rejected. To Brzezinski, like Lenin, the ends justified the means.

In addition to the premium that Carter put on his brain, Brzezinski had a key situational advantage over Vance: his West Wing office was just a few feet from the Oval Office. He and Carter would sometimes meet ten or twelve times in a day. Vance's offices were more than a mile away. He saw the president at most three or four times a week, often with Brzezinski present. Brzezinski knew that in a presidential system, power, like real estate, was about "location, location, location." Or as George Ball, borrowing a line from Ian Fleming, put it, "Nothing propinks like propinquity." Locational advantage also helped Brzezinski to build esprit de corps among his staff.

In their first week, Carter addressed the NSC staff as a group and did so several more times during his presidency. That instilled in them a feeling of inclusion and privilege. Brzezinski encouraged his staff to think of themselves as the president's "Praetorian Guard." Unlike many previous national security advisors—but similar to Kissinger—Brzezinski rarely took staff members to Oval Office meetings. He guarded his presidential face time with a rottweiler's ferocity. Every NSC staff member, however, had good access to Brzezinski. Their weekly Friday meeting on the third floor of the Old Executive Office Building was more like a freewheeling seminar. Brzezinski would share the president's thoughts and disclose classified information. He warned that if there were any leaks, he would terminate the practice. None occurred.[48] The meetings continued until their last Friday in office. Every night, every staff member was required to send him a daily activity report, including journalists they had met. The next day the memo would be back on their desk, often with comments.

Though his team was dominated by PhDs and included three or four female officers, it was not above frat house humor. During the transition, staff members drew up a spoof employment application form that lampooned Carter's born-again persona. Among the questions were "What is your favorite nut? How many times have you been 'born'? Who made you? To what magazines do you subscribe? Who is the greatest president since Ford? What country is Noo Yawk in? Does Jesus turn you on?"[49] Carter was not above such repartee. On his fifty-third birthday on October 1, 1977, Brzezinski's staff sent him a congratulatory telegram purportedly from Brezhnev: "The Soviet government remains disappointed by the rigid and one-sided position taken by the United States." In the margin, Carter scribbled, "It's my staff." The spoof Brezhnev continued, "As a step toward greater trade between us, I propose that you let me have your Assistant Mr. Brzezinski for a few weeks; I would personally take care of his human rights and return him to you in a deserving condition." Carter wrote, "OK, but will not take him back."[50]

The NSC team was small enough for Brzezinski to host regular weekend social events. After Muska and the children—Ian, by now fourteen; Mark, age twelve; and Mika, just turned ten—joined Brzezinski in June 1977, he often hosted his colleagues at home. With Madeleine Albright's help, the Brzezinskis found a rambling, historic country house in McLean, Virginia. It was a thirty-minute drive from the White House, about as long as it had taken him to get there on foot from the Harrimans' Georgetown residence. Spring Hill had a tennis court, a pool, and a garden large enough for sprawling picnics. At such gatherings Brzezinski would often propose a game of soccer with his colleagues. Though of limited talent he had a decisive edge over the other players. Having turned up in sandals or flip-flops, his staff lacked any willingness to tackle him. He would go inside just before the game and emerge in an intimidating pair of combat boots.[51] The others learned to keep out of his way. He always played to win.

A few weeks before Carter won the 1976 Democratic nomination, Brzezinski took an educational trip to Israel. His visit coincided with the hijacking of an Air France plane at Uganda's Entebbe International Airport. The lives of ninety-four Israeli and Jewish passengers and twelve crew members were in imminent jeopardy. Israelis could focus on nothing else. The Palestinian hijackers, members of a group called the Popular Front for the Liberation of Palestine, demanded a $5 million ransom and the release of fifty-three prisoners in exchange for the hostages' lives. The hijackers were assisted by members of Germany's Baader-Meinhof Gang, which gave their mission an added menace. In the midst of this, Brzezinski was invited to dinner at the home of Shimon Peres, Israel's defense minister.[52] Peres kept having to leave the room to take calls. Somewhat flippantly, Brzezinski quipped to Peres that Israeli commandoes should storm the airport and free the hostages. Peres gave Brzezinski an enigmatic stare and went silent. The following day it became obvious why he had kept his counsel: Israeli forces raided the airport in one of the most daring rescue operations in modern history. Though the unit commander, Yonatan Netanyahu, was killed, Israel had shown what a highly skilled counterterrorist force could accomplish. The raid stuck in Brzezinski's mind.

His other big takeaway was a long conversation with Menachem Begin, Israel's hard-right opposition leader who had led Irgun, the extremist Jewish underground movement that fought the British in the late 1940s. Although Begin was Israel's most hawkish leader, he and Brzezinski hit it off. Indeed, their shared hawkishness may even have helped. Begin was surprised by Brzezinski's deep knowledge of Irgun's activities.[53] Begin had notoriously plotted the 1946 terrorist bombing of Jerusalem's King David Hotel that killed ninety-one people. He and Brzezinski met at his apartment, where he had hidden from the British three decades earlier. There was something about Begin's inveterate nationalism that struck a romantic chord in Brzezinski. That both men had been born in Poland—although raised in very different milieus—helped. They could switch easily from English to Polish. Their shared compendious knowledge of the Polish Home Army's wartime resistance and the Warsaw Uprising gave them plenty to talk about. Begin had been imprisoned for part of the war by Stalin's NKVD, which meant that they also shared an allergy to communism. Their discussion ranged to Ze'ev Jabotinsky, the Jewish Polish father of revisionist Zionism, who had been Begin's mentor. Neither man could have imagined how many more conversations they would have.

As had become typical of Democratic presidential nominees, Carter received 70 percent of the Jewish vote in the election a few months later. There was nevertheless disquiet about Carter's pro-Israeli credentials among Washington's leading Jewish organizations, particularly at the increasingly powerful American Israel Public Affairs Committee (AIPAC). As a candidate Carter had declared his hopes of brokering peace in the Middle East—the "land of the Bible." He had mentioned his support for Palestinian self-determination in the primaries but scaled back his rhetoric during the general election. Americans had no experience of a president who was a born-again Christian, let alone one who made such a spectacle of it. Carter repeatedly underlined his support for the Jewish people's sacred right to their homeland. But he also sympathized with the Palestinians' plight. Eizenstat, who was Carter's most senior Jewish advisor, thought that Carter viewed the Palestinian struggle in much the same way as he did the African American civil rights movement.[54] In a strange way, Carter saw the Palestinian cause as an opportunity to redeem his somewhat patchy civil rights record in Georgia.

There were also forebodings about Brzezinski's views on Israel. In 1975, Brzezinski had participated in a controversial Brookings Institution study that said that the US should sponsor a broad Arab-Israeli settlement that would include Soviet participation and would result in self-determination for the Palestinians. Carter incorporated the report into his campaign. Brzezinski's motives for contributing to the Brookings study had been twofold. First, he wanted to offer a far bolder alternative to Kissinger's incremental "step-by-step" approach in the Middle East. Kissinger's shuttle diplomacy had wrought a cease-fire and disengagement between Israel and Egypt after the 1973 Yom

Kippur War. But the situation was uneasy and could unravel at any time. In his view, the US should go for a comprehensive settlement; incrementalism was out. Second, he saw almost everything through a Cold War lens. An Israeli-Palestinian settlement would rob the Soviets of their most potent anti-imperialist rallying cry in the Arab world. To bring the Arab parties to the table, however, the Soviets would need to be given a stake in the process.

The first sign of Jewish unease took place a week before Carter's inauguration when Brzezinski chose William Quandt to be the NSC's Middle East director. Quandt, who was a professor at the University of Pennsylvania, had directed the Brookings study and was perceived to be pro-Palestinian. Brzezinski got a call from the executive director of AIPAC, Morris Amitay, complaining about Quandt's appointment.[55] Brzezinski was also visited by Richard Stone, a senator from Florida and prominent Jewish American Democrat. Brzezinski denied that there was anything in Quandt's background that implied an anti-Israel bias. On Brzezinski's first day in office, Stone dropped by again. This time he was holding a piece of paper with a list of a hundred or so officials across the federal government, but mostly at the Pentagon, who were allegedly biased against Israel. He wanted them all fired. It was a remarkably audacious demand. Quandt was present. After Stone left, Brzezinski scrunched up the paper and threw it into the wastepaper basket.[56] A few weeks later, Quandt was overheard at a party discussing Stone's "hit list" and what Brzezinski had done with it. Quandt's indiscretion surfaced in a *Washington Post* report a few days later. Stone called Brzezinski to request that he issue a denial of the *Post*'s article. "There's one problem," said Brzezinski. "It's true." Stone hung up.[57] It was not a promising start.

In contrast to the Carter administration's theological divisions over the USSR, there was unity among its key figures on the Middle East. Carter, Brzezinski, and Vance were all of one mind. Brzezinski had maneuvered to ensure his own outsized influence over SALT II and other Soviet-related matters. Most Soviet issues were overseen by the SCC committee that he chaired. Because they were like-minded on the Middle East, Brzezinski made no objection to Vance's leading that portfolio on the NSC's other body, the Policy Review Committee, which Vance chaired. Vance's first overseas visit as secretary of state was to the Middle East in mid-February. He came back feeling pessimistic. The Israelis had chewed him out about Carter's decision not to sell cluster bombs to Israel on humanitarian grounds. Carter feared that Israel would use the devastating antipersonnel bombs in Lebanon, where the

PLO and its militias were headquartered. Civilians could die. Yitzhak Rabin, Israel's prime minister, was also angry at the Carter administration's refusal to permit Israel to export its Kfir combat jets to Ecuador. The planes contained a General Electric engine, which gave the US a veto. In the campaign, Carter had vowed to reduce US conventional arms sales and crack down on nuclear proliferation. Israel's supporters on Capitol Hill bombarded the White House with complaints.

The US-Israeli mood took another bad turn during Rabin's unsuccessful visit to the White House in early March. That it went so wrong played a part in Rabin's resignation a few days later and the Labor Party's general election defeat to Begin's Likud Party in May. For some reason, Carter and Rabin's chemistry was off. When Carter suggested to Rabin that they slip out early from the formal White House dinner to look in on his daughter, Amy, in the president's upstairs living quarters, Rabin responded with a gruff "No."[58] That convinced Carter that Rabin was cold and unyielding.

Had Carter and his briefers, notably Brzezinski, done more research, he would have cut Rabin more slack. Israel's leader was facing possible electoral oblivion and was also dogged by a financial scandal. He was in no position a few weeks before the election to embrace the new president's ambitious framework, especially in light of Carter's already negative reputation in Israel. Two days after their frosty encounter, at an event in Clinton, Massachusetts, Carter said he supported a "Palestinian homeland." No US president had used that sort of language before. Amid a media uproar, Brzezinski and Vance met to discuss how they might defuse Carter's comment. Before they could thrash out a line, they got a message from Carter, who was returning to DC on Air Force One. It said that "no clarifications or elaborations were to be issued" to Carter's wording.[59] A bruised Rabin, now back in Israel, was quoted in the Israeli media describing Brzezinski as "anti-Israel." Rabin issued a denial that he had said that, but Brzezinski's standing with Jewish American groups was already damaged.

Carter's closest Jewish advisors, including Eizenstat and Gerald Rafshoon, an advertising executive from Atlanta, knew how clear the president was in his own mind about the Middle East. "Carter was the real hard-liner," Rafshoon said.[60] Brzezinski told Carter that he had become the administration's fall guy on Israel. The president seemed half amused by Brzezinski's discomfort. He laughed and said, "This is exactly what we want you to be— the fall guy."[61] There was a blurry line between saying that Brzezinski was anti-Israel and accusing him of anti-Semitism, which was taking hold in some Jewish-American circles. Eizenstat, who insisted that Brzezinski did "not have an anti-Semitic bone in his body,"[62] set up several meetings with leading Jewish organizations to douse the rumors. Those interactions had only modest effects. "Stu Eizenstat is an extremely serious, extremely able, and highly competent person, whose integrity and judgment I would very confidently rely on," Brzezinski wrote.[63] Yet Eizenstat could do little to assuage Brzezinski's notoriety.

There was nothing Brzezinski could do about his Slavic accent, which instantly reminded people of Poland's historical anti-Semitism. In other respects, Brzezinski was his own trip wire. His impatience with domestic politics, which he started out seeing as unrelated to foreign policy, was an unforced error, particularly when it came to Israel. He would sometimes ask Madeleine Albright why they had to make the trek to Capitol Hill for meetings with senators. Shouldn't it be the other way around? he asked. "No, because they're elected, Zbig, and you're not," she would reply. Albright set up dinner parties at her Georgetown home to better acquaint Brzezinski with prominent legislators and journalists. She had to school him to couch his disagreements politely, which did not always happen. Instead of saying, "Senator, I have a slightly different view," he would say, "You're wrong." Albright kept trying—largely in vain—to get Brzezinski to "stroke, not punch."[64] Brzezinski's instinct was to go for the rhetorical kill.

In that respect Walter Mondale was Brzezinski's opposite. To Brzezinski's frequent irritation, the vice president always gave priority to the domestic impact of any foreign policy move, especially regarding Israel. In Mondale's mind, foreign policy substance came second to electoral calculations. Yet Mondale's politically attuned ear was a helpful counterbalance to Carter, who more than once told Brzezinski that he would be prepared to sacrifice a second presidential term on the altar of a Middle East peace deal. He said the same about his parallel drive to secure a new Panama Canal Treaty, a campaign promise that consumed much of his first year in office. On Israel, Carter was even more tone deaf to the effect of his language than Brzezinski. Against advice that he later belatedly took, Carter preached at a Sunday school in the First Baptist Church a few blocks north of the White House. Twice in his first few months, he said something that could be construed as endorsing the early Church's anti-Semitic doctrine of deicide (pinning the murder of God on Jews). In the first, he told the story of Jesus driving the moneylenders from the Temple in

Jerusalem: "[Christ] had directly challenged in a fatal way the existing church, and there was no possible way for the Jewish leaders to avoid the challenge. So they decided to kill Jesus." In a second incident, he explained the story of Jesus raising Lazarus from the dead. By revealing himself as the Messiah, Jesus knew that he was risking death "as quickly as it could be arranged by the Jewish leaders, who were very powerful," he said.[65]

The White House was inundated with complaints from the Anti-Defamation League and other Jewish organizations. Eizenstat, who used the latest uproar to get Carter to quit his Sunday school teaching, was beside himself. How, he asked, could an American president be "so insensitive to the way his impolitic Bible lessons would be received?" Eizenstat just managed to avert another PR disaster by dissuading Carter's younger sister Ruth Carter Stapleton, a prominent evangelist, from speaking at a Jews for Jesus event.[66] Most Jewish Americans had little patience with the proselytizing outfit. The only light relief to the worsening narrative between the White House and Jewish Americans came when Carter's quirky and widely beloved mother, Lillian, accepted a humanitarian award from the United Jewish Appeal, a Jewish humanitarian organization. "Miss Lillian," as she was fondly known, had in her late sixties become a Peace Corps volunteer at a leper colony in India. On accepting the award, the president's mother told the audience, "I have never been with so many Jews before in my life." She got a standing ovation.[67]

Eizenstat, Mondale, Jordan, and Bob Lipshutz, another senior Jewish figure in Carter's White House, tried to dilute Carter's missionary zeal on the Israel-Palestine question. They had only limited impact. But Brzezinski was a convenient foil. Politics dictates that a president's detractors blame a senior figure for an unpopular stance, rather than the president directly. In the case of Israel and the pro-Israel lobbies, Brzezinski took most of the flak. In public, he claimed not to be bothered. One of his most persistent critics was Rabbi Alexander Schindler, president of the Conference of Presidents of Major Jewish Organizations, whom Brzezinski knew was telling people around town that he was an anti-Semite. Brzezinski told the *New York Times*, "'If you don't agree with us,' they are saying, 'we're going to stamp you as an anti-Semite.'" Such tactics would not succeed in knocking the Carter administration off course, he said; "I've decided to grit my teeth and bear it. What we're doing is in the national interest of the United States and is central to Israel's survival."[68]

In private, Brzezinski was distraught. He went to see Eizenstat in his

White House office, where he unburdened his angst about the injustice of the innuendos against him. A sympathetic Eizenstat did his best to counter the gossip. But it rarely let up. At one point Mondale was so worried about its impact on Brzezinski that he dropped by to ask how he was bearing up. The vice president would usually slip into Brzezinski's office when he was not there to pinch a Cuban cigar from his copious supply; Brzezinski figured at least ten had gone missing.[69] On that occasion, Mondale was genuinely checking on Brzezinski's morale.

Carter's Middle East gamble took on far higher stakes when Begin gained power in May. After thirty uninterrupted years of Labor rule, Likud's victory was seismic. Though Begin was an Ashkenazi Jew (of European roots), Likud took most of the Sephardic vote. Sephardic Israelis were generally more implacably anti-Arab than other groups. Several hundred thousand Sephardic Jews had been expelled from Arab-majority countries after Israel's creation in 1948. The consensus in Washington, which included Carter, was that Begin's victory was a blow to Carter's Middle East ambitions. Brzezinski was the sole dissenting voice. He argued that Begin's win could be a blessing in disguise.[70] Carter now had a hard-line counterpart in Tel Aviv. In the spirit of Nixon-goes-to-China, Begin would be better placed to sell a peace settlement to the Israeli public than a moderate leader. Moreover, his extremism would make it easier for Carter to win over a "significant portion" of the Jewish community in the US. That was neither Brzezinski's first nor last bout of wishful thinking about Carter's ability to appeal over the head of Washington's Israel lobby. But Brzezinski had found an unlikely sometime-friend in Begin.

In the buildup to Begin's first meeting with Carter in mid-July, AIPAC launched an intensive campaign against Carter's peace initiative.[71] There was also an ominous uptick of references to Brzezinski's Polish Catholic background in the media's Middle East reporting. Brzezinski felt particularly singled out by two journalists, CBS's Marvin Kalb and Joseph Kraft, a syndicated columnist with whom he had first become acquainted in the 1960s.[72] Carter inflamed matters by saying that in any peace settlement, Palestinian refugees should get reparations for the loss of their ancestral homes. He also reiterated his support for a Palestinian homeland. Brzezinski felt that Carter had "gone too far."[73] But he was the media's chief villain. With Averell Harriman's support, Kalb had lobbied Carter to be his ambassador to Israel. He did not get the job, which both Carter and Brzezinski believed had created bitterness. Kalb claimed in one report that Brzezinski had told Carter that he "owes nothing to the Jews."[74] Brzezinski told the *New York Times* that it was not the kind of thing he would say. "Zbig, Kalb is not interested in accuracy. He wanted to be an ambassador," wrote Carter on the margins of a transcript of one of Kalb's evening reports that Brzezinski had passed on.[75] On a few occasions, Brzezinski had to prod the State Department to issue factual rebuttals.

On the second morning of Begin's visit, the Israeli prime minister invited Brzezinski for breakfast at Blair House, the elegant guest lodging opposite the White House, where foreign leaders are often put up. To Brzezinski's astonishment, the Israeli prime minister had invited a gathering of photographers and reporters to record the moment. Begin then handed him documents from the Jerusalem "golden book" that chronicled how Tadeusz Brzeziński had supplied hundreds of passports and exit visas to German Polish Jews when he was Poland's consul general in Leipzig more than four decades earlier. Brzezinski was profoundly moved.[76] In the context of so many insinuations about his background, Begin's gesture exhibited public and timely generosity; it tapped into Brzezinski's earliest childhood memories. Begin also wrote a personal letter to Tadeusz in Montreal that concluded, "May I add that your son and I are good friends. We respect him highly." That could hardly fail to melt Brzezinski, Jr. They spent the next hour and a half going over Carter's framework for the peace talks. As Carter had discovered the day before, Begin did not show much flexibility and was militantly opposed to ceding Israeli sovereignty over the ancient Jewish lands of Judea and Samaria, as he called the West Bank. They discussed Jabotinsky again. Brzezinski's familiarity with Begin's teacher and Zionism's most inflexible advocate was his mode of seduction. The rapport between the two Polish-born figures would endure.

An irony of the media flap about Brzezinski is that he was not the spearhead of the administration's Arab-Israel effort. Vance and Carter were far more directly involved. At their first NSC meeting on Israel in February, Brzezinski took a dominant role in arguing that Carter's first year was the time to strike.[77] His political capital would deplete and his ability to take risks on the Middle East would fade as his presidency went on, he said. Brzezinski also won the argument that they should aim high. Vance favored a more cautious start.

Since then, however, Vance had taken detailed custody of the process. It was Vance, not Brzezinski, who shuttled Kissinger-style from Tel Aviv to Cairo and often also to Amman, Damascus, and Riyadh. As Begin dug in his heels, Vance also became increasingly stubborn. Prior to Begin's visit, both Vance and Carter had argued that the US should oppose all Israeli settlements in the occupied territories. Brzezinski felt that exceptions could be made, especially for religious settlements. They were all outraged, however, when Begin legalized three Israeli settlements within days of his White House visit during which they thought he had agreed to a freeze. "Son of a bitch," said Carter.[78] Begin had found a semantic loophole to exploit. In August, he unveiled a batch of completely new settlements. Begin seemed to be poking Carter in the eye. Carter told Brzezinski that America had for years been "financing their conquests" and that Israel was continually "making a mockery of our advice and our preferences."[79] The process was unraveling before it began.

Nor was Begin swayed by Carter's strenuous efforts via intermediaries to get Yasser Arafat, the Palestinian leader, to endorse UN Resolutions 242 and 338, which would mean the PLO's recognition of Israel's right to exist. Kissinger had given Israel assurances that the US would not deal with the PLO until it had recognized Israel. Carter had inherited Kissinger's promise. Unlike Rabin, Peres, and others from Israel's supplanted establishment, Begin did not much care whether the PLO recognized Israel since he had no intention of ceding a homeland to the Palestinians. His goal was to strike a bilateral deal with Egyptian president Anwar Sadat and leave the Palestinian issue on the White House cutting-room floor. Sadat, however, to whom Carter instantly warmed—it was "love at first sight," according to Brzezinski—was fighting for his political survival. Much of the Arab world had turned its back on Sadat after he had expelled the Soviets from Egypt. His surprise 1973 Yom Kippur War could in retrospect be seen as a cry for help—a plea to be taken seriously by Israel and the United States.

With Begin intransigent, Arafat elusive, and an emotional Sadat always on the cusp of losing patience, Carter took a risk. After a long meeting with Andrei Gromyko, the Soviet Union's poker-faced foreign minister, the Soviets and Americans issued a joint statement on the Middle East. They unveiled it on October 1 as world leaders were gathering in New York for the annual UN General Assembly. The superpowers called for a grand Middle East conference in Geneva that they would cochair, which would aim for a regional peace settlement and address the "legitimate rights of the Palestinians." Carter's hope, supported by Vance and Brzezinski, was that would pressure Begin to make the kind of concessions he would never contemplate on his own. It would also provide cover for Palestinians to sit at the same table as the Israelis, even if they were part of a larger Arab delegation or in the Jordanian contingent. But Carter made an expensive error: he did not brief Congress or

Jewish organizations in advance about his dramatic move.[80] That the US and the USSR were now apparently on the same side was shocking enough. But their joint endorsement of Palestinians' "legitimate rights" created a furor.

On reading the joint statement, Moshe Dayan, Israel's foreign minister, exploded. A hero of the 1967 Six-Day War, Dayan had lost an eye that he covered with a patch, which gave him a piratical air. "I may only have one eye but I am not blind," he said.[81] The US domestic reaction, which was primed by Dayan and Simcha Dinitz, the Israeli ambassador in Washington, whom Brzezinski saw as untrustworthy (every private conversation between the two had found its way into the media in distorted form), was visceral. When Carter arrived at a Wall Street helipad in New York, he was met by Ed Koch, a candidate for mayor of New York and prominent Jewish Democrat. Koch handed Carter a letter accusing him of abandoning America's "commitments to peace, to Jewish refugees, to the protection of Israel." Coming from a member of Carter's party, a candidate who had been seeking the president's help in his mayoral campaign, Koch's move was tantamount to a middle finger. Bizarrely, Carter chose to interpret it as a "friendly" gesture.[82]

Amid the firestorm, Carter faced a choice of standing firm or retreating. To Brzezinski's and Vance's consternation, he chose the latter. In a statement that Carter, Vance, and Brzezinski wrangled over with Dayan in a hotel suite until the small hours of the morning, Carter climbed down. He did not dilute America's negotiating framework for Geneva. But the impression, particularly in the Arab world, was that he had caved in to Israeli and Jewish American outrage. Brzezinski wrote that Dayan had "effectively blackmailed"[83] Carter by threatening to make their differences public unless he agreed to a US-Israeli statement clarifying the Soviet one.

In the weekly report that Brzezinski gave Carter that Friday, he summarized a lunch conversation he had with James Reston, the *New York Times* columnist who was close to Brzezinski and sympathetic to Carter's Middle East goals. Carter was too easily "intimidated by a highly organized constituency," Reston had told Brzezinski. Carter also lacked any clout with Congress.[84] In fact, Reston had been far blunter than what Brzezinski passed on to Carter. "If [you] do not take the Jewish lobby head-on, Carter will get chopped to pieces and in the end will not have any effective leadership," he said.[85] A few weeks later, Brzezinski warned Carter that his poll ratings were slipping. There was a growing impression that Carter backed down too easily. "To put it simply and quite bluntly [your foreign policy] is seen as 'soft,'" he wrote. Carter, he advised, should make a decision "that has a distinctly 'tough' quality to it."[86] Carter understood Brzezinski's point, which was not just about the Middle East; he was also seen to have softened his stance on the USSR and human rights. In the margin of Brzezinski's note, as though trying to steel himself, Carter wrote, "Don't chicken out."

Throughout his presidency, Carter's sense of resolve would go up and down like a yo-yo. At that moment of impasse it was Sadat's courage that saved the day. The Egyptian president was almost as skeptical of Carter's US-Soviet Geneva plan as Begin. Neither wanted Moscow to have a formal role in the Middle East. Sadat decided to short-circuit Carter's approach. In early November, he announced that he would visit Israel and address the Knesset in a dramatic attempt to win over Begin and the Israeli public. No Arab leader had set foot in the country since its formation. In the absence of a Palestinian homeland, such a move was unthinkable. When Carter heard the news, he abandoned work on a big energy speech he was planning. Sadat's gamble was so "sensational and exciting" that he could think of nothing else.[87]

Sadat was isolated and running out of time and options. Egypt was not a democracy. But Sadat's power depended on upholding his authority with the army and Egypt's religious leaders, neither of which was keen on peace with Israel. He was also bailing out Carter, whose peace efforts had reached an early dead end. Watching it on TV in the White House, Brzezinski saw the unfolding pageant in Jerusalem as "living history." Sadat was betting that Israel would be sufficiently responsive to make up for the accusations of betrayal by the Arab world. On a public relations level it worked; he won the hearts of the Israeli public the moment he stepped on the airport tarmac. There he came face to face with Golda Meir, the former Israeli leader and Egypt's enemy. Sadat broke into a broad smile and embraced her. His courage and warmth melted even the most critical onlookers.

Judging, however, by Begin's continuing inflexibility in the trip's aftermath, Sadat's gesture was initially an anticlimax. Carter, who told Brzezinski that his heart had grown cold to Begin, was always at the point of writing off Israel's prime minister. He thought that Begin had come across as unyielding in response to Sadat's greathearted overture; the Israeli leader should have offered immediate concessions. Brzezinski argued that Begin must be allowed more time. He was learning that nothing in the Middle East happened easily or according to Brookings Institution blueprints. All of them, especially Carter, felt indebted to Sadat. "One cannot help but admire a leader who is willing to take such risks on behalf of a higher cause," Brzezinski wrote. "My only regret is that Carter is not doing it."[88]

Carter was also facing escalating criticism over his part in the nose-diving US-Soviet relationship. Much of the media coverage bore Kissinger's finger-prints, on Brzezinski's reading. One *New York Times* piece ran an unflatter-ing front-page comparison of Kissinger's methods with Brzezinski's that was sprinkled with quotes from a former senior official.[89] In early May 1977, a "peeved" Kissinger telephoned Brzezinski to complain that he kept hearing secondhand that he was being blamed by Brzezinski as a source for many of the stories attacking Carter's foreign policy.[90] Those criticisms were unfair and hurtful, he said.

Brzezinski reminded Kissinger that he was privy to all of the diplomatic cables. At a recent Kissinger lunch with Dobrynin the former had complained that the Carter administration was "too anti-communist." Brzezinski was a "theoretician of anti-communism without practical experience in interna-tional relations," Kissinger said. Dobrynin recalled, "I could almost feel [Kis-singer's] personal satisfaction at the administration's [SALT II] failure." Carter was "so bent on doing things his own way that he would not even repeat the good moves made by his predecessors," Kissinger told the Soviet ambassador. Brzezinski's hint that he was reading such transcripts put Kissinger on the de-fensive. Their call ended with an injured Kissinger protesting his loyalty to Carter.[91]

A few weeks later, Kissinger sought an urgent Oval Office meeting with Carter on a personal matter. Since Kissinger requested that it be private, Brzez-inski did not sit in on the meeting, as he usually would. Afterwards Brzezinski asked Carter what their conversation had been about. Carter laughed. "Oh yes, he came to complain about you, how you are saying that he is critical of our foreign policy and how embarrassing this is to him etc." Brzezinski thought Carter was teasing him. What was Kissinger's real agenda, Brzezinski pressed. "I just told you," Carter said.[92] Kissinger's goal was to continue to get face time with Carter, which he succeeded in doing. He was playing a delicate game. He would be coruscating about Carter in private but said nothing in public that could jeopardize his Oval Office access, which was critical to sustaining his image as an insider.

Towards the end of 1977, Brzezinski was invited to give the traditionally humorous address at Washington's Gridiron Dinner. "Only Churchill could describe how well I've done," he said.[93] "Never in the course of human history have so many been alienated by so few." The widespread notion that he and Vance had fallen out was false, he insisted. "Those stories are unfair. Besides I gave them on deep background." On his relations with Israel, he insisted that Israeli leaders genuinely did like him: "When Moshe Dayan was here, he brought me a present: two eye patches." Likewise, "Former Prime Minister Rabin offered to help me handle my bank account." There was also a joke about his Polishness. He summarized Carter's foreign policy in a string of indigestible Polish phrases. His biggest laugh line, however, was about Kissinger. "There are some things that get me down, like how everybody tries to compare me to Henry Kissinger," he said. "We are old friends and my admiration for him is as enormous as his is for me." He ended with this summary of Carter's foreign policy philosophy: "Henry Kissinger, *moze byc, innedo zdania* [it may be different to your opinion]."[94]

At a meeting with Carter at around the same time, Kissinger offered his services to Carter as an envoy on "diplomatic missions," presumably in the Middle East. Brzezinski warned Carter that he would be "digging his political grave" if he hired Kissinger to play an official role for him. "If Kissinger succeeded, his would be the credit. If he failed, Carter would be blamed."[95] Carter saw the point, but Kissinger did not relent. Turning down Kissinger's recurring application to be Carter's envoy was one issue on which Brzezinski and Vance were viscerally united. Kissinger had far more room and inclination to attack Brzezinski than Carter directly. In a piece in *Esquire*, he was quoted describing Brzezinski as an "opportunist." That was mild compared to what some others were saying. A long *Newsweek* article published in early May 1977 noted Stanley Hoffmann's views at length: "Brzezinski, to use Kissinger's favorite phrase, is not a conceptual thinker. Brzezinski thinks he is but I don't believe it. He is an activist and a highly tactical man. What is lacking in him is the one thing Kissinger had, whatever his flaws—the notion of an overall strategy."[96]

That was false. Whether it was a good one or not, Brzezinski possessed a strategy, and it had been largely unchanged for almost thirty years. Unlike Kissinger, however, who had had carte blanche from Nixon to run foreign policy without regard to the rest of the administration, Brzezinski was in a constant war of attrition with Vance's State. In Carter's first two years, Brzezinski won some battles and lost others. He succeeded in nearly doubling the budget of Radio Free Europe, which had been dying a slow death over the previous eight years. Kissinger saw the broadcaster as an irritant to the Soviets.

The Left thought that the radio operation was an outdated propaganda outlet. Senator Fulbright dismissed RFE as a "relic of the Cold War."[97] Since RFE was not a weapons system, the hawkish Right paid it little attention. Vance's State distrusted anything that could upset SALT II. As a result, the service was in decline and needed considerable investment to break through the Warsaw Pact's increasingly effective jamming systems. Brzezinski secured it. Jan Nowak, the former head of the Polish section, dubbed Brzezinski "the patron saint of RFE."

Also against State's opposition, Brzezinski convinced Carter to issue a presidential directive that laid out his strategy for direct diplomacy in Eastern Europe, rather than through Moscow. This was a sharp departure from the previous eight years. PD-21 said that the US would make overtures to the more flexible Eastern European regimes, including Poland, Hungary, and Romania. The Czechs and East Germans were considered too hostile to be worth engaging. The new presidential declaration added nothing to the budget but signaled a marked shift in Cold War tactics.

Brzezinski's efforts at peaceful engagement earned him a new enemy: the West German chancellor, Helmut Schmidt of the Social Democratic Party (SPD). Though they had been running across each other for years at conferences without incident, their relationship degenerated into a feud after Carter took office. Their first clash was in London in May 1977. It was Carter's coming-out party on the global stage: a G6 summit followed by a NATO one, both hosted by James Callaghan, Britain's Labour prime minister. Carter already knew about Schmidt's criticisms of him from the German media and through third parties (Callaghan had written a "personal and secret"[98] letter warning Carter about Schmidt). During the 1976 campaign, the West German chancellor had said publicly that he hoped Ford would be reelected, which was a breach of diplomatic protocol.[99] Since Ford's defeat, he had criticized Carter's "missionary zeal"[100] and his aggressive opening offer on SALT II. He was close to Brezhnev, whose cooperation he needed for the success of *Ostpolitik*, Bonn's charm offensive on East Germany.

The rules of *Ostpolitik* dictated that Bonn make no criticisms of East Germany's domestic repression. Schmidt and Brezhnev kept up an eccentric running dialogue via exchange of cassette tapes on which they each recorded their private thoughts. Schmidt also offered Carter his services as an intermediary between the White House and the Kremlin. On Brzezinski's advice, Carter turned him down. Schmidt's bottom line was that he needed full-blown détente to maximize the chances of Germany's reunification. The new US president was getting in the way of that. Carter's meeting with Soviet dissidents broke "the code of détente," which said that Western leaders should not kick up a fuss about what was going on behind the Iron Curtain. Schmidt was Europe's Kissinger but without the guile.

When Schmidt's name arose during a prep session for the London trip. Carter said, "He's been quite obnoxious to me."[101] To Carter's annoyance, Brzezinski pointed out that Schmidt might feel the same way about him. A few weeks earlier, with little warning, Carter threatened to halt shipments of nuclear fuel from the US to West Germany, thus jeopardizing a large German business deal to build an enrichment plant in Brazil. At a time when West Germany and others were trying to shift to civil nuclear power at home to insure themselves against OPEC's weaponization of oil, Carter's preachiness about nuclear safeguards was not going down well. It could have been far worse. In March, the State Department's Richard Holbrooke and Joseph Nye, Jr., had pleaded with Brzezinski to intervene with Carter at the last minute to stop him from making an even more sweeping proclamation on nuclear proliferation.[102] Since the allies had not been given advance notice, Carter's statement would cause diplomatic harm. Europe was increasingly grumbling about America's "technological imperialism." There was also friction with Britain and France over the new supersonic Concorde's US landing rights, which had been suspended by a local judge after protestors converged on JFK Airport complaining of noise pollution.

Vance, who was a conflict avoider, did not want a showdown with the president, though the objections were coming from his people. At Holbrooke and Nye's urging, Brzezinski agreed to confront the president. He arm-twisted an irritated Carter into delaying the announcement so that US diplomats would have more time to soften the impact with America's allies. "Mark this one down," Carter told Brzezinski. "This one is for you and it won't happen too often." Zbig told Nye, "You can tell Cy [Vance] that I pulled his bacon out of the fire this time but I won't do it all of the time."[103] Privately, he said that he was "appalled at Cy's unwillingness to take Carter on when he feels strongly about a subject." More generally, he deplored the tendency of Carter's team to "nod their heads and agree with everything he says."[104] He had not come that far to be a yes-man.

The back-to-back London summits were a success. The British media and most of Carter's fellow leaders hailed him as a man of the people and a US leader who had caught the mood of the times—"a breath of fresh air in the Western world," in Callaghan's words. He was also an unexpected hit with the UK tabloids. "Jimmy Stars in the Big Summit Show" was the *Daily Mirror*'s welcoming headline. Carter flattered his hosts by saying it was no accident that his first overseas trip as president was to the land of his ancestors. Large crowds greeted him wherever he went. His itinerary included a side trip with the prime minister to Newcastle, the most depressed city in England's Northeast.

Carter signaled that the United States was returning to the heart of NATO following years of neglect under Ford and Nixon. He promised major new US military commitments. His goal was to reassure his counterparts that the Nixon shocks and Kissinger's widely derided "year of Europe" were behind them. Carter was already retreating from his campaign pledge to cut defense spending by between $5 billion and $7 billion. The Pentagon's budget had fallen in real terms by almost 40 percent in the previous eight years.[105] Carter's U-turn on military spending was slow but cumulatively dramatic. The London trip was the first public glimpse of Carter's grudging change of mind. Later that year, he denied to Brzezinski that he had agreed to a 3 percent real annual increase in the Pentagon's budget. Brzezinski insisted that he had as part of a collective NATO pledge. Carter lost his cool and said that he would "kiss [your] fanny" if Brzezinski could find proof.[106] Evidence was duly supplied. Against his instincts, Carter restored US military spending to pre-Nixon levels.

Callaghan, or "Sunny Jim," as he was known because of his chirpy persona, wanted some of Carter's high approval ratings to rub off on him. The Labour Party was sinking in the polls. Carter met with Callaghan's nemesis, Margaret Thatcher, the opposition Conservative leader, at Winfield House, the US ambassador's London residence, where he was staying. The rest of the team, including Vance and Brzezinski, had rooms at Claridge's. Thatcher made the mistake of telling Carter that she had read many of Brzezinski's books. Brzezinski winced inwardly. "She might have done better had she mentioned Carter's own book," he noted.[107] At a second meeting later that year, Brzezinski found Thatcher to be "tough, outspoken but rather shallow. . . . She really was better at articulating slogans than dealing with issues."[108] Carter had asked her what she thought about British participation in the nuclear test ban treaty. Thatcher looked blank. After Carter explained what he was talking about, Thatcher said, "Oh, yes, of course, of course."[109]

Brzezinski and Carter usually had the same reading of other leaders. Carter did not seem to mind their occasional stand-up fights. He would often say that apart from his family, Brzezinski was always his first choice as seatmate on long flights because he had so much to say. "We might argue, but I would never be bored," Carter wrote.[110] Their affinity went further than a shared yen for policy debate. While the presidential motorcade whisked through London, they caught each other staring at "a rather striking black-haired woman in a white dress." Having been caught ogling, Carter laughed sheepishly. He had already admitted to the world that he had sometimes lusted in his heart; Brzezinski found it amusing that his grace-saying boss had "an eye for good-looking women."[111]

Carter felt an element of dread about his first meeting with Helmut Schmidt. The media were building it up to be a clash. It did not go well. When they met in London, Brzezinski irritated Schmidt by addressing him as "Helmut" in response to the West German leader's informal "Hi, Zbig." During the meeting, a visibly anxious Schmidt kept reaching for his snuffbox. He suggested that Carter and Brezhnev hold a summit soon in a neutral country. Turning to Vance, Carter said that was a good idea. Brzezinski interrupted to say that it was Brezhnev's turn to come to America. The last US-Soviet summit had been held in Vladivostok in 1974. Brezhnev had visited the US in 1973, and Nixon went to Moscow in 1972. It was almost three years since a summit had been held anywhere.

To Schmidt's annoyance, Brzezinski said Alaska would be a more fitting venue. He and Schmidt then clashed over Radio Free Europe, which the West German leader asked Carter to move to another country. Brzezinski replied that the fate of RFE's Munich operation "could not be decided unilaterally or outside the larger security context."[112] Should the radio station have to move, he said, other US assets might follow. Schmidt tore into Brzezinski, saying that RFE was "contrary to détente" and hinting that he would cancel RFE's license to broadcast from West German soil. Carter and Brzezinski shared private jokes about Schmidt's platform shoes, which made him an inch taller than the US president. At five foot eight, he was actually two inches shorter. "Schmidt has in some ways become more and more of a poseur," Brzezinski thought.[113]

The Carter White House's relationship with Schmidt only worsened. Schmidt thought that Brzezinski "presented himself unabashedly as the self-assured agent of a world power."[114] That was not far off. Brzezinski, in turn, said that Schmidt, from their "very first encounter, adopted a patronizing attitude, mixed with less than persuasive protestations of friendship."[115] Ditto. In his diary, meanwhile, Carter wrote that Schmidt's fluctuating moods reminded him that "women are not the only ones that have periods."[116] Menachem Begin often enraged Carter. But Schmidt was the only foreign leader he genuinely detested. By contrast, Carter and Brzezinski found Callaghan "genial" and France's Valéry Giscard d'Estaing "engaging" though occasionally "monarchical."[117] The problem went deeper than a clash of personalities. "Schmidt acts as if détente were his private preserve and openly castigates the US human rights policy," wrote Bill Odom in a note that Brzezinski included in Carter's weekly briefing.[118] Part of Schmidt's angst was that West Germany's opposition Christian Democrats were increasingly critical of *Ostpolitik*. It was no longer paying high dividends.

Schmidt was just one voice, albeit a weighty and often vinegary one, among a growing chorus urging Carter to get détente back on track. At White House meetings, Brzezinski and Vance were relatively cordial and often able to cut through the amplified strains between their staffs. They set up a weekly meal that included the Pentagon's Harold Brown, which was known as the VBB (Vance, Brown, Brzezinski) lunch. At Carter's request, they also instituted a foreign policy breakfast every Friday, which Carter said was his favorite event of the week. The president would ask someone to say grace before the meal. Often he would turn to Vance, Brown, or Mondale. Brzezinski's grace-saying skills were judged to be poor. In four years, Carter asked him to do it only once. The breakfast soon expanded to Hamilton Jordan after he complained that domestic politics were being given short shrift. Each of the attendees was billed $1.75. For the time being, relations between Vance and Brzezinski were manageable.

Since the Moscow debacle in April, Vance had regained a measure of control over the SALT II process. The plan was for talks to proceed at three levels: among technical experts in Geneva, between Vance and Gromyko in regular bilateral encounters, and between Carter and Brezhnev if the talks hit a roadblock. Carter was keen on a summit with Brezhnev but kept being brushed off by Moscow. Like many leaders, he had deep faith in his ability to win the day with the sincerity of his case. Brzezinski thought that Carter came across as too keen for a summit, which betrayed a whiff of desperation. The Soviets kept saying that they would agree to a summit only after a SALT II treaty had been nailed down. Carter thought that was backwards; his personal impact could yield a breakthrough.

What the Americans did not know was that Brezhnev had suffered a stroke two years earlier. It had happened shortly after the Vladivostok summit. Indeed, the Soviet leader blamed his physical setback on the strains of that meeting with Ford.[119] This was partly why he was so obdurate in his insistence that Carter stick to the nuclear limits to which he and Ford had agreed. In his mind, negotiating those concessions had cost him his health. He was also drinking heavily and taking various medications, which meant that he was now routinely slurring his words. He could scarcely preside over a Politburo meeting, let alone hold his own with a new president who played tennis and jogged every day. To the rest of the world, he seemed to be freezing Carter out for psychological effect. In reality, the Politburo was keeping him out of view for medical reasons. The thorniest issues would have to be settled between Vance and Gromyko.

Brzezinski thought that Vance's disastrous Moscow meeting had been positive for the US on two counts: it revealed to the world that the USSR was opposed to serious arms reductions, and it put Moscow on the defensive over human rights. America now wielded a weapon that was just as potent as the Soviet Union's international class struggle. As it happened, 1977 was the year that Amnesty International, the human rights group, won the Nobel Peace Prize. Brzezinski's assessment had some merit. But a rattled Carter now wanted to correct course with Moscow. He gave Vance license to pursue SALT II on much softer terms. The outline of what Vance and Gromyko began to negotiate fell somewhere between what had been decided upon at Vladivostok and the ambitious package that Moscow rejected. As the arms talks went on, it became clear that Carter's opening bid had set him up for possible failure. Carter's first offer had established an ambitious benchmark against which whatever deal Vance negotiated would be compared. Getting the Soviets to agree to some kind of nuclear deal was one thing; persuading skeptical senators to ratify a treaty by a two-thirds majority was quite another. As Vance's talks went on, the latter became the bigger headache. Every concession Vance made cost Carter another potential Senate vote.

Carter further damaged his cause on Capitol Hill in June when he canceled the Pentagon's prized B-1 bomber program, which was to replace the storied B-52. At more than $100 million per plane, the B-1 was too extravagant for Carter's tastes. He also knew but could not publicly disclose that the Pentagon's forthcoming B-2 stealth bomber would render the B-1 obsolete. At the same time, he said he would accelerate America's new cruise missile program, which had far more strategic punch. His move nevertheless fueled the image of a president too easily pulled in contrasting directions. The B-1 cancellation had been a campaign promise. Both Brzezinski and Vance agreed with Carter's decision to honor it. In this instance Brown was the odd one out. If two of the three agreed, Carter usually sided with the majority. As time went on, Brown and Brzezinski would increasingly join forces, particularly over the game-changing potential of America's next generation of nuclear weapons. Mondale, Jordan, and sometimes Eizenstat could force a domestic calculation into Carter's mind. In general he reacted badly to being told that doing the right thing would lose him votes. The ax on B-1 meant instant loss of ten thousand high-paying jobs. It would also sacrifice Carter's credibility with more hawkish senators, such as Scoop Jackson and Georgia's Sam Nunn. Senate opposition to SALT II was growing and could prove fatal.

Another example of Carter's harmful tendency to vacillate was the "neutron bomb," an enhanced-radiation weapon. The bomb relied on a low-yield thermonuclear blast to spread radiation. Carter hated the idea of it. Technically the neutron bomb had nothing to do with SALT II, which was exclusively about strategic (long-range) nuclear weapons. Tactical weapons, such as the neutron bomb, were for short-range army use on the battlefield. Intermediate-range nuclear weapons, such as the Soviet SS-20s, were also outside the parameters of SALT II. As the only nonnuclear power among Europe's big three—France and Britain each having its own arsenal—West Germany felt vulnerable. It also hosted more US troops than the rest of Europe combined. Schmidt called the arrangement a "master-vassal relationship."[120] West Germany thus had the least say in Europe's nuclear future yet the most at stake. He had a point.

In a high-impact speech in late October to London's International Institute for Strategic Studies, Schmidt complained that America's nuclear umbrella over Europe was leaky. The US and the USSR were negotiating a reduction in the ICBMs that targeted each other, but America was ignoring the huge buildup of Soviet intermediate-range missiles aimed solely at Europe. The United States had nothing to match them. Schmidt was playing on an old European fear of America decoupling its nuclear strategy from Europe. As de Gaulle had once put it, "Would you risk Chicago for Bonn?" Though the neutron bomb was a short-range tactical weapon and therefore had no impact on Schmidt's concern about Europe's "theater of operations" or America's "Euromissile" gap with the Soviets, its fate turned into a kind of bellwether of the transatlantic relationship.

In June 1977, Brzezinski's old friend Walter Pincus, who had taken part in his effort to sabotage the Soviet youth festival at Vienna eighteen years earlier, introduced Americans to the neutron bomb. Almost no one had heard of it before Pincus's front-page piece in the *Washington Post* titled "Neutron Killer Warhead Buried in ERDA [Energy Research and Development Administration] Budget."[121] From then on the weapon was a public obsession, especially in Europe. The neutron bomb terrified people because it killed by radiation, rather than blast. That meant it preserved buildings while incinerating enemy soldiers. Its deployment would help deter the Soviets' massive advantage in conventional forces in Europe. Since it largely left property intact, the Soviets ingeniously dubbed it the "capitalist bomb." Brzezinski was furious about Pincus's scoop. At a White House briefing for reporters, Pincus turned up late. As he was walking to his seat, Brzezinski said, "I was just telling everyone about how you and I were in Vienna for the CIA."[122] This was not a friendly act towards a self-respecting journalist. Pincus had in fact gone to Vienna at his own expense, not the CIA's. Their friendship lapsed for several years after that. But Pincus's front-page stories kept coming. Years later, Harold Brown said that the neutron bomb would have been quietly deployed had it not been for Pincus's reporting.

Brzezinski and Brown now had a problem. Not only was European public opinion becoming more antinuclear, but Carter's heart seemed to be with the protestors. After several agonizing Oval Office sessions, Brzezinski, Brown, and others persuaded him to go ahead with the neutron bomb if Schmidt would publicly ask Carter to deploy them. In so doing, Carter was passing the responsibility on to Bonn. Schmidt's foreign minister, Hans-Dietrich Genscher, flew to Washington to insist that another European power also make the request; West Germany could not take such a stand in isolation. Carter suggested Britain. Genscher insisted that he needed another "continental European" power.[123] Carter volunteered the Dutch and the Danish because of their proximity to the Iron Curtain.

In September, Brzezinski toured the European big three. He met for two hours apiece with Giscard at the Elysée Palace and Callaghan at 10 Downing Street and had a long session with Schmidt at his more modest offices in Bonn. Alighting from his military jet to be greeted by US ambassadors was clearly to Brzezinski's taste. On this occasion he and Schmidt got along and agreed to call each other by their first names. Brzezinski's trip, amid a flurry of lower-level ones, helped bring Schmidt on board. All the German leader now had to do was to get parliamentary approval to host the neutron bomb. A few months later, he secured it. A day after that, a conscience-stricken Carter announced that he was deferring production of the neutron bomb. Schmidt had done everything Carter had asked of him. Then Carter buckled. Brzezinski, who had done his utmost to persuade Carter "not to waver," was unhappy. He described it as Carter's worst decision in his fourteen-month presidency. He tried to persuade Carter to think again. "Zbig, I must say you never give up," Carter wrote.[124] Schmidt never trusted either of them again.

In an Oval Office meeting, Carter complained to Brzezinski and Brown that the bureaucracy was constantly putting the brakes on decisions and second-guessing ones he thought he had already made. He was livid and holding a paper-cutting knife while he was talking. Brzezinski said he hoped Carter was not planning to use it.[125] His quip broke the tension. In a handwritten note to Brzezinski about cruise missiles, Carter said, "Zbig, you have obviously tried time after time to change my decision and with varying words have succeeded to some degree." Brzezinski replied, "I profoundly resent your statement which more than implies that I deliberately distorted your position. That is simply not true."[126] Carter acknowledged Brzezinski's point and backed off. But he was feeling the pressure. The media portrayed Carter's vacillation as the product of contrasting advice from Vance and Brzezinski. But the ultimate battle was taking place inside his head. As a former nuclear submarine officer, he understood the technicalities of weapons systems better than any of his advisors, except for Brown. Brzezinski had little clue about the science. Jessica Tuchman once had to draw him a diagram of the nuclear fuel cycle to help him grasp a paper on nonproliferation that she had written.[127]

Carter needed no such instruction. But he was also a preacher. Sunday school Carter and naval engineer Carter were in conflict. His way of tackling his policy dilemmas was to absorb as much detail as possible. He took his reading habits to self-parodying lengths. In late 1977, Brzezinski gave Carter a long and abstruse paper about the reorganization of the US intelligence community. The underlying document was so long that the covering memo ran to six pages. Brzezinski told him just to read the executive summary and sign at the bottom. A day later, Carter returned the document to Brzezinski with a covering handwritten memo. The president had read the whole document and was complaining about the paragraph numbering. He even disputed its system of subnumbering, as well as the usual grammatical errors. "The President doesn't know when to stop reading," Brzezinski thought.[128] Carter frequently complained about being overloaded. But he was author of his overwork. In periodic discussions about the Carter reading problem, Brzezinski and other advisors, including Vance, concluded that the patient was past the point of healing. Some presidents are unburdened by their ignorance. Carter was haunted by his, even on issues about which he knew far more than his advisors.

In April 1977, Carter had enthusiastically signed off on a ten-point plan of the administration's first-term foreign policy goals drawn up by Brzezinski's staff. The list was closely held; Vance did not receive a copy, and it was never leaked to the media. Whenever Carter wavered in his resolve, Brzezinski would brandish the document to remind him of his goals. Among its items were a strategic arms *reduction* with the Soviets, as opposed to arms *limitation*, a normalization of US relations with China, a Middle East comprehensive settlement, and a curb on the global armaments trade. The first item on the list was to bind Western Europe and Japan into a network of closer political and economic co-operation. It was vintage Trilateralism. Brzezinski included it both a riposte to Kissinger's great-power obsession and to signal strategic encirclement of the USSR. Carter's first overseas visit to London had broadly advanced that goal.

Many of the Trilateral Commission's other priorities, including trade liberalization, monetary coordination, and a strengthening of NATO were part of that first item. Beyond that, the commission's shadow quickly faded. As both Ford and Nixon had done, Carter hosted its members at the White House when the group met in Washington. Brzezinski, to the annoyance of Kissinger, who had joined the commission's executive committee, also addressed the group's annual meeting in Bonn in late 1977. Brzezinski's key line was that "human rights is an idea whose historic time has come."[129] But he also dwelt on the "broader malaise" that had afflicted the West in the previous few years. Kissinger complained to Carter and others that Brzezinski's speech was too critical of Carter's immediate predecessors.[130] Brzezinski had welcomed new Trilateral Commission members, including Henry Kissinger. "Be patient, there's hope for you also!" he needled. Kissinger's complaint was about Brzezinski's allegedly disrespectful substance, not that quip. As was now almost metronomically predictable, Brzezinski and Kissinger struck an amicable but short-lived cease-fire a couple of weeks later over lunch at Sans Souci.

In the public's mind, the Trilateral Commission's tentacles were spreading. From Lyndon LaRouche's cultists to various evangelical figures, it was now the leading bugbear of every conspiracist. In a widely read three-part series for *Penthouse* that ran in late 1977 and early 1978, the investigative journalist Craig S. Karpel claimed to show proof that David Rockefeller's group was now running the world. "Watergate was someone named Martinez breaking into the office of the Democratic National Committee in the dead of night," he wrote.[131] "Cartergate is David Rockefeller breaking into the Oval Office in broad daylight."

In the week before Carter was inaugurated, the *Washington Post* reported that Trilateral Commission members were dominating his senior appointments.[132] That was an understatement, said Karpel. "The Trilateral Commission *is* the Carter administration."[133] The man in control was not Carter but Brzezinski. He and Rockefeller had picked a pliable, unknown governor from Georgia and groomed him for the White House. Their plan had worked. They were now in charge. The second part of the *Penthouse* series anointed Brzezinski as "the Real President."[134] Karpel's third (and final) consecutive story had a cartoon of Brzezinski in a Mao suit on the cover under the headline "Chairman Brzezinski's Thoughts."[135] Though Karpel was from the left, the Trilateral trope grew in equal bounds on both extremes. It would be deployed to some effect by Ronald Reagan in the 1980 campaign. Reagan's chief rival, George H. W. Bush, resigned from the commission in advance of the 1980 primaries to inoculate himself against Reagan's attacks.

In practice, differences between former members of the Trilateral Commission bedeviled the Carter administration. The recently Trilateralized Kissinger's ongoing polemic from the sidelines further exacerbated those breaches. One such issue was the itinerary of Carter's first lengthy foreign trip as president. Other than his spring summits in London, he did not leave the United States during his first eleven months in office. Brzezinski persuaded him that his first full-blown foreign trip should be a global tour of "regional influentials" to deepen America's ties with rising new powers, such as India, Iran, Saudi Arabia, Nigeria, and Venezuela. As an evangelist, Carter had no trouble signing on to Brzezinski's expansive idea. The goal of "strengthening North-South relations" was third on his list of foreign policy priorities. It was the result of Brzezinski's evolved thinking over the previous decade in which he aimed to broaden America's horizons beyond the "East-West" prism and to recognize that the Cold War's front lines were shifting to the Third World.

Ceding control of the Panama Canal was part of that agenda. It also fit into Brzezinski's idea that the US should abandon the long-standing Monroe Doctrine, by which Washington asserted its sphere of influence over the

Western Hemisphere. The US could hardly dispute the USSR's claim to its own spheres of interest in Europe and central Asia while America was clinging to its own. Giving the tiny nation of Panama sovereignty over the vast canal that traversed its territory would demonstrate America's principled new approach to hemispheric relations. But the North-South idea proved too hazy for most of the rest of the bureaucracy, including the State Department. Foggy Bottom saw it as a distraction from Carter's big priorities. Carter's six-nation tour, which was meant to start before Christmas, kept being knocked off the agenda. Brzezinski kept putting it back on. Eventually, he got his way. The first nation on Carter's itinerary—and the destination of his first official state visit as US president—was Poland.

Confusion over the purpose of Carter's nine-day excursion drowned out the strategic import of the Polish leg. It was also the most contested part of the itinerary within the administration. Because it was Poland and because Brzezinski had been raised there, the media wrote it off as a concession by Carter to his national security advisor's sentiments. A few days before they left, Brzezinski undertook a torturous media briefing session in which he failed to make his point about the significance of what Carter wanted to accomplish in Poland. The visit would include the first open press conference by a US president on Warsaw Pact soil. Brzezinski would also drop by for a meeting with the Polish Catholic primate, Cardinal Stefan Wyszyński. It would also be the first time a US president had visited a Warsaw Pact country without having first been in Moscow. Brzezinski failed to convey Poland's "peaceful engagement" context to the media. "I can't improve on what I've tried to do for about an hour," the exasperated Brzezinski said after a journalist asked how Carter's trip to Poland differed from that of Nixon or Ford. "I am sorry. I will just have to leave you unsatisfied."[136]

By contrast, the State Department grasped Poland's significance and tried to remove it from the itinerary. Vance saw Carter's visit and his plans to showcase human rights as a needless provocation to the Soviets and another risk to SALT II. Human rights dominated the running feud between Vance and Brzezinski. After Vance had returned from his unhappy opening trip to Moscow in April, he gave a well-publicized speech implicitly criticizing Carter's emphasis on human rights. Those, he said, should be pursued "less stridently" and through quiet diplomacy. He also enraged Brzezinski by declaring that Brezhnev and Carter had "similar dreams and aspirations about the most fundamental issues."[137] They clashed again that summer over the significance of the meeting in Belgrade of the Conference on Security and Cooperation in Europe (CSCE), a product of Helsinki. Vance wanted his deputy, the mild-mannered, conciliatory Warren Christopher, to lead the US delegation. Brzezinski persuaded Carter that the more outspoken Arthur Goldberg, a former Supreme Court justice and civil rights advocate, should take the position.[138] As a result of Goldberg's grandstanding, Moscow was on the defensive throughout the conference. The US led the way in pointing out the USSR's failure to live up to its Helsinki commitments on human rights.

Little of what took place in Belgrade caught the US media's attention. But it was followed very closely by dissident groups in the Warsaw Pact countries. Poland's leader, Edward Gierek, released several dissidents shortly before the Belgrade conference. His priority was to secure the US trade credits and soft loans that Carter was dangling. He also pushed hard for Carter to visit Poland, which he knew would help unlock some of the economic relief Warsaw so desperately needed. Vance's State chose to overlook Poland's growing open-mindedness. The US ambassador to Poland, Richard Davies, a career Foreign Service officer, protested stridently against the first lady's plan to visit Cardinal Wyszyński on the trip. "This is wrong! No, no, no!" he said.[139] Davies was repeating the standard line that the US delegation should do nothing to antagonize the host government. Visiting a Church leader and preaching about human rights would enflame the Polish Communists and break with US diplomatic precedent, Davies said. Neither Nixon nor Ford had made his hosts uncomfortable. Nor should Carter. That was the end of Davies's career. Carter fired him. In Brzezinski's eyes, Davies had committed the unforgivable sin of representing Poland's government to the United States rather than vice versa. Even by that metric, however, Davies had erred; he had failed to observe the Polish government's willingness to be flexible with Carter.

Carter's two-day visit to Poland in late December 1977 is best remembered for the mistakes of the State Department's hapless interpreter, Steven Seymour. On his arrival at Warsaw's Okecie Airport, Carter gave opening comments to the assembled Polish dignitaries. Unfortunately, his words were misinterpreted. In English, he said that he was glad to be in Poland. In the Polish translation, he was rendered as having said he had abandoned America and come to live in Poland. In English, he then said that he wanted to get to know the Polish people better. In the Polish translation, he was rendered as having expressed the desire to have sex with Poles. Though Seymour was an accomplished multilingual interpreter, he conflated his primary

Russian-language skills with his secondary Polish one. His gaffes dominated media coverage.[140]

Aside from that distraction, Carter's Poland visit had a profound impact on Poland's nascent civic opposition. In contrast to East Germany and Czechoslovakia, where the regimes kept a tight grip on religion and civil society, Poland's Catholic Church was virtually untouchable. In spite of decades of Communist rule, Poland's deep nationalist spirit was undimmed. Partly with Rockefeller Foundation funding, Poland's Communist government had permitted the reconstruction of Warsaw's royal castle, which had been razed by the Nazis—a project that had only just been completed. Unlike other Warsaw Pact nations, Poland had strong links between its workers and intellectuals, who, together with the Church, presented a formidably challenging trifecta to a regime that claimed a monopoly on political legitimacy. In other Communist states, a flare-up by workers or dissidents could be dealt with separately. Churches had also been closed down or co-opted. Poland was not only the largest Eastern European nation by far; for Carter's foreign policy purposes, it was also Washington's easiest target. Carter's goal, incited by Brzezinski and doggedly opposed by Vance, was to take the ideological offensive to the Soviets. It worked in Poland yet went largely unnoticed in the US. In contrast to Nixon and Ford's stopovers on their way back from Moscow, Warsaw did not lock up any dissidents in advance of Carter's visit.

Brzezinski withheld knowledge until the last moment of Rosalynn Carter's addition to the Wyszyński meeting. Even the cardinal was caught unawares, at first mistaking the first lady for Brzezinski's wife. The three chatted amiably for ninety minutes about Poland's delicate situation. Brzezinski handed Wyszyński a letter from Carter that said, "I share your faith. I admire what you represent. I seek the same goals."[141] The real significance was that they had met at all. It was also in Carter's unabashed support for human rights, which he enunciated at the press conference and in his speech at the state dinner. His visits to the Tomb of the Unknown Soldier, the Warsaw Ghetto, and the Monument to the Heroes of Warsaw (also known as the Nike monument) attracted large crowds. Regime supporters were among them. Brzezinski steered Carter to the spontaneous sections of onlookers who were chanting "Carter, Carter!" Some of them were even yelling "Brzezinski!" In his memoirs, Hamilton Jordan wrote that Vance did not possess an ounce of ego, while Brzezinski had several pounds.[142] Carter's Poland visit did nothing to disabuse that contrast. Vance played a dutiful background role as accompanying senior

dignitary, allowing Brzezinski to soak up attention. While Vance remained si-
lently in place, Brzezinski broke the ranks to banter with veterans of the Polish
Home Army.[143]

Comic misinterpretations aside, the opening Polish leg of the world tour
delighted Carter. On New Year's Eve, the presidential delegation arrived in
Tehran for the second stop of his six-nation itinerary. History records the Iran
part of his trip somewhat differently from how his delegation experienced it
at the time. They should have realized that something was amiss by the sheer
volume of security that greeted their arrival. Iranian soldiers and police lined
the entire route between the national airport and downtown Tehran, their
backs turned to the motorcade so they could be alert to potential trouble. Ten
days after Carter's visit to Iran, protests broke out that would not subside until
Carter's host, Shah Mohammed Reza Pahlavi, fled into exile thirteen months
later. On the last day of 1977, Carter, Brzezinski, and the rest were oblivious
to Iran's ominous undercurrents. In a toast that evening at the state banquet
at Tehran's Niavaran Palace, Carter hailed the shah as a beloved leader of his
people. "Iran is an *island of stability* [my italics] in one of the more troubled
areas of the world," he said.[144] These were the most infamous words he uttered
as president.

The Sands of Ogaden

In mid-1978, a journalist asked Brzezinski why the State Department objected so strongly whenever Carter raised human rights with the Soviets. "Because they are concerned that the Soviets might become so irritated that they will be unwilling to accept our concessions," Brzezinski quipped.[1] Evans and Novak were only too happy to use that quote. By the start of Carter's second year, the war of attrition between Foggy Bottom and the NSC's corner of the West Wing was threatening to degenerate into full-pitched battle. The rough verdict on Carter's first year was that his foreign policy was adrift and likely heading for the rocks. The United States and the Soviet Union were at loggerheads; the SALT II negotiations were going nowhere; and the Middle East initiative had stalled. In spite of Sadat's historic trip to Jerusalem, Begin was continuing to expand Israeli settlements in the occupied territories. There was a growing risk, meanwhile, that the Senate would reject the Panama Canal Treaty, which could prove fatal to Carter's parlous authority. The bottom line was that Carter lacked a clear foreign policy win. His temperament was coming under the microscope: one day he blew hot; the next day, cold. It was getting harder to ignore that he was hopelessly torn between Vance and Brzezinski. Sooner or later, one would surely have to go. A Washington straw poll would undoubtedly have awarded that honor to Brzezinski.

Brzezinski was aware that he was the media's number one target. Yet he only fought his corner harder. He could often rely on support from Carter's

political team, led by Hamilton Jordan and backed by White House press secretary Jody Powell. Carter's reputation for second-guessing himself was harming his public standing. Harold Brown, who was in many respects the swing
vote, was also siding more often with Brzezinski against Vance. In his second
weekly report to Carter of 1978, Brzezinski assessed where the administration
had gone wrong and what it had done right. He conceded that they had under-
estimated the strength of America's pro-Israel lobby. "Part of the problem is of
our own making," he admitted. They had also failed to anticipate the depth of
Soviet aversion to Carter's stances on arms control and human rights, which
had "stiffened their resistance."

On the plus side, Carter had lifted America's profile in the Third World,
particularly sub-Saharan Africa and Latin America. And he had made overtures to the more flexible regimes behind the Iron Curtain. In spite of the mis-
translations, his visit to Poland had been a win. Brzezinski's big takeaway was
that Carter needed to stiffen his resolve. "We can even gain some political
support if, from time to time, we seem to be adopting a somewhat tougher
conservative posture," he wrote.[2] He recommended two courses of action for
the coming year. First, it was time to play the China card. "I should visit Peking," he wrote. Second, Carter needed to spell out to Brezhnev that "there
is no such thing as a selective and compartmentalized détente." The Soviets
must not be allowed to think that they could quarantine SALT II from their
ongoing sponsorship of international revolution.

In early 1978, the administration's chief fault line ran through the Horn of
Africa, which threatened to host the world's next big proxy war. In late 1977,
Somalia's president, Mohammed Siad Barre, had expelled Soviet advisors after
war broke out with neighboring Ethiopia. Confusingly, both were Marxist client regimes; Ethiopia's revolutionary leader, Mengistu Haile Mariam, had in
1974 overthrown Emperor Haile Selassie. The Soviets responded to Ethiopia's request for military support after Somali forces occupied Ethiopia's sand-
swept Ogaden region in mid-1977. Much as in Angola, to which Fidel Castro's
Cuba had sent thirty-six thousand soldiers and civilian personnel to support
its Communist insurgency, Moscow was letting the Cubans take the lead in
Ethiopia. But the Soviet presence was escalating. Somalia had swapped the
USSR's patronage for America's; Moscow was now doubling down on Ethiopia. By early 1978, there were a thousand uniformed Soviet personnel in the
country and several thousand Cubans. The airlift of tanks and rockets from
Moscow to Addis Ababa was ratcheting up alarmingly. At one point, a Soviet

plane landed every twenty minutes.[3] America's friends in the region, including Saudi Arabia and Egypt, feared Soviet designs on the Arabian Gulf's oil resources and shipping choke points. Moscow and Havana were also increasing their aid to the Communist regime in South Yemen.

There were two ways of looking at events in the Horn of Africa. The first was to treat the region as a local quagmire of no global significance; Carter should encourage diplomacy between Mogadishu and Addis Ababa but nothing further. That was the State Department's view. As ever, Vance was determined not to let anything interfere with the prize of a SALT II deal. The second, articulated by the outnumbered Brzezinski, was that the USSR's military expansion in Africa should not go unopposed. Moscow and Havana had paid no price for their intervention in Angola, chiefly (to Kissinger's frustration) because Congress had blocked further covert action. Moscow took Washington's inaction as a green light for adventurism elsewhere. Carter warned Ethiopia not to cross the border into Somalia once it had recaptured Ogaden. Ethiopia's victory was only a matter of time given the scale of Soviet military assistance.

Brzezinski argued in vain that Washington should back up Carter's warning by sending an aircraft carrier to the Indian Ocean.[4] The debate became so heated that at one point Vance lost his cool, his face reddening.[5] State Department leaks against Brzezinski were turning into an almost daily event. In Foggy Bottom the joke was that "Zbig is always looking for a smoking [Cuban] cigar."[6] Tony Lake, Vance's head of policy and planning, would dismiss Brzezinski as Carter's in-house champion of "globaloney"—the practice of filtering every local event through an all-purpose ideological prism. In practice, neither the Soviets nor the Americans had much grasp of the realities on the ground. Carter could more effectively win over Africa by trying to see the continent's problems the way Africans saw them rather than through a Cold War lens, Lake and other senior State Department officials argued. America's smartest counter to Soviet Third World clientelism would be to take the higher road.

In Brzezinski's favor was the fact that the Soviets were stonewalling claims of their involvement in the Horn of Africa in spite of clear evidence to the contrary. Carter found such lying unconscionable. In one Oval Office encounter, the Soviet foreign minister, Andrei Gromyko, enraged Carter by flatout denying the presence of Soviet generals in Addis Ababa.[7] By that point there were two thousand Soviet officers on the ground in Ethiopia, including several generals, in addition to almost twenty thousand Cubans. Gromyko lied to Carter's face. Soviet archives suggest that the truth about Moscow's designs lay somewhere in between Brzezinski and State's reading of them. Politburo ideologues, notably Mikhail Suslov, its chief propagandist, believed that America's humiliating exit from Vietnam in April 1975 and the realities of détente had created "additional opportunities for struggle against imperialism," he told Castro in late 1975. There was a growing "correlation of forces" (the Soviet version of globaloney) favoring revolutionary action across the Third World.[8] "In Africa we can inflict a severe defeat on the entire reactionary imperialist policy," Castro told Erich Honecker, his East German counterpart, in Berlin in 1977.[9]

At a conference of key Soviet and American figures at Georgia's Musgrove Plantation many years later, Anatoly Dobrynin insisted that the Soviets had not been fomenting revolution in the Horn. "So it was just an act of international philanthropy?" Brzezinski asked. Dobrynin demurred.[10] In his memoirs, the former Soviet ambassador revealed that he had pressed Moscow to supply him with a plausible defense of the USSR's strategy in Africa. In return, he had received an "abracadabra" of verbiage about the "historical inevitability" of anticolonial uprisings. That had left him powerless to counter America's impression that Moscow was prosecuting a "broad offensive . . . for control of Africa."[11]

Brzezinski nevertheless lost the internal debate for a show of US force off the Horn of Africa. Key to that was the opposition of Harold Brown and the Pentagon service chiefs. He described the debate as "like pulling teeth."[12] But Brzezinski was making headway in his larger battle for a bold move on the chessboard. In an NSC meeting in early March 1978, the defense secretary came out in support of Brzezinski's feeling that the time was ripe for a US overture to China.[13] Carter was still unsure. Brzezinski had been pestering him for the go-ahead to lead a delegation to China. He was testing Carter's patience to the limit. "I favor you instructing me to visit China some time in March or April. . . . We have shown excessive sensitivity to the Soviets," he wrote in early February. Next to that Carter scrawled "No."[14]

A few weeks later, Brzezinski launched a full-blown polemic about where the Carter administration's foreign policy was going wrong. The clear implication was that Carter was too weak; he should draw on a little more Machiavelli and a little less Sunday school. Carter could do that, he suggested, through a "demonstration of force" or steps "to infuse fear" into America's adversaries. Use of "black propaganda" and "deception" should not be ruled out. "I will be developing some ideas for you regarding the above," he concluded. In the margins Carter scribbled, "You will be wasting your time."[15] Next to Brzezinski's bullet points, the irritated president had written, "Lying?" "Proxy war?" Strained relations between the president and his foreign policy guru coincided with Carter's decision to suspend production of the neutron bomb, which caused angst in Europe and further crystallized the Capitol Hill hawks' skepticism about Carter. Brzezinski had used every means at his disposal to get Carter to make a different decision or at least water down the one he wanted to make. After one such contentious meeting, Carter sent an oddly passive-aggressive complaint to Brzezinski. It was a line he used on several occasions: "Zbig, I have to say that you never give up."[16]

When the two were alone in the Oval Office one morning in mid-March, a "perplexed and concerned" Carter admitted to Brzezinski that he wanted to check Soviet aggression in the Horn of Africa but felt that he had no good options. Sending a nuclear-armed battle group to the area would be too risky. Doing nothing would only invite further Soviet meddling around the world. Brzezinski said there were other moves available. Carter stood up from his armchair and walked across to the fireplace. After a pause he said that he had decided in favor of Brzezinski's going to China. He would write a note to Vance to that effect. But the bureaucracy was a step ahead of Carter.

That afternoon, Vance dropped by Brzezinski's White House office to say that Walter Mondale had agreed to go to China and that he had recommended to the vice president that he take Brzezinski along for part of the trip. Brzezinski's deputy, David Aaron, found out that Mondale would prefer to undertake his China outreach alone. A despondent Brzezinski concluded, "It looks like I will be maneuvered out of this trip altogether."[17] The next morning, Brzezinski asked Carter what he really wanted. "Why do you suppose Vance is so opposed to you going?" Carter asked. Brzezinski replied that it was the "pygmies" around Vance, notably Richard Holbrooke and Philip Habib, the undersecretary of state for political affairs, who were agitating against him. "Don't talk to the Vice-President about this," Carter said. "I'll decide and let you know." Brzezinski returned to his office. Five minutes later, Susan Clough, Carter's Oval Office secretary and gatekeeper, handed Brzezinski a copy of a letter that Carter was about to send to Vance and Mondale. It stated, "I have decided it would be better for Zbig to go to China."[18]

Brzezinski's persistence had paid off. Getting Carter's sign-off was an internal coup that wrenched China policy from Vance's hands. The seeds of

Brzezinski's idea that it should be he who led the China initiative had been planted the previous October at a lunch with Lee Kuan Yew, Singapore's prime minister. Lee told Brzezinski and his accompanying Asia officer, Michel Oksenberg, that the time was ripe for normalization of relations with China. Brzezinski knew that Vance would bitterly oppose such a move. On their walk back to the White House after the lunch, Brzezinski asked Oksenberg whether he could arrange an invitation from China's Washington mission for him to visit China. "Jesus, Zbig, of course I could," said Oksenberg. "They would love to have you." Oksenberg asked whether Brzezinski had obtained Carter's go-ahead to short-circuit the State Department on China. "No problem," said the grinning Brzezinski. "Just get it."[19] Three weeks later, at a goodbye lunch for China's departing mission chief, Huang Zhen, Oksenberg delivered on his promise. Within intentional earshot of Mondale, Vance, and the media, Huang invited Brzezinski to visit China. At the private lunch afterwards, he repeated the invitation twice more.

It was as though war had been declared. After the goodbye lunch, Holbrooke called Oksenberg and yelled, "Have you been playing games?" An incandescent Habib also telephoned. "What the hell have you been doing?" Vance called Brzezinski "in considerable agitation" to protest that this invitation would undercut the administration's China policy.[20] Brzezinski told Vance that he was appalled that "these two little puppies [Holbrooke and Habib] would immediately run to him with such a story."[21] The invitation to visit China had been casual and low-level, said Brzezinski—as had been his polite acceptance. In fact, no turf battle could have been less casual. It took Brzezinski another four months to secure Carter's final blessing. During that time, State's rearguard actions—particularly by Holbrooke and Habib— were unrelenting. But Brzezinski had two advantages: not only did he have unrivaled access to the president, especially during those key early-morning sessions when Carter's mind was most active; unlike Vance, he had also developed a strategic case. Vance's position on China was to stick to the status quo. His preference was to restore US relations with Vietnam, which Holbrooke was in charge of negotiating.

Given the growing enmity between China and Vietnam, Carter could have one kind of normalization or the other, not both. Mending ties with Vietnam would help to salve liberal America's conscience. But State failed to supply a strategic rationale. Such a step might help improve the atmosphere with Moscow; Vietnam was a client state of the USSR. But it would go against the grain of US public opinion, which was clamoring for Hanoi to repatriate alleged American prisoners of war and MIAs. That year, the movie *The Deer Hunter* was released; *Rambo* came out three years later. Having already pardoned Vietnam draft law violators on his second day in office, Carter could ill afford to stir more ghosts of Vietnam amid America's brewing culture war. China normalization was an opening waiting to be seized. It would be a momentous step, requiring sharp elbows and determination. Once Carter's mind was made up, it made little sense to assign that role to anyone other than Brzezinski.

Brzezinski treated the role of national security advisor much the same way he played tennis. In Jordan's telling, he would either return a low winner at missile speed or hit the ball way out of court, and not much in between.[22] He approached the chessboard with similar bravado. "He would bring out his queen very early in the game," said Peter Jay, the British ambassador, son-in-law of James Callaghan and Brzezinski's frequent chess partner.[23] By contrast, Brzezinski's China maneuver was more like a lob over Vance's head or an obscure feint with his knight; it took time and tactical guile to execute. Like Kissinger, Brzezinski cornered the China portfolio and never let it go. Unlike Kissinger, who was initially skeptical about what had been Nixon's idea, he had to school the logic of China normalization into his president. The move went against many of Carter's instincts. Most glaringly, it undercut the goal of bringing human rights into the heart of his foreign policy—at least insofar as it applied to countries beyond the Soviet Bloc.

With twenty thousand executions in 1977, China had arguably the harshest regime on the planet—far bloodier than the Soviets'. When there was a clash between Carter's ideals and his political interests, more often than not his ideals would at least in some respects prevail. He restricted arms sales to the juntas in Argentina and Brazil on human rights grounds, even though they were Cold War allies. He likewise slapped curbs on West Germany's civil nuclear industry in spite of Bonn's critical importance to the Western alliance. His support for black majority rule in South Africa and Rhodesia was a smart Cold War shift in contrast to Kissinger's indifference to southern Africa's political arrangements. That was partly Brzezinski's rationale. To Carter, ending apartheid was a nonnegotiable matter of principle. His decision to restore Panama's sovereignty over its canal made no sense at all in terms of domestic politics or even diplomatically. To Carter it was the honorable course of action. In 1903,

Theodore Roosevelt's administration had rammed an unequal treaty down Panama's throat, having effectively expropriated its sovereign territory. In 1976, Ronald Reagan had said, "We bought it, we paid for it, we built it, and we intend to keep it."[24] Polls showed that a large majority of Americans agreed with Reagan. Carter's view was that America had stolen it from Panama. "It's obvious that we cheated the Panamanians out of their canal," he wrote in his diary.[25]

To get the two Panama Canal Treaties passed would require a two-thirds majority in the Senate. Carter's stand cost him a vast chunk of the credit he had built up on Capitol Hill over his first fifteen months. It was a politically exorbitant act of US diplomacy and a big gamble that swallowed a large chunk of the White House calendar. Though Panama was by no means Brzezinski's project—it was Vance who converted Carter to the cause—his hawkish reputation made him Carter's most valuable salesman. Night after night, Carter asked Brzezinski to brief groups of lawmakers in the White House or to take questions from visiting state delegations. At one session on Capitol Hill, Brzezinski was asked what the US could do if the Panamanian government announced that it would be closing the canal for maintenance and repairs. "In that case, according to the provisions of the neutrality part of the Treaty, we will move in and close down the Panamanian government for repairs," he said to uproarious laughter.[26] In that instance, Carter's Gradgrindian urge to read everything worked in his favor. To secure the vote of one of the Senate holdouts, California's Samuel Hayakawa, Carter read his tome *Language and Thought in Action*, a highly abstract book on semantics. When Carter told Hayakawa that he had read every page, the suspicious senator quizzed the president on his thesis. Carter passed the test. "I think it was this encounter that got his vote," he concluded.[27] The Neutrality Treaty and Panama Canal Treaty scraped through the Senate by votes of 68 to 32, one more than was needed.

It was no coincidence that Carter agreed to Brzezinski's China trip on March 16, 1978, the same day the Neutrality Treaty passed the Senate. Carter could now exhale. Having just pulled off a narrow defeat of the Senate hawks on Panama, led by Republicans Barry Goldwater, Jesse Helms, and Strom Thurmond, he now had bandwidth for an unavoidable confrontation with the same figures over Taiwan. Encouraged by Reagan, the Republican hawks had defeated Kissinger's attempts at China normalization during the Ford administration. By its end, a demoralized and exhausted Kissinger said that he had never believed normalization was possible. That was misleading; Kissinger had told China's new leader, Deng Xiaoping, that he would pursue normal-ization after the 1976 election, assuming that Ford won. At the same time he vowed to Goldwater that normalization would never happen. On China, Kiss-inger's self-contradicting promises had caught up with him.[28]

During a tense meeting with Deng in mid-1975, the diminutive Chinese leader lost his cool and accused Kissinger of appeasing the Soviets. He com-pared Kissinger to Neville Chamberlain and the Helsinki Final Act to the 1938 Munich sellout. Deng's invective so shook Kissinger that he asked to take a break. He thereafter referred to Deng as "that nasty little man."[29] Mat-ters deteriorated further during Ford's ill-fated visit to China in late 1975 for a meeting with the ailing Mao, who would die a few months later. Mao was clearly feeling Nixon's absence. He expressed impatience with Ford and Kissinger's inability—or reluctance—to complete the sale. Both Deng and Mao were exercised by the interim SALT II deal that Ford had struck with Brezhnev in Vladivostok the previous year. Like Brzezinski, they saw it as too generous to the Soviets. Deng had berated Kissinger for supplying the USSR with US technology that was helping its weapons modernization program and vast shipments of midwestern grain that were feeding the Soviet people. The Chinese leadership's astute hunch was that America had been dangling the threat of China normalization to bind the Soviets more deeply to détente. The near-cadaverous Mao told Ford that God had sent him an invitation. Ford misunderstood Mao's allusion to his impending death. "I hope you get your invitation soon," he replied.[30] It was a tone-deaf response to a relationship that since its dramatic opening had been heading steadily in the wrong direction.

Given the secrecy with which Nixon and Kissinger had pursued America's surprise opening to China, Beijing put a high premium on personalized di-plomacy. Nixon's resignation had been a blow to Mao. Chinese premier Chou Enlai's death in early 1976 had been an equal setback to Kissinger. Urbane, silky, and erudite, Chou was the ultimate mandarin and Kissinger's ideal coun-terpart. Nixon and Mao had struck the opening chords; Kissinger and Chou sustained the duet. Chou's replacement by Deng robbed Kissinger of his most cherished interlocutor. It was precisely the qualities that Kissinger most dis-liked in Deng—the Chinese premier's blunt, sometimes uncouth, manner and his impatience with euphemisms—that most appealed to Brzezinski. Their shared sense of urgency and mutual allergy to the Soviets would be the propel-lants of Carter's China shift. Neither the Chinese premier's well-used spittoon nor his chain-smoking of Lesser Panda cigarettes could lessen Brzezinski's deep respect for him. Deng was "a man tiny in size but great in boldness," he thought.[31] His rapport with China's four-foot, eleven-inch leader was instant.

Preparations for Brzezinski's May 1978 China trip were as filled with intrigue as his battle to make it happen. Having lost the argument that Carter's outreach should be led by Mondale or not take place at all, State tried to cram Brzezinski's plane with as many of its officers as it could. Over a long lunch, Holbrooke begged Brzezinski to include him in his delegation. His chief point was that it would be harmful to his image if he was left out. Brzezinski told Holbrooke that he needed to come up with a better rationale than his personal reputation. At Vance's request, Brzezinski had already agreed to add Holbrooke but wanted to make him sweat a little. "He is actually very bright, and in many respects a nice guy, but terribly pushy and self-centered," Brzezinski thought.[32] Having secured his own inclusion, Holbrooke then tried to inveigle more State colleagues onto the manifest and get hold of the instructions Carter had written for Brzezinski. In reality, Brzezinski had written his own very open-ended instructions. Carter had signed off on them without modification. Brzezinski was not going to share his talking points with a leaky State Department. Holbrooke was undeterred. Brzezinski called Holbrooke at dawn one day to reprimand him. "I have never heard such a vile, profane man," Holbrooke complained to Oksenberg. "Zbig yelled at me over the phone so loud that it woke up my wife!"[33]

In their opening meeting in Beijing's cavernous Great Hall of the People, Deng's first aim was to ascertain that it was Brzezinski, not Vance, who spoke for Carter. The secretary of state had conducted an exploratory visit to China in August 1977 that seemed jinxed before it began. Carter had not given Vance license to explore a normalization with China that in any case Vance would not have pursued with any conviction. Carter worried that any concessions to China on Taiwan would jeopardize the Panama Canal's prospects in the Senate. Carter later described Vance's trip as "a failure."[34] It had been the kind of box-checking diplomacy guaranteed to annoy the Chinese at that juncture of the Cold War. To Deng's consternation, Vance had taken a "step backward" from what Ford and Kissinger had discussed two years earlier. Vance said that in the event of China normalization, Washington would maintain a US diplomatic presence in Taiwan. Vance's words were anathema to Deng and in breach of China's three bedrock principles for normalization: that the United States sever its relations with Taiwan, reaffirm the One China policy, and repudiate the US-Taiwan mutual defense treaty.

The transcript of the two-and-a-half-hour Deng-Brzezinski dialogue is a remarkable historical document. Years later, Kissinger would publicly compliment Brzezinski's skill in his handling of the Chinese leader. Deng's negotiating tactics and constant probing for Brzezinski's weaknesses was just as striking. "The US has made up its mind," Brzezinski declared at the start. He had to repeat the line several times; Carter had decided to normalize relations with China. Roughly an hour later, Deng said, "We are looking forward to the day when President Carter makes up his mind." Brzezinski replied, "I have told you before, President Carter has made up his mind." Deng replied, "So much the better." The Chinese premier knew that he and Brzezinski had similar views about the "polar bear," Deng's term for the Soviet Union. Yet he had been well briefed. Was Brzezinski speaking for the whole of the Carter administration? "Your spokesmen have consistently justified and apologized for Soviet actions," Deng said. "To be candid with you, whenever you are about to conclude an agreement with the Soviet Union, it is the product of concession on the U.S. side to please the Soviet side."

Brzezinski told Deng that it was not helpful for China to keep on accusing America of being an "appeaser" of the polar bear. If the US wrapped up a SALT II treaty, which, Deng insisted, would be another climbdown, it would be because it was in America's interest to cooperate with the USSR in some areas and compete in others. "I can assure you that my inclination to be fearful of offending the Soviet Union is rather limited," Brzezinski said. "I would be willing to make a little bet with you as to who is less popular in the Soviet Union—you or me." Deng replied, "It is hard to say. But one thing is certain. The main target of the Soviet Union is the U.S."

In spite of Deng's formal skepticism, the two could finish each other's sentences on Moscow's imperialist agenda. Brzezinski admitted that there were different schools of thought within the Carter administration. His objective was to satisfy Deng that it was Brzezinski's posture, not Vance's, that would prevail. "I think it is fair to say that in my country there is some division of opinion regarding Soviet motives," Brzezinski said. "My own view is that the American-Soviet relationship will remain for a very long time to come fundamentally a competitive and in some respects a hostile relationship."[35]

Brzezinski somewhat brutally kept Holbrooke out of the Deng meeting. Like Kissinger, who had excluded William Rogers, Nixon's secretary of state, from the China dialogue, Brzezinski regarded State as the enemy within. Any advance in China normalization would come at the expense of its goal of rapprochement with Vietnam. Carter agreed. He assigned the task of negoti-ating normalization to Leonard Woodcock, a former United Auto Workers union leader and chief of the US mission in Beijing. At Brzezinski's urging and in a major snub to State, Carter instructed Woodcock to report directly to the White House, cutting out Vance. At Holbrooke's behest, Woodcock nevertheless tried to get him into the meeting with Deng. Brzezinski refused. The next day, during a tour of the Forbidden City, another State official, Wil-liam Gleysteen, urged Brzezinski to relent on Holbrooke. "Zbig, this is totally wrong. You are destroying the processes of government." Zbig replied, "Screw you. I'm not going to."[36]

Brzezinski found out that Vance had phoned Dobrynin to inform the Soviets of his impending trip to China an hour before the White House an-nounced it. He was not about to risk his grand chessboard move for the sake of interagency niceties. On a tour of the Great Wall of China, Brzezinski again raised State Department hackles when he told his Chinese escorts, "Last one to the top fights the Russians in Ethiopia!" He also reminded his hosts that their forebears had built the wall to keep out the northern barbarians. On being told of Brzezinski's comments, Vance grimaced. It was the kind of media stunt he abhorred. When Brzezinski reached the nearest summit of the ancient wall, he encountered a group of friendly Chinese sailors who asked to have their picture taken with him. "Do you know you are posing with an im-perialist?" he asked. No, they replied, "We are having a photograph taken with the polar-bear tamer."[37] That became Brzezinski's moniker in China. Deng had found the American with whom he could do business.

The two agreed to rapid normalization. The US accepted China's three principles. Meanwhile, China would not demand that America cancel its ex-isting arms sales to Taiwan, nor would it contradict a US statement calling for peaceful resolution to the Taiwan problem. Deng had given Brzezinski the perfect stick to poke the polar bear. The three-day trip was also a boon for Muska, who, with Carter's permission, had accompanied her husband. At the official banquet given by Huang Hua, China's foreign minister, she caused a minor diplomatic flap by jumping up to propose a toast—a breach of protocol by an official's wife, even though Mao had often referred to women as hold-ing up half the sky. Huang looked mortified until his wife broke the silence by endorsing Muska's right to speak and "women's lib."[38]

Brzezinski spent eleven hours in formal talks with Deng, Hua Guofeng, China's titular premier, and Huang, not including a private dinner with Deng on the penultimate evening at the Fang Shan restaurant overlooking a lake bathed in moonlight. "The atmosphere was out of this world," he said.[39] He likened his first visit to Beijing to an American astronaut visiting the moon. Amid escalating toasts with *maotai*, Brzezinski spelled out the expected opposition from Washington's Taiwan lobby and how they could help each other to overcome it.

The seventy-four-year-old vice premier kept referring to the fact that he had only three years left, so time was in short supply (as it turned out, he had another nineteen years to live). Brzezinski laid out the benefits of a full-blown relationship, including sharing US satellite intelligence about Soviet deployments along the Russia-China border and US technology transfer that would propel China's economic and military leap forward. In their formal meeting, they had conducted a global *tour d'horizon*, listing areas of Soviet weakness that they could jointly exploit. Both agreed that Moscow was behind the recent bloodthirsty coup in Afghanistan. Kabul was now in the hands of a pro-Soviet faction and would likely turn into "the Cuba of the East," Deng warned.

Brzezinski's China trip was a turning point in the Carter administration. Having so often been paralyzed between radically opposing sets of advice, Carter was shifting crablike, although with deep misgivings, towards Brzezinski's approach. Brzezinski was careful never to use the media term "tilt to China" or "playing the China card." But he managed to purge Vance's preferred description of America as being "even-handed" between the Soviets and the Chinese. Such code language belonged to the Kissinger era.

In the Brzezinski era, the Soviets were being encircled. On the air force plane back to Washington, Holbrooke's frustration tipped over into an infamous incident. Brzezinski had refused to give him the memcon of his Deng meeting, saying that Carter should read it first. Holbrooke tried to wrestle a copy of the transcript from Mike Oksenberg, who refused to give it up. A shouting match ensued during which Holbrooke seized Oksenberg by his shirt collar. Oksenberg grabbed him back. Others had to pry them apart. Gleysteen later said that in a quarter of a century in government, he had never seen anything like it.[40] That high-altitude fracas was a fitting summary of the tenor of NSC–State relations.

At an Oval Office meeting a few days after their return, the Soviet delegation, led by Gromyko, seemed almost as unhappy about Brzezinski's China trip as Holbrooke. Many of the Russians were "strikingly cold" and looked away when they shook hands with Brzezinski. "Oh you're back already," said

Gromyko. "Yes I was on a little trip," said Brzezinski. During the meeting Brzezinski and Brown, the only other Carter principal who spoke Russian, exchanged sarcastic comments and periodic snickers as Gromyko delivered a "mendacious" lecture about why the US was mistaken about Africa and human rights.[41]

Gromyko also complained bitterly about reports that Brzezinski had briefed the Chinese about the state of SALT II. Carter's awareness of Gromyko's lying about the Soviet presence in Ethiopia contributed to the frosty atmosphere. To restore the impression of balance, Vance had tried to put the meeting with Gromyko on Carter's calendar while Brzezinski was in China. Brzezinski had persuaded Carter that a rival Soviet meeting would undermine his message to Deng. It was hard to avoid the impression that there was now a China camp inside the Carter administration and an opposing Soviet one.

A few weeks earlier, on April 12, the *New York Times* columnist William Safire, a former speechwriter for Nixon, had written a column dripping with sarcasm about the "Mr. Softee Faction" inside the Carter administration, masterminded by Marshall Shulman, Vance's chief Sovietologist, and the "Woody Woodpecker Faction," led by Brzezinski. The column, which was written as a spoof article by Georgi Arbatov, the Kremlin's lead Americanologist, was based on two actual leaks. The first revealed a call that Shulman had made to the Soviet Embassy in March, telling its staff to pay no attention to a hard-line speech Carter was about to give at Wake Forest University—his most hawkish address to date as president. Carter's speech was meant for domestic consumption, Shulman reassured the Soviet diplomats; Moscow should discount it.

The second leak was a draft letter in which State had proposed to Carter that he inform Brezhnev before the US public or America's allies of his decision to cancel the neutron bomb. "I have decided that the U.S. will not proceed with production of the reduced-blast enhanced-radiation warhead," said the proposed Carter letter to Brezhnev, which was never sent. "I believe it is important to foster a general climate propitious to arms control and conducive to mutual restraint." Safire's piece was particularly damaging to Vance, as it said he had approved Shulman's friendly heads-up to the Soviets. Safire also alleged borderline disloyalty by State given the Soviets' massive tactical and theater nuclear advantage over the Americans in Europe, which the "capitalist" neutron bomb would have only partially redressed. The article concluded, "If we can restrain the Woodpeckers and seduce the Softees, we will make Mr. Carter the best U.S. President the Soviet Union has ever had."[42]

Vance lost his temper and demanded that Brzezinski fire Sam Huntington, who, he claimed, had been the leaker. Brzezinski questioned Huntington
and concluded that Vance's charge was false.[43] He said the breach must have
come from State or Defense. Whoever leaked the material behind Safire's polemic, relations between State and the NSC were getting steadily more toxic.
Safire's column echoed a hardening sentiment against SALT II on Capitol
Hill. Carter's cancellation of the B-1 bomber and the neutron bomb played
into a growing impression among hawkish senators, such as Scoop Jackson,
Bob Dole, and Sam Nunn, that Vance and Warnke were making too many
concessions to the Soviets.

As the talks progressed, the final SALT package was beginning to resem-
ble the Vladivostok deal that Carter had rejected during his first weeks in office. In fact, this was misleading. US negotiators were pushing hard for tough
new verification protocols and sticking firm to its plans to exclude its new
cruise missile from the talks' parameters. But the trade-off between getting a
modest deal with Moscow and the vast expense of capital that it would take to
get it through the Senate was starting to look like a poor one.

Carter was still desperate for a summit with Brezhnev. To Brzezinski and
Jordan's irritation, he repeated that desire to Gromyko, thus negating the effect of the more hawkish message he had just delivered.[44] Jordan, meanwhile,
wrote Carter a memo suggesting that they postpone SALT II until after the
midterm elections that November. He also urged Carter to fire State Department officials for giving the Soviets almost routine advance notice about
upcoming White House announcements, including Brzezinski's China trip.
Was State representing America to the Soviets or vice versa? Jordan's note to
Carter, which Brzezinski helped him write, implied the latter.[45]

The combined forces of Jordan and Brzezinski, and increasingly of
Brown, were tipping the balance. At a Friday foreign policy breakfast in
early June, Carter agreed that China normalization should now take prece-
dence over SALT II ratification. His decision reflected both the slow pace
of the nuclear talks as well as Carter's evolving disillusion with Moscow.
Vance had no choice but to agree. The media was starting to take note of
Brzezinski's ascendancy. *Newsweek* put Brzezinski's face on the cover next
to the question "A New Cold War?"[46] The headline on the *Economist*'s cover
story, which also came out in early June, was "Going Brzezinski's Way" with
a suitably hawkish picture of him. A few weeks earlier, to Brzezinski's pleasure, *U.S. News & World Report* had called him the seventh most powerful

figure in the United States and Vance fourteenth. It was a reversal of the magazine's 1977 rankings.[47]

There was also a corresponding escalation of attacks on him. In a lengthy *New Yorker* essay filled with anonymous quotes from easily recognizable Foggy Bottom sources, Brzezinski was depicted as a lone aggressor inside Carter's administration: impulsive, ideological, brash; a figure always wanting "to appear tough without thinking through the consequences." The piece's main example was Brzezinski's agitation over the Horn of Africa and human rights in the USSR, which was putting détente at risk. In spite of having decried Kissinger's linkage-based handling of the Soviet relationship, Brzezinski was linking progress over SALT to Soviet restraint in Ethiopia. The *New Yorker* quoted Vance as saying, "I come to SALT as the most important item in our [Soviet] relationship. It is life or death." Brzezinski was getting in the way of that. "It is not a question of Brzezinski's views," the piece concluded. "It is a question of his temperament and judgment."[48] In reality, however, it was mostly about Brzezinski's views.

George McGovern, the Minnesota senator and 1972 Democratic presidential nominee, also piled on. Brzezinski, he said, was conducting US foreign policy as though "every stirring in Africa, Asia and the Indian Ocean is another Cuban missile crisis." In so doing, Carter's firebrand advisor was jeopardizing nuclear talks aimed at preventing our "mutual extinction." Even Britain's usually chummy prime minister, Jim Callaghan, was getting in on the act. "There seem to be a number of Christopher Columbuses setting out from the United States to discover Africa for the first time," he told the Washington media during the NATO summit in early June. "It has been there a long time." Brzezinski found the Carters and the Callaghans chatting amiably on the White House portico. He showed Carter the transcript of Callaghan's words.[49] The British prime minister blushed. Carter dismissed it as a trifle. He was nevertheless under relentless pressure to declare where he stood between Vance and Brzezinski. "It would appear that as of the moment we do not have a coherent foreign policy, but a collection of conflicting voices," McGovern said in a Senate speech. "I pray that in the contest for the mind of the president, calm and common sense will prevail over the strategy of crisis and confrontation."[50]

Carter's answer to the escalating clamor was to give his own speech. In his case, addressing the public was rarely a good move. He had a habit of disconcerting his speechwriters by smiling at unsuitable moments and putting rhetorical emphasis on the wrong passages. On television he looked like a "plucked chicken," said one unkind observer. Unlike Safire with Nixon or Ted Sorensen with Kennedy, Carter lacked a close relationship with any of his speechwriters.[51] Effective presidential addresses generally get one simple message across: "Tear down that wall," "Bear any burden," "The era of big government is over," and so forth. Carter's instinct was to cram in lots of medium-sized points. They read better in hindsight than how they were received at the time.

His address on June 7 at the US Naval Academy in Annapolis, from which he had graduated as a midshipman three decades earlier, was no exception. He asked for input from Brzezinski and Vance and then effectively stapled their drafts together. His clashing head and heart were both on full display. Far from resolving the confusion about where he stood, Carter's speech seemed to confirm his administration's short-fused ambivalence. The Soviets had long since developed a habit of writing "CV" or "ZB" alongside passages in Carter's speeches to indicate which lines had come from his secretary of state and which from his national security advisor. In that case Carter made it easy for the Soviets; he had created the textual version of a Minotaur. They divided his Annapolis speech in half.[52]

On paper, Carter was laying out a rational fork in the road for Moscow. The choice was theirs. "The Soviet Union can choose either confrontation or cooperation," he said.[53] "The United States is adequately prepared to meet either." In practice, Americans detected yet more indecision; the Soviets heard only Polish-accented bellicosity. A *Pravda* editorial detected "the aggressive hand of Brzezinski" in Carter's speech.[54] At a Politburo meeting a few days later, Brezhnev blamed Carter's Polish advisor for what increasingly looked like the return of the Cold War. Brzezinski's reputation in Moscow was now entering the realm of legend. Back home he was a feisty advisor with a growing share of the president's mind. To the Politburo, he was the mastermind of a new ideological war on the USSR.

Fidel Castro thought the same way, in June publicly blaming his tensions with Carter on Brzezinski. "[Castro has] joined the Soviets and the Israelis and everyone else when they have a problem with me to blame it on Zbig," Carter wrote in his diary.[55] There was also a comic side to Brzezinski demonization. At an arms control meeting in Moscow, Reginald Bartholomew, an NSC staffer, moved a malachite box standing on the desk of Georgy Kornienko, the Soviet deputy foreign minister. It triggered a piercing alarm throughout the Soviet Foreign Ministry. "Quick, quick, call Zbig and tell him it was a mistake," said Dobrynin, who was in Moscow at the time.[56]

As was by now almost habitual, the Soviets were overestimating Brzezinski's omnipotence. He tried and repeatedly failed to get Carter to take a tough stand over the highly publicized trials of the world-famous refuseniks Natan Sharansky and Aleksandr Ginzburg for treason and "anti-Soviet agitation," respectively. In the buildup to Vance's next SALT II negotiations with Gromyko in Geneva, State wanted to downplay the trials, which were taking place in a court more than a hundred miles outside Moscow.

On this occasion, Brzezinski took a nuanced position. He argued against freezing SALT II, which Jordan and most of Carter's political team now saw as a hopeless cause. Paul Nitze, Richard Perle, and others on the Committee on the Present Danger were depicting Carter's nuclear talks as the next Munich. Brzezinski dismissed this as hyperbole. But he insisted there had to be some US response to the refusenik trials. His recommended course was to cancel a forthcoming trip of an American technology delegation to the USSR and freeze export of the Cray supercomputer, the most advanced such hardware in existence.

Carter was conflicted. His Jewish advisors Stu Eizenstat, Jerry Rafshoon, and Bob Lipshutz eventually persuaded him to take Brzezinski's advice. Even then, Brzezinski spent weeks combating the State, Treasury, and Commerce Departments' attempts to water down the president's new trade restrictions. Michael Blumenthal, the treasury secretary, was throwing up even more obstacles than Vance. "Tell Mike to support my policies," Carter told Brzezinski, who promptly called the startled treasury secretary to relay Carter's order.[57] The media treated Carter's actions as half-hearted and belated. The trials, which resulted in a fifteen-year jail sentence in Siberia for Sharansky and eight years for Ginzburg, were depicted by Israel's Menachem Begin as a "blood libel" against Jews. In the face of a worldwide media glare and Carter's now-plummeting approval rating, senior members of his domestic team were veering close to rebellion. "I'm pissed off, I'm just pissed off, I don't know what's the matter with him," Ham Jordan told Brzezinski.[58] Even the normally optimistic Stu Eizenstat seemed to be succumbing to fatalism. Brzezinski walked in on Eizenstat and Lipshutz in a state of acute despondency. "[Carter] has bought the soft line entirely," Eizenstat said. Your credibility is now close to zero, Rafshoon told the president.[59]

Carter's seeming paralysis turned out to be the proverbial darkness before dawn. While his senior advisors were sniping at one another or complaining about him, he was busy making grandiose plans. Brzezinski walked in on

Carter early one morning to find him pensively spinning the Oval Office's vast globe. He was trying to figure out the best historical site to hold a make-or-break Middle East peace summit with Begin and Sadat. Nobody was pressuring him to take such a gamble. The odds were poor that he would get Sadat and Begin to agree on anything. Yet his mind was set; the only question was about the location.[60] He and Brzezinski discussed Spain, Morocco, Portugal, and Norway. Each had pros and cons. Casablanca had a particular resonance. After several days of back-and-forth, Carter finally settled on Camp David, the president's official Maryland retreat. That way the Americans could have full control over the logistics. Brzezinski and Vance both saw Carter's move as bold, noble, and the right thing to do. If it failed, however, it could be politically suicidal. One this issue, at least, the two advisors were in agreement. Going for broke in the Middle East had not been their idea. But both admired Carter for his boldness.

Brzezinski convinced Deng Xiaoping of Carter's tenacity by citing two bills he had just railroaded through Congress against all odds. The first example was the Panama Canal Treaties. The second was a big arms package of F-15 fighter jets to Israel, Saudi Arabia, and Egypt. AIPAC's executive director, Morris Amitay, Brzezinski's bête noire, had pulled out all stops to delink Israel's plane deliveries from those to its big Arab neighbors—fighter jets that Begin said could be turned against Israel. Neither Carter's nor Vance's protestations that they would be used for defensive purposes swayed the Israel lobby. They knew that the real reason Carter was traducing his own strict rules on arms sales was Cold War related. Both Egypt and Saudi Arabia needed to be kept inside the American camp. Since an alliance of conservative Republicans and Kennedy liberals would doubtless defeat the Arab military transfers in a stand-alone vote, the White House lumped all the sales into one package. Carter was daring Congress to vote against sending arms to Israel. The campaign against the bill targeted Brzezinski as its main culprit.

Brzezinski kept up his usual bravado but suffered inner turmoil over the torrent of accusations, often seeking Eizenstat's counsel. He even wrote Eizenstat a long memo detailing his history of encounters in the Middle East.[61] The invective hit a nadir in May when a Republican senator, Lowell Weicker, seemed to compare Brzezinski to Hitler. "We know from history that time and time again, when national leaders ran into difficulties, they found it convenient to blame their problems on the Jews," Weicker told the AIPAC conference in

Washington, DC. "If there is a meaningful distinction between those historical proclivities, and the signals which Brzezinski is sending today, I don't know what it is. I can tell you if I were President, and I had a national security adviser who singled out American Jews as an impediment to my policies, I would have his resignation before sundown, and his reputation for breakfast."[62] This was the most scurrilous attack on Brzezinski to date. But its outlandishness was almost helpful. Weicker was widely viewed as having miscued. His remarks triggered revulsion from Jewish organizations and condemnatory editorials in the *New York Times* and *Washington Post.* Carter also went out of his way to say that Brzezinski was being unfairly targeted by "special interests." In reality, he was a useful decoy.

Against that backdrop, Carter's ambitions for the Camp David talks were beyond extravagant. He decided to gamble everything: he would either achieve a sweeping deal or collapse. In preparation for the summit, he studied theories of negotiation, ordered in-house psychological profiles of Begin and Sadat, and devoured histories of the Middle East conflict.[63] For a change, Vance and Brzezinski's teams worked seamlessly, using Averell Harriman's Virginia retreat for preparatory sessions. Carter's decision was to lock the two leaders and their teams into his wooded retreat in Catoctin Mountain Park until he had brokered a deal or failed. He limited each delegation to principals plus a handful of aides.

Apart from one brief photo op, the media were kept off-site. Outside communications were impossible except via the phones in the cabins, which both the Israelis and the Egyptians wrongly assumed were bugged. In that fashion, Carter maintained silence about the state of the talks for almost two weeks. The delegations totaled forty-four people with another eighty or so support staff. They were all packed into the complex, sleeping on hastily assembled cots in rooms designed for one or two. Brzezinski shared a room with Hamilton Jordan. His daughter, Mika, now eleven, bunked with Amy Carter. The girls spent the first few days of the summit swimming, biking, and watching movies. To them it was a holiday camp. By contrast, to the recalcitrant Begin, the accommodation was "concentration camp deluxe."[64] After several days, everyone started complaining of cabin fever.

Carter saw the Israeli and Egyptian delegations as mirror images of each other. Begin was by far the most obdurate and legally hairsplitting member of his team. Carter often turned to Moshe Dayan, the Israeli foreign minister, and Ezer Weizman, the defense minister, to find ways around their leader.

They often obliged. At one fraught moment, Weizman and Dayan telephoned Ariel Sharon, Begin's tough agriculture minister, to get his support for dismantling Israeli settlements in the Sinai Desert. Sharon agreed to the move as long as it was put to the Knesset. Only then did Begin accede.[65]

Sadat's team, conversely, was filled with hawks. Poetic, emotional, and serially impulsive, Sadat was everything lacking in Begin; frequently, however, his flexibility and willingness to be swayed by Carter's appeals to history alienated him from his own delegation. At 4:15 a.m. one morning, Carter woke Brzezinski on his cabin phone and asked him to come over. The president was paranoid about Sadat's security. He had inadvertently disclosed to one of Sadat's most hawkish negotiators a big concession the Egyptian leader had made to him in a private meeting. At ten o'clock the previous evening when Carter walked over to Sadat's cabin, he was told the Egyptian leader was asleep even though the lights were still on. Since Sadat was a famous night bird, he feared the worst. "Zbig, I am very much concerned for Sadat's life," said Carter, who had awakened with a terrible premonition.[66] Brzezinski quickly tightened security and had all the comings and goings from Sadat's cabin monitored.

During a postdinner chat Brzezinski had one evening with Weizman and Boutros Boutros-Ghali, Egypt's deputy foreign minister, the latter disclosed his view that Sadat should not sign the draft deal being hammered out. Its provisions for Palestinian autonomy were too vaguely worded; Sadat would be putting himself at severe risk both in the Arab world and at home.[67] His forebodings were prophetic. For the same reason, Boutros-Ghali's boss, Mohammed Ibrahim Kamel, resigned before the summit was over (though he agreed to keep it private until afterwards). Kamel had been in place only a few months; his predecessor had quit in protest at Sadat's trip to Jerusalem. Most of the business with Sadat was conducted privately by Carter.

After three days, Carter concluded that nothing would be achieved with the Israelis and Egyptians in one room. At their supposedly collective meals in the Aspen cabin, the Egyptian and Israeli delegations sat at separate tables. The only exception was when Weizman shifted ostentatiously to the Egyptian table to prove a point. "There was a lot of bantering, laughing, exchanges of anecdotes," Brzezinski observed. "Dayan sat at the other table sulking, obviously irritated by Weizman's little coup."[68] Begin ate kosher food prepared by the camp's Filipino cooks, alone in his cabin.

Carter therefore switched from playing broker to taking charge of parallel bilateral talks. He himself drafted many of the outlined texts. Neither before nor since has a US president involved himself in a negotiation so closely and over such a long period of time. Brzezinski's contemporaneous jottings during the Carter years were often critical of Carter, although rarely scathing. Throughout the Camp David summit, his admiration of Carter's mastery of detail and refusal to give up is striking. "His textual criticisms are as good as by any expert," he thought. Carter's voracious appetite for detail was in other contexts a handicap; at Camp David it was indispensable. One morning, he spent almost four hours alone with the Israeli and Egyptian legal experts reviewing the document he had drawn up. "I am immensely impressed by the amount of determination and concentration on detail that the President has been displaying," Brzezinski wrote.[69]

For the most part, Brzezinski and Vance worked well together, although the latter's tendency to agree with everything Carter said was an annoyance. Vance was too much of a yes-man for Brzezinski's taste. To Rosalynn, Carter described Begin as a "psycho."[70] The coldness between them was tangible. Towards Sadat, on the other hand, Carter had deep affection. Again and again, the Egyptian leader pulled Carter's irons out of the fire. At one US-only gathering, Carter was elaborating on the vast differences between the two leaders. His praise for Sadat was emphatic. "My chemistry with him is good," he said. "I feel with him the way I feel with Cy Vance." Vance replied, "Yes because Cy accommodates you the way Sadat does, isn't that right?" Everyone laughed. Pointing at Brzezinski, Carter added, "Yes and you're just like Begin." Brzezinski took that as a compliment. "I think this remark was in some respects quite true," he noted to himself.[71]

When Carter could no longer face talking to Begin, he sent Vance. But he insisted that Brzezinski accompany the secretary of state to ensure a tough line was upheld. Brzezinski was the chief Begin handler, helped by their shared Polish background and love of chess. One afternoon, he challenged Begin to a game on his cabin porch. Begin grumbled that he had not played since he was interrupted in the middle of a game in 1940 when he was arrested by Stalin's NKVD. During his first encounter with Brzezinski, Mrs. Begin inconveniently turned up and blurted out, "Menachem just loves to play chess!"[72] Brzezinski lost the first game after he gambled his queen too soon. In the second he took a leaf from Begin's playbook and consolidated his defense first. He equalized. Over the following days, they played twice more, ending at two games apiece. At one tense stage of the talks, Begin asked Brzezinski to accompany him on a walk. He said he had always defended Brzezinski from unfair attacks in the Israeli and US media. He therefore felt wounded to hear that Brzezinski was referring to the Israeli West Bank settlements as "a form of colonialism." He also heard that Carter had been using the same vocabulary. Begin described the idea that the settlements could be dismantled as "fantasmorphic."[73]

If Begin could not be moved on the Israeli settlements, the whole endeavor would come to naught. Sadat's readiness to risk being the first Arab leader to recognize Israel was predicated on Begin's willingness to agree to eventual Palestinian self-determination, even if the timeline stretched to several years. Though the term *two-state solution* was never used, that was Carter and Sadat's implicit goal. Sadat made it clear that the first part of the deal, in which Israel would gradually withdraw from the Sinai Peninsula in exchange for Egypt's diplomatic recognition, had to be linked to an agreed-upon mechanism that would result in a Palestinian homeland. In spite of Carter's best efforts and various runarounds via his Israeli colleagues, Begin would not budge.

He and Carter spent hours arguing about UN Resolution 242, which stated the "inadmissibility of the acquisition of territory by war." Carter took the mainstream view that the language applied to the West Bank, which Israel had occupied in the 1967 Six-Day War. Begin insisted that the UN wording should not apply to the territories of what he called Judea and Samaria. Carter privately began to question the Israeli leader's sanity. Unbeknownst to him, Sadat had already decided to quit the negotiations. On day eleven, Vance rushed in ashen-faced with the news that Sadat had ordered a chopper to take him to Dulles International Airport. The Egyptians were packed and ready to go. It was the second time Sadat had threatened to bolt; on the first, Carter had physically blocked him from leaving the room.[74] This time, Carter had to think of something more drastic; he threatened to downgrade relations with Egypt, which would risk pushing it back into the Soviet orbit. Their friendship, and possibly even Carter's presidency, would come to an end if Sadat quit. "I was dead serious and he knew it," Carter wrote in his memoirs.[75]

Sadat wanted to know how Carter would ensure that Israel would commit itself to genuine substance on Palestinian autonomy, including language on East Jerusalem's sovereign status. Carter improvised a novel pledge; he told Sadat that if any part of the deal was abrogated, the whole package would unravel—an all-or-nothing promise to stop Israel from backsliding that he vowed he would publicize were it to happen. That pledge was enough for

Sadat. After a lengthy pause, he promised to stick with Carter to the end.[76] It is hard to imagine the two Middle Eastern leaders enduring twenty-four hours of negotiation with each other in Carter's absence.

The final documents were a master class in linguistic sleight of hand. The Egypt-Israel part of the deal was relatively straightforward since both leaders wanted it. Carter nevertheless had to sweeten the pot by offering Sadat a large consignment of wheat and maize; with Begin, he agreed that the United States would finance two new airstrips inside Israel in exchange for Israel's giving up the two it had built in the Sinai. Carter's jujitsu lay in the second part of the deal. The wording on Palestinian autonomy was so imprecise that it would be child's play for a legal hairsplitter such as Begin to reinterpret.

The package nearly came undone at the last minute when Begin objected to the provision on Jerusalem that had been part of Sadat's price for not quitting. Carter rushed over to Begin's cabin with pictures of himself for each of the Israeli leader's grandchildren. On each he had written, "With love and best wishes." To Carter's concealed delight, his gesture triggered deep emotion in Begin. The Israeli leader's eyes filled with tears as he talked of each of his grandchildren, one by one.[77] He waved through the next draft of the Jerusalem side letter, which was only slightly more anodyne than the one he had so adamantly rejected. Such are the idiosyncrasies that can bridge the gap between failure and success.

When it became clear the deal was done, Carter sent Brzezinski back to Washington ahead of the others to brief the media. Most of the last-minute hitches and technicalities were handled by Vance and Carter. Though he had ably played the role of lieutenant, Brzezinski was a strategic thinker, much happier sketching out grander themes than haggling over legal terminology. The details came more naturally to Vance the lawyer and Carter the engineer. At about 5:30 p.m. on Monday, September 18, Vance told Carter, "I think you have it." Carter reclined in his chair with a wistful smile. "No one spoke up, no one cheered, there was a sense of genuine admiration for what Carter had achieved," Brzezinski wrote. At that moment a great storm hit Camp David. Flashes of lightning and thunderclaps added to the sense that history was being made. Once the winds abated, Brzezinski was the one who unveiled the deal to the world. He took a chopper to the White House and then briefed the media. Only then did he realize what a coup Carter had pulled off. Having been sealed off from the outside world for so long, he had forgotten that almost no one had a clue about what had been going on. "There was an audible gasp when I announced the conditions of the Egyptian-Israeli agreement," he wrote. "The sense of excitement mounted steadily as the briefing went on."[78]

What followed were parallel movies in which Washington, both houses of Congress, and the world's media feted Carter as a master negotiator. Blessed are the peacemakers, he said, pointing at Begin and Sadat to bipartisan whoops and applause. Muska had joined Rosalynn Carter and Gay Vance next to them in the congressional gallery. In the other movie, meanwhile, Begin was celebrating only the Egypt-Israel portion of the deal. He put his own stamp on a clause in which Israel promised that no new Israeli settlements would be built in the West Bank and Gaza Strip "during the negotiations." Carter and everyone else had taken that pledge to cover the upcoming five years of talks on Palestinian autonomy. But Begin declared that the freeze would hold only for the three months of negotiations needed to wrap up the final details of the Egypt-Israel treaty. His switch was a blow to Carter and especially to Sadat. It was an act of bad faith that Carter never forgave. A few weeks later, Sadat and Begin won a joint Nobel Peace Prize. "Sadat deserved it," wrote Carter. "Begin did not."[79] Dayan and Weizman both expressed embarrassment to Carter and Brzezinski about Begin's actions.

For the time being, however, all bitterness was set aside. At a celebratory cocktail party at Mondale's official residence, Brzezinski was the toast of the American Jewish community. Though his role had been secondary, he took undisguised pleasure in his newfound popularity. The smiling AIPAC leader, Morris Amitay, told Brzezinski that if Begin and Sadat could shake hands, they surely could, too. Brzezinski laughed, and they made peace.[80] The following day, the New York Times' Scotty Reston called Brzezinski to confirm a story going around town that Sadat had been packed and ready to go and had been dissuaded from leaving by secret promises from Carter. Having no idea what Carter had promised to Sadat, Brzezinski told Reston he had to hang up as the president was calling.[81] Carter then called him over to his office and related the details of his conversation with Sadat. He had told only Rosalynn and Vance about its content. Brzezinski was moved by Sadat's readiness to place his trust in Carter. "You know the implication of this is that you have to be very steadfast on the settlements," he told Carter.[82] The president replied, "I hadn't thought of that but that is true." Tragically, Carter's inability to enforce part two of Camp David would play a role in Sadat's assassination just three years later.

·   ·   ·

During less frantic phases in Brzezinski's career, Muska would be his editor and fiercest critic. If she could not understand the meaning of his words, he was failing the test. His formal communication skills improved only slightly while he was in office. The *New Yorker* would even lampoon his excessive abstractions and pregnant subclauses in a spoof called "Brzezinski's Tips for Teens." On love and sex: "What we have failed to grasp adequately, in my judgment, is the organic connection between love and sex. The two are fundamentally linked and in any attempt to grasp what's happening to your very complex yet intersecting processes of growth you cannot separate them."[83] Now that Brzezinski had a bureaucracy to support him and the kids were happily settled in local Virginia schools, Muska could indulge her passion for art full-time. With twelve sprawling acres of woodland, their home in McLean was ideal for her particular line in sculptures. She built a large art studio in their garden— more like a carpentry workshop—where she worked on her carvings. They were made from giant pieces of driftwood that were often dragged home by her husband and the children. Her other style, which was unique, was to take molds of trees with latex and convert them into plexiglass sculptures.[84]

All the various admiring media profiles of Muska noted her dislike for the Washington social circuit. Being a spouse meant playing the wallflower. "I dislike it when I feel obliged *not* to participate," she told one newspaper.[85] Her exhibitions were nevertheless local media events.[86] From the first lady downwards, other wives showed up. Ambassadors also turned out in strength. The wife of the Japanese ambassador, Fumihiko Togo, bought *Springhill Locust* for $3,000 on the opening night of Muska's exhibition at Osuna Galleries in early 1979. Morocco's Mrs. Ali Benjelloun bought *Englewood Maple* for $900. Muska's style was inimitable and personalized. "She told me about it once at Camp David but I couldn't visualize it," Mrs. Carter told the *Washington Star*. Brzezinski would try and fail to stay in the background. "I inspired it all. I'm the essence of negative space," he joked to the attendees. It being Washington, Muska knew she could never separate her art from her public husband. "We'll invite her to the Soviet-American summit," said Anatoly Dobrynin. "She can show the leaders how to carve their way through the trees."

The Brzezinski family's relationship with the Carters was in some ways a substitute for the president's threadbare social life. To the disdain of Georgetown and to his political cost, Carter spurned the cocktail party set, much as Muska did. That gave him a reputation for both aloofness and provincialism. He frequently hosted movie nights in the White House's subterranean theater. He also invited families, including the Vances and the Brzezinskis, for weekends at Camp David, where he spent nearly a quarter of his presidency, considerably more than any president before or since.[87] There was a lot of swimming, hiking, tennis, and movies. In keeping with Carter's puritanical bent, almost no alcohol was consumed. One evening, the Carters invited themselves over for dinner in McLean. It was a relaxed meal; no one stood on ceremony.

To the children, hanging out with world leaders, senators, and ambassadors was a routine part of their upbringing. Dobrynin and Britain's ambassador, Peter Jay, were regulars. The Brzezinskis' close neighbor was Richard Lugar, a Republican senator from Indiana. The youthful Joe Biden often dropped by. At family dinners, Brzezinski would propose topics for debate, then subject his children to the same merciless interrogation as he did his subordinates. Motions such as whether to abolish capital punishment would be laid down at the start of the meal. "What did I think of inflation? I didn't know what I thought of inflation. I was a child." Mika later recalled. All of the children said that when their father won a debate, he would be happy. If he was outnumbered, he would be downcast.[88] For the most part, Muska kept up an amused tolerance.

But family dinners were becoming a rarity. Brzezinski's days were long, and he was seldom free of crisis. The Carter years were turning into a rolling foreign policy emergency. By the autumn of 1978, the ambassador with whom Brzezinski was spending most time was Iran's Ardeshir Zahedi. Since Carter's glittering stopover in Tehran the previous New Year's Eve, Iran's simmering unrest had barely registered. To the distaste of State's newly created Bureau of Democracy, Human Rights, and Labor, Carter had continued the settled practice, with only small modifications, of waving through whatever outsized military orders the shah requested. Other than the controversies around that, which were mostly about Carter's double standards—the shah's regime being neither a democracy nor a paragon of human rights—Iran issues rarely appeared in his in tray.

That changed on September 8 when Iranian troops fired on a large demonstration in Tehran's Jaleh Square, killing at least a hundred protestors and probably far more. The shah had declared martial law two days earlier. Carter, Vance, and Brzezinski were in the thick of Middle East negotiations at Camp David and had little time to pore over the cables from Tehran. After a brief call with the shah, Carter issued a rote statement of support for his efforts to restore stability and press on with political reform.[89] Given Carter's level of distraction, he could be forgiven for missing the significance of the massacre. In hindsight, Jaleh Square was the point of no return. Considering Carter's devotion to human rights, however, his reflexive backing of a repressive autocrat was worse than mere oversight; it was a giant stain on his presidency. Brzezinski and Vance were caught just as unawares as their boss.

To be fair, almost every part of the system, from the intelligence agencies to State and especially the US Embassy in Tehran, was oblivious to the gravity of Iranian events. William Sullivan, the US ambassador, had just returned to Tehran after having spent an eye-popping three months out of the country on vacation. Before his vanishing act, he had in May sent a note on the shah's outlook. "Iran has now reached the position of a stable and moderate middle-level power," he wrote. "There are no outstanding issues of such serious magnitude that they need to be identified in this memorandum."[90] At a lunch in early July with Brzezinski and Gary Sick, the NSC's Iran aide, Sullivan had underlined his serene confidence in Iran's stability.[91] The US ambassador was in good company. In September, the Defense Intelligence Agency said that the shah "was expected to remain actively in power over the next ten years."[92] The system's serial blindness on Iran amounts to one of the most egregious failures in the history of America's diplomatic, security, and intelligence apparatus. As Sick would later conclude, US intelligence reports about Iran were "sheer gobbledygook masquerading as informed judgment."[93]

Brzezinski's friendship with Ardeshir Zahedi was a critical factor in America's evolving response to the crisis in Iran. As the son-in-law of the shah, Zahedi was as close as it got to being a plenipotentiary ambassador. Perhaps even more significantly, his father, General Fazlollah Zahedi, had been the head of the Iranian army in 1953 when the CIA overthrew Iran's nationalist prime minister, Mohammed Mossadegh, and restored the young shah to the throne. As a reward for Zahedi's role in the coup, the shah appointed him prime minister. As the Iranian crisis unfolded in late 1978, his son became Brzezinski's ideal back channel. He was also the face of what Washington loved about the shah's Iran. Zahedi's parties at his gilded official residence on Massachusetts Avenue's Embassy Row were in a decadent class of their own.[94] Champagne flowed like water, Caspian Sea caviar was placed next to edible flower arrangements, and movie stars such as Barbra Streisand and Liza Minnelli lolled on leopard skin–covered chaise longues. Drugs were consumed on the premises. On party nights, the road outside was gridlocked with limousines. Though married to the shah's daughter, Zahedi dated the actress Elizabeth Taylor and the *Washington Post*'s star reporter Sally Quinn. His residence was the closest DC came to New York's Studio 54.

Through successive administrations, Washington's power brokers had been so seduced by the shah that to them, he was Iran and Iran was the shah. In 1971, the cream of DC had decamped to Persepolis in Iran's Fars province, where the shah had hosted a neo-Caligulan celebration of twenty-five hundred years of the Iranian monarchy, styling himself "King of Kings,"[95] thus linking himself to Cyrus the Great. He laid on caviar, roast peacock, champagne, and raspberries from Paris's Maxim's restaurant to entertain his three thousand mostly foreign guests. Nixon's vice president, Spiro Agnew, represented the United States. Britain's Queen Elizabeth II was advised to steer clear. She sent her husband, Prince Philip, in her stead. The Philippines' first lady, Imelda Marcos, was there, as well as Ethiopia's Haile Selassie, North Korea's Kim Jong Il, and nearly every sheikh and emir from the region. The Shah's bout of conspicuous self-indulgence coincided with the beginnings of a famine in the same province, which in turn sparked the protests that would convulse Iran on and off for the remainder of the decade. The Western media were as clueless about the brewing crisis as the CIA. On November 4, 1974, *Time* put the shah on the cover, describing him as a man who had "brought Iran to a threshold of grandeur that is at least analogous to what Cyrus the Great achieved for ancient Persia."[96] Iran's surface allure was fueled by its swelling oil revenues after the OPEC embargo in 1973. The shah recycled most of his oil proceeds into lavish spending on the latest US military hardware.

Following Nixon and Kissinger's trip to Tehran in 1972, Kissinger issued a directive exempting the shah's military order book from normal Washington security reviews.[97] The shah, in effect, was given the unique privilege of securing whatever hardware he wanted. His shopping list included more than a hundred F-14 fighter jets, the AWACS early-warning radar system, and Iran's nascent civil nuclear program. Between 1972 and 1977, Iran accounted for almost half of US military exports.[98] Iran's cocktail of sumptuous hospitality, rolling defense industry contracts, and America's geostrategic myopia was a reality that Carter inherited. The shah was the most prized exemplar of the Nixon Doctrine, in which Nixon had outsourced regional security to key local allies. To Nixon and then Ford, Iran's ruler was their man in the Middle East. Iran was also the toast of Grumman Aerospace, Lockheed Martin, Boeing, AT&T, Chase Manhattan, and much of the rest of the Fortune 500. Kissinger, as ever, personified the relationship. In a Tehran nightclub during their 1972 visit, a belly dancer, Nadia Parsa, danced on Kissinger's table, then sat on his lap. "She was a charming girl and very interested in foreign policy," Kissinger quipped.[99]

Such was the backdrop of the revolution that convulsed Carter's presidency. Exotic dancers and risqué embassy parties were not Brzezinski's style; power was. At a dinner that Zahedi hosted for Iran's crown prince, the shah's eighteen-year-old son, Reza Pahlavi, in late October 1978, Brzezinski was the American guest of honor.[100] After the customary banter and toasts, Brzezinski and Zahedi sequestered themselves from the other guests in an adjoining room. There they reviewed their options. It was a critical moment in the unfolding saga. A few days later, Zahedi returned to Tehran on a mission to stiffen the shah's resolve. Because of his frequent flights back and forth, he became known at State as Brzezinski's man in Tehran.[101]

To Carter and Brzezinski's surprise and contrary to their urgings, Iran's ruler had been impassive in the face of disintegrating order in the weeks since the Jaleh Square massacre. Vance was too preoccupied with Middle East shuttle diplomacy to be closely involved. Nobody could understand the shah's inaction. At a Security Coordination Committee meeting on November 2, Brzezinski reviewed a range of possible responses. State wanted the shah to enter into a coalition with the opposition parties, including Shiite radicals representing the exiled Ayatollah Ruhollah Khomeini. Brzezinski saw the project as a pipe dream. His knowledge of revolutions, especially the Bolshevik one, convinced him that reform in the midst of a chaotic power vacuum was likely to precipitate a revolution. The system must first establish order before politics could be liberalized.

The November 2 SCC meeting had been triggered by an urgent cable from Ambassador Sullivan, who said that the shah was in desperate need of Washington's guidance. Iran's ruler seemed to be paralyzed with indecision. Brzezinski argued that the US should back the shah in whatever actions he deemed necessary to restore order. In the middle of the meeting, Carter called from Air Force One. Brzezinski secured his approval for that message. The following morning, he called the shah to convey the gist of it. "He sounded very alone, not very forthcoming, quite depressed and concerned," he thought. "Rather revealingly, he asked me whether the ambassador [Sullivan] had been briefed on the substance of the message, thereby further conveying the impression that the US embassy may have been pushing in the opposite direction."[102] That same morning, Brzezinski received the latest CIA report. "Good news!" he wrote to Carter in a memo. "[According to the CIA,] Iran is not in a revolutionary or even a 'pre-revolutionary' situation."[103]

The next day, protestors stormed the British Embassy in Tehran and partially burned it. The British ambassador, Anthony Parsons, moved briefly into Sullivan's residence. With great reluctance, the shah formed a military government and flooded Tehran with security forces. Nelson Rockefeller, whose family-owned bank, Chase Manhattan, was Iran's largest creditor, telephoned Brzezinski to congratulate him on his resolve, which, he said, had saved the day. For a short while it seemed as though the shah had regained control. "I shudder to think what would have happened had the State Department line prevailed," Brzezinski wrote on November 7. "We would have had a first-class crisis on our hands."[104]

Brzezinski and Rockefeller were sorely misinformed. The shah's military was by design as divided as the rest of the country. Always paranoid about a coup, the shah had ensured that his top generals were at loggerheads with one another. Any prospect of a coherent military stance was delusional. Iran's generals were as impassive as the shah in the face of turmoil on Tehran's streets. On November 9, Sullivan dropped the diplomatic equivalent of a bombshell with a cable entitled "Thinking the Unthinkable." He laid out his preferred scenario, in which the now-discredited shah would leave the country along with his senior generals. After that, the younger pro-Western Iranian military officers would form an alliance with the repatriated Ayatollah Khomeini. The ayatollah would play a "Gandhi-like" role as the spiritual leader of Iran's new arrangement without involving himself in day-to-day politics.

The Carter administration was confused, to put it mildly. On Iran, its mind was as divided as the shah's. State, led by its Iran desk officer, Henry Precht, was pushing for a coalition government and a new constitution in which Iran's now-figurehead monarchy would be subject to a referendum. Precht's other obsession was Brzezinski. The State Department's loathing for Brzezinski was reaching almost "pathological proportions," thought Gary Sick.[105] Ambassador Sullivan, who was turning rogue and ignoring Washington's instructions, thought he could fashion his own solution based on his frequent contact with the shah. Brzezinski wanted a military crackdown. None of those remedies was realistic. Brzezinski's was too bloody for Carter and, it turned out, also for the shah. Zahedi's efforts to find the right generals to lead a pro-shah regime were coming to naught. Brzezinski's key aide,

Gary Sick, thought that Zahedi wanted a replay of the 1953 coup in which he would emulate his father and be rewarded with the prime ministership. But there were no generals able or willing to take control. The supposed secular opposition to the shah was equally weak and in disarray. Most of its key figures had been exiled or jailed. The notion of a civilian national front was thus also based on fantasy. Sullivan, meanwhile, had convinced himself that Ayatollah Khomeini's return would have a benevolent impact; the Shiite leader would provide a calming influence as Iran's spiritual guide.

Only Carter could cut through the three wildly clashing Iran policies and impose a clear line. He never did. Had he been given accurate intelligence, things might have turned out differently. Carter's team was blinded on two critical fronts. The first was the potency of the Iranian mullahs. Nobody in the US government had any experience of a religious overthrow; theocratic revolution simply did not feature in anyone's playbook. Neither Carter nor Brzezinski yet understood the difference between Shia and Sunni Islam. If intelligence operatives had read Khomeini's freely available tomes or listened to his recorded messages distributed on cassette tapes via Iran's mosques, they would never have mistaken him for a nonviolent Shiite version of Mohandas Gandhi. Few of them took Khomeini's words seriously. The shah was also ignorant of the mullahs' appeal. He had swallowed his own propaganda that Iran was a modernizing society in which women's freedoms were secure and social progress was popular. Having robbed Iran of its secular critics, the Shah had unwittingly ensured that the mosques were the only remaining hubs of dissent.

The second key missing piece of intelligence was on the shah's ill health. Unknown to the CIA but likely known to French intelligence, the shah had been suffering from lymphoma for several years and was in a worsening physical condition. He had been diagnosed by two French physicians in 1974, possibly earlier. Either way, by 1978, he was in no state physically or mentally to get a grip on Iran's security crisis, which Brzezinski was continuing to urge him to do. If Carter and Brzezinski had known of the shah's short life expectancy, they might have gone back to the drawing board. As it happened, the US did have a huge intelligence presence in Iran. Yet the agency's Iran operations were focused solely on gathering data from its listening posts on the Soviet-Iranian border. For reports on Iran's internal situation, the CIA and others relied almost exclusively on information fed to them by SAVAK, the shah's notorious secret police. SAVAK told the shah and Langley what they wanted to hear about Iran's domestic stability.

In November 1978, Brzezinski woke up to the scale of America's vast intelligence failure. He got Carter to write a letter to Stansfield Turner, urging him to fill in the gap.[106] But it was too late for the CIA to cultivate the assets required to produce useful insights into Iran. Brzezinski's other move was to persuade Carter to appoint George Ball, a former UN ambassador and member of the Georgetown set, to conduct a lightning inquiry into Iran policy. After a two-week scramble, Ball's conclusions were very much in line with the State Department's. He called for a "Council of Notables" to take charge in Iran. Brzezinski admitted to himself that he had broken the cardinal rule of not finding out what Ball thought before he commissioned his services.

In addition to upholding State's view, Ball told Vance that Brzezinski was running a separate Iran policy through Zahedi. That "snake-like" behavior appalled Brzezinski. "I have learned my lesson," he wrote. "We will never use him again."[107] Ball also scotched Carter's plan to send Brzezinski to Tehran, which he described as "the worst idea I had ever heard." It turned out that nobody had any good ideas. Ball told Arthur Schlesinger, Jr., that he had never seen a Washington policy mess quite like it. "Zbig made two miscalculations: about the Shah and about me," he said. But he assigned the primary blame for the Iranian mess to Kissinger. It was under Kissinger and Nixon that "the all-out embrace began," Ball said. "It wasn't a failure of intelligence. It was a failure of policy."[108]

Kissinger, meanwhile, was reveling in Brzezinski's discomfort. "[Kissinger] detests Brzezinski, likes Vance but thinks him ineffective and thinks Carter is highly intelligent but intolerably self-centered," wrote Schlesinger following a dinner with Kissinger.[109] Everyone seemed to be feasting on Carter's Iran woes. His ordeal was only just beginning.

At one of their periodic lunches shortly before Christmas, Kissinger struck a markedly different note with Brzezinski than he had with Schlesinger or in his regular chats with Dobrynin: Kissinger told Brzezinski that he was in roughly the same position as he had been after two years on the job. Brzezinski was getting about the same amount of credit and attracting a similar intensity of attacks. "He urged me to keep my cool, not to respond, to let attacks develop, and then to strike back when the other side makes a truly tactical error."[110] The "other side" in that case was the State Department. A few days earlier, Brzezinski had sealed his China coup. On December 15, to the surprise of the State

Department, the Soviets, and the world's media, the White House announced the normalization of relations with China.

The final stages of the negotiations had been kept secret. Only a handful of people other than the chief negotiator, Leonard Woodcock, had been privy to the talks. Vance and his team were given a few hours' notice. "This news came as a shock," Vance wrote in his memoirs.[111] Holbrooke was also oblivious to what had been happening. The Soviets were stunned; all color drained from Dobrynin's face when Brzezinski broke the news to him in his White House office.[112] Restoring relations with Vietnam would have to wait another seventeen years. Both Nixon and Kissinger asked Brzezinski to pass on their congratulations to Carter. Kissinger had once told Nixon, "We should be able to have our *maotai* and drink our vodka too."[113] He was now apparently shifting towards Brzezinski's Cold War logic. China normalization would be politically helpful to Brzezinski, he said.

The deal almost unraveled at the last minute. After having been given almost no warning, Vance's deputy, Warren Christopher, insisted that Holbrooke be included in the final hours. Brzezinski said that Holbrooke was a leak risk since he was dating the CBS reporter Diane Sawyer.[114] Carter and Oksenberg also opposed bringing Holbrooke into the loop. After a testy exchange with Christopher, Brzezinski relented. On hurriedly reading the draft US-China communiqué, Holbrooke noticed that there was no language covering US arms sales to Taiwan following the specified one-year moratorium. Woodcock had to hurry back to Deng Xiaoping to get his sign-off on the missing language. The Chinese leader lost his temper but was mollified when Woodcock assured him that any military transfers would take place in secret. Brzezinski knew that it would be impossible to maintain secrecy on arms sales and conveyed that to Chai Zemin, the Chinese representative in DC. Having heard nothing back from Chai, he took Deng's silence as acquiescence. That it was Holbrooke who spotted the potentially fatal oversight was beyond ironic. "When he sets his mind to a problem, he does have useful and thoughtful points to make," Brzezinski conceded.[115]

The announcement went ahead without further hitch. Holbrooke helped brief the media as if he had been in on the act all along. Brzezinski considered China normalization his biggest feat so far. "That this event represents a momentous shift in the geopolitical order is, I think, self-evident," he wrote.[116] Carter, who was famously parsimonious with credit, called Brzezinski that weekend to commend him. "You were genuinely the driving force," Carter said. "Whenever

I wavered you pushed me and pressed me to go through with this."[117] Carter always maintained that China normalization was his proudest accomplishment.[118]

The task of officially breaking relations with the Taiwanese fell to Christopher. "There was little competition in the upper echelons of the administration for the assignment," Christopher drily recalled later.[119] After he arrived in Taipei, his motorcade was attacked by an angry mob. CARTER SELLS PEANUTS—ALSO FRIENDS read one banner. The Taiwanese police did nothing to restrain the protestors. All the windows of his official car were shattered, and he was covered with broken eggs and tomatoes. He was lucky to escape with a few cuts and bruises. The hapless Christopher was then assigned the job of shepherding the new Taiwan Relations Act through Congress. Ronald Reagan had branded the deal a "betrayal"[120] and scheduled his own trip to Taiwan. Jesse Helms said that Carter was planning to "sell Taiwan down the river."[121]

The news about China landed with a thud in Geneva, where Vance's negotiators were finalizing SALT II details with their Soviet opposites. Moscow was enraged by the language against "hegemony" in the US-China communiqué. That term had long been Beijing's preferred taunt against the Soviets. The two negotiating teams had developed a spirit of camaraderie. At their weekly socials, the Soviets drank Kentucky bourbon and the Americans consumed Russian vodka.[122] Progress had been modest and painstaking. But the outlines of a deal were now in sight. A conclusion would set up Carter's much craved summit with Brezhnev.

Brzezinski and Vance had been in a race to see which would happen first: a visit by Deng Xiaoping to the US or Carter's summit with the Soviet leader. Brzezinski had at several moments in the previous weeks spurred Deng to accelerate the talks by saying that a SALT II deal and a visit by Brezhnev to Washington were imminent.[123] Brzezinski's methods could have come straight from Kissinger's playbook. There were still details to iron out in Geneva. The White House was worried that Vance's team was paying too little attention to ways of verifying the treaty's limits on missile testing and deployment. The Senate's distrust of Soviet behavior since SALT I meant that the new treaty had to include robust constraints on telemetric encryption to ensure that the Soviets did not cheat again.

To Brzezinski and Carter's concern, Vance was not pressing that forcefully enough with Gromyko. As the joke went, the Soviet position was that "gentlemen did not read each other's telemetry."[124] Without strong verification mechanisms, the treaty would likely be doomed in the Senate. Carter had long since lost Scoop Jackson's support. Public opinion was also skeptical of Soviet promises, as Jordan kept reminding him. Five days before Christmas, Carter convened a lunch of his principals in response to a lengthy complaint he had received from Vance that Brzezinski had routinely been undermining him.[125] The atmosphere was jittery as they settled down to the meal in the Roosevelt Room. Carter asked Vance to go first. He launched a sharp attack on Brzezinski's tendency to portray the State Department as soft, about his back-channel contacts with ambassadors, the fact that it was Brzezinski who summarized the minutes even of NSC meetings that Vance chaired, and the exclusion of Vance's State from the China negotiations. Carter then asked Brzezinski to respond.

Brzezinski pointed out that Carter had given him responsibility for China and Vance the lead on SALT II and that each kept the other about equally well informed. Nobody had complained about any slant in the NSC minutes that Brzezinski's staff provided to Carter (on that question Harold Brown later weighed in on Brzezinski's side). Meanwhile, the torrent of leaks by State against Brzezinski were on a scale far worse than the other way around. Carter came down strongly in Brzezinski's favor. As his surrogate, Brzezinski had been the target of constant attacks, he said. Among the worst leakers were Gelb and Holbrooke. Vance interrupted Carter to protest that he had done all he could to stem their leaking but had not fully succeeded. Carter said he had given Brzezinski the China portfolio because the Chinese had more confidence in him than in Vance. Moreover, he wanted to keep the NSC minuting system as it was. He did not like the idea of outsiders meddling in White House business. The latter was another pointed reference to State Department leakers. Carter's summation was anything but evenhanded. Nobody present could miss his sharp rebuke to State. "He sure leaned towards you, didn't he?" Jordan said to Brzezinski after the meeting.

A bruised Vance returned to Geneva that night to finalize SALT II. His triumphant hour was potentially at hand. The prospect that he could tie up the deal and announce a summit with Brezhnev in mid-January—before Deng's now publicly agreed trip to the US at the end of the month—offered some Christmas cheer after his recent humiliations. Yet the thorny question of encryption would not go away. Vance had agreed with Gromyko that they would ban the encryption of missile tests "wherever it impedes verification."[126] The issue reached a climax on the night of December 22. Vance cabled the White House with what he thought was the final language on encryption. All he needed was Carter's sign-off and SALT II would be done. Paul Warnke and Marshall Shulman were so confident that the deal was complete that they stayed up most of the night drinking whiskey. Years later, Shulman would joke that he was still suffering from a hangover.[127]

But the Vance-Gromyko formula did not go down well with Harold Brown and Stansfield Turner. Muska Brzezinski and David Aaron's wife, Chloe, were waiting outside the British Embassy to go into its Christmas party.[128] Their husbands had to rush back to the White House for a meeting with Brown and Turner. The wives went into the reception without them. After a long, hairsplitting meeting, the officials concluded that Vance would have to go back to Gromyko the next morning and nail down more concrete language. Brzezinski called Carter, who was in Plains, Georgia, for Christmas and in bed suffering from a painful case of hemorrhoids, to get his agreement. Brzezinski cabled Vance at midnight, which was 6:00 a.m. in Geneva. An agitated Vance telephoned Brzezinski and pleaded that he be left with on-the-ground discretion to conclude the deal.[129]

This time Brzezinski had to awake Carter, who reiterated that Vance must stick to the language that Brown and Turner had drafted. By the time Brzezinski could return Vance's call, the secretary of state was already at the Geneva negotiating center, which was hosted in a Soviet building. They spoke on phones that were likely tapped by the Soviets. Referring elliptically "to that earlier conversation," Brzezinski told Vance that "the previous instructions stand." Vance was by now "livid and close to mutiny," according to one aide.[130] As Vance feared, Gromyko bristled at having to reopen an issue he had thought was settled. The Soviets retaliated with a host of abstruse new demands. It would take another three months for SALT II to be completed. Brzezinski had won the battle of sequencing. Carter's summit with Brezhnev would have to wait.

Deng, on the other hand, was ready for the big stage. At the White House Christmas reception for the media, Brzezinski was slapped on the back, congratulated, flattered, and wooed. Big media names offered to write profiles of Brzezinski and requested exclusives. After a year of being the media's favorite bugbear, Brzezinski found the sudden change "rather sickening." He wrote, "Just as I didn't deserve all of the brickbats, I certainly don't now deserve all of the praise. But the China affair is being turned into a personal success for me. Since it won't last, I may as well lap it up."[131] He had no trouble doing that. With the assistance of Deng, who became an instant celebrity in the United

States and an unexpected object of public affection, he arranged the grandest possible China coming-out party. The pint-sized Communist was the first Chinese leader in history to visit the US. He spent a week in the country. Against all protocol, his first evening on American soil was spent in McLean at a boozy dinner with the Brzezinskis. This time they toasted US-China friendship with vodka—Russian vodka that had been Dobrynin's Christmas gift to Brzezinski. Deng laughed for a long time when he was told the vodka was Brezhnev's preferred label.[132]

To preempt complaints from Foggy Bottom, Brzezinski also invited Vance and Holbrooke to the dinner at his home. Just before Deng's motorcade arrived, the main living room was engulfed in acrid smoke; the Brzezinskis had forgotten to open the chimney flue. As Brzezinski was greeting Deng at the door, Muska, Oksenberg, and the children were trying to waft the smoke out of the room with old magazines and newspapers. The evening was a success. No caterers were involved. Apart from Dobrynin's caviar, Muska prepared the American meal. The children served.

At one point, Mika spilled caviar into Deng's lap, then tried to scoop it up with a napkin. Having almost run over Menachem Begin in a golf cart that she was driving the previous summer, Brzezinski's eleven-year-old daughter was turning into a diplomatic liability. Deng laughed it off. His wife, Zhuo Lin, was particularly taken with Mika and her brothers. In the following days, Zhuo and Deng won Carter's heart by the attention they paid to Amy. At the dinner, Brzezinski teased Vance by telling Deng that the secretary of state had banned Muska from taking any more overseas trips after she made the faux pas of proposing a toast in China. The Muska travel ban was an invention. Deng wagged his finger at Vance and said, "You are denying her her human rights."[133] They also touched on substance. Deng made an ominous reference to Vietnam. In the following days, China's imminent plans to invade its neighbor would dominate the conversation. Brzezinski also referred to domestic controversy over Deng's visit and asked whether he had encountered any trouble in China. "There was some opposition in the province of Taiwan," he replied.

The following day, Carter hosted the most lavish state dinner of his presidency. Deng's interactions with Carter went like a charm; the president told Brzezinski that he liked Deng almost as much as he did Sadat. Over the objections of Mondale (who came "storming in" to the Oval Office to protest), but at Deng's request, Brzezinski persuaded Carter to invite Richard Nixon to the state dinner.[134] It was the former president's first visit to the White House since he had left in disgrace four and a half years earlier. Brzezinski had been providing Nixon with national security briefings, a courtesy normally extended to former presidents. Brzezinski had a showdown with Mondale, who was enraged by Nixon's invitation. It would inflame the Left and help rehabilitate him, said the vice president. On the phone, a grateful Nixon said it was an act of political courage on Carter's part. He was bracing for the backlash. "I must say that I feel sorry for Nixon," Brzezinski wrote.[135]

At the state dinner, Nixon greeted Brzezinski like an old friend. Nixon's attendance was a useful political cover for the looming showdown over Taiwan. Kissinger, who was moving to the right in tandem with the rise of Reagan, was also invited. Contrary to the feedback he had given Brzezinski, Kissinger was now going around town telling people that he opposed China normalization.[136] His apparent change of mind made its way back to Carter. Brzezinski sent word to Kissinger that there was plenty in the secret transcripts of Kissinger's conversations with his Chinese counterparts that had not been publicly disclosed, which succeeded in quieting him.[137] An exuberant Nixon somewhat overplayed his conversational hand. He was seated at Brzezinski's table and took up his new lease of airtime with extended pontifications. "As a consequence, it was difficult to have a serious and sustained discussion," Brzezinski wrote.[138] At the end of the dinner, Nixon got the guests to autograph the bilingual menus as a memento for Pat Nixon, the former first lady.

That evening, Carter took Deng to the John F. Kennedy Center for the Performing Arts, where the country singer John Denver introduced a local school choir that had learned to sing one of Deng's favorite songs, "I Love Tiananmen Square," in Chinese. That was followed by a rendition of "Getting to Know You" in English.[139] As with much else about Deng's US tour, the symbolism would look different from a later vantage point. At the time, though, Deng's evident delight in the performance won over the audience. After Deng kissed the schoolchildren, most of whom were taller than him, Paul Laxalt, a Reaganite senator from Nevada, turned to Brzezinski and said, "You've got us beat."[140] On his trips to Detroit, where he visited a Ford plant; Atlanta, where he dropped in on Coca-Cola's headquarters; Houston, where he toured the Johnson Space Center; and Seattle, where he visited a Boeing factory, Deng showed a savvy media touch. Photos of him donning a ten-gallon hat at a Texas rodeo had a priceless effect on China's image. It was hard to spot the Chinese leader underneath it. "In one simple gesture, Deng seems to not only end thirty years of acrimony between China and America, but to give his own people permission to join him in imbibing American life and culture," observed Orville Schell, a noted Sinologist.[141]

But Deng and Carter nearly stumbled over the question of Vietnam. On Christmas Day a few weeks earlier, Vietnam had invaded Cambodia and ejected the genocidal Pol Pot regime. It came a few weeks after Vietnam finalized a treaty of friendship with the Soviet Union, which Deng saw as aimed at China. The treaty stoked China's paranoia about Soviet encirclement. It would also likely entail the transfer of America's former naval base in Cam Ranh Bay to the Soviet navy. "Our general view is that we must disrupt Soviet strategic dispositions," said Deng.[142] If human rights were the yardstick, the Carter administration would have given Vietnam a standing ovation. The Khmer Rouge had run the most bloodthirsty dictatorship in the world.

But *realpolitik* governed Carter's response along the lines Brzezinski was advising. Deng told Carter that Vietnam was like a naughty child: "It is time it got spanked." He informed Carter that China planned to teach Vietnam a "limited lesson" with a brief invasion that would send a clear message to the Soviets. The People's Liberation Army (PLA) would be in and out within ten to twenty days, he promised. Carter was uncomfortable but knew that Deng's mind was made up. All he could do was counsel restraint. Brzezinski was anxious only because China's actions in Vietnam would complicate normalization. At the same time, he was impressed with Deng's style of operating, which was the opposite of lawyerly. As the two leaders galloped through a checklist of global issues, Deng would say "Agreed" and move on to the next one. When Carter raised human rights in China, which in his Soviet-conditioned frame of mind was bound up with the right to emigrate, Deng offered to send 10 million Chinese to the US. "He was decisive, crisp, and to the point," thought Brzezinski.[143]

Predictably, Brzezinski and Vance tussled over the wording in the concluding US-China statement. Vance did not want *hegemony* to surface again; it would be a needless provocation to the Soviets. Brzezinski suggested "domination" as a substitute. The Chinese were unhappy with that. Brzezinski came back with "hegemony *or* domination over others." That tweak satisfied the Chinese. To Brzezinski's surprise, Vance acceded. His staff were clearly upset. The following day, Vance went to the president with a draft statement that stressed a balanced approach between China and the USSR. It looked forward to a conclusion of SALT II and a summit with Brezhnev. Carter asked, "Is this another apology?"[144] He picked up his pen and proceeded to draw heavy lines

through Vance's more evenhanded passages before passing the heavily edited
sheet of paper back to him. Brzezinski suspected that Vance had been put
up to it by Shulman. When it became clear that neither Mondale nor Brown
would speak up for him, Vance gave up. There was no need for any statement
at all, he somewhat mournfully declared.

Having put China normalization on the road, Brzezinski now pressed
on the accelerator. Vance kept trying to apply the brakes. A few weeks
later, the treasury secretary, Mike Blumenthal, visited China. At first Vance
wanted to cancel Blumenthal's trip in protest over China's invasion of Vietnam; two hundred thousand PLA troops had poured across the Vietnam
border on February 15. To Brzezinski's surprise, Holbrooke backed his view
that Blumenthal's trip should go ahead regardless.[145] Having lost that battle,
Vance wanted to combine China's most favored nation trading status—the
promise that its goods would receive the same terms as those from other
countries—with the Soviet one. Since there was zero chance that Congress
would approve MFN for the Soviets, Brzezinski insisted they must be de-
linked. Vance lost that one, too.

Blumenthal went to China with the MFN offer in hand. While in China,
he said repeatedly that America condemned China's invasion of Vietnam.
Brzezinski got Carter to send him a cable asking him to confine his remarks
to trade.[146] That time Vance acquiesced. Almost every night of China's high-
casualty operation—an estimated twenty thousand PLA troops were killed
and probably more Vietnamese—Brzezinski held clandestine meetings with
Chai Zemin,[147] China's redesignated ambassador to the US. He fed Chai with
the CIA's latest data on Soviet deployments on China's northern border. One
evening, he passed on to Chai new data from weather stations in the Soviet far
east. That morning the stations had altered their normal reporting protocols;
they were now providing detailed forecasts on upper air layers and surface
weather across the entire frontier.[148] To everyone's relief, the Soviets did not
draw China into a two-front war.

China withdrew from Vietnam a few weeks later, having both given and
received a bloody nose. Carter, meanwhile, lost even more standing with
State's human rights bureau. In addition to his tacit green light for Deng's
invasion, he issued a statement calling on Vietnam to pull out of Cambodia and China simultaneously to withdraw from Vietnam. When Gromyko
asked Carter whether Deng had given him advance notice of China's plans,
Carter denied it. During his campaign, Carter had promised never to lie to

the American people; he had made no such vow about communications with the Soviets.

The most significant follow-up trip to China was made by Mondale. Although some of the language was tougher than the White House wanted, the Taiwan Relations Act passed Congress in March with less kerfuffle than Brzezinski and Carter had feared. Christopher's low-key advocacy on Capitol Hill helped to drain some of the drama from the switchover. Deng's popularity had also changed the political climate in America. Sensing that mood shift, Mondale was especially keen to make his own pilgrimage. But he needed a reason to go. Brzezinski had something very strategic in mind: he proposed that China host two new CIA listening posts on the Mountains of Heaven in Xinjiang province, which bordered the Soviet Union. Brzezinski had told Deng that the US could be China's "eyes and ears."[149] Staff from the CIA and the National Security Agency, America's signals intelligence agency, would train their Chinese counterparts, who would receive the same information from the eavesdropping operations as the Americans. It was a bold escalation—and it happened with remarkable alacrity. Mondale's trip was a hit with the Chinese.

Almost every principal in the Carter administration was now clamoring to get in on the act. The exception was Vance. Stansfield Turner visited China the following year to finalize details of the new listening posts. The CIA director wore a false mustache in the hope he would not be recognized.[150] A delegation of American technology companies, the largest in US history, also visited in late 1979. The following year, Harold Brown joined the roster with a large Pentagon and defense-industrial entourage bearing plenteous gifts of dual-use hardware. What had begun as a trickle turned into a flood. Having started out in a lonely camp of one, Brzezinski was now the ringmaster of the unfolding of what would later turn into the most critical bilateral relationship in the world. Towards the end of the Carter administration, Leonard Woodcock, who had become America's first ambassador to what had once been demonized as "Red China," voiced a rare note of disquiet. Was anyone looking at the long-term impact of America's deepening military ties with China? he asked.[151] The answer was no.

The immediate effect of China normalization on the USSR was as Brzezinski had foreseen. A few weeks after China's PLA withdrew from Vietnam, Gromyko and Vance concluded the SALT II treaty. Far from alienating the Soviets, the China card seemed to incentivize them. At worst, it did nothing to derail the nuclear deal. For his part, Vance saw the merit of the China listening posts. The US had just been forced to abandon its two key eavesdropping sites on Iran's eastern border, Tacksman I and Tacksman II, which for years had been America's clearest window on Soviet missile tests. The new sites in China could be even more useful since they were closer to Kazakhstan, where most of the Soviet nuclear tests were carried out. By one of those odd quirks of fate, Ayatollah Khomeini had made his dramatic flight back to Tehran on the same day that Deng Xiaoping left Washington. The ayatollah's return led to the CIA's flurried departure from Iran. The agency quickly fled the country. When one door closes, another one opens.

It is a truism to which both Kissinger and Brzezinski subscribed that figures in senior roles have no time to replenish their stock of intellectual capital; their job is to spend it. Even by that measure, global turmoil made spendthrifts of Brzezinski and his colleagues. The confluence of China normalization, the final stages SALT II (with a Soviet summit to prepare for as well), the specter of the unraveling of Carter's Camp David Accords, and a rash of regional crises from war in the Horn of Africa to revolution and social upheaval in Central America would tax the best stocked of brains. The Iranian Revolution seemed like one crisis too many.

8

Twilight of the Doves

A few weeks into the new year, Carter summoned senior State officials for a dressing down. In spite of his recent exhortations, the war of leaks between Foggy Bottom and the White House had only escalated. "It feels like I am a referee of two opposing teams instead of like a captain of one team," he said.[1] The obvious riposte was that key members of his team were implacably at odds; if he truly wanted to fix the problem, he should fire either Brzezinski or Vance and some of their lieutenants. He had been ignoring that advice since late 1976, when he had picked both; he was unlikely to change his ways now. His second-best move was to issue ever sterner warnings, which was what he did. They were mostly in vain.

Brzezinski's inimitable weekly notes to Carter each Friday evening would sometimes reprise the tutor-student role in which their relationship had been forged. In several such memos, as well as orally, he approvingly cited Niccolò Machiavelli's *The Prince*.[2] The medieval Florentine philosopher had made a distinction between *fortuna*, the fickle and uncontrollable nature of events, and *virtù*, a leader's ability to exert some sway over destiny through his qualities of courage, skill, and ruthlessness. Carter relished his rolling symposium with Brzezinski. Their morning dialogue stretched to literature, classical music, ballet, and theology. As far as Machiavelli was concerned, Brzezinski's guidance was wasted. It is hard to think of a leader less susceptible to the Florentine's wiles. Carter was not feared by his subordinates.

Tony Lake, State's director of policy planning, knew that Carter's next reading of the riot act would be considerably testier than the last. He shared a car to the White House with Les Gelb, head of the Bureau of Political-Military Affairs. "If this was the Soviet Union we would ask the driver to take us straight to the border," Lake joked.[3] Carter tore into the assembled State officials. They were chronic leakers who seemed more enamored of the Georgetown circuit than their duties as government servants, he said. The next time they leaked, he would fire them. As regards their criticisms of Brzezinski, he was sometimes too feisty but never lacked a plan or ideas. "It is a rare occasion when I received an innovative and helpful suggestion from State," Carter said. "Either be loyal or resign."[4] Then he got up and left. A flushed Vance was given no chance to respond.

To lend a veneer of balance, Carter then addressed a group of NSC staffers. His message hardly qualified as a rebuke. "Once I have made a decision, I have to demand full support and loyalty," he said. "I have not had a sense of disloyalty from you but sometimes I think you are too competitive with State."[5] That was the harshest thing he told Brzezinski's staff. For the second or third time, Vance was on the verge of resigning. To make Vance feel better, Carter reassured him that he had been "very severe with the NSC people." But he was despondent about the quality of advice he was getting from State, which, he complained, was tired, predictable, and oracular. Indeed, the president was so annoyed by Foggy Bottom's jargon that he sent Brzezinski a spoof of how one of State's memos would read: "Zbig, I think, in the future, if you agree, perhaps it might be possible, if no unforeseen obstacles arise, under some circumstances, for you to permit me to express my opinion that I might know if it is your reading on the subject that both of us might benefit in texts of letters, including those to heads of state, some circumlocutions could be avoided—unless Cy and you think otherwise."[6]

Carter's latest air clearing, which took place on February 7, had been triggered by the downwards spiral in Iran. The previous day, CBS's Marvin Kalb had reported that State officials were saying that Iran's moderate government, led by Prime Minister Shapour Bakhtiar, would collapse within a couple of days. Carter was livid.[7] That directly contradicted his orders, which had been hashed out with Vance, Brzezinski, and others. Carter's line was that the United States stood behind Bakhtiar. He was urging the Iranian army to do what was necessary to shore him up. Ayatollah Khomeini had been greeted by millions as a prophet and savior on his return to Tehran the previous week. Brzezinski had hurriedly left the state dinner with Deng Xiaoping to call William Seawell, chief executive officer of Pan American World Airways, to ensure the ayatollah would not go back on an American plane.[8] The shah had fled to Egypt two weeks before that. With each shift in the dynamics, Carter had tried to overcome the confusion of what seemed like at least two conflicting administration policies. Constant leaks were making that impossible. Carter's word seemed to be just one among several. The most recalcitrant actor was Ambassador Sullivan. Since late 1978, he had been holding secret talks with Khomeini's allies and was trying to stitch together a broad opposition group that included the mullahs. That went against Carter's express wishes. Khomeini had been declared off limits. Nobody had been aware of Sullivan's freelancing.

In early January, Sullivan persuaded Vance that the US should send an emissary to Paris to open a dialogue with Khomeini.[9] At a meeting on January 10, Brzezinski convinced Carter and Vance that such an outreach could blow up in their faces. Carter was trying to steel the Iranian military to restore order and support Bakhtiar, an opposition moderate who had been appointed prime minister by the shah. They agreed instead to ask the French to act as emissaries to Khomeini on America's behalf. On hearing that his advice had been ignored, Sullivan sent an explosive rebuke to Washington deploring Carter's decision as "a gross and irretrievable mistake" and pleaded for "sanity." Carter's instinct was to fire Sullivan for insubordination. He picked up the phone to Vance. "Why don't you read the telegram again, Cy," he said. "This man says that I am insane."[10] Somehow Vance managed to talk Carter out of dismissing Sullivan. Carter had missed yet another chance to reassert his authority.

The conflict between Vance and Brzezinski on Iran became steadily more heated. Vance thought that Khomeini could be brought into a broad coalition that would stabilize a post-shah Iran. Brzezinski argued that any government that included Khomeini would lead to an eventual bloodbath. He wanted Iran's military to launch a coup, which, he insisted, would be the lesser of two evils. Carter refused to support an explicit coup. But he wanted Iran's generals to be made aware that they would have his backing if they got their act together. The problem was that nobody could identify a plausible general for the role. Moreover, Sullivan was ignoring Carter's instructions.

The lines of authority were further blurred by the appointment in early January of General Robert "Dutch" Huyser, the deputy commander of America's European command, as the Pentagon's emissary to Tehran. Huyser's boss,

General Alexander M. Haig, Jr., promptly resigned as Supreme Allied Command for Europe in protest. He had wanted the Iran role. Haig had been urging Washington, in vain, to deploy an aircraft carrier in the Persian Gulf as a signal of America's resolve.[11] In effect, Washington now had two ambassadors. The first, Sullivan, seemed to answer only to himself and was on a solo mission to forge an alliance with Khomeini's forces. The other, Huyser, reported to Harold Brown. His role was to stiffen the Iranian military's spine. Each night Sullivan and Huyser headed to the US Embassy's secure communications unit to report over the voice scrambler to their respective bosses. Sullivan would call Vance; Brzezinski would usually join Brown on the Huyser call. Though the situation was fraught and rapidly deteriorating, it was not without its comic moments. "If you ever want a real test of your faculties, you should try to understand Dr. Brzezinski on one of our vintage secure phones," Huyser recalled.[12] Most people sounded like Donald Duck over the scrambled lines. With his rapid-fire Polish accent, Brzezinski's voice beggared description. One evening David Newsom, a senior State official, called Sullivan to relay Brzezinski's questions about prospects for a coup. Brzezinski could "go fuck himself," said Sullivan. After a pause, he added, "Does he want me to translate it into Polish?"[13]

Brzezinski never stopped pressing the military option. His case was that a coup would be less bloody than the alternatives. His advice offended Carter's deepest convictions. It was also at odds with the broader Democratic view that overthrowing foreign governments was not what their party was about; coups were the tool of unscrupulous figures such as Kissinger and John Foster Dulles. Brzezinski's detractors insisted that the shah was the problem. Once he was out of the picture, they said, new Iranian forces would coalesce. "We seem to have become captive to the demonology of the Iranian mobs, who believe that once the exorcism of the Shah's departure has been performed all will be well," Brzezinski wrote in a memo to Carter. The president replied, "Zbig: After we have made joint decisions, deploring them for the record doesn't help me."[14]

Two days later, the shah fled Iran. Brzezinski felt that Carter had misunderstood his point. He had reluctantly agreed with everyone else that the shah had to go. But he still faced the dilemma of finding someone who could restore order or "wash our hands" of Iran, Brzezinski said. Carter asked which historical analogies best fit the Iranian situation. Brzezinski cited Russia in 1917.[15] Following the overthrow of the Russian czar, Alexander Kerensky, a non-Bolshevik socialist, had tried to stabilize the postrevolutionary situation with a moderate coalition. After a few months, the Bolsheviks got rid of him. The implication was that Bakhtiar was Kerensky and Khomeini was Lenin. Another example was Georges-Jacques Danton, a relative moderate of the 1789 French Revolution, who had been executed in Maximilien Robespierre's reign of terror. Revolutions do not stop halfway, said Brzezinski. Neither would Iran's.

A few days after Khomeini's return, Huyser quit his post. Over a long meeting in the Oval Office, the general spelled out his differences with Sullivan, who was still on the ground. Tehran was now in a tense limbo between Bakhtiar, who was backed by the military, and Mehdi Bazargan, who was Khomeini's rival prime minister. Huyser told Carter that Sullivan was wooing Khomeini's faction while he had fruitlessly been trying to aid Bakhtiar's.[16] In spite of the fact that Khomeini had given interviews making it clear that he would play the strongman and that blood would flow, Sullivan continued to believe that he would be a "Gandhi-like" handmaiden of a brighter Iranian day. Sullivan's efforts were being stymied by his "badly informed superiors" (as he was quoted in the media as saying). "Sullivan thought we ought to permit Khomeini to take over, that it would lead to democracy," the incredulous Carter recorded in his diary.[17] Still the president would not remove him. Within a few days, Khomeini won the standoff; Bakhtiar fled into exile. The revolution started to gather speed. The situation was neatly captured by the US defense attaché in Tehran, who cabled, "Army surrenders; Khomeini wins. Destroying all classified."[18]

Even had a coup been desirable, would it have been feasible? It is impossible to say. Huyser believed he was never given the chance to pursue that avenue. Sullivan was trying to encourage Iran's top brass to follow the shah into exile. It was little wonder that Huyser's crosscutting overtures led to confusion. Iran's military leaders could never be sure where the United States really stood. "I had been encouraging the generals to make a move," wrote Huyser. "The only official in the White House who seemed interested in that option was Dr. Brzezinski." For what it is worth, the general believed that a coup could have been arranged if the administration had been unified. "If America wills the end, then it has to will the means," he concluded.[19] Carter's will could not be imposed because it was never resolved in his own mind. Brzezinski bemoaned what he saw as Carter's philosophical "distaste for the use of force." Sometimes there were only unpalatable choices. "World politics," he noted, "is not a kindergarten."[20]

Tehran was now flooded with mobs burning the Stars and Stripes and shouting "Death to America!" The US Embassy was briefly occupied by radical students. Washington had lost whatever marginal scope it had had to shape events. The execution of generals, SAVAK agents, and opposition figures was starting in earnest. Women's liberty evaporated. In the immediate future, Washington's focus was on the consular emergency. The urgent priority was to evacuate US nationals, of whom there were an estimated ten thousand still in Tehran. "The more I hear of what is going on, the more depressed I am that I did not get the US government to approve and, if necessary, initiate an Iranian military coup," Brzezinski wrote in late February. "I suppose I went as far as it was possible . . . without isolating myself as a madman."[21] As he had predicted, the revolution kept devouring its children. Bakhtiar moved to France, where he lived for the next twelve years before falling to assassins' bullets. Bazargan joined him in exile a few months later. His successor, President Abolhassan Bani-Sadr, in turn fled to France a year after that.

The temptation to declare US foreign policy as being "in disarray" is a natural one. No report would make the front page if it found Washington to be in array. On Iran, however, the Carter administration was truly in chaos. Its approach to the rest of the Middle East was more consensual. Menachem Begin was in the process of purging the *s* from the Camp David Accords—with the second part on Palestine left out. Barely a week passed without a new Israeli settlement being waved through. Anwar Sadat was on the cusp of giving up on the accords altogether. In late February, Brzezinski told Carter that Begin's ultimate objective was to ensure that Carter was not reelected. Hamilton Jordan echoed Brzezinski's diagnosis of the Israeli leader's malign intentions towards Carter. Begin was in a particularly rejectionist frame of mind during his visit to Washington the following week. "If he wasn't my guest I would have asked him to get the hell out of my house," said Carter.[22] Whenever the Palestinian issue arose, Begin would say, "It is not written," "We shall never agree," "It is unacceptable." The most he would permit was the creation of weak administrative councils in the West Bank and Gaza Strip. An elected legislative body was out of the question.

After Begin had left, a dispirited Carter said he would draft a speech to the nation saying that the peace process had failed. That evening, Brzezinski attended a Shabbat dinner at Blair House. He was emotionally struck by the religious songs and patriotic atmosphere. Though he strongly objected to Begin's vandalism of both the spirit and letter of part two of Camp David, he could not help but admire his iron will. There was something of the Polish cavalry charge in the Israeli leader's spirit. "There is no doubt that in the negotiations, Begin knows exactly what he wants and is quite unyielding in seeking it," he observed. "Our objectives tend to be vaguer and our determination weaker."[23]

As ever, it was Sadat who revived Carter's spirits. The Egyptian leader told Carter that he was coming to Washington and would go before Congress to denounce Begin. Brzezinski was terrified that Camp David's collapse would radicalize the Arab world and throw it back into Soviet arms. Saudi Arabia was signaling that it would establish diplomatic relations with atheist Moscow. Jordan's King Hussein, meanwhile, was publicly berating Carter whenever he got the chance. Carter rediscovered the grit that he had shown the previous summer. He declared he would visit Cairo and Jerusalem in a last-ditch effort to salvage the accords. Brzezinski would go first to "soften up" Sadat. Brzezinski mentioned that it meant he would miss the confirmation of his son Mark. Carter offered to go to Mark's church service in Brzezinski's stead. The offer was gratefully declined.[24]

Brzezinski spent hours with Sadat at Qubba Palace talking through the implications of failure. No arm-twisting was necessary. With his usual dash of gallantry, Sadat proved to be more than willing to respond to Carter's pleas. Brzezinski underlined the benefits that would flow if Egypt and Israel restored relations. Among them would be a US-Egypt defense relationship worth hundreds of millions of dollars a year. A few weeks later, Brzezinski increased Egypt's defense credit from an annual $500 million to $1.5 billion to bring it closer to Israel's $3 billion.[25]

Bob Gates, Brzezinski's intelligence aide, learned two things about his boss during the trip. The first was that Brzezinski presented his junior staff as colleagues, not as staff. That was how he introduced Gates to Sadat. Kissinger treated his staff as minions; Brzezinski's loyalty to those who worked for him was almost uniformly reciprocated. The second was that Brzezinski was very conscious of his media image. On a visit to the pyramids, Gates tried to shield Brzezinski from the cameras. He thought Brzezinski wanted a private moment with the Sphinx. Afterwards Brzezinski put his arm around Gates and said, "You're doing a great job, but don't ever get between me and the cameras again."[26]

Carter's trip could now go ahead. Over the following days and in spite of Begin's continued inflexibility, Carter managed to piece Camp David back together. "You are my brother," Sadat told Carter. "I will represent your interests as though they were my own."[27] A few weeks later, Sadat and Begin signed the Accords and made their historic handshake at a ceremony in the White House East Room. In his remarks, Sadat said that the road was now set for Palestinian statehood. Israel's defense minister, Ezer Weizman, groaned and said, "Now you will see the Polish character in Begin assert himself and he will rebut."[28]

That day, however, Begin was the epitome of charm. He praised both Sadat and Carter. "Peace can be contagious," Brzezinski thought. Until the end of his life, Weizman maintained that Carter had done more than any other US president to strengthen Israel's security. Though Carter extracted the barest of concessions from Begin to win Sadat's support, he now pursued the quest for Palestinian autonomy with renewed vigor. The president's new flurry of activity led to two more resignation threats by Vance. The first came when Carter suggested that Kissinger would be a good presidential envoy to the Middle East. On the inadvisability of appointing Kissinger, Brzezinski and Vance remained as one. The second came when Carter chose Robert S. Strauss, the former chairman of the Democratic National Committee and a prominent Jewish American, as his special envoy for Palestinian autonomy talks.[29]

Strauss wanted cabinet rank and insisted that he report directly to Carter, not Vance. His office would be in the Old Executive Office Building, not in Foggy Bottom. Carter entrusted Mondale and Jordan with the delicate task of negotiating the division of authority between Vance and Strauss on the Middle East. Their awkward compromise was never to Vance's satisfaction. Strauss was an ebullient character and egomaniac. He told Carter that he had awakened his wife, Helen, in the middle of the night to tell her, "You know, Carter is right in appointing me. If there's anybody in this country who can solve this problem, it's only me."[30] But even Strauss could not seduce Begin into making concessions on Palestinian autonomy.

At a White House discussion on how Carter could get the Palestinian Liberation Organization (PLO) to recognize UN Resolution 242, the president said that such decisions should be left to Strauss. Vance lost his temper. "Do you want me literally to do nothing?" he shouted. "Mr. President, I am not going to be a figurehead for you. If you don't want me to do this, I might as well resign as Secretary of State."[31] Carter talked Vance out of quitting. The one resignation he did accept was that of Andrew Young, his UN ambassador, a civil rights icon from Carter's home state of Georgia and the most prominent African American in his administration. Against US policy, Young had met with a PLO official, then denied to State that he had done so. Brzezinski and Vance were also united on that; both advised Carter to fire him. Though Young was ejected for having defied presidential authority, his exit was a fitting coda to a Palestinian trail that was rapidly going cold.

On SALT II, however, Vance's tireless efforts finally paid off. On May 8, Vance reported to Carter that "the long, arduous SALT II negotiations were completed."[32] It was Carter's long-awaited chance to work his political faith healing on the Soviet leader. He had been craving a summit since day one of his presidency. Earlier in the year, Brzezinski had talked him out of giving a speech on SALT II at the Georgia Institute of Technology in Atlanta. Were Carter to hold forth on the unfinished nuclear talks while he was in the throes of an Iran crisis, Americans would think he was living in a dreamland, he said. Carter saw the point and dropped the plan. Three months later, he now had a deal.

He launched into preparations with his unique diligence, conscientiously going through every technical memo that Vance, Brown, and Brzezinski threw at him. Dobrynin worried that Brezhnev's grasp of detail would be no match for Carter's. Doctors had advised the Soviet leader against taking the long flight to US. His respiratory and neurological disorders were too dire. They wanted Carter to come to Moscow instead. As a compromise, Brzezinski suggested Vienna, which the Soviets accepted.[33] Even then, they fretted about the Soviet leader's stamina. Partly because of his need for stronger medication, Brezhnev's slurred speech was getting worse, as was his memory. He was also ignoring his doctors' advice to cut down on drinking and smoking. Dobrynin took Brzezinski aside and pleaded with him to keep the summit agenda light. "Stick to one or two issues and don't embarrass the old man," he implored.[34]

A few days before the June summit, Brzezinski was reminded of the depth of Carter's hatred of nuclear weapons. The SALT II agreement allowed each superpower to develop one new long-range missile. The Pentagon had developed the MX, which was as significant a leap forward in ICBM technology as the now-aging Minuteman had been in its time. Brown and Brzezinski had to get Carter's sign-off on the new missile's production. Carter kept trying to evade the decision. It reminded them of his agonizing cat-and-mouse game over the neutron bomb, which he had ended up canceling. Brzezinski lacked technical mastery of missile technology. His staff, led by David Aaron and James Thompson, supplied him with what he was missing. Brown was a genuine expert. Brzezinski's job was to keep Carter interested in both MX and the intermediate-range Pershing II missile to be deployed in Europe, which was also under development. Continuous involvement would minimize the risk that he would undergo a last-minute change of mind.

Brzezinski impressed on Carter that the Joint Chiefs of Staff were already skeptical about SALT II, which, they were grumbling, would enshrine Soviet parity. If Carter wobbled on the MX, he might lose the Pentagon altogether. Carter said that he wished he could break the spiral of superpower nuclear competition. "How can I reach Brezhnev?" he asked Brzezinski one morning. "How can I ever communicate with them and get them to understand the futility of it all, the waste of it all?" Brzezinski suggested that Brown could open more ambitious new talks with his Soviet counterparts. "Shit, Harold Brown will only agree with the Soviets that we need more nuclear weapons," Carter replied.[35] At the same time, Carter was deeply aware of America's "vulnerability gap" to a Soviet first strike, as Brown kept reminding him. Nowhere more than on nuclear weapons were Carter's head and heart further apart. After much agonizing, he gave the go-ahead to the MX.

The public relations goal in Vienna was to show Carter securing the toughest deal possible. It was touch-and-go whether Congress would ratify the treaty. Centrist Democrats, such as Sam Nunn, were on the fence. "I thought SALT could be helpful on the margins but not a slam dunk," he said.[36] Scoop Jackson was militantly opposed. He compared Carter's journey to Vienna with Chamberlain's to Munich. "The failure to face reality today, like the failure to do so then—that is the mark of appeasement," he said.[37] Carter was so paranoid about the Munich analogy that he banned anyone in his delegation from bringing an umbrella to Vienna, given its association with Chamberlain. The infamous British prime minister's nickname had been "Umbrella Man" since he had always had one with him. "I'd rather drown than carry an umbrella," Carter said.[38] Lieutenant General Edward Rowny, the Joint Chiefs of Staff's representative in Vienna, declined Carter's invitation to the signing ceremony in protest at what he saw as America's needless concessions.[39] Brzezinski joked about taking the views of Washington's pro- and anti-SALT lobbies with a "pinch of salt." He entitled one memo to Carter "Saltcumgranosalis."[40] He was in neither camp. Brzezinski did not see SALT II as transformative, as Carter and Vance believed it would be; with or without the treaty, superpower rivalry would continue. But he thought that Jackson, Nitze, and the rest were intoxicated by their own rhetoric. It was better to have a modest nuclear deal than nothing.

Partly in compensation for what he saw as Carter's inflated expectations for the Vienna summit, Brzezinski professed not to be looking forward to it. When it happened, though, he basked in his notoriety. Brzezinski was Moscow's bête noire. His ability to converse in Russian gave him an edge. "Oh, I've heard a lot about you," said Brezhnev when they were introduced on the first night at the Vienna State Opera.[41] It was a performance of Mozart's *The Abduction from the Seraglio*. Brzezinski was placed behind the Soviet leader and his defense minister, Dmitry Ustinov. Most of them were too jet-lagged to enjoy the opera: "The smaller the country, the longer the opera," Brezhnev's aide whispered loudly to Brzezinski. "Have you ever been to Luxembourg?" Brzezinski replied.

Noticing that the Soviet leader was sweating, Brzezinski opened the doors to the box to let more air in. "That will cost you fifty Backfires," he told Ustinov. The Backfire was a Soviet supersonic nuclear-capable jet that was in the SALT negotiating mix. The defense minister had to repeat the whispered repartee to Brezhnev, who had trouble hearing. "Oh, you're bargaining already?" Brezhnev responded after he understood Brzezinski's joke. The wife of one of the Austrian ministers then irascibly asked them to shut up. Both Brezhnev and Carter left after the first act. Jody Powell joked that he feared that Carter would exploit the Viennese custom of circling the opera house's rotunda during the interval to go jogging.

The eleventh US-Soviet summit was a modest success. "God will not forgive us if we fail," Brezhnev told Carter, to the visible shock of some of his henchmen.[42] Though Brezhnev was ailing, he had enough wits during the opening stages to appear to be in charge. Every now and then he would turn plaintively to aides to check that he was doing okay. "*Khorosho* [fine]," they would reply. Possibly against the advice of Gromyko, who was constantly at his side, Brezhnev agreed after Carter's repeated pressing that the Soviets would limit their production of Backfires to thirty. Like the cruise missiles, the Backfire was a so-called gray-area system, since it had long-range capability and could thus be defined as strategic. Carter and Brezhnev also settled gray-area production ceilings and nailed down the final details on telemetry. The Soviets listened to a tough lecture by Carter about their lack of regional restraint, particularly over Cuba's proxy global adventurism in Africa, Central America, and increasingly the Caribbean. Brezhnev, in turn, made it clear that it would be foolish for either superpower to try to "remodel" the other's domestic affairs. He also delivered a violently worded screed against China.

It was clear to Brzezinski, as well as to SALT's critics in Washington, that the treaty would have no restraining effect on Soviet behavior. Vienna yielded no advance in prospects for reciprocal détente.

The summit also dashed Carter's hope of establishing a personalized connection with Brezhnev. Even without the language barrier, the Soviet leader's speech was too halting and rigid to permit a meeting of souls. When Carter met Brezhnev alone, the Soviet leader routinely turned for help to his interpreter, Viktor Sukhodrev, when Carter pushed him for answers. Following each question, Sukhodrev reached into his folder, then handed Brezhnev a sheet of paper from which he haltingly read out the answer. At their larger meeting, Carter laid out his hopes for SALT III, which would involve far more dramatic nuclear cuts along the lines of his doomed SALT II opening bid in the opening weeks of his presidency. This time the Soviets were respectful, taking detailed notes on yellow pads as Carter spoke. But there could be little papering over the nugatory reach of SALT II. During their opening session, when Brezhnev was musing about the world's clamor for détente, he pointed at Vance and said, "Only he doesn't believe in it."[43] He meant Brzezinski. The joke united both sides in laughter. That morning, the Soviet leader was alert and capable of humor. By the end of the summit, he struck the Americans as senile.

Carter's media operation strongly emphasized the US president's vigor. He was filmed jogging each morning. At the signing ceremony on the last day at the historic Hofburg Palace, where leaders from across the continent had in 1815 forged the Concert of Europe, Carter bounded up the entrance steps; Brezhnev took an elevator. The two sat in the same brocaded chairs that Nikita Khrushchev and John F. Kennedy had used during their ill-fated 1961 summit. The Soviets had a mischievous response to Carter's stress on his youthfulness. At a press conference with the Soviet spokesman, an American journalist asked about Brezhnev's physical health. The spokesman took his next question from an *Izvestia* reporter who sarcastically inquired about Carter's "political health." Moscow could read Carter's poll numbers. His Gallup approval rating had recently dropped below 30 percent. They knew he would face an uphill struggle getting the treaty through Congress. By the time of their farewells, Brezhnev's speech was barely decipherable. "He is the one who fears us," the Soviet leader said to an aide when he was shaking hands with Brzezinski. "Not you," Brzezinski replied. He confessed, however, that he may have misunderstood what Brezhnev had been trying to imply.

The Soviet leader kissed Carter on the cheek and later remarked that the US president was "quite a nice guy after all."[44] After their return to Washington, Carter's overriding priority was Senate ratification. As with the Panama Canal Treaties, Brzezinski's reputation made him a key asset in the SALT-selling operation on Capitol Hill. He and Carter had gradually won over Robert Byrd, the Democratic majority leader, to the deal's importance. Too many legislators were still undecided, though. The Republican minority leader, Howard Baker, was an almost certain no. The White House could draw on the services of Averell Harriman, who turned his Georgetown residence into the unofficial headquarters of the ratification drive. Among the "wise men" and the doves, who were by now almost indistinguishable, the nuclear treaty took on an almost talismanic quality. "I live for SALT II," Harriman told Holbrooke.[45]

Harriman had created ripples a few months earlier by going to Moscow for what he thought would be a valedictory dinner. Having known Stalin during the war, when he was US ambassador to Moscow, Harriman, now eighty-seven, was one of the few Americans left who could draw on direct memories of the dictator. Their relationship had been so warm that on Harriman's departure in 1946, Stalin had made him a gift of two chestnut Russian Thoroughbreds, which Harriman had shipped to New York. He called the horses "Fact" and "Boston."

At the December 1978 dinner in Moscow, which was hosted by Brezhnev, Harriman remarked both on Stalin's "extraordinary brutality" and on his "extraordinarily able leadership." After an awkward pause, he received a standing ovation. Harriman's support for SALT II was a reminder to the Soviets of their soft spot for American aristocrats. Of Vance, Gromyko wrote, "He was always correct in his behavior, even at the worst moments in US-Soviet relations. . . . He is simply one of those rare people in American public life who do not look at the world through the narrow window of profit or money-grubbing." Of Carter, the veteran Soviet diplomat observed, "He was not overburdened with foreign policy expertise."[46] He conspicuously offered no reflections on Brzezinski.

Almost before the ink was dry on SALT II, it began to fall apart. Ironically, it was Frank Church, the notably liberal chairman of the Senate Foreign Relations Committee, who did the most harm to the nuclear deal's prospects. He was facing a tough reelection battle in Idaho the following year. America's political winds were blowing in a conservative direction. Church's Republican opponent, Steve Symms, had been disseminating old photographs of Church embracing Cuba's dictator, Fidel Castro. Carter had received a crash course in Church's political insecurity in early 1979. Shortly after Church took over the Foreign Relations Committee, Carter invited him to lunch in the Oval Office. The senator's lack of foreign policy nous stunned the president. Carter told aides that Church was "just plain ignorant." The world of 1979 was uncertain and riven by crisis. The only thing that Church wanted from Carter was that he make a presidential visit to Spain. Idaho was home to a community of former Basque shepherds; a trip to Spain by Carter, Church felt, could help his campaign. "Church really needs education," said Carter. "I was just amazed."[47]

In mid-July, the National Security Agency circulated an internal report that it might have discovered a hitherto unknown Soviet military unit in Cuba. Brzezinski was alarmed and told Carter that if the news leaked it "could most adversely affect SALT."[48] No public statement was issued. The details were vague. Brzezinski pressed Stansfield Turner to step up Langley's efforts to find hard intelligence. On August 10, the CIA came back with much more troubling news: it had found a Soviet militarized rifle brigade numbering up to three thousand men conducting combat exercises on Cuba's San Pedro Beach. Although such a brigade would pose no direct threat to the United States, it would be in breach of the USSR's commitments following the 1962 Cuban Missile Crisis. It was also further evidence of Moscow-sponsored Cuban adventurism.

The finding coincided with a left-wing revolution in Nicaragua in which Cuba was the chief backer of the victorious Sandinistas. The guerrillas had taken the capital, Managua, in mid-July. Still, Carter made no public statement. In late August, when most politicians were out of town on vacation, including Brzezinski, who was in Vermont with the family, the *National Intelligence Digest* used the fatal phrase "Soviet combat brigade." The quickly leaked digest, which had an administration circulation of about four hundred people, became the spark of a political wildfire based on two false premises: that the Soviet brigade was new and that it was active. Neither was true.

At this point, the Carter administration could have extinguished the fire with cold water. Ironically, it was Vance, wanting to appear tough to help his advocacy of SALT, who fanned the flames. He chaired an NSC meeting that agreed to issue a démarche to the Soviets over the brigade. He also instructed aides to brief the key senators, including Church, about the brigade's existence. Ordinarily, senators would keep the content of such briefings to themselves; that is the implicit bargain of being in the loop. But

Church was desperate to repair his reputation. On August 30, he called a press conference in Boise, Idaho, in which he revealed the brigade's existence. "The United States cannot permit the island to become a Russian military base, 90 miles from our shores," he said; the Soviets would use it as a springboard for revolution in the Western Hemisphere.[49] Church's alarmism was echoed by Richard Stone, a Democratic senator from Florida, who was also facing an uphill reelection battle and needed to keep the hawkish Cuban American community on his side. What should have been a nonstory was turning into a forest fire.

At a press conference a few days after Church's jaw-dropping statement, Vance referred to the Soviet presence as a "combat brigade" and a "matter of serious concern."[50] By that point, everyone, including Brzezinski, knew better. But the White House had lost control of the narrative. An overstretched CIA had forgotten about the brigade's existence. The information had been released in garbled, piecemeal fashion into a Washington already awash in rumors about Cuba's regional arson. To the enemies of SALT, the story was a gift that they put to immediate use.

Ronald Reagan called for the US to cease all contact with Moscow until it withdrew the brigade from the island. Scoop Jackson muttered about appeasement. Church suspended hearings on SALT II until the end of September. That lost the White House a crucial month in which to push its flagship treaty through the Senate. To save face, Carter needed the Soviets to do something. Short of withdrawing the nonexistent combat brigade, they could announce that they would "disaggregate" it, Brzezinski suggested. Or they could say that it was there for training purposes, which had been true for at least seventeen years. But the Soviets were unbending. Dobrynin made clear to Vance that the story was a phony one. "My advice to you: drop this whole affair," Brezhnev told Carter over the White House hotline.[51] In this instance, Brezhnev's counsel was impeccable. But it was too late. For the sake of SALT, Carter needed to sound tough.

Knowing that the brigade story was a mistake, Brzezinski nevertheless urged Carter to take a hawkish line with the Soviets. He should exploit the moment to push through defensive military sales to China, approve Harold Brown's trip to China, identify the growing security threat in the Caribbean, and stress that Cuban adventurism had to stop. Instead, Carter convened a meeting of foreign policy "wise men." It included the usual suspects, notably McGeorge Bundy, Clark Clifford, George Ball, Henry Kissinger, and James Schlesinger, who had been Ford's secretary of defense and most recently Carter's secretary of energy. Brzezinski tried to dissuade Carter from convening the elders by saying that Truman, Kennedy, and Nixon did not convene panels before taking big decisions. Carter ignored him. Most of the eighteen-member group was aghast at how the White House could have allowed a nonissue to spiral out of control. Only Kissinger went against the consensus. He took the hawkish line that Carter should blow the whistle on Soviet worldwide activism. Kissinger's metamorphosis into full-blown Reaganite was picking up speed.

Carter gave a prime-time address on October 1 in which he downplayed the significance of the brigade and called for a renewed drive to pass SALT. It was too late. The treaty's hope of ratification that year was all but dead. It would have to wait until early 1980. A despondent Brzezinski for the first time considered resigning. Though he knew the Cuban brigade was a fiction, he thought Carter had once again missed an opportunity to draw a red line for the Soviets. Moscow's activism was showing up elsewhere, including most ominously in Afghanistan. Brzezinski was now frequently referring to "an arc of crisis." From the Hindu Kush to the Bosphorus, he said the Soviets were fueling a widening rim of instability. In a showdown, a livid Carter told Brzezinski that he had "no intention of going to war over the Soviet brigade in Cuba."[52] For a day or two, Carter and Brzezinski barely exchanged a word. Events robbed their antagonism of any space to fester. Machiavelli's *fortuna* kept intervening.

The Cuba brigade crisis was a self-created fiasco. As was sometimes the case, Washington's instinct to reach for historical analogy was an unhelpful prism through which to filter real-time events. In Vienna, Carter had been shadowed by Munich 1938. Over the Horn of Africa, Vance and others were haunted by Vietnam. With the phony Soviet brigade, everyone was in thrall to the 1962 Cuban near miss. The big winners were Reagan and the Committee on the Present Danger. Brzezinski, like Vance, could have downplayed the crisis before it got out of control. They flubbed their chance. Vance gambled that striking a tough pose over a phantom brigade could boost his SALT II leverage on Capitol Hill; Brzezinski saw it as an opportunity to press his larger Soviet agenda. Carter again came out looking weaker.

After he retired, Frank Church confided to his son, Forrester, that his Cuba move had been "the biggest mistake of my life." His stunt did not even work; he lost his seat at the next election. As did Stone. To Vance, the debacle was close to the final straw. The treaty that had defined his tenure was slipping away with each passing week. Brzezinski observed several times how tired and despondent Vance was looking. Earlier in the summer, Vance had taken Brzezinski aside and told him, "This is an awful town."[53] He could not wait to leave Washington. Carter's beleaguered chief diplomat had long since lost his reputation for being even-tempered. In that year's *U.S. News & World Report*'s power rankings, Brzezinski jumped to fourth place, while Vance slipped to nineteenth.

The same day that Carter addressed the nation on Cuba, Pope John Paul II touched down on US soil for the first time as pope. To Carter and Brzezinski, the pontiff's visit was a gift from heaven. Brzezinski had already met Karol Wojtyła at a Harvard conference in the summer of 1976, when he gave a talk on "Participation or Alienation."[54] To Brzezinski's surprise, the Polish then cardinal had made a special effort to ensure that Brzezinski was there. He was in Maine with the family and decided "for some reason" that he should accept Wojtyła's invitation. It was like buying Microsoft stock before anyone had heard of the company.

Over tea and cake, the two chatted about events in Poland. That modest investment of time with a relatively unknown prelate from Kraków led to a lifelong friendship with the most influential pope of the modern era. Brzezinski had no idea that Wojtyła would be the next pontiff but one. Italians had monopolized that role for almost half a millennium. When Wojtyła was elected vicar of Rome in October 1978, an ecstatic Brzezinski broke the news to Carter. The president embarrassed Brzezinski by telling the media that John Paul II was a "friend" of Brzezinski, though they had met only once. Brzezinski jointly headed the US delegation to John Paul II's investiture in Rome a few days later. Tip O'Neill, the Irish American Speaker of the House, was the delegation's cochair.

The Soviets were convinced that Brzezinski had fixed the pope's election. The propagandistic setback of having a notoriously activist prelate from Poland (of all places) running the Vatican was too big to be a coincidence. Stalin once mockingly queried how many divisions the Vatican had. Under a figure such as Wojtyła, at a moment when the USSR's human rights record was turning into a global PR disaster, the Vatican could mobilize the moral equivalent of force. An Italian journalist with close Kremlin ties said that the Soviets would rather have Aleksandr Solzhenitsyn as UN secretary-general than a Pole in the Vatican.[55]

The head of the KGB, Yuri Andropov, cobbed together a report that claimed to prove that Brzezinski had rigged Wojtyła's election.[56] The KGB's

theory was that Brzezinski conspired with John Joseph Krol, the Polish American cardinal and archbishop of Philadelphia, to work with German cardinals
for his elevation. In practice, the Italian and Spanish cardinals were dead-
locked and Wojtyła emerged as the compromise figure. Years later, Russian
diplomats still clung to the belief that Brzezinski had manipulated the outcome. No proof has emerged to support the KGB's claim. In the White House
the following joke did the rounds: "The cardinals could not make up their
minds so they took a poll."[57] After the investiture, Brzezinski and the O'Neills
were invited to an audience with the pope. "Thank you, professor," John Paul II
joked to Brzezinski. "I understand that I owe my job at the Holy See to you."

The Soviets were right to worry. John Paul II was the equivalent of a geopolitical windfall for Carter, Brzezinski, the West in general, and East Bloc dissident groups in particular. The pope had arrived in Boston a few days earlier.
When he arrived at Andrews Air Force Base by helicopter on October 6, Brzezinski and Muska were at the head of the greeting line. The pope asked Brzezinski to join him for dinner that evening at the Vatican's embassy (the Apostolic
Nunciature of the Holy See) on Massachusetts Avenue.[58] Without checking
Brzezinski decided to bring his family along. Muska had to extricate a mud-
splattered fifteen-year-old Ian from an athletic event in suburban Virginia, then
clean him up for the Holy Father. Mark and Mika were located more easily. The
pope gave blessings and rosaries to each of the Brzezinskis, including to ones
not there, notably Leonia, Brzezinski's ailing mother, who was by far the most
devout in the family. Then he and Brzezinski talked politics. John Paul II said
that he saw himself as the pope of all the Slavs, not just the Catholic ones.

A few months earlier, John Paul II had electrified Poland and caused
heartburn in Moscow on an exultant trip to his native land. Some Catholic
scholars claim that the 1979 papal visit was the beginning of the end of the
Soviet Union. That is an exaggeration. But it is hard to overstate the energy
he injected into civic Poland. John Paul II was the informal patron saint of the
Solidarity movement born the following year. On his arrival, he knelt down
and kissed Polish soil. That became his signature move. Nobody could mistake his calls to freedom in Poland for quietist sermonizing. "Be not afraid,"
he had said in his inaugural address in Rome the previous year.[59] "Open, I say
open wide, the door to Christ. To his saving power, open the boundaries of
states, economic and political systems, the vast fields of culture, civilization
and development."

In the pope's afternoon meeting with Carter a few months later, the president had intended to discuss society's moral problems. Politics did not feature. By contrast, in their conversation at the residence of the Apostolic Nunciature, Brzezinski and John Paul II talked mostly about the Cold War. Coincidence had led to the bizarre overlap of history's first Polish-born pope and America's first Polish-born grand strategist. It was the start of a political collaboration between Rome and Washington conducted almost entirely in Polish. Over their light supper, Brzezinski joked that Carter was more like a religious leader and the pope was more like a world statesman. John Paul II threw back his head and laughed.

It was in Qom, a Shia holy city from which Ayatollah Khomeini was directing Iran's revolution, not in Rome, that Carter's fate was being written. Since the shah had fled to Egypt in January, Carter had been under virtual siege from the exiled sovereign's friends to admit him into the US. David Rockefeller, Brzezinski's erstwhile sponsor and chairman of Chase Manhattan Bank, Iran's largest creditor, spearheaded the lobbying drive. The shah had spent a few months in Egypt, then brief spells in Morocco and the Bahamas, before ending up in a walled estate in Mexico. Among Rockefeller's most loyal allies in his quest to bring the shah to the United States was Henry Kissinger, who thought Carter was behaving dishonorably towards America's old friend. Kissinger was also chairman of Chase Manhattan's International Advisory Committee. The other key figures in what Rockefeller dubbed "Project Eagle" were Richard Helms, a former CIA director who had been Nixon's ambassador to Iran, and John McCloy, a venerable leading WASP and future chairman of Chase. Their plan was to make contact with a senior Carter official at least once a week. Brzezinski was their sole ally inside the White House.

To Carter's growing annoyance, Brzezinski raised the shah's fate with him at regular intervals. Carter knew that a key element of Khomeini's street appeal was that Iranians saw him as their bulwark against the widely believed expectation that the Great Satan was plotting to reinstate the shah. Bringing Mohammad Reza Pahlavi to America, he felt, would feed Iranian paranoia. Carter "became quite furious" when Brzezinski first broached the shah's asylum in late March.[60] If Brzezinski felt so strongly about America's honor, he heatedly inquired, why had he not raised it earlier? He refused to entertain the idea. But it kept cropping up. In early April, Rockefeller got onto Carter's schedule. He prepared a one-page memo in which he accused Carter of "uneven application" of his human rights policy.[61]

Rockefeller's chief evidence of Carter's double standards was his refusal
to grant asylum to the shah. His only other example of Carter's uneven human
rights policy was the impact of China normalization on the people of Taiwan.
After reading the memo, Carter withdrew into an icy fury and cut the meeting
short. "He was clearly irritated," Rockefeller observed.[62] Given the shah's poor
human rights record, Rockefeller's rap sheet against Carter was eccentric. Nor
was it clear how denying asylum breached the shah's rights. He was no less safe
in Mexico or the Bahamas than he would be in the Hudson Valley. But there
was a likely financial motive for Rockefeller's complaint. With a syndicated
loan to Iran of $1.7 billion and about $860 million in additional Iran deposits
and direct loans, Iran was the jewel in Chase Manhattan's international portfolio. It was turning into a potential albatross on its balance sheet.

Carter hoped the shah's supporters would get tired and move on. But Project Eagle never let up. "The Shah should not be treated like a flying Dutchman
who cannot find a port of call," Kissinger told the media.[63] He was also in the
thick of the debate on "Who lost Iran?" His private but widely shared view was
that Carter's "ill-timed" human rights policies had undermined the shah. This
was an idiosyncratic take on what had gone wrong. In practice, Carter had
largely spared Iran from the human rights conditions he imposed on transfers
of military materials to countries such as Brazil and Argentina. In late July,
he complained that Rockefeller, McCloy, and Kissinger were waging a constant campaign against him—and that Brzezinski was also bugging him daily.
Brzezinski protested. "Well, not every day, but very often," Carter replied.[64]

He did not want pictures of the shah playing tennis in the US published
while Americans in Tehran were under threat of being kidnapped or worse,
he said. There had been a minor attempt to storm the US Embassy in February. By July, Rockefeller and others had persuaded Mondale that it would
be politically wise to admit the shah. Carter's image was suffering. In early
October, they finally won over Vance. Rockefeller's doctors revealed to the
State Department's doctors that the shah was severely ill and could die at any
moment. His cocktail of medical complexities—lymphoma and other can-
cers combined with severe jaundice—could be treated only in a New York
hospital, they asserted.

Given the risk that the shah could die abroad after being abandoned by
his former US patrons, Carter relented. He had been the last holdout. "You're
opening a Pandora's box with this," Iran's foreign minister, Ebrahim Yazdi,
warned Bruce Laingen, the US chargé d'affaires in Tehran, who had been

holding the fort since Sullivan's departure (the ambassador had retired to Mexico, not far from where the shah was staying).[65] During the debate over whether to admit the shah, Carter asked, "What are you guys going to advise me to do if they overrun our embassy and take our people hostage?" When no one spoke up, he went on, "On that day, we will all sit here with long, drawn, white faces and realize we've been had."[66] But even he acknowledged the political specter of the exiled shah dying. Jordan imagined the fuss Kissinger would create if the shah passed away abroad: "First you've caused the shah's downfall, and now you've killed him."

Rockefeller's doctors told Carter and his team that the shah's only hope of staying alive was to be treated in an American medical facility. Only later did they learn that he could just as well have received care in Mexico or Europe. In hindsight, it seems obvious that Carter should have either said no or made it a condition of the shah's asylum that he renounce all claims to the Peacock Throne. In the melee, nobody thought of that simple precaution. On October 22, the shah, his family, and their four dogs arrived on a private charter plane at Fort Lauderdale, Florida, en route to New York's LaGuardia Airport. "The eagle has landed!" said Joseph Reed, Jr., Rockefeller's assistant.[67] The initial response in Tehran was muted. Iran's quiescence seemed to confirm State's view, particularly that of its Iran desk officer, Henry Precht, that the revolution was abating. Precht thought that Mehdi Bazargan's relatively moderate government had a grip on the situation. Carter, Vance, and Brzezinski had been preoccupied with China, SALT, Brezhnev, and the Cuban brigade crisis. Precht had effectively been running Iran policy since February.

Brzezinski grabbed the chance to meet Bazargan and Yazdi a week later at the twenty-fifth anniversary celebration of the launch of the Algerian Revolution. He had just read Alistair Horne's *A Savage War of Peace: Algeria 1954–1962* and was a fervent admirer of Algeria's liberation struggle against France. He asked to be given a tour of the Casbah, where much of the resistance had been based. The gathering at the celebration's opulent reception included a "remarkable collection of lesser-known terrorists, guerrilla leaders, and representatives of various national liberation movements," Bob Gates recalled.[68] Among those were Vo Nguyen Giap, one of Vietnam's leading generals; Libya's autocrat, Muammar Gaddafi; the PLO's Yasser Arafat; Cuba's vice president, Raúl Castro, Fidel's brother; and Iran's civilian leaders. Brzezinski relished the frisson of his entrance into the Middle East's version of the bar in *Star Wars*.

He had no idea quite how much he would generate. *"J'admire votre courage,"* he told Giap.[69] He caused a minor flap in Washington by shaking Arafat's hand. It was either that or snubbing him, Brzezinski cabled back.

Bob Gates and Madeleine Albright accompanied Brzezinski to meet Bazargan and Yazdi in one of the Iranians' hotel rooms. There were large bowls of pistachios. Gates struggled to keep up with his note taking of what Brzezinski called a "humdinger of a conversation."[70] To his surprise, Brzezinski found his Iranian interlocutors likable. When they protested the shah's presence in the United States, however, he responded sharply; the United States would always stand by its traditions, which included freedom of residence, he asserted. Neither Brzezinski nor Gates and Albright thought much of it when Iranian photographers took a snapshot of him shaking Bazargan's hand. It was November 1, nine days since the shah had arrived in New York. It also happened to be the first day of organized mass protests in Tehran against the shah's arrival in America. Two million people turned out.

Precht had led the White House and Vance to believe that Bazargan and his ministers had sidelined Khomeini. The moderates were in fact locked in a power struggle with the mullahs. The picture of Brzezinski shaking Bazargan's hand was splashed on the front page of Iran's newspapers the next day. Brzezinski's face gave the radicals the pretext they wanted; here was proof that Bazargan was in league with the Great Satan. Two days later, on November 4, they occupied the US Embassy and took sixty-six Americans hostage. The storming of America's Embassy was initially an internal power move against the moderates. It worked. An empowered Khomeini ousted Bazargan and his ministers a few weeks later. Iran's Kerensky fled into exile. Brzezinski had been an unwitting catalyst of Bazargan's demise.

The US public's initial response was to rally behind the president. Carter's approval rating rose by the high double digits to 51 percent in early December. But as the impression of paralysis started to set in, his numbers began to sag. The White House's internal divisions were wholly predictable. Brzezinski, sometimes backed by Brown, wanted a display of US might. The superpower, he said, could not allow itself to be humiliated by a bunch of crazy radicals. Options included bombing Iran's oil fields, mining its harbors, and isolating it commercially. Vance, mostly backed by Mondale, preferred to tread softly. Any military action could endanger the lives of the hostages, he said. Carter leaned towards the latter.

At the NSC meetings in the wake of the occupation, there was unanimity on appointing envoys to reach out to Khomeini. No US emissary ever got near him. Over the coming weeks, a variety of intermediaries, including the UN secretary-general, Kurt Waldheim, an envoy from the pope, and even Yasser Arafat, would also return from Iran empty handed. A series of freelance characters, including the Texas businessman Ross Perot, volunteered ideas to exfiltrate the hostages. Iran's aging religious leader sent mixed signals, mostly negative. His only positive one was to release the thirteen women and African Americans among the hostages, which reduced the total to fifty-three. But it was increasingly obvious that Khomeini did not have full control over the student radicals.

Within days of the embassy takeover, Carter, Vance, and Mondale were persuaded that it would be better if the shah left America. Brzezinski was aghast. He saw this as "abject capitulation" and "acquiescence to blackmail."[71] To Carter's chagrin, both Rockefeller and Kissinger also thought the time had come for the shah to go back to Mexico. Rockefeller reluctantly concluded that "the situation had reached a point where private citizens could no longer deal with it."[72] Rockefeller's change of mind came several days after Carter had ordered that all Iranian assets held in the US financial system be frozen. That allowed Chase Manhattan to use Iran's deposits to service the Iran loans on its books. The bank was secure.

Kissinger now embarked on a campaign to blame the hostage crisis on Carter's human rights agenda. "The disintegration of America's ability to shape events cannot be an accident," he told a gathering of Republican governors on November 20.[73] "Could it be that there is no penalty for opposing the United States and no reward for friendship to the United States?" Having helped bring about the hostage crisis by insisting on giving the shah asylum, he was now washing his hands of personal responsibility. His private assurances of support to Carter had counted for nothing. In an inversion of the Lord Acton dictum, Brzezinski joked about Kissinger, "I conclude that, although power corrupts, the absence of power corrupts absolutely."[74]

Carter's patience with Kissinger was close to snapping. The criticisms coming from the US statesman who had done the most to build up the shah's delusions of grandeur were too much for Carter. He instructed Vance to bring Kissinger into the State Department to "read him the riot act." Vance should let Kissinger know what Carter thought of his double-dealing. "I told Cy not to trust him or say anything that Kissinger could twist around, and to have a witness present," he wrote in his diary.[75] After reading Vance's account of the meeting, he scrawled in the margin, "This sounded, according to the newspapers, more like an apologia."[76]

The aftermath of the embassy storming was also the nadir of the Carter-Brzezinski relationship. Several times Carter said that Brzezinski and Kissinger were to blame for having forced him to admit the shah. Brzezinski replied that if his advice on Iran had been heeded a year earlier, none of it would have happened. Unlike Kissinger, though, Brzezinski did not disown his Iran views. Whatever the failings of his Iran advice, which was arguably seminal in Carter's blunders, Brzezinski's counsel did not vary with his audience. On the first Saturday in December, Brzezinski called Carter from home to pass on his advisors' consensus that Egypt would not be a good refuge for the shah; the shakiness of Sadat's grip meant it would risk a dangerous backlash. A frayed Carter snapped and launched into a tirade about Brzezinski's culpability, Vance's uselessness, and everyone's inertia. Then he hung up. It was the only time that happened. "He was absolutely outraged: really sputtered on the phone," Brzezinski wrote that night. "I must say that I am really disgusted by the fearful way in which this whole matter is being handled."[77]

Brzezinski's bottom line was that the US was turning into a helpless giant. Carter had met the families of the hostages and promised he would do nothing to endanger their lives. Though he announced his reelection bid in early December, he opted for the "Rose Garden" strategy, which meant he would shun the campaign trail for the duration of the emergency. There would be no lights on the White House Christmas tree that year. To Brzezinski, national prestige mattered even more than the hostages' lives. Their fate should not become the sole arbiter of US actions. "From every public contact I have had, I sense a strong desire for U.S. honor to be reasserted and for American power to be demonstrated," he wrote in a memo to Carter. The worst outcome would be "endless litigation, transforming the crisis into a prolonged malaise."[78]

In spite of Brown's support, Brzezinski could not persuade Carter to take tougher measures. Brown backed Brzezinski's argument that the time had come for the United States to mine Iranian harbors. Vance's view was that if the Pentagon was going to take charge, State would first need to extricate its people from the Muslim world. The US Embassy in Islamabad, Pakistan, had recently been stormed and burned; two Americans were killed. Military action against Iran would trigger copycat assaults on any number of US diplomatic missions elsewhere, said Vance. Brzezinski replied that it would be better to double embassy security; abandoning them would "undermine our strategic position in the entire region." On the meeting's transcript, Carter wrote, "I agree."[79] Nothing happened.

As the impasse wore on, Carter's mindset began to harden. Hamilton Jordan once more became one of Brzezinski's few allies in the daily wrangling. In a reorganization a few months earlier, Jordan had become Carter's first and last official chief of staff, a belated move that satisfied no one, partly because of Jordan's undisciplined habits. Unlike Brzezinski, Jordan had played no role in admitting the shah to the US. Carter thus gave him a longer rope, though not that much longer. In late November, Khomeini said he was considering putting the American hostages on trial for espionage. Given the escalating level of killing in Tehran and what Laingen had cabled was an atmosphere of "dangerous emotional frenzy," Khomeini's threat was plausible. Executions of Americans could not be ruled out. The sight of apostates and other enemies of the revolution being hung from the ends of cranes was not uncommon. At an NSC meeting, Carter's team debated how best to talk the ayatollah off the ledge. One option was to threaten a disruption of Iranian commerce if the hostages were put on trial. Vance opposed that as too provocative. Jordan, along with Brzezinski, was in favor of threatening unspecified military action. Carter tilted towards getting tougher. They issued a statement to that effect. Khomeini stopped mentioning the trials. To Brzezinski, here was evidence that the threat of force was effective. Carter remained conflicted.

Again over Vance's objections, the president agreed to divert the aircraft carrier USS *Midway* to the Persian Gulf. He also sent helicopters to the Diego Garcia naval base in the Indian Ocean. But his instinct was to solve the crisis by negotiation. As the crisis wore on, bitter experience taught Carter that he could not reason with a fanatic whose power grew with every act of defiance against the Great Satan. "At least a portion of our government has operated for almost a year on the assumption that the U.S. could work with Khomeini," Brzezinski told Carter. That was a "dangerous fallacy."[80] In a memo titled "Taking a Toll on Your Presidency," Jordan laid out the damage to Carter's reelection prospects if he continued in the same timid fashion. In a recurring sideswipe at Vance's legal background, Brzezinski that same week had labeled his diplomacy "contractual-litigational."[81] Vance had thrived on Wall Street by being congenial; that would not work with Khomeini. "The American people, who have been supportive to date, will soon begin to sour on the situation," Jordan wrote in the memo to Carter, "and we will see increased support for extreme measures from giving the Shah back to wiping Iran off the face of the earth." Letting Iran off lightly would only invite more attacks on America, such as the recent incineration of the embassy in Islamabad. There had also been an assault on the US Embassy in Tripoli, Libya. "As a people and as a nation, we desire to be loved and respected," Jordan concluded. "As a result, we are neither."[82]

In a larger replay of the battle between Brzezinski and Vance, the national debate was also pulling Carter in two directions. On the right, there was contempt for his perceived weakness, in spite of the recent boost in his approval ratings. The shah's departure to Panama (Mexico had refused to take him back) was depicted as a betrayal. From the left, Ted Kennedy denounced Carter for having admitted the shah in the first place. It seemed that Carter could do nothing right. Three days after the Tehran embassy's storming, Kennedy launched a primary challenge to unseat Carter for the 1980 Democratic presidential nomination. Uncharacteristically for Carter, who tried to see the best in people, he felt contempt for Kennedy. At the dinner in the Brzezinski home to which the Carters had invited themselves the previous September, the president had shared his dark reading of Kennedy's character. He cited the youngest Kennedy brother's cheating on his college exam in the early 1960s, his behavior in the Chappaquiddick tragedy, and "his character in general."[83] Brzezinski pointed out in a subsequent memo that Kennedy's voting record was the most liberal in the Senate—to the left even of McGovern. Still, few observers could figure out exactly what Kennedy's candidacy was about.

In an infamous interview with CBS's Roger Mudd, Kennedy seemed unable to answer the simple question of why he wanted to be president. This confirmed to some that he was spurred by dynastic entitlement. He challenged Carter to a debate about the shah, which Carter's advisors told him to ignore. In early December, Kennedy said that the shah had run "one of the most violent regimes in the history of mankind."[84] Brzezinski thought that was "asinine."[85] Carter chose not to respond. In reality, Iran under the shah had just made it into the top twenty human rights abusers in the State Department's ranking. According to the Red Cross, in 1978 Iran had 2,100 political prisoners and carried out two political executions. In the early 1970s, the picture had been considerably worse. Between 1963 and 1977, an estimated three thousand political opponents had been killed. SAVAK had tortured hundreds of political detainees. Even then, however, Iran's record could not begin to compare with the genocide of 2 million to 3 million people in Cambodia, the thousands executed in China every year, the slaughter of 300,000 in Idi Amin's

Uganda, or even the scale of civilian "disappearances" in the Argentinian jun-
ta's "dirty war."

The shah was exorbitantly corrupt, vainglorious, in love with weapons,
contemptuous of dissent, and capable of brutality. But Iran was no killing
field. Under the Islamic regime, Iran shot up the rankings of global human
rights violators, which included robbing the female half of its population of
their basic civil rights. In late 1979, Brzezinski managed to dig out the State
transcript of Ted Kennedy's visit to Iran a few years earlier. Kennedy had not
raised human rights in his meeting with the shah. Brzezinski offered to let the
cable fall out of his pocket somewhere along Pennsylvania Avenue. "Carter
was delighted by the idea," he wrote.[86]

The record states that it was Carter who lost Iran. In late 1979, he did not
have the luxury of second-guessing his administration's blunders. The previous July, he had given his so-called malaise speech—though that word did not
feature. His portentous address followed several days of Camp David seminars with diverse groups of scholars, civic activists, spiritual figures, and political advisors in what was a prolonged spell of secluded reflection. Brzezinski
had not been involved: it was a domestic retreat. Carter's long contemplation
had been about the "crisis of the American spirit."

He had originally planned to talk about America's latest energy crisis,
which had been triggered by the Iranian Revolution. During the chaos, much
of Iran's refining capacity had gone offline. Snaking lines of American cars
waiting for gas were becoming a feature of his presidency. Between April 1979
and April 1980, the price of a barrel of oil doubled. The more Carter reflected
on the energy crisis, the more he was drawn into the idea of national malaise.
"We were sure that ours was a nation of the ballot, not the bullet, until the
murders of John Kennedy and Robert Kennedy and Martin Luther King, Jr.,"
Carter told the nation. "We were taught that our armies were always invincible
and our causes were always just, only to suffer the agony of Vietnam. We respected the Presidency as a place of honor until the shock of Watergate."[87] His
basic message was that Americans needed to reach deep into their collective
soul for renewal.

For a week or two, Carter's address rallied the citizenry and lifted his poll
numbers. Here was a president who could hold up a mirror to his country
without flinching. Then people started to turn away. In hindsight, his words
seemed almost prophetic. Much like the solar panels he installed on the White
House roof, they were ahead of their time—or perhaps too self-sacrificing for

any era. Carter had defined the energy challenge as the "moral equivalent of war." But it was his fate to be defined by the Iran hostage crisis. The two were, of course, connected.

One aspect of Carter's character that Brzezinski admired—though on Iran it caused him conniptions—was his stubborn instinct to do what he thought was right, even if it damaged his reelection prospects. Handing back the canal to Panama had been one such example. The Camp David Accords and the fight with American Jewish organizations were others. Another was his decision in August 1979 to appoint the hawkish inflation-slaying Paul Volcker as chairman of the Federal Reserve, a move that Carter knew would lead to sky-high interest rates. Killing inflation was the right course, he believed, even if the short-term pain coincided with the election. Iran was the latest example of Carter's political self-harm. No matter how stridently Brzezinski, Jordan, or the pollster Patrick Caddell urged Carter to take action, he recoiled from any hint of force. Striking Iran could have done wonders for his image. "The worst thing you could say to Carter was that something was good for his poll numbers," said Gerry Rafshoon.[88]

Less than a month after the hostages were seized, Harold Brown warned Carter that the hostage situation was starting to normalize. In mid-January 1980, the hallowed CBS anchor Walter Cronkite added a time count to his broadcast sign-off. It was the fiftieth day of the hostage crisis. Cronkite's evening reminder of their growing length of captivity did Carter more drip-drip harm than anything his political opponents could have devised. It was a clock that hung over his presidency. ABC's Ted Koppel launched *Nightline* as a nightly report on the hostage crisis. Rafshoon later calculated that the broadcast networks devoted more minutes to the Iran hostage crisis than they had spent on the entire Vietnam War. Fifty-eight thousand Americans died in Vietnam. The lives of fifty-two Americans in Tehran were at stake. Cold cost-benefit analysis could not explain why the fate of the hostages weighed quite so heavily on the nation. As the fifteenth-century French philosopher Blaise Pascal said, "The heart has its reasons of which reason knows nothing." Carter's heart—and Americans' obsession—was with the hostages. Their fate was burned into the nation's consciousness.

Brzezinski's inner compulsions were very different; his job was to focus on America's strategic calculus. The US government machinery was gearing towards a slow tightening of sanctions on Iran. Brzezinski argued that they would be useless. Khomeini would not bend to commercial threats. Devoted

1

2

Portrait of Leonia Brzezinski (née Roman), Warsaw, late 1920s.

Zbigniew Brzezinski with his mother, Leonia, at a Warsaw train station, 1932.

3

Leonia in a fur coat next to an off-road car and consular chauffeur, Germany, circa 1933.

Zbigniew (*center*) and Adam with their parents, Tadeusz and Leonia, in a Warsaw park, 1935.

4

A young Zbigniew (*right*) and Adam Brzezinski, probably in Leipzig, Germany, circa 1932.

5

Passenger manifest for the Brzezinski family's October 1938 journey on MS *Batory* from Gdynia to New York; Brzezinskis and traveling servants top the list.

6

List 6.
Diplomatic Visas & Passp. Visas

LIST OR MANIFEST OF ALIEN PASSENGERS FOR THE UNITED
ALL ALIENS arriving at a port of continental United States from a foreign port or a part of the insular possessions of the United States, and all aliens arriving at a port of said insular possessions from a foreign port, a part of continental United

S. S. m/s "Batory"   Passengers sailing from   Gdynia   Oct. 12th 1938, 19

No. on List	HEAD-TAX STATUS	Family name	Given name	Age Yrs. Mos.	Sex	Married or single	Calling or occupation	Able to— Read / Read what language	Nationality	Race or people	Place of birth Country / City or town	Last permanent residence
1	DIPLOMAT	Brzezinski	Dr. Tadeusz	42	m	m	gov.off.	yes polish	yes Poland	Polish	Poland Klosnow	Poland Warsaw
2	DIPLOMAT	Brzezinska	Leonja	38	f	m	"	yes polish	yes Poland	Polish	Poland	
3	DIPLOMAT	Brzezinski	Zbigniew	10	m	s	child	yes polish	yes Poland	Polish	Poland Warsaw	
4	DIPLOMAT	Brzezinski	Adam	9	m	s	child	yes polish	yes Poland	Polish	Lille	
5	DIPLOMAT	Brzezinski	Lech	1½	m	s	child	no child	yes Poland	Polish	Warsaw	
6	DIPLOMAT	Zylinski	Jerzy	17	m	s	gov.off.	yes polish	yes Poland	Polish	Warsaw	
7	DIPLOMAT	Berthold	Lidja	24	f	s	servant	yes polish	yes Poland	Polish	Aleksandrow	
8	DIPLOMAT	Gorzynski	Jozef-Jerzy	17	m	s	teacher	yes polish	yes Poland	Polish	Aooin	
9	DIPLOMAT	Ostark	Halgodor	58	m	m	gov.off.	yes polish	yes Poland	Polish	Konin	Germany Stettin
10	DIPLOMAT	Ostark	Aniela	50	f	m	"	yes polish	yes Poland	Polish		
11	DIPLOMAT	Ostark	Janina	27	f	s		yes polish	yes Poland	Polish	Lodz	
16	NOT COUNTED	Antosiewicz	Feliks	28	m	s	Lime's employe	yes polish	yes Poland	Polish	Poland Warsaw	Poland Warsaw
18	EXEMPT	Csako vel Czaszkowski	Jozvid	49	m	m	industr.	yes polish	yes Poland	Hebrew	Bialystok	Bialystok
19	EXEMPT	Grabowski	Jerzy	43	m	s	journalist	yes polish	yes Poland	Polish	Warsaw	Warsaw
15	NOT COUNTED	Horse	Marja	49	f	m	h'wife	yes polish	yes Poland	Polish	Warsaw	Pittsburgh, Pa.
17	DIPLOMAT	Buerer	Vilma	24	f	s	actress	yes german	yes Germany	Hebrew	Walk	Prague
		Marczynska	Marja	38	f	m	h'wife	yes polish	yes Poland	Polish	Krakow	Warsaw
18		Perlmuter	Lejb	52	m	m	merchant	yes polish	yes Poland	Hebrew	Sokol	Sokol
20	EXEMPT	Homar	Aleksy	31	m	m	manager	yes polish	yes Poland	Polish	Orla	
21		Szafir	Icchok	44	m	m	merchant	yes polish	yes Poland	Hebrew	Lubor	Warsaw
22		Wysowiemski	Mieczyslaw	18	m	s	student	yes polish	yes Poland	Hebrew		Warsaw
23		Wysowiemski	David	50	m	m	merchant	yes polish	yes Poland	Hebrew	Loza	Lodz
		Wysowiemska	Rachela	50	f	m	h'wife	yes polish	yes Poland	Hebrew		Lodz

OCT 23 1938

7

Brzezinski (*middle, in white blazer*) at Newman House School, summer 1941.

Brzezinski hitchhiking near
Boston, circa 1951.

Zbigniew and Muska on
their wedding day, Boston,
June 11, 1955.

The newlywed couple
of Zbigniew and Muska
coming out of the church.

Top to bottom:
Brzezinski with Henry Kissinger, Pratt House,
Council on Foreign Relations, 1965.

Faculty, fellows, and associates of the Center
for International Affairs, Harvard University
(1959–1960). At the front is Robert Bowie. To
his left is cofounder Henry Kissinger. Behind
Kissinger's left shoulder is Brzezinski.

Brzezinski on *Meet the Press* facing four journalist
interrogators, circa 1965. Brzezinski appeared
regularly on this show throughout the 1960s
and onward. *Left to right:* Bob Abernethy, NBC
correspondent; Carl Rowan, nationally syndicated
columnist; Elizabeth Drew, of *The New Yorker*;
Bill Monroe, moderator of *Meet the Press*.

14

Brzezinski with
Hubert Humphrey,
Washington,
DC, 1967.

15

Brzezinski with
President Lyndon
Baines Johnson,
Oval Office, 1967.

Brzezinski in Maine with one of
the family's menagerie of ducks
and other pets, early 1970s.

16

17

Brzezinski with family in Maine, early 1970s.

Brzezinski and President Jimmy Carter bantering in the Oval Office.

Brzezinski with Cyrus Vance and Jimmy Carter, Oval Office, 1977.

Israel's prime minister, Menachem Begin, showing Brzezinski papers related to Tadeusz Brzezinski's role in providing passports to Germany-based Polish Jews, Blair House, July 1977.

Brzezinski and Begin playing chess at Camp David, September 9, 1978.

Brzezinski meeting China's leader Deng Xiaoping for the first time, Beijing, May 21, 1978.

Brzezinski at the Great Wall of China, with a group of Chinese sailors, May 23, 1978.

Brzezinski jogging with President Carter in Seoul, South Korea, June 1979. Brzezinski was rarely able to keep up.

Brzezinski with Cyrus Vance on a golf cart at Camp David during the marathon Israel-Egypt peace talks, September 1978. Though the two were usually at loggerheads, they saw eye to eye on the Arab-Israeli dispute.

Carter giving Brzezinski a surprise cake on Air Force One to Caracas, Venezuela, on his fiftieth birthday, March 28, 1978.

27

Brzezinski toasting Deng at Spring Hill, January 29, 1979. On Deng's right is Cyrus Vance; to Vance's right is Zhuo Lin, Deng's wife. To her right is Richard Holbrooke. In the foreground facing Brzezinski is Michael Oksenberg, the NSC China advisor.

Brzezinski with West German chancellor Helmut Schmidt, Bonn, September 27, 1977.

Deng Xiaoping shaking hands with Mark Brzezinski, as Muska watches on. Spring Hill, January 29, 1979.

30

Jimmy Carter and Soviet leader Leonid Brezhnev at the signing ceremony of the SALT II treaty, Hofburg Palace, Vienna, June 18, 1979. Brzezinski is behind Carter's left shoulder.

32

31

Brzezinski as national security advisor, undated.

33

Brzezinski playing tennis on the White House "Supreme Court," undated.

Brzezinski playing tennis in his sardonic NSC-emblazoned gear.

34

Brzezinski with
Egypt's president,
Anwar Sadat,
Oval Office,
July 1977.

35

Brzezinski with
President Carter,
Oval Office, 1977.

36

Brzezinski reading
on the porch of
Tranquility Base,
the family summer
home in Maine's
Northeast Harbor.

37

Muska and Zbigniew Brzezinski (*far right*) on the White House ballroom dance floor with First Lady Rosalyn and President Jimmy Carter, December 1980.

38

The Brzezinski family on the Maine shore, circa 1975.

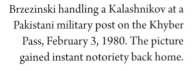

39

Brzezinski handling a Kalashnikov at a Pakistani military post on the Khyber Pass, February 3, 1980. The picture gained instant notoriety back home.

40

41

Top to bottom:
Brzezinski playing chess with Leonard Woodcock, former head of the United Auto Workers and first US ambassador to China, on a plane to China, May 1978.

Zbigniew and Muska Brzezinski greeting Pope John Paul II at Andrews Air Force Base, October 6, 1979.

Brzezinski and Pope John Paul II, with Mika and Ian looking on, October 1979.

42

43

Brzezinski at a White House lunch with President Ronald Reagan, 1981.

44

45

Brzezinski with his daughter, Mika; son Ian; and pony, Strawberry. Spring Hill, 1983. One of Strawberry's tricks was to drink shots of Polish vodka.

Brzezinski with Muska at their tennis court at Spring Hill, Virginia, early 1980s.

Brzezinski with his daughter, Mika, and her cohost,
Joe Scarborough, attending a bust-unveiling
ceremony for the late Czech leader Václav Havel in
the Capitol's Statuary Hall, November 19, 2014.

Brzezinski with Henry Kissinger
at Spring Hill, circa 2010.

Brzezinski onstage with Kissinger in Oslo, at the Nobel Peace Prize Forum in December 2016—his
last overseas trip. It was moderated by Olav Njølstad, director of the Norwegian Nobel Institute.

Brzezinski with President Barack Obama in the Situation Room. *From left of the president:* Brent Scowcroft, Bud McFarlane, Colin Powell, Dennis Ross, Sandy Berger, Frank Carlucci. September 1, 2010.

Brzezinski on the set of *Morning Joe* with Mika and Scarborough, 2010.

Brzezinski in the last year of his life.

actors who believed in their cause could tolerate indefinite economic pain. Rhodesia's racist white minority had withstood roughly a decade of economic sanctions. Shortly before Christmas, Brzezinski recommended to Carter that the US occupy three Iranian islands until the hostages were released.[89] The US military options to date had only been an extension of the sanctions plan, he said. Jordan added that any commercial hit to Iran should be big and immediate, as opposed to the incremental schedule that State was working on. Carter dismissed both ideas. Such actions would only rally Iranians around Khomeini, he said.

Carter did allow work on a hostage rescue operation to get under way. As early as November 6, two days after the embassy was stormed, Brzezinski had raised this scenario with Carter. On Thanksgiving, which that year was a normal working day in the White House, Brzezinski sent his military aide, Lt. Col. William Odom, into the Oval Office, where he laid out for Carter the twin plan of a hostage rescue operation and retaliatory air strikes on Iran.[90] Brzezinski knew that many hostages could die during a rescue mission, since they were being held in a densely populated urban environment. Any operation, he felt, should be accompanied by larger military percussion. "A massive strike would . . . obviate the likely failure of the operation by itself," he said.[91] Moreover, Carter agreed that hostage rescue planning should be done in a small subcommittee without State's involvement. For the time being, only Brown and General David Jones, the chairman of the Joint Chiefs of Staff, would be included, along with Brzezinski.

The daily crisis meetings, which often got diverted down endless byways, were starting to grate on Carter's nerves. His principals held long discussions about the best legal strategy for handling Iranian assets in the United States, on the mechanics of how Iran's Washington embassy should be closed and its diplomats expelled, and on the legal rights of radical Iranian students at American universities. The White House tirelessly litigated the shah's peregrinations. To Brzezinski, this was like discussing deck chair arrangements on the *Titanic*. After one long session, an exhausted Carter was more receptive than usual to Brzezinski's sense of urgency. "I don't blame him," Brzezinski wrote. "All efforts by me to direct discussion toward the larger issue, namely should we strive to effect a significant change in the character of the political regime in Iran, was deflected by Vance and others. Vance is not prepared to do anything decisive, and Brown always comes out on both sides of every issue."[92]

On the last Friday before Christmas, Brzezinski finally got Carter to agree that the grand ayatollah was "not interested in a compromise."[93] Action could now be contemplated. In tandem with economic pressure, the White House should start working on a plan to remove Khomeini. Brzezinski created a sub-committee to pursue covert action against the ayatollah's regime. Its decisions would be secret and its scope broad. Among the potential tools would be assistance to the Iranian opposition and separatist groups. In post-Watergate Washington and in Carter's heart, CIA "black ops" were taboo; they belonged to the era of Nixon and Kissinger. Frank Church's Senate investigative committee had shut them down. In 1979, Brzezinski brought covert action back to life. In these circumstances, Carter grasped their utility. As the White House staff dispersed for a decidedly unmerry Christmas, Brzezinski took some solace from that.

Brzezinski's—and Carter's—most fraught public moment was yet to come. But in the bleak spell leading up to Christmas, Brzezinski's resilience was tested in other ways. On December 19, one of the *Washington Post*'s star writers, Sally Quinn, who had recently married the newspaper's editor in chief, Ben Bradlee, dropped the journalistic equivalent of a chemical weapon. The first of her three-part series on Brzezinski, which was run in the paper's Style section, was headlined "The Politics of the Power Grab: Nine Rules of Notoriety." The piece was a character assassination that depicted Brzezinski as a ravenous power seeker with unseemly appetites. Many of the quotes were from unnamed sources, though there could be little mistaking the fingerprints of State Department spokesman Hodding Carter. Other wild guesses included Les Gelb and Richard Holbrooke. There were plenty of quotes from people "close to Kissinger."

There were also a couple of devastating on-the-record takedowns of Brzezinski. "He's a very, very arrogant, self-opinionated man," said the Republican senator and former presidential candidate Barry Goldwater. "He should be my kind of guy. But he is arrogance with a capital A." From former Democratic presidential candidate George McGovern: "I endorse Barry." The unsourced quotes portrayed Brzezinski as a man who craved the limelight and had no real agenda other than to put his name in lights; his real goal was to become secretary of state. "Zbig has always been in a position where he has felt an enormous need to attract attention that came to Henry normally," said a person who was "very close to Kissinger." Quinn also cited Kissinger's wife, Nancy, as saying that Ardeshir Zahedi, the shah's former ambassador, told her that Brzezinski was the only person who had asked him to send him Iranian caviar. They went nicely with the Cuban cigars that he got from Shirley MacLaine.

Not only was Brzezinski a shallow opportunist, he was also lacking in courage, Quinn implied. In the thick of the Iranian hostage crisis, he was nowhere to be seen. His "self-aggrandizement problem" was thus in temporary suspension. "There are no Russians involved and he is lost without an anti-Soviet stance," Quinn observed. A few weeks before Quinn's piece came out, Brzezinski had been in a scrap with Ben Bradlee. He refused to grant an interview to Quinn because he thought her piece would be a "hatchet job."[94] He told his press secretary, Jerry Schecter, to deny Quinn permission to travel with him to Algeria. Bradlee and Schecter had a shouting match over the phone. Schecter held fast. Quinn's end product was an exquisitely composed essay of acidic vignettes. "But even men who have been despised in some quarters in Washington during their careers will inspire loyalty or affection or admiration in some group, no matter how small," she wrote. "Not Brzezinski."[95]

Many of Quinn's observations were within the bounds of fair comment: Brzezinski was indeed obsessed with the USSR; he seemed to go out of his way to cultivate unpopularity with the media; his rivalry with Kissinger was kinetic (though she did not mention that it was two-way); unlike Kissinger, Brzezinski's humor often miscued; and he was undoubtedly arrogant. Other claims were wrong. From from being missing in action, Brzezinski had been in the thick of the Iran debates, though his advice went against the White House consensus, much to Carter's annoyance. He also made clear that he was in the job he had always wanted. Since Carter had effectively decided to be his own secretary of state, Brzezinski had agitated to be the president's senior advisor. Had he hypothetically been offered both roles—as Kissinger had been but which Carter would never have considered—he would doubtless have been delighted to become secretary of state as well. But if he could pick one job, he was already in it. Brzezinski also had a sizable group of admirers, including his NSC staff, as well the extensive network of those he had taught as a professor. If Quinn had stopped at those criticisms, her piece would not have entered the annals of journalistic legend, though its lively prose stood out. As Carter kept observing, Brzezinski had been the target of more negative media than anyone else in the administration. He was used to it.

But Quinn went a big step further. She insinuated that Brzezinski was a sexual predator. "It is a scurrilous article, one which ends with the clear implication that I am some sort of pervert," Brzezinski stated.[96] Her piece ended

with an anecdote from a female magazine reporter who had profiled Brzezinski. At the end of their interview, Brzezinski showed her around the Oval
Office. The official photographer took a picture of Brzezinski gesticulating.
It purportedly showed him playfully unzipping his fly. "Shortly afterward,
the reporter received a photograph of the private moment they had shared,
captured for eternity. It was inscribed by Zbigniew Brzezinski." That was
how Quinn's piece ended. The White House was not a calm place that morning. Carter's senior counsel, Lloyd Cutler, picked up the phone and yelled at
Bradlee, as did Jody Powell, Carter's spokesperson. They tracked down the
reporter, who signed a deposition saying that Quinn's claim was a fabrication.
She also handed over the picture. The next day, the *Washington Post* printed a
full retraction.

Given the unusual nature of its statement and the article's impact on
Brzezinski, it is worth quoting in full:

> In yesterday's story about Zbigniew Brzezinski, it was stated that at the end
> of an interview with a reporter from a national magazine—as a joke—Brzez-
> inski committed an offensive act, and that a photographer took a picture
> "of this unusual expression of playfulness." Brzezinski did not commit such
> an act, and there is no picture of him doing so. A photograph of Brzezinski
> and the reporter was made, and Brzezinski autographed it at the reporter's
> request. The poses, shadows and background of this picture create an ac-
> cidental "double entendre," which Brzezinski refers to in his caption. The
> magazine reporter states that nothing in the interview or the autographed
> picture offended her. The Washington Post sincerely regrets the error.[97]

The White House did not dispute that Brzezinski had mailed the photo
to the reporter and had written a joke on it. How bad or ill-advised the joke
was is a matter of speculation. Quinn's error was not to have taken a copy of
it before her article went to press. The impression that Brzezinski was some
kind of Casanova has no corroboration. Several decades later, that was also
Quinn's candid admission. "Zbig was very smart, with a mordant wit, and all
the hostesses wanted him at their parties," she said. "When Zbig walked into
a room, it was about Zbig. But he had sharp elbows and pissed a lot of people
off." She said that in retrospect she had been persuaded that Brzezinski was
probably not a predator.[98]

Quinn's piece had a rallying effect on Brzezinski's friends and allies, who flooded him with sympathetic notes. The same day the *Post* corrected it, James "Scotty" Reston ran a column in the *New York Times* complaining that journalists focused too much nowadays on personality at the expense of substance. His prime example was a piece by the "highly talented and sometimes recklessly provocative" Sally Quinn. The rift between Vance and Brzezinski was almost the oldest story in Washington, he wrote. Yet it was a reasonable topic to write about. "But she has also tried to psychoanalyze Brzezinski's ambitions, his motives, and even his sexual urgings, which is rather original, because Brzezinski may be the most faithful, old-fashioned, square family man in town."[99] Brzezinski had made more than his quota of enemies in DC and beyond. None publicly attempted to counter Reston's characterization.

The Brzezinskis stayed home in McLean that Christmas. Their holiday was not a restful one. On the evening of December 24, the Soviet Union invaded Afghanistan. By Christmas night, Soviet commandos had taken control of key military and communications sites in Kabul; the Soviets were airlifting paratroopers into major Afghan cities. Soviet *spetsnaz* (special forces) murdered Afghanistan's president, Hafizullah Amin, in the presidential palace on December 27. Moscow replaced him two days later with Babrak Karmal, an Afghan Communist more congenial to its wishes. Somewhat careless of the timeline, Karmal's puppet government retroactively requested Soviet intervention. By New Year's Day, there were forty thousand Soviet troops in Afghanistan. By the end of January, that number had doubled. Détente was over.

To Brzezinski, little of this was a surprise. Carter was in Camp David with the family. Over the phone, Brzezinski reminded him that the Soviets had been beefing up the number of "military advisors" in Afghanistan during 1979.[100] The Red Army was now suddenly within three hundred miles of the Persian Gulf. Carter, who felt betrayed by the Soviets, and sickened by the threat to world peace, withdrew SALT II from the Senate. There was no going back. His fondest diplomatic hope was over. When Brzezinski saw his military aide, Bill Odom, in the White House on December 26, he reportedly clenched his fist and said, "They have taken the bait!"[101] The Soviets would now have their Vietnam.

It remains an open question whether Brzezinski lured the Soviets into Afghanistan, as a number of scholars and journalists have claimed. A lot of work is required of the word *lure*. Throughout 1979, he had been pushing for US covert action to fuel Afghanistan's growing insurgency against the country's

Communist regime. The Communists, under party leader Nur Muhammad Taraki, had taken power in a brutal coup in April 1978. The man they toppled, Mohammad Daoud Khan, was a cousin of the Afghan king, Mohammad Zahir Shah, whom he had sent into exile five years earlier. The 1978 putsch was far bloodier. Daoud and twenty-seven members of his family, including his grandchildren, were slaughtered.

Both Brzezinski and Deng Xiaoping, whom he had first met in China a few weeks earlier, thought the Soviets were behind the coup,[102] though the evidence was inconclusive. Either way, Moscow had acquired an ideological sibling in Kabul. Brzezinski stepped up his warnings about an "arc of crisis." He told Carter that the political upheavals in the Horn of Africa, Yemen, Iran, Afghanistan, and Southeast Asia were connected. On February 12, 1979, ten months before the invasion, he told an SCC meeting that failure to act would only invite further Soviet interventions. "We acquiesced to Soviet-Cuban intervention into Africa; we have now acquiesced into the collapse of Afghanistan and Iran," he said. "The cumulative effect of this is bound to be destructive."[103]

Two days later the US ambassador to Afghanistan, Adolph Dubs, was killed after being dragged from his car at gunpoint by a group of uniformed Afghans. It was Valentine's Day. They bundled him into a nearby hotel and barricaded themselves into a room. US Embassy officials rushed to the scene. In a blur of hurried consultations, they urged the Afghan police not to attempt a rescue until they could find out the identity of the captors and what they wanted. Soviet advisors at the hotel seemed to countermand that advice. In the resulting shootout, Dubs and his abductors were killed. Brzezinski repeatedly stated that Dubs's death "involved either Soviet collusion or ineptitude."[104]

A few days later, he accompanied Carter to Andrews Air Force Base to receive Dubs's remains. He shivered as they stood there awaiting the coffin; it was the coldest day of the year. Whether it had happened by accident or design, the ambassador's killing created the conditions for covert action. Brzezinski asked the CIA to draw up a menu of options, which it supplied in early March. Kabul had provoked a "tribal" uprising in rural Afghanistan by launching a brutal campaign of land reform, in which the regime also closed mosques and arrested mullahs. Feudal Afghanistan was in rebellion against the cities. In late March, Pravda and other Soviet organs accused the US of fomenting the Afghan insurgency. The accusation, which was false, enraged Carter.[105] But it was a revealing window on Moscow's paranoia. Brzezinski set about trying to stoke Moscow's anxiety.

In Soviet parlance, the correlation of forces in Afghanistan was ripe. The infamous "graveyard of empires" bordered the Soviet republics of Uzbekistan, Tajikistan, and Turkmenistan. Since 1977, Brzezinski had played on Soviet fears of internal Muslim revivalism by intensifying Voice of America broadcasts to the USSR's central Asian republics. He had done so without fuss or internal debate. He continued to believe that simmering nationalisms were the USSR's Achilles' heel. Before the revolution, there had been thousands of mosques in the Soviet republic of Azerbaijan, for example; following the crackdown, there were only twenty-four.[106] Moscow's fear of restive Islam at home increasingly fused with its neuralgia about the Muslim insurgency in Afghanistan. Afghanistan's rural uprising wakened deep fears in Brezhnev that it was a dagger held to the USSR's underbelly.

In early July 1979, six months before the Soviet invasion, Brzezinski pushed through a "presidential finding" that authorized up to $695,000 in nonlethal aid to Afghan rebel groups.[107] The money was spent on communications equipment, such as radios; VOA broadcasts in Dari and Pashto; propaganda leaflets; and contacts with people in Afghan refugee camps in neighboring Pakistan. He pushed the package through over State's objections. Warren Christopher's counterargument was that the president, if asked, ought to be able to answer truthfully that he had not approved any covert action. Dismissing State officials as "mush heads," Brzezinski replied, "Is the only covert activity that we are able to undertake the one that no one asks about?"[108]

The deeper paranoia in Moscow was that the Americans were angling to put a military base in Afghanistan and even plotting to locate US nuclear weapons there. Again, Soviet fears were wildly inaccurate, particularly in the wake of the 1978 "Red coup." Brzezinski nurtured that paranoia. In September, the Afghan government's increasingly powerful number two, Hafizullah Amin, ousted his former comrade Nur Muhammad Taraki in another brutal coup. Taraki was probably smothered to death with a pillow. Brezhnev, who viewed Taraki as the poet of the Afghan Revolution, was distraught over his murder.[109] Taraki had just passed through Moscow, where Brezhnev had urged him to rein in his comrade. Amin had survived one Soviet assassination attempt; his coup against Taraki was preemptive.

The KGB suspected that Amin was on the CIA's payroll or was at least looking for opportunities for "political reorientation to the West."[110] He had twice studied in the United States, including at Columbia University in the early 1960s, when Brzezinski was there as a professor. At Columbia, Amin joined the Afghan Student Alliance, which was indirectly funded by the CIA.[111] There is no record of Brzezinski having met Amin. Either way, the Soviets suspected a connection. In the weeks leading up to the Soviet invasion, Amin met three times with the US chargé d'affaires in Kabul, which only deepened Soviet paranoia. At the urging of Andrei Gromyko; Yuri Andropov, head of the KGB; Mikhail Suslov, chief Soviet propagandist; and the Soviet defense minister, Dmitry Ustinov, a reportedly drunk Brezhnev gave the go-ahead for the invasion on December 8. He took the fateful step after strong pressure from party ideologues and civilian officials. Soviet combat generals were opposed.[112] They knew a quagmire when they saw one. So did Brzezinski.

It would be outlandish to conclude that Brzezinski tricked the Soviets into invading Afghanistan. That was Moscow's decision. There is no secret memo that could somehow prove that Brzezinski duped Brezhnev into a war that would contribute to the unraveling of the Soviet Union. Yet there is a whiff of T. S. Eliot's cat Macavity about Brzezinski in the thicket of diplomatic cables, White House memos, SCC minutes, and CIA reports on Afghanistan leading up to the invasion. Like the cat, Brzezinski seems always just to have vanished from the scene. Robert Gates, Brzezinski's former aide who had returned to the CIA in late 1979, emphasized that Washington set up the mujahideen logistics pipeline months before the Soviet invasion.[113]

In an interview years later with France's *Le Nouvel Observateur*, Brzezinski said, "We did not push the Russians into intervening, but we did knowingly increase the chances that they would do so."[114] Brzezinski insisted he had been inaccurately quoted and asked the French paper to retract it. But his actions in 1979 fit with those offending words. On July 24, Brzezinski predicted to Carter that the Soviets would try to eject Amin. "On my instructions this will be publicized in order to sow discord between the Soviets and Amin," he wrote.[115] Two months before the invasion, he had breakfast with the British ambassador, Sir Nicholas Henderson. According to Henderson's memo for the UK Foreign Office, Brzezinski dropped hints of US "preparedness to do something to make life difficult for the Soviets in Afghanistan."[116]

Brzezinski wasted no time making good on those hints as the invasion got under way. This time he had no trouble persuading Carter to take his advice. Carter was an altered man. "The action of the Soviets has made a more dramatic change in my opinion of what the Soviets' ultimate goals are than anything they've done in the previous time that I've been in office," he said on New Year's Eve.[117] Conservatives accused Carter of naiveté; where had he been for the past thirty years? Liberals accused him of exaggerating; was the Soviet invasion of Afghanistan really more of a threat than the Cuba crisis?

But Carter had traveled a reverse Damascus. Having given Brezhnev the benefit of the doubt for so long and in so many ways, he felt the invasion of Afghanistan as a personal betrayal. He littered the statement Brezhnev sent over the Kremlin hotline with sarcastic comments. Where Brezhnev stated that the Afghan government had invited the Soviets in, Carter wrote, "The leaders who 'requested' Soviet intervention were assassinated."[118] When Brezhnev referred to "external aggression" against Afghanistan, Carter asked, "From where?" Writing years later, Dobrynin described what he called the "KGB operation"[119] as a gross miscalculation. Moscow had assumed that Washington would react in the same way it had to the 1968 invasion of Czechoslovakia: a flurry of condemnations, then a return to business as usual. Détente flourished in spite of Czechoslovakia. It died in Afghanistan. The Soviets had badly misread Carter. He, in turn, projected too much goodwill onto the semicatatonic Brezhnev. Moscow was now being run by the ideologues. Some observers were saying the same about Washington.

To Brzezinski, Afghanistan was a vindication. Since 1977, he had incessantly challenged State's view that the USSR was a status quo power that had given up on global revolution. Four more countries—Yemen, Cambodia, Ethiopia, and Afghanistan—had been added to the Soviet Bloc since Carter had taken office. From now on, Brzezinski would be far harder to oppose. One of Carter's first steps was to kill the nuclear treaty. Brzezinski declared, "SALT lies buried in the sands of Ogaden."[120] If Carter had taken his advice to oppose the USSR in the Horn of Africa, the Soviets might not have invaded Afghanistan, Brzezinski kept telling people. Others countered that SALT lay buried in the sands of Afghanistan's Kandahar province. Somalia had not even been a sideshow. To Brzezinski, that did not qualify as a serious rebuttal; he maintained that America's passive reaction to Soviet moves in the Horn of Africa and elsewhere gave Moscow the confidence to invade Afghanistan. Indeed, that inertia extended to Afghanistan as well. As late as December 14, when signs of Soviet plans were evident, a State official tried to stop Brzezinski from giving a background media briefing on Afghanistan. The department's objection was that any publicity would be seen by Moscow as US meddling in Afghan affairs. "That remark conveys well the flavor of much of the State Department thinking on tough international issues," Brzezinski wrote.[121]

In the aftermath of the invasion, Brzezinski's tussle with Vance was mostly over China and the boycott of the 1980 Summer Olympics in Moscow. To Carter and Brzezinski's surprise and to Mondale's distaste, Vance favored restricting grain sales to the Soviets.[122] Mondale objected that that would damage Carter in Iowa, where Carter was to face his first contest with Kennedy in the Democratic in late January. Hurting midwestern grain producers would be a surefire way of losing Iowa. To everyone's surprise—and Mondale's outrage—Vance was also in favor of restoring the military draft. The idea was never seriously considered.

The Afghanistan emergency boosted Carter's standing. Having been running neck and neck with Kennedy for most of late 1979, he won the Iowa caucuses in January by a margin of two to one. Brzezinski's most serious rift with Foggy Bottom was over China. Harold Brown was about to go on a previously scheduled trip to Beijing. His visit now took on greater significance. The time had come to make defensive arms sales to China, Brzezinski argued. Vance did his best to block those. He also insisted that it would be impractical to limit the number of Soviet diplomats in Washington to the same total as China's delegation—one of the symbolic measures that Carter was planning. "I am asking for sacrifices from farmers, from businessmen, from the whole country, but you feel that diplomats shouldn't make any at all," Carter told Vance.[123]

Brown got Carter's permission to give Deng Xiaoping over-the-horizon radar equipment, on the grounds that it was more of an intelligence tool than a military weapon. At a briefing for a group of national leaders in Washington, Vance said that the United States would not be selling arms to either China or the USSR. Donald Rumsfeld, who had been Gerald Ford's defense secretary, asked whether anyone had seriously proposed selling arms to the Soviets. Vance had no response.[124] As expected, Deng's comments to Brown could have been taken verbatim from Brzezinski. China's leader said that the Soviets were on a southward drive to seize warm-water ports in the Gulf of Oman and the Indian Ocean. It was not an isolated military action. Afghanistan must become the USSR's quagmire, as Vietnam had been for the US, said Deng.

In Moscow, Brezhnev was in shock over Carter's retaliatory measures. By mid-January, that included a near-total ban on technology-related sales to the USSR, grain export restrictions, efforts to move the Olympics to another city, such as Montreal, and full-blown ideological warfare. It is a measure of Brezhnev's isolation that he was taken aback by America's response. In an interview with *Pravda*, he said that US efforts to "poison" relations would come back to haunt it "like a boomerang."[125] A few days later, an unnamed Afghan rebel group received the first consignment of US military aid. It consisted of a modest fifty AK-47 rifles and fifty thousand rounds of ammunition.[126] The CIA reported that another US-funded shipment containing fifty RPG-7 rocket launchers, two thousand pounds of explosives, and five hundred AK-47s was on the way from Saudi Arabia. After a slow start, America's clandestine response was increasing geometrically.

In late January 1980, the bureaucratic infighting shifted to the content of Carter's looming State of the Union address. Carter's instincts were idealist. He wanted to be a liberal internationalist president in the mold of Woodrow Wilson. Brzezinski said he would first have to play the role of Harry S. Truman. "He kind of agreed with it, though reluctantly, and said he would hope to come back to his more idealistic agenda in the second term," Brzezinski recorded.[127] Truman had proclaimed his eponymous doctrine in 1947 in a speech to Congress, declaring that it was in America's national interest to defend any country from Soviet takeover wherever it happened in the world. Truman's speech followed Great Britain's withdrawal from Greece and Turkey. Carter now faced a comparable challenge in the Persian Gulf. Declaring warm-water ports off limits to the Soviets must be the Carter Doctrine, Brzezinski argued. Carter should unveil it to Congress in his State of the Union address. Carter was uneasy about associating his foreign policy legacy with a philosophy of military deterrence. He had wanted SALT II to be his first term's signature achievement. Since any kind of nuclear deal with the Soviets was now a pipe dream, he allowed Brzezinski to run with his doctrine.

Until the last moment, Brzezinski and State fought their own version of guerrilla warfare over key passages in the speech. Vance excised the paragraph announcing the Persian Gulf "regional security framework." Along with the creation of a new rapid reaction force—the Rapid Deployment Joint Task Force, later renamed the United States Central Command, or CENTCOM— that was the meat of the Carter doctrine. A frantic Brzezinski intercepted Jody Powell on the way to the Oval Office a couple of hours before Carter was to give his address. Powell was clutching the final draft of the speech. Brzezinski persuaded Powell to reinsert the passage that Vance had cut, with slightly modified wording.[128] This was the message Carter delivered on Capitol Hill that night. Foreign policy is often forged in momentous debates over principles and methods. It is also about proximity; the last person to see the draft wins.

The Soviet invasion of Afghanistan "could pose the most serious threat to the peace since the Second World War," Carter said. "An attempt by any outside force to gain control of the Persian Gulf region will be regarded as an assault on the vital interests of the United States of America, and such an assault will be repelled by any means necessary, including military force." That was the Carter Doctrine. The mostly positive coverage the next day embarrassed Brzezinski, since the media correctly attributed the content to him. Like the Soviets, US journalists had developed the habit of marking "CV" or "ZB" next to passages in Carter's speeches. The press marked down the whole of Carter's State of the Union foreign policy content as ZB's. In addition to State, Brown called Brzezinski to accuse him of planting such stories in the media. These were not helpful to Carter since they implied he was under somebody's influence, Brown said.[129] Brzezinski denied having leaked anything. Brown backed down.

A bruised Ted Kennedy, who was suffering in the polls after his Iowa loss ahead of a clutch of New England primaries, came out strongly against the Carter Doctrine. "Is this really the gravest threat to peace since World War II?" he asked. "Is it a graver threat than the Berlin blockade, the Korean War, the Soviet march into Hungary and Czechoslovakia, the Berlin wall, the Cuban missile crisis, or Vietnam? Exaggeration and hyperbole are the enemies of sensible foreign policy." Kennedy could have stopped there. He had couched his critique within a powerful historical context. But he was trying to occupy the whole spectrum. Carter, he added, had not been tough enough in response to the discovery of a Soviet brigade in Cuba the previous autumn. By failing to draw a line in Cuba, he said, Carter "may have invited the Soviet invasion of Afghanistan."[130]

Carter dismissed Kennedy's speech as unserious. The Massachusetts senator stayed in the race, but money was tight. His campaign was closing offices across the country. Carter's priority was increasingly to protect his right flank for the general election, which meant he would soon be in need of Brzezinski's services. To Jordan's amusement, Brzezinski was getting more and more involved in Carter's campaign strategy. Over the coming weeks, Carter dispatched Brzezinski to give hawkish foreign policy speeches in key states. Jordan, in turn, was devoting most of his time to trying to get the US hostages released from Iran—donning wigs and fake mustaches to meet shadowy intermediaries in Panama and Paris. "We ought to swap jobs, Dr. Strangelove," Jordan joked. "Could I use nuclear weapons in the presidential campaign?" Brzezinski replied.[131]

The next Brzezinski-Vance showdown was over Pakistan. The NSC realized that comparing Soviet woes in Afghanistan to America's Vietnam disaster was not at all helpful to its cause. State was using the analogy to argue that the Soviets had blundered terribly and would now learn their lesson, much as the Americans had in Vietnam. All the US needed to do was to sit back and watch. Marshall Brement, Brzezinski's staff person for the region, summarized the line that State was taking on the Hill and with journalists. "Some public testimony, in addition to much background briefing, leaves the implication that the pendulum will swing back in due course and that within several months we can expect 'business as usual' with the Soviets," he wrote. It made a mockery, he said, of Carter's claim that Afghanistan posed the greatest threat to world peace since the Second World War.

"Excusing the Soviet invasion or laying the blame for it on the feebleness of our diplomacy and the lack of wisdom of specific actions taken by the President undercut the President's leadership, question his judgment, and are not appropriate analyses from high officials of the Carter Administration."[132] In a memo to Carter, Brzezinski argued that the Vietnam comparison was misplaced. Unlike Vietnam, which is five thousand miles from US shores, Afghanistan borders the Soviet Union. That would make it far easier for the Soviet military to beef up its operations and quash the rebels. Moreover, the Soviets had sustained the Vietnamese Communists with regular military airlifts. Finally, North Vietnam had supplied the Vietcong with continuous arms via the Ho Chi Minh Trail. In view of those stark differences, the Vietnam comparison made no sense. Afghan rebels lacked an equivalent sanctuary. Only Pakistan could play such a role.

The debate over Pakistan's part in the Afghan war created a migraine for Carter. In his view, Pakistan was a rogue nation that was in breach of US nuclear nonproliferation rules and thus ineligible for US arms transfers. The country was known to be working on a nuclear device. Its strongman, President Muhammad Zia-ul-Haq, who had been educated at Sandhurst, the UK's military academy, had in 1978 ordered the execution of Zulfikar Ali Bhutto, Pakistan's president, after ousting him in a coup. India and Pakistan were always one trip wire away from another war. There could be no guarantee that Pakistan would not redeploy US-supplied arms meant for Afghanistan against India. Moreover, India's recently reelected prime minister, Indira Gandhi, was supporting the Soviet line on Afghanistan at the UN. According to New Delhi, the Soviets were acting in self-defense against foreign interference (Pakistan in the mind of the Indians; America in the eyes of the Soviets). Making friends with Zia would put Carter into a quandary. Not only would he need to suspend his human rights rules and circumvent congressional restrictions on arms sales to potential illegal nuclear states; if he was not careful, he could also trigger another Indo-Pakistani war. That was also State's concern.

Brzezinski urged Carter to look at the bigger picture. Without Pakistan's cooperation, he said, the US would be unable to supply the Afghan rebels; Carter should brush aside Vance's concerns about Zia. "Let us not recreate in Zia's mind the same ambiguity that clearly existed in the Shah's mind last year," Brzezinski argued.[133] In a separate note to Carter he wrote, "*The basic decision* for you is whether to jeopardize a number of your present policies (arms transfers, nuclear proliferation, and arms control) and make a comprehensive long-term response to check Soviet power, *or* to treat the Afghanistan affair as a minor episode in the competitive-cooperative mix of US-Soviet relations. . . . I strongly urge you to make this a turning point."[134] After several hotly contested debates with Vance and others, Carter took Brzezinski's advice. That this was the backdrop to Brzezinski's early-February trip to Pakistan.

Brzezinski's public relations stunt in the Khyber Pass on the Pakistan-Afghanistan border earned him further notoriety with his detractors at State. He was photographed pointing a Chinese-made Kalashnikov in the direction of Afghanistan. To Mondale's and Vance's anguish, the *Washington Post* and *New York Times* carried the picture on their front pages. Brzezinski's excursion to Pakistan also acquired retrospective notoriety after the 9/11 attacks on New York's World Trade Center in 2001, when conservative and liberal groups dubbed him "the godfather of Al Qaeda." Brzezinski's goal in Pakistan was to persuade a doubtful Zia that Carter would supply arms to the mujahideen and shore up Pakistan's defenses against a possible Soviet attack.

Zia had made his task much harder by having already dismissed the $400 million in proposed US aid as "peanuts"—an unhelpful swipe at Carter's family business.[135] Brzezinski and the CIA's solution to congressional restrictions was to buy Soviet-made weapons in the arms bazaars of Cairo, Tunis, Istanbul, and elsewhere. They would funnel them through Saudi Arabia to Afghan rebel groups in the refugee camps. There would be no direct US arms sales to Pakistan. Zia had been hoping for American F-16s, which Brzezinski made clear was not on the menu. Although he liked Zia, who was practical and carried a "strong British veneer," their bargaining was contentious.[136] Warren Christopher was Brzezinski's State counterpart on the trip.

After Islamabad, Brzezinski and Christopher were helicoptered from Peshawar to a large Afghan refugee camp close to the Afghan border. At the tented city in the hills of the North West Frontier Province, hundreds of refugees, mostly women and children, mobbed them. A large share of the men were away fighting the Soviets. Spokespersons for the refugees told them that they did not need any more American beds or blankets. They wanted weapons. Unbeknownst to the accompanying American press contingent, US-financed rockets and guns were already finding their way into Afghan hands. Brzezinski made his way to the top of a small hillock bedecked in Afghan carpets. There he delivered an address to the Afghan refugees. Pointing north, he said, "That land over there is yours and you will go back one day because your cause is right and God is on your side. You should know that the whole world is outraged. Not only the world of Islam but the world of Christianity is outraged."[137]

In his State of the Union address the previous week, Carter had said, "We respect the faith of Islam, and we are ready to cooperate with all Moslem countries." The goal was to bring down the Soviet Union. Brzezinski saw the USSR's enemies as America's friends. The United States sought, and secured, the Organisation of Islamic Cooperation's unanimous condemnation of the atheist Soviet Union's war on the Muslim faithful. Brzezinski was warming to that kind of appeal. On his way back to Washington, he stopped for two days in Riyadh for secret talks with King Fahd and Crown Prince Saud. The frictions of previous years, particularly over Riyadh's concern that Carter was backtracking on a Palestinian homeland, had evaporated. The Saudi leaders gave Brzezinski a royal welcome. The foreign minister, Saudi bin Faisal Al Saud, invited Brzezinski to use his pool at dawn each morning, which he gladly accepted.[138] The head of Saudi Arabia's intelligence agency, Saud's brother Prince Turki, participated closely in Brzezinski's meetings with the king and crown prince. Turki was the key conduit between the CIA and Pakistan's Inter-Services Intelligence (ISI). He thought Brzezinski's negotiating style was "laser focused." Amid Bedouin hospitality and lavish banquets, they nailed down the details of the American-Saudi part of the three-way secret pipeline to the mujahideen. "They told us exactly what they are prepared to do for the Pakistanis," wrote Brzezinski.[139]

He returned to a chorus of tut-tutting in Washington. An irritated Mondale told Brzezinski that his "Khyber Pass imagery" had been awful.[140] Vance could barely meet his gaze in a meeting. Carter seemed indulgently amused.

Whenever he sent Brzezinski overseas, controversy erupted. Personal frictions aside, Brzezinski had grounds to feel chipper, as did Carter, whose Gallup rating had hit a recent peak of 55 percent. Kennedy was on course to losing the primaries. Carter's gritty response to Afghanistan had reduced Republican scope to paint him as soft and dithering. Reagan was still seen by most of the media as a warmonger. Kissinger, meanwhile, had gone uncharacteristically silent. Carter's election prospects still looked fair. But he was increasingly haunted by the plight of the US hostages in Iran. Cronkite had recently clocked up day seventy-five of the hostages' captivity. But there, too, were grounds for optimism. Though Carter was not yet persuaded, Brown and Jones had been working on a hostage rescue plan. They told Brzezinski that the operation stood a good chance of success. The dress rehearsals at various mock urban warfare sites had gone well. As Carter contemplated the final months of his first term, Khomeini seemed to be the chief obstacle in the way of his second. As always, but especially now, Brzezinski's goal was to convince Carter that fortune favored the brave.

9

The Ayatollah and the Pope

At around 3:00 a.m. on June 3, 1980, Brzezinski was startled awake by his and Muska's bedside phone. "Sorry, sir, but we are under nuclear attack," reported Bill Odom, Brzezinski's senior military aide.[1] Thirty seconds earlier, the Soviets had fired 220 ICBMs and submarine-launched ballistic missiles at the United States, he said. Under America's nuclear engagement rules, Brzezinski had a heart-stoppingly small window in which to verify that America was indeed facing Armageddon. He had a maximum of seven minutes before he would need to awaken the president. A minute later, Odom called back. He told Brzezinski that there were in fact more than two thousand Soviet missiles heading for America. This second call was incomprehensibly worse: the human story was within thirty minutes of changing forever. Brzezinski still had another couple of minutes before he would have to wake Carter to engage the legendary nuclear football. In the meantime, he told Odom to instruct Strategic Air Command to scramble two hundred jets to prepare for US retaliation. "I was going to make sure we had lots of company," he later said.[2] He was about to pick up the phone to Carter when it rang a third time. It had been a false alert, said Odom. He could go back to sleep.

There are two arresting details in this incident. The first was the incompetence of the North American Aerospace Defense Command (NORAD). One of its staff had put a simulation training video into the computer system at its mountain silo in Cheyenne, Wyoming, that had somehow flashed up on

Strategic Air Command's live screens. That happened on at least three occasions. The first was during the day on November 9, 1979. "I think you will agree with me that there should be no errors in such matters," Brezhnev told Carter in a civic-minded Kremlin hotline communication after one near miss had surfaced in the US media.[3] The next, which occurred on the night Brzezinski was awakened, took place in the small hours of June 3, 1980. The third happened on June 6. In those eight months, the bureaucracy had been unable to fix a basic glitch in a 46-cent computer chip that could trigger a decision that would incinerate much of the human species. The other striking quality of the incident was Brzezinski's sangfroid. Since they would all soon be dead, he saw no need to awaken Muska and the kids. Why ruin their last half hour of life? "Fortunately, the military quickly identified the problem as a computer failure, but it could have been a close call," he wrote matter-of-factly the next day.[4]

The last year of Carter's term was fraught even by US postwar standards. The Cold War was back with a vengeance. Carter had located his inner zeal on the Soviet Union. At the top of Brzezinski's in tray were Afghanistan and Iran. The simultaneous upheavals in the two neighboring counties were interacting in subtle but dynamic ways. In spite of their new climate of mutual loathing, Iran and the US had similar reactions to the Soviet invasion of Afghanistan; each wanted the USSR to be defeated. Much as America was supplying the Sunni Afghan groups in Pakistan, the Iranians were funneling small arms to Afghan Shia rebel forces.

Satellite reports of Soviet military exercises in the USSR's Transcaucasus region bordering Iran were also surfacing.[5] The Soviets had a record in the region; Stalin's forces occupied northern Iran during the Second World War. Brzezinski thus took the risk of Soviet intervention in Iran very seriously. That specter complicated the White House debate over how to respond to the hostage situation. Any US military action in Iran would undermine Carter's efforts to unite Muslim countries against the Soviets. A US economic blockade of Iran would be tantamount to an act of war since ships or planes in breach of the quarantine would have to be sunk or shot down. Mining Iran's harbors or striking its oil refineries would not be much better. There had to be some way of extracting the hostages without bloodshed.

That left two options. The ideal one would be their release by negotiation. The first hundred days of their captivity had made clear that Ayatollah Khomeini, now the supreme leader of Iran's theocratic Council of Guardians, had no interest in parlaying with the American devil. One small ray of light was that Iran had just elected a civilian president, Abolhassan Bani-Sadr. He represented the nonfanatic wing of the Iranian revolution. Bani-Sadr and his foreign minister, Sadegh Ghotbzadeh, wanted to end the hostage crisis since it was blocking Iran's ability to reengage with the world. Brzezinski doubted that Iran's secular front had the authority to secure the hostages' release. But he was briefed on Hamilton Jordan's secret negotiations with the two French lawyers Bani-Sadr had authorized to act as his intermediaries.

The sequence of steps the French lawyers laid out that would result in the hostages' release was improbable. Jordan compared it to a billiard shot in which the ball had to bounce off five sides before it went into the pocket.[6] A key part of Jordan's plan was that a UN commission would travel to Iran to hear its complaints about the shah's crimes and America's responsibility for them. The notables would also visit the hostages to check that they were alive and safe. The US government would also account for Iran's assets in America and prepare to unfreeze them. At some point, the student radicals, who had renamed themselves "The Muslim Student Followers of the Imam's Line in the Den of Espionage," would transfer the hostages to government custody. Following a statement of contrition by Carter, they would be sent home.

But Jordan's intermediaries kept switching the billiard balls. A new condition was that the hostage transfer and release would have to be approved by the Majlis, Iran's legislative assembly, which would be elected only in late March. Even then, the legislature's composition might not be settled. Runoff elections in seats without a majority were scheduled for April. Nor was it clear that the Majlis would approve of such a move. Though Jordan was indefatigable in his quest for a deal, Brzezinski and others doubted his French interlocutors had any sway with the revolutionaries. Brzezinski thought that the talks would end in a "fiasco."[7] The electoral clock was ticking. There were two further complications. The shah, who was close to dying, urgently required an operation on his spleen. Panama would not allow the procedure to take place in the US-controlled Panama Canal Zone, since that would be a slight on the isthmus state's medical competence. The shah wanted to return to Egypt and be treated there. That would provoke the ayatollahs, given Egypt's proximity to Iran.

· America's European allies were also resisting Carter's package of sanctions. Even Britain was slow-walking Carter's entreaties. Margaret Thatcher, whom both Carter and Brzezinski had come to admire, was not delivering. Influential banks in London, Frankfurt, and Geneva were too exposed to

Iran to agree to arbitrary write-offs. Even were the US to cobble together a united front to isolate Iran's economy, Brzezinski thought, imposing sanctions would be clutching at straws. The tightening screw would take time to work and could even be counterproductive. "Graduated escalation" simply inoculated the other side, he argued.[8] The media were getting impatient. One reporter sarcastically told Gary Sick, Brzezinski's Iran aide, that everyone was waiting for the White House to unsheathe its next noodle. The US public viewed Carter's Iran policy as a flop, Brzezinski told him in mid-March. "The polls are accurate," Carter wrote in the margin.[9]

By late March, a reluctant Carter was ready for a full briefing on the rescue plan. It was a weekend. The air turbulence on the way to Camp David was so severe that David Aaron, Brzezinski's deputy, vomited. Brzezinski was too absorbed in conversation with Harold Brown to notice.[10] General Jones briefed the group on the multiple-stage Operation Eagle Claw on which the Pentagon had been working. Though it was a logistical headache, Jones told the group that the rescue plan stood a high chance of succeeding. This was the unanimous view of the other chiefs as well, he said.

The operation would involve sixteen US aerial vessels operating over two days at four sites.[11] In the first stage at Desert One, eight helicopters would rendezvous at night in the Iranian desert. They would then be refueled by eight C-130 transport planes before heading to a spot in the mountains above Tehran, where they would spend the rest of the night and the following day under camouflage. The next night, the Delta Force that had been brought in on the choppers would storm the embassy and take the hostages to an abandoned sports stadium nearby, from where the waiting choppers would whisk them to Desert Two for the final leg. From there they would be flown out of Iran on C-130s. It was a forty-eight-hour operation across several theaters, including a highly risky extraction from the heart of a teeming metropolis. It was the opposite of the Israeli Entebbe raid a few years earlier, which had only one leg spanning a couple of hours.

Brzezinski acknowledged the risk of a "messy and bloody" outcome but felt Carter had no choice.[12] Vance's preference was to wait for Iran's theological fever to break. Eventually the hostages would be released, he argued. Carter was still not ready to commit. After several tantalizing false dawns with Jordan's back-channel negotiations, he finally came around to the plan on April 11. Earlier that day, Sadat, who was again playing host to the shah, visited the White House. He wanted to know what was taking Carter so long. He told Carter that his delay in acting was harming America's reputation. Carter, who, Brzezinski noticed, always glowed when Sadat was around, finally tipped. "Our national honor is at stake," he told Brzezinski, Jordan, Powell, and Rosalynn in the Oval Office after Sadat left. "We will go with the rescue. We have to mislead everyone, including people in the White House if necessary."[13] The earliest possible date for the rescue was April 24, the Pentagon said. In the meantime, the circle of those in the know should be highly restricted. The plan was to fool the Iranians by persisting with back-channel negotiations and deceive America's allies by continuing to press for collective sanctions.

Brzezinski pressed hard for accompanying military strikes on Iran in the event that the rescue either failed or involved heavy loss of life. He wanted punitive action even if the rescue went seamlessly. Carter rejected that option; he could not countenance a single casualty. He also had to remonstrate with the near-despairing Vance, who requested several one-on-one Oval Office meetings. Vance could not be won around to the gamble. As the only Carter principal with any combat experience—Vance had served in uniform in World War II—his voice should have carried greater weight. But his doubts were trumped by the Pentagon's confidence and everyone else's impatience. Brzezinski knew that if the operation worked, many people would get credit, including Carter, Brown, Jones, and Turner. "If it fails," he wrote, "I have not the slightest doubt that the press will finger me as the architect of the operation and as the person responsible for getting the president to adopt it."[14]

A few days before the rescue mission, Carter gave his sign-off. Vance, who was on vacation in Florida, was not consulted. On his return, he insisted on having another private session with Carter. Once again, Vance pressed the president to reconsider. At least a third of the hostages could die, he warned. Carter told Brzezinski that he thought that Vance had been "burned out by the Vietnam war."[15] Brzezinski agreed. In confidence, Carter added that Vance had told him he would be resigning. Even then, Carter tried to give Vance a way to stay in his job: he could honorably keep his position even while publicly declaring that he did not support the rescue mission. Vance was not interested. He was now losing almost all foreign policy battles with Brzezinski and saw no upside to staying on. Marshall Shulman, Vance's closest advisor, summarized his tenure as having achieved "success in modest ways but failure in the great sweep of things."[16] Vance agreed to withhold his announcement until after the operation.

A few days before the scheduled rescue date, the British, whose suspicions had been aroused, began to make inquiries. US forces were using Oman, where the British had a large military presence, as one of their assembly points. Any leak would kill the operation. Brzezinski nevertheless "strongly objected" to bringing Thatcher into the loop.[17] Carter overruled him. He dispatched Warren Christopher to brief Thatcher and her foreign secretary, Lord Carrington, about the mission. Christopher met them secretly at Chequers, the British prime minister's countryside retreat.[18] He was carrying a handwritten note from Carter to Thatcher that laid out the basics of Operation Eagle Claw. Thatcher read the note, then threw it into the fire. To Christopher's relief, she pledged Carter her enthusiastic backing. She did not permit Christopher to go home until he had sampled her rhubarb crumble.

Thursday, April 24, was the longest day of Brzezinski's life. The military had reported fair weather conditions, so the operation could go ahead. The day began with Carter's usual morning briefing. He had decided to carry on the routine White House schedule to avoid raising suspicion. At 10:35 a.m. Eastern Time (6:35 p.m. in the Persian Gulf), Brzezinski briefed Carter that eight RH-53D helicopters had left USS *Nimitz* in the Gulf on their five-hundred-mile journey across the Iranian desert to the isolated landing strip. They would fly at high speed beneath the radar through the night. Carter and Brzezinski had to sustain their poker faces over a long lunch with Senator Robert Byrd, the Democratic majority leader, who talked nonstop for more than half an hour. Congress had not been briefed on the covert mission. Carter had been tiring of Byrd's eccentric habits, which included playing his fiddle for excruciating lengths of time to captive audiences, including White House staff. Aides pulled Brzezinski out of the lunch to take a call from Brown.[19] Two of the eight choppers had been forced to turn back. Since the operation needed a minimum capacity of six helicopters to carry all the hostages, it could afford to lose two. One had suffered a rotor blade problem; the other had turned back in the midst of a heavy sandstorm.

Desert One was now more than two hours behind schedule. This was potentially troubling, since the helicopters could not fly to the next site in daylight. Everything else was still going roughly to plan, however, when Brzezinski next checked in with Brown at 3:30 p.m. Four choppers were now at the first site and being refueled. The other two were on the way. At 4:45 p.m., Brown called again. "I think we have an abort situation," he said.[20] A third helicopter had suffered hydraulic problems. There were now three "sick birds," which meant that the operation had fallen below its threshold. Brzezinski asked Brown to double-check with the ground commander, Colonel Charles Beckwith, whether they could press on with five choppers. The answer was no. Carter was talking to Christopher and Lloyd Cutler in the Oval Office. When he saw Brzezinski's expression, he asked them to clear the room. "Damn, damn," said the president after Brzezinski relayed the news.[21] Carter picked up the phone to Brown. After listening to the same account, he said, "Let's go with his recommendation," and hung up. For a few moments he cradled his head in his hands over the Oval Office desk. Then he asked Brzezinski to summon the rest of the team. "I felt extraordinarily sad for the country, for him, and for the people involved," Brzezinski wrote.

There was more bad news to come. Over the next hour, Carter, Brzezinski, Brown, Vance, Mondale, Powell, and Jordan discussed damage-limitation measures. Carter's idea was to issue a statement saying he had ordered a training exercise for a rescue mission that had been called off because of technical difficulties. He was also insistent on a news blackout until the entire team had been extricated. Turner's CIA ground staff in Tehran also needed time to make themselves scarce. Both of Carter's improvised suggestions made sense. Every effort should be made to avoid engaging with Iranian planes, he said. He was desperate to avoid loss of life.

Fate had other ideas. At 5:58 p.m., Jones called the Oval Office with worse news: a helicopter had collided with a C-130 at Desert One, and the resulting conflagration had killed eight Americans. There was no means of cleaning up the site. The corpses and wrecked choppers would have to be left there for the Iranians to pore over. The mood in the room abruptly changed. The enormity of the failure was sinking in. People seemed to be avoiding one another's eyes. "Perhaps I was being too sensitive, but I had the feeling at that stage that I was very much alone," Brzezinski wrote.[22] The news was not made public until one in the morning. At 7:00 a.m., Carter gave a brief and sober address to the nation taking full personal responsibility for the disaster.

It was also the worst day of Brzezinski's career. When he went home to snatch a couple of hours' sleep, his family noticed that his face had turned gray. "That was the only time I ever saw him like that," said his oldest child, Ian.[23] Back in the White House two hours later, a suddenly reenergized Brzezinski called Odom and Sick into his office. "We must go back in," he declared. His nearly instant rebound did not surprise either of his aides. After a brief pause, Brzezinski's adrenaline had redoubled. The next day, a Saturday, he told Carter that he had set up a meeting on Monday with Turner and Jones to thrash out a possible second rescue attempt. He expected Carter to fall off his chair or kick him out of the room. Carter replied, "Before this meeting I called Brown and Jones and told them to be in my office at 10:30 a.m. to plan another operation." Brzezinski beamed in relief. "That is exactly the right kind of spirit," he told the president.[24]

The aftermath of the failed attempt was bleak on many levels. Planning for a second mission ran aground. The logistics were just too complicated and the risk of another failure too great. The charred corpses of the Americans who had died in the failed first attempt were put on macabre display in Tehran. The Stars and Stripes was again being burned on the streets of Iran. The ayatollah's ubiquitous visage seemed to mock American impotence. Vance's resignation only fueled chatter about Carter's haplessness.

In Carter's defense, Operation Eagle Claw was his only chance of freeing the hostages in the foreseeable future. Such a mission has only two possible outcomes: failure, which makes its authors look like idiots; or success, which turns them into geniuses. Whenever he was asked if he had any regrets about his presidency, Carter would joke that he wished he had added two more helicopters to Operation Eagle Claw. Perhaps he should have been thankful for their absence. Inquiries into the debacle were scathing about the military's planning. To maintain the strictest secrecy, the team never conducted a full dress rehearsal. Each leg was practiced in isolation, which meant that many of the operation's members would be meeting one another for the first time at Desert One. Few military plans withstand first contact with reality. If one element fails, the whole thing falls apart. It is remarkable that it was ever attempted.

Much of the blame, however, lay with the Joint Chiefs of Staff. Lacking in any feasible diplomatic option, Carter made a political choice to rescue the hostages. His decision was based on the military's operational confidence. Had Jones and his team expressed doubts about whether it would work, Carter would almost certainly not have gone ahead. Yet he and Brzezinski desperately wanted to believe in the plan's viability. They deserved much of the opprobrium that came their way. The episode prejudiced Brzezinski's attitude to the armed services for many years. Later he would routinely screen out military applicants to his graduate classes.

A few weeks after quitting, Vance delivered the commencement address at Harvard's graduation ceremony. He spoke more in sorrow than in anger. In keeping with his deep sense of honor, he singled out no one by name, though he deplored the "dangerous fallacy" of believing that force could substitute for diplomacy. The meat of his speech was a quixotic appeal for Carter to ratify SALT II. The Soviet invasion of Afghanistan should not prevent the United States and the USSR from working together for long-term peace. "When the historian of 1990 looks back upon the year 1980, I believe a profound mistake may well be identified: a failure to ratify the SALT II treaty," he said.[25]

Carter took Vance's resignation personally. He felt he was being kicked when he was down. Rosalynn, who was more instinctively hawkish than her husband and had always had a soft spot for Brzezinski, was particularly stung by Vance's timing. Though Cy and Gay Vance were closer to the Carters than anyone else in Washington—spending many more weekends at Camp David than the Brzezinskis—a part of Carter was also relieved. "Among all my cabinet officers, Cy Vance was philosophically closest to me, but his first loyalty was to the State Department bureaucracy," he wrote in his diary. "Its primary role seemed to be to put brakes on any proposal that originated elsewhere."[26]

State's habits did not alter under Ed Muskie, whom Carter picked as the new secretary of state over Warren Christopher, the first choice of both Vance and Brzezinski. In 1976, Carter had only narrowly opted for Mondale over Muskie to be his running mate. Following the Desert One disaster and with an election looming, he thought the senator from Maine would lend his administration much needed star power. Muskie would also give him the heft on Capitol Hill that he had been lacking. Madeleine Albright, who had worked in Muskie's Senate office, reassured Brzezinski that he and Muskie would get along. Muskie was in his midsixties and would be no match for Brzezinski's energy, she said. He was also quaintly old-fashioned. At Albright's Senate goodbye party, he thanked her for "bringing sex into the office." Albright responded, "I think you mean gender, Senator."[27] Muskie had also half-jokingly warned Albright that with Brzezinski she should not forget that "he is Zbig and you are Zmall."[28]

The senator from Maine was a New England Yankee who happened to be a Polish American Catholic, Albright thought; Brzezinski, on the other hand, was a Pole who happened to be an American. Carter almost immediately regretted his choice. The first signs that Muskie could be a problem were apparent at his swearing-in at the State Department. His speech went on for much longer than Carter's and was unsubtly political. "Is he running for president?" Vance whispered to Brzezinski.[29] Until the eve of Carter's presidential convention in August, there was speculation over whether Muskie would jump into the race.

Brzezinski's chief worry was that Muskie was an even softer touch than Vance. In his *New York Times* column shortly after Muskie took over, James Reston warned that the new Polish American secretary of state would be "Poles apart" from Carter's national security advisor. The freewheeling senator could easily be captured by the Foggy Bottom bureaucracy. "Finding your way through the maze that is called the State Department takes even longer than learning to spell Zbigniew Brzezinski," he wrote. A few days after he took the job, Muskie sent his draft recommendation for a speech Carter was about to give. Brzezinski thought it was "mushy." Al McDonald, a senior Carter military aide, said it "made the Quakers sound war-like."[30]

Carter went with Brzezinski's version. A few days after that, Muskie had his first meeting with Gromyko. He excluded Brzezinski's two aides, David Aaron and Marshall Brement, from their meeting in Vienna. Muskie's instructions were to hit Gromyko hard on Afghanistan. Instead, he seemed to apologize for America's resolve. Carter was facing reelection, so he had to sound tough for domestic reasons, Muskie told Gromyko. After reading the Muskie-Gromyko memo, Carter agreed with Brzezinski's view that it "made Vance look like a cold warrior." He added, "They [Muskie's words] are horrible. They are just horrible. . . . I will have to speak to him." As Brzezinski was leaving, Carter added, "Zbig, we can't let State push us around."[31]

The previous evening, Carter and Muskie had spoken to a congressional delegation at the White House. Muskie was supposed to follow Carter with a five-minute pep talk. Twenty minutes into Muskie's oration, Carter conspicuously walked out of the room. A *New York Times* piece that week quoted people close to Muskie as saying that he had a political base of his own. If Carter tried to impose his will, Muskie would resign and bring about his defeat in the general election. "I have the feeling the president did not appreciate that," Brzezinski wrote.[32] As a condition of accepting the job, Carter had agreed to Muskie's demand that State officials would write up the minutes of NSC meetings that he had chaired. Brzezinski slapped his own covering note on top. In a later interview, he said, "[Muskie] gained nothing from it."[33]

With Vance gone and Muskie already sidelined, Brzezinski ought to have been in a strong position. If anything, however, the media's disenchantment with him was deepening. Its negativity echoed the Brzezinski verdict of the Democratic Party's Kennedy wing and Vance's loyalists. The two groups overlapped. "While Mr. Vance played by Marquis of Queensberry rules, it might be said that Mr. Brzezinski was more of a street fighter," wrote Les Gelb, Vance's former aide. "The battle was never over, Mr. Brzezinski would never stop."[34] In a cover story headlined "Almost Everyone vs. Zbig," *Time* held nothing back. "Brzezinski was more mistrusted and even despised than ever at the State Department and among career diplomats," said the piece, written by Strobe Talbott. Brzezinski's foreign policy philosophy was "geostrategic gobbledygook"; his labels "too often seem facile, even interchangeable, and his theories too flexible, too clever by half"; most of all, however, he had "shown poor judgment in indulging his visceral anti-Russian sentiments and his combative, provocative personality." Because of those character flaws, Brzezinski had exacerbated "the impression so widespread at home and abroad of an Administration that is impetuous and in disarray. In that sense, Brzezinski is unquestionably part of Carter's overall political problem."[35]

The *New York Times*' Anthony Lewis, meanwhile, concluded that Brzezinski was "not a hawk, or a dove, but a jay: vain, noisy, and interfering." His column ended with the unforgivable insult that Brzezinski was "nothing but a tinpot Kissinger."[36] Brzezinski put Lewis down as one of the "ZB haters." By mid-1980, that club was quite large. "One has to develop a thick skin and simply ride this out," he told himself.[37]

Carter's immediate headache was his enduring split with the Kennedy wing of the party. Because of his hawkish reputation, Brzezinski was Carter's foreign policy lightning rod to the disenchanted Left. Over lunch a few weeks before the Democratic National Convention in New York, Pat Caddell, one of Carter's political advisors, told Brzezinski that Carter should be more liberal on domestic policy and more conservative on world affairs; that would better fit with the mood of the nation. Caddell was also summarizing Brzezinski's views. The president's economic philosophy could not easily be described. He detested budget deficits, always sought to purge wasteful spending, and was an anti-inflation hawk. He had little affection for unions and was an enthusiast for deregulation.

His small-c conservatism alienated the Left and many blue-collar voters. His investments in clean energy were far ahead of their time. Following the Three Mile Island nuclear accident in late 1979, in which one of the reactors melted down in America's largest commercial nuclear leak, Ted Kennedy had promised to convert all US nuclear plants to coal. Carter, by contrast, was on a mission to wean the US off fossil fuels. He provided public seed money for alternative fuels that would reach commercial scale only years later. Yet he could not resist being preachy about it. He wore cardigans in lieu of turning up the White House heating and lectured anyone within earshot about energy conservation. In addition to a low temperature in the winter, he ordered the White House thermostat to be set high during the summer months. Brzezinski would defeat Carter's parsimony by placing his space heater under the thermostat to trigger the air-conditioning.[38]

Carter's background of naval engineer and Sunday school preacher made for a spasmodic case-by-case approach to policy. Regardless of its merits, Brzezinski's systematic bent of mind filled a yawning gap in his president's worldview. Carter worried over parts; Brzezinski lobbied for the whole. Moscow's adventurism and the direction of world events helped make much of Brzezinski's case for him. After an evenhanded first eighteen months, the pendulum swung to Brzezinski during the second half of Carter's term. That was the ultimate cause of Vance's resignation, though Brzezinski's take-no-prisoners approach to policy disputes and Washington's in-built institutional tensions also played a big role.

On the economic side, Carter lacked both a Brzezinski and a Vance. Nobody coined the phrase "Carternomics," since it would have been so hard to define what it meant. Carter's tension with Ted Kennedy drew partly on the Democratic Left's fear that the age of the New Deal and the Great Society was fading—worse, that a Democratic president was performing the funeral rites. The two candidates' tension was also personal. On June 4, Carter's victory over Kennedy in the Ohio primary tipped him over the threshold. When Brzezinski walked into the Oval Office the next morning, Carter was grinning broadly. "Congratulations: You really whipped his ass," Brzezinski said. "And it's been a pleasure," Carter replied. He had telephoned Kennedy twice the previous evening—once at 6:30 p.m. and again at 10:00 p.m.—to congratulate his opponent on the fight. On both occasions, Kennedy's aides told Carter that the senator was resting. No conversation occurred: Kennedy did not concede to Carter.[39]

As the convention approached, the Kennedy-Carter war shifted to a battle over delegates. Kennedy wanted an open process, meaning that pledged delegates could switch their loyalty regardless of whether their state's residents had voted for the other candidate. Kennedy hoped this rule change would conjure victory out of defeat. Carter's delegate operation, led by Tom Donilon, a twenty-five-year-old White House aide who would go on to become

Barack Obama's national security advisor, insisted that the delegates were bound. After a feverish buildup, Carter narrowly won the vote to uphold the "faithful delegate."

In his lyrically grudging concession speech, Kennedy mentioned Carter just once. Judged by his body language and the content of his address, it was clear that he had not accepted his defeat. New York 1980 was no Chicago 1968. But the party was still disunited. Kennedy had apparently been planning to make a more rousing endorsement. Then he had seen a statement by Hamilton Jordan that Carter could defeat Reagan without Kennedy's help. "He doesn't matter so much himself, but his people do," said Jordan.[40] To shouts of "We want Teddy!" Kennedy delivered an implicit rebuke of the president. "For me, a few hours ago, this campaign came to an end," he said. "For all those whose cares have been our concern, the work goes on, the cause endures, the hope still lives, and the dream shall never die." For Carter, Kennedy's passive-aggressive endorsement meant that the nightmare would never die. It was the speech of Kennedy's life.

In 1980, Brzezinski made an exception to his habit of avoiding conventions. He should have stuck to his resolution. To his surprise, Jody Powell steered him clear of both the media and the podium. Brzezinski's brand was too aggressive for the moment and outright toxic to the Kennedy wing of the party. On the final evening, Robert Strauss, who was running the convention, called the members of Carter's cabinet to the stage one by one. When Brzezinski's name was announced, it elicited loud boos. Brzezinski thought that the noise came chiefly from the Massachusetts and Pennsylvania delegations. He was nevertheless shaken. "I had not expected this, but I kept smiling and waved to the crowd," he wrote.[41] Watching it on TV, his oldest son, Ian, who was approaching seventeen, was marked by that moment. He resented the mob that was booing his father.[42] Ian was the only Brzezinski child who would go on to become a Republican.

Carter then gave a mediocre address in which he pleaded a little too cravenly for Kennedy's support. "Ted," he said, "your party needs you—and I need you. . . . We'll make great partners this fall in whipping the Republicans." Kennedy seemed to be in a very different frame of mind. In the closing peak viewership moments, he unsmilingly entered the stage and gave Carter and Rosalynn perfunctory handshakes. The former rivals were expected to embrace and hold each other's arm aloft in a symbol of unity. Carter's team tried to attribute Kennedy's disdainful body language to confusion over the timing of his entrance. But the awful visual could not be unseen. Brzezinski thought it was "graceless and petulant."[43]

Brzezinski's poor image was further harmed by his dealings with Billy Carter, the president's bucktoothed, wayward younger brother. Twelve years Jimmy's junior, Billy had been declared an accident by their mother. At various points in his presidency, it seemed as though Carter's youngest sibling had been brought into the world solely to embarrass him. As the brand ambassador of Peanut Lolita, a short-lived 53 proof whiskey-and-peanut-based liqueur that played on the Carter farm business, Billy was not shy about monetizing his brother's name. After Peanut Lolita, he endorsed Billy Beer, a midwestern brewery that played up his image as a southern good ol' boy. Among his antics was urinating on an airport runway in full view of the media.

By 1979, Billy was trying to do business in Libya. Three weeks after the hostages were seized, Brzezinski asked him to set up a meeting with Libya's ambassador. The idea originated with the first lady. Billy sat in on the meeting.[44] Brzezinski asked the ambassador to pass on a request to Libya's strongman, Muammar Gaddafi, who had ties to Ayatollah Khomeini: Would Gaddafi press Iran's leader to release the hostages? Gaddafi received Brzezinski's message and relayed it to Khomeini. It had no discernible effect.

A few months later, an intelligence report came across Brzezinski's desk stating that Billy was acting as a paid advocate of a US energy company that wanted to enlarge its oil quota in Libya. That could be damaging both to the US government and to Jimmy Carter's reputation. Brzezinski picked up the phone and warned Billy that his activities could cause acute embarrassment to his older brother. Billy reacted furiously, told Brzezinski to mind his own business, and made an anti-Semitic remark that Brzezinski did not specify ("some comments about American Jews").[45] That was their last interaction.

Unbeknownst to Brzezinski, however, the Department of Justice was investigating Billy. Even more awkwardly, Billy had taken a $220,000 loan from the Libyan government and had recently, on the rushed advice of his lawyers, registered as a foreign agent for Libya. Thus, in mid-July 1980, a few weeks before the Democratic convention, "Billygate" was born. An investigative Senate panel was set up. Brzezinski was its main witness; Stansfield Turner also testified. Preparation for his Capitol Hill grilling swallowed vast chunks of Brzezinski's time. Carter, who was fuming over Billy's follies, had to spend hours with White House lawyers going over every contact with his younger brother, what he had known and when. But Brzezinski was the chief target.

On Kissinger's advice, Brzezinski hired one of Washington's top lawyers, William Rogers from the Arnold, Fortas & Porter law firm as his personal counsel at considerable expense.[46] White House counsel Lloyd Cutler's team advised Brzezinski on his public response.

The Senate panel failed to turn up evidence of criminal wrongdoing on Brzezinski's part, though it explored several avenues. The most dangerous one was Brzezinski's alleged criminal misuse of classified intelligence to warn Billy Carter off his Libyan pursuits, in effect misusing intelligence for Carter's domestic benefit. The committee also accused him of freelancing as Carter's political troubleshooter and usurping the State Department's role of dealing with foreign ambassadors. Each inquiry ran into a dead end. Vance helped Brzezinski by confirming that he had approved Rosalynn's idea for Brzezinski to contact Gaddafi. In a statement, Carter said, "I am deeply concerned that Billy has received funds from Libya and that he may be under obligation to Libya. These facts will govern my relationship with Billy as long as I am president. Billy has had no influence on U.S. policy or actions concerning Libya in the past, and he will have no influence in the future."[47]

But Brzezinski took the main hit. He won the questionable distinction of becoming the first national security advisor to testify under oath before Congress. Carter waived his executive privilege. The toll on Brzezinski's time, reputation, and bank account was steep. It further soured his view of the White House press corps, which was considerably more excited about Billygate than the war in Afghanistan, US nuclear modernization, and even the briefly quiescent Iran hostage crisis. "I wish I was negotiating with Brezhnev on serious matters and not being dragged in the mud with this buffoon from Georgia," he wrote.[48] Billygate was one of those periodic squalls that convulses Washington, then vanishes without trace.

By contrast, Carter's across-the-board modernization of the US nuclear arsenal and war-fighting doctrine gathered pace slowly and only rarely sparked controversy. The policy reached a peak in 1980 with a flurry of momentous decisions. Carter began his presidency with the dream of a nuclear-free world; he ended it having laid the basis for Reaganism. His evolution was a tale of sudden changes of mind, contradictory impulses, and a running inner dialogue between his New Testament idealism and his practical mindset. Shock over the USSR's blunders, particularly its invasion of Afghanistan, and the pincerlike lobbying impact of Brzezinski and Harold Brown, over time converted him to the merits of nuclear modernization. State was almost completely shut out.

Brzezinski's first move was to instruct Sam Huntington—"Zbig's Zbig"—to conduct a net assessment of US and Soviet power. Huntington's paper, Presidential Review Memorandum 10, or PRM 10, established a template for almost every strategic investment in the rest of the Carter years.[49] Huntington divided the Cold War into "Era One" and "Era Two." In Era One, which had lasted until the mid-1960s, the US had dominated the USSR with its nuclear superiority. America's nuclear doctrine of massive retaliation had fit that reality. In Era Two, which had reached its apogee in the mid-1970s, the USSR had achieved parity and would soon be in a position to launch a devastating first strike on the United States: a winnable nuclear war.

Huntington's 360-degree evaluation of the two superpowers' relative strengths concluded that the US had the decisive advantage over the Soviets by every other yardstick, notably in the strength of its economy, the quality of its technology, America's world-class higher education, and its widely emulated culture. Moscow would thus be tempted to lean on its military prowess to compensate for its growing deficiencies in the nonmilitary spheres. In popular American imagery, the USSR was already something of a punch line. Long gone were the days of *Sputnik* and fears of Soviet economic convergence. The tedium of Soviet life was now familiar to Western television audiences. The Soviets, for their part, saw US society as decadent and its people as ignorant. In Brezhnev's view, Americans were addicted to a shallow entertainment culture. They did not even read. "They only watch TV, and that only if the programs are interesting," Brezhnev remarked to a colleague.[50]

Paranoia about Soviet nuclear intentions was nevertheless acute in the Pentagon and the US intelligence agencies, especially among the Committee on the Present Danger's hawks. Later research into the Soviet Union's murky nuclear doctrine showed that the Politburo did not think the country could win a nuclear war. Brezhnev, in particular, was mortified by the idea of nuclear exchange. At the time, that was not obvious to Washington. Moscow's plans to help its civilians survive a nuclear exchange were far more advanced than America's.

To his horror, Brzezinski discovered that the USSR had the ability to protect as much as 10 to 20 per cent of its population in nuclear shelters. Moscow's postholocaust survival plan mirrored the almost total lack of US civil defense planning. Even Washington's continuity-of-government plan was substandard. Brzezinski instructed the military to conduct several drills and was disturbed to find out that the rehearsals took way longer to complete than the missile warning time. The president and the rest of his team would be dead before they could regroup.[51] The Soviets, meanwhile, would be secure in a vast complex of well-stocked bunkers. The shock of discovering that asymmetry of post–first strike planning led Brzezinski to overhaul the emergency procedures. On the civil side, Carter agreed to the creation of the Federal Emergency Management Agency (FEMA). The newly created Department of Energy would take responsibility for nuclear weapons. CENTCOM would extend US Cold War doctrine to the Middle East.

Carter's most important nuclear directive was PD-59, which finally retired what Huntington had dubbed America's Era One doctrine of massive nuclear retaliation. Under Carter, mutually assured destruction embraced and extended the flexible nuclear war–fighting plan that had been adopted in the 1960s. This permitted tactical strikes on moving Soviet military assets. US nuclear planners would no longer target Soviet cities and other population centers. Instead, Strategic Air Command would pinpoint shifting Soviet targets on the battlefield.[52] To PD-59's critics, including Muskie, the shift made nuclear war more likely. Carter was substituting the unthinkable scenario of Armageddon-plus with the much more versatile scenario of Armageddon-minus.

Brzezinski argued that PD-59 lessened the risk of nuclear war because it made US deterrence more credible. The "very likelihood of all out nuclear war is increased if all out spasm war is the only kind of nuclear war we can fight," he said.[53] In his mind, PD-59 was his era's NSC-68, the landmark Truman strategic framework for fighting the Cold War. NSC-68 operationalized George Kennan's doctrine of containment. That was now obsolete. PD-59 reflected Brzezinski and Brown's diagnosis of a declining Soviet Union that would be increasingly tempted to lash out. In reality, though, it was consummating a strategic shift that was years in the making.

Carter's decision was so classified that even Ed Muskie did not know about it. This revelation triggered a media storm and an internal inquiry by Lloyd Cutler to find out whether State had been excluded deliberately. Cutler's conclusions were ambivalent. He found that officials at State had been kept abreast of the new concept but had failed to brief Muskie about it in the confusion after Vance's departure. But they had known nothing about the shift in nuclear targeting. The operational side of PD-59 was jealously guarded by the Pentagon; only Carter and Brzezinski were fully briefed. Muskie was furious. State officials told the media that he had been deliberately cut out of a critically important process. "There was no particular reason to bring him on board," Brzezinski thought, but the White House had "no design to embarrass or undercut or bypass Muskie."[54] In the event, Cutler's investigation, which irritated Brzezinski, since it felt to him like a witch hunt into a process that he thought he had managed by the book, split the blame between Brown, who was supposed to keep Muskie briefed, and Muskie's staff, who knew more than he did. Brzezinski was implicitly absolved, though not in the eyes of the media.

At one of their weekly lunches, renamed MBB (Muskie, Brown, Brzezinski), in late August 1980, Muskie and Brown got into a shouting match over PD-59. "I was inclined to sit back and enjoy this but after a while I couldn't resist and joined in," Brzezinski wrote that evening.[55] The meeting ended amicably. That became the pattern: showdown followed by relaxed banter. Brzezinski enjoyed Muskie's bluntness, in contrast to what he saw as Vance's strangulated angst. In reality, Muskie was no match for his weekly lunch partners. The new secretary of state took long vacations in Maine and did not like to be disturbed on weekends. At the end of that heated exchange, Muskie put his arm around Brzezinski, who punched him playfully in the stomach. In a meeting with Carter a few days later, Muskie agreed to go on a Sunday-morning show and say that Foggy Bottom officials had been aware of PD-59's foreign policy implications. He agreed not to specify that State would continue to remain in the dark about the Pentagon's nuclear targeting plans. Muskie seemed delighted by the compromise. To Brzezinski's relief, he was proving to be less of an obstacle than Vance.

Carter's other nuclear controversy was his long-simmering feud with West Germany's Helmut Schmidt. In 1980, their relationship degenerated into an open breach. Brzezinski pinpointed 1980 as the low point in postwar US–West German relations. Schmidt, like France's Giscard, believed that Carter was overreacting to the Soviet invasion of Afghanistan. Not only had Carter banned grain exports to the Soviet Union and boycotted the Moscow Summer Olympics, he was pressuring allies to match his actions with a sweeping embargo on technology sales. The French could get away with taking a softer approach to Moscow because that was the French way. Washington tolerated the unending Gallic quest for an America-free Europe as a permanent feature of the landscape. To Carter's irritation, however, Giscard pressed ahead with a Brezhnev summit in March 1980, less than three months after the Soviet invasion. France also refused to pull out of the Olympics. Britain did not join the boycott, either, although Thatcher had tried to persuade the British Olympic Association to match its American counterpart. In the event, only West Germany, Japan, and China heeded Carter's call. The boycott, which both Mondale and Jordan fought hard to prevent, made Carter so unpopular with US athletes that in 1996 he had to withdraw from his torch-carrying role in the Atlanta Olympics.

Alone among the European allies, West Germany complied with Carter's request. But Schmidt firmly resisted Carter's pressure to abandon or even slow down his country's multibillion-dollar Siberian pipeline project that would deliver Soviet gas to Western Europe. This was the crown jewel of *Ostpolitik*, which Schmidt was not ready to abandon. Schmidt treated the pipeline's collateral financial benefits to the Soviet defense budget as a manageable side effect. Western investment would moderate Moscow's behavior, he believed. To Brzezinski, this was worse than wishful thinking. The idea that the USSR's global stance could be tempered by German mercantilism was preposterous, in his view. He worried that Bonn was becoming more vulnerable to "Finlandization," or de facto neutrality.

At heart, every West German leader had German unification as his ultimate dream. Reuniting Germany's two halves could realistically take place only under highly evolved conditions of détente. It followed in Bonn that almost nothing should be allowed to disrupt good relations with Moscow. West Germany's east-facing emollience inevitably led to clashes with Washington, particularly with Brzezinski. Yet it was Bonn's enduring political reality. Trade statistics reveal the extent to which Schmidt did not bend to Carter's pressure. In 1980, West German–Soviet trade soared; US-Soviet trade plummeted.

Schmidt was also grappling with rising disaffection from the left of his Social Democratic Party, which was in open rebellion over the nuclear arms race. In December 1979, NATO approved the deployment of hundreds of US Pershing II and Tomahawk cruise missiles in Europe, the largest share of which would be stationed in West Germany (with the UK taking most of the rest). The deal ought to have been a triumphant moment for Schmidt, who had been arguing for years that America should stop treating Europe as an afterthought. Europe's anxieties about the buildup of Soviet medium-range missiles—notably its massive rollout of SS-20s, all targeted at Europe—were being ignored, he complained. SALT II had addressed only long-range missiles, which left a vast disparity in what Schmidt dubbed "eurostrategic" missiles. He hated the Pentagon's term "Theater Nuclear Forces" (TNF), which implied that Europe was the main stage of life-and-death superpower decisions. It also implied that the nonnuclear West Germany would never be consulted.

But the West German public's visceral reaction to the planned nuclear deployments wrong-footed Schmidt. In practice, he was deeply conflicted. At a small gathering in Guadeloupe in early 1979, Carter, Giscard, Callaghan, and Schmidt had taken the plunge on agreeing to deploy the euromissiles. Brzezinski, not Vance, accompanied Carter to that informal beachside summit. Nuclear weapons did not entirely dominate their agenda. Three of the leaders referred so often to the abundance of topless women on the beach in front of them that Callaghan complained that his chair was facing the wrong way.[56] The otherwise convivial gathering of the so-called Quad was marred by Schmidt's unquenchable anxiety about the nuclear question. As leader of the Quad's only nonnuclear power, perhaps it could not have been otherwise. "Throughout, [Schmidt] was the one who was most concerned about the Soviet nuclear threat in Europe and the least inclined to agree to any further response," Brzezinski concluded.[57]

By mid-1980, Schmidt was casting around for a solution to a problem that was almost insoluble. There was no coherent way he could continue to combine his deep fear of the USSR's missile stranglehold over Europe with strong distrust of America's planned matching deployments. At his party conference in Essen, Schmidt hinted thickly that he would call for a three-year freeze or moratorium on both Soviet and US nuclear missile deployments in Europe. He asked Senator Joe Biden, a rising Democratic star who was close to Carter, to visit Bonn for a briefing. For two hours, Schmidt harangued the senator from Delaware about Carter's disrespect for West German sensitivities and Brzezinski's alleged anti-German bias. As he had done with others, Schmidt told Biden that Carter should fire Brzezinski. Biden, as intended, passed all of it on to the Carter administration.[58] It was a brazen interference by a foreign leader in a US president's staffing choices. Even the Soviets had not requested that Brzezinski be fired, though they would surely have been delighted if Schmidt had gotten what he wanted.

Of far greater concern to Carter and Brzezinski was Schmidt's gravitation towards a nuclear freeze. Not only would that unravel the delicately constructed NATO consensus, it would also guarantee Soviet nuclear dominance over Europe. The USSR had already deployed two hundred SS-20s, which was two hundred more missiles than the Americans had in place. The new US missiles would not be ready until 1983. An alarmed Carter wrote to Schmidt in early June, warning against any talk of a freeze on superpower deployments. The letter was leaked to the West German and US media. Carter's request that Schmidt postpone his planned summit with Brezhnev until after the Moscow Summer Olympics had already irritated Schmidt. He had reluctantly complied with Carter's wishes. The leaked Carter letter felt like one slight too many. In his memoirs, Schmidt wrote that it had to have come from "someone who was eager to vent his spleen—someone who had never been able to decide whether the Germans or the Russians were the arch enemy of the Polish people from whom he was descended."[59] In his diaries, Brzezinski denied having been its source.

Either way, Schmidt was facing a tight general election in October and in a state of rising panic. When Schmidt met Carter at the G7 summit in Venice in late June, he could no longer contain himself, launching into a litany of complaints about how badly Carter had treated him. He was the most loyal of America's allies, he said, and was being taken for granted. Unlike Thatcher, Britain's reputed Iron Lady, Schmidt had put sanctions on Iran and boycotted the Olympics, he said. Yet his loyalty to the US had been rewarded with contempt. After listening to about forty minutes of Schmidt's tirade, Brzezinski intervened to point out that Carter had not once summoned West German legislators to Washington to hear tirades against Schmidt. "In speaking to Senator Biden, you were critical of American policy in general and figures in the American government in particular," he said. Schmidt replied, "If necessary, I can fight with the best of them." Brzezinski responded, "And we know how to fight back."[60] Carter waved at Brzezinski to be quiet.[61] Somehow the contretemps had cleared the air. Carter and Schmidt agreed to appear before the media to say that they were of one mind on European nuclear deployments and against the Soviet invasion of Afghanistan. They took no questions.

About three weeks later, Schmidt invited Bob Strauss, Carter's campaign manager and maestro of the forthcoming Democratic convention, to Bonn. The chancellor reiterated his visceral hope that Brzezinski be fired. Brzezinski wanted to know every detail of what Strauss reported back to Carter. "Well he [Schmidt] just dumped all over you," said the smiling president. "Most of it was a denunciation of you, how incompetent you are, what a cold war warrior you are, and it went on and on for about two hours. What have you ever done to him?" Brzezinski replied that he had friendly relations with Schmidt for a long time. Their tone had changed for the worse about three years back, after he started working for his new boss. Carter laughed.[62] By now Carter and Brzezinski had a running banter about what they most disliked about Schmidt. The chancellor's most glaring trait was his habit of complaining about Carter and his national security advisor to anyone who would listen. This included invited Democratic figures, the West German and American media, visiting Republicans (among them Henry Kissinger), and even Brezhnev. Most of his complaints filtered back to the White House. Both Brzezinski and Carter detested him.

To their surprise, they agreed that Thatcher was the Western leader with whom Carter got along the best, despite her failure to deliver on Iran and the Summer Olympics.[63] Britain was nevertheless the only European ally that had agreed to send arms to the Afghan mujahideen. When they met in Venice, Thatcher told Carter that a large cache of British rifles would soon be on its way to Pakistan. Carter disclosed that several Soviet helicopters had been shot down by US-supplied SA-7s, the Soviet predecessor to the Lockheed Martin–made Stinger missile. The Stinger would become the mujahideen's most devastating tool in the jihad against the Soviets (they would first be fired by British forces in the 1982 Falklands War).

Partly because of Thatcher's help, Carter got the Venice G7 wording on Afghanistan that he wanted (in addition to a unified stance on OPEC and coordinated fiscal stabilization). By putting their Afghanistan differences to one side, the communiqué slowed the pace of parallel West German and French attempts to revive détente. "The summit has demonstrated firm unity, which is much more than we ever had the right to expect," Brzezinski thought. It turned the Venice meeting into an unexpected success. But the Washington-Bonn drama rarely flagged for long. In late September, about a week before the West German federal election and six weeks before the US presidential election, Schmidt told a local newspaper that he expected Carter would fire Brzezinski in his second term. At this point Carter was within striking distance of Reagan in the polls. The syndicated columnist Rowland Evans called Brzezinski for his reaction. On background, Brzezinski dismissed the German leader's prediction as "Horse-Schmidt."[64]

To Brzezinski, the summit in Venice was only the second most important leg of Carter's Italy trip. The most interesting bit had taken place in Rome the day before. Over the previous year, Brzezinski and Pope John Paul II had been conducting a regular handwritten correspondence in Polish. Brzezinski wanted the pope's help in releasing the US hostages from Iran.[65] John Paul II obligingly instructed Hilarion Capucci, a Syrian bishop and the papal nuncio in Tehran, to appeal to Ayatollah Khomeini. Capucci was highly popular with Iran's Revolutionary Council since he had been convicted by Israel of smuggling arms to the Palestinians. The pleas of a fellow prelate did not sway Khomeini.

The pope, in turn, wanted Brzezinski's help in persuading Beijing to allow the Catholic Church to resume its mission in China. "I will be very grateful if you could become concerned with this matter for which you seem to be particularly well placed," he wrote. Millions of Chinese Catholics had sustained their fidelity to the Church in the most difficult of circumstances, the pope wrote. "I feel I do not have to add how much it is on my heart."[66] Brzezinski brokered a correspondence between the pope and Hua Guofeng, China's premier. "My relations with [China's leaders] are very good, and I intend to take advantage of that," Brzezinski replied. Though China was obliging enough to receive a papal delegation to discuss the matter, the pope's hopes kept stumbling over the Holy See's relations with Taiwan. Brzezinski tried to persuade the pope to match Carter by normalizing relations with China. But the pope could not bring himself to abandon Taiwan.

Their dialogue was turning into a significant back channel—and a unique one in the annals of Washington's dealings with the Vatican. John Paul II upheld his American tour the previous year as definitive. "The entire stay in the US exceeded my expectations," he wrote. "I asked myself for the reasons regarding such a reaction on my part. The conversation that we had helped me to clarify that issue, at least partially."[67] In one letter, which Brzezinski wrote in black ink on White House letterhead, he apologized for the quality of his Polish. "Probably some of the expressions above are amusingly nongrammatical," he wrote. "But I lived in Poland for only three years, and I never attended Polish school. So please forgive me!"[68]

In his reply to the "Respected and Dear Doctor," the pope told Brzezinski not to worry about the written quality of his Polish, which, he said, was very good. He was more concerned about getting as much time as possible with Brzezinski during Carter's forthcoming trip to Rome. He wanted to talk about China, Iran, Central America and, of course, Poland. "We are trying to arrange the program in such a way as to make time for all of this," he wrote.[69] Carter was due for a papal audience at 11:00 a.m. on June 21. The night before, the pope invited Brzezinski to come several hours earlier for breakfast and Mass. Brzezinski arrived at 7:00 a.m., accompanied by his special military assistant, Les Denend, who had replaced Bob Gates. They had hoped to enter by stealth through a back entrance to keep the media from knowing. The Vatican had other ideas; the two Americans were met by a police escort who handed them over to a full complement of the Swiss Guard. Two priests, one Polish and one Irish, then whisked them to the pope's private chapel.[70]

There Brzezinski and Denend were given a Mass for the ages. There were four nuns with the pope. During their private service, the two priests acted as the servers while the nuns were the respondents to John Paul II's liturgy. Brzezinski and Denend were the sum total of his congregation. The pope then invited them to join him for breakfast in a private adjoining room. Denend, who had flown combat missions over Vietnam, was so nervous that he spilled his coffee over the table. When they were leaving, the pope grabbed Denend's arm and told Brzezinski, "I should have a colonel as my assistant, not you. I am keeping him."[71] Apart from a one-hour break for the papal audience with Carter and the first lady, Brzezinski and John Paul II spent seven hours in conversation. They continued talking while he gave Brzezinski and Denend a private tour of the Sistine Chapel.

Most of their focus was on the internal situation in Poland, which had been restive since the pope's historic visit a year earlier. But he was also troubled by the turmoil in El Salvador, where the widely revered Óscar Romero, the archbishop of San Salvador, an icon to liberation theologists across the region, had been assassinated in his cathedral by a right-wing death squad a few weeks earlier. To Brzezinski's surprise, the pope thought that Romero had become unsound in his judgment; Romero's deeply felt beliefs had led him astray. Moreover, John Paul II believed that Romero had probably been murdered by the Left, which had "staged the assassination as a right-wing killing as a deliberate provocation."[72]

That was untrue, yet revealing. To Poles and others behind the Iron Curtain, John Paul II was a progressive figure who took the side of the masses against power. But to many Latin Americans, he was a reactionary bulwark of the landed Catholic establishment. In a letter to Brzezinski, the pope wrote, "I spoke with [Romero] a few weeks before his death when he was here in Rome. Assuredly—in this case as in others—correct pastoral concern for people socially deprived easily becomes the object of manipulation and political games."[73]

Poland, not Romero, was what Brzezinski wanted to discuss. The pope repeated his joke that his audience with Carter had resembled a meeting of two religious leaders. Brzezinski replied that their own dialogue was like "two political leaders consulting together." The pope agreed. Their conversation about Poland was extensive, tactical, and deeply political—and deliberately not recorded by note takers on either side. Yet it was a mere hors d'oeuvre to their division of labor over the events that were about to convulse the country of their birth, which would in turn assist in the unraveling of the Soviet Union. Both men saw Poland as a key to bringing down the Iron Curtain. A few weeks after their Vatican meeting, Brzezinski instructed his assistant to add "P" for "Pope" to his White House phone.[74] It was his personal Vatican hotline.

In a memo in early August, Brzezinski warned Carter that the Reagan campaign was worried that he was planning an October surprise. "Republicans are very much concerned that you will stage some sort of foreign policy coup . . . shortly before the election," he wrote.[75] There were no prizes for guessing which turn of events Reagan most feared. As Cronkite was continuing to remind viewers night after night, the US hostages were approaching three hundred days in captivity. Yet there were precious few signs that State was making headway via its third-party probes to Khomeini. "My impression is not much is being done," Brzezinski thought after Warren Christopher had given the National Security Council an overview of its desultory negotiations.[76] The shah died in Egypt in late July. After much wrangling, Carter reluctantly allowed the US ambassador to Egypt to attend the funeral. Richard Nixon caught most of the attention. Speaking at Cairo's airport, the former president rehearsed familiar gripes about America having abandoned a loyal ally.

In addition to the steady corrosion of Carter's ratings, Brzezinski worried about Soviet designs on Iran. In late August, General Jones, chairman of the Joint Chiefs of Staff, told Brzezinski's NSC committee that Moscow was preparing for an invasion.[77] The Soviets would exploit Tehran's revolutionary turmoil to occupy northern Iran, as Stalin had done more than three decades earlier. Much of the summer was taken up by contingency planning for that specter. Since the Pentagon deemed it suicide for the US to intervene directly against the Soviets in Iran, Brzezinski focused on the need to "escalate horizontally."[78] That would include blockading Soviet ports, such as Vladivostok and Murmansk, and possibly carrying out air strikes on Cuba and Yemen. On several occasions Muskie accused Brzezinski of preparing for World War III. Iran could not be defended, he said, so the United States must confine itself to diplomatic warnings. Brzezinski said that America should not restrict itself to an all-or-nothing choice, which would inevitably result in its doing nothing. In 1948, the US had also been in a seemingly hopeless position to defend West Berlin against the Soviet blockade and a likely follow-up military occupation, he said. The Truman administration had nevertheless blunted the Soviet embargo with the Berlin airlift.

Iraq's invasion of Iran on September 22 added an unexpected dimension to the internal debate. For a while, it looked possible that Iraq's secular strongman, Saddam Hussein, might have inadvertently saved Carter's skin. The Iranian military had been badly depleted by the revolution. In addition to mostly grounding the country's air force, the revolutionaries had purged twelve thousand officers from the Iranian army, which had left it rudderless and demoralized. The mullahs were now desperate for spare parts so that Iran could operationalize its mostly US-supplied stock of hardware, particularly its F-4 fighter jets, against Saddam. Carter now had the leverage he had so desperately been craving. This new Iraqi dimension caused Republican jitters; Reagan accused Carter of having fomented the Iran-Iraq War.

A few days before the Iraqi invasion, Khomeini put out feelers to Carter on releasing the hostages. The ayatollah's doctors had apparently given him months, possibly only weeks, to live (he actually survived another eight years), which lent an added urgency to ending the hostage crisis. Khomeini had three conditions for their release: that the US would unfreeze Iran's financial assets; that Carter would pledge not to intervene militarily in Iran; and that Washington would deposit the shah's US-held assets into an Iranian account. Of those, only the last was unacceptable. In their debate over Khomeini's terms, Carter could barely suppress his delight. "It could be a critical turning point not only in our relations with Iran but in the elections here," wrote Brzezinski. "No wonder the president was absolutely elated."[79] After the Iraq invasion, Khomeini added a fourth condition: that the US supply Iran with the military spare parts for which it had already paid. The mesmerizing prospect of an electorally game-changing October hostage release was within Carter's grasp.

The remaining six weeks until the presidential election was a tense cat-and-mouse game between Washington and Tehran, punctuated by premature celebrations that a deal had been clinched followed by despondency when it evaporated. The seesaw negotiations bore an uncanny resemblance to LBJ's frantic efforts to achieve peace in Vietnam during the 1968 presidential election. Nixon had dreaded the specter of a breakthrough during the Paris peace talks. As was later exposed, his campaign meddled in the process to stop that from happening. Kissinger had played a role in that. The Nixon campaign's method was to promise South Vietnam a better deal if it waited out the Johnson administration.

The parallels between the 1968 and 1980 campaigns are striking. It was in Reagan's interest that the American hostages not be freed before November 4. Their release would be an "October surprise," a term coined by Reagan's running mate, George H. W. Bush (and retrospectively applied to 1968). The question is whether Reagan "pulled a Nixon" by promising the Iranians that they would get a better deal from him on military supplies than what Carter was offering. Brzezinski's former aide Gary Sick was convinced that Reagan's people did strike a deal with Iran to do so. Sick's 1991 book, *October Surprise: America's Hostages in Iran and the Election of Ronald Reagan*, provided strong circumstantial evidence of that theory.

Carter was also convinced that Reagan's campaign made such a deal with Khomeini, but he felt that it would be counterproductive to say so in public.[80] After leaving office, Carter learned from PLO leader Yasser Arafat that he had been asked in 1980 by Reagan's campaign manager, William J. Casey, to be a conduit to Iran. In 2023, the *New York Times'* Peter Baker uncovered even stronger evidence for Sick's theory. It came from Ben Barnes, who had been the speaker of the Texas House of Representatives and lieutenant governor to former governor John Connally, Jr.[81] In the summer of 1980, Connally and Barnes had made a tour of Middle Eastern capitals in a Standard Oil Company jet. They asked every regional leader from Sadat to King Hussein to pass on to Khomeini that he should hold out for a better hostage deal after the election. On their return, they reported their findings to William Casey in a meeting room at Dallas Fort Worth airport.

As Sick reported, Casey had met with senior Iranian officials in Madrid in late July 1980 to pitch the bargain directly.[82] The gist was that US arms would flow to Iran via Israel after Reagan's inauguration. That was precisely what occurred. Separate bipartisan congressional investigations in the early 1990s failed to turn up proof of the theory, notably Casey's secret side trip to Madrid. Two decades later, a *Nightline* reporter unearthed a US Embassy cable from Madrid confirming Casey's presence in Spain on those exact dates in 1980. The cable had conveniently been mislaid during the congressional probes. For his part, Barnes said, he would go to his grave believing the truth of the Reagan hostage deal. After Carter entered hospice care in early 2023, Barnes's conscience got the better of his partisan loyalties. "I just want history to reflect that Carter got a little bit of a bad deal about the hostages," he told Baker. "He didn't have a fighting chance [of winning reelection] with those hostages still in the embassy in Iran."[83]

As polling day loomed, Brzezinski got more involved in the drive to secure the hostages' release. Neither he nor Carter could understand why the Iranians were holding out against their offer of spare parts to reboot its military. Tehran kept insisting that it wanted new hardware rather than spare parts, which would have breached the arms ban that Carter had imposed on Iran. In all other respects, the hostage release was ostensibly a done deal. Unknown to Carter at the time, however, he was involved in what Sick described as a "three-cornered bidding contest" in which Reagan's people were offering something better to Iran. In mid-October, according to Sick, Casey and other Reagan campaign staff met with Iranian and Israeli officials in a hotel in Paris. They agreed in detail on the kind of hardware that Iran would get in early 1981 after Reagan's inauguration.[84]

On October 21, a few days after that meeting, Iran declared that it was no longer interested in new US military equipment. Brzezinski was at a loss to explain why Tehran was blowing hot, then cold. "The Iranians are continuing to nibble on our offer of spare parts," he wrote on October 8. "It looks like there could be a deal. I will keep my fingers crossed because we have been burned so many times before."[85] Almost certainly in error, he blamed Iran's latest retreat on Carter's hopeful public statements about the possibility of the hostages' release. "I said [to Ham Jordan] that a couple of weeks ago the Iranians seemed to be extremely eager for a settlement," he recorded. "Now that we are conveying that impression, and [sic] the Iranians, being essentially carpet merchants, will up the ante."[86]

A stunning quality of the 1980 election is how close it was until the last moment. Political lore does not remember it that way. It was as though Americans were waiting for something to make up their minds for them. Then it was a landslide. Carter's ratings had continued to bleed over the summer. Six weeks of Billygate followed by another curdled Democratic convention had given Reagan a lead as high as thirty points in one late-summer poll. Here was a sitting president who could control neither his family nor his party, let alone the fate of fifty-two blindfolded Americans somewhere in the Middle East. But the forces of gravity pulled Reagan back down to earth during the campaign. Five days before the election, the *Washington Post* gave Carter a five-percentage-point lead over Reagan. Gallup put Reagan a single point ahead.

Two things changed. First, most pundits thought Carter lost the single debate he had had with Reagan a week before election day. By appearing genial and nonbelligerent, Reagan quelled widespread fears that he would be a warmonger. The American public had rejected Barry Goldwater in 1964 because of those same fears. Reagan duly packaged himself as the un-Goldwater. Carter had come across as nervous and phony. When he mentioned that his thirteen-year-old daughter, Amy, told him that "nuclear weaponry and the control of nuclear arms" were her biggest concerns, his campaign team groaned. "Oh my God—not *that*," said Jerry Rafshoon. "It's so bad it's almost funny."[87] But on the substance, Carter's team thought he had held his own. Brzezinski was not alone in thinking that his boss had triumphed. They had no idea how low Reagan's bar was.

The second change was the fate of the hostages. Nothing stings quite as much as dashed hopes. Three days before the election, Iran's Majlis voted through four conditions for the release of the hostages. Carter deemed the move serious enough to fly back to DC at dawn on Sunday, November 2, from a last-minute campaign stop in Chicago. Brzezinski met him at the steps of the chopper on the White House lawn and handed him the text of the Iranian conditions. Carter took the paper wordlessly and marched grimly to the Oval Office while reading it. Christopher told him that the Iranians were planning on a full release. Admiral Turner said the CIA had pictures of empty buses waiting outside the US Embassy in Tehran.

It was another Iranian false dawn. Nothing came of the Majlis vote. But Iran's cruel tease guaranteed that the last three days of the campaign would be dominated by media coverage of Iran. The *Washington Post* ran a five-day front-page series on the crisis, which recounted in painful detail the year since the hostages had been taken—from the initial storming of the embassy to the failed rescue mission, Vance's resignation, and the months of paralysis since then. Instead of showing the closing rallies of Carter's and Reagan's campaigns, the networks were dominated by reels of Khomeini addressing fanatical crowds chanting "Death to America!" The blanket coverage could not fail to remind voters of America's unavenged humiliation.

As late as the day before the election, Pat Caddell's polls still showed a close race. Late Monday afternoon, he predicted to Brzezinski that undecided voters would break Carter's way. Then Caddell saw the eve-of-election data.[88] At 2:00 a.m. he awoke Ham Jordan to pass on his findings. The election was over, he told Jordan; Carter was going to lose by around ten points. "We are getting murdered," Cadell said. "All the people that have been waiting and holding out for some reason to vote Democratic have left us. I've never seen anything like it in polling. Here we are neck and neck with Reagan up until the very end and everything breaks against us. It's the hostage thing."[89] Election day turned into a White House wake.

In an early postmortem with Jordan, Powell, Caddell, and Rafshoon, Brzezinski and the rest agreed that the latest Iran twist had delivered Carter's coup de grâce. "The revival of the resentment and frustration over the hostage issue simply boomeranged against us" was Brzezinski's summation. The following morning, he lingered outside the Oval Office with his presidential daily briefing. Carter was sitting by the fire reading a newspaper. Instead of the usual rundown, they discussed what had gone wrong the day before. Brzezinski said that the vote for Reagan had been driven by escapism and nostalgia. Carter replied that his actions on the Panama Canal, the diplomatic overtures to Africa, including opposing apartheid, and China normalization had earned him nothing. "There were subtle racial undertones in the rejection of some of the things we did," he said.[90]

In the briefing papers that he left with Carter, Brzezinski slipped in a handwritten note: "Mr. President and Rosalynn, Life is fully of mystery and victory is often followed by defeat, and then again by victory. But you have already won the greatest victory of all; you have touched and improved the lives of thousands and thousands of people in prisons abroad and underprivileged at home, ignored and slighted or just forgotten. You made love of others into a tool of power, and those who have worked with you have also come to love you. I will always be grateful and personally better because of you. Fondly, Zbig."

His note struck home. Its message reflected Carter's truest aspirations rather than what Brzezinski had often advised him to do. On more than one occasion, Brzezinski had pointed out to Carter that there had been no combat deaths during his presidency; not one US soldier had lost his life in conflict. The eight who died during Operation Eagle Claw were killed by accident. Carter's bloodless record was, and remains, unique among post–World War II presidents. On the evening of election day, White House staff lined up to say goodbye to the Carters as they headed off for a long weekend at Camp David. Carter shook their hands one by one. At Brzezinski he lingered, clasped his hands, and said, "God bless you, Zbig."[91]

In the aftermath of Carter's defeat, a quip circulated that he had lost because of the "three K's": Khomeini, Kennedy, and Koch. The last K, Ed Koch, the Democratic mayor of New York City, stood in for the Jewish vote, which moved decisively for Reagan. Carter had won 71 percent of the Jewish vote against Ford. That percentage dropped to just 45 percent in 1980, which contributed to his loss of New York State to Reagan. It was the last time a Democratic candidate got less than half the Jewish vote. Koch's influence was considerable. Earlier in 1980, the United States had voted for a UN resolution that condemned Israeli settlements in the occupied Arab territories, "including Jerusalem." Brzezinski was assured by Donald F. McHenry, America's UN ambassador, and separately by Vance, that the language on Jerusalem had been removed from the text. He was misinformed. Strauss and Mondale had persuaded Carter to issue an apology for America's vote, which implied that Jerusalem was not a Jewish city. "The whole affair makes the entire administration look like a bunch of idiots," Brzezinski wrote.[92]

A few days later, Koch told the *Washington Post* that the Carter administration had a "Gang of Five" who were "anti-Israel." They were Brzezinski, Vance, McHenry, Andrew Young (McHenry's predecessor), and State's Harold Saunders. McHenry, whom Koch described as "Third World–oriented and viciously anti-Israel," dismissed the allegation as unfounded. Like Young, McHenry was African American and a key face of the Carter administration's outreach to southern Africa's repressed black populations. Like Young, McHenry sympathized with the Palestinian cause. Vance called Koch's allegations "absolute baloney. Ed Koch knows damn well . . . that I am not anti-Israel, never have been, never will be."[93] Brzezinski declined to comment.

Carter spent much of his final year in office agonizing over the collapse of the second part of the Camp David Accords. Even Mondale, who constantly worried about the Jewish vote and tried to water down Carter's reactions to Israel's new settlements, was convinced that Menachem Begin wanted Reagan to win the election. The issue peaked in midsummer over a vote in the Israeli Knesset to declare Jerusalem, including Palestinian-claimed East Jerusalem, a united capital. Israel was also musing about annexing the Golan Heights, which had been taken from Syria in the 1967 Six-Day War. Those actions would be the death blow to Camp David's second agreement.

Carter felt that he had lost whatever sway he once had over the Israeli prime minister. "Begin is devious to the point of lying," he told Brzezinski. Mondale added that Begin was skillfully maneuvering the US Jewish vote into Reagan's camp.[94] Brzezinski rehearsed the case for a tougher response to Begin. Mondale, sometimes backed by Bob Strauss and Sol Linowitz, who had replaced Strauss as Middle East envoy, would point out the domestic fallout of taking a hard line. Carter would generally split the difference, pleasing no one. "I can tell that the president has no stomach for a direct confrontation with the Israelis," Brzezinski wrote. "Privately he makes extremely tough noises about them. But it is clear that in public he is not prepared to take them on because it would cost too much politically."

Carter's Herculean efforts had brought about the first recognition of Israel by an Arab nation—none less than Egypt, which posed by far the biggest military threat to Israel. Carter could argue that no US leader had done more for Israel's security than he had. In late 1980, such a case would have moved few. Begin's clear preference for Reagan and Carter's reputational hit with Washington's pro-Israel advocacy groups helped seal Carter's fate in November. Brzezinski was a big part of Carter's image problem with Jewish Americans; Koch and others made sure of that.

But there was a larger contributor to Carter's defeat: Paul Volcker, the chairman of the Federal Reserve. At the end of Carter and Reagan's sole debate, Reagan looked into the camera and asked, "Are you better off now than you were four years ago?" Because of Volcker's tough medicine, most voters answered in the negative. When Carter took office, the prime interest rate was 6.25 percent; in December 1980, it hit a record high of 21.5 percent. That Carter had appointed Volcker in full knowledge of his hair-shirt remedy earned him no credit with voters. The Left hated draconian interest rates. The Right mythologized Reagan as the inflation slayer. That became the conventional wisdom. A moral of Carter's presidency is that virtue must be its own reward. History is a biased judge.

Carter's most overlooked foreign policy success was the Soviet Union's 1980 noninvasion of Poland. The situation reached a climax in the transition period after Carter lost to Reagan. Unrest had been building among Polish workers for most of the year. On July 22, Brzezinski warned Carter that agitation against the Polish regime could get out of hand. "We could thus have a serious crisis before too long," he said.[95] Polish crises had historically tended to be sparked by worker restiveness over rising prices, which then spread to other parts of society. At that point Soviet intervention loomed.

In 1970, Poland's leader, Władysław Gomułka, was ousted from power after ordering the suppression of a strike at the regime's showpiece Lenin Shipyard in Gdańsk. At least forty-four workers were killed. The strike had been sparked by food price rises. His successor, Edward Gierek, had no better luck in defying the logic of centrally planned economies. Saddled with ever-rising foreign currency debts, Poland could not generate the growth to service its loans. As a result, the regime was constantly tempted to cut the country's generous food subsidies, which helped keep Polish society quiescent. In 1979, Poland had negative growth, the first instance for any Soviet Bloc nation since the Second World War.

In mid-1980, the Polish government again raised food prices. On August 14, in solidarity with a worker who was fired just months before she was due to retire for belonging to an illegal trade union, workers at Lenin Shipyard went out on strike. It began on the same day Brzezinski was booed at the Democratic convention. That was the moment of peak Brzezinski infamy on the left and simultaneously the start of arguably his greatest service to America. The Gdańsk strike struck an instant chord across Poland. Labor unrest rapidly spread. Two weeks later, Warsaw caved in to most of the workers' demands. Gierek recognized the union and its right to strike. The Solidarity movement was born.

Solidarność, or Solidarity, was led by Lech Wałęsa, a charismatic thirty-six-year-old unemployed electrician. His handlebar mustache gave him a resemblance to Józef Piłsudski, the pre-Communist founder of independent Poland. Wałęsa's Solidarity was openly Catholic; Pope John Paul II's portrait was ubiquitous on factory floors. Polish flags also covered the Gdańsk shipyard's walls. In the Soviet mindset, a trade union that was both religious and nationalistic was a contradiction in terms. According to Marxist-Leninist orthodoxy, unions were superfluous since the socialist state already represented workers' interests. In reality, the material gap between the privileges awarded to Poland's apparatchiks, who could buy subsidized foreign goods at Party commissaries, and the conditions of the ordinary Polish worker made a mockery of the regime's class pieties.

Solidarity posed a clear ideological threat to the USSR. Not only had it broken the Communist monopoly on worker representation, which brought Poland a step closer to multiparty democracy; it was also a patriotic groundswell against Russia's overlordship. Solidarity's membership swelled to 10 million in the year after its birth, close to a third of Poland's population. It included intellectuals such as Brzezinski's cousin Andrzej Roman, a sports journalist, who, as Brzezinski's intimate friend kept him abreast of Warsaw's rumor mill. It also had the open support of the Catholic Church. The Soviets and their satellite states could crush rebellions with relative ease if they were confined to one segment of society. When disparate groups combined, as they did under Wałęsa, the threat turned existential. In addition to the workers, priests, and intellectuals, Solidarity could draw on the behind-the-scenes support of the pope and the US president's national security advisor. John Paul II and Brzezinski being in those roles at that moment was a historic stroke of good fortune for Poland.

Brzezinski's goal was to ensure that Solidarity would provide no pretext for the Soviets to invade. He was arguably the world's leading expert on where the US had gone wrong in the buildup to the 1956 Soviet invasion of Hungary and its 1968 invasion of Czechoslovakia. He lost no opportunity to tutor Carter about Washington's history of signaling indifference to looming Soviet occupations of erring satellites, the so-called Brezhnev Doctrine. The most pressing lesson from the past, he said, was to ensure that the Polish government did not allow the situation to get out of hand, as Imre Nagy had done in Hungary and Alexander Dubček had allowed in Czechoslovakia.

"Gradual changes in Poland are very much in our interest," he argued in late August. "From our point of view, a Soviet intervention, especially now, would be catastrophic. It would essentially illuminate American impotence and play into Reagan's hands."[96] Accordingly, in early September, Carter agreed to more than double Poland's US credit to $670 million. He also agreed to sound the alarm in letters to Thatcher, Giscard, Schmidt, and the pope. Brzezinski pleaded with Lane Kirkland, the gung ho anti-Communist leader of the AFL-CIO, not to go public about the union's financial aid to Solidarity. Kirkland did it anyway. "I admire him for his guts but I think his judgment is poor," Brzezinski thought.[97]

Kirkland's grandstanding triggered another Brzezinski spat with Muskie. In early September, the State Department issued a bland statement about the situation in Poland. On Brzezinski's reading, it implied that America "couldn't care less as to what is happening in Poland." Muskie also called in the Soviet chargé d'affaires to inform him that the US government had nothing to do with the AFL-CIO's pro-Solidarity declaration. That doubly annoyed Brzezinski: first, because Muskie should have delivered the message to Poland's ambassador—giving it to the Soviets suggested that the US saw Poland "as a vassal of the Soviet Union"; second, because Muskie's implicit deference to Moscow's sphere of interest repeated Dulles's errors in 1956 and LBJ's in 1968. Foggy Bottom's studied indifference would only make a Soviet intervention more likely, Brzezinski thought. He was also irked with Carter, and let him know it, for having cleared Muskie's emollient statement.[98] An annoyed Muskie grudgingly agreed to issue a new one and speak to Poland's ambassador.

Reagan, meanwhile, spotted a chance to retrieve some of the Eastern European votes Carter had siphoned from Ford in 1976. On Labor Day 1980, he kicked off his official campaign with an "ethnic picnic" in front of the Statue of Liberty.[99] A display of Eastern European flags, Poland's most prominently, decorated the rally. Reagan's chief guest was Bolesław Wałęsa, Lech's father, who had emigrated to the United States a few years earlier. He was now working in a Jersey City lumberyard. Reagan told the crowd that Wałęsa's son had "provided the kind of leadership that Carter failed to deliver."[100] In practice, Carter was doing a lot to prevent the worst from happening. It made no difference in November; Americans of Eastern European heritage made up a large part of the blue-collar "Reagan Democrats" who switched their loyalty to Republicans.

A week after Reagan's picnic, Gierek was ousted as general secretary of the Polish Communist Party by Stanisław Kania, an apparatchik who was far more amenable to Soviet ways. But Kania did not yet feel secure enough to confront Solidarity. Moscow kept stepping up the pressure on him to end the strike and liquidate Solidarity's leaders. In early October, Brzezinski warned Carter of the mounting risk of a Soviet military intervention. Unbeknownst to the State Department, Brzezinski was receiving gold-plated intelligence from a CIA agent on the Polish Army's general staff. Indeed, Ryszard Kukliński, whose agency code name was "Jack Strong," was the star in Langley's firmament. The CIA's Soviet Division chief had in 1977 described him as "the agency's best placed and most productive source within the Soviet bloc."[101]

In April 1980, Stansfield Turner awarded Kukliński the CIA's Distinguished Intelligence Medal without naming him. Kukliński had sent roughly twenty thousand pages to Langley in the preceding years. Because of the information pipeline from Kukliński, Brzezinski and the CIA had long since been familiar with the Soviet Union's invasion plans for Western Europe. Poland was defined as a "second-echelon" country (the USSR was "first echelon") through which Warsaw Pact forces would attack NATO. Among other motivations, Poland's Soviet-allotted role as a dispensable nuclear target had prompted Kukliński to offer his services to the CIA. His motive was patriotic, not financial. The Soviets rated Kukliński so highly that he was invited to train at the K. E. Voroshilov Military Academy in Moscow, the USSR's elite military school.[102] His specific job was the Polish general staff's chief liaison to the Soviet military, which meant he was privy to some of the USSR's most valuable operational secrets. Years before Solidarity sprang into existence, Brzezinski was armed with firsthand intelligence of Soviet offensive planning. Kukliński was often the author of the documents that he was leaking.

Kukliński's chilling reports, which Brzezinski insisted on receiving without analytical filter in their original Polish, kept the White House a step ahead of Brezhnev. Langley sent them to the White House in blue-bordered folders, which indicated that they were raw intelligence. Washington had high confidence that it knew what the USSR was planning to do next. Kukliński was so trusted that on October 30, the Polish defense minister, Wojciech Jaruzelski, asked him to devise plans for the imposition of Polish martial law. After drawing them up, Kukliński deposited a copy in his usual American drop box. Brzezinski was his premier customer. Kukliński had insisted that the CIA give him a cyanide pill, which he put into a fountain pen that he kept close at all times.[103]

His reports gave Brzezinski added confidence in dismissing State's default position that the USSR's priority was peace and stability. He encountered the same arguments from Muskie in late 1980 as Soviet divisions amassed on Poland's borders. More than once, Brzezinski bulldozed through Muskie's objections to holding emergency NSC committee meetings on the Poland crisis. As an added benefit, the CIA officer overseeing the USSR and the Soviet Bloc was Bob Gates, Brzezinski's former protégé. Brzezinski also recruited Jan Nowak to join his staff. On several occasions he dialed "P" for "Pope." "Do we have our own telephone number?" John Paul II whispered to his Polish aide, Monsignor Stanisław Dziwisz, when Brzezinski first asked for it.

Brzezinski gave Carter layered advice on how to deter the Soviets. The outgoing president took most of Brzezinski's suggestions without question. Both saw the prospect of a Soviet invasion of Poland as a disaster that could set back US-Soviet relations by decades. Their only goal was to prevent that from happening. Brzezinski did so by sending two apparently contradictory signals to Moscow. The first was that the US had no intention of interfering in Poland's internal politics, let alone encouraging it to leave the Warsaw Pact. The second was to set out explicitly how a Soviet invasion of Poland would harm East-West relations: it would trigger far worse reverberations than the Soviet invasion of Afghanistan. At the same time, he urged senior Polish officials, including the country's ambassador in Washington, to discourage further radical steps by Solidarity. He telephoned Solidarity leaders to give them the same message. With the big exception of Kukliński, the consensus in Poland was that the Soviets would not dare to invade. In contrast to Hungary in 1956 and especially Czechoslovakia in 1968, Soviet troops would encounter stiff resistance from Polish citizens and probably from elements of the Polish Army.

Such complacency worried Brzezinski. In contrast to the Soviet invasion of Afghanistan, which Brzezinski had known was coming and relished, he thought America should do all it could to stop the Red Army from reoccupying Poland. A Soviet invasion would increase the risk of World War III. At the very least, it would push West Germany further towards neutrality. In late August, the Solidarity outburst had forced Helmut Schmidt to cancel a planned summit with East Germany's leader, Erich Honecker. It would have been the first trip by a West German leader to East Germany in years. That was irritating enough to Schmidt. At a meeting of Quad senior officials in late October, the Germans insisted that a Soviet invasion of Poland could not be allowed to disrupt détente. At stake was a $5.5 billion West German loan for the construction of a three-thousand-mile-long gas pipeline from Siberia to Western Europe. "This is the best proof yet of the increasing Finlandization of the Germans," Brzezinski told Carter.[104] It meant that Bonn was taking a softer line than most of Western Europe's Communist parties, which sided strongly with Solidarity.

In late November, Schmidt flew to Washington to meet President-Elect Reagan. After a lot of wrangling with his staff, a reluctant chancellor agreed to request a meeting with Carter, as protocol required. "He did everything possible to get out of it," said Wolfgang Ischinger, an embassy official.[105] At their meeting, Schmidt rebuffed Carter's attempts to talk about Poland. "He did not want to discuss any serious issues at all," said Carter. Brzezinski thought that the ensuing goodbye lunch for Schmidt was the most awkward official reception he had ever attended. Jody Powell refused to show up. "I don't want to have lunch with that son of a bitch," he said.[106] Attempts at conversation were perfunctory. Though Schmidt was a nondrinker, he protested against Carter's one-glass policy by turning his wineglass upside down.[107] At the two leaders' brief joint press conference after, Brzezinski walked off once Carter had finished talking. Schmidt had just started. Since Brzezinski was standing behind Carter, his gesture of contempt was caught on camera. A year later, after martial law had been imposed on Poland, Schmidt got his much-delayed summit with Honecker. The two leaders were filmed throwing snowballs at each other. When asked about martial law in Poland, Schmidt said, "Herr Honecker is as dismayed as I am *that this was necessary* [my italics]."[108]

On December 1, Kukliński passed on the Soviet Union's plan to invade Poland. Fifteen Soviet divisions, two Czech, and one East German would move in simultaneously from Poland's east, south, and west within the next few days. His intelligence was more timely than usual because blanket cloud cover was blocking America's satellite view. Soviet divisions were conducting an exercise, Soyuz 80, as a decoy for the impending invasion of Poland. Since it would be preceded by a Polish Army crackdown on Solidarity, Kukliński had real-time access to the plans and dates. "I believe the Soviets are readying their forces for military intervention," Stansfield Turner wrote in a cover note on top of a CIA alert for the president.[109]

Brzezinski persuaded Carter to send Brezhnev a stern warning over the Kremlin hotline. "I wish to convey to you the firm intention of the United States not to exploit the events in Poland, nor to threaten legitimate Soviet security interests in that region," Carter told Brezhnev. "At the same time I have to state that our relationship will be most adversely affected if force is used to impose a solution on the Polish nation." A few hours later, he issued a similar statement publicly.[110] At Brzezinski's urging, Carter rallied fellow world leaders, including the pope, to send like-minded messages to Moscow in private or in public. Thatcher and Giscard were as firm as Carter; Schmidt was the outlier. With Brzezinski's encouragement, the pope privately beseeched Solidarity to avoid doing anything that could be taken as a pretext for the Soviets to invade.

On Friday, December 4, Kukliński relayed that Soviet divisions would be ready to move by the following Monday. Washington was also receiving satellite images of military hospitals being set up in Kaliningrad and reports of the partial closure of the East German–Polish border. Radio Moscow was hyping claims that the US was the animating force behind the Polish protests. Soviet outlets singled out Brzezinski by name as chief US troublemaker. On December 7, Brzezinski convinced Carter to issue a far more explicitly worded statement. He also sent a memo to Harold Brown instructing the Pentagon to draw up a list of US weapons that would be sold to China if the Soviets invaded Poland. His note was intended to be leaked.

Brzezinski's various steps, which for the first time specified to Moscow the precise harm it would incur from invading another country, helped deter the USSR from invading Poland. Signs that the Poles would fight back and the Soviet army's mounting casualty rate in Afghanistan also weighed on the Politburo's deliberations. The Soviet decision was a close call. In a hurried summit, Warsaw Pact leaders offered Brezhnev their support on December 4. Apparently oblivious to the effect that occupying German troops would have on the Polish psyche, Honecker was the most enthusiastic of them all. A tired and increasingly unpredictable Brezhnev pulled back at the last moment.

There can be no doubt that Brzezinski played a serious role in convincing the Soviets that the country of his birth would be indigestible. The pope did, too. Poland was made to look like a porcupine. Even without John Paul II doing anything, Polish adulation of the pontiff would probably have inspired resistance. There can also be no doubt that Kukliński was a once-in-a-generation asset to the US. His intelligence gave Carter the confidence to act with calculated and timely clarity. Another CIA officer described him as "possibly the most productive single human source against the Soviet/Eastern European military the Agency has ever had."[111] A year after the Soviet noninvasion and eleven months into Reagan's presidency, General Jaruzelski imposed martial law on Poland. Kukliński passed Warsaw's advance plans to the CIA, now headed by William Casey. Reagan chose not to warn Moscow either in public or private against Poland's upcoming crackdown. The White House saw Poland as far too rhetorically useful an example of Soviet oppression to try to stop martial law from being imposed.

That was Kukliński's final dispatch to Langley. Believing he would be caught imminently, he arranged for the CIA to exfiltrate him from Poland two days before martial law was declared. Brzezinski met the Polish CIA agent in person for the first time in late November 1981, a few days after he had arrived in the United States and ten months after Carter had left office. The two men—one a long-standing naturalized American, the other a terrified asylum seeker who would be branded a traitor to Poland—met at the Four Seasons hotel in Georgetown. It was Kukliński's first time in America. His wife and two sons had also been spirited out by the CIA. The family was living in a safe house in Virginia. Having lost his homeland and technically betrayed it, the Polish mole was in a state of high anxiety. As they shook hands, Brzezinski said, "*Pan sie dobrze Polsce zasłużył!*"—"You have served Poland well!"[112] Those are the words that accompany the decoration of a Polish hero.

In keeping with so much of his presidency, Carter's final weeks were dominated by Iran. To Carter it was a matter of honor and conscience that he do everything possible to ensure the hostages' release while he still had the power to do so. But Iran had mysteriously lost its sense of urgency. Brzezinski was only peripherally involved in the bargaining over the amount and timing of the transfer of Iran's frozen assets and the hostages' concomitant release. Algeria's government played the role of third party. Warren Christopher, who shuttled back and forth from Europe and the Middle East, was Carter's chief negotiator. Brzezinski, as ever, felt that America would get nowhere if it treated the talks as a stand-alone negotiation. The threat of US power had to be part of its bargaining kit. On that, however, State's line prevailed.

There was also friction with the Reagan transition team. Carter could not understand why Reagan's people did not want to meet with their outgoing Carter counterparts. Brzezinski struck up a rare productive relationship with Richard Allen, the head of Reagan's foreign policy transition team, whom people assumed would be his national security advisor. Allen was expected to be offered that role by Nixon in 1968 only to be supplanted by Kissinger. Allen thought that he would become Reagan's NSC director but with far less power than Brzezinski or Kissinger had. Reagan was "primarily a disposer rather than a decider," he told Brzezinski.[113]

Reagan, in other words, would not be a hands-on president. Big foreign policy decisions would be made by State and the Pentagon. Some things, however, did not change. Kissinger was lobbying Reagan's people for a big role. He told Dobrynin that Reagan was considering making him an all-purpose envoy. Having watched Kissinger morph from being the chief apostle of détente to a Reaganite loyalist who believed the US was not tough enough on the USSR, the Soviet ambassador was dubious about Kissinger's speculations. "You could see that he is still an unprincipled politician, and a political chameleon who only cares about staying visible in the US public life and returning to power," Dobrynin wrote in a cable to Moscow.[114]

Kissinger, meanwhile, told Brzezinski that Reagan had been going to pick him as his secretary of state but was talked out of it by his advisors. Brzezinski passed that intelligence on to Allen. "Bullshit, bullshit," Allen replied.[115] Kissinger had about as much chance of being the next secretary of state as the pope had of becoming Iran's next ayatollah, he said. "Kissinger would betray his mother to get a headline," Allen later recalled.[116] Reagan's pick for Foggy Bottom was Alexander Haig, the former general who had served Kissinger in the NSC and was an equally strident Kissinger detractor. Mere mention of Kissinger's name agitated Haig almost as much as it did Allen. Over a White House breakfast, Haig told Brzezinski that he almost always detected Kissinger's fingerprints on newspaper criticisms of him.[117] Kissinger was on a trip to the Middle East that he told people he was undertaking on Reagan's behalf. Neither Haig nor Allen was aware of any such request by the president-elect. At Carter's insistence, Brzezinski did persuade Reagan's team to issue separate statements on Poland and Iran—in both cases to quash any ideas in Moscow or Tehran that they could exploit a power vacuum between the two administrations. It was a rare point of cooperation between teams that barely communicated.

Carter was visibly depressed after his defeat. Brzezinski would find him listening to classical music in his private study adjoining the Oval Office, reading the newspapers, or just staring out of the window. He was also vexed by what he thought a Reagan presidency would mean for America. In a memo to the president, Brzezinski listed what he thought would be Reagan's impact on the world. He mentioned seven areas. The first was the growing polarization in Central America, particularly since the Cuba-backed Sandinistas had come to power in Nicaragua. The second was that Africa, notably the black majorities in South Africa and Zimbabwe, would turn hostile to the United States as Reagan backed off from a principled majority-rule stance. The third was that Carter's Camp David deal would come unstuck, particularly the second part, regarding the Palestinians. Begin and Reagan were ideologically similar. Fourth, US-China relations would suffer as Reagan made warmer overtures to Taiwan and resumed arms sales. Fifth, Europe's Left would become far more anti-American. Sixth, there would be an accelerated US arms race with the USSR. Finally, there would be renewed Third World hostility to America. Most of those forecasts were borne out. What Brzezinski missed was the extent to which Reagan's Cold War policies would be a continuation of the last two years of Carter's administration. Indeed, Reagan made it clear that he was a fan of Brzezinski. "When Brzezinski spoke, Reagan listened, which was very rare for him," Allen recalled.[118]

Shortly before Christmas, Jimmy and Rosalynn Carter hosted a large dinner for White House staff. Nancy Reagan had annoyed the Carters by asking that they move into Blair House before the January 20 handover. Mrs. Reagan had already made it clear that she would be a powerful first lady, as attentive to detail as her husband was not. There was also media speculation about how the White House was about to become far more elegant with its incoming Hollywood crowd after the dowdiness of the Carter years. Carter told Brzezinski that he found such media gossip "sickening."

At his one sit-down with Reagan, Carter had been unable to move beyond platitudes. Reagan would never be interested in detail, he feared. In his Christmas toast, Carter jokingly thanked his staff for coming to the Blair House annex, which lightened the mood since the Carters had no intention of moving out of the White House early.[119] After dinner Brzezinski and Muska waltzed beside Carter and Rosalynn. Brzezinski handed the first lady a rose and planted a kiss on her cheek. During Brzezinski's low points, when State, the media, West Germany's chancellor, and others were agitating for his removal, he always knew he could rely on Rosalynn to stiffen her husband's resolve. She was the Carter family's hawk. "You certainly were the lightning rod for Jimmy, and I want you to know that you were always one of my very special persons," Rosalynn told Brzezinski.[120]

At one of their final morning briefings, a concerned Carter asked Brzezinski how he was holding up. If anything, the media criticism of him was even more savage as he was leaving power than it had been at its height. Brzezinski reassured Carter that he had a thick skin. But he had brought some of the brickbats on himself. Shortly after Carter's defeat, he gave an interview to the *New York Times* in which he said that Reagan's victory showed that the American people were ready for "a policy of assertive competition" with the Soviets. The Carter administration should have drawn the line in 1978 when the Soviets and Cubans were moving into the Horn of Africa, he said. The interview was when Brzezinski first publicly used his phrase "SALT lies buried in the sands of Ogaden." Had the US responded more robustly, he said, Soviet troops would not now be laying waste to Afghanistan. When asked why he was so unpopular in the Democratic Party, he replied, "It is not a popular thing to remind people that power is important, that it has to be applied, that sometimes decisions which are not fully compatible with our concepts of what the world ideally ought to be like need to be taken." The American Right was mesmerized by "nostalgia" for an age of untrammeled US power, he said; the Left was guilty of "escapism." Perhaps most pointedly, he volunteered that US-Soviet relations had become too bogged down in the narrow and technical "litigation of issues," a sideswipe at Vance's trial lawyer's approach to geopolitics.[121]

Brzezinski's comments jolted Vance into an uncharacteristic public rejoinder. Brzezinski was talking "hogwash," he said. In Vancespeak, that was as damning as it got. Brzezinski put far too much emphasis on "the use of military power, or bluff, ignoring, in my judgment, the political, the economic, and the trade aspects of our relationship with the Soviet Union." Vance's riposte paled against the splenetic reactions of people in his circle. His former spokesman Hodding Carter, who Brzezinski thought was a "snake" and whom he saw as the chief source of negative leaks about him, wrote a riposte to Brzezinski in *Playboy*. Hodding Carter had resigned a couple of months after Vance. Brzezinski, he said, was a "second-rate thinker in a field infested with poseurs and careerists." Brzezinski thought of himself as another Kissinger but "had neither Kissinger's intellect nor his political savvy.... Like a rat terrier, he would shake himself off after a losing encounter and begin nipping at Vance's ankles, using his press spokesman and chief deputies as well as himself to tell the world that he had won or that only he, Zbigniew Brzezinski, hung tough in the national-security game as a foreign-policy realist."[122]

President Carter knew that Brzezinski had often been the proxy for attacks on him. But the problem was more subtle than that. Because Carter's mind was so often in contention with itself—or prone to what Hodding Carter called his "willful inconsistency"—there was everything to play for. Carter had no neat way of reconciling Brzezinski's Soviet perspective with that of Vance or those who worked for him at State. Events had settled the president's mind for him. Brzezinski reassured Carter that he had accomplished more on foreign policy in four years than many presidents do in eight. "I was only doing what you told me to do," Carter joked.[123]

The WASPs held Brzezinski in even lower esteem when he was leaving office than when he had begun. Though Harriman had gone out of his way to host Brzezinski for his first few months in DC, the grand "wise man" was indiscreet to the point of obsession about what he thought of the "traditionally anti-Russian Jesuit." Dobrynin, who was an honorary member of the Georgetown set and who would often go for weekends to Harriman's Virginia estate, was given a running commentary. "Appointing Brzezinski, a Pole, to the role of the main advisor on Russian affairs is like appointing an Irishman the President's advisor on England," Harriman told the Soviet ambassador. At a dinner with the Schlesingers in mid-1978, Harriman complained that Brzezinski was putting SALT in jeopardy with his flap about Soviet intervention in the Horn of Africa. "[The Soviets] have always made it clear that they would of course continue to back liberation movements around the world," he said.[124]

That Brzezinski, unlike most of his detractors, spoke Russian did not apparently weigh on their appraisals. A few months before the 1980 election, Harriman told Dobrynin that Carter had been "hypnotized" by his "loquacious advisor."[125] Schlesinger, meanwhile, was so upset with Carter that he voted for John B. Anderson, the third-party independent candidate. Anderson took almost 7 percent of the vote, largely from Carter, which helped turn Reagan's already-big margin into a landslide. A couple of weeks before the election, Schlesinger bumped into the great conductor Leonard Bernstein, who was obsessed with the threat of "fascism" posed by Reagan. A vote for Anderson would be a vote for Reagan, Bernstein insisted. "Do you really want four more years of Zbig Brzezinski?" Schlesinger retorted.[126] In practice, Reagan left most of Carter's Soviet policies in place. His one big change was to redeem his promise to Iowa's farmers by lifting America's grain embargo on the USSR.

A few days before Carter left office, Brzezinski gave a "valedictory speech" to the French Institute of International Relations in Paris. Giscard asked him to come to the Elysée Palace for a farewell chat. Brzezinski loved taking limousines with police escorts to see heads of state in their gilded chancelleries. At a supposedly incognito visit to the three European leaders the previous year, during which Carter had asked him to secure a consensus on European nuclear weapons deployments, Brzezinski asked his traveling aide, Robert Blackwill, whether he was hungry. They had just visited Giscard in secret. Brzezinski insisted that they book a table at La Tour d'Argent, one of Paris's gastronomic treasures—and a venue where people went to be seen. Aren't we supposed to be on a secret trip? Blackwill asked. Brzezinski just smiled.[127] One of his incognito meetings with Britain's Jim Callaghan had been decidedly less glamorous. Britain's prime minister was at the Labour Party's annual conference, which was taking place in Blackpool, a seaside resort that had seen better days. Callaghan's hotel room was so small that Brzezinski had to sit knee to knee with him on a chair facing his bed.[128] In Brzezinski's final conversation with Giscard, they agreed that a weakening West Germany was their primary worry.

Two weeks before Reagan's inauguration, Iran upped the price for the hostages. Instead of $7.3 billion, it was now demanding $9.5 billion. Carter told Christopher to stick to his guns. "I am afraid we will now leave office with the hostages still under detention," Brzezinski thought.[129] There followed days of haggling as the US navigated the logistical complexities of how to transfer gold and Federal Reserve certificates to Algeria in time for the hostages to be released. The final figure was $7.75 billion. Iran kept Carter guessing until the last moment. Carter's advisors were still huddled in the Oval Office talking about the hostages on the morning of January 20, just hours before Reagan's inauguration. "The tragedy, which so poisoned everything about the presidency, continues to dominate," Brzezinski wrote.

The White House confirmed that two Algerian planes were at Tehran International Airport awaiting the hostages. At 11:18 a.m., forty-two minutes before Reagan's swearing-in, the Swiss ambassador in Tehran announced that the hostages had reached the airport. Still they waited. And waited. The hostages finally got airborne at 12:05 p.m., five minutes after Carter's presidency had ended. It was Ayatollah Khomeini's final twist of the knife in Carter. One small consolation was that Reagan loaned Air Force One so that Carter could greet the hostages at the US military base in Wiesbaden, Germany. Carter asked Brzezinski to accompany him. Brzezinski declined, fearing that his presence might prove controversial.

But he enthusiastically accepted Carter's offer to travel with the Carters to Atlanta on Air Force One and from there by helicopter to Carter's hometown. There Carter said his farewells. The weather was grim, and the planned barbecue was washed out. Plenty of well-wishers turned out to watch the ex-president and first lady return home. "The atmosphere in Plains was strange," Brzezinski thought. "It was as if a whole circle had been turned."[130] Both the Carters shed tears, Rosalynn repeatedly. "You know what you meant to me," the ex-president told Brzezinski with a glance that said more than words. Then they hugged.

Thus ended Brzezinski's time in government. Similarly to Kissinger, who had been fifty-three when he had left office, never to return, Brzezinski was fifty-two. To Brzezinski, serving Carter had been the honor of a lifetime. It was one of the least likely yet most consequential relationships between a US president and his advisor. Carter's meeting with Brzezinski was the first one on his schedule on January 20, 1977, and his last as president on January 20, 1981. Brzezinski never criticized his former boss in public. Nor did his NSC staff hear him demean or joke about the president. In the coming years, he would devote a lot of energy to defending Carter's intense one-term presidency from critics on both left and right.

Carter was an orphan of history, disowned by his party. In the eyes of the Left, he sold out to the hawks. To the Right, he was a hopeless dove. In Brzezinski's mind, he was a uniquely moral figure who had overcome deep inner qualms to make tough calls. He had rewritten the Cold War in America's favor. Reagan inherited those terms. As Deng Xiaoping had kept pressing, Carter did make up his mind about the USSR. Yet his proudest boast was that no "combat" deaths had occurred on his watch. The most concise and widely quoted summary of the Carter years was supplied by Mondale, his loyal number two: "We told the truth. We obeyed the law. We kept the peace."[131]

10

The Conservative Years

Brzezinski's return to academia could have gone badly. Shortly after Kissinger had left office in 1977, the Columbia University administration rescinded its offer of a specially endowed chair for him in its Political Science Department. So much had changed since 1968 that Harvard was not even an option. Labeling Kissinger a "war criminal," 130 Columbia professors and roughly a thousand students had signed petitions opposing his appointment. Among Columbia's leading agitators was Noam Chomsky, the linguistics philosopher turned biting critic of US foreign policy, who described Kissinger as a "pseudo-academic." "There is no place at Columbia for Henry Kissinger," said an editorial in the *Columbia Spectator* on April 28, 1977.

Whatever his notoriety, which continued to suppurate among liberals, Brzezinski could console himself that Kissinger's was worse. Having been a stalwart Columbia institutionalist for the best part of sixteen years, his return triggered fewer protests, though activists still called him "Carter's Darth Vader." Although Brzezinski would resume teaching only part-time in September, he agreed to give a one-off lecture at Columbia in early April. The auditorium was so packed that people had to be turned away. That remained the case with his lectures as long as he continued to teach. In a *New York Times* interview he confessed to being a little nervous about going back to academia. None of his predecessors had successfully returned to the fold, he said.[1] It was obvious he had one person in mind, although his observation also applied to McGeorge Bundy.

In his talk, Brzezinski referred to the previous week's assassination attempt on Ronald Reagan by a lone gunman in Washington, DC. Alexander Haig had controversially turned up at the White House to announce that he was "in charge." Brzezinski came to Haig's aid, saying he was better placed in the Reagan pecking order to handle crises than Vice President George H. W. Bush. That role in Carter's chain of command would naturally have fallen to Brzezinski, he said, describing himself as Carter's "alter ego." In contrast to the Carter and Nixon administrations, which had dominated foreign policy from the White House, Reagan was a laissez-faire president; it made sense that his national security advisor would be the de facto secretary of state, he said. The following week, he starting teaching two postgraduate classes, one on American foreign policy, the other on US-Soviet relations. Students had to apply for his US-Soviet relations class because too many showed up. Brzezinski could take his pick from the applicants. Those with a military background learned to downplay or exclude that detail from their résumés.[2] Brzezinski took years to overcome his feeling of having been bamboozled by the top brass's exaggerated confidence about Operation Eagle Claw.

For most of the 1980s, Brzezinski divided his routine between Washington and New York. The family remained in McLean while Brzezinski commuted on Amtrak to New York on Mondays and Tuesdays during term time. He stayed in a campus apartment. His Washington professional home was Georgetown University's Center for Strategic and International Studies, a latecomer to the capital's major think tanks that was strictly bipartisan. CSIS unapologetically pitched itself as the home of future and former members of US administrations. Brzezinski fit right in.

His first priority was to write his White House memoir. He asked Madeleine Albright to be his assistant. A natural linguist, Albright learned Polish, which she felt would improve her rapport with Brzezinski. She also used her newly acquired language to research a paper on the Polish media. They spent much of the next two years going through his diaries and sifting out classified from unclassified memos and cables for his book. Brzezinski would often tease Albright about having been born a Czech. In his repeated telling, the Poles fought while the Czechs surrendered. "Why do you think this city looks so intact?" he asked Albright on a trip to Prague. "I learned to humor his Czech-Polish rivalry," Albright said. When Poland declared martial law, she told Brzezinski, "At least the Czechs didn't invade ourselves."[3] Having studied under Brzezinski at Columbia and served him at the NSC, Albright was highly attuned to his punitive work schedule.

That was nevertheless the period when the Brzezinski children got reacquainted with their father. The White House years had swallowed most of his time. Because of his schedule, which had begun with the Carter briefing each morning before the children had arisen and often ended after their bedtime, as well as consuming most of his weekends, Muska had been the sole day-to-day parent.

The family's only pure stretches with Brzezinski were during the two or so weeks he spent with them in Maine or Vermont every summer. Pleading long hours, he had circumvented Carter's ban on White House perks to get his own car and driver, supplied by the Pentagon. Carter had had to issue a waiver for Brzezinski, who liked to boast that no one else was given that privilege. The kids also got accustomed to the lurking Secret Service detail, who stayed in a mobile home nearby. Brzezinski would usually dictate his White House diary into a Dictaphone on his evening ride home. His lifelong assistant, Trudy Werner, typed the entries up after he left office. Brzezinski had seen even less of Muska than might have been expected because of her allergy to playing Washington spouse. She strongly disdained the Georgetown dinner party circuit and the wallflower role that she was expected to fill. Instead of sporting perms and pearls, the tousled Muska could usually be found dressed in overalls, chain saw in hand, in her McLean garden workshop.

Muska was always happy, however, in her ramshackle way, to do almost all the work of hosting her husband's periodic gatherings of visiting notables, friends, peers, and colleagues. They almost never used outside caterers. Strawberry, the family pony, would often stroll nonchalantly into the kitchen. One of Brzezinski's party tricks was to give Strawberry a shot of Polish vodka. Having downed the spirit, the pony's lower lip would quiver in cartoonish appreciation. The Brzezinski residence was a bespoke gentleman's farmyard. In addition to Strawberry, there were ducks, chickens, dogs, cats, and often hanging deer carcasses, either shot by the boys or picked up as roadkill. His neighbor Senator Dick Lugar would sometimes complain that Strawberry roamed into his garden and ate his flowers. At one of the Brzezinskis' weekend lunch parties, Pamela Harriman complimented Muska on the quality of the venison. Was it from Virginia? she asked. In fact, it was roadkill that the boys dragged from two miles down the road, Muska replied. She could tell by the tire marks that the offending car had been a Mercedes-Benz. Harriman reportedly turned green and spat the deer meat onto her plate.[4]

Muska was nominally in charge of handling family discipline. Brzezinski's parental mien was outwardly stern, yet he rarely meted out formal punishment. His approach was to sit the offending adolescent down and trot out three or four reasons why his or her behavior had been irrational and self-defeating. He was convinced that reasoning worked better than fear. Family dinner talk continued to be dominated by Brzezinski's debate topics. Typical questions were "When is abortion defensible?" and "Were we wrong to go into Vietnam?" If he thought he had won the debate, Brzezinski would compliment Muska on her cooking. When he lost, he would not. Brzezinski once addressed Mark's seventh-grade class. He left the gathering of twelve-year-olds in a state of high confusion about the finer points of détente and SALT II. It was the first time they had heard of either.[5]

When Brzezinski returned to normal life, Ian was eighteen, Mark fifteen, and Mika thirteen. The boys were more assiduous students than Mika. They both attended good local public schools: first Cooper Middle School, then Langley High School. Mika was more of a challenge. She was embarrassed by the secondhand clothes her mother made her wear and the messy state of her family home. Plates were left piled in the kitchen overnight. Deer meat was often seen twisting on hooks. With her Farrah Fawcett hairstyle, Goth eye shadow, and ripped denims, Mika was not the academically focused offspring her father wanted her to be. Her teachers complained that she did not take her studies seriously. One afternoon, Brzezinski called Mika down the corridor to his study. With a glint in his eye, he congratulated her on her acceptance to the Madeira School, a private, somewhat snooty girls' boarding school a few miles down the road.

Madeira was the choice of a rich set that included the daughters of Middle Eastern sheikhs and local equestrian WASPs. Its stables were state of the art. Brzezinski felt that Mika's new setting would supply her with much needed social and pedagogical discipline. He also wanted to take boys out of the equation. A few weeks after she started there as a day student, Madeira's headmistress was arrested for homicide.[6] She had killed her celebrity dietologist partner in New York after discovering that he was having an affair. Brzezinski turned the scandal into a family dinner debate: "Are crimes of passion justified?" With Muska and Mika's affirmative answer, Brzezinski lost the motion.

In the real world, Jean Struven Harris was convicted of manslaughter. Mika fared well at her new school.

The children saw their grandparents often. "Moun," their Czech grandmother, had lived in Florida for a few years after the family had moved from New Jersey to Virginia in Carter's first year as president. After a few years, she moved once again to be close to her Brzezinski grandchildren, taking an assisted-living apartment in Virginia a few miles from Spring Hill. The Brzezinski grandparents, meanwhile, lived in a Montreal-based home for seniors run by the Polish Canadian Welfare Institute. By the early 1980s, they had entered their maudlin winter years. Though they never formally split, they decided to live in separate quarters. Leonia had become ever less reconciled to their émigré circumstances as time went by. She remained as frustrated with her downgraded fortunes as Tadeusz was phlegmatic. She would often hector her husband for no apparent reason.[7]

Both of Brzezinski's parents "worshipped the ground he walked on," in the words of one grandchild.[8] But Leonia never fully warmed to Muska. During one summer visit to Maine, the whole family fell victim to food poisoning. It turned out that Muska had picked the wrong mushrooms that day in the woods. A subtle distinction in hue was the difference between a tasty fungus and a potentially fatal one. The badly afflicted Leonia was convinced that it was an assassination attempt by Muska. She was also mortified by the state of Muska's kitchen. Tadeusz, meanwhile, was riveted by every twist in his oldest son's career. His collection of newspaper clippings about his son filled many cartons.[9] Every year or so, Brzezinski would send a donation of $1,000 to their assisted-living home. Brzezinski's youngest brother, Lech, provided far more regular support from his nearby home in Montreal, where he ran his own successful engineering business. Their half brother, George, predeceased both Leonia and Tadeusz, dying of cancer, aged sixty-two, in a Montreal hospital in 1985. In spite of his harsh ill luck, he never sacrificed his sense of fun and did not lose his artistic spirit. He was buried with military honors in the Polish Canadian cemetery.

The early eighties ought to have been the time of Brzezinski's peak cachet. He had gone as far as he could in his adopted homeland, rising higher and achieving more power than any Eastern European–born American in history. More important, he was one of America's foremost Cold War strategists. Democratic Washington, however, had not been inclined to treat him with the slightest veneration. The antipathy was mutual. Republican Washington, on the other hand, was receptive to his strategic advice on the USSR. Reagan even toyed with the idea of asking Brzezinski to be his national security advisor. It would have broken precedent for the outgoing foreign policy strategist of one party to be retained by the other.

Whether Reagan was planning to make Brzezinski a serious offer remains a matter of conjecture. What is true is that he wanted Brzezinski, rather than one of his principals, to stand in for him during a three-day nuclear war games exercise shortly after he took office. Reagan was to turn up only for the brief opening and closing sessions. In the meantime, he asked Brzezinski to assume the president's role. "Reagan saw Brzezinski as being his best surrogate," Richard Allen said.[10] Brzezinski was flattered but wanted to check first with Edwin Meese III, Reagan's counselor, whether his selection had been run past Alexander Haig at State or Caspar Weinberger at the Pentagon. A few hours later, a sheepish Meese called back to say that their plan had altered; Bill Rogers, Nixon's secretary of state, would take the role. Brzezinski often wondered what would have happened had he accepted Reagan's invitation without checking.[11]

Reagan did call Brzezinski in for regular chats. These were not probing discussions. A rival California politician once remarked, "If you walked through Reagan's deepest thought you wouldn't get your ankles wet."[12] But there was something about Brzezinski that appealed to Reagan. He fit the new president's idea of how an anti-Communist crusader should sound. At one lunch of former national security advisors, Brzezinski was seated next to Reagan. The president was supposed to be soliciting their advice on how to convince Congress to agree to the sale of AWACS to Saudi Arabia. In practice, Reagan showed no interest in the topic. After exhausting every policy angle in an effort to coax a monosyllabic Reagan into chatting, Brzezinski mentioned a recent visit to California's Napa Valley. The lunch suddenly came alive. Reagan opened up in rich detail about the relative merits of the wine-making region's varietals.[13]

In 1986, amid great White House turmoil, Reagan for the second time thought of asking Brzezinski to be his national security advisor, according to William Casey, who was still the CIA director.[14] Again, Reagan's advisors quashed the idea. It is doubtful that Brzezinski would have accepted the job at the start of Reagan's presidency, still less in his second term. His loyalty to Carter was total. By 1986, he knew that Reagan's Iran-Contra-besieged White House was a nest of intrigue. Revelations of the White House's scheme to break the law by using the proceeds of arms sales to Iran to fund Nicaragua's Contra rebels had entangled Reagan's team in congressional probes. Reagan had been through four national security advisors in five years, none of whom left a strategic mark. But Brzezinski kept up a good relationship with Reagan. A year after Reagan retired, Brzezinski sent him a copy of his latest book. "I started with page 243 as you suggested," Reagan wrote in his thank-you note. "And then went back to page one. I have only just begun but assure you I'll read it from cover to cover and not put it down until I've done so."[15] At a meeting with George Shultz, who had replaced Haig as secretary of state, Shultz told Brzezinski that he would have been more ideologically at home in Reagan's administration than Carter's. "Yes, but they needed me more," Brzezinski replied.[16]

After leaving office, making money was Brzezinski's most pressing concern. In early 1981, he was struggling to meet the mortgage payments on their McLean home. With three teenage children and an unexpectedly steep legal bill resulting from the Billygate affair, his government salary of $56,000 had not stretched far enough. In addition to his Columbia and CSIS stipends, he boosted his income with paid speeches, book advances, and the occasional consultancy. Trudy Werner, who organized much of his and Muska's lives for several decades, had control of their bank accounts. She paid their utility bills, settled school bills, and alerted the couple to any financial issues.

Muska was too ethereal to cope with the accounts. She received a monthly allowance. Brzezinski was highly money conscious but uninterested in equities or any kind of investment other than Treasury bonds. He saw the stock market as a casino. After he left government, Trudy insisted that he replace his hundred-dollar suits from Filene's Basement with clothing more befitting his station. Getting Brzezinski to sign an $800 check at Saks Fifth Avenue was like trying to get blood out of a stone. He kept the family vehicles going for at least ten years. And he imposed a $50 upper limit on family birthday and Christmas gifts.[17] As the 1980s went on, he attained financial comfort almost in spite of himself.

Trudy occupied a special role in the Brzezinskis' world. She knew everything about them and was trusted as a family member. A child of recent German immigrants, Werner and her family had been interned for three years during the Second World War. On her parents' advice, she spoke to no one about their wartime incarceration. In 1977, when the Secret Service vetted Trudy for the White House job, Brzezinski had to bail her out. The agents pointed out that her internment made her a security risk. "So you're telling me she was a dangerous toddler?" Brzezinski replied. "That's nothing. I was born in Poland and have been back there frequently." That closed the subject.[18]

Brzezinski was as tightfisted as they come. Much of that had been imprinted on him by his parents' abrupt wartime change in fortunes. On National Secretaries Day, Trudy persuaded him to take her out for lunch. At the end of their McDonald's meal, he asked, "So how much do I owe you for my share?" Lunches with colleagues, including junior ones, were always split. When he dined with fellow members of the Metropolitan Club, he often suggested that they flip a coin to decide who would sign for the meal.[19] If he lost, he would insist on best of three. The most glaring exception to his parsimony was Muska's art studio. Any equipment she wanted, he was happy to buy. The other exception was supporting impoverished relatives, including his parents. The Brzezinskis also sent money to Andrzej and Dagmara Roman in Warsaw and would smuggle in luxury goods for them on their near-annual visits.

As an attractive single blonde, Trudy was a self-declared expert on the misdirected attentions of married men. She saw Brzezinski as a fanatically loyal husband. She and her fellow secretaries in the NSC pool dubbed Brzezinski "Vitamin Z" for his indefatigability. He never spoke to Trudy inappropriately or inquired about her love life. He did not swear. Even the famously unprofane Carter had once used the F-word when he had said "Fuck the shah" to Brzezinski and other staff at a fraught moment during the Iranian Revolution.[20] Brzezinski's vocabulary was even more proper than his born-again president's. "I don't think I even heard him use the word *shit*," said Rick Inderfurth, his special assistant.[21] The only speculation about Brzezinski's fidelity was over his relationship with Kathy Kemper, an attractive young tennis coach whom Brzezinski had met at a dinner party in Bethesda.[22] She became Brzezinski's regular instructor on the White House court, at the Chevy Chase Club, and on the Brzezinskis' less manicured home court in McLean. Because of Brzezinski's introductions, "Coach Kathy" turned into the unofficial White House tennis director.

Her client roster was a Washington power list, beginning with Carter and stretching to Alan Greenspan after he became chair of the Federal Reserve. Kemper coached Brzezinski so often that on one occasion a sawdust-flecked Muska marched furiously past the starchy club receptionist and straight onto the court. "Stop trying to wreck my marriage," she said to Kemper. She then escorted Brzezinski off the premises. Muska's protest was about Brzezinski's time priorities rather than an implied affair. Kemper would continue to coach Brzezinski, often in McLean, for decades with Muska's approval. In 1983, *Tennis* magazine featured him and Kemper promoting a proposal to handicap the way tennis was scored. Though the method never caught on, their "ZBalanced Handicap System" showed how much Brzezinski cared about the game. The *New York Times* observed that Brzezinski's tennis style was better known for its tenacity than its finesse. "There is nothing like devastating your opponent with a good, clean shot with precision and power," Brzezinski said. Or losing the ball in the trees.[23]

In contrast to Kissinger, Brzezinski was unsophisticated in business. Trudy persuaded him to set up an advisory firm called Z.B. Inc. as his sole earnings vehicle. He was the president, Muska the vice president, and Trudy the secretary-treasurer.[24] He had barely any long-term clients, partly because that would have meant forcing himself to see the world through a corporate lens. He preferred to tell company boards what he thought of global trends, and that would be that. One-off consultancies were often glorified versions of a paid speech. The content was often indistinguishable from what he told his graduate students. He served for long spells on the boards of W. R. Grace, a Maryland-based chemicals producer, and Morrison-Knudsen, an Idaho-based civil engineering company. But he spent the bulk of his time teaching; writing books; meeting with visiting world leaders, Washington figures, and journalists at his CSIS office; and writing essays for *Foreign Affairs* and other publications. He did not look for clients; business contracts came as unexpected windfalls.

Kissinger, meanwhile, was pioneering his booming model of geopolitical consultancy. He launched Kissinger Associates with former national security advisor Brent Scowcroft in 1982. Clients paid between $150,000 and $420,000 annually to hear from Kissinger or one of his executives four times a year.[25] Additional services, such as putting a chief executive in touch with a central banker in China or Turkey's prime minister, cost considerably more. In the company's early days, Kissinger attracted flak for his apparent conflicts of interest. As a member, along with Brzezinski, of Reagan's President's Intelligence Advisory Board, which received classified information, Kissinger was personally accused of misusing inside knowledge for commercial purposes.[26]

Among his clients was ITT, which had defense industry contracts. His roster also included Volvo, Lehman Brothers, American Express, Heinz, Merck, the Rio Tinto Group, Chase Manhattan, Fiat, and Coca-Cola. Those names, which Kissinger himself never made public, leaked out over the years. Clients were contractually obliged not to disclose their ties to him. A key element of Kissinger's business model was to retain access—and a reputation for easy ingress—to the corridors of power, be they in the White House, European capitals, Beijing's Zhongnanhai complex, and later the Kremlin. Kissinger's sphinxlike pronouncements, which were the geopolitical version of Greenspan's oracular monetary testimonies, were designed not to jeopardize such access. As Kissinger's prospects of returning to high office receded, his public commentary increasingly dovetailed with whatever the current administration's stance might be. Where his opinions diverged, he was felicitous in how he couched his criticisms. His maxim was implicit: the more controversial one's views, the shorter one's client list.

Brzezinski wanted more money. He charged $20,000 a speech in the 1980s and frequently picked up consultancies.[27] But he also put a high value on the freedom to speak his mind, even when he came across as implacable. He was willing to sacrifice access to administrations that he did not admire; Kissinger, on the other hand, almost never offered his criticisms in public. Brzezinski did not mind being disliked; those who knew Kissinger best, including most of his biographers, concluded that he was at heart deeply insecure. One theory is that the Holocaust wipeout of almost all of Kissinger's family who had stayed behind in Bavaria had instilled in him a lifelong yearning for stability. That horrific legacy had driven his quest for order. Whether that psychoanalysis accurately captured Kissinger, his lodestars were balance and stability. When asked whether he put a higher value on justice or order, he chose order.[28] In most contexts, Brzezinski would have picked the reverse. Brzezinski's core trait was a deep self-confidence that often spilled over into arrogance. That made him less easy to like than Kissinger. It also made him more transparent. The two lifelong frenemies continued to seek each other's views over lunch or dinner. "Dear Henry, get well soon!" Brzezinski wrote in 1982. "Your friends miss you; your enemies need you."[29]

During the Reagan years, most of Brzezinski's public feuds were with his own side. A colleague asked him whether there was still room in the Democratic Party for a hawkish centrist. Brzezinski said that the Democratic Party's Truman wing had dwindled to a small minority. But that meant there was greater value in upholding it.[30] He was also publicly contemptuous of what he saw as the poor quality of the US media's foreign policy coverage. A few months after leaving office, he gave a long and widely cited interview to

George Urban of Britain's *Encounter* magazine in which he tore into the media. His basic lesson from the Carter years was that foreign policy rarely lent itself to the binary simplicities that journalists craved. History was the product of neither design nor conspiracy but the "reflection of continuing chaos." The role of contingency made dealing with the world inherently complex. Explaining the meaning of *comprehensive and reciprocal*, for example, did not meet the test of supplying one news line on détente or the other. "I would frequently give speeches or make statements of an analytical kind," he said. "Invariably, in briefing newsmen, I or my colleagues would be asked: 'What's new in it?' If you told them, 'Well, this is an attempt to explain the meaning of America's position in the world—to emphasize a number of continuing themes underlying American foreign policy,' they would ignore it. What they find more appealing are the either-or presentations of world issues, 'good guys' versus 'bad guys,' 'hawks' versus 'doves' and personal gossip and power plays."[31]

Such observations did not endear Brzezinski to influential journalists. When his memoir, *Power and Principle: Memoirs of the National Security Adviser, 1977–1981*, came out in 1983, he got payback. The book, which was dedicated to his NSC colleagues, was panned. By Washington standards, his account was frank. Brzezinski paid a lot of pro forma compliments to Vance and other rivals. But his depiction of their styles was unsparing. "Vance seemed to be the quintessential product of his own background," he wrote. "As a member of both the legal profession and the once-dominant WASP elite, he operated according to their values and rules, but those values and rules were of declining relevance." Again: "[Vance] was successful on Wall Street because he was methodical and congenial. But the contractual-litigational approach which works so successfully in a large law firm was less suited for shaping a foreign policy."[32]

Brzezinski approvingly quoted a comment by Harold Brown that "Secretary Vance was persuaded that anything that involved the risk of force was a mistake." The only lead character spared sharp criticism in Brzezinski's account was Carter. He mostly eluded blame for his administration's rolling confusions. Mondale came across as shallow and obsessively political; Brown was often prevaricating. Aside from the occasional tactical error, Brzezinski emerged as invariably right. Vance's State, and to a lesser extent Muskie's, took the brunt of the criticisms. "Vance was representative of an elite that was no longer dominant either in the world or in America," he wrote. "Carter certainly never was part of that America, and it certainly was not easy for me to relate to it either."

Most memoirs are self-serving. Brzezinski's was far from being an exception. However, *Power and Principle* did give an unusually detailed and intellectually coherent rendering of Brzezinski's version of what happened, much of it owing to Albright's restless pursuit of the paper trail. He gave her the title "Empress of Research."[33] It is fair to say that Brzezinski's reviewers were not appreciative. Here are the opening lines of the *New York Times* review: "Fated to follow, if not to fill, the footsteps of Henry Kissinger, Zbigniew Brzezinski has delivered his memoirs. . . . Just as his career has been less grand than Mr. Kissinger's, so is his prose less magisterial. Where Mr. Kissinger was eloquent, Mr. Brzezinski is earnest." The reviewer added, "Like an old performer digging out his press releases, Mr. Brzezinski quotes every scrap of compliment that the President ever threw his way on a ceremonial occasion. After a while, this courtierlike performance provides a laugh or two in a book that is not rich in wit."[34] And so on. Meanwhile, *Time*'s Strobe Talbott thought Brzezinski's memoir offered yet more evidence of his weakness for "glibness" and "gobbledygook." More damningly, he added, "[Brzezinski] does not seem to realize how often his candor, when directed at others, looks like malice and, when directed at himself, looks like shameless egotism."[35] It was scant consolation that no one, including the key players, disputed Brzezinski's accuracy.

Brzezinski affected bravado in proclaiming himself to be unruffled by the scathing reviews. But the self-centeredness of his account caused him reputational harm. It also overshadowed what was valuable about his memoir, not least its analytical clarity about the global context of the Carter years. Harold Brown told the *Washington Post*'s Elisabeth Bumiller, "Other people may find the world as portrayed in his book distorted because he'll be at the center and around the edges as well, but that doesn't mean it's not a valuable book." David Rubenstein, the future private equity titan who had worked on the Carter White House domestic staff, said, "This is a book by somebody who is not looking to go back to government." Bumiller did find one unequivocal defender among Brzezinski's former colleagues: Stu Eizenstat, who had returned to private law practice in DC. She also pointed out that Eizenstat was now Brzezinski's lawyer. "It is an honest book," Eizenstat told her. "I think it is the best book that will come out of the Carter administration."[36]

Brzezinski's career reflects a person who only occasionally bore grudges. He would happily work with onetime enemies if their interests overlapped. Disputes were rarely personalized. His memoir was a glaring exception. It is a measure of his lack of introspection that the general reaction to the book surprised him. Bumiller's piece included an interview with Brzezinski that offered a raw snapshot into his spirit of defiance and braggadocio. "America is not a country in which people who are prepared to make waves and to stand for something usually get a second chance," he told her. "America could have a terrific government composed, let's say, of Jim Schlesinger, and Melvin Laird, in some ways John Connally, Henry Kissinger, perhaps myself. But if you're controversial, you don't make it again in America. You only make it if you're safe."[37] In practice, he was talking about Washington, DC, not the United States.

Towards the end of the Reagan administration, Bob Woodward, the investigative co-maestro with Carl Bernstein of the Watergate scoops, brought out *Veil: The Secret Wars of the CIA*. Woodward's trademark exposé offered an insider's account of William Casey's period as CIA director, which had ended in 1987. The narrative begins in the late Carter years and includes the Iranian Revolution and America's early support for Afghanistan's mujahideen. Brzezinski did not come off well. Casey was the star of the book. Stansfield Turner also emerged positively. Woodward interviewed Casey forty-six times in the course of his research, Turner "more than twenty times."[38] He interviewed Brzezinski just once over lunch. It was not for lack of trying. With a journalist as influential as Woodward, researching a book that was likely to become a best seller, Brzezinski's insouciance was unusual. Most Washington figures would have grabbed at the chance to depict themselves in a positive light. In the early 1980s, more than ever, Brzezinski did not appear to give a damn about what people thought of him. He took perverse pride in his indifference to popularity.

Three weeks after Reagan took office, Wojciech Jaruzelski, Poland's defense minister, took power in Warsaw. Though the threat of a Soviet invasion had receded, the Solidarity crisis continued to rage. To Brzezinski's frustration, Reagan's people had no interest in Polish events. Reagan professed shock when Jaruzelski declared martial law on December 13, 1981, and rounded up Solidarity's leadership. Thousands of protestors were jailed or put under house arrest. Reagan's team had known in advance the precise details of Jaruzelski's martial law plan from the CIA mole Ryszard Kukliński.[39] It had chosen not to publicize that knowledge.

In that respect, Reagan's approach was the opposite of Carter's a year earlier. By using intelligence preemptively, Carter had helped to stave off the invasion of Poland. Later Al Haig would complain that Reagan's advisors had rebuffed his attempts to follow Carter's lead. They did not want to discourage any moves by Moscow that would "inflict mortal, political, economic, and propaganda damage on the USSR."[40] Poland was dispensable. There is still debate in Poland about whether Jaruzelski had a disguised patriotic motive for imposing martial law. By clamping down so harshly, he might have forestalled a Soviet invasion, some argue. Around the same time, the Soviets had been conducting Soyuz 81, another ominously armor-heavy war exercise, on the Polish-Soviet border.

In practice, as later testimonies bore out, Moscow gave Jaruzelski little choice. But the Polish leader, who Brzezinski discovered had been a class below his half brother, George, at their Catholic primary school in Warsaw in the 1920s, was in an impossible situation. His aim was to placate Moscow while avoiding a Polish bloodbath. That he roughly achieved. Three years later, the short-lived Soviet leader Konstantin Chernenko decorated him with the Order of Lenin on Moscow's Red Square. Aware of how most Poles saw him, Jaruzelski made sure that the photo of the ceremony did not appear in the Polish media.

Brzezinski was publicly critical of Reagan's response to the imposition of martial law in Poland. "Poland is a powerful signal that the Soviet bloc is starting to disintegrate," he wrote. Washington's best stance, he felt, would be to encourage the highly indebted Poland to reform by admitting it to the International Monetary Fund, then restructuring its debt to the West. In contrast, he complained, Reagan's people clearly believed in "the worse, the better." A Polish collapse could prompt the unforced error of a Soviet invasion. "This simple-minded anti-Communist perspective is both tragically wrong and blind to the long-range opportunities for a better East-West relationship inherent in the Polish situation," he wrote.[41]

At that point in his presidency, Reagan had little interest in the complexities of dealing with the "the evil empire." The Kremlin was mired in gerontocratic stasis. A comatose Brezhnev had turned seventy-five. His potential successors seemed almost as decrepit. What Brzezinski had long before described as a dictatorship of "clerks" was still firmly in place. The effect of the country's ossified leadership was to leave Moscow's foreign policy adventurism on autopilot. The Soviet war in Afghanistan was getting worse, as was a rash of proxy fights between Cuban- and US-backed forces across Central

America. The Soviets walked out of talks with the US on intermediate-range missiles in Europe.

For the time being, it suited Reagan's political needs to keep matters simple. His Manichean Cold War rhetoric did not leave much scope for entrepreneurial diplomacy. Tom Kahn, the director of the AFL-CIO, said that Reagan had treated Polish martial law as an opportunity for a "rhetorical holiday, lighting candles for the suffering Polish people . . . and mounting a mass anti-communist campaign without adverse consequences."[42] But Brzezinski kept chipping away at friends on the inside. In a meeting with Casey at Langley, he complained that Washington had cut off all support for Polish dissident groups. The next day, an unidentified man showed up in Brzezinski's CSIS office. He was carrying a briefcase containing $18,000 in cash. "Give it to your Polish friends," he said before walking out.[43]

The stark reality of Polish repression was also a jolt to many on the US Left. Others downplayed it as a sideshow. At a gathering of leftist groups in New York's City Hall in February 1982 to discuss the crackdown on Solidarity, the writer Susan Sontag was loudly booed when she said that martial law revealed the bankruptcy of the Soviet system.[44] Growing up in the 1950s, she had come to distrust any demonization of the Soviets as the product of Joe McCarthy's Red scare, she said. She had then become a prominent activist against the Vietnam War. But the American Left had been deluding itself for years about the true conditions behind the Iron Curtain, she said. The crackdown on Polish workers was only the latest proof of the Soviet Union's darkness and "villainy." Her speech was highly unpopular. She was still in a minority. The satirical writer P. J. O'Rourke wrote about a Soviet-hosted Black Sea cruise to which it had invited left-wing Americans in the early 1980s. Many American academics accepted the invitation, then packed their own toilet paper. One of the reasons Brzezinski had returned only part-time to academia, and then mostly because he enjoyed interacting with students, was because of his disenchantment with academics, particularly Sovietologists.

Right through the 1980s, the "revisionist" school of US Sovietology continued to downplay Stalin's crimes and argue that his brutal path to industrialization had been necessary. The most prominent revisionist was Jerry Hough, a political science professor at Duke University, who insisted that Stalin had killed only ten thousand people. The true figure was in the tens of millions. To add to Brzezinski's disenchantment, Hough had been given authorship of the new edition of his mentor Merle Fainsod's classic *How Russia Is Ruled*.

Hough retitled it *How the Soviet Union Is Governed*. Fainsod's original classic had had sixty references to Soviet labor camps. Hough's edition had none. One of Brzezinski's colleagues, the British historian Robert Conquest, whom he had helped recruit as a fellow at Columbia University's Russian Institute, was the revisionists' most biting critic. Conquest caricatured their exclusive focus on the material betterment of Stalin's masses as a dereliction of scholarship. American historians wrote about the galloping rate of Soviet electrification, its soaring metals output, and the mundanity of the workers' improving social conditions—indeed, any topic other than Stalin's political terror. "This involved studying everything that was happening to people except for their being starved to death, executed or sent to camps," Conquest wrote.[45]

In May 1981, a Turkish assassin shot Pope John Paul II twice in Saint Peter's Square in Rome. Brzezinski was in his CSIS office when he heard the news on the TV. He spent hours trying to get through to the Vatican. Eventually a nun told him that the pope would pull through. One of the two bullets that had entered his body had just missed his vital organs. Whether the Kremlin plotted the attempt on the pope's life has been an unresolved debate ever since. Both Brzezinski and Kissinger publicly supported the view that it was a KGB assassination attempt carried out through Communist handlers in Bulgaria, which was reliably Moscow's most obedient satellite. The assassin, Mehmet Ali Ağca, claimed he had been paid by the Bulgarians. Their motive was to kill the spiritual head of Poland's Solidarity movement, he said.

The ensuing trials, Italian commissions of inquiry, and journalistic investigations left a murky picture. In a Vatican letter to Brzezinski, the pope's secretary categorized the attempt as a *mysterium iniquitatis*—an inexplicable crime.[46] But it is clear that the pope thought the plot was hatched by the KGB. He forgave Ağca and persuaded the Italian state to show clemency. Ağca returned to Turkey. The pope's narrow escape only heightened the world's focus on Poland. In a letter to the pope while he was still in recovery, Brzezinski wrote, "I am doing everything in my power to stimulate the interest of the new administration in Polish affairs—with some degree of success."[47] A month later, the pope replied with "heartfelt gratitude to you, Dear Professor, for everything that you have done and continue doing for the sake of our nation that is very determined to defend the common good and is intent on advancing the renewal process [democratization]."[48] Almost every time they met, the pope would repeat his joke that Brzezinski had elected him.

Brzezinski kept up his own semiauthorized efforts to ease the situation in Poland. Reagan was happy to deploy Brzezinski as an envoy to the Vatican. Frank Shakespeare, the US ambassador to the Holy See, described one such meeting between Brzezinski and the pope: At the end of a long table sat "Giovanni Paolo Secondo," flanked by half a dozen red-hatted cardinals. At the other sat Brzezinski, Shakespeare, and several US diplomats. To the growing consternation of both the red hats and the Foreign Service officers, the conversation was conducted almost entirely in Polish. Only two men understood what they were telling each other.[49] Throughout the 1980s, the pope and Brzezinski regularly exchanged tips, gossip, and suggestions on what to do about Poland.

On one such visit, Brzezinski showed the pope a photograph of a ten-foot crucifix that Muska had shaped from driftwood and coated with all-weather bronze. The pope asked what she had done with it. Brzezinski told him that she had tried to donate it to McLean's Saint Luke Catholic Church, their local place of worship. But the diocese had turned her down. It had dismissed the piece as too modern. "I think they will have a revelation," the pope commented.[50] The following week, Saint Luke telephoned Muska to say it would be delighted to install her sculpture. Muska's *Mystical Body of Christ* stands there today on an outer wall of the church. For the most part, however, the pope and Brzezinski talked about Poland. Both strongly felt that their homeland was in acute danger.

In 1985, General Jaruzelski unexpectedly requested a meeting with Brzezinski. Though he had by then lifted martial law, Poland was still at a nearly ungovernable impasse. It was even further enmired in economic stagnation. Jaruzelski's crackdown on Solidarity had solved nothing. His lifting of martial law had won him no credit at home or from Reagan, who did not relax US sanctions on the country. Poland's military leader was seeking a way out. Their meeting took place in a New York hotel during the United Nations' annual General Assembly, a gathering of world leaders. David Rockefeller hosted the event.[51]

Brzezinski's former benefactor wanted Jaruzelski to approve the creation of a foundation that would invest in Polish agriculture. Up to $200 million was in the offing. Rockefeller insisted that his venture be tied to a separate Catholic Church–led one. Before the meeting began, Jaruzelski took Brzezinski by surprise by enthusiastically recollecting their first meeting during Carter's 1977 trip to Poland. Then he handed Brzezinski a thick folder of documents about his family. The Polish leader's staff had taken a lot of trouble to chase down the Brzezinski letters, genealogical trees, and parental birth certificates in the file. Jaruzelski's collection even included a handwritten note by the nine-year-old Brzezinski to his aunt.

Jaruzelski told Rockefeller that there were problems with the Polish Church foundation's paperwork; parish priests were trying to import Mercedes-Benzes duty free. Brzezinski interrupted to say that he refused to believe Jaruzelski's story about the Polish Church's luxury car scam. The dictator backed off. Though the meeting ended without the breakthrough Rockefeller was seeking, it was the start of a much more fruitful dialogue between Brzezinski and Jaruzelski. Brzezinski invited Lawrence Eagleburger, a former undersecretary of state for political affairs under Reagan, now president of Kissinger Associates, to the meeting. His plan was for the two of them to continue a dialogue with Jaruzelski under bipartisan colors. Reagan had little interest in details and was happy to outsource the initiative. They kept George Shultz informed. Brzezinski's confidence in that most unlikely of relationships had been boosted by Jaruzelski's gift of Brzezinski family documents. He compared the gesture to the time when Begin, in 1977, had presented him with Tadeusz's record of helping Leipzig's Jews. Jaruzelski's gift was a "deliberate signal."

Two years later, their back-channel conversation began to pay off. Vice President George H. W. Bush contacted Brzezinski for advice about his forthcoming visit to Poland. The 1988 election was looming, and Bush was trying to establish a foreign policy record before launching his presidential bid. He asked Brzezinski to act as his go-between with Jaruzelski to ensure that his visit yielded fruit. After years of biting US sanctions, which, against Brzezinski's advice, had not been eased, Poland was desperate for economic relief. It was clear by then that no help would be forthcoming from Moscow. Brzezinski's advice to Bush was to link the offer of US debt relief to the relaxation of political and economic conditions in Poland. After talking to Brzezinski, Jaruzelski agreed that Bush could meet with Lech Wałęsa and Church leaders. He could even visit the grave of Father Jerzy Popiełuszko, a Solidarity priest murdered by Polish security forces in 1984. After visiting Popiełuszko's grave with Wałęsa, the two men went out onto a balcony to wave to the crowd. Bush had wrapped the Solidarity colors around his shoulders. The onlookers chanted, "Solidarity! Lech Wałęsa! Long live Bush! Long live Reagan!" The trip's boost to Bush's profile was largely Brzezinski's doing.[52]

By that point, Brzezinski's estrangement from the Democratic Party was almost complete. He mostly kept aloof from the 1984 presidential campaign, although he had endorsed Walter Mondale, Reagan's Democratic opponent, a few weeks before election day. But there was precious little affinity between the two. In his memoir, Brzezinski said that underneath Mondale's "genial demeanor" was "some inner tension and insecurity." Mondale's chief contribution to foreign policy debates had been to fret about their domestic impact. The implication was that he was a shallow poll-obsessed figure without strong principles. Brzezinski added, "I was also amused by the loving way he would comb his hair in front of the mirror in his office before proceeding to any meeting."[53] Mondale made his view of Brzezinski's book clear. "I don't think kiss-and-tell books have much to do with history," said his press secretary, Maxine Isaacs.[54] Mondale's relatively dovish 1984 platform was conditioned by the fact that both of his late-surging challengers, Jesse Jackson and Gary Hart, had come from the left of the Democratic Party. Mondale nevertheless held the line on sustaining US defense spending and keeping overseas military bases. But he promised to scrap the MX nuclear missiles that Carter had approved and also to cancel the stealth bomber.

Most worrying to Brzezinski was Mondale's support for a superpower nuclear freeze. In 1983, Reagan had thrown the cat among the nuclear pigeons by coming out with his Strategic Defense Initiative (SDI), generally known as "Star Wars." Reagan said that SDI would end the specter of nuclear Armageddon. Critics said that the new era of space-based missile defense would dangerously upend both sides' nuclear calculations. Britain's foreign secretary, Geoffrey Howe, likened Star Wars to a "new Maginot Line of the 21st century," the infamous French Second World War defense that Hitler's Panzer divisions had easily skirted.[55] Mondale described Star Wars' promise of ending the nuclear specter as "a great hoax."

After Mondale came out in favor of a nuclear freeze at the 1984 Democratic National Convention, Brzezinski said, "We never had a major party before advocating a hoax as foreign policy. I think the nuclear freeze is a hoax." He added, "Yet we're committed to it because of an activist wing of the party." He risked little with his jibes against Mondale. He thought that the Democrats had succumbed to "naive escapism."[56] Either way, Mondale never got close to Reagan in the polls. Reagan's landslide was the second-heaviest Electoral College victory since 1820, even greater than Nixon's victory over McGovern in 1972. Mondale carried just one state, his native Minnesota, and then only by a hairsbreadth.

Brzezinski annoyed a far wider group of Democrats with his endorsement of George H. W. Bush in 1988. Though few had much inkling at the time, it was the last US presidential election of the Cold War. It is perhaps fitting that it was also the first time that Brzezinski and Kissinger appeared on the same platform. The two great rivals and Brent Scowcroft, Ford's national security advisor, were announced as cochairs of Bush's foreign policy task force on September 12, 1988.[57] The news went down very badly with Brzezinski's former colleagues, most of all Madeleine Albright. She was the campaign foreign policy coordinator for Michael Dukakis, the Democratic nominee. Brzezinski and Albright, who had risen fast in the Democratic foreign policy world and ran her own version of a Georgetown salon from her home in its West Village, fell out over his switch of loyalties. He did not even give Albright advance warning.

At the same time, neither she nor Dukakis approached Brzezinski to ask him to advise their campaign. "I was suspicious that Zbig had been promised a big job with Bush," she later said.[58] At the time, she downplayed it. Either way, there was not much contest between the foreign policy credentials of the two candidates. Bush had been US envoy to China, director of the CIA, and vice president for eight years. Dukakis was the governor of Massachusetts. As a Greek American he had an encyclopedic knowledge of the Turkish-Greek dispute. But he had not once in his life set foot in Great Britain, France, or West Germany, America's closest allies.

Dukakis could never shake off a lingering prejudice that he did not pass the macho test. Efforts to fix that only made things worse. At what was one of the most unintentionally funny photo ops in modern presidential campaigns, Dukakis scheduled a big event at an M1 Abrams tank factory in Michigan (candidates were banned from campaigning on military bases). The journalists assembled on the bleachers outside the hangar dissolved into laughter when Dukakis emerged in an outsized helmet at the helm of a large tank. As one observer quipped, it looked as though an accountant was heading into battle. Brzezinski was unsparing about why he did not think Dukakis was fit to be commander in chief: "Dukakis's comments during the course of the primary campaign revealed a combination of extensive ignorance and very strong anti-militarist impulses," he said. He pointed out that he had offered his support to the Bush campaign in July, when Dukakis had been polling seventeen points ahead.[59] That he cited to refute charges that he was angling for a job with Bush: "I've already done my national service," he said. Dukakis retorted that Brzezinski had been a "lousy national security advisor with an ego as big as a house."[60]

As part of his negotiations with the Bush campaign, Brzezinski sought reassurance that Bush would not target Carter. He wrote to Carter to explain his decision, pointing out that it was Bush, not Dukakis, who aligned better with Carter's foreign policy.[61] Bush would go ahead with the MX rollout. Dukakis wanted to kill the new line of ICBMs. He would also cut defense spending. Carter did not feature much in Bush's rhetoric. But Brzezinski was nevertheless accused of disloyalty. "It is inexplicable how someone could support George Bush when George Bush is running against Jimmy Carter's foreign policy," said David Aaron, Brzezinski's former NSC deputy.[62] "The man who considers himself the architect of that policy is libeling the very work he did in government." Brzezinski had little trouble justifying his endorsement in purely foreign policy terms. The USSR had become a much more flexible negotiator under the comparatively youthful Mikhail Gorbachev, who had taken the helm in 1985. But the Warsaw Pact was still intact, and its massive conventional-weapons advantage in Europe was unchanged. Europe's nuclear playing field was now roughly level since Reagan had deployed the Pershing II and cruise missiles in the early 1980s, the process begun by Carter. But now was not the time for America to cash in Dukakis's implied peace dividend, said Brzezinski.

The part that came least naturally to him was defending Bush's choice of Dan Quayle, an Indiana senator, as his running mate. Quayle was a notorious butcher of the English language. A former professor of Quayle's said that if you looked into his eyes you could see straight to the back of his head. Even at its most mangled, however, his language was possible to decipher. "The Holocaust was an obscene period in our nation's history," he once said. "I mean in this century's history. But we all lived in this century. I didn't live in this century." Brzezinski would have agreed with his first ten words: "We are on an irreversible trend toward democracy and freedom—but that could change."[63]

On being pressed, Brzezinski grudgingly conceded that Quayle would be "marginally" better as commander in chief than Dukakis. "I would prefer Bush sitting across from Gorbachev," he said.[64] If forced, however, he would also pick Quayle over Dukakis. It was a measure of Brzezinski's hardened reputation that it was Kissinger, rather than he, who stirred conservative discomfort when Bush unveiled his big endorsers. Republican voters still recalled Reagan's late-1970s vow not to hire Kissinger if he became president. "They can be really turned off if they think Bush would revive Kissinger," Paul Weyrich, the hard-line cofounder of the Heritage Foundation, told the *Washington Times*.[65]

"Brzezinski has been far more sound on major foreign policy questions than has been Kissinger." Their announcement partly drowned out the resignation of Fred Malek as deputy chair of the Republican National Committee. It had been revealed that in 1971, on Nixon's orders, he had investigated the loyalties of the staff of the Bureau of Labor Statistics. Nixon had been convinced that the BLS was run by a "Jewish cabal."[66]

Brzezinski's record of picking winners was upheld in 1988. Bush won forty states and 426 Electoral College votes, making it yet another Republican landslide, though slightly less crushing than in 1972 and 1984. Brzezinski's relationship with Bush stayed close. Bush wrote handwritten replies to Brzezinski's periodic memos, often extending to two or three pages. They spoke frequently, though Brzezinski was never offered a big job. The only one Bush suggested was US ambassador to Japan.[67] That would have taken him and the family too far away. Besides, to Brzezinski it would have felt like a demotion. A couple of developments helped nudge him back into the Democratic fold. After a few months of silence, Albright reached out to Brzezinski to try to rekindle their friendship. She approached him through their mutual friend Charles Gati at the Johns Hopkins School of Advanced International Studies (SAIS).

A few years earlier, Brzezinski wrote recommendation letters for both Gati and Albright for the same Eastern European teaching position at Georgetown University's School of Foreign Service. Albright had narrowly won the job. Brzezinski and Albright's social circles, which included Gati and his wife, Toby, another former Brzezinski doctoral student, were too overlapping for the two to remain estranged for long. Brzezinski told Gati that he would be waiting for Albright's call. The Gatis were among Brzezinski's closest Washington friends. The only comparably close non-Washington ones were Sam Huntington and Bill Odom. On the Gatis' living room mantelpiece is a framed picture of them standing with Brzezinski. He inscribed it "To my true friends—in the 'European' sense of the term." That was meant as a jibe at Washington, where friendship is infamously pragmatic. Brzezinski had many enemies. With the fleeting exception of Albright, his network of loyal friends stayed intact.

He relished his cameo moments in presidential campaigns. But they were a relatively minor call on his time compared to his unceasing machinations behind the Iron Curtain. His grasp of Kremlinology had always been deeper than his feel for US politics. The peaceful collapse of the USSR and the West's

Cold War victory helped consummate his rehabilitation among Democrats. It could hardly have been otherwise: 1989 brought the crystallization of his life's work. For the better part of three decades, Brzezinski had been predicting the demise of the USSR. As the 1980s wore on, his forecasts became more precise. Apart from one uncharacteristically pessimistic book, *Game Plan*, which he brought out in 1986, he had not altered his view of the Soviet system's waning shelf life. *Game Plan* was something of an aberration since it was premised on a long-term struggle with the Soviet Union for control of Eurasia. The slim volume attracted polite reviews but left only a faint mark on the Cold War debate.

Both before and after that book, Brzezinski stuck to strong forecasts of the USSR's coming collapse. In January 1988, he gave the prestigious Hugh Seton-Watson Memorial Lecture at London's Centre for Policy Studies. He predicted that 1988 could be another year of European upheaval on a par with the 1848 wave of national revolutions. He was a year early. "It is not an exaggeration to affirm that there are five countries now in Eastern Europe all of which are ripe for revolutionary explosion," he said. "Nor is it an exaggeration to say that this could happen in more than one simultaneously."[68] In March 1989, he published *The Grand Failure: The Birth and Death of Communism in the Twentieth Century*. It was an elegant obituary of a system that even Gorbachev's bold revisionism could not bring back to life. He started writing the book in mid-1987, the seventieth anniversary of the Bolshevik Revolution. He finished in mid-1988, when the effectiveness of Gorbachev's twin policies of *glasnost* (openness) and *perestroika* (restructuring) were still in the balance.

Brzezinski gave Gorbachev almost no chance of succeeding. "We are all witnesses to a truly monumental historic process: the waning and final agony of a doctrine that generated the world's most bloody and costly social experiment," he wrote. "The massive failure of that undertaking means that Communism, which dominated much of the 20th century, now appears unlikely to survive it." The very tools of Gorbachev's reform efforts were being used to dig the USSR's grave, he argued. *Perestroika* meant decentralization to the regions, which had ended Moscow's iron grip over the Soviet national republics. *Glasnost* gave the USSR's restive minorities an unprecedented outlet to express their frustrations. Both *glasnost* and *perestroika* were bringing the nationalist genie back to life. Only a highly improbable return to Stalinist terror could squeeze it back into the bottle. Whether he knew it or not, Gorbachev was dissolving the Russian Empire.[69]

Brzezinski's reputation for being prophetic—a term he spurned—owes as much to the fact that he correctly set out why the USSR would fail, not just that it would fail. Much as with the USSR as a whole, *perestroika's* Achilles' heel was the non-Russian nationalities. The mask of Marxist-Leninism could not forever obscure the Great Russian chauvinism beneath. The nature of the Soviet Union's unraveling also crowned Brzezinski's lifelong opposition to America's revisionist school of Sovietology. Jerry Hough saw Gorbachev as proof of his long-standing assertion that the Soviet system was inherently pluralist. Some of Brzezinski's colleagues had denied there was any longer such a thing as real nationalities left in the USSR. Marshall Shulman, in particular, had argued that there were Soviet citizens just as there were US citizens. In both cases their ancestral identities had been transcended by their new one. Students and colleagues alike adored the avuncular Shulman. In Brzezinski's view, though, he was guilty of the unpardonable sin of naiveté. "[Shulman's views] struck me as totally absurd and the reflection of an embarrassing lack of knowledge," he told the French historian Justin Vaïsse. "For centuries there had been Georgians, Ukrainians etc. He was a particular kind of Soviet expert, that is to say, in my view, without any real gut feeling for the Soviet Union." Brzezinski's favorite retort to the Shulman line was "So do they speak Soviet?"[70]

Publication of Brzezinski's death notice for communism and the dizzying pace of events in the year after its release settled half of his life's intellectual disputes in one go. His volume was slim, forensic, and merciless. The extirpation of religion from Soviet life had left nothing in its place, he said. During the 1980s, there had been a steady revival of the Russian Orthodox Church. The quiet return to piety was a sign of collapsing faith in the official creed. After Stalin's successor, Georgy Malenkov, died in 1987, he received a Christian burial.[71] Military deferment for the sons of senior officials in the USSR's "international proletariat war" in Afghanistan combined with the rising death toll of ordinary Soviet troops was another blow to the system's legitimacy.

Even the upsides to Gorbachev's reforms, such as new market freedoms, were backfiring politically. Rents in urban areas had been frozen since 1928, the year of Brzezinski's birth. The Russian working class was thus a short-term victim of Gorbachev's price liberalization. One barometer of the USSR's rapid ideological slippage was the April 1988 meeting hosted by the *World Marxist Review*, Moscow's residual organ for global ideological instruction.

The meeting, held in Prague, was chaired by Anatoly Dobrynin. After nearly a quarter of a century, he had finally quit his Washington ambassadorship and had been a foreign policy advisor to Gorbachev since 1986. In Brzezinski's words, the gathering's doctrinal debates were "tepid, listless, and largely formalistic."[72] He took a measure of satisfaction in the fact that it was his old chess partner who presided over the moribund ritual. Dobrynin did his best to give coherence to Gorbachev's neo-Leninism, but there was no orthodoxy to propagate.

Many reviewers treated Brzezinski's book as a minor gem. One admiring skeptic was Margaret Thatcher. She made a point of reading all of Brzezinski's books and essays; he made a habit of sending her copies. After each one she wrote him detailed letters from 10 Downing Street explaining where she did and did not agree. In 1985, she took exception to Brzezinski's generalizations about weak European defense in a *Foreign Affairs* essay entitled "The Future of Yalta." She complimented his overall take; "I am disappointed, however, that you appear to ignore Britain's contribution to Europe's defence, which is considerably more significant than the Franco-German cooperation to which you do refer."[73] About *The Grand Failure*, Thatcher could only agree with Brzezinski's declaration of communism's bankruptcy, but she thought he was too optimistic about how soon it would end. "I wonder how susceptible to change communism will prove to be," she added. Up until the collapse of the Berlin Wall, Thatcher's skepticism was the norm. Even Brzezinski thought the Communist system could limp on until the year 2000. Once the wall came down, fears of a brutal Soviet U-turn were quickly supplanted by euphoria that liberal democracy would universally prevail.

The debate quickly shifted to how soon Communist China would fold. To Brzezinski, such expectations were based on a giddy misreading of what was different about China. There could be no doubt that China suppressed minorities within its borders—in Xinjiang, Tibet, Inner Mongolia, and elsewhere. But the Han-dominated nation-state could not be compared to the USSR's thinly veiled Russian Empire. Russians made up barely half of the USSR's population; ethnic Chinese accounted for more than 90 percent of China's. Beijing therefore suffered from no comparable Achilles' heel. Moreover, Deng Xiaoping, with whom Brzezinski had retained a close relationship, was a maestro of thoughtfully sequenced reform.

Deng had first liberalized the rural sector from state control, then created free-trade zones in pockets of China. *Glasnost* did not feature in Deng's vocabulary. In contrast to Gorbachev, who was throwing radical new policies against the wall in the hope that one of them would stick, China had unshackled its economy gradually, after study. Deng's approach was inkblot; successful reforms would spread to other parts of the country. "The reform of Chinese communism is probably fated to be successful," Brzezinski wrote in *The Grand Failure*.[74] "In the course of the next several decades, a more modern and more powerful China will likely become a major political and economic player on the world scene." China's global rise would be driven by the "emerging state-sponsored commercial class." The USSR would fall apart. Red China would adapt and survive.

Poland played a starring role in the Soviet endgame. In February 1989, Jaruzelski sat down with Solidarity leaders at Poland's seminal Round Table Talks. Knowing that Gorbachev could not bail him out of Poland's almost $40 billion in Western debt, he had little choice but to make political concessions at home. That was the only way he could win Western relief. Poland's simmering crisis had culminated in a tenacious wave of strikes the previous year. Like a coach on the sidelines, Brzezinski offered a constant stream of advice to Solidarity during the two months of negotiations with Jaruzelski. He was in Warsaw for five days at the conclusion of the talks in spring 1989. While there, he wandered into a festival-like atmosphere at Solidarity's election headquarters. The building teemed with potential voters. At the nearby Polish United Workers' Party election HQ he found "two biologically retarded types" sitting alone. Where are all the voters? he asked. "Out in the street," one replied.[75]

Solidarity invited Brzezinski to address a rally; it felt more like a rock concert. People mobbed him, asking for his autograph. The Communist rally that Brzezinski planned to attend later the same day was canceled; he was the only person to show up. Contrary to his firebrand reputation and the one-way direction of the popular tide, Brzezinski advised Solidarity's leaders not to back Jaruzelski into a corner. They should be practical and nonrevolutionary in their demands, he said. Though the two sides could not know it at the time, they were discussing the terms on which communism would be buried. After the talks wrapped up in early April, Wałęsa flew to Rome for an audience with the pope. John Paul II was keeping as close an eye on the Polish situation as Brzezinski was.

On paper, what the two sides agreed to sounded modest. Parliamentary elections would be held in June. All the seats in Poland's new Senate would be openly contested. Just a third of the more powerful lower-house Sejm would be up for grabs. The results shocked everyone. Solidarity took 99 of the 100 Senate seats (the other went to an independent) and swept all 35 percent of Sejm seats that it was allowed to contest. Jaruzelski had originally planned a Communist-led coalition in which Solidarity would be given a few token ministries. The Polish voters' emphatic verdict in the country's first real election since the 1930s made that plan impossible.

Brzezinski was in Warsaw to watch the results. He was as swept away in the euphoria as the victors. After another two months of wrangling, Jaruzelski caved in to Solidarity's demand that it be allowed to form a government. He made sure to get Gorbachev's approval first. On August 24, the Solidarity advisor and Catholic intellectual Tadeusz Mazowiecki became prime minister. Though Jaruzelski was now Poland's president, the Communist dam had broken. Solidarity called it the "Your president, our prime minister" arrangement. Jaruzelski, whom history would assess more positively than anyone could have imagined a few years earlier, became a latent collaborator in Poland's peaceful revolution. He stepped down without fuss a year later. "We are dealing here with an epochal event. . . . For once, words like 'watershed' and 'turning point' are no overstatement," Brzezinski told the *New York Times* in late August 1989.

Three weeks later, Leszek Balcerowicz, Poland's first post-Communist finance minister, turned up at Brzezinski's home in McLean. Over lunch and serial cups of coffee, he was given a crash course by Brzezinski and Jan Nowak on how to woo the IMF.[76] Polish inflation was running at 30 percent a month. Without Western help, the Polish economy would soon collapse. To qualify for Western aid, Warsaw would need to convince its creditors that there would also be an economic revolution. On the advice of the Harvard economist Jeffrey Sachs, Balcerowicz had drawn up a "shock therapy" plan that would almost overnight end price control and shift Poland to a market economy. Brzezinski impressed on President Bush, Treasury Secretary Nicholas Brady, and legislators on Capitol Hill the urgency of coming to Poland's aid.

Sachs described Brzezinski as a "real gentleman" for his advocacy in Bush's White House and with other G7 governments.[77] Brzezinski also tutored Balcerowicz in his English-language presentation. Balcerowicz had been reading the Polish underground translations of Brzezinski's writings for years. "To me Brzezinski was a legend," he said.[78] Now he was Balcerowicz's coach and advisor. Their efforts paid off. The IMF stamp of approval was a green light to Poland and its creditors. In the coming years, the Paris and London clubs (of official and private credits) would forgive roughly half of Poland's national debt. Balcerowicz became "Poland's Ludwig Erhard" (West Germany's postwar finance minister who was credited with its economic miracle). The "Balcerowicz plan" was its template. Poland became the star performer of the post-Soviet bloc.

Three weeks later, Brzezinski joined a small delegation of Americans to Moscow, led by his old sparring partner Charles Gati. The party included scholars such as William Griffith, Angela Stent, and Michael Mandelbaum. Among the journalists was Strobe Talbott. It was the first time in fifteen years that the figure dubbed by Moscow as the "notorious Brzezinski" had set foot in the USSR; Carter had repeatedly turned down Brzezinski's request to go there on his behalf. The delegation arrived at the Soviet capital's airport amid the surreal turmoil of Gorbachev's revolution. They were struck by how broken down everything seemed, starting with Moscow's dust-filled airport. They were put up at a Soviet Pioneer camp outside Moscow. The floors were dirty, the air reeked, and the showerhead barely dripped water. Next to Brzezinski's room was a small closet "masquerading as a toilet."[79]

Brzezinski was so upset with the facilities that a couple of days later he moved to Spaso House, the US ambassador's residence. There he wallowed in the bathtub and inhaled the scent of freshly washed linen. At a dinner with US correspondents that evening, his former aide Rick Inderfurth (now with ABC News) presented him with an impressively lifelike mask of Brezhnev.[80] Brzezinski donned the mask before he reentered the embassy. Once the Soviet guard at the residential gate had grasped whose face was behind it, he couldn't stop laughing. A photo of Brzezinski's meeting with Alexander Yakovlev, who had been Soviet ambassador to Canada and was now the head of Communist Party propaganda, made the front page of *Pravda* the next day.[81] While in Canada, Yakovlev had asked Tadeusz Brzeziński why his son was such "an anti-Soviet hawk." He is still young, Tadeusz had replied.[82] Brzezinski turned sixty in 1988. Either way, it was clear to the US delegation that Moscow's polluted air felt freer.

Though the USSR was still Communist run, its recently established Congress of People's Deputies was dominated by a diverse cast of opposition figures, among them Andrei Sakharov, the Nobel Peace Prize–winning dissident. Nobody had a firm grasp on where or whether Gorbachev would draw the line on reforms. In addition to allowing Poland to form a Solidarity government, a few days earlier, he had engineered the replacement of East Germany's Erich Honecker, the Soviet Bloc's last hard-line Stalinist. In June, on the pretext of budget cuts, Hungary's government had lifted all border restrictions with Austria. East Germans had since been streaming to Hungary in tens of thousands and from there into Austria and West Germany. Meanwhile, the bedraggled Soviet army had completed its pullout from Afghanistan. A few days earlier, Gorbachev's foreign minister, Eduard Shevardnadze, had called the Soviet invasion "an illegal and immoral" act.[83] Yet there were still 380,000 Soviet troops stationed in East Germany. Given the pace of events, nothing could be ruled out—including a coup against Gorbachev.

Brzezinski was invited to address the Diplomatic Academy of the Ministry of Foreign Affairs. Until a few months earlier, the academy had been off limits to foreigners. No other American figure could quite match the ogre-like role that Brzezinski played in the Soviet imagination. To the American party's surprise, every inch of the amphitheater-shaped lecture hall was occupied. It was built for a seated audience of 150. That evening's count was 500. Behind Brzezinski loomed a huge illuminated white bust of Lenin. The audience included a large section of KGB officers and members of the Communist Party's Central Committee. Along the dimly lit avocado-colored walls to the inner sanctum were pictures of Lenin and Gorbachev—but tellingly, no portrait of any Soviet leader in between. Gorbachev had said that nothing good had happened in the USSR since 1921, when Lenin had launched his New Economic Policy. (Stalin abandoned it the year Brzezinski was born, in 1928; Gorbachev was born in 1931.) That span included the wasted "era of stagnation" under Brezhnev. Yet Gorbachev still clung to Lenin. He would spend long stretches at one of his dachas on the Caspian Sea poring over the Bolshevik leader's works for inspiration on what he should do. Vladislav M. Zubok, a leading scholar of that era, described Gorbachev as the "last true Leninist believer." The Soviet leader's faith in the salvaging potential of his neo-Leninist reforms, he said, was "genuine and heartfelt."[84]

Amid the outpouring of nationalist fervor in the USSR and its satellites, Gorbachev's stubborn loyalty to Lenin served as a fallback orthodoxy of sorts. In his speech, Brzezinski bulldozed straight through it. He spelled out the steps the USSR would need to take to achieve Gorbachev's dream of a "common European home"—a vision that triggered a muscle-memory hostility in the Bush administration. Figures such as Scowcroft and his deputy, Bob Gates, saw Gorbachev's rhetoric as an age-old ruse to separate America from Western Europe. Bush's skepticism struck a widely noticed contrast to Reagan, who had shared Thatcher's view of Gorbachev as a man with whom they could do business. To the audience's surprise, Brzezinski chose to take Gorbachev's vision at face value. He described the idea of a common European home as a noble appeal to universal ideals. He then laid out the transformation such a vision would require: Moscow would have to embrace multiparty democracy at home and permit it in all the Warsaw Pact countries; the USSR should permit the reunification of Germany, move to a market economy, and create a loose confederation of Soviet republics. The time had come for Moscow to take the leap to genuine democracy and friendship with the West. Brzezinski's hosts, in other words, should liquidate their system with deliberate haste.

Other than the clicking of cameras and Brzezinski's voice, the room was silent throughout his speech. The audience remained still. To Russian eyes and ears, here was a Pole stamping on the embers of Marxist-Leninism. When he finished, the audience leapt to its feet in boisterous applause. To many of the Americans present, it was the moment the Cold War was over. No one, least of all Gorbachev, who had a visceral aversion to violence—a quality that Reagan sensed in him before most others—had the stomach to put Humpty Dumpty together again. That was the diplomatic piece of Brzezinski's message.

At a private meeting afterwards with senior Party officials and Soviet diplomats, Brzezinski shredded their last ideological comfort blanket. "I am struck by the preoccupation with Lenin," he told them.[85] "I am not saying that he was not an interesting man. But to keep referring to him, not only in the search for legitimacy, but as a guide to policy, is absurd. You make yourselves prisoners of the past." Stalin, he insisted, had been a natural outgrowth of Lenin. It was Lenin who had founded the gulag and killed thousands of people for belonging to the wrong class. You could not reject one without also rejecting the other. To cope with today's problems, the country must renounce the last vestiges of Leninism. At the end, Brzezinski's demoralized Soviet interlocutors quietly shuffled out of the room. Some of them had tried to defend the founding icon of their revolution. Others fell silent. They had neither the energy nor the self-belief to match Brzezinski's merciless onslaught. After reading the transcript of Brzezinski's exchanges, Jimmy Carter wrote of his pride in his former national security advisor's analysis. But, he added, "You might have given [Gorbachev] more credit."[86]

The next day, Brzezinski took an overnight train to Smolensk. The US ambassador, Jack Matlock, Jr., went with him. From the station they drove to the site of the Polish mass graves in Katyn. Brzezinski was twelve when he heard about the cold-blooded execution of thousands of Polish officers in that forested corner of western Russia. The Soviets said it was Hitler's doing. In his diary on that wintry Canadian night, Brzezinski had pinpointed the Soviets as the true culprits. As the USSR was by then allied with the West, Stalin's line went unchallenged in London and Washington. Since history is written by the victors, the Soviet version was still intact. At the site's entrance they saw a large black granite monument with the inscription "In memory of the Polish officers murdered by the Nazis in 1941."

At one of the graves away from the monument, Brzezinski laid down a basket of flowers with a large sheet of paper saying "For the victims of Stalin and the NKVD." He signed his name underneath. That day was also the first time the Soviets had permitted Polish relatives of the dead to visit the site in a large group. Above the word *Nazis* on the monument, one of them had scrawled a sign saying "NKVD." All of it was recorded by Soviet camera crews and broadcast on the evening news in Moscow and nationwide.[87] A moved Brzezinski avoided mentioning Lenin in his interviews. "Russians and Poles, tortured to death, lie here," he told the BBC. "It seems very important to me that the truth should be spoken about what took place, for only with the truth can the new Soviet leadership distance itself from the crimes of Stalin and the NKVD."[88]

Two weeks after they returned home, the Berlin Wall fell. The sudden opening of the Iron Curtain's most infamous symbol was in fact an accident. An East German border guard either misheard or simply ignored an instruction to open Checkpoint Charlie to a specific party as an order to open the gate to everyone. A rapid surge of East Berliners into the West made it impossible to rectify his error. The resulting orgy of historic vandalism, as crowds dismantled the wall with shovels and pickaxes, instantly became the worldwide symbol of a dying system. Brzezinski described the Soviet Bloc's unraveling as a journey that had begun in Gdańsk in 1980 and ended in Berlin in 1989.

The American political scientist Francis Fukuyama wrote that it was "hard to imagine an individual more vindicated by the actual course of historical events" than Brzezinski.[89] In a congratulatory telegram to Brzezinski after reading his account in *Foreign Affairs* of the Soviet Bloc's dissolution, Richard Nixon wrote, "It also demonstrates your skills as a prophet since you have been predicting such developments long before others saw them coming."[90] Even long-standing critics acknowledged that Brzezinski had been right about the USSR's innate weakness and likely demise. In a *Time* article entitled "Zbigniew

Brzezinski: Vindication of a Hard-Liner" that came out in mid-December 1989, Strobe Talbott gave Brzezinski his due in an interview. Brzezinski took some pleasure in the fact that it was Talbott who composed that headline. The two became belated friends. "You've always been a strong critic of the Soviets," said Talbott, "yet just in the past month you have been given a standing ovation at the Diplomatic Academy in Moscow, you've been respectfully interviewed in *Pravda* and even given prime-time coverage on Soviet television. What has it been like for you personally?" Brzezinski said, "Well, I wouldn't be human if I didn't confess to a certain amount of ego gratification." Everything that Brzezinski had been forecasting for decades—often in a minority of one—had come to pass with remarkably little violence. In 1989, Brzezinski's theory of peaceful bridge building stood redeemed.

One of Brzezinski's more improbable friendships was with Richard Nixon. The disgraced ex-president had not forgotten Brzezinski's invitation to the state dinner for Deng Xiaoping in 1979. It had been his first step towards rehabilitation since his iniquitous exit almost five years before. It was also the start of a long correspondence between the two. Their readings of global events were strikingly alike, though Brzezinski did not hesitate to complain when he felt that Nixon had been unfair to Carter. The increasingly settled stereotype of Carter was that his presidency had been a weak, confusing interlude between the waning era of Nixon-Ford détente and the new era of Reaganite Cold War decisiveness. Those condensed accounts annoyed Brzezinski. In his view, the sidelining of Carter was the product of expertly induced amnesia by the Reagan PR machine. Even Nixon fell prey to it.

Taking issue with one such piece, Brzezinski complained that Nixon had attributed the MX decision to Reagan. Not only was that inaccurate—MX had been initiated by Carter; "I rammed the initiative through the NSC myself"—it also overlooked the fact that Reagan had then cut the MX deployment in half, to a hundred missiles. Moreover, the Soviets had not achieved nuclear parity with the US when Carter was president, as Nixon claimed, but as a direct result of concessions that Nixon had made in the SALT I deal in 1972. "Historical accuracy requires some acknowledgement that it was under President Carter that defense spending for the first time started to go up during peace time, and that important decisions regarding the MX, the RDF, and a 3 percent per annum increased NATO defense spending were taken," he added.[91] Nixon conceded that he stood corrected.

Their correspondence led to regular weekday lunches in New York and dinners at their respective homes in New Jersey and Virginia. At a dinner that Brzezinski hosted for Nixon in McLean in 1988, the hosts' ignorance about what they had in their own wine cellar floored the ex-president.[92] Brzezinski emerged with the last remaining bottle of a case they had been given years earlier. Seeing the label, Muska airily remarked that she had used the other eleven bottles for cooking. It turned out to be 1961 Château Cheval Blanc, one of Saint-Émilion's finest, that retailed for hundreds of dollars or more a bottle. All of it had been drowned in venison stew. "It was the Bordeaux of the century," Nixon wrote a few days later. "But what impressed me the most was your family. Mrs. Z, your two sons and your daughter were the key players in making the evening one we will always remember—not the usual official 'Washington dinner' but as an intimate family gathering."[93]

Nixon double underlined his point about the wine by throwing an "Honoring Brzezinski" dinner at his home in Saddle River, New Jersey, the following year. Among the guests were the financier Felix Rohatyn, AIG chairman Maurice "Hank" Greenberg, and CNN anchor Bernard Shaw. Brzezinski's main recollection of the dinner, though, was the 1961 Château Lafite-Rothschild that Nixon had dug out for Brzezinski. "I must admit that I felt that one or two of the guests did not know what they were sipping," Brzezinski wrote with the judgmentalism of a recent convert.[94] Nixon took a bottle of the same wine to his next dinner with the Brzezinskis in Virginia.

Other than Carter, Bush, and Thatcher, no Western leader read Brzezinski's output quite as avidly as Nixon. Some of their affinity doubtless sprang from being fellow victims of unpopularity, though Brzezinski's early-1980s reputational nadir had come nowhere close to Nixon's lifelong disgrace. They also shared a take on Reagan as being hopelessly devoid of strategic direction. Some of it reflected their mutual bias towards a White House–centered foreign policy. By contrast, the principals who gathered at the daily 7:00 a.m. breakfast led by Shultz and Weinberger (and later Frank Carlucci) made most of the meaty foreign policy decisions without troubling the president. On the rare occasions when Reagan's lieutenants disagreed, they took the conflict to the Oval Office. Reagan's foreign policy management was as laissez-faire as his economics.

On one big issue, however, Reagan knew his own mind and ignored the contrary advice of almost everyone around him: he trusted Gorbachev. History looks kindly on Reagan's leap of faith in the USSR's last leader. Brzezinski and Nixon shared the skeptical consensus on Gorbachev. Each was more preoccupied with the probable failure of Gorbachev's reforms than with his moral sincerity. On the short life expectancy of Gorbachev's reforms, their doubts proved to be right; on Gorbachev's character, Reagan was vindicated.

Perhaps their most enduring meeting of minds was on the need to sustain good US relations with China no matter what. Brzezinski went to some lengths to maintain his chemistry with Deng Xiaoping. At Deng's invitation, the Brzezinski family spent three weeks in China in the summer of 1981, their first long family trip since Brzezinski had left office. At Brzezinski's request, they were given a guided tour of the route of Mao Zedong's legendary 1930s Long March. Being treated like VIPs in China's hinterlands was a remarkable experience for the Brzezinski adolescents. Over dinner with Deng in Beijing after their tour, China's leader complained about Republican rhetoric in favor of the Taiwanese government. "You are very precise about the use of words— you are in the Marxist-Leninist and Chinese tradition," Brzezinski told Deng. "But the American tradition is not to pay attention to words. We tend to throw out words like garbage."[95]

Brzezinski's commitment to the US-China relationship was put to a severe test when Deng ordered tanks to open fire on Tiananmen Square protestors on June 4, 1989. It was a bitter twist of fate that the cold-blooded slaughter of several hundred or more Chinese students took place on the same day that Poland held its history-altering first free election. It was even odder that China's mass antiregime protests coincided with Gorbachev's presence in Beijing, the first visit to China by a Soviet leader in decades. "My father thinks that Gorbachev is an idiot," one of Deng Xiaoping's sons told an American journalist.[96] Brzezinski often characterized Gorbachev's rule as "all glasnost and no perestroika"; Deng's, meanwhile, was "all perestroika and no glasnost." The pope was so taken by Brzezinski's clever phrasing that he asked if he could plagiarize it.[97]

Ten days after the Tiananmen bloodbath, Brzezinski wrote a letter to Deng and copied President Bush.[98] Bush said that Brzezinski's message fit in with what he was trying to do.[99] Brzezinski also recommended that Bush use Nixon as an unofficial message-carrier to China. To Deng, Brzezinski wrote, "Let me express the hope that forces interested in undermining the relationship will not gain the upper hand, and that young Americans and young Chinese will not again be separated by political barriers. I write this in the same spirit in which I came to Beijing and with which I was privileged to welcome you to my house."[100] A week later, Bush called Brzezinski and "warbled enthu-siastically" about his letter to Deng.[101] They strategized on how Bush might strike a balance "between the needed moral condemnation and the impera-tive of keeping our options open." Bush took the advice to deploy Nixon, who visited China in late 1989. The former president was treated like royalty. He came back with a seven-page memo on how Bush should handle US-China relations.

In Nixon's view, which Brzezinski shared, China's human rights abuses in Tiananmen Square were nowhere near as bad as they had been in 1971, dur-ing Nixon's opening to China, or in 1979, when Carter had normalized rela-tions. That observation was factually correct. Yet it is impossible to imagine Brzezinski reacting with equanimity had even a tenth the number of Poles or other Eastern Europeans been gunned down by Communist troops. No coun-try more than China illustrates the degree to which Brzezinski treated human rights as a selective tool rather than a universal standard.

The same applied to Bush. In spite of publicly suspending contact with China after Tiananmen Square, his national security advisor, Brent Scow-croft, took a highly secret fence-mending trip there a few weeks later. He went again in December 1989, this time publicly. On his second visit, Scowcroft was caught on camera raising a convivial glass to his Chinese hosts by can-dlelight.[102] The outrage over Bush's double game carried through to the 1992 election. To great effect, Democratic candidate Bill Clinton was widely quoted as having attacked Bush for indulging "the butchers of Beijing." Scowcroft's of-ficial and incognito trips had been the spark. "[They] make a mockery of our profession of concern for human rights and the stated ideals of our democratic system," said George Mitchell, a Democratic senator from Maine.[103]

Sometime between the end of the Cold War in 1989 and the dissolution of the Soviet Union in 1991, Brzezinski misplaced his geopolitical cheerful-ness. Until that triumphal denouement, his mind was dominated by the Cold War. His view was that the Soviet model was doomed and that the US sys-tem was inherently superior. Kissinger was the pessimist; Brzezinski was very much the optimist. Once the bipolar postwar order collapsed, Brzezinski's at-tention shifted to problems at home.

He was also becoming disenchanted with Bush. Much of that arose from Bush's reluctance to offer serious help to the post-Soviet republics, Ukraine in particular. Brzezinski felt that Bush was ambivalent about the unraveling of the USSR and instinctively preferred order to uncertainty. That created in

Bush a bias towards Moscow's perspective. Bush also felt personally indebted to Gorbachev, who had shocked everyone, including the Kremlin, by accommodating Bush's foreign policy agenda. The Soviet leader had allowed a reunified Germany to be absorbed into NATO; he had put up minimal resistance to the independence of the three Baltic republics; he had withdrawn Soviet forces from Eastern Europe without a fuss; and he was acquiescent in Bush's US-led war to liberate Kuwait.

Saddam Hussein's Iraqi forces invaded Kuwait on August 2, 1990. In keeping with Bush's wishes, the United Nations authorized the use of force to liberate Kuwait. Partly because of Bush's good chemistry with Gorbachev—and that of James Baker, his secretary of state, with his Soviet counterpart, Eduard Shevardnadze—the USSR did not impose its veto. The US-dominated Desert Storm coalition was assembled in Saudi Arabia over the coming months. To the surprise of many, Brzezinski was critical of Bush's countdown to war. In congressional testimonies and op-eds, he cautioned against an attack on Iraq. He also criticized the Bush administration's shifting rationale. "Not oil, not Kuwait—but Iraq's nuclear program has become the latest excuse for moving toward war," he told the Senate.[104] Whatever the justification, a war in Iraq could radicalize the Middle East and trigger a bloodbath, he warned. Nothing of the sort happened. With the aid of vastly superior weapons technology, the US-led coalition chased Iraq's military out of Kuwait in barely seventy-two hours. The ensuing "turkey shoot" of what remained of Saddam's supposed crack units in southern Iraq crystallized America's new status as the world's unchallenged colossus. Its so-called Vietnam syndrome was exorcised. A unipolar world was already in sight. Moscow was putting no obstacles in its way.

A grateful Bush visited Moscow for a summit in late July 1991. He and his wife, Barbara, stayed with Mikhail and Raisa Gorbachev in their dacha outside Moscow. Bush agreed with Gorbachev that it was not in either of their interests for the Soviet Union to collapse. He promised the Soviet leader that he would deliver that message to the Ukrainians on the next leg of his trip. The moment was historically critical. One by one, former Soviet republics were threatening to break off from the USSR or had already left. Moscow could withstand the departure of Georgia, Kazakhstan, and the Baltics. Ukraine, however, was indispensable to the survival of the Soviet state. Bush took the USSR's side. In a speech in Kiev to Ukraine's Supreme Soviet, its parliament, Bush warned the restive Ukrainians against any rash plans to break away. He pointedly refused to meet Ukraine's independence leaders on his stopover in Kiev. "Americans will not support those who seek independence in order to replace a far-off tyranny with a local despotism," Bush told the Ukrainian assembly. "They will not aid those who support a suicidal nationalism based on ethnic hatred."[105]

The columnist William Safire dubbed Bush's address the "'chicken Kiev' speech."[106] A protestor dressed as a chicken followed Bush throughout his 1992 presidential campaign. Some of Bush's fears over Ukraine were motivated by the breakup of Yugoslavia, which was starting to take an ominous turn. The term *ethnic cleansing* entered the lexicon. Gorbachev convinced Bush that Yugoslavia's descent into warring ethnic parts was a small foretaste of what could happen with the USSR. But Bush spectacularly misjudged the mood in Ukraine. Before the end of the month, Ukraine's assembly voted overwhelmingly for independence. The vote was ratified by a 92 percent "yes" vote in a national referendum in December 1991. The newly independent republic of Georgia issued a stunningly undiplomatic riposte to Bush's "chicken Kiev" address: the Tblisi communique accused Bush of betraying America's ideals.[107]

Yet Bush had been right to fear for Gorbachev's future. Three weeks after Bush's meeting with Gorbachev, the Red Army launched a coup. Gorbachev was on vacation in the Crimea. Within forty-eight hours, the last twitch of the old system fell apart. The coup's ringleaders were arrested. Soviet soldiers refused to fire on the sea of demonstrators led by Boris Yeltsin, Gorbachev's chief rival and president of the hitherto ornamental Russian Socialist Federative Soviet Republic. Three days after that, Ukraine voted for independence.

Because of their relationship, Brzezinski's public criticisms of Bush were relatively muted. Privately he was outraged by what he saw as Bush's bad misreading of the flowering of suppressed nations. "The West should no longer coddle a hesitant Gorbachev," he wrote in the *Washington Post* in August 1991, "(and President Bush would do well to stop speaking of 'the Soviet people'—a phrase from the odious past)." Misplaced notions of keeping the Soviet empire together would only set back the efforts of those such as Yeltsin who were fighting for Russian democracy, he argued. Washington should grasp that there was only one road to a democratic, nonimperial Russia: the dissolution of the USSR. "Western statesmen will now have to display the courage of commitment so vividly demonstrated by Boris Yeltsin," he concluded.[108] The Moscow coup precipitated Ukraine's rush to independence. That in turn set

the pace for Russia itself to quit the USSR. Collectively the former Soviet republics agreed to dissolve what was left of the union. On Christmas Day 1991,
Gorbachev was out of a job.

The following October, Brzezinski joined the effort to put George H. W.
Bush out of a job. His endorsement of Bill Clinton came three weeks before
the 1992 presidential election. "Four years ago I supported President Bush,"
he said. "I did so because I believed at the time—with the Cold War entering
its climactic phase—that the defining issue in the elections was foreign policy.
Today the defining issue is the renewal of America. . . . There is a yearning in
America for younger and dynamic leadership—and I believe that Governor
Clinton can provide it."[109] Clinton was grateful. He brandished Brzezinski's
endorsement in a speech to the Polish American Congress the next day.

Brzezinski again picked the right horse. With the help of Ross Perot's
third-party candidacy, Clinton comfortably won the Electoral College, though
he garnered far less than half of the popular vote. Following the bad blood of
1988, Brzezinski was now back in with the Democrats. But he saw a world
of problems awaiting Clinton. A few weeks before the election, he submitted
Out of Control: Global Turmoil on the Eve of the 21st Century, his first book of
the post–Cold War era, to his publishers. It was dedicated to Jimmy Carter,
a man whose name most Democrats, including Clinton, could hardly bring
themselves to utter. Brzezinski was one of the few who stuck by Carter's side
and defended his record. The former president loved *Out of Control*. "I read
every word, underlined passages, and have begun to plagiarize your ideas and
information," he wrote to Brzezinski.[110]

Brzezinski's latest book struck a discordant note amid the post–Cold War
triumphalism of the early 1990s. Though he did not mention Francis Fukuyama's best-selling *The End of History and the Last Man*, which had come out
earlier in 1992, Brzezinski's thesis was in some ways its counterpoint. Fukuyama believed that the world had reached an ideological end state with the
collapse of the USSR. The enemies of liberal democracy, he said, had failed.
Brzezinski did not necessarily disagree with Fukuyama's take, which was far
more nuanced than often presented. Indeed, the two had become friends and
colleagues.

In the late 1980s, Brzezinski had given up his weekly commute to New
York. To Muska's relief, he switched from Columbia to teaching at the Johns
Hopkins University School of Advanced International Studies (SAIS) in
Washington, DC. Fukuyama was a regular at the seminar-style "brown bag

lunches" that Brzezinski hosted at SAIS. Brzezinski agreed with Fukuyama that the Marxist-Leninist experiment was over, although not in China. But he warned that the specter of fascism in new guises was lurking. "This book is not a prediction but an urgent warning," he wrote. "History has not ended but has become compressed."[111]

Brzezinski's fear was that an arrogant and hedonistic West would squander its chances to build what Bush had dubbed "the new world order," something that he had not defined to anyone's satisfaction. Whenever Brzezinski sat down with the pope, their discussion would turn to the West's spiritual emptiness. They deplored the materialism, consumerism, and "permissive cornucopia" of Western societies. In that respect, Brzezinski was starting to sound like the aging George Kennan, who spent much of his last decades denouncing modern America's ugliness and philistinism. To some degree their cultural pessimism overlapped. In Kennan's case, however, the gloom extended to democracy itself, which he felt Americans were neither spiritually mature nor educated enough to handle.

Brzezinski never questioned the democratic system, but he was rapidly losing patience with American exceptionalism. In *Out of Control*, he warned that America might be too self-congratulatory and navel gazing to manage the global threats that he saw looming. He had never feared that communism would triumph. He always believed the Marxist God would fail. The threat of "global anarchy," on the other hand, was all too plausible. *Out of Control* was the plea of a Cassandra, the Trojan priestess who issued dire prophecies destined never to be believed. While Americans were napping, global politics would veer out of control. Russia continued to play a starring role in Brzezinski's thoughts.

His immediate dread was that the US would mess up the post-Soviet world's transition to democracy. Several years later, the term *Washington consensus* was coined to describe the tool kit that the United States prescribed for all economies at all times. Brzezinski thought that that one-size-fits-all approach would boomerang in Russia, which had no tradition of private property or entrepreneurialism to draw upon. The West seemed to be saying that there was only one way of doing things: the Western way. The flow of knowledge could go in only one direction. "The West considers itself to be inherently superior," he wrote. "Inherent in that attitude is the assumption that historical development is unilinear, and that imitation of the West is the only positive option open to others."[112]

The West's insistence on one-size-fits-all reform not only was tone deaf; it could backfire terribly. On the geopolitical front, the risks were visible to Brzezinski in 1992. A weakened and humiliated Russia would try to rebuild the empire it had lost. The key piece of Russia's lost domain was Ukraine. A thriving independent Ukraine could help bring Russia into the European orbit; an unstable Ukraine would kindle Russian revanchism. "If the socio-economic difficulties of the newly independent Ukraine become acute, the large Russian minority of some 10 million people (out of a total population of about 52 million), concentrated heavily in the key industrial regions of Kharkov [the Polish spelling of Kharkiv] and Donetsk, may become openly disaffected," he wrote. "That will then tempt the Kremlin to apply pressure on Ukraine, first to obtain for this minority a special status and then perhaps even to exploit its grievances as the leverage for destabilizing Ukrainian statehood. The makings of a serious collision are inherent in this situation."[113]

Early-1990s Washington was not receptive to such bromides. Those who had failed to anticipate the collapse of communism were now trumpeting the universal victory of American-style capitalism. Brzezinski's use of the word *fascism* was also out of kilter with the moment. In *Out of Control*, he warned that the "intensifying crisis of the Russian spirit" could lead it into virulent nationalism. That would be a particularly big risk if Boris Yeltsin's economic reforms failed. In 1992, the Russians were suffering from the equivalent of America's Great Depression, he said. If the market economy failed in Russia, democracy would soon crumble. The new fascism would not be as totalitarian as Nazism, or as racially obsessed. But it would pose a serious authoritarian danger to its neighbors.

"The reincarnation of the Fascist phoenix in Russia would not only repre-sent a supreme historical irony," he wrote. "With its potential for contagion . . . It would represent a catastrophically infectious failure of the democratic alterna-tive as the path to the future."[114] Such a Russia would also jeopardize America's sway over Eurasia, which remained the key to global supremacy. Specifically, a vengeful Russia could align with an autocratic China and a resentful Iran to challenge the American-led world. "To some extent, such a triple alliance would thus resurrect the old Sino-Soviet bloc, but with formal ideology replaced by a generalized rejection of the inequitable global status quo and with Beijing and Moscow reversing their previous hierarchical relationship."[115]

Out of Control's prescience was uncanny. As ever, though, Brzezinski's abstract style detracted from his message. If he had written with the poetic touch of a Kennan or the anecdotal liveliness of a Kissinger, he would have won many more readers. His nonacademic books were short and to the point. Their meaning was clear. What they possessed in clarity, however, they lacked in style. In this respect, as in so many others, he was Kissinger's opposite. Brzezinski's book sales were respectable, but they never approached Kissinger's celebrity heights. The latter wrote with the general reading public in mind; Brzezinski's prime audience was policy wonks. In 1994, Kissinger brought out his best-selling book *Diplomacy*. It was widely and justly pronounced a tour de force. At 912 pages, it was also quadruple the length of Brzezinski's typical book. The sweeping history, which takes the reader from the birth of the nation-state in the 1648 Peace of Westphalia right up to the end of the Cold War, falters only when Kissinger's own role starts to crop up near the end. At that point, his history lapses into special pleading. Until then it is magisterial. *Foreign Affairs* captured that disjointedness well. The headline on its review of *Diplomacy* was "The World According to Henry: From Metternich to Me."[116] Brzezinski's name is not mentioned in the book.

In 1997, Brzezinski converted his CSIS office into a temporary courtroom. As part of the think tank's deal to retain Brzezinski, he was given a suite of rooms in its new 1800 K Street headquarters in downtown Washington. He arranged his office to look like a mini–State Department. Trudy's reception area was at the entrance with a sitting room to the left. There was another side room, a larger conference room, then Brzezinski's ambassadorial office. In the reception area was the archetypal power wall of photographs of Brzezinski with an array of world leaders and his face on framed magazine covers and newspaper front pages.

Trudy's daily telephone messages give a flavor of the degree to which Brzezinski was scheduled to within an inch of his life. Visiting foreign government heads, especially from the former Soviet republics, wanted to drop by. Global and US media telephoned daily to solicit his views on everything from the war in Chechnya to the health of the pope. Muska would also leave regular updates. "She has gone out to pick strawberries" was a typical missive.[117] On more than one occasion, the Chinese ambassador's secretary called to wriggle her boss out of a tennis date with Brzezinski. The Chinese diplomat had not been on a court for decades, but he wanted Brzezinski to know that he was a strong swimmer. "I think he's really worried about this; it's at least the 4th time we've gotten this message," Trudy wrote.

In April 1997, Brzezinski set aside his meeting room for the "prosecuto-rial hearing" of Ryszard Kukliński, the Polish double agent who had fled with his family to the US in 1981. Brzezinski had kept in occasional touch with Kukliński. The Polish colonel's American exile had not been a happy one. Both of his sons had died in the early 1990s: one in a drunken boating tragedy off the Florida Keys, the other after being hit by a car in a Florida parking lot. In 1984, he was convicted in absentia as a traitor to Poland and sentenced to death. Lech Wałęsa, who was elected Poland's first post-Communist presi-dent in 1990, converted Kukliński's capital sentence into a twenty-five-year jail term. Brzezinski could not persuade Wałęsa to overturn the original Com-munist verdict. Poland's president was still nervous about the loyalty of Po-land's armed forces, which had not been fully reformed by Solidarity. Wałęsa said that he would consider commuting Kukliński's sentence at a later date. To both Brzezinski and Kukliński, Wałęsa's response missed the point. A com-mutation would imply that Kukliński had been guilty; Kukliński's argument was that he had been loyally serving Poland. "Was it an authentic Polish state or an imposed satellite?" Brzezinski asked the Polish American Congress in a 1992 speech. "Was opposition to it therefore legitimate or illegitimate?"[118] His question was rhetorical. In reality, as Brzezinski told every visiting Pol-ish leader and made sure to repeat on his visits to Warsaw, Kukliński was a national hero.

Brzezinski's campaign to exonerate Kukliński was an offshoot of his sup-port for Poland's application to join NATO. At first, Clinton was uninterested in NATO expansion. The young president seemed to inherit some of Bush's indifference to the fate of the former Soviet republics, including Ukraine. Cri-ses in Somalia, Haiti, Rwanda, and particularly the former Yugoslavia dom-inated the first two years of Clinton's first term. Given the heaviness of his domestic agenda, including his health care reform, led by the first lady, Hil-lary Clinton, the wobbly foundations of many post-Communist governments were easy to overlook. Like Bush, Clinton feared that what was happening in Bosnia could be a portent of the former USSR's future.

Two weeks after Clinton was elected, Brzezinski added his name to a let-ter from Ford, Thatcher, Reagan, and others, warning of a bloodbath in Bos-nia. "We are now witnessing in Bosnia a replay of one of the darkest eras of modern history: the invasion of one sovereign nation by another," the letter said.[119] The Clinton administration was nowhere near being of one mind on Bosnia. For most of Clinton's first two years, he hesitated to act in the face of pincer Serbian and Croatian nationalist assaults on secular Bosnia. As Sarajevo came under siege and evidence mounted of brutal ethnic cleansings of Muslims across the landlocked nation, Clinton's inaction became harder to justify.

The president initially sided with the doves. In a strange replay of the splits inside the Carter administration, Warren Christopher, Clinton's secretary of state, appointed Cyrus Vance, his former boss, to colead the Geneva-based Bosnian peace talks with Britain's David Owen, who had been James Callaghan's foreign secretary. In Brzezinski's mind, the resulting Vance-Owen ratification of Bosnian Serbs' battlefield gains merely rewarded the aggressors. Without the threat of NATO force, the West could not hope to wrest concessions from Serbia's virulent nationalists, let alone achieve a fair settlement, he said. "Hogwash," said Vance in his by now familiar word of choice about Brzezinski's criticisms.[120]

With Sarajevo under constant bombardment and in danger of toppling at any moment, Brzezinski stepped up his pressure on Clinton. In a public letter in July 1993 cosigned by Frank Carlucci, a former defense secretary; and Lane Kirkland, a former head of the AFL-CIO, they urged Clinton to lift the West's arms embargo on Bosnia. Clinton should also use US airpower to target Bosnian Serbian positions around Sarajevo. "The US failure to act decisively has already gravely damaged the political and moral credibility of American leadership," they wrote.[121] Clinton replied to Brzezinski a few days later, saying that he shared Brzezinski's view that the situation in Bosnia "has become dire." He was looking for new ways to bring America's "considerable energy and resources to bear."[122]

The Clinton administration's echoes of the Carter debates also came with a twist. Tony Lake, Clinton's national security advisor and formerly a senior advisor to Vance, was deeply sympathetic to Brzezinski's stance on Bosnia. Clinton eventually appointed Richard Holbrooke as his Bosnia envoy. Holbrooke, who had served Vance with fierce loyalty in the Carter years, but with a dash of Brzezinski-style freelancing, brought the war to an end in his marathon and heroic peace talks at a US Air Force base near Dayton, Ohio. Crucially, Holbrooke had US airpower at his disposal. That upended Serbia's calculations. Vance and Christopher lost their argument that diplomatic carrots alone would be enough to bring around the Serbs. The war claimed 200,000 Bosnian lives, roughly a tenth of the country's population. Holbrooke's 1995 Dayton Accords made up for the time lost in Geneva. In spite of their combustible history, Holbrooke did not hesitate to accept Brzezinski's offer of help. "Dear Dick, I enjoyed our lunch and really do strongly applaud your efforts," Brzezinski wrote to Holbrooke in mid-1995.[123]

Brzezinski also helped to win Clinton and Lake around to the goal of NATO expansion. Poland was at the front of Brzezinski's mind. In 1994, Jerzy Koźmiński, a former aide to Prime Minister Balcerowicz, became Poland's ambassador to Washington. His relationship with Brzezinski grew so close that Brzezinski would lightheartedly refer to Koźmiński as his third son.[124] In the five years between Koźmiński's arrival and Poland's 1999 accession to NATO (along with Hungary and the Czech Republic), they met for strategy planning breakfasts at the Polish residence once or twice a week. The other participant was Jan Nowak, who, though now in his eighties, was as activist as ever. Nowak was paranoid that Poland might be sold out again, as it had been by Churchill and Roosevelt at Yalta in 1945. They dubbed him "AWACS" after the early-warning system. Brzezinski, whose Polish vocabulary came across to Koźmiński as belonging to a quainter era, would mimic Nowak's catastrophism. The slightest rumor would trigger a panicked phone call from Nowak. "Catastroph! Catastroph!" he would cry.[125]

Nowak's great fear was that Strobe Talbott, who was Clinton's State Department envoy to Russia, would somehow contrive to bury Poland's dreams in the greater good of helping Russia's Yeltsin. Nowak also suspected that was Christopher's instinct. The NATO campaign received a decisive boost in 1997 when Christopher was replaced as secretary of state by Madeleine Albright, who had been Clinton's ambassador to the United Nations during his first term. When NATO leaders agreed in mid-1997 to the historic expansion at a summit in Madrid, Brzezinski was the first person Albright telephoned with the news. "He earned the right to be the first to know," she said.[126] Clinton also appreciated Brzezinski's support. His next hurdle was Senate ratification. "It is comforting to know that I have your support on an issue of such great importance," he wrote to Brzezinski.[127]

One of the last obstacles to the Senate's ratification of Poland's NATO accession was Kukliński's guilty verdict. Among others in the national security establishment, people at the CIA were outraged by Kukliński's continuing pariah status in Poland. Kukliński's former CIA handler, David Forden, who spoke fluent Polish, publicly highlighted the injustice to Kukliński.[128] A number of Republicans picked up Forden's message. Unless Poland expunged Kukliński's sentence, the Senate might fail to muster the required two-thirds majority for it to join NATO. Overturning a foreign court's verdict is not easy.

Partly over fears for his personal safety, Kukliński would not agree to risk a retrial in Poland. Without a retrial nothing could happen, said the Poles. Brzezinski and Koźmiński then had a lightbulb moment: Polish judges should hear Kukliński's appeal at Brzezinski's CSIS offices in Washington, DC. They could issue their verdict back in Poland. One evening in DC, Brzezinski sold the idea to Leszek Miller, Poland's minister of interior and administration. They toasted it with cognac.[129]

The election in 1995 of a new Polish president, Aleksander Kwaśniewski, lifted hopes for that plan. His worldview was much less psychologically challenging than that of the narrowly defeated Wałęsa. More than once, the pope complained to Brzezinski that Wałęsa was a "blabbermouth."[130] The Solidarity hero was not a good listener. Kwaśniewski, a youngish Social Democrat and former academic, was eager to clear whatever obstacles blocked Poland's path to NATO. The new Polish president's relationship with Brzezinski could have started on a very different footing. In the early 1990s, Brzezinski had come under growing pressure from his friends in Warsaw to run against Wałęsa for the presidency. That would have meant taking on Kwaśniewski as well. A leading Polish newspaper had given Brzezinski a 12 percent advantage in the polls in spite of the fact that he lived in DC and had expressed no interest in running for office anywhere.

Brzezinski's response to the question that Polish journalists often threw at him was Shermanesque: "I am a Polish American, but my loyalty is to America." He told friends that any such gamble would risk making a fool of himself. Having not lived in Poland since he was ten, he would be branded a carpetbagger. Moreover, it would cast retrospective doubt on his loyalty to the United States. Though Poland treated Brzezinski as an icon whenever he visited, he never seriously entertained the idea.

Kukliński's trial was a secretive affair. Two Polish judges traveled incognito to Washington. Koźmiński collected them at Dulles International Airport. In Koźmiński's correspondence with the Polish government, the procurators were referred to as "travelers"; Kukliński was "our friend"; and Brzezinski was "the professor."[131] There was still a significant Polish faction that saw Kukliński as a traitor. The hearing lasted for three days and included a ringing testimony from Brzezinski. He sat at one head of the table, Ambassador Koźmiński at the other. The two judges faced Kukliński and his lawyer in the middle. The conclusion looked favorable from the moment the judges met Kukliński. The Poles clicked their heels and called him "colonel."

It took several more months for the judges to uphold Kukliński's claim that he had acted from the patriotic motive "of higher necessity." That elegant formula enabled them to expunge a verdict that had been technically accurate under Polish law at the time. It was a neat solution that removed a block to Senate ratification of Poland's NATO accession a year later. Kukliński was now free to visit his homeland, where he was awarded honorary citizenship by several cities. He died of a stroke in Tampa, Florida, in 2004 at seventy-three. He was given full CIA honors at his funeral in Fort Myers. Brzezinski described Kukliński as Poland's "first officer in NATO." He was buried in Warsaw along with the remains of one of his sons in the Powązki Military Cemetery's row of honor.[132]

The twentieth century's closing years were an emotional peak in Brzezinski's life. He had been raised in the unshakable belief that Poland was a civilizational part of the West. Partitioned, betrayed, and sidelined over the centuries, Poland was the West's eternal orphan. Finally now, as he turned seventy, the country of his birth was coming into the light. The age of Yalta had ended. At the White House signing ceremony for the Senate ratification deal in 1998, Brzezinski's was the first name that Clinton called out in thanks. Poland had entered NATO and was on track to join the European Union. Albright said that Poland's membership would have been "unthinkable without Brzezinski."[133] His only regret was that his parents were not alive to see it. Leonia had passed away in her sleep in 1985 at the age of eighty-seven. Tadeusz had lived long enough to see the collapse of communism. He died of pneumonia in a Polish nursing home in Montreal in January 1990, two months after the fall of the Berlin Wall. The exiled Habsburg gentleman was ninety-three. Leonia and Tadeusz were laid to rest beside Adam in the Polish cemetery they had created a few miles down the road from the Canadian farm they had so loved.

11

Autumnal Battles

B rzezinski was in Beijing having dinner with former German chancellor Helmut Kohl when he learned of the September 11, 2001, terrorist attacks. The ordeal of getting home was his first taste of 9/11's aftereffects. Because of the closure of US airspace, it took him a full week. During that time, his daughter, Mika, was continuously at Ground Zero reporting for CBS on the collapse of the Twin Towers and its aftermath. Seeing the tragedy close up marked her for life. That included a lingering mistrust of cloudless blue skies.[1] The other jolt to Brzezinski was his first serious exposure to the dark side of the internet. Sites cropped up almost overnight demonizing him as the "Godfather of Al Qaeda."[2] They drew a straight line from the start of America's support for the mujahideen in Carter's last year in office to the current global terrorist menace. The 9/11 shock triggered a national soul-searching on many levels. Did the Muslim world resent the US because of its freedoms, or was Islamist terrorism a distinct menace linked to specific grievances? Who should take the blame for failing to act on the CIA's warnings about a terrorist plot? Was the US government too cozy with Saudi Arabia's Wahhabi-backed ruling family? Had America been too supportive of the Afghan jihad in the 1980s? The national trauma unleashed a wave of retrospective finger-pointing.

Brzezinski was unfazed by the claim that he had somehow given birth to Al Qaeda. Osama bin Laden had formed the terrorist group in 1988, seven years after Carter left office. Moreover, the price for supporting Afghan jihadi groups was far outweighed by the damage they had done to America's Cold War adversary, he argued.[3] The United States' chief failing had been to leave an unstable Afghanistan to its own devices after the Soviet withdrawal in 1989. It had become a haven for Al Qaeda and other Islamist groups. The US was paying the price for having washed its hands of Afghanistan. His defense was entirely logical within his larger Cold War perspective. He omitted to mention that both he and Carter had put a starkly religious framing on the Afghan jihad against the godless Soviets. Reagan had gone even further, hailing the mujahideen commanders as "valiant and courageous freedom fighters."

But the debate that really mattered was what America should do now. A few days after the 9/11 attacks, Brzezinski sent a fax to Donald Rumsfeld, George W. Bush's secretary of defense, advising him to get in and out of Afghanistan quickly and be wary of the risks of a Soviet-style quagmire. He should use the Special Forces to take out Al Qaeda and the Taliban leadership if necessary but avoid putting regular troops on the ground. In an op-ed for the *Wall Street Journal* on September 25, Brzezinski warned against depicting the struggle in civilizational terms. The object, he said, should be to isolate extremists from their host populations, not to tar whole religions and societies with guilt. "The current struggle is not against 'Islamic terrorism' just as the struggle against the IRA is not against 'Christian terrorism.'" He was clear, however, that removing Saddam Hussein "would not only be justified but required" should Iraq's government be found to have colluded with Al Qaeda.[4]

In spite of backing US military action in theory, Brzezinski was already swimming against the tide. A couple of rhetorical tropes coined by the Bush administration irritated him in particular. The first was to present the battle against Al Qaeda as a "global war on terror" (GWOT). It was logically nonsensical to go to war against a tool of warfare, he argued. It would be like the British in 1940 saying that they were waging war on the *Blitzkrieg* rather than against Nazi Germany. Such "quasi-theological formulations," he said, were blinding the Bush administration to obvious steps it should take. Chief among those, in his view, was settling the Arab-Israeli dispute and counteracting broader Middle Eastern resentment about America's role in the region. "It is as if terrorism is suspended in outer space as an abstract phenomenon, with ruthless terrorists acting under some Satanic inspiration unrelated to any specific motivation."[5]

A year later, he was still making the same point. "We need to ask who is the enemy, and the enemies are terrorists. But not in an abstract, theologically defined fashion, people, to quote again our highest spokesmen, 'people who hate things, whereas we love things,'" he said in a speech to a Washington conference. "Not to mention the fact that of course terrorists hate freedom. I think they do hate. But believe me, I don't think they sit there abstractly hating freedom."[6] His advice had no impact on the White House, although it was picked up by Bush's critics.

To Brzezinski's consternation, Bush's war on terror was taken as carte blanche by unsavory regimes around the world to brand any group they disliked as terrorists. Russia linked rebel forces in Chechnya to Al Qaeda. China did the same for separatists in its northwestern province of Xinjiang. By pretending not to notice such opportunism, Bush was unwittingly boosting terrorism, Brzezinski said. Such license was being abused by America's friends as well. For example, India's Hindu nationalist–led government cracked down on its Muslim-majority province of Kashmir; Turkey stepped up operations against minority Kurdish groups; and Israel's prime minister, Ariel Sharon, linked the latest Palestinian intifada to Al Qaeda.

Unsurprisingly, Washington's indulgence of Russia was Brzezinski's biggest complaint. Even before 9/11, he had been alarmed by Clinton and Bush's eagerness to find reasons to like its new leader, Vladimir Putin. An ailing and frequently inebriated Boris Yeltsin had handpicked Putin as his successor in 2000. Their deal was struck a year after Yeltsin had made the recently appointed KGB (FSB) head Russia's prime minister. Yeltsin had also put Putin in charge of the war in Chechnya. Putin wrapped it up in short order by razing its capital, Grozny, making it by far the bloodiest conflict in the former USSR. To Brzezinski's horror, Clinton said that Russia's aim had been "to liberate Grozny."

Far from being the first democratic transfer of power in a thousand years of Russian history, as Clinton officials were claiming, the terms of the Yeltsin-Putin handover had been a de facto coup, Brzezinski said.[7] In exchange for inheriting the presidency, Putin would let Yeltsin retire in peace. In March 2000, Putin easily won election for the Russian presidency. "The people of Russia once again demonstrated their intense commitment to democracy," said Clinton in his statement congratulating Putin.[8] Brzezinski thought that Washington's stamp of approval on Russia's increasingly illiberal turn was a serious blunder. Clinton had made a choice to hear no evil and see no evil.

Throughout the 1990s, Washington had been bankrolling Moscow with billions of dollars in aid. Yet the truth was plain to anyone who looked. Putin was boasting that his personal hero was his grandfather, who had been both a cook and a security person for Lenin and Stalin.[9] Brzezinski repeatedly defined Putin and those around him as the product of the Soviet era. George W. Bush's approach to Russia was a continuation of Clinton's. Three months before 9/11, Bush had met Putin for the first time at a bilateral summit in Slovenia. "I looked the man in the eye," Bush had said in the press conference afterwards. "I found him to be very straightforward and trustworthy. . . . I was able to get a sense of his soul."[10] Most people, including Brzezinski, thought that Bush had been played by Putin. During the summit, the Russian leader wore a crucifix dangling conspicuously from his neck.

Bush's second post-9/11 rhetorical blunder, in Brzezinski's view, was to declare that "either you are with us or you are against us." Vladimir Lenin had coined that phrase about Russia's Social Democrats in 1917. Two years into the war on terror, Brzezinski counted ninety-nine instances in which either Bush or his senior officials had repeated those words. "I strongly suspect the person who uses that phrase doesn't know its historical or intellectual origins," he said. Its effect was to fuel the impression of a superpower "intensified by a fear that periodically verges on panic that is in itself blind."[11] He did not comment in detail on the USA PATRIOT Act that Congress had passed by huge margins in both houses six weeks after 9/11. The law gave US law enforcement sweeping powers to investigate and detain suspected terrorists.

As the war in Afghanistan progressed, Brzezinski feared that pictures of suspects in orange jumpsuits held without trial at Guantánamo Bay, Cuba, would replace Ground Zero as America's image in the world. From New Delhi to Paris, foreigners had declared "We are all Americans now" after the Twin Towers came down. Bush was squandering that goodwill in a flurry of missteps. The United States now faced a troubling paradox. "American power worldwide is at its historic zenith. American global political standing is at its nadir," Brzezinski said in his October 2003 speech. "Maybe the explanation is that we are rich, and we are, and that we are powerful, and we certainly are. But if anyone thinks that this is the full explanation [for 9/11] I think he or she is taking the easy way out."[12]

Bush's people were not fans of Brzezinski. He was particularly disliked by the team around Dick Cheney, Bush's vice president. Cheney had amassed a foreign policy staff of thirty, almost as large as Brzezinski's NSC. By contrast, Mondale, as vice president, had made do with just one advisor. The size of

Cheney's team raised fears of a shadow administration that was really making the decisions. Brzezinski was not alone in his disdain for Bush's jingoistic chorus. More vexing to the Bush-Cheney team were Brent Scowcroft's public criticisms. The retired general had been Bush senior's national security advisor and was a close Bush family friend. Any doubts that Scowcroft expressed about the actions of "Bush 43" were, rightly or wrongly, presumed to be have been approved by "Bush 41." On top of questions about Cheney's grip over the White House, there was parallel chatter about the Bush family psychodrama. Scowcroft was its lightning rod. "Like father unlike son," wrote William Safire. "Poppy Bush Finally Gives Junior a Spanking" was the title of a Maureen Dowd op-ed.[13]

Both Scowcroft and Brzezinski were appalled by Bush's January 2002 State of the Union address in which he proclaimed that there was an "axis of evil" consisting of Iraq, Iran, North Korea, and their terrorist allies. "We have known freedom's price," he said. "We have shown freedom's power. And in this great conflict, my fellow Americans, we will see freedom's victory." Few doubted that Iraq was first among equals in Bush's axis. In early summer 2002, Bush officials started to make the case for "regime change" in Iraq. With the help of US Special Forces, the Taliban had easily been overthrown by Afghan rebel groups, led by the Northern Alliance. The remnants of Al Qaeda, including Osama bin Laden, had been allowed to slip through the net in the cave complex of Tora Bora. Bush was nevertheless switching from what critics later called America's "war of necessity" in Afghanistan to its "war of choice" in Iraq.

At that point, few leading Democratic or big media voices made serious efforts to push back against an Iraq invasion. One prominent exception was Ted Kennedy. Another was former vice president Al Gore. Here and there, other Democratic progressives were also raising doubts. Among them was a young Illinois legislator named Barack Obama, who said he opposed "dumb wars," not all wars. Only in retrospect would his misgivings win national attention. The pipes of war were getting louder. On the national stage, Scowcroft and Brzezinski were the coming invasion's most visible skeptics.

In mid-August 2002, Scowcroft published a *Wall Street Journal* op-ed with the headline "Don't Attack Saddam."[14] There was no evidence of any link between Saddam and Al Qaeda, nor of Iraqi weapons of mass destruction, he wrote. "An attack on Iraq at this time would seriously jeopardize, if not destroy, the global counterterrorist campaign we have undertaken." Two days later, Brzezinski fired a similar broadside in the *Washington Post*. The headline was "If We Must Fight . . . " His message was that the United States had every right to remove Saddam if terrorist links or WMD could be proved. In their absence, an invasion would be reckless. "War is too serious a business and too unpredictable in its dynamic consequences—especially in a highly flammable region—to be undertaken because of a personal peeve, demagogically articulated fears or vague factual assertions," he wrote.[15]

In the countdown to the Iraq War and beyond, the two former national security advisors could almost finish each other's sentences. Scowcroft and Brzezinski had become the Jack Lemmon and Walter Matthau of US foreign policy, in the memorable description of one Washington insider; the unlikely pair were America's leading "dissidents."[16] Kissinger was for the most part a Bush apologist. If he had any doubts about the looming invasion, he failed to air them in public. In late 2002, Bush appointed Kissinger to chair the National Commission on Terrorist Attacks upon the United States, more commonly known as the 9/11 Commission, which had been set up by Congress to investigate US intelligence failures. Under its conflict-of-interest rules, members of the ten-strong panel were required to disclose any clients that had paid them more than $5,000 in the previous year. Kissinger tried to negotiate a separate deal in which he could avoid revealing his client list, which was widely presumed to include Saudi and other Gulf figures. Breaking confidentiality agreements, he said, could destroy his consulting business. As an appointee of the executive branch, he should be excused from the transparency required of the other nine congressionally appointed members. Democrats and families of the 9/11 victims refused to drop their demand that Kissinger abide by the same rules. Two weeks after his appointment, Kissinger withdrew his name.[17]

The countdown to war also put a strain on the Brzezinskis. Ian Brzezinski, the only Republican in the family, was a senior official in the Bush administration. As deputy assistant secretary of defense for Europe and NATO policy, he was working in the Pentagon for Rumsfeld and his deputy, Paul Wolfowitz. Dealing with European governments, particularly France and Germany, both of which were opposed to the Iraq War, was often a thankless task. German chancellor Gerhard Schröder became persona non grata in Bush circles. Rumsfeld praised the "new Europe," which was typified by gung ho Poland, and dismissed "old Europe," by which he meant Germany and France. The political scientist Robert Kagan would later typecast Europeans as being from pacific Venus and Americans as coming from warlike Mars. Such was the

ill-feeling towards old Europe that the priceless epithet "cheese-eating surrender monkeys" was lifted from a 1990s episode of *The Simpsons* and applied to
France. Other terms of abuse included "axis of weasels." On the eve of the war
in March 2003, two Republican legislators got all House of Representatives
cafeterias to rename French fries "freedom fries."

Continental Europeans were easy to stereotype. It was far harder to pass
off Brzezinski and Scowcroft as free-riding peaceniks. The *Weekly Standard*,
which was effectively the in-house organ for neoconservatives, branded
Brzezinski "demented." He suffered from *"algoreitis simplex*, the mysterious
brain infection so named for its most obvious manifestation: the eagerness
of its victims to indulge in ludicrously exaggerated condemnations of George
W. Bush's war on terrorism."[18] The strength of resentment against Brzezinski
inside the Pentagon put Ian Brzezinski into an awkward position. Wolfowitz,
in particular, felt targeted by Ian's father. The two had become friendly in the
1990s when Wolfowitz was dean of the Paul H. Nitze School of Advanced
International Studies, where Brzezinski was teaching. After Wolfowitz's marriage broke up, Brzezinski had tried to lift his morale by taking him to a movie
and dinner in Georgetown.[19] But such ties counted for little in the fetid climate of post-9/11 Washington. As a participant in the Project for the New
American Century, a neoconservative think tank set up during the Clinton
years, Wolfowitz had argued for "preemption" and "unilateralism." Those glorified impulses became key parts of the Bush Doctrine.

Wolfowitz's idea that America should unilaterally strike an enemy before
it posed a serious threat was tailor made for Iraq. Both Rumsfeld and Wolfowitz argued for a quick pivot to Iraq in the first NSC meeting after 9/11.
Wolfowitz became a bugbear of the Brzezinski parents. Ian had several full-
blown arguments with them about Iraq. Even Muska, who usually tried to
pour balm on heated discussions, was hard to placate. She said she would spit
on Wolfowitz's name.[20] Mark Brzezinski also got in on the act. A few months
after the invasion, he coauthored a piece in the *New York Times* attacking the
Bush administration's cavalier treatment of its new central European partners.[21] Poland had provided a brigade to the "coalition of the willing" in Iraq.
The Czechs and the Ukrainians supplied chemical warfare experts. No companies from those countries had won a bid to rebuild postwar Iraq, Mark
observed. All the big contracts were scooped up by Halliburton, Bechtel, and
other US contractors.

In defense of his own role and the Pentagon he served, Ian argued that no responsible US administration could ignore the risks of a nuclear, biological, or chemical warfare attack in the wake of the Twin Towers. On that key point, his father did not disagree. Brzezinski, Scowcroft, and Kissinger were invited to a briefing on Iraq's secret weapons program by General Colin Powell, the secretary of state. The meeting took place at the Pentagon in early February 2003, a couple of days before Powell delivered the same (instantly notorious) presentation to the United Nations. Rumsfeld and Condoleezza Rice, Bush's national security advisor, were there.

Brzezinski found Powell's evidence persuasive. After the speech, Brzezinski spoke up for Powell. "I thought he made a very impressive presentation," he told PBS's *NewsHour* that night. But in the following weeks, the Bush administration's refusal to give UN weapons inspectors more time to probe Powell's claims on the ground tilted Brzezinski against the war. "We are the number one power," he told CBS on March 10, nine days before the invasion. "We have to lead. But our leadership depends also on being viewed as legitimate. We have to mobilize people on behalf of shared principles. And this is where we have really fallen down."[22]

It did not take long after the invasion for Brzezinski to realize that the evidence Powell laid out had been cherry-picked and exaggerated. It was ultimately shown to have been false. Powell later conceded that Bush's decision to go to war had already been made, whether or not his PowerPoint presentation changed the minds of the three veto-wielding UN skeptics, France, China, and Russia. Moreover, a somewhat embarrassed Rice admitted to Powell that his speeches' claims had been inserted by Cheney's staff. Neither the State Department nor the CIA could back them up. Powell had allowed himself to be the credible face of an erroneous policy. Somewhere in the six weeks between the start of the invasion and Bush's "Mission accomplished" message from the deck of the USS *Abraham Lincoln*, Brzezinski's skepticism turned into righteous anger. The only proof he needed that Iraq lacked the nuclear, chemical, and bacteriological weapons that Powell claimed it had was America's easy military walkover. Saddam would surely have used some of his WMD had he possessed them.

In mid-July, four months after the invasion, Brzezinski appeared with Kissinger on Wolf Blitzer's CNN show to discuss the absence of such weapons. Brzezinski called for the removal of intelligence agency heads if the failure was indeed theirs or for senior Bush figures to resign if they had distorted the intelligence, as he suspected they had. Kissinger disagreed. "I don't think anyone should resign," he said. "We should analyze where the problem arose, but I don't think this was a central element in making the decision." He suggested that Saddam might perhaps have destroyed the weapons after the US invasion. Either way, Kissinger was fully on board. "I believe that, in essence, [Bush] was right, even if it now turns out that some of these weapons may have been destroyed," he said. Brzezinski's fury was barely controlled. "The United States stated, at the highest level, repeatedly, without any qualification whatsoever, that Iraq was armed with weapons of mass destruction," he said. "And that's why we went to war. This is what we said to the world. This is what we said to the American people. . . . It's clear that they weren't armed with these weapons. They didn't use them. We defeated their army in the field. We have control over their arsenals. We haven't found them. We're now maintaining that they may be hidden somewhere, *which is kind of comical, actually* [my italics]."[23]

In spite of that, Democratic leaders were still reluctant to question the basis for Bush's invasion. They were a long way from calling for a US withdrawal from Iraq. That would only begin in earnest three years later, on the eve of the 2006 midterm elections. The Democratic House minority leader, Nancy Pelosi, endorsed a timeline for a US troop withdrawal in October 2006. Brzezinski had called for that in 2004, though he had already implicitly done so in 2003, within weeks of the invasion. His frustration with the Democrats' caution manifested itself in the advice he gave John Kerry, the 2004 Democratic presidential nominee. With some reluctance, Brzezinski endorsed Kerry, though he felt no obligation to pick a Democrat. He had declined to endorse Al Gore in 2000 because of what he saw as Gore's appeasement of Russia. He did advise Arizona senator John McCain, who made Bush sweat in the Republican primaries. There, for the second and last time, Brzezinski found himself on the same team as Kissinger. "It is revealing that the two most distinguished creative minds in foreign policy—Henry Kissinger and Zbigniew Brzezinski—one who served Republicans, the other who served Democrats, are both supporting McCain," said Richard Burt, a former ambassador to West Germany who was on McCain's campaign team.[24]

After McCain's "straight talk express" ran into the ditch in the South Carolina primary—Bush trouncing him in one of the dirtiest campaigns in memory—the sparring partners went their separate ways. Kissinger endorsed Bush; Brzezinski sat on the sidelines. In 2000 he had also been annoyed that Gore was Clinton's main cheerleader for accommodating and financing

Yeltsin's Russia. Gore was also in the go-slow camp on NATO. In a Post-it note that Brzezinski stuck on a *Washington Post* article, "Gore Wins Russia's Endorsement," he wrote, "NATO—a formula for delay, disappointment, deceit."[25] Brzezinski's sole 2000 endorsement was for the reelection of Senator William Roth of Delaware. That Ian Brzezinski was serving on Roth's Senate staff was not unrelated. "While I have not taken a public position regarding the national elections, I do feel that Senator Roth's leadership in shaping a bipartisan foreign policy and especially his decisive role in NATO enlargement, make his re-election a matter of national importance," said Brzezinski.[26]

In 2004, nothing was more important to Brzezinski than Bush's defeat. The 9/11 attacks had turned the world upside down. One of its more ironic aftereffects was to make Brzezinski a lodestar to America's Left. Brzezinski's Darth Vader had morphed into Obi-Wan Kenobi. Former enemies, notably Harvard's Stanley Hoffmann, who had been bitingly critical of Brzezinski during the Carter years, ended their estrangement.[27] The two resumed their Harvard-days friendliness as if nothing had happened. As James Mann, author of *Rise of the Vulcans: The History of Bush's War Cabinet*, a seminal book on Bush's foreign policy team, pointed out, Brzezinski became an overnight hero to the Left. That made him an ogre on the right.

"The Democratic Party is beginning to sound like an echo chamber for Zbigniew Brzezinski," wrote Reuel Marc Gerecht in the *Weekly Standard* several years after the war began.[28] A *Wall Street Journal* article stated, "We get even Zbigniew Brzezinski, who spent his career fighting for the freedom of his native Poland, dismissing its prospects in Baghdad. What a disappointing spectacle."[29] Brzezinski's journey from liberal bugbear to hero was complete. In January 2004, he was the keynote speaker at the Center for American Progress's conference on US national security. The think tank, which had been set up by John Podesta, Clinton's last White House chief of staff, epitomized liberal Washington.

Brzezinski's disgust with Bush was so intense that he would have backed almost any Democratic opponent, possibly even a McGovern-like figure. But he liked Kerry. In May 2004, the prospective Democratic nominee invited Brzezinski to his sumptuous Washington residence on Georgetown's O Street for a briefing. Brzezinski entered via the back door to avoid the cameras.[30] Brzezinski found Kerry "quite refined, intellectually bright, and very well spoken." The candidate listened to Brzezinski's case for painting Bush as a reckless extremist who was harming America's interests around the world. Brzezinski suggested that Bush had been "lethargic before 9/11, missing during 9/11, and reckless after 9/11." Kerry liked that framing and wrote it down.

Over the coming months, however, Brzezinski felt let down by Kerry's reluctance to go for Bush's jugular. In July, he complained to Rand Beers, Kerry's foreign policy advisor, that Kerry was fuzzy whereas Bush had clarity. "In foreign affairs we are getting beat!" he wrote. "The Rs have made progress in defining JK as a waffler and they are ruthless in doing so." To Brzezinski's chagrin, Republicans were persuading some in the media, and even a handful of Democrats, that the intelligence agencies were to blame for the debacle over Iraq's missing WMDs. "This is music to Rep ears," Brzezinski wrote. In terms of electoral rhetoric, he said, Bush was miles ahead. "Compare the two: B's is clear, focused, and leaves a direct message. JK's is complex, and the listener has to ask, what was he telling me exactly[?]"[31]

Before one of the autumn 2004 presidential debates, Brzezinski sent Kerry a three-page memo suggesting attack lines designed "to rattle W." His summary was that Bush's Russia policy had been a "strategic failure," that he had "been divisive and destructive of trust" with Europe, that he had set the Middle East "on fire—hatred of America is massive," that he had abandoned the Israeli-Palestinian peace process, and that he had squandered post-9/11 global solidarity.[32] Kerry never quite lived up to Brzezinski's hopes. In spite of taking a softer approach than Brzezinski wanted, he held his own in the three debates. Bush was mocked for having retorted, "Well, actually, he forgot Poland," after Kerry said that only three countries—the United States, the United Kingdom, and Australia—had been part of the invading coalition.

"You forgot Poland" became a Bush-mockery trope for a few days. Poland had contributed two thousand soldiers. But Bush's riposte was prompted by the kind of argument Brzezinski did not want Kerry to make: that Bush should have assembled a larger "coalition of the willing." Kerry could not bring himself to declare the Iraq invasion a mistake. The 2004 election was the first time since Hubert Humphrey's 1968 campaign that Brzezinski picked the loser. He did so knowing that Kerry was the underdog.

Yet it could easily have gone the other way. Had sixty thousand people in Ohio voted differently, Kerry would have become president. With just 286 Electoral College votes, and 50.7 percent of the popular vote, Bush's victory was touch-and-go. "Bush was beatable," Brzezinski said a few weeks after the election. "Since 9/11, the Democratic leadership has been in disarray and essentially following the president's lead, with some of its top leaders actually acting as cheerleaders for the president's demagogically defined war."[33] The US electorate in its wisdom usually got it right, he said. In this case Americans had been frightened into making the wrong choice.

A fine autumn is often described as golden. In Brzezinski's case, that adjective would be too serene. His alleged waning years were a riot of New England colors. Brzezinski's seventies and eighties were marked by the kind of strenuous policy debates that would have exhausted many younger people. He kept fit and played tennis on most days well into his eighties. At one lunch party at his home in McLean, Brzezinski boasted that his doctor assured him that he had the tennis-playing physique of a forty-year-old. "He didn't tell you that you have the mental age of a fourteen-year-old?" Muska replied.[34]

The Brzezinski parents had good reason to feel happy about their progeny's careers. By accident more than design, their three children covered pretty much every Washington base: Ian was a Republican working for Bush; Mark was a Democrat who had served as a Europe specialist on Clinton's national security staff; and Mika was becoming a television superstar. Having jumped around various networks, including ABC, CBS, and MSNBC, in 2007 Mika found her permanent home as the cohost with Joe Scarborough and Willie Geist of *Morning Joe*. It was MSNBC's flagship political morning show, watched closely inside the Capital Beltway and by political junkies nationwide. It turned her into a Washington celebrity. Brzezinski would often joke that he was only the second-best-known person in his family. More than once when he had signed a restaurant bill, the server asked, "So are you Mika's dad?"

Brzezinski became a regular on *Morning Joe*. His appearances did not necessarily go smoothly. Scarborough, a lively anchor with an outsize personality, who had been a Republican congressman from Florida and remained a conservative, did not always hit it off with his cohost's father. In one viral encounter in late 2008, Brzezinski clashed with him over Israel. Scarborough asked why Brzezinski was not coming to Israel's defense after it was hit by rocket attacks from Hezbollah in Lebanon and by Hamas from the Gaza Strip. Brzezinski told Scarborough that he was asking the wrong question. "No, it's not the wrong question," said Scarborough. "You can't blame what is happening in Israel right now on the Bush administration." Yes, you can, Brzezinski replied. The breakdown, he said, was the direct result of Bush abandoning attempts to broker a settlement with the Palestinians. To Mika's visible discomfort, Brzezinski then scornfully interrupted Scarborough's account of Yasser Arafat's having walked away from Bill Clinton's attempted deal in 2000—Washington's last such stab at a settlement. "You know you have such a stunningly superficial knowledge of what went on that it's almost embarrassing to listen to you," Zbigniew told Scarborough. With Mika nervously darting glances at the camera, the producers tried to fade out by playing Stevie Wonder's "Superstition" at escalating volume. But Scarborough and Brzezinski could not stop going at each other. "It's helpful to know a little bit about this subject," Brzezinski said. "It's very exciting, Chief, that you know things that the rest of the international community doesn't know," Scarborough replied. With Mika now burying her face in her hands and periodically muttering, "Oh, no," her father replied, "If you're going to judge your knowledge by the collective standards of three hundred million people, then don't be surprised if you're embarrassed." Mika eventually managed to shift to the commercial break. In spite of that exchange, her father kept being invited back on.[35]

Brzezinski's father-son relationships were perhaps fated to be more complicated. Both sons were fiercely proud of their father and the Brzezinski name. But he could sometimes be harshly judgmental. As the youngest and a girl, Mika had somehow managed to make light of the rigid expectations that each of her older brothers felt, though her dad could be scornful with her. Brzezinski's argumentative style was to spare no one's feelings. His academic colleagues and the staff who reported to him in the White House were often surprised to find that their apparently worthless points surfaced in Brzezinski's speeches or lectures the next day. In oral arguments, he would test his interlocutor to destruction. "If you really wanted him to think calmly about what you were saying, you always had to put it on paper," said Bob Gates.[36] He took the same approach to his offspring, who did not have the luxury of writing concept papers in advance. His retorts could sometimes sting to the quick. In one instance, he told the teenage Mark that the eight bodies of US servicemen returned from the failed Iran rescue operation had more honor than what he was arguing. "He probably didn't realize it, but these lines stuck in your head for a long time," said Mark.[37]

In that regard, Brzezinski was far from being a typical American parent. Just as his students rarely got A's, his children were not brought up on praise. But he took a detailed interest in what they were doing. Both Ian and Mark felt the pull of Poland and Eastern Europe in general. Ian attended Williams College as an undergraduate and did his postgraduate studies at Harvard's

Kennedy School. In the early 1990s, he spent three years living in Ukraine as a military advisor to its fledgling government. Though Ian never learned Polish, he did pick up serviceable Ukrainian. He saw his father frequently during that stint.

Brzezinski was running a frenetic "track-two" US-Ukrainian advisory group. He led several delegations to Kyiv. On one such trip, he flew over with Henry Kissinger on the private plane of the American publishing billionaire Steve Forbes. On each trip, Brzezinski would hold talks with Ukrainian leaders. He developed close, almost mentoring, relationships with both Leonid Kuchma and Leonid Kravchuk. Their consecutive presidencies lasted from Ukraine's independence in 1991 to 2005. Both knew that Brzezinski was intensely lobbying the Clinton administration to shore up Ukraine's fragile independence. During the 1990s, Brzezinski's efforts on behalf of Ukraine came second only to his advocacy of Poland's NATO membership. Both causes were offshoots of his larger concern about the new threat of a revanchist Russia.

In a 1993 letter to Clinton, Brzezinski underlined his case that if Washington ignored Ukraine, the whole post–Cold War situation could unravel. "If Ukraine fails, Russia will have no choice but to again become an empire," he wrote.[38] He pulled out all the stops to bring Tony Lake, Clinton's national security advisor, on board. Whenever Russia is cited, "Ukraine should always be mentioned by name," Brzezinski advised him.[39] Lake needed little persuading. In 1994, Clinton and Yeltsin negotiated the so-called Budapest Memorandum. Ukraine agreed to give up its share of the former Soviet nuclear arsenal in exchange for Russia's recognition of its sovereignty. It is difficult to measure, yet hard to overstate, Brzezinski's efforts to keep Ukraine in officials' minds at a time when many around Clinton sympathized with Russia's concerns over its "near abroad." In practice, Brzezinski kept pointing out that "near abroad" was Moscow's code for its sphere of influence over Russia's former empire. He could draw on the support of a bipartisan group of senators including Biden, McCain, Roth, and Lugar.

The debate within the Clinton administration was between those such as Gore, Talbott, Christopher, and the Pentagon who wanted to massage Russia's pride and others, notably Lake, and to some degree Albright, who feared that overindulgence of Russia's sensitivities would only fuel its worst instincts. Clinton leaned both ways. There was no obvious right answer to the question of how to handle post-Soviet Russia. It is debatable whether Yeltsin would have acquiesced in NATO's expansion if Clinton had removed the kid gloves.

Yet in hindsight, the larger goal of bringing Russia into a broader European home evidently failed. The argument would pick up more heat in 2014 when Putin's Russia annexed Crimea. During the 1990s, Brzezinski was in the rare position of interpreting Ukraine to Washington and vice versa. In that regard, Ian's feedback was of particular interest to his father.

In early 1993, Brzezinski took the family on a trip to Kyiv. Ian met them at the airport. They were treated as celebrities.[40] On arrival, each Brzezinski was interviewed for Ukrainian newspapers. As part of their grand tour, government officials took the family to Kolkiev, a town near Lviv, where the authorities had discovered the 1880s graves of Brzezinski's paternal great-grandparents. In the period in which they lived there, parts of what later became modern-day Poland and Ukraine had belonged to the same province of the Austro-Hungarian Empire. At the end of World War I, Tadeusz had fought against the Ukrainians in Lviv. There were terrible massacres on both sides during World War II. In a letter to the mayor of Przemyśl, the original family home, Brzezinski awarded a $1,000 annual prize for good citizenship for students of the town gymnasium (high school). "Let me add my expressions of hope that the citizens of Przemysl will display the needed tolerance of their Ukrainian brethren," he wrote. "A democratic Poland cannot be built on the basis of religious or national prejudice towards others."[41]

Mark, who had studied at Dartmouth College in New Hampshire and graduated from the University of Virginia School of Law, was interested primarily in Poland. He won a Fulbright scholarship to spend time there in the 1990s to research his PhD dissertation on the history of Polish constitutionalism. Poland's first constitution dated back to the eve of his ancestral country's late-eighteenth-century partition by Russia, the Habsburgs, and Prussia. Whenever Jan Nowak visited Poland, he would check in on Mark. Nowak was like an uncle to the Brzezinski children. "We beam with pride when we hear Nowak rave about your Polish," his father wrote.[42]

Mark completed his PhD at Oxford University. His father said that attending Oxford would open up new intellectual horizons. But he cautioned Mark not to ape his hosts. "You should be careful to avoid the trap that many Americans fall into: that of mindlessly pretending to be English in order to emulate their sophistication and snobbery," he wrote. In the same epistle, he warned Mark against becoming too ambitious, which made people "unhappy, driven and one-dimensional." Oddly, he omitted himself from that category. Mark's Polish expertise paid off. In 2007, Polish president Lech Kaczyński decorated Mark with Poland's Officer's Cross "for outstanding contributions to the development of Polish-American relations."

Mark's father had long since been inundated with Polish honorary degrees, keys to cities, and various medals of freedom. They came with such frequency that Brzezinski asked Jerzy Koźmiński, the former ambassador to the US who was now running Warsaw's richly endowed Polish-American Freedom Foundation, to shield him from any more. Each time he was honored, Brzezinski had to cross the Atlantic and write another speech. He was a household name in Poland. A square in Kraków was named after him, as were streets in Warsaw and Lublin. On a visit to Gdańsk, Brzezinski and Koźmiński bumped into Jennifer Lopez in a hotel lounge. She was on a European tour. To Koźmiński's surprise, Lopez recognized Brzezinski and greeted him. "Who was that?" Brzezinski inquired after she had left.[43] On each visit, Brzezinski stayed at Warsaw's storied Bristol Hotel in the heart of the old city. After checking in, he would take a shower and immediately head out. His itineraries were minutely planned. Even in his eighties, he did not appear to suffer from jet lag.

Guests invited to the Brzezinskis' for lunch or dinner knew they had to prepare rigorously beforehand. After a shot of Polish vodka, they would sit down to a meal prepared by Muska and a single-table conversation moderated by Brzezinski. It would be a mix of senators, foreign leaders, ambassadors, and the occasional journalist. McCain, Lugar, Biden, Nunn, and John Warner of Virginia were his most frequent senatorial guests. The focus was mostly transatlantic; the meal's flavor usually rustic. The conversational focus was a mix of earnest Washington policy talk and émigré intellectual banter. Another regular was Aleksander Kwaśniewski, who had defeated Lech Wałęsa for the Polish presidency in 1995 and been reelected in 2000. He stepped down five years after that. At Brzezinski's suggestion, Kwaśniewski then took a part-time sinecure at Georgetown University, which offered a parachute to many a retiring foreign leader. Kwaśniewski had been grateful for Brzezinski's public validation of his controversial decision to send Polish troops to Iraq. Though Brzezinski disapproved of the war, he also emphasized that Poland should redeem its NATO membership at the first opportunity. "Brzezinski's comments [on Polish TV] made my job easier," said Kwaśniewski. Radek Sikorski, Poland's young deputy foreign minister, said, "Zbig and I agreed that the Iraq War was a disaster but that Poland's participation was essential."[44]

There was little change to the McLean formula at an eightieth birthday celebration that Brzezinski hosted for himself in 2008. After a few toasts, the talk pivoted to the future of Europe. Brzezinski conspicuously seated Kwaśniewski between the Russian and German ambassadors. "As a Pole, you know this is your destiny," he said.[45] He then subjected the Russian ambassador, Yuri Ushakov, to a merciless cross-interrogation. The German ambassador, Wolfgang Ischinger, who had been a junior embassy official in Washington during the Carter years, had become a good friend of Brzezinski after the Iraq invasion. Because of Germany's opposition to the war, Ischinger was frozen out by Bush's people for a time. He relied on Kissinger, Scowcroft, and Brzezinski for ambassadorial intelligence collecting. In April 2006, Ischinger hosted an all-day sixtieth birthday party for himself. A group of male guests, led by Brzezinski, held a foosball competition in the German Residence's basement. Most of the guests approached it as harmless fun. Only Brzezinski took it seriously. "When he won, he danced around with his arms in the air," said Ischinger. "I have never seen an old man take such delight in winning a game."[46]

Every three or four years, Brzezinski would come out with another book. Concision was his leitmotif; they rarely ran longer than 250 pages. His most enduring was 1997's *The Grand Chessboard: American Primacy and Its Geostrategic Imperatives,* which set the stakes for the post–Cold War struggle. This new era would be won by whichever power dominated the Eurasian landmass, Brzezinski argued. Ukraine was key. His thesis was an updating of the theories of Alfred Thayer Mahan, a late-Victorian American strategist who compared the United States to Great Britain. America, he said, would be the balancing and controlling offshore power to the Eurasian landmass. Among Brzezinski's later-in-life books, *The Grand Chessboard* was the most often cited. "Potentially, the most dangerous scenario would be a grand coalition of China, Russia, and perhaps Iran, an 'anti-hegemonic' coalition united not by ideology but by complementary grievances," he wrote. "It would be reminiscent in scale and scope of the challenge once posed by the Sino-Soviet bloc, though this time China would likely be the leader and Russia the follower."[47]

Brzezinski's manuscript submission process was brutally straightforward: he would write a book, then invite publishers to bid for it. His editor at Basic Books, Paul Golob, first met Brzezinski at his CSIS office in Washington. Trudy ushered him into a side room to read *The Grand Chessboard* and was sternly told not to remove the manuscript from the room.[48] The book was available on a take-it-or-leave-it basis. Only the mildest of line editing would be tolerated. Having speed-read the manuscript, Golob told Brzezinski that he interpreted it as the *Grand Choice* for the post–Cold War world. "You have understood it," said Brzezinski. Golob got the contract.

After 9/11, Brzezinski's book sales went from respectable to best seller, though he never matched Kissinger's commercial success. As they aged, the two became even more bracketed in people's minds. In 2004, Brzezinski came out with *The Choice: Global Domination or Global Leadership,* which laid out America's stakes in the post-9/11 world. "Among the handful of practitioners who write seriously and often about U.S. foreign policy, only Henry Kissinger (another import) can compare with Brzezinski in terms of historical knowledge and imagination," wrote Walter Russell Mead in *Foreign Affairs* of Brzezinski's latest monograph.[49] "When it comes to what might be called the 'philosophy' of foreign policy—the relationship of U.S. power and policy to broader historical and cultural trends—no statesman of Brzezinski's generation is in his league. And no Democrat of any age can match Brzezinski's grasp of the national interest and its sometimes difficult relationship to the values of liberal society."[50]

Brzezinski's voice took on new currency in the wake of the attack on the World Trade Center. In practice, he swapped his WASP enemies on the left for a new generation of neoconservative foes on the right. There was never a phase of contemplative repose when he did not have an easily identifiable and highly provoked group of enemies. It is a recurring irony of Brzezinski's odyssey that detractors accused him of having dual loyalty to Poland and the US. Yet he generated hostility among Jewish Americans for implying that they had a divided loyalty to Israel and America. That in turn triggered hints that Brzezinski was anti-Semitic.

Brzezinski's often irascible exchanges with the Iraq War's backers was closely tied up with the related debate over Israel. That was often simplified to the view that the road to Baghdad lay through Jerusalem, according to Brzezinski, while his opponents argued that in fact the road to Jerusalem went through Baghdad. As the fallout from the Iraq War intensified, Brzezinski stepped up his calls for a new peace process between the Israelis and Palestinians. If that running sore could be healed, Al Qaeda, ISIS, and other Salafist terror groups would be deprived of a vital recruiting tool, he said. Nonsense, said the neoconservatives; the Palestine question was both a red herring and a dead end. Arafat's autocratic PLO would be engulfed in the wave of change generated by a newly democratic Iraq.

After 9/11, Brzezinski's mind switched to Israel with the same alacrity as Wolfowitz and others linked it to Iraq. "There is a nearly unanimous global consensus that United States policy has become one-sided and morally hypo-critical, with clear displays of sympathy for Israeli victims of terrorist violence and relative indifference to the (much more numerous) Palestinian civilian casualties," he wrote in the *New York Times* in early 2002. "At risk is America's ability to maintain international support for the war on terrorism."[51] His ur-gent tone ramped up as the situation in Israel deteriorated during Ariel Sha-ron's premiership, which ended in 2006. It further sharpened after the return to power of Binyamin Netanyahu in 2009. "There was an edge in the way he spoke about Israel and its American supporters that made me uncomfortable and caused me to pull back from dealing with him," said a former SAIS col-league who served in the Bush administration.

One person's prejudice is another's impolitic style of advocacy. In the feverish climate of Bush 43's presidency, harsh criticisms of Israel were in-terpreted by some as dislike of Jews. In a town so deeply aligned with Israel, Brzezinski's qualified Zionism and the often brutal wording of his criticisms were easy to depict as hostility to the Jewish homeland. His Polish accent, which never faded, did not help. His views, which had remained virtually un-changed since the 1967 Six-Day War, won a far readier audience in Tel Aviv than in Washington or New York. They revolved around four principles that he had set out in his 1975 coauthored Brookings paper, which Carter had adopted wholesale as his Arab-Israeli plan: the parameters of a settlement would mean no right of return for Palestinians to their pre-1947 homes; Jeru-salem should be the joint capital of Israel and the Palestinian homeland; Israel should return to its 1967 borders with mutual adjustments; and there should be an independent but demilitarized Palestinian state. There is nothing anti-Zionist about those parameters. Brzezinski never altered them.

It would be fair to question how deeply Brzezinski was motivated by con-cern for Israel's security in its own right, as opposed to wanting to excise the Arab world's chief grievance against the US. During the Cold War, especially the Carter years, Brzezinski's Israel stance had been animated by his larger aim of sapping the USSR's regional allure. In the wake of the Cold War, he was a strong backer of Bush 41's Madrid peace talks. "I am delighted that you sup-port my recent stand regarding loan guarantees," Bush senior wrote to Brzez-inski in September 1991. "I have no intention of 'wavering.'"[52] Brzezinski had urged Bush to stand firm on his threat to withdraw loan guarantees to Israel if it persisted with the building of new illegal settlements. "I know from bitter personal experience that you will take a lot of heat on this issue," Brzezinski wrote to Bush 41. "A significant period of tension with a significant portion of the American Jewish community is inevitable. However, its sensible members realize that the hard liners in Israel would like to have their cake and eat it too. . . . We can only help the moderates in Israel—and the majority of Israeli people are moderate and decent—by being tough on the hard liners."[53] After 9/11, Brzezinski saw the Palestinian grievance as a festering sore that was also a recruiting sergeant for global terror groups.

Many thought Brzezinski crossed a line in 2006 when he endorsed an essay, "The Israel Lobby," by John Mearsheimer and Stephen Walt. As tenured scholars of international relations at Chicago and Harvard, respectively, Mearsheimer and Walt could have easily found a publisher on almost any other subject. After more than a year of hunting for an American outlet, they gave up.[54] A prominent US magazine had commissioned them to write the essay, but the editors killed it after having asked for several rewrites. Eventually the *London Review of Books* agreed to run their essay.[55] Their thesis was that pro-Israel lobby groups had hijacked US foreign policy for the benefit of a foreign country. That had led to the Iraq War and could also lead to war with Iran. The essay in the left-of-center and (to American readers) obscure British publication was downloaded 300,000 times in its first few weeks, mostly by American readers. Its virality proved the declining relevance of a publication's geographic location in the age of the internet. Their piece sparked a massive and furious reaction in America, giving it a dramatic backdoor entrance into the US market.

Two months later, Moises Naim, editor of *Foreign Policy*, which Brzezinski had helped launch more than three decades earlier, held a symposium about the piece. Naim published four scholars' responses to Mearsheimer and Walt. Brzezinski was the only one to come to their defense; the other three laid into the authors with varying degrees of savagery. Princeton University's Aaron Friedberg described what they had written as a "stunning display of intellectual arrogance . . . At a minimum, this is a slanderous and unfalsifiable allegation of treason leveled at individuals whose views of the Middle East differ from the authors'. At worst, it is an ugly accusation of collective disloyalty, containing the most unsavory of historical echoes." Dennis Ross, a former Clinton official, pointed out that the decision to invade Iraq had been made by Bush, who was far less close to the Israel lobby than Al Gore. He had been opposed to the war from early on. Even Shlomo Ben-Ami, a former Israeli minister of foreign affairs, said the authors' claims were "grossly overblown."

Many of their criticisms had obvious merit. The Iraq War "decider" was Bush. His two most influential lieutenants were Cheney and Rumsfeld, neither of whom was Jewish. Nor did they have closer ties to AIPAC than some of the war's critics did. Indeed, in some cases, it was the opposite. Without endorsing all their arguments, Brzezinski said that Mearsheimer and Walt had "rendered a public service by initiating a much-needed debate on the role of the 'Israel lobby' in the shaping of U.S. foreign policy." He conceded that some of their arguments could be labeled anti-Israel, a stance he did not share: "But an anti-Israel bias is not the same as anti-Semitism," he argued.

Brzezinski couched his defense in the context of the rising assertiveness of "ethnic or foreign-supported lobbies" at a time when Congress was inserting itself more and more into day-to-day foreign policy. Given such groups' fundraising prowess and legislators' unquenchable thirst for money, that gave them a growing sway over US foreign policy. He ranked the clout of the Cuban American and Armenian American lobbies alongside the pro-Israel groups with the Taiwanese American and Greek American ones trailing behind. What triggered Brzezinski was the censorious nature of the public reaction to the Walt and Mearsheimer article. Israel's influence in Washington should not be off limits as a subject, he said. Yet the response in leading US publications had been to question the authors' motives. "Sadly, some even stooped to McCarthyite accusations of guilt by association, triumphantly citing the endorsement of Mearsheimer and Walt's views by vile, fanatical racists as somehow constituting proof of the authors' anti-Semitism," he wrote.[56]

Brzezinski's intervention was an egregious display of principled rashness. He had no need to get embroiled in a zero-sum debate. By any measure of Washington's mood, he could only lose friends and influence. Yet he had no qualms about risking insinuations of anti-Semitism. When he was on the rise in the 1960s and 1970s, he and Kissinger had been objects of disapproving commentary about the new era of the gun-for-hire professionals: ambitious players who built their careers on advising presidents. Unlike traditional foreign policy practitioners, the brash new breed of geopolitical strategists made their living in government.

By 2006, Brzezinski had long since achieved wealth and status. He was almost eighty. It would have been a natural time to retreat into the role of genteel ex-statesman. He could have spent his time on eminent boards, given hortatory commencement addresses, and slipped into a softer mien befitting his advancing years. But that went against his nature. Some people's characters are mutable; Brzezinski's was not. His integrity often outstripped his wisdom. In his clashes over Israel, he also betrayed a lingering resentment at the way he had been treated by AIPAC and a handful of journalists during the Carter years. That gave his discourse an edge that could be presented as bigoted. He could rarely resist throwing the final punch. At the end of his defense of Walt and Mearsheimer, he wrote, "Of course, stifling such debate is in the interest of those who have done well in the absence of it. Hence the outraged reaction from some to Mearsheimer and Walt."

Eighteen months later, he made his last winning bet on a US presidential derby: he endorsed Barack Obama. In fact, they chose each other. Brzezinski's endorsement took place at a fluid stage in the epic battle between Obama and Hillary Clinton in the Democratic primaries. Obama's most devastating critique of Clinton was over her 2002 vote for the Iraq War. Like many of her colleagues, Clinton had voted for Bush's agenda and had only recently been won around to the merits of a US withdrawal—a "Johnny come lately," in Brzezinski's words. The excitement Obama generated among younger and more educated Democrats was partly because he personified a new generation of political outsider. He offered hope, while the Clintonesque insiders traded in cynical positioning. In addition to Obama's impressive intellect and soaring eloquence, part of his appeal stemmed from his unusual biography and mixed-race background.

Brzezinski was an instant fan. Obama had read several of his books and admired the fervor of his opposition to the Iraq War. Obama also admired Brzezinski's most recent short book, *Second Chance: The Presidents and the Crisis of American Superpower*, in which he had given Bill Clinton's presidency a grade of C and George W. Bush's an F (Bush 41, by contrast, received a B). Obama read it carefully. The Iraq War's "only saving grace is that it made Iraq the cemetery of neocon dreams," Brzezinski wrote. "Had the war been more successful, America by now might be at war with Syria and Iran."[57]

After they met for lunch in Washington's Metropolitan Club in May 2007,[58] Brzezinski told anyone who would listen that Obama excited him more than any presidential candidate since John F. Kennedy. In so doing, he conspicuously skipped over Carter. Yet he worried that Obama too often sounded diffident. In an email to Obama, Brzezinski wrote, "My sense is just as Bush succeeded in defining Kerry while Kerry refrained from defining

Bush (contrary to my advice), Clinton is defining you (inexperienced etc) while you are not defining her (opportunistically cynical on Iraq, deliberately misleading in her explanations of her vote, and out of tune with the global imperatives of her age)."[59]

Two days later, Obama emailed Brzezinski to ask him to comment favorably on a foreign policy speech he had given. "Obviously you may feel constrained to avoid a formal endorsement of my candidacy, but for you to offer an honest assessment of my foreign policy approach would carry considerable weight," he wrote.[60] After his wife, Michelle, appeared on *Morning Joe*, Brzezinski emailed Obama to compliment him on how "fantastic" she had been. Obama replied, "Michelle is vastly superior to me. She's just too smart to want to be president. She would rather tell the president what to do! Michelle very much enjoyed being on with Mika by the way—they seemed to have much in common. What's your take on where we are in Pakistan?"[61]

In August 2007, Brzezinski offered to endorse Obama at a particularly uncertain moment in his contest with Clinton. She was leading Obama both in the national polls and in Iowa. The other candidates, including former senator John Edwards, Joe Biden, and New Mexico governor Bill Richardson, were lagging far behind. In one of the Democratic debates, Clinton had accused Obama of being naive when he had said he would talk without preconditions to the leaders of Iran, Cuba, North Korea, and other rogue states. Later her campaign ran a hard-hitting ad that asked whom Americans should trust to take a 3:00 a.m. White House call.

In the midst of the cross fire, Brzezinski timed his endorsement for maximum effect. The Obama campaign was jubilant at Brzezinski's validation. Nobody could accuse him of being faint-hearted, particularly at 3:00 a.m. Moreover, he had earned genuine street cred with liberals. Dismissing Clinton as a "very conventional" figure who was regurgitating Bush's stance, Brzezinski told Bloomberg's Al Hunt that Obama had the "guts and intelligence" to help America turn the page. Obama was "clearly more effective" than Clinton. Refusing to talk to enemies was a sign of weakness, not strength, Brzezinski said; "What it in effect means is that you only talk to people who agree with you. So what's the hang-up?"[62]

A few days later, Brzezinski flew to Davenport, Iowa, to introduce Obama. The candidate was delivering a set-piece address called "Turning the Page in Iraq." Given the virtually nonexistent differences on domestic policy between Obama and Clinton, media attention was dominated by their clashing temperaments and their implications for foreign policy. Clinton claimed that Obama was not ready for prime time. Obama said that Clinton would deliver more of the same fare that had so harmed America under Bush. "The next president must be one who understands, even personalizes, the global quest for dignity and diversity," said Brzezinski in his introduction. "*Personalizes.* A person who has shown that even without extensive intelligence briefings he knew from the beginning that a solitary war resented by our friends by mobilizing our enemies is a fool's enterprise. . . . And so, good people of Iowa, you have a unique historical opportunity to take the lead in the election of our next president, and thus to change the world. I give you Barack Obama."[63]

Brzezinski's help at that low point in Obama's fortunes was "a huge deal," said Ben Rhodes, one of Obama's speechwriters and foreign policy advisors, who wrote Obama's address. "It was a validation from someone who didn't want a job and had real credibility—an unconventional hawk. He stuck his neck out for Obama at the right moment."[64] It did not take long, however, for Brzezinski's controversial views on Israel to surface and be used against Obama. After Obama won Iowa in January 2008, dark rumors began to surface about his past. Detractors started to refer to him as "Barack *Hussein* Obama." Fox News kept reminding viewers that Obama's Kenyan father had been a Muslim. Several times he had to correct claims that he had been schooled in a *madrassa* when he had lived with his mother in Jakarta for a couple of years.

During a call with Hillary Clinton's donors, Ann Lewis, a senior Clinton advisor, said that Brzezinski was Obama's "chief foreign-policy advisor."[65] Any mention of Brzezinski was a red flag to many Jewish groups. As it happened, the Jewish Democratic vote was split between Obama and Clinton in the primaries, although she took the lion's share in her home state of New York. The Jewish American vote was by no means monolithic. But Clinton had her own reputation to refurbish, having famously kissed Suha Arafat, the PLO leader's wife, in New York several years earlier. Obama was also dogged by his ties to the Reverend Jeremiah Wright, whose South Chicago church was depicted as a hotbed of anti-Israel (and anti-American) radicalism. Wright was an admirer of the Nation of Islam's leader, Louis Farrakhan, who was widely seen as anti-Semitic. At the urging of his campaign staff, Obama rejected Farrakhan's endorsement.

Obama also kept having to fend off inquiries about Brzezinski. Since some people thought Brzezinski was anti-Semitic, Obama's pro-Israel credentials were also suspect. With Brzezinski's acquiescence, Obama publicly disavowed him. The last thing Brzezinski wanted was to become a liability. But Obama was unexpectedly brutal in the way he distanced himself. "I do not share [Brzezinski's] views with respect to Israel," he told reporters in February 2008. "I have said so clearly and unequivocally. He's not one of my key advisers. I've had lunch with him once. I've exchanged e-mails with him maybe three times. He came to Iowa to introduce me for a speech on Iraq."[66] From then on, Brzezinski's name did not appear on any Obama campaign literature. Obama's official foreign policy advisors were Tony Lake, Susan Rice, Greg Craig, and Ivo Daalder. Yet the email exchanges between the aging Polish American statesman and the young senator from Illinois did not flag. Brzezinski sent Obama a suggested statement that said he had never spoken to Obama about Israel and that for thirty years his views on an Israel-Palestinian settlement had been on the record.

"That is fine," Obama replied from his BlackBerry thirty minutes later. "I tried to diffuse the issue without hampering our ability to communicate regularly."[67] A few weeks later, Brzezinski warned Obama that his Middle East advisor, Robert Malley, would cause him problems. Malley, like Brzezinski, favored holding direct talks with Hamas. "Sorry Zbig, what's this in reference to (I rarely read my own press nowadays)?" Obama replied. "Is this something related to Rob Malley, my Harvard classmate?"[68] Brzezinski filled him in. A day later, Obama fired Malley. Obama's public distancing stung Brzezinski, though he agreed with its logic. Unable to help himself, he told the UK's *Daily Telegraph*, "It's not unique to the Jewish community—but there is a McCarthy-ite tendency among some people in the Jewish community. They operate not by arguing but by slandering, vilifying, demonising. They very promptly wheel out anti-Semitism. There is an element of paranoia in this inclination to view any serious attempt at a compromised peace as somehow directed against Israel."[69]

Brzezinski's comments only inflamed the wound. Obama continued to seek his advice as if nothing had happened. This being Brzezinski's first campaign where he used email, the flow of missives was far less formal than with previous candidates. Obama sought Brzezinski's views before his July 2008 trip to London and Berlin, which was designed to showcase his popularity in Europe. Brzezinski urged Obama in his Berlin speech to move beyond the impression he was a "global celebrity" by offering policy substance.[70] Several weeks before the election, Obama asked Brzezinski to suggest a plan for his White House foreign policy line of authority. Brzezinski's response assumed (correctly) that Obama would be a hands-on foreign policy president like Nixon and Carter. After winning, Obama appointed Mark Brzezinski as US ambassador to Sweden. When Obama visited Mark in Stockholm in 2013, he waxed lyrical about his father. "He could not speak highly enough of my dad," said Mark.[71]

Obama did not heed Brzezinski's tough counsel on Israel. Early into Obama's presidency, Brzezinski urged him to convene talks on a final Israel-Palestine settlement. That was in accordance with Brzezinski's long-held view that a step-by-step process would inevitably unravel. Instead, Obama called for a freeze on new Israeli settlements. Israeli prime minister Binyamin Netanyahu immediately called Obama's bluff by creating new "facts on the ground" with a green light to another round of settlements. In that first eyeball-to-eyeball with Israel's leader, Obama blinked. "In hindsight, our proposed settlement freeze was a mistake," said Rhodes. "It was like getting half pregnant."[72] Brzezinski was peeved. He warned Obama that this would happen.

In some ways, Brzezinski did mellow in his later years; a hint of begrudging fondness crept into his relationship with Kissinger. In a long discussion on the future of US foreign policy in a turbulent world, PBS's Charlie Rose invited Kissinger, Brzezinski, and Scowcroft—a rare trio—onto his show. It was 2007. They were America's last surviving twentieth-century grand strategists. George Kennan had died two years earlier at the age of 101. Kissinger gave an oracular opening answer. The horizon he sketched was grand, although his specific views were hard to pin down. Brzezinski replied, "I don't disagree with what Henry said, but . . . " "Agree? Agree?" Rose interrupted in mock incredulity. "I don't disagree," Brzezinski emphasized. "But my perspective . . ." "I've made great progress," Kissinger interrupted. "Don't be too optimistic," said Brzezinski. "I take what I can get," said Kissinger.[73]

The two continued to meet for lunch and write to each other. In one exchange, Kissinger complained that he had tried to get through to Brzezinski three times without a return call. He was researching a history of China, to be titled On China, and wanted details about Brzezinski's 1978–79 negotiations with Deng Xiaoping. In the meantime, the Jimmy Carter Presidential Library in Atlanta had given Kissinger what he needed. "My conclusions will be very complimentary so you could have risked a conversation which is now unnecessary," Kissinger wrote.[74] Brzezinski replied by email, "Henry, You are getting grumpy! We called you back twice, and in spite of your letter I am not grumpy but forgiving." When Kissinger's book came out in 2011, he sent a copy to Brzezinski. His inscription read, "To Zbig Brzezinski, who traveled a parallel road with distinction. From his friend (we'll keep that a secret), Henry Kissinger."[75]

In March 2008, friends of Brzezinski hosted a lavish eightieth birthday party for him at Washington's Metropolitan Club. The host was Bill Odom. Brzezinski's closest friends were beginning to die off. Odom died of a heart attack in May at his home in Vermont aged seventy-five; Sam Huntington passed away at eighty-one in December in Martha's Vineyard. Brzezinski was laid low by both losses. Odom, in particular, had become a kind of alter ego. The former West Point instructor and Cold War hawk had been appointed by Reagan to head the National Security Agency, which sifts through the United States' rolling avalanche of signals intelligence. Odom was as scathing a critic of Bush's Iraq War as Brzezinski. Both Odom and Charles Gati, who had a weekly lunch with Brzezinski, thought that the militancy of Brzezinski's opposition to the Iraq War came partly in atonement for having backed the Vietnam War. Though Brzezinski did eventually turn against the Vietnam War, his earlier support embarrassed him more as time went on. Odom, an inveterate hawk on most questions, had opposed Vietnam from the start. "Zbig was a bit jealous!" Gati recalled.

Brzezinski and Odom would also call each other at least once a week, often talking for an hour or two, to ruminate on the state of the world. Odom called it their "continuous net assessment." After Odom's passing, the weekly lunch turned into a Gati-Brzezinski date. Brzezinski gave the oration at Odom's funeral. Brzezinski's eightieth birthday party was packed. "There's a lot of love for you in this room," Rick Inderfurth, Brzezinski's former NSC assistant, told him. Brzezinski looked startled. "Really?" he said. Yes, insisted Inderfurth.[76] *Love* was not a word often associated with Brzezinski.

Through his eighties, Brzezinski's routine remained unchanged. That was also true of his idiosyncrasies. Every summer, he and Muska would load up their station wagon and a U-Haul and drive for twelve hours straight to their vacation home in Maine. Their vehicle was laden with venison, dogs, ducks, mountains of files, a powerful computer, a printer, and a small library of books. Mika, who was in the throes of a divorce, finally decided that her parents were too old to make the journey by road. She and her cohost, Joe Scarborough, hired a jet to fly them to a small private airport near Northeast Harbor. At the end of the summer, Brzezinski sent Mika a receipt for her soda bill from the local club. It amounted to $13.00.[77] Though he had long since become a multimillionaire, Brzezinski remained the child of émigré Polish austerity. About a year after he had lent $20 to Wanda Brzezinski, his Canada-based sister-in-law, she got a letter from Brzezinski. It consisted of a stamped self-addressed return envelope and a receipt for what she owed him.[78]

Nor did Brzezinski's Washington routine slow down. Each weekday was still scheduled to the hilt. The media demand for him did not flag during the Obama years. In addition to *Morning Joe*, he appeared on other shows regularly, churned out op-eds at his usual clip, and came out with new books. He remained a habitué of the international circuit. In November 2009, he was invited by Hillary Clinton, Obama's first secretary of state, to join the US delegation to Germany to celebrate the twentieth anniversary of the fall of the Berlin Wall. In his memo of the event, another habit that did not fade, he wrote that the commemoration was even more moving than the original event. He spoke straight after Clinton. In a private chat with her afterwards, Brzezinski complained that Obama's Middle East policy was "a shambles." Clinton agreed. She admitted that they had no plan for what to do when Netanyahu rejected Obama's proposed freeze, as he privately noted after their conversation.[79]

The next morning in the hotel lobby, a strange-looking man approached Brzezinski. He was elderly, stocky, wearing a black leather zippered parka, and accompanied by a young blond woman. The man extended his hand to Brzezinski, who wordlessly reciprocated. Then Brzezinski recognized him: "Mikhail! Mikhail!" he said, hugging the USSR's last leader. Shunned at home as an embarrassment, Gorbachev took to the overseas lecture circuit as often as he could. The West was where he was most appreciated. The two had met only after the Soviet Union had dissolved. They had come to relish each other's company. "Zbiiiiiig. Zbiiiiiig!" Gorbachev yelled across a Paris hotel lobby in the early 2000s.[80] Any guests who might have recognized the two would have been bemused to see the USSR's implacable enemy and its final leader embrace like long-lost comrades.

On April 10, 2010, Poland suffered a national tragedy in its worst-ever air disaster. A major slice of the country's establishment, including President Lech Kaczyński, died when the plane collided with a treetop in dense fog as it approached Smolensk Airport in Russia. Everyone on board was killed. Among the ninety-six victims were the chief of the Polish general staff, eighteen members of parliament, the president of the National Bank of Poland, and aging relatives of victims of the 1940 Katyn Massacre. They were flying to Smolensk to commemorate the seventieth anniversary of the Soviet mass executions. Poland's initial reaction was a unified spirit of shock and mourning. Russian president Dmitry Medvedev and prime minister Vladimir Putin both flew to the site and spoke in rare tones of Russian-Polish solidarity. A few months later, the Russian Duma for the first time formally acknowledged Russia's culpability for the Katyn Massacre. Given that Putin had approved the Duma's resolution, which acknowledged that Stalin had personally ordered the killings, it was a remarkable moment of Russian-Polish national reconciliation. "It is possible that future historians will see . . . the beginning of a truly significant turning point in Polish-Russian relations," Brzezinski wrote a few days later.[81] He was sorely mistaken.

Separate Polish, Russian, and international crash investigations all reached the same conclusion: a mix of bad weather and pilot error had caused the accident. Yet conspiracy theories spread. Endorsed by the dead president's twin brother, Jarosław Kaczyński, who was a stalwart of Poland's right-wing Law and Justice Party (PIS), the theory took hold that the crash had been an assassination plotted by Russia and covered up by Poland's Civic Platform, allegedly led by Donald Tusk, who was prime minister at the time. No serious evidence was supplied to back up the rumors. Yet they had a life of their own.

In general, Brzezinski had little patience with conspiracy theories. At one of his sessions with Deng Xiaoping, he had corrected the Chinese leader about Czar Peter the Great's last will and testament, which had laid out Russia's plans to dominate all of Europe. Peter's so-called will was an early-nineteenth-century forgery, Brzezinski told Deng. In terms of its stubborn persistence, the Smolensk conspiracy theory was modern Poland's version of that. By pouring scorn on the conspiracy theorists, Brzezinski made an enemy of PIS and the Polish Right. "There are people who, consciously or subconsciously, maybe because they're sick, divide society and undermine the credibility of the state, of the government, and of justice," he said.[82]

The Polish government's decision to bury Kaczyński and his wife, Maria, in Kraków's hallowed Wawel Cathedral further antagonized Brzezinski. It was the resting place of Poland's Jagellonian Dynasty and of Marshal Józef Piłsudski, the nation's most cherished figures. The Kaczyńskis were buried in a sarcophagus in an antechamber to Piłsudski's tomb. Brzezinski thought that a plaque to all the Smolensk victims would have been more appropriate. Instead the Kaczyńskis were given a separate honor they did not merit, in his view. When PIS returned to power in 2015, it returned the favor. Brzezinski became a face of the liberal cosmopolitanism that the Polish Right reviled. In an interview with the Polish media, Brzezinski said that only psychiatrists could explain why people clung to the Smolensk myth with such stubbornness. The PIS government quickly shelved plans to install a monument to Brzezinski in Warsaw alongside those of other luminaries of the Polish diaspora, such as Joseph Conrad and Marie Curie. Brzezinski's scornful diagnosis turned him from hero to pariah in some circles.

At the opening of Poland's Emigration Museum of Gdynia in May 2015, Brzezinski recalled how he had left the country of his birth from that same port almost eight decades earlier. He told those present how he had tried to get his father to promise they would return within a year. "It was not until many years had passed that I returned, by then an adult, a US citizen, a Polish American, bearing a Polish surname, loyal to the United States of America," he said. "Yet all those long years I was aware that a large part of my identity is formed by what follows from Polish history. Therefore, Poland was with me every step of the way—also when I served as a high-ranking official of the United States government."[83]

Dread of Russia was a nonoptional piece of that Polish identity. Even before the Berlin Wall had fallen, Brzezinski was issuing jeremiads about Russia's desired revenge on history. "We'll probably see a turn toward some highly nationalistic form of dictatorship, perhaps what I call a 'Holy Alliance' between the Soviet Army and the Russian Orthodox Church," he told Strobe Talbott in 1989. "It could be a very ugly picture."[84] Twenty years later, he was making the same warnings of a new generation of Russian "black-shirted youth" infected "with a bacillus that could be quite ominous."[85] Yet as the 2000s progressed and his dark expectations of Putin's Russia were borne out, he began to look for ways to bring Russia into the West. If Russia became a junior partner to China, it would "lose the Far East some day, perhaps cataclysmically," he warned. The West should do what it could to welcome it into a larger European home. Ukraine must therefore *not* be admitted into NATO; that would only push Russia into China's arms. Ukraine should instead embrace a "Finland option" and become a buffer state between Europe and Russia.[86]

Brzezinski's counsel of restraint triggered a new round of heated arguments with his son Ian, who insisted that Ukraine should be admitted into NATO. Even after Putin annexed Crimea in 2014 and poured lightly disguised troops into Ukraine's Russian-speaking Donbass, Brzezinski was looking for an off-ramp. At the same time, he could not resist contrasting Ukraine's relatively stunned initial response to Putin's aggression with the way the country of his birth would have acted. "I can't imagine 20,000 Polish troops; foreigners come in, try to take power, and nobody shoots. Hell, they would have been in one big fight instantly."[87]

During the Bush 43 administration, Brzezinski had often half-seriously called for regime change in America. He would then add that Europe lacked any kind of regime to overthrow. Given Germany's east-facing mercantilism, he was pessimistic that Europeans could ever speak with one voice. At a dinner with a senior executive of the German engineering giant Siemens, he got into an argument about the merits of German economic diplomacy. The Siemens executive said that he had just been in Moscow, where the company had big investments. Brzezinski's colleague Robert Zoellick, who had served in several Republican administrations, interrupted. What percentage of your global sales involves your deal with Russia? he asked. Two percent, the executive replied. And what share comes from the United States? Twenty percent. "There was silence in the room," said Brzezinski. "And of course everybody got the message. You [Germany] better learn how to calculate what your interests are."[88]

As the Obama years wore on, Brzezinski did not try to muffle his disillusion. In addition to Obama's half-hearted stab at an Israeli-Palestinian peace process, Brzezinski opposed his 2009 Afghanistan troop surge. Obama's vice president, Joe Biden, was the surge's chief in-house critic. The US was committing billions of dollars to train Afghanistan's National Army. But who was training the Taliban? Brzezinski asked rhetorically. The answer, of course, was nobody. The highly motivated insurgents were continuing to get the better of Kabul's forces.

When Obama called in the "wise men"—now regularly including one woman, Madeleine Albright—he would open the meeting by first laying out his views. Brzezinski queried the purpose of those sessions since Obama's mind seemed already settled. He also questioned Obama's habit of crafting big and important speeches, then moving on. In his address in Cairo in 2009, Obama laid out a compelling case for recalibrating US relations with the Middle East. But there was little White House follow-up. Obama's weakness was to confuse speech with action, he thought. "The question is, 'Does Obama have it in his guts to strategize as well as sermonize?'" Brzezinski asked. "I don't know the answer to that. I really don't know."[89]

Underlying Brzezinski's disquiet about global trends and the rise of what he dubbed the "global Balkans" was pessimism about the future of US democracy. Regardless of its faults, only the US had the power and prestige to stop the world's descent into a lethal era of great-power conflict. The alternative to the US was not China but chaos. China could never emulate America's universal appeal. It was the opposite of an immigrant nation. Nor could China replicate the network of alliances that the US had built since the Second World War. Talk of China's coming economic dominance was also overblown, he felt. He treated such forecasts with a disdain similar to predictions of Japan as the coming superpower in the 1970s and 1980s. The US was the only nation capable of enforcing a global order. But it urgently needed to address problems at home.

In his final book, *Strategic Vision: America and the Crisis of Global Power*, which came out in 2012, Brzezinski laid out why there was nowhere other than America to look. Europe was turning into "a comfortable retirement home."[90] The City of London was the "Las Vegas of global corruption," the money-laundering choice of the world's kleptocrats. India was too beset with internal religious, language, and caste divisions to project power globally. And Latin America barely got a mention. Brzezinski shared with Kissinger a remarkable lack of curiosity about the rest of the Western Hemisphere. Somewhat confoundingly, both also tended to be dismissive of India. Brzezinski's sketch of a "receding West" meant that America's global preeminence was vulnerable to the rising "alliance of the aggrieved," chiefly Russia, China, Iran, and North Korea.

His book was a restatement of what he had been saying for years. During the 2000s, he often made fun of Washington's hair-trigger paranoia by signing himself in as "Osama bin Laden" at the concierge desk of grand Washington buildings.[91] He claimed that nobody had caught him out. The depth of America's fear of terrorism made US politics susceptible to demagoguery, a predictable offshoot of what he saw as the US electorate's shocking ignorance. "Americans don't learn about the world, they don't study world history, other than American history in a very one-sided fashion, and they don't study geography," he said. "If the US doesn't revitalize at home, it will fail internationally. If it does, we may not necessarily fail internationally—but we will have to be intelligent to succeed. But if we continue to fail domestically, we will have no chance internationally, even if we do the right things."[92]

By that point, I had known Brzezinski for several years. In 2012, I brought out my own dramatically less noticed book on America's relative decline called

Time to Start Thinking: America and the Specter of Decline. Brzezinski told me to send twenty copies to his home in McLean. He would invite some friends over to discuss it. Only when I arrived did I realize whom he meant by "friends."

The dinner guests included Madeleine Albright, John Kerry, Stephen Hadley, who had been George W. Bush's national security advisor, and a few ambassadors and heads of think tanks. That was daunting enough. Then he introduced me. "Here's Ed's book, *Time to Start Thinking*," Brzezinski said, holding up a copy. "You've got ten minutes to tell these people what they should be thinking. Then we can tell you what we think." To my surprise, many of those present thought I was too optimistic. Kerry was in an especially Spenglerian frame of mind. Albright kept her counsel. Brzezinski's view was that the US had the means to remain the top dog globally but was giving a good impression of trying to destroy itself from within. Acute inequality, deteriorating infrastructure, falling education standards, congressional gridlock, and a culture of instant gratification were rendering it incapable of thinking seriously about its challenges.

Around the same time, I invited Brzezinski to do "Lunch with the FT," in which the interviewee picks his or her favorite restaurant for the interview. The conversation is recorded. This format's appeal is that its informality gives free rein to its subject's idiosyncrasies. Although Brzezinski had dined numerous times at his chosen venue—Teatro Goldoni, an Italian restaurant on Washington's K Street—he seemed puzzled by the menu.

> "Remind me again, what is linguine?" he asks the waiter, who launches into a detailed description. "And what kind of meat do you have in your lasagna?" he continues. The waiter explains that "as usual" it's ground beef. Before ordering food, we had both chosen the same drink. "You know that red drink that they have before lunch in France?" asks Brzezinski. "Perhaps wine?" the waiter suggests. "No, no, it's stronger than that." Remembering my maternal grandfather, who loved aperitifs, I have an epiphany. "Dubonnet?" I suggest. "Yes, yes, I'll have a Dubonnet," Brzezinski says. "It's really a very good drink."[93]

That lunch took place a few months before Obama was reelected. He defeated former Massachusetts governor Mitt Romney in November 2012. It was a period of marked despondency in Brzezinski's mood. It was no longer easy to contrast his cheerful outlook with Kissinger's pessimism. At lunch he quoted a senior Chinese official who had reportedly said of the United States, "Please don't decline too quickly." He then lampooned the standard American candidate's response to any talk of decline, which is simply to assert that America's greatness will return if only people would believe in it. "'Help is here. Smile a lot. Everything will disappear. It will be fine'—well, sad to say, it doesn't work that way. People are ignorant and scared. It will take more than that."

What struck me most about that encounter was the contrast between Brzezinski's near helplessness in navigating the world's daily challenges and his paragraph-by-paragraph fluency in describing the world in abstract. That applied as much to simple technology—his inability to operate a microwave on the rare occasions when Muska was away—as to the ingredients of dishes he must have ordered dozens of times. For fifty-seven years, Muska had been arranging everything practical at home. And for most of the previous four decades, Trudy had been overseeing their household finances.

> When our main courses arrive, Brzezinski looks suspiciously at his steaming plate of duck ragù pasta. "It's quite a large portion," he says to the waiter, who does not reply. "And your plate of lasagna is also very big," he says, pointing at my dish.

I was almost as amused by Brzezinski's confusion as the waiter. At eighty-four, Brzezinski was still reveling in his life. Physically lean and mentally sharp, he boasted that he was still playing tennis almost every morning. Apart from the deep etchings on his weathered face, he betrayed few signs of his age.

In May 2014, the media power couple Tina Brown and Harold Evans hosted a book party for Emilie Brzezinski in their Sutton Place apartment on Manhattan's East River. Muska's coffee table book *The Lure of the Forest: Sculpture, 1979–2013* showcased more than three decades of her unique wood sculptures.[94] In the brief speeches, Mika made fun of her mother's taste in clothes from T.J.Maxx. Muska was wearing a white-belted trench coat and black knee-high boots. "I get all my clothes there except the occasional piece which I would buy abroad," Muska replied. Mika joked about being the difficult child in the family. "I was the hardest one to raise," she said.

A few months earlier, Mika had appeared on the cover of the Polish magazine *Wysokie Obcasy* in a sultry pose with stylized tousled hair and a white satin top. A few days later, she received a ripped-out copy of the cover in the mail from her mother, who had scrawled the word "YUK" over it.[95] It included a note: "How on earth did you manage to get this perfectly hideous cheep [*sic*] trashy common image of yourself on the front page of Wysokie Obcasy?" she asked. "The hair, did you roll in bed for a couple of hours to get it just like that? How can you permit it? Don't you have any control????? It takes a pervert to get you up that way and put you on the cover." Mika framed Muska's cover along with the note and hung it at home in a conspicuous spot.

Even in middle age, the Brzezinski children knew better than to expect praise from either parent. The Brzezinskis managed to be inveterate Washingtonians yet exemplars of a fading central European upper class. Mika had a knack of foiling their criticisms with humor. To her cohost, Joe Scarborough, the Brzezinski style of communication always came as something of a jolt. Yet he learned to see beneath Mika's parents' ornery exteriors. In spite of their inauspicious beginnings, Scarborough often turned to Mika's father for advice. A mutual respect developed. Brzezinski came to appreciate the demands of Scarborough's punitive morning vocation; Scarborough came to admire Brzezinski's directness. In very different ways, they shared an adoration of Mika, as well as the occasional overlapping frustration.

One Christmas not long after his marriage had ended, Scarborough telephoned Brzezinski in a slough of despond. In addition to his divorce, Scarborough's father had just died. His mother was suffering from dementia, and he was struggling to keep up the seasonal spirit for his young children. Nat King Cole was playing in the background. Scarborough poured out his woes to Brzezinski. "Isn't it wonderful that God has trusted you to take care of other people?" Brzezinski said. "What an extraordinary gift." Scarborough ended the call in better spirits.[96]

A couple of years later, Mika separated from her husband. She had married James Hoffer, a fellow TV reporter, in 1993. They had two daughters. There had been rumors for a while of a relationship between the *Morning Joe* cohosts. By that point, Scarborough knew both Brzezinski parents well. He bristled when they criticized their daughter, whether it was for wearing high heels, having the wrong guests on the show, or something amiss that she had said on the air. After hearing Mika berated one too many times, Scarborough could no longer hold back. "What are you all doing?" he asked. "Don't insult the woman I love. If this is going to continue, we're going to leave." Both the Brzezinski parents broke out into sheepish smiles. "This calls for a toast," said Brzezinski as he fished out a bottle of Polish vodka. "Stop calling me Dr. Brzezinski—I'm Zbig," he said. "And I'm Bumba," said Muska.[97] Scarborough also learned to emulate Mika's humorous mode of deflection.

When he mentioned his future father-in-law, he would often remind viewers that Brzezinski had called him "stunningly superficial."

In late 2014, Muska was given a three-month exhibition at the Kreeger Museum in Washington's leafy Palisades.[98] It was also titled *Lure of the Forest*. The chief sponsor was the chain saw manufacturer Stihl, whose equipment Muska had been using for many years. The centerpiece was her most recent work, a maple sculpture called *Ukraine Trunk*. Inside the hollowed-out wood, she had molded dozens of photos of Ukrainians from the Donbass. Not a single face is smiling.

The opening night was packed. After standing in line for hours greeting the stream of arrivals, Muska's celebration suddenly turned into a medical emergency: Brzezinski passed out. He was rushed to Sibley Memorial Hospital's emergency room, where he was diagnosed with heart arrhythmia.[99] He was out of the hospital the next day. Yet it took weeks for his family to persuade him to accept the doctors' advice to insert a pacemaker. The idea offended Brzezinski in several ways; it would be a memento mori—a reminder of his shortening life expectancy; the procedure entailed technology, to which he had an instinctive aversion; worst of all, the device would upload data to a receptor that could open him to compromise. The Russians would be able to hack into his medical information. "You know, I think Putin has enough on his plate right now to be worrying about your medical data, Dad," Ian told his father.[100] After considerable persuasion, Brzezinski relented. The pacemaker was installed. He was discouraged from playing tennis.

Around this time, Brzezinski sent an unusual note to Jimmy Carter. The two had regularly been in contact since they had left office. Carter often asked Brzezinski to help out with public events in Atlanta or DC, to contribute to his fundraising drives, or to give him feedback on something that he was thinking. By 2015, the cliché had long taken hold that Carter had been a mediocre president but was the best ex-president ever. Brzezinski did not dispute the latter. The former he vigorously contested. In contrast to many of his peers, Carter did not seek to enrich himself after leaving office. He and Rosalynn continued to live in the same modest-sized home in Plains, Georgia. They did not socialize with celebrities. The idea of cultivating their brand would have been alien to both. Brzezinski loved that the Carter Center had led the way in virtually eradicating Guinea worm disease from Africa and river blindness from sub-Saharan Africa and most of the Americas—a feat that in 2002 helped win him the Nobel Peace Prize.

"For four years we had a formal hierarchical relationship as the above salutation, 'Dear Mr. President,' testifies," Brzezinski wrote to Carter in September 2015. "Yet I also felt there was a special personal bond, which survived some tensions and occasional frictions. You protected me—or so I felt. And in the last several weeks I have felt the need to address you just once informally and to share these very personal feelings for an extraordinary president and post-president and human being who is an example to all of us. So dear Jimmy, with profound affection and respect, both of which have grown over the years, Zbig."[101] A couple of days later, the ninety-three-year-old Carter replied, "Zbig, you will never realize how much this means to me. You were always much more than a national security advisor, and you know from experience that I also trusted you implicitly, Jimmy."[102]

For a while, Brzezinski kept up his pace of engagements. Yet he would periodically become lost and forgetful. Mental decline can show up one day and vanish the next. With someone of Brzezinski's acuity, though, any trace of verbal imprecision is instantly noticeable. At the same time, Muska was diagnosed with incipient dementia. The two carried on their routines as if nothing had happened. Brzezinski continued to put on a suit every morning and go to his stately CSIS office. Without being explicit about it, John Hamre, the CSIS president, minimized the demands on Brzezinski's time.[103] To some extent, everyone went through the pretense of maintaining a normal routine. Whenever Brzezinski agreed to a TV interview, Trudy would fret. But he usually managed to rise to the occasion. No "senior moment" was caught on camera. One day in advance of the 2016 tax deadline, he called Trudy into his office three times so she could explain the difference between dividend and capital gains income. Even by the standards of Brzezinski's unbusinesslike mind, that level of confusion was egregious. It brought Trudy to tears.[104]

In spite of Brzezinski's technophobia, he had set up a Twitter account a few years earlier. He continued to sprinkle it with one-line aphorisms after his medical downturn. In total he tweeted 337 times, roughly once every three days. His first tweet on April 4, 2013,[105] linked to an op-ed he had written in the *Financial Times* about the need for new rules of engagement in the age of cyberwarfare. His second linked to a piece by his old friend Walter Pincus in the *Washington Post*. His third said, "I'll be on @Morning_Joe tomorrow circa 7:15AM." Given his facility with the platform—he typed out and pressed "send" on his own tweets—the suspicion arises that his technophobia was selective. Heating up prepared meals was beyond his ken; composing digital pronouncements came easily.

After his pacemaker was put in, he tweeted about once a week. The medium is a platform for instant opinion. A trawl through Brzezinski's tweets is stranger than going through faded 1940s correspondence. "The road to peace between the Israelis and Palestinians will be full of zig-zags, setbacks, and time bombs . . . and no shortcuts," he tweeted in November 2015 as John Kerry, who had replaced Hillary Clinton as secretary of state, embarked on the latest forlorn drive at a settlement. "Refusing to take refugees only reinforces the [Islamic State] narrative. Together with other NatSec leaders, I deplore xenophobia," he wrote in December 2015. "Putin's bitterness over the breakup of the USSR has led him to blame Lenin for the 'nonsense' creation of nationally defined republics," he tweeted in February 2016.

His first reference to Donald Trump was indirect. It came in February 2016: "With some exceptions, the current electoral contest is becoming for American democracy a global disgrace." Only once did he cite Trump by name. "Trump with no coherent grand strategic design and Mrs. Clinton favoring traveling over strategizing raises global uncertainty about America," he tweeted in February 2016.

Two days after Trump's victory in November 2016, Ashton Carter, Obama's outgoing secretary of defense, awarded Brzezinski the Department of Defense Medal for Distinguished Public Service, the Pentagon's highest civilian honor. As is befitting on such occasions, Ashton Carter's speech was fulsome. Appropriately, given the setting, the anecdote he emphasized was about Brzezinski being awakened in the dead of night in June 1979 to receive the nuclear alert. "And with that Zbig, our one-man deterrent, made sure the Strategic Air Command bombers were taking off," he said.[106]

Brzezinski's brief thanks were disquietingly wayward in syntax and flow. Though he was nattily attired in a sleek gray suit, his face was noticeably drawn. "There was a sadness in his eyes," said David Ignatius, the *Washington Post* columnist and a close friend of Brzezinski. The meaning of his brief talk was nevertheless plain: the United States had just elected someone who was manifestly unqualified to be president. Every other leader in the country must do what they could to protect America's interests from the dangers that lay ahead. Listening to Brzezinski's warning and taking note of his shaky condition left Ignatius in a deep sense of gloom about his fading health and that of America. "It was like history in a fever dream," he recalled.[107]

Brzezinski's cognitive slide was also apparent at a Nobel Prize event in Oslo a few weeks later. The committee gave Brzezinski the equivalent of a life-time achievement award: an invitation to be the keynote speaker at its first an-nual Nobel Peace Prize Forum. To Brzezinski's annoyance, they had expanded the solo invitation to include Kissinger. "Henry will overshadow me but it will enrich the event," he said. Both were now being honored equally. Brzezinski spoke first. He mentioned that he had first met Kissinger at Harvard in 1950 when the rotund German-accented research assistant had put him off sign-ing up for William Yandell Elliott's government course. Thereafter, they had tracked each other's careers. Kissinger said, "We have had some controversies over the years, but what I know most about Zbig is what I have learned from him." After both had made their remarks, they sat down to a moderated dis-cussion. No longer relying on his written text, Brzezinski at moments seemed lost for words. His expression betrayed uncharacteristic bewilderment.[108] It would be his final trip overseas. He did not seem to enjoy it.

He delivered his last public address at Columbia University on April 2, 2017, five days after his eighty-ninth birthday. He was receiving the Colum-bia School of International and Public Affairs' Lifetime Achievement Award. Mark Brzezinski introduced his father. This time, Brzezinski was fluent. He spoke without notes for twenty-five minutes. It was the final testament of a man who was starting to sound remarkably like a dove. In today's dangerous situation, he said, the US had no margin for geopolitical error. But the stakes for all humanity were too great for geopolitics to continue as normal. The world's three big powers—China, Russia, and the US—had to act in concert to prevent the proliferation of WMD and tackle humanity's common dangers, including climate change. Humanity could no longer afford to indulge in geo-political enmity. "Remember this is Brzezinski talking," he quipped. He made just one allusion to Trump. "This will require patience and intelligence and a president who doesn't use public appearances for entertainment but is pre-pared to discuss the global problems we now confront." The standing ovation after he sat down elicited a beatific smile. His capacity to enjoy the limelight was undimmed.

Over lunch at Washington's Tabard Inn a few weeks later, Brzezinski caught up with Rick Inderfurth. Brzezinski's former NSC assistant had a nagging sense that this might be one of their last meetings. In preparation, Inderfurth had rummaged through his basement to find Brzezinski memora-bilia from decades earlier that he presented to his former boss. Chief among them was a bumper sticker that read "God bless Brzezinski." Brzezinski was delighted. As was customary, they split the bill. "We must do this more often," Brzezinski said as they shook hands.[109]

A couple of weeks later, Brzezinski collapsed and was rushed to Inova Fairfax Hospital in Virginia. With all of his organs failing, this time there was no hope of discharge. He spent his last few weeks in a semicoma at the hospital with his family by his side. Occasionally he would awaken and say something in Polish. One morning, to check whether he was still conscious, the nurse asked Brzezinski to say his name. He answered correctly. And do you know where you are? "In Heaven," he replied.[110] At one point, Scarborough joined Mika and Muska at their bedside wake. Brzezinski had not opened his eyes for days. Scarborough greeted his future mother-in-law by kissing her on the forehead. A surgical glove hit him in the chest. Brzezinski had somehow managed to strike his target without opening his eyes. It was a valedictory in-joke.

Towards the end, Brzezinski awoke and asked Mika how she was doing. Her divorce had only just gone through. Though she was now engaged to Scarborough, Brzezinski knew she had not yet made her peace with her ex-husband. Brzezinski was fond of his former son-in-law. He asked Mika to call him. "Jim, it is so good to see you," he said when they put the phone in front of his face. "Life is so short, we should all just be happy and get along." His words had the desired effect. They were also his last. He died the next day, May 26, 2017.

Brzezinski's formal funeral was a grand affair in Washington's baroque Saint Matthew's Cathedral. The keynote speakers were Jimmy Carter, Madeleine Albright, CSIS's Dr. John Hamre, and Ian, Mark, and Mika. "He seduced the Chinese leaders as much as he seduced me," Carter said. People had often overlooked Brzezinski's sense of humor, he said. In one Oval Office meeting, he told Carter that the Soviet Union under Lenin had been like a revival meeting; under Stalin it was like a prison; under Khrushchev it was a circus; and under Brezhnev it resembled a United States Post Office.

Carter counted 552 entries on Brzezinski in his diary; keeping it was a daily habit that Brzezinski persuaded him to adopt. He repeated his line that on long flights there was no one, other than Rosalynn, that he would prefer to have sit next to him. Albright described her former PhD supervisor and White House boss as the biggest influence on her life other than her father. Brzezinski approached the world as a "realistic optimist," she said. The big absence from Brzezinski's funeral was Kissinger, who was unwell. Unaware of how sick Brzezinski had been, Kissinger asked to see him one last time in the hospital. Brzezinski's family told him that a bedside visit would be impractical. Kissinger sent the following letter to Muska and Mika:

I learned of Zbig's passing while leafing through some books in my library late at night. I was stunned. How central Zbig's presence had been to my image of a world worth living in and defending hit home with unexpected force. So my first reaction was a good cry. I mention this because my reaction was a surprise in the face of a relationship which, despite great mutual respect, was also shadowed by a certain competitiveness. . . .

But that night, I felt as if a sustaining pillar of the structure of the world I cared about had disappeared. For my entire intellectual life, Zbig had been one of the few who called us tirelessly to our duties far beyond the exigencies of the moment. He strove to provide structure to a world ever tempted by chaos and confusing mirages with vision. He was forever challenging his time with concepts of peace and freedom. . . . The world is an emptier place without Zbig pushing the limits of his insights.

We shared, I like to think, our cause, if not always our ambitions. It is important to me that you understand how much I shall miss Zbig.[111]

When Carter appointed Brzezinski as his national security advisor, the Belgian newspaper *Le Soir*'s headline was "Polish Aristocrat Follows German Jew." Technically, in fact, Brzezinski followed Scowcroft in that job. Scowcroft died in 2020 at ninety-five. Kissinger died in November 2023, six months after he had become a centenarian. Brzezinski was always five years behind Kissinger, except in death. In Kissinger's final years, he agreed to several interviews for this biography. The first observation he shared was that Brzezinski's death had been untimely and tragic. But Brzezinski was eighty-nine when he had died, I pointed out. That is my point, Kissinger replied.[112]

When I asked where Brzezinski would rank among America's national security advisors, Kissinger said he would be in the top two in terms of strategic thinking. Assuming that Kissinger had, not uncharacteristically, meant himself for the number one slot, what set them apart? "As immigrants we knew about the fragility of societies and we had an instinct for the transitoriness of human perceptions," he said. "The question is whether Americans can ever understand that they are living in a continuous experience that has no end and that you can never segment life into different problems. . . . Europeans knew that we were living in a continuous history. It never comes to an end." The difference between the two, he said, was that Kissinger had come from Germany but was not defined by it; Brzezinski had been defined by Poland, though that had not set limits on what he became. Were they friends? "Actually no," said Kissinger. "He was always somewhat competitive with me, although also somewhat respectful of me. When he died, it was a really sharp pang—it was a part of the world that mattered to me that disappeared. I never reacted to anyone else's death like that."

Four years after Brzezinski died, Mark Brzezinski got a call from the Oval Office. Joe Biden had been inaugurated as president three months earlier. Would Mark like to be ambassador to Poland? Biden asked. Mark accepted. He had been preparing for a job like that all his life. "Your father is looking down from Heaven and smiling as we talk," said Biden.[113] Poland's Law and Justice government nevertheless put obstacles in Mark's way. Under an antiquated Polish law, he and his siblings were legally Polish citizens, they said. That disqualified him from representing a foreign country. Getting around that legal roadblock added months to the process. Mark's lawyers dug up a 1930s Polish-Czech treaty that said if the mother was from Czechoslovakia, the offspring were in fact Czech citizens. It worked. But Brzezinski senior had evidently not been rehabilitated in the eyes of the Polish Right. They still clung fast to the Smolensk conspiracy theory. In the same way that declaring the 2020 US presidential election was stolen became a form of loyalty oath in Trump's Republican Party, acceptance of the Smolensk theory became a litmus test on the Polish Right.

It was only in late January 2022 that Mark arrived in Warsaw as US ambassador. Russia invaded Ukraine a few weeks later, on February 24. As Ukraine's most important NATO neighbor, Poland instantly became the front line for the US-led supply of Ukraine's resistance against Putin's forces. Most US ambassadors do not receive one presidential visit in four years. Biden visited Warsaw twice in Mark's first year. On his first visit, a month after the Russian invasion of Ukraine, Biden and his Polish counterpart, President Andrzej Duda, gave speeches at the Polish airport that had become the delivery hub for most of the West's supplies. At the start of his speech, Biden pointed at Mark and said, "We've sent you the best. We've sent you Brzezinski."[114] In the new context, Poland's Right and Left were suddenly able to unite on the Brzezinski name.

Three months later, Emilie Benes Brzezinski—the hidden key to Zbigniew's life, his truest editor, and the one who had done what it took to make sure that their family always held together—passed away.[115] She was ninety. Following her husband's death, Muska had moved to Florida to live next door to Joe and Mika. The cohosts married in early 2018. The Brzezinskis' McLean home was bought by the township and converted into a building for artists in residence. The capacious studio in which Muska had wielded her chain saw and carved her pieces lives on as a workshop for future artists. Brzezinski loved to boast about Muska's creativity, though he had scant artistic sensibility. Muska spent much of her life trying to keep her husband grounded. Brzezinski's material was soaring geopolitics; Muska's was tree trunks. "To the casual observer, a tree is vertical and straight," she said. On intimate inspection, however, it had turned out that even the biggest trunks could bend. "I am more often exhilarated by dealing with their monumental presence than afraid of it."[116]

Brzezinski was once asked which thinkers had had the greatest impact on his mind. He mentioned four: Merle Fainsod, Carl Friedrich, Barrington Moore, Jr., and Pierre Teilhard de Chardin.[117] The first three were Harvard mentors and colleagues. Teilhard, a French Jesuit who had found his path to God through science, was the odd one out. Many in the Catholic Church saw the scientific priest as a borderline heretic. In conversation with Pope John Paul II, Brzezinski would often mention Teilhard's teachings. The quality that most appealed to Brzezinski about him was his definition of faith. You did not need to find God, Teilhard had said; the act of searching was faith enough.

Dropping the French theologian's name was Brzezinski's way of telling the pope that he harbored doubt. The pope, to Brzezinski's surprise, endorsed Teilhard's unorthodox path to faith. It was nevertheless a shock to some of Brzezinski's family that he was not buried in the traditional Catholic way. His brother Lech hoped that he would be laid to rest in the Polish cemetery that his parents had carved out in the Laurentian Mountains.[118] On this question, Brzezinski was uncharacteristically silent. He left no instructions.

Brzezinski's ashes were scattered in a small ceremony in a Virginia forest. He had taken his sons deer hunting in the Appalachian foothills on many occasions. Much as with his search for God, Brzezinski loved to hunt but would often fail to locate his target. His sons were better shots. There is no Brzezinski gravestone or epitaph. Perhaps none could pin down such a relentless soul.

Acknowledgments

I was initially very skeptical about embarking on a full life biography of anyone, let alone a figure as big as Zbig. Sustaining a hectic day job at the *Financial Times* is not easily compatible with such an all-consuming project. There can be no cutting corners with a life; you research it comprehensively or not at all. Then I started to dip into the voluminous diaries Brzezinski kept as national security advisor that were sent to me by Mark Brzezinski. His father's rough first take on a period of history that continues to shape today's world—and in many ways is echoed by it—was exclusively mine if I wanted, and without conditions. Once I began to dig, I could not stop.

Along with Mark, his siblings, Ian and Mika, gave me everything that I requested, from their extensive family correspondence and diaries to photo albums and diverse miscellany. Being a biographer is relentlessly intrusive. All three Brzezinski offspring and Joe Scarborough, Mika's husband, a former congressman and her television cohost, and Ginny Brzezinski, Ian's wife, unfailingly tolerated repeated demands on their time and private memories. Lech Brzezinski, Zbig's surviving sibling, supplied additional boxes of speeches, newspaper cuttings, and other collated moments from his brother's life. Lech and his wife, Wanda, also kindly received me in the Laurentian Mountains, where Zbig had spent many a youthful summer. Mika and Joe hosted me at their lovely Tranquility Base vacation home in Maine's Northeast Harbor, which Mika's parents bought in the late 1960s. My deep and abiding thanks to all the family.

Several books' worth of material had to be translated from the original Polish. I am immensely indebted to Michael Perkinson, a former student of

Brzezinski's and a naval intelligence officer, now a Santa Monica–based investor, for funding a large share of the translation costs. On hearing of the biography, Michael got in touch sight unseen with his exceptionally kind offer. His recollections of Brzezinski as a teacher were also invaluable. Most of the remaining costs were covered by Stephen B. Heintz, president of the Rockefeller Brothers Fund—again with no strings attached. I will never stop marveling at how readily American philanthropic funding is available for serious projects. Both Perkinson's and Heintz's generosity also enabled me to hire Gibbs McKinley, a bright young American St. Andrew's graduate, as my research assistant. Without Gibbs I doubt I would have been able to complete this book. Her diligence, thoughtfulness, sharp brain, and technological savvy were indispensable. She spent many a weekend at the Library of Congress downloading material from the Brzezinski collection. Gibbs has a bright future and richly deserves it. My profound thanks to her. Both of us were struck by the care and speed of Andrzej Grzadkowski, our Warsaw-based translator. Thanks also to the John Hopkins School of Advanced International Studies for facilitating the research.

This biography also benefited from the kindness of strangers. Jerzy Koźmiński, president of the Polish-American Freedom Foundation, and former ambassador of Poland to the United States, was a font of ideas and encouragement. Jerzy shared copious documents, speeches, and archival material related to Brzezinski—including the Polish secret police files on Brzezinski and his remarkable correspondence with John Paul II, the Polish pope. Jerzy also set me up with a fascinating Polish itinerary that included unforgettable interviews with Lech Wałęsa in Gdańsk and Cardinal Stanisław Dziwisz in Kraków. Jerzy's colleague, Maciej Makulski, was also a great help. In Poland I also benefited from lengthy conversations with Dagmara and Zbigniew Roman, the widow and son respectively, of Brzezinski's oldest friend and first cousin, Andrzej Roman. I am also hugely indebted to Justin Vaïsse, a French diplomat and scholar, who wrote Brzezinski's excellent first full biography (*Zbigniew Brzezinski: America's Grand Strategist*, Harvard University Press, 2018, translated by Catherine Porter). In spite of his being a nominal competitor, Vaïsse's only instinct was to be helpful. He saved me a lot of time by sharing his comprehensive files of everything that Brzezinski had published as well as the transcripts of dozens of interviews with Brzezinski and his contemporaries, among them Henry Kissinger, Samuel Huntington, and Stanley Hoffman. I cannot thank Vaïsse enough for his generosity.

This biography is enriched and animated by interviews with about a hundred of Brzezinski's contemporaries, many of them repeatedly. Some of them have since passed away. Not every observation is cited in the endnotes, but their recollections suffuse the book. I would especially like to thank Trudy Werner, Zbig's near-lifelong assistant, whose company was as delightful as her memories were rich. Trudy was far more than a secretary to Brzezinski but took pleasure in joking that the first six letters of that role spell "secret." She provided intimate glimpses into the Brzezinski world. I would also like to single out Karl F. ("Rick") Inderfurth, Brzezinski's NSC special assistant, for his endless supply of vivid anecdotes and material. George Weigel, the definitive biographer of John Paul II, went to great lengths to dig up material relevant to the Brzezinski relationship, including the KGB's outlandish conspiracy theory about how the pope was chosen. My thanks to him. My huge thanks also to my friend Steve Clemons for sharing his revealing interviews with Brzezinski in his soon-to-be-released documentary, *A Chessman in Winter*.

In no particular order, my deep thanks to the late Emilie ("Muska") Brzezinski (née Benes), who was generous enough to share memories in the twilight of her life, the late Henry Kissinger, the late Madeleine Albright, the late Jerrold Schecter, the late Peter Jay, Robert Gates, Paul Golob, William Overholt, Robert Hunter, John Kornblum, Stu Eizenstat, George Packer, James Fallows, Gary Sick, David Rothkopf, William Quandt, Frank Wisner Jr., John Hamre, Gerald Rafshoon, David Owen, Thomas Wright, Kurt Campbell, "Coach" Kathy Kemper, Janusz Onyszkiewicz, Gordon Goldstein, Joe Nye, Walter Pincus, Niall Ferguson, David Ignatius, Michael Klare, Sam Nunn, Jessica Matthews (née Tuchman), Tony Lake, Patrick Vaughan, Steven Larabee, Richard Allen, Aleksander Kwaśniewski, Charles and Toby Gati, James Thomson, Angela Stent, Robert Blackwill, Wolfgang Ischinger, Sally Quinn, Moisés Naím, Stephen Walt, Charles Freeman, Charles Heck, Ivo Daalder, Tom Donilon, Robert M. Kimmitt, David Rubenstein, Les Denend, Matthew Nimitz, Ben Rhodes, Jeffrey Sachs, Francis Fukuyama, James Mann, Bill Moyer, John Rielly, Jonathan Alter, Jon B. Alterman, Strobe Talbott, Stephen Cook, Marvin Kalb, Susan Glasser and Peter Baker, Mike Abramowitz, Jane Harman, Paula Dobriansky, Brigadier General Mark W. Odom, Timothy Garten Ash, Radek Sikorski, Anne Applebaum, Kai Bird, Bob Woodward, President Jimmy Carter, Cardinal Dziwisz, Eliot Cohen, Lech Wałęsa, Leszek Balcerowicz, Daniel Fried, Odeh Aburdene, Alan Wolff, Matthias Matthijs, Steve Clemons, Colonel Mark Odom, Matthew Brzezinski, Elise Zylinska,

Lech and Wanda Brzezinski, Ian, Ginny, Mark and Mika Brzezinski and Joe Scarborough. I would also like to thank the SAIS scholar Sergey Radchenko for so readily sharing Soviet archival material with me and an advance copy of his book, *To Run the World: The Kremlin's Cold War Bid for Global Power* (Cambridge, UK: Cambridge University Press, 2024). Huge thanks also to the staff at the Library of Congress and the Jimmy Carter Presidential Library in Atlanta.

Several experts and friends kindly read the manuscript in whole or part and provided indispensable feedback and spotted errors of fact or judgment. These include Stu Eizenstat, Karl Inderfurth, Timothy Garten Ash, Jerzy Kozminski, Charles and Toby Gati, David Rothkopf, Kori Schake, Flora McEvedy, Julian Haber, Anne von Finckenstein, and Jon B. Alterman. My father, Richard Luce, and father-in-law, Joe King, happily volunteered to be guinea pigs for the general reader. My *FT* friend and colleague Peter Spiegel not only read and commented on the first draft with his keen editorial eye but was also a militant enthusiast for my taking this project on. Much gratitude also to my friend Roula Khalaf, editor of the *Financial Times*, for tolerating so many leaves of absence to research and write this book. I was also highly fortunate to have Ben Loehnen as my editor at Simon & Schuster. Ben's skills as an editor and his faith in this project have been a delight. In publishing terms, I hit the jackpot. I also greatly enjoyed working with Ben's highly patient and helpful assistant, Carolyn Kelly. My deep thanks also to Alexis Kirschbaum at Bloomsbury—my British publisher. Likewise, huge thanks to my New York and London-based agents, Elyse Cheney and Natasha Fairweather, both of whom propelled this book forward with constant advice and encouragement. Great thanks to both of them.

This book is dedicated to my wife, Niamh King. Living with me is hard enough. Living with both me and Zbig for several years is beyond any reasonable expectation, even for a marriage as strong as ours. So consumed was I by the project that Niamh would joke that if she asked me to pass the salt, I would reply, "SALT I or SALT II?" Both Niamh and my beloved daughter, Mimi, were highly tolerant of my being "locked in the attic" for prolonged spells as I worked on this book. Niamh was also the hidden editor, advisor, evangelist, propagator, and nurturer of this biography. Without Niamh, I would never have left the starting blocks. My undying gratitude and love to her.

Notes

PROLOGUE

1. Zbigniew Brzezinski, diary, May 8, 1945 (henceforth "Zbigniew Brzezinski, diary"). All translations of Brzezinski's diary from Polish to English were done by Andrzej Grzadkowski. Diary is privately held by Brzezinski's family.
2. Zbigniew Brzezinski, interview with Justin Vaïsse, May 2011.
3. Zbigniew Brzezinski, diary, January 17, 1945.
4. Charles Gati, "Zbigniew Brzezinski: The Professor-Strategist," *Politico*, December 28, 2017.
5. Zbigniew Brzezinski, interview with the author, January 2012.
6. Patrick G. Vaughan, "Zbigniew Brzezinski: The Political and Academic Life of a Cold War Visionary" (PhD dissertation, West Virginia University, 2003), 34.
7. Zbigniew Brzezinski, "Russo-Soviet Nationalism" (master's thesis, McGill University, 1950), box I: 84.5, Zbigniew Brzezinski Papers, Manuscript Division, Library of Congress, Washington, DC (henceforth "Brzezinski Papers, LoC").
8. Characterized by Vaughan, "Zbigniew Brzezinski," 6.
9. Robert M. Gates, *From the Shadows: The Ultimate Insider's Story of Five Presidents and How They Won the Cold War* (New York: Simon & Schuster, 2006), 95.
10. Quoted in Gates, *From the Shadows*, 96.
11. Description of Brzezinski by President Askar Akayev of Kyrgyzstan, diary of Central Asia-Georgia trip, Thursday, December 9, 1993, box I: 103.6, Brzezinski Papers, LoC.
12. Mikhail Zygar, *All the Kremlin's Men: Inside the Court of Vladimir Putin* (New York: PublicAffairs, 2016), 342.
13. Quoted in Walter Isaacson and Evan Thomas, *The Wise Men: Six Friends and the World They Made* (New York: Simon & Schuster, 2014), 728.
14. Quoted in Isaacson and Thomas, *The Wise Men*, 736.
15. Aleksandra Ziolkowska-Boehm, *The Age of Brzezinski*, box II: 248.9, Brzezinski Papers, LoC.

1: INTERBELLUM WARSAW

1. Winston Churchill, *The Second World War*, vol. 6, *Triumph and Tragedy* (Boston: Mariner Books, 1986), 622.

2. Much of the Polish history in this chapter is drawn from Joshua D. Zimmerman, *Jozef Pilsudski: Founding Father of Modern Poland* (Cambridge, MA: Harvard University Press, 2022); John Connelly, *From Peoples into Nations: A History of Eastern Europe* (Princeton, NJ: Princeton University Press, 2020); Timothy Snyder, *Bloodlands: Europe Between Hitler and Stalin* (New York: Basic Books, 2016); Timothy Snyder, *The Reconstruction of Nations: Poland, Ukraine, Lithuania, Belarus 1569–1999* (New Haven, CT: Yale University Press, 2003); Norman Davies, *White Eagle, Red Star: The Polish-Soviet War 1919–20 and "the Miracle on the Vistula"* (London: Pimlico, 2003 [1972]); Norman Davies, *God's Playground: A History of Poland*, vol. 1: *The Origins to 1795* (New York: Columbia University Press, 2005); Wacław Jędrzejewicz, *Piłsudski: A Life for Poland* (New York: Hippocrene Books, 1990).

3. Aleksandra Ziolkowska-Boehm, *The Age of Brzezinski*, box II: 248.9, Brzezinski Papers, LoC.

4. Józef Frankiewicz, *Kazimierz Brzeziński 1866–1924*, "Studia Przemyskie" 2004, t. 2, s. 230–235 [Kazimierz Brzeziński, curriculum vitae], translated, box III: 58.8, Brzezinski Papers, LoC.

5. Tadeusz Brzeziński, curriculum vitae, photographs of album before deconstruction, trans. Andrzej Grządkowski, box II: 246.4, Brzezinski Papers, LoC.

6. Roman family history, private collection, Lech Brzezinski, trans. by Andrzej Grzadkowski.

7. Speech that Tadeusz Brzezinski gave in Montreal in 1940, private family collection.

8. Tadeusz Brzezinski speech, Montreal, 1940.

9. Ziolkowska-Boehm, *The Age of Brzezinski*.

10. Leonia Brzezinski, diary, December 24, 1934, trans. by Andrzej Grzadkowski.

11. Karen De Witt, "Brzezinski, the Power and the Glory," *Washington Post*, February 4, 1977.

12. Leonia Brzeziński, diary, December 19, 1933.

13. Leonia Brzeziński, diary, October 7, 1933.

14. Leonia Brzeziński, diary, February 24, 1934.

15. Aleksandra Ziolkowska-Boehm, *The Age of Brzezinski*, box II: 248.9, Brzezinski Papers, LoC.

16. Ziolkowska-Boehm, *The Age of Brzezinski*.

17. Leonia Brzeziński, diary, May 28, 1934.

18. Leonia Brzeziński, diary, December 24, 1933.

19. Leonia Brzeziński, diary, January 21, 1934.

20. Juliette Bretan, "The Glittering Nightlife and Thriving Culture of Interwar Warsaw," Notes from Poland, May 28, 2021, https://notesfrompoland.com/2021/05/28/the-glittering-nightlife-and-thriving-culture-of-interwar-warsaw/.

21. Leonia Brzeziński, diary, August 15, 1934.

22. Leonia Brzeziński, diary, August 15, 1934.

23. Leonia Brzeziński, diary, February 1, 1935.

24. Thomas Jefferson to Horatio Gates, February 21, 1798, Founders Online, https://founders.archives.gov/documents/Jefferson/01-30-02-0083.

25. Leonia Brzeziński, diary, May 14, 1935.

26. Patrick G. Vaughan, "Zbigniew Brzezinski: The Political and Academic Life of a Cold War Visionary" (PhD dissertation, West Virginia University, 2003), 18.

27. Zimmerman, *Jozef Pilsudski*, 414.

28. Leonia Brzeziński, diary, May 11, 1937.

29. Zbigniew Brzezinski, interview with Justin Vaïsse, May 2011.

30. From transcript of Polish TV documentary *Father and Son*, trans. Andrzej Grządkowski.

31. Leonia Brzeziński, diary, March 18, 1938.

32. Leonia Brzeziński, diary, March 18, 1938.

33. Richard M. Langworth, "Churchill's Words: Choosing Between War and Shame—and Getting Both," Hillsdale College Churchill Project, October 11, 2019, https://richardlangworth.com/war-shame. Churchill is often quoted as having told Chamberlain, "You were given the choice between war and dishonour. You chose dishonour, and you will have war." No record of such a remark can be found.

34. Jerzy Koźmiński, interview with the author, January 2021.

35. Leonia Brzeziński, diary, October 20, 1938.

36. Leonia Brzeziński, diary, October 20, 1938.

2: BETWEEN TWO WORLDS

1. Lech Brzeziński, private family paper.

2. Zbigniew Brzezinski, diary, November 3, 1938.

3. Leonia Brzeziński, diary, November 14, 1938.

4. Interview with Zbigniew Brzezinski, *The Gazette* (Montreal), July 30, 1983.

5. Elaine Kalman Naves, "The Open Closed Society," *Books in Canada*, November 1996.

6. Leonia Brzeziński, diary, May 8, 1939.

7. Leonia Brzeziński, diary, March 15, 1939.

8. Leonia Brzeziński, diary, May 16, 1939.

9. Leonia Brzeziński, diary, June 25, 1939.

10. Zbigniew Brzezinski, diary, September 1, 1939.

11. Leonia Brzeziński, diary, September 2, 1939.

12. Zbigniew Brzezinski, diary, September 29, 1939.

13. Leonia Brzeziński, diary, September 2, 1939.

14. Leonia Brzeziński, diary, September 2, 1939.

15. Leonia Brzeziński, diary, November 26, 1939.

16. Leonia Brzeziński, diary, December 27, 1939.

17. Newman House yearbook, 1939–1940.

18. Zbigniew Brzezinski, diary, August 19, 1940.

19. Chris Bowlby, "Josef Frantisek: The Battle of Britain's Czech Hero," BBC News, September 14, 2018, https://www.bbc.com/news/stories-45516556.

20. Aleksandra Ziolkowska-Boehm, *The Age of Brzezinski*, box II: 248.9, Brzezinski Papers, LoC.

21. Zbigniew Brzezinski, diary, August 20, 1941.

22. Leonia Brzeziński, diary, February 2, 1940.

23. Leonia Brzeziński, diary, March 19, 1940.

24. Leonia Brzeziński, diary, December 15, 1940.

25. Leonia Brzezinski, diary, January 7, 1941.

26. Zbigniew Brzezinski, diary, January 7, 1941.

27. Quoted in Martin Gilbert, "What Did the United States Mean to Winston Churchill?," The Churchill Project, Hillsdale College, July 17, 2015, video, https://winstonchurchill.hillsdale.edu/what-did-the-united-states-mean-to-winston-churchill/.

28. Leonia Brzeziński, diary, December 20, 1940.

29. Leonia Brzeziński, diary, December 15, 1940.

30. Newman House yearbook, 1941–1942.

31. Jan Karski, *The Karski Report*, interviews with Claude Lanzmann, 2010, video. Original interviews conducted in 1978.

32. "Albright, Brzezinski, Polish Ambassador Pay Tribute to Jan Karski," Georgetown University, March 19, 2013, https://www.georgetown.edu/news/albright-brzezinski-polish-ambassador-pay-tribute-to-jan-karski/.

33. Zbigniew Brzezinski, "Afterword," in Jan Karski, *Story of a Secret State: My Report to the World* (Washington, DC: Georgetown University Press, 2014 [1944]), 401.

34. Karol Karski, "The Crime of Genocide Committed Against the Poles by the USSR Before and During World War II: An International Legal Study," *Case Western Reserve Journal of International Law* 45, no. 3 (2012): 710.

35. Downing Street, formal reply, private collection, Ian Brzezinski.

36. Newspaper clipping from Lech Brzezinski's private collection, undated.

37. Zbigniew Brzezinski, diary, July 5, 1943.

38. Leonia Brzeziński, diary, November 7, 1944.

39. Zbigniew Brzezinski, "The Future of Yalta," *Foreign Affairs* 63, no. 2 (Winter 1984/85): 279–302.

40. Leonia Brzeziński, diary, January 21, 1945.

41. Zbigniew Brzezinski, diary, May 19, 1945.

42. Leonia Brzeziński, diary, January 21, 1945.

43. Karen De Witt, "Brzezinski, the Power and the Glory," *Washington Post*, February 4, 1977.

44. Zbigniew Brzezinski, diary, June 22, 1944.

45. Zbigniew Brzezinski, diary, May 24, 1947.

46. Zbigniew Brzezinski, diary, August 16, 1945.

47. Brzezinski family private collection, Lech.

48. Brzezinski family private collection, Lech.

49. Zbigniew Brzezinski, diary, April 4, 1950.

50. Zbigniew Brzezinski, diary, November 11, 1948.
51. Zbigniew Brzezinski, interview with Justin Vaïsse, June 2011.
52. Zbigniew Brzezinski, diary, December 11, 1947.
53. Zbigniew Brzezinski, diary, March 3, 1950.
54. "Brzezinski: Power-Player from McGill," *The Gazette* (Montreal), August 6, 1980.
55. "Brzezinski: Power-Player from McGill."
56. Stanley Grossman, letter to the editor, *The Gazette* (Montreal), September 16, 1980.
57. Leonia Brzeziński, diary, February 20, 1949.
58. Leonia Brzeziński, diary, February 20, 1949.
59. Zbigniew Brzezinski, diary, June 21, 1947.
60. Zbigniew Brzezinski, diary, August 28, 1947.
61. Author interviews and email exchanges with Lech Brzezinski, 2021–24.
62. Matthew Brzezinski, interview with author, March 2021. Matthew is Lech and Wanda's son.
63. Leonia Brzezinski, diary, undated entry, 1948.
64. Memoirs: Forty Years Among Polish Canadians, Tadeusz Brzezinski, trans. Irma Zaleski (Brzezinski family private collection, Lech).
65. Zbigniew Brzezinski, diary, October 28, 1949.
66. Zbigniew Brzezinski, diary, January 25, 1950.
67. Zbigniew Brzezinski, diary, May 28, 1950.
68. Zbigniew Brzezinski, diary, August 25, 1947.
69. Aleksandra Zilkowska-Boehm, *The Roots Are Polish: A Conversation with Zbigniew Brzezinski* (Toronto: Canadian-Polish Research Institute, 2004).
70. Zbigniew Brzezinski, diary, January 18, 1948.
71. Norman Davies, *Europe at War, 1939–1945: No Simple Victory* (London: Pan Books, 2008), 195.
72. Brzezinski, "Russo-Soviet Nationalism," 3.
73. Brzezinski, "Russo-Soviet Nationalism," 62.
74. Brzezinski, "Russo-Soviet Nationalism," 60.
75. Brzezinski, "Russo-Soviet Nationalism," 24.
76. Brzezinski, "Russo-Soviet Nationalism," 121–22.
77. Brzezinski, "Russo-Soviet Nationalism," 92.
78. Brzezinski family private collection, Ian Brzezinski.
79. Zbigniew Brzezinski, diary, April 4, 1950.
80. Zbigniew Brzezinski, diary, June 16, 1950.
81. Zbigniew Brzezinski, diary, August 26, 1950.
82. Zbigniew Brzezinski, diary, September 19, 1950.
83. Brzezinski, interview with Justin Vaïsse, June 2011.
84. Leonia Brzeziński, diary, September 29, 1950.
85. McGill University yearbook, 1950, https://yearbooks.mcgill.ca/viewbook.php?campus=downtown&book_id=1950#page/24/mode/2up.

3: A POLE IN CAMBRIDGE

1. Justin Vaïsse, *Zbigniew Brzezinski: America's Grand Strategist* (Cambridge, MA: Harvard University Press, 2018), 48

2. Karen De Witt, "Brzezinski, the Power and the Glory," *Washington Post*, February 4, 1977.

3. John M. Chang to Zbigniew Brzezinski, July 13, 1950 (private collection of Ian Brzezinski).

4. W. J. Harlan to Zbigniew Brzezinski, July 13, 1950 (Brzezinski family private collection, Ian).

5. Zbigniew Brzezinski, letter to parents, April 5, 1951, from Acc. 25, 124 Letters to Parents 1950–1963, World Tour 1962–1963, box I (removed), trans. Andrzej Grządkowsk, Brzezinski Papers, LoC.

6. Vaïsse, *Zbigniew Brzezinski*, 47.

7. Nobel Prize, *Nobel Peace Prize Forum Oslo 2016 with Dr. Henry Kissinger and Dr. Zbigniew Brzezinski*, YouTube, December 14, 2016, https://www.youtube.com/watch?v=H7xJN1tbNMc.

8. David C. Engerman, *Know Your Enemy: The Rise and Fall of America's Soviet Experts* (New York: Oxford University Press, 2009), 1.

9. Engerman, *Know Your Enemy*, 3.

10. Zbigniew Brzezinski to parents, March 1, 1951.

11. Zbigniew Brzezinski to parents, February 2, 1951.

12. Zbigniew Brzezinski to parents, February 2, 1951.

13. Zbigniew Brzezinski to parents, November 1, 1950.

14. Zbigniew Brzezinski to parents, February 15, 1951.

15. Zbigniew Brzezinski to parents, October 9, 1951.

16. Zbigniew Brzezinski to parents, March 6, 1951.

17. Zbigniew Brzezinski to parents, February 17, 1951.

18. Zbigniew Brzezinski to parents, March 9, 1951.

19. Zbigniew Brzezinski, interview with Justin Vaïsse, 2011; Richard Hatton, Vaïsse interview, February 2012.

20. Zbigniew Brzezinski to parents, April 2, 1951.

21. Zbigniew Brzezinski to parents, October 9, 1951.

22. Zbigniew Brzezinski, "Party Controls in the Soviet Army," *Journal of Politics* 14, no. 4 (November 1952): 565–91.

23. Zbigniew Brzezinski, diary, March 14, 1951.

24. Zbigniew Brzezinski to parents, October 1, 1951.

25. Zbigniew Brzezinski, *The Permanent Purge: Politics in Soviet Totalitarianism* (Cambridge, MA: Harvard University Press, 1956), 3.

26. Zbigniew Brzezinski to parents, May 15, 1953.

27. Zbigniew Brzezinski, diary, November 23, 1953.

28. Zbigniew Brzezinski to parents, October 3, 1951.

29. Zbigniew Brzezinski, diary, August 13, 1952.

30. Zbigniew Brzezinski to parents, June–August 1953.

31. Zbigniew Brzezinski, diary, April 6, 1953.
32. Zbigniew Brzezinski, diary, January 20, 1952.
33. Zbigniew Brzezinski, diary, January 20, 1952.
34. "1938: Chamberlain Addresses the Nation on Peace Negotiations" (BBC Archive, https://www.bbc.com/videos/c999nrjj8jgo.
35. Muska and Mika Brzezinski, author interview, May 2021.
36. Emilie Beneš, diary, December 27, 1954 (private collection of Mika Brzezinski).
37. Emilie Beneš, diary, December 31, 1954.
38. Emilie Beneš, diary, January 20, 1954.
39. Zbigniew Brzezinski, diary, March 15, 1954.
40. Leonia Brzeziński, diary, August 3, 1955.
41. Zbigniew Brzezinski to parents, August 18, 1958.
42. Matthew Brzezinski, interview with author, March 2021.
43. Zbigniew Brzezinski, diary, May 11, 1954.
44. Muska Benes, diary, August 17, 1954.
45. Vaïsse, *Zbigniew Brzezinski*, 30.
46. Brzezinski, *The Permanent Purge*, 165.
47. Brzezinski, *The Permanent Purge*, 161; Zbigniew Brzezinski, "The Pattern of Political Purges," *Annals of the American Academy of Political and Social Science* 317, no. 1 (1958): 85.
48. Zbigniew Brzezinski to parents, February 28, 1955.
49. Zbigniew Brzezinski to parents, February 28, 1955.
50. Zbigniew Brzezinski to parents, February 17, 1955.
51. Emilie Beneš, diary, March 30, 1954.
52. Rosovksy, interview in Polish documentary *Strateg* ("Strategy"), TVN, 2013, trans. by Andrjez Grzadkowski.
53. "Emilie Anna Benes Is Wed in Massachusetts," *Boston Globe*, June 14, 1955.
54. Zbigniew Brzezinski, diary, June 13, 1955.
55. Edward Taborsky, review of *The Permanent Purge: Politics in Soviet Totalitarianism*, by Zbigniew Brzezinski, *American Political Science Review* 50, no. 3 (September 1956): 872–73.
56. Carl Friedrich to Zbigniew Brzezinski, December 20, 1955, box I: 9.9, Brzezinski Papers, LoC.
57. Zbigniew Brzezinski to Carl Friedrich, June 28, 1956, LoC.
58. All citations from Brzezinski's 1956 Russia trip are from a diary he kept in Brzezinski family private collection, Ian.
59. From Brzezinski's Soviet journal.
60. William Ebenstein, "The Study of Totalitarianism," review of *Totalitarian Dictatorship and Autocracy* by Carl J. Friedrich and Zbigniew K. Brzezinski, *World Politics* 10, no. 2 (1958): 278.
61. Ebenstein, "Study of Totalitarianism," 275.
62. The phrase was coined by Lev Dobriansky, a Ukrainian American professor of economics at Georgetown University.
63. Louis Menand, "The Devil's Disciples," *New Yorker*, July 20, 2003.

64. Carl Friedrich to Zbigniew Brzezinski, December 6, 1961, box I: 9.9, Brzezinski Papers, LoC.

65. Drawn from Brzezinski's unpublished diary of his 1957 Poland trip (Brzezinski family private collection, Ian).

66. SB, Zbigniew Brzezinski ("Ogiński"), UB/SB files, Warsaw, marked SECRET, trans. Andrzej Grzątkowski, September 21, 1963.

67. Zbigniew Brzezinski ("Ogiński"), UB/SB files, trans. Andrzej Grzątkowski, May 23, 1957.

68. Zbigniew Brzezinski ("Ogiński"), UB/SB files, Memo file 10, February 1965, by "Rudzki."

69. Zbigniew Brzezinski ("Ogiński"), UB/SB files, November 25, 1964, by "Rudzki."

70. When Poland's secret police files were opened after the fall of communism, Roman declined to look at his. He did not want to know which friends had betrayed him. Dagmara Roman, his widow, interview with author, Warsaw, June 2022.

71. Dagmara Roman, interview with the author, Warsaw, June 2022.

72. Zbigniew Brzezinski, Poland diary, July 1958.

73. Bennett Kovrig, *Of Walls and Bridges: The United States and Eastern Europe* (New York: New York University Press, 1991), 93.

74. Zbigniew Brzezinski, "U.S. Foreign Policy in East Central Europe—a Study in Contradiction," *Journal of International Affairs* 11, no. 1 (1957): 60.

75. Zbigniew Brzezinski, Poland diary, July 1957.

76. Fred Holborn to Zbigniew Brzezinski, July 29, 1957, box I: 16.6, Brzezinski Papers, LoC.

77. General correspondence with John F. Kennedy, July 29, 1957; "Remarks of Senator John F. Kennedy in the Senate, Washington, D.C., August 21, 1957: The Struggle Against Imperialism—Part II," John F. Kennedy Presidential Library and Museum, https://www.jfklibrary.org/archives/other-resources/john-f-kennedy-speeches/washington-dc-19570821.

78. "Remarks of Senator John F. Kennedy at the Annual Awards Dinner of the Overseas Press Club, New York, New York, May 6, 1957," John F. Kennedy Presidential Library and Museum, https://www.jfklibrary.org/archives/other-resources/john-f-kennedy-speeches/overseas-press-club-nyc-19570506.

79. John F. Kennedy to Zbigniew Brzezinski, August 23, 1957, box I: 16.6, Brzezinski Papers, LoC.

80. McGeorge Bundy to Zbigniew Brzezinski, June 24, 1957, box I: 3.7, Brzezinski Papers, LoC.

81. Zbigniew Brzezinski to parents, February 13, 1956.

82. Zbigniew Brzezinski to parents, January 1, 1956.

83. Zbigniew Brzezinski to parents, January 1, 1956.

84. Zbigniew Brzezinski to parents, November 19, 1958.

85. Zbigniew Brzezinski to parents, May 6, 1958.

86. Zbigniew Brzezinski to parents, March 12, 1958.

87. Zbigniew Brzezinski to parents, July 6, 1958.

88. Drawn from Mika Brzezinski's unpublished collection of her parents' papers.

89. Emilie Brzezinski, letter to Zbigniew, August 15, 1958 (Brzezinski family private collection, Mika).

90. Emilie Brzezinski, letter to Zbigniew, August 17, 1958.

91. Vaïsse, *Zbigniew Brzezinski*, 59.

92. Vaïsse, *Zbigniew Brzezinski*, 32.

93. Patrick G. Vaughan, "Zbigniew Brzezinski: The Political and Academic Life of a Cold War Visionary" (PhD dissertation, West Virginia University, 2003), 29.

94. Henry Rosovsky, *Strateg*, author interview with General Mark Odom, son of the late William H. Odom, June 2023.

95. Vaïsse, *Zbigniew Brzezinski*, 59–62.

96. Walter Pincus, interviews with author, February 2021 and July 2023.

97. Inge Schneier, interview with Justin Vaïsse, December 4, 2009.

98. Zbigniew Brzezinski, *The Soviet Bloc: Unity and Conflict* (Cambridge, MA: Harvard University Press, 1960), 512.

99. Stephen D. Kertesz, review of *The Soviet Bloc: Unity and Conflict, Ideology and Power in the Relations Among the USSR, Poland, Yugoslavia, China, and Other Communist States,* by Zbigniew K. Brzezinski, *The American Slavic and East European Review* 20, no. 1 (February 1961): 123–25.

100. Alexander Dallin, "In Unity, Diversity," *New York Times*, July 3, 1960.

101. Cyril Black, review of *The Soviet Bloc: Unity and Conflict,* by Zbigniew Brzezinski, *Russian Review* 19, no. 4 (October 1960): 400.

102. Robert Legvold, review of *The Soviet Bloc: Unity and Conflict,* by Zbigniew Brzezinski, *Foreign Affairs* 76, no. 5 (September–October 1997): 231.

103. Zbigniew Brzezinski to parents, May 4, 1958.

104. Walter Isaacson, *Kissinger: A Biography* (New York: Simon & Schuster Paperbacks, 2005), 76.

105. The account draws heavily on Vaïsse, *Zbigniew Brzezinski*, 63–66.

106. Kissinger interview cited in Vaughan, "Zbigniew Brzezinski," 53.

107. Vaïsse, *Zbigniew Brzezinski*, 80.

108. Zbigniew Brzezinski, interview with Justin Vaïsse, transcript, February 15, 2011.

4: FALLING TOWARDS WASHINGTON

1. Adam Garfinkle, "The Strategic Thinker," in *Zbig: The Strategy and Statecraft of Zbigniew Brzezinski,* edited by Charles Gati (Baltimore: Johns Hopkins University Press, 2013), 194.

2. Justin Vaïsse, *Zbigniew Brzezinski: America's Grand Strategist* (Cambridge, MA: Harvard University Press, 2018), 54–55; Robert Novak, "Kennedy's Brain Trust: More Professors Enlist but They Play Limited Policy-Making Role," *Wall Street Journal,* October 4, 1960.

3. Vaïsse, *Zbigniew Brzezinski*, 54–55.

4. John F. Kennedy to Zbigniew Brzezinski, August 5, 1960 box I: 220.4, Brzezinski Papers, LoC.

5. Speech of John F. Kennedy, Polish American Congress, Chicago, October 1, 1960, The American Presidency Project, https://www.presidency.ucsb.edu/documents/speech-senator-john-f-kennedy-polish-american-congress-chicago-il.

6. David B. Truman to Zbigniew Brzezinski, January 20, 1960, box I: 5.4, Brzezinski Papers, LoC.

7. Zbigniew Brzezinski to Alexander Dallin, July 29, 1962, box I: 6.9, Brzezinski Papers, LoC.

8. Zbigniew Brzezinski to Alexander Dallin, July 29, 1962, box I: 6.9, Brzezinski Papers, LoC.

9. Vaïsse, *Zbigniew Brzezinski*, 68.

10. Zbigniew Brzezinski to Alexander Dallin, July 29, 1962, box I: 6.9, Brzezinski Papers, LoC.

11. Vaïsse, *Zbigniew Brzezinski*, 95.

12. Kai Bird identifies McCloy as the epitome of the postwar establishment in his biography, *The Chairman: John McCloy and the Making of the American Establishment* (New York: Simon & Schuster, January 2017).

13. Zbigniew Brzezinski, "America in a Hostile World," *Foreign Policy* no. 23 (Summer 1976): 65–96.

14. Walter Isaacson and Evan Thomas, *The Wise Men: Six Friends and the World They Made* (New York: Simon & Schuster, 2013), 593.

15. Fred Bergsten, interview with author, March 2023.

16. Zbigniew Brzezinski and William E. Griffith, "Peaceful Engagement in Eastern Europe," *Foreign Affairs* 39, no. 4 (July 1961): 642–54.

17. Henry Kissinger to Zbigniew Brzezinski, July 24, 1961, box I: 16.18, Brzezinski Papers, LoC.

18. Arthur Schlesinger, Jr., to Zbigniew Brzezinski, box IV: 9.1, Brzezinski Papers, LoC.

19. John F. Kennedy, "Address at the Free University of Berlin," June 26, 1963, American Presidency Project, https://www.presidency.ucsb.edu/documents/address-the-free-university-berlin.

20. Zbigniew Brzezinski to Charles "Chip" Bohlen, October 5, 1962, box I: 2.14, Brzezinski Papers, LoC.

21. Zbigniew Brzezinski to Charles "Chip" Bohlen, October 9, 1962, box I: 2.14, Brzezinski Papers, LoC.

22. Madeleine Albright, interviews with author, January 2021 and March 2021.

23. Several of Brzezinski's students and acquaintances reported this to the author, including Madeleine Albright, Gordon Goldstein, Michael Perkinson, and Toby Gati.

24. Stephen F. Szabo, *Zbig: The Strategy and Statecraft of Zbigniew Brzezinski*, edited by Charles Gati (Baltimore: Johns Hopkins University Press, 2013), 212.

25. All the details from Brzezinski's world tour come from his lengthy letters to his parents. There are roughly seventy letters in total.

26. Zbigniew Brzezinski to parents, November 20, 1962, from "World Tour," 1962–1963, box 1, Brzezinski Papers, LoC.

27. Zbigniew Brzezinski to parents, December 14, 1962, from "World Tour," 1962–1963, box I, Brzezinski Papers, LoC.

28. Zbigniew Brzezinski to Arthur Ochs Sulzberger, December 30, 1963, box I: 29.15, Brzezinski Papers, LoC.

29. David C. Engerman, *Know Your Enemy: The Rise and Fall of America's Soviet Experts* (New York: Oxford University Press, 2009), 46.

30. Engerman, *Know Your Enemy*, 67.

31. Interview with the author, January 2012.

32. Zbigniew Brzezinski, *The Soviet Bloc: Unity and Conflict*, rev. and enlarged ed. (Cambridge, MA: Harvard University Press, 1967), xiii.

33. Engerman, *Know Your Enemy*, 224.

34. Zbigniew Brzezinski to Henry Kissinger, May 19, 1961, box 1: 16.18, Brzezinski Papers, LoC.

35. Henry Kissinger to Zbigniew Brzezinski, October 24, 1963; Zbigniew Brzezinski to Henry Kissinger, October 30, 1963; Henry Kissinger to Zbigniew Brzezinski, November 8, 1963, box 1: 16.18, Brzezinski Papers, LoC.

36. Henry Kissinger, interviews with author, March 2021 and April 2023.

37. Henry Kissinger to Zbigniew Brzezinski, January 23, 1964; Zbigniew Brzezinski to Henry Kissinger, January 30, 1964, box 1: 16.18, Brzezinski Papers, LoC.

38. Josef Korbel, "Changes in Eastern Europe and New Opportunities for American Policy," review of *Alternative to Partition: For a Broader Conception of America's Role in Europe*, by Zbigniew Brzezinski, *World Politics* 18, no. 4 (July 1966): 759.

39. David McClellan, review of *Alternative to Partition: For a Broader Conception of America's Role in Europe*, by Zbigniew Brzezinski, *Political Research Quarterly* 18, no. 4 (December 1965): 900–901.

40. Transcript of the debate provided by the Chicago Council on Global Affairs (courtesy Ivo Daalder).

41. McGeorge Bundy to Brzezinski, December 22, 1965 (Brzezinski family private collection, Ian Brzezinski).

42. Niall Ferguson, *Kissinger: 1923–1968: The Idealist* (New York: Penguin, 2015), 389.

43. William A. M. Burden to Zbigniew Brzezinski, June 24, 1965, box I: 3.9, Brzezinski Papers, LoC.

44. William A. M. Burden to Zbigniew Brzezinski, August 14, 1967, box I: 3.9, Brzezinski Papers, LoC.

45. William A. M. Burden to Zbigniew Brzezinski, May 11, 1966, box I: 3.9, Brzezinski Papers, LoC.

46. Zbigniew Brzezinski, diary, August 23, 1966, "Policy Planning Staff, 1966–7" (Brzezinski family private collection, Ian).

47. Zbigniew Brzezinski, diary, August 23, 1966.

48. Zbigniew Brzezinski, policy planning diary, January 5, 1967 (Brzezinski family private collection, Ian).

49. Oral history transcript, Zbigniew Brzezinski, interview 1 (I), November 12, 1971, by Paige E. Mulhollan, LBJ Library Oral Histories, LBJ Presidential Library, accessed

October 23, 2024, https://www.discoverlbj.org/item/oh-brzezinskiz-19711112-1 -82-1.

50. Zbigniew Brzezinski, policy planning diary, September 13, 1966.

51. Zbigniew Brzezinski, policy planning diary, August 15, 1967.

52. Lyndon B. Johnson, "Remarks in New York City Before the National Conference of Editorial Writers," October 7, 1966, The American Presidency Project, https://www .presidency.ucsb.edu/documents/remarks-new-york-city-before-the-national-confer ence-editorial-writers.

53. Zbigniew Brzezinski, policy planning diary, October 18, 1966.

54. Zbigniew Brzezinski, policy planning diary, September 16, 1966.

55. Zbigniew Brzezinski to Muska, undated (Brzezinski family private collection, Mika).

56. Zbigniew Brzezinski to Muska, "composed in the skies between DC and NYC," June 21, 1972 (Brzezinski family private collection, Mika).

57. "Organizations: The Card Caper," *Time*, December 21, 1962.

58. Zbigniew Brzezinski, policy planning diary, January 12, 1966.

59. Zbigniew Brzezinski, policy planning diary, June 13, 1967.

60. Sean Wilentz, "Lone Star Setting," *New York Times Books*, April 12, 1988.

61. Zbigniew Brzezinski, policy planning diary, May 18, 1966.

62. Harry McPherson, *A Political Education: A Washington Memoir* (Austin: University of Texas Press, 1995), 294.

63. Zbigniew Brzezinski, policy planning diary, May 18, 1967.

64. Oral history transcript, Zbigniew Brzezinski, interview 1 (I), November 12, 1971, by Paige E. Mulhollan, LBJ Library Oral Histories, LBJ Presidential Library, accessed October 23, 2024, https://www.discoverlbj.org/item/oh-brzezinskiz-19711112-1-82-1.

65. Oral history transcript, Zbigniew Brzezinski, interview 1.

66. Zbigniew Brzezinski, policy planning diary, December 14, 1967.

67. Zbigniew Brzezinski, policy planning diary, November 27, 1967.

68. Zbigniew Brzezinski to Secretary of Defense Clifford Clark, unpublished memo (Brzezinski family private collection, Ian).

69. John Rielly, memo to Bob Nathan, Subject: Financial arrangements for Professor Brzezinski, June 19, 1968, box I: 94.5, Brzezinski Papers, LoC.

70. Roy Reid, "Humphrey's Advisers Critical of War," *New York Times*, July 14, 1968.

71. "Chairmen of Humphrey Foreign Policy Task Forces Announced," News from United Democrats for Humphrey, July 15, 1968, box I: 94.6, Brzezinski Papers, LoC.

72. Jospeh A. Loftus, "Humphrey Maps War Position with Aid of Specialists on Asia," *New York Times*, July 24, 1968, box I: 94.6, Brzezinski Papers, LoC.

73. Robert Dallek, *Lyndon B. Johnson, Portrait of a President* (New York: Oxford University Press, 2004), 340.

74. Brzezinski to Humphrey, July 16, 1968, box I: 94.6, Brzezinski Papers, LoC.

75. John Rielly, interview with author, November 2023.

76. Hubert H. Humphrey interviewed by Sam Donaldson and Bob Clark, *Issues and Answers*, ABC, August 11, 1968, 6, Minnesota Historical Society, http://www2.mnhs .org/library/findaids/00442/pdfa/00442-02664.pdf.

77. Patrick G. Vaughan, "Zbigniew Brzezinski: The Political and Academic Life of a Cold War Visionary" (PhD dissertation, West Virginia University, 2003), 119.

78. Lyndon Baines Johnson, *The Vantage Point: Perspectives of the Presidency 1963–1969* (Holt, Reinhart and Winston, 1971).

79. Bennett Kovrig, *Of Walls and Bridges: The United States and Eastern Europe* (New York: New York University Press, 1991), 114.

80. Kovrig, *Of Walls and Bridges*, 113.

81. Zbigniew Brzezinski to Hubert H. Humphrey, August 14, 1968, box I: 94.7, Brzezinski Papers, LoC.

82. Hubert H. Humphrey, "Address Accepting the Presidential Nomination at the Democratic National Convention in Chicago, August 29, 1968, The American Presidency Project, https://www.presidency.ucsb.edu/documents/address-accepting-the-presidential-nomination-the-democratic-national-convention-chicago-2.

83. Zbigniew Brzezinski to Hubert H. Humphrey, Subject: Teddy Kennedy for Vice President: "Heads You Lose, Tails He Wins," July 19, 1968, box I: 94.7, Brzezinski Papers, LoC.

84. Hubert H. Humphrey to Zbigniew Brzezinski, August 6, 1968, box I: 94.7, Brzezinski Papers, LoC.

85. Hubert Humphrey, *The Education of a Public Man: My Life and Politics* (New York: Doubleday, 1976), 276.

86. Norman Mailer, *Miami and the Siege of Chicago: An Informal History of the Republican and Democratic Conventions of 1968* (New York: New York Review Books Classics, 2008, ebook, location 2612.

87. "Losers: Weepers or Walkers," *Newsweek*, September 9, 1968.

88. Zbigniew Brzezinski to George Kennan, January 31, 1968, box I: 16.3, Brzezinski Papers, LoC.

89. Zbigniew Brzezinski, "Revolution and Counter-Revolution (but Not Necessarily About Columbia!)," *New Republic*, June 1, 1968.

90. Mark Rudd, "Reply to Uncle Grayson," *Up Against the Wall*, April 22, 1968.

91. Zbigniew Brzezinski, letter to the editor, *Washington Post*, April 17, 1968.

92. Zbigniew Brzezinski, interview with Justin Vaïsse, April 2011.

93. Michael Klare, interview with author, February 2021.

94. Much of this account is drawn from Vaughan, "Zbigniew Brzezinski."

95. Vaughan, "Zbigniew Brzezinski," 98.

96. Isaacson and Thomas, *The Wise Men*, 656.

97. Isaacson and Thomas, *The Wise Men*, 656.

98. Isaacson and Thomas, *The Wise Men*, 660.

99. Isaacson and Thomas, *The Wise Men*, 661.

100. Walter Isaacson, *Kissinger: A Biography* (New York: Simon & Schuster Paperbacks, 2005), 124.

101. Zbigniew Brzezinski, interview with Justin Vaïsse, April 2011.

102. Henry Kissinger, interview with author, March 2021.

103. Vaughan, "Zbigniew Brzezinski," 131–32.

104. Isaacson, *Kissinger*, 133.

105. Among those who harbored that suspicion was Robert Hunter, who served on Humphrey's campaign. Robert Hunter, interview with author, February 2024.

106. Zbigniew Brzezinski to Hubert H. Humphrey, "A Strategic Memorandum: A Humane Way to Renewal and Reconciliation," September 9, 1968, box 1: 94.7, Brzezinski Papers, LoC.

107. Vaughan, "Zbigniew Brzezinski," 135.

108. Zbigniew Brzezinski to Hubert H. Humphrey, November 22, 1968, box I: 13.2, Brzezinski Papers, LoC.

109. Brzezinski repeated this frequently told anecdote at the Nobel Peace Prize Forum in December 2016, a few months before he died.

110. Isaacson, *Kissinger*, 132.

5: THE WARRIOR DOVE

1. Henry Raymont, "Intellectuals Gather to Discuss Nixon's Problems," *New York Times*, December 1, 1968.

2. Israel Shenker, "Kennan Analysis Coolly Received," *New York Times*, December 4, 1968.

3. Shenker, "Kennan Analysis Coolly Received."

4. Walter Goodman, "The Liberal Establishment Faces the Blacks, the Young, the New Left," *New York Times*, December 29, 1968.

5. Stanley Hoffmann, "Gulliver's Troubles," Council on Foreign Relations, New York 1968 (as cited in Patrick G. Vaughan, "Zbigniew Brzezinski: The Political and Academic Life of a Cold War Visionary" [PhD dissertation, West Virginia University, 2003], 75).

6. Goodman, "The Liberal Establishment."

7. Zbigniew Brzezinski to Muska Brzezinski, June 15, 1968 (Brzezinski family private collection, Mika)

8. Author interview with Elise Zylinska, August 2023.

9. Jiri Valenda, *Soviet Intervention in Czechoslovakia, 1968* (Baltimore: Johns Hopkins University Press, 1979), 34.

10. "Brzezinski Accused," *New York Times*, July 16, 1968.

11. Erwin Weit, *At the Red Summit: Interpreter Behind the Iron Curtain*, trans. Mary Schofield (New York: Macmillan, 1973), 203–4.

12. *Neues Deutschland* article, Reactions to Brzezinski, box I: 101, Brzezinski Papers, LoC.

13. Vaughan, "Zbigniew Brzezinski," 118.

14. SB memo by "St," US/SB "Oginski files," trans. Andrjez Grzadkowski, March 31, 1966.

15. SB memo by "W," June 19, 1966.

16. SB memo by "R," May 10, 1966.

17. SB memo by Senior Operations Officer of Unit IV, Dept I, or Ministry of the Interior, October 17, 1966.

18. Zbigniew Brzezinski, "Victory of the Clerks," *The New Republic*, November 14, 1964.

19. That characterization is from Vaughan, "Zbigniew Brzezinski," 69.

20. Alexander Krivitski, "Mr. Brzezinski's Fruits of Enlightenment," March 26, 1969, box I: 101.1, Brzezinski Papers, LoC.

21. Reactions to Brzezinski, box I: 101.

22. Reactions to Brzezinski, box I: 101.

23. Quoted in Michael Dobbs, *Madeleine Albright: A Twentieth-Century Odyssey* (New York: Henry Holt, 2000), 197.

24. Zbigniew Brzezinski, letter to the editor, "Probing Panther Attack," *New York Times,* December 21, 1969.

25. Dobbs, *Madeleine Albright,* 215.

26. Zbigniew Brzezinski, *Between Two Ages: The Global Impact of the Technetronic Revolution* (New York: Viking Press, 1970), 24.

27. John G. Stoessinger, "Recent Books on International Relations," *Foreign Affairs* 48, no. 4 (July 1970), 782.

28. Richard Burt, "Zbig Makes it Big," *New York Times Magazine,* July 30, 1978.

29. Brzezinski, *Between Two Ages,* 133.

30. Hal Brands, *The Twilight Struggle, What the Cold War Teaches us about Great Power Rivalry Today* (New Haven, CT: Yale University Press, January 25, 2022), ebook, 168.

31. Brzezinski, *Between Two Ages,* 138.

32. Gerry Argyris Andrianopoulos, *Kissinger and Brzezinski: The NSC and the Struggle for Control of US National Security Policy* (London: Palgrave Macmillan, 1991), 29.

33. Zbigniew Brzezinski to Henry Kissinger, July 30, 1968, box I: 16.18, Brzezinski Papers, LoC.

34. Zbigniew Brzezinski to Henry Kissinger, July 30, 1968.

35. Zbigniew Brzezinski to Henry Kissinger, December 22, 1970.

36. Zbigniew Brzezinski to Richard Nixon, October 22, 1969, box I: 16.18, Brzezinski Papers, LoC.

37. Zbigniew Brzezinski to Richard Nixon, Key Elements of the Speech on Vietnam, October 22, 1969, box I: 16.18, Brzezinski Papers, LoC.

38. Zbigniew Brzezinski to Henry Kissinger, January 26, 1970, box I: 16.19, Brzezinski Papers, LoC.

39. Zbigniew Brzezinski, Memo on Conversation with Henry Kissinger, May 23, 1970, box I: 16.19, Brzezinski Papers, LoC.

40. See, e.g., Walter Isaacson, *Kissinger: A Biography* (New York: Simon & Schuster Paperbacks, 2005), 172–265.

41. Zbigniew Brzezinski "The Cambodian Crisis," May 25, 1970, box I: 16.19, Brzezinski Papers, LoC.

42. Zbigniew Brzezinski, "Isolationism and Fragmentation," *Newsweek,* February 9, 1970.

43. Zbigniew Brzezinski, Memo on Conversations with Henry Kissinger, May 23, 1970, box I: 16.19, Brzezinski Papers, LoC.

44. Zbigniew Brzezinski, diary, June 3, 1971.

45. Henry Scott Stokes, "Say Sayonara to Certainty in Japanese Political Life," review of *The Fragile Blossom: Crisis and Change in Japan* by Zbigniew Brzezinski, *New York Times,* April 9, 1972.

46. General Correspondence, Zbigniew Brzezinski to Abraham Brumberg, November 23, 1960, box I: 3.3, Brzezinski Papers, LoC.

47. Zbigniew Brzezinski, "Sayonara to Certainty," *Newsweek,* September 20, 1971.

48. David Rockefeller, *Memoirs* (New York: Random House, 2003), 216–17.

49. Justin Vaïsse, *Zbigniew Brzezinski: America's Grand Strategist* (Cambridge, MA: Harvard University Press, 2018), 165.

50. Zbigniew Brzezinski, diary, April 1972.

51. Rockefeller, *Memoirs*, 216–17.

52. Rockefeller to Brzezinski, May 12, 2009, private collection, Ian Brzezinski.

53. Vaïsse, *Zbigniew Brzezinski*, 171.

54. Fred Bergsten, interview with author, March 2023.

55. Quoted in Rockefeller, *Memoirs*, 415.

56. Cited in Vaïsse, *Zbigniew Brzezinski*, 216. Brzezinski to Smith, Owen, Franklin, "Some Brutal Reflections on the State of the Commission," December 16,1974, folder "Gerald Smith file—Atlantic Institute," Box 33.7, Brzezinski Collection, Jimmy Carter Library, Atlanta, Georgia.

57. Board of Trustees of the Trilateral Commission, summary of the meeting, February 8, 1975, New York City, Gerald Smith file, Atlantic Institute, box 33: 1, Brzezinski Collection, Jimmy Carter Library.

58. Edmund Muskie to Zbigniew Brzezinski, August 10, 1972, box I: 94.13, Brzezinski Papers, LoC.

59. Hubert Humphrey to Zbigniew Brzezinski, July 17, 1972 box I: 94.9, Brzezinski Papers, LoC.

60. Rowland Evans and Robert Novak, "McGovern's Odd Braintrust," *Washington Post*, September 3, 1972.

61. Zbigniew Brzezinski, "Not in Agreement," letter to editor, September 3, 1972, box I: 94.11, Brzezinski Papers, LoC.

62. Zbigniew Brzezinski to Cord Meyer, October 12, 1972. box I: 94.11, Brzezinski Papers, LoC.

63. Zbigniew Brzezinski, to Hubert Humphrey and Edmund Muskie, 1972 (undated), box I: 94.9, 94.13, Brzezinski Papers, LoC.

64. Zbigniew Brzezinski to Max Kampelman, Re: Hubert's speech on Nixon's and McGovern's foreign policies, May 6, 1972, box I: 94.9, Brzezinski Papers, LoC.

65. Zbigniew Brzezinski to Max Kampelman, May 6, 1972.

66. Zbigniew Brzezinski to Hubert Humphrey, March 16, 1970, box I: 13.3, Brzezinski Papers, LoC.

67. Robert Novak revealed the source of this quote as Senator Tom Eagleton; see Timothy Noah, "'Acid, Amnesty, and Abortion'": The Unlikely Source of a Legendary Smear," *The New Republic*, October 21, 2012.

68. Jonathan Alter, *His Very Best: Jimmy Carter, A Life* (New York: Simon & Schuster, 2020), 198.

69. Carter used this phrase repeatedly in his published memoirs and on the stump.

70. Vaughan, "Zbigniew Brzezinski," 192.

71. Vaughan, "Zbigniew Brzezinski," 193.

72. Alter, *His Very Best*, 204.

73. Alter, *His Very Best*, 221.

74. Zbigniew Brzezinski, *Power and Principle: Memoirs of the National Security Adviser, 1977–1981* (New York: Farrar, Straus and Giroux, 1983), 5.

75. Alter, *His Very Best*, 221.

76. Zbigniew Brzezinski, interview with Justin Vaïsse, February 2011.

77. Brzezinski, *Power and Principle*, 6.

78. Attributed to the legendary *New York Times* reporter R. W. "Johnny" Apple.

79. Jurek Martin, "Carter: The Favourite Who Could Defeat Himself," *Financial Times*, July 17, 1976.

80. Madeleine Albright loved repeating this quip.

81. For the best description of this period, see Martin Indyk, *Master of the Game, Henry Kissinger and the Art of Middle East Diplomacy* (New York: Knopf, 2021). Also read my review of Indyk's book in the *Financial Times*, "Kissinger's Perilous Middle East Balancing Act," December 2, 2021.

82. Edward Luce, "Kissinger's Perilous Middle East Balancing Act."

83. Luce, "Kissinger's Perilous Middle East Balancing Act."

84. Zbigniew Brzezinski, "Crisis and Parity," *Newsweek*, March 1, 1972.

85. Henry Kissinger to Zbigniew Brzezinski, October 19, 1973, box I: 16.19, Brzezinski Papers, LoC.

86. Zbigniew Brzezinski, "The Deceptive Structure of Peace," *Foreign Policy* 14 (Spring 1974): 35–55.

87. Brzezinski, "Deceptive Structure of Peace," 35–55.

88. Henry Kissinger to Zbigniew Brzezinski, March 23, 1974, box I: 16.20, Brzezinski Papers, LoC.

89. Henry Kissinger to Zbigniew Brzezinski, March 23, 1974.

90. Al Kamen, "Kissinger Calls Brzezinski 'a Total Whore,'" *Washington Post*, October 16, 2012.

91. Kamen, "Kissinger Calls Brzezinski 'a Total Whore.'"

92. Kamen, "Kissinger Calls Brzezinski 'a Total Whore.'"

93. Zbigniew Brzezinski, unpublished personal diary, August 13, 1975 (Brzezinski family private collection, Ian).

94. Stu Eizenstat, interview with the author, March 2022.

95. Zbigniew Brzezinski, 1976 campaign diary, July 12, 1976 (Brzezinski family private collection, Ian).

96. Zbigniew Brzezinski to Jimmy Carter, October 28, 1975, box I: 38.10, Brzezinski Papers, LoC.

97. Zbigniew Brzezinski to Jimmy Carter, November 3, 1975, box I: 38.10, Brzezinski Papers, LoC.

98. R. W. Apple, Jr., "Carter Appears to Hold a Solid Lead in Iowa as the Campaign's First Test Approaches," *New York Times*, October 27, 1975.

99. Alter, *His Very Best*, 219.

100. James Reston, "When Jimmy Pretends," *New York Times*, March 19, 1976.

101. Jimmy Carter, "Relation Between World's Democracies," June 23, 1976, Office of the Historian, https://history.state.gov/historicaldocuments/frus1977-80v01/d6.

102. June 29, 1976, Carter administration campaign internal memoranda, June 1976, box I: 39, Brzezinski Papers, LoC.

103. Hal Brands, *The Twilight Struggle: What the Cold War Teaches Us About Great-Power Rivalry Today* (New Haven, CT: Yale University Press, 2022), 144.

104. Gerald R. Ford, "Remarks and a Question-and-Answer Session at the Everett McKinley Dirksen Forum in Peoria, March 5, 1976, The American Presidency Project, https:// www.presidency.ucsb.edu/documents/remarks-and-question-and-answer-session -the-everett-mckinley-dirksen-forum-peoria.

105. Isaacson, *Kissinger*, 700.

106. Drew Middleton, "Zumwalt, in Book, Says Kissinger Sees a Lack of U.S. Stamina," *New York Times*, March 17, 1976.

107. John Nordheimer, "Reagan, in Direct Attack, Assails Ford on Defense," *New York Times*, March 5, 1976.

108. Jimmy Carter, "Our Foreign Relations," March 15, 1976, Office of the Historian, https://history.state.gov/historicaldocuments/frus1977-80v01/d4.

109. Alter, *His Very Best*, 233.

110. Emma Hurt, "How Jimmy Carter and Joe Biden Built an Enduring Friendship," Axios, March 1, 2021, https://www.axios.com/2023/03/01/jimmy-carter-joe-biden-friend ship, quoting Joe Biden's video tribute to Jimmy Carter in which he quoted the words he used during his March 26, 1976, endorsement of Carter.

111. Zbigniew Brzezinski, diary, July 17, 1976.

112. Zbigniew Brzezinski, diary, July 17, 1976.

113. "Transcript of Carter Address Accepting Democratic Nomination for the Presidency," *New York Times*, July 16, 1976.

114. Alter, *His Very Best*, 263.

115. Zbigniew Brzezinski, campaign diary, July 29, 1976.

116. Lee Dembart, "Carter's Comments on Sex Cause Concern," *New York Times*, September 23, 1976.

117. Carter Campaign Briefing Books, Foreign Policy Debate, 1976, box I: 35, Brzezinski Papers, LoC.

118. Zbigniew Brzezinski, campaign diary, October 7, 1976.

119. William Safire, "Super Yalta," *New York Times*, July 28, 1975.

120. Ronald Reagan, "To Restore America," March 31, 1976, Ronald Reagan Presidential Library and Museum, https://www.reaganlibrary.gov/archives/speech/restore-america.

121. Transcript of the Musgrove Conference of the "Carter-Brezhnev Project," Saint Simon's Island, Georgia, May 6–9, 1994, quoted by Viktor Sukhodrev, former Brezhnev interpreter, 45.

122. Zbigniew Brzezinski, campaign diary, October 7, 1976.

123. Patrick G. Vaughan, "Zbigniew Brzezinski: The Political and Academic Life of a Cold War Visionary" (PhD dissertation, West Virginia University, 2003), 265.

124. Debate transcript, "October 6, 1976 Debate Transcript," The Commission on Presidential debates, https://www.debates.org/voter-education/debate-transcripts/october-6 -1976-debate-transcript/.

125. Vaughan, "Zbigniew Brzezinski," 266.

126. Brzezinski family private family collection, Ian.

127. Saturday Night Live, "Debate '76," October 1976, https://www.youtube.com/watch?v=xu2vdE0z7ds.

128. Isaacson, *Kissinger*, 703.

129. Zbigniew Brzezinski, campaign diary, November 3, 1976.

130. Zbigniew Brzezinski, campaign diary, November 29, 1976.

131. Zbigniew Brzezinski, campaign diary, November 29, 1976.

132. Zbigniew Brzezinski, Carter campaign diary, December 7, 1976 ("dictated on plan [*sic*] back from Atlanta").

133. Anatoly Dobrynin, *In Confidence: Moscow's Ambassador to Six Cold War Presidents* (Seattle: University of Washington Press, 1995), 368.

134. George Packer, *Our Man: Richard Holbrooke and the End of the American Century* (New York: Knopf, 2019), 170.

135. Quoted in Rudy Abramson, *Spanning the Century: The Life of W. Averell Harriman, 1891–1986* (New York: William Morrow, 1992), 688–90.

136. Abramson, *Spanning the Century*, 688–90.

137. Abramson, *Spanning the Century*, 690.

138. Zbigniew Brzezinski to Averell Harriman, June 21, 1974, box I: 12.2, Brzezinski Papers, LoC.

139. Averell Harriman to Zbigniew Brzezinski, July 2, 1974, box I: 12.2, Brzezinski Papers, LoC.

140. Arthur M. Schlesinger, Jr., *Journals, 1952–2000* (New York: Penguin Press, 2007), 448.

141. Betty Glad, *An Outsider in the White House: Jimmy Carter, His Advisors, and the Making of American Foreign Policy* (Ithaca, NY: Cornell University Press, 2009), 26.

142. Zbigniew Brzezinski, diary, December 15, 1976.

143. Walter Isaacson and Evan Thomas, *The Wise Men: Six Friends and the World They Made* (New York: Simon & Schuster, 2013), 726.

144. Zbigniew Brzezinski, diary, December 19, 1976.

145. Zbigniew Brzezinski, Carter campaign diary, December 19, 1976.

146. "Brzezinski Excelled in Politics, Says Father," *Toronto Star*, October 23, 1976.

6: ZBIG HEAVEN

1. Charles Heck, interview with author, February 2023.

2. Zbigniew Brzezinski, diary kept while holding the role of US national security advisor, 1977–1981, unpublished, January 11, 1977, henceforth referred to as "NSA diary."

3. Rick Inderfurth, interview with author, January 2021. Inderfurth was Brzezinski's special assistant.

4. NSA diary, January 11, 1977.

5. NSA diary, January 20, 1977.

6. Ian, Mark, Mika, and Matthew Brzezinski, interviews with author. Matthew is Lech Brzezinski's son.

7. Hamilton Jordan, *Crisis: The Last Year of the Carter Presidency* (New York: Berkley, 1983), 39.

8. NSA diary, January 21, 1977.

9. Zbigniew Brzezinski, *Power and Principle: Memoirs of the National Security Adviser, 1977–1981* (New York: Farrar, Straus and Giroux, 1983), 66.

10. Anatoly Dobrynin, *In Confidence: Moscow's Ambassador to Six Cold War Presidents* (Seattle: University of Washington Press, 1995), 368.

11. Dobrynin, *In Confidence*, 375.

12. Dobrynin, *In Confidence*, 377.

13. Dobrynin, *In Confidence*, 377.

14. Cyrus Vance, *Hard Choices: Critical Years in America's Foreign Policy* (New York: Simon & Schuster, 1983), 45–48.

15. Dobrynin, *In Confidence*, 386–87.

16. NSA diary, February 28, 1977.

17. "Letter from Soviet General Secretary Brezhnev to President Carter," February 25, 1977, in *Foreign Relations of the United States, 1977–1980*, vol. 6, *Soviet Union*, edited by Melissa Jane Taylor (Washington, DC: US Government Printing Office, 2013), document 12.

18. NSA diary, February 28, 1977.

19. Strobe Talbott, *Endgame: The Inside Story of SALT II* (New York: Harper Torchbooks, 1980), 52.

20. Dobrynin, *In Confidence*, 391.

21. "Letter from President Carter to Soviet General Secretary Brezhnev," March 4, 1977, in *Foreign Relations of the United States, 1977–1980*, vol. 6, document 13.

22. NSA diary, March 4, 1977.

23. Talbott, *Endgame*, 58–60.

24. Talbott, *Endgame*, 48.

25. Warren Weaver, Jr., "Senate Confirms Warnke 58–40; Vote Falls Short of Carter's Hopes," *New York Times*, March 10, 1977.

26. NSA diary, March 18, 1977.

27. Henry Kissinger to Anatoly Dobrynin, *In Confidence*, 397.

28. NSA diary, April 3, 1977.

29. Jerry Schecter, interview with author, February 2022; NSA diary, April 5, 1977.

30. NSA diary, April 5, 1977.

31. Trudy Werner, interview with author, January 2021 (Werner was Brzezinski's secretary for most of his life); NSA diary, March 28, 1977.

32. Jordan, *Crisis*, 41.

33. NSA diary, March 28, 1977.

34. NSA diary, May 23, 1977.

35. NSA diary, May 23, 1977.

36. Charles Fenyvesi, "A Cold, Analytical Mind," *Jerusalem Post*, October 28, 1976.

37. "Zbigniew Brzezinski Oral History Transcript," UVA Miller Center, https://millercenter .org/the-presidency/presidential-oral-histories/zbigniew-brzezinski-oral-history.

38. Zbigniew Brzezinski, Memorandum for the President, "Personal and confidential," May 8, 1978 (Brzezinski family private collection, Mark).

39. Jimmy Carter, *White House Diary* (New York: Farrar, Straus and Giroux, 2010), 24.

40. NSA diary, February 1, 1977.

41. NSA diary, February 7, 1977.

42. Stu Eizenstat, interview with the author, March 2022.

43. Madeleine Albright, interview with author, February 2021.

44. Brzezinski, *Power and Principle*, 147.

45. Brzezinski, *Power and Principle*, 13.

46. Jimmy Carter, *Keeping Faith: Memoirs of a President* (Fayetteville: University of Arkansas Press, 1995), 56.

47. NSA diary, September 11, 1978.

48. Rick Interfurth, Bob Gates, Robert Hunter, Madeleine Albright, and other former NSC staff, interviews with author, 2020–2024.

49. Copy provided to author by Rick Inderfurth.

50. Copy provided to author by Rick Inderfurth.

51. Former NSC staffers, interviews with author.

52. Brzezinski, *Power and Principle*, 84.

53. Brzezinski, *Power and Principle*, 84.

54. Stu Eizenstat, interview with author, March 2021.

55. Brzezinski, *Power and Principle*, 77.

56. William Quandt, interview with author, March 2022.

57. William Quandt, interview with author, March 2022.

58. Stuart E. Eizenstat, *President Carter: The White House Years* (New York: Thomas Dunne Books, 2018), 426.

59. NSA diary, March 18, 1977.

60. Gerald Rafshoon, interview with author, March 2021.

61. NSA diary, June 21, 1977.

62. Stu Eizenstat, interview with author, March 2021.

63. NSA diary, February 16, 1978.

64. Madeleine Albright, interviews with author, January and March 2021.

65. Eizenstat, *President Carter*, 447–49.

66. Eizenstat, *President Carter*, 489.

67. Carter, *White House Diary*, 108.

68. Bernard Gwertzman, "Jewish Leader Says Mideast Policy Makes a 'Question Mark' of Carter," *New York Times*, March 10, 1978.

69. NSA diary, December 16, 1977.

70. NSA diary, May 19, 1977.

71. NSA diary, June 9, 1977.

72. Brzezinski, *Power and Principle*, 98.

73. NSA diary, May 30, 1977.

74. Marvin Kalb, "The New Face of Israel," *New York Times*, July 17, 1977.

75. Jimmy Carter to Zbigniew Brzezinski, private collection, Mark Brzezinski.

76. NSA diary, July 20, 1977.

77. "Minutes from a Policy Review Committee Meeting," February 4, 1977, in *Foreign Relations of the United States, 1977–1980*, vol. 8, *Arab Israeli Dispute, January 1977–August 1978*, edited by Adam M. Howard (Washington, DC: US Government Printing Office, 2013), document 3.

78. NSA diary, August 17, 1977.

79. NSA diary, August 17, 1977.

80. That was the unanimous view at the time, supported in hindsight by author interviews in 2021 with William Quandt and Stu Eizenstat.

81. Eizenstat, *President Carter*, 94.

82. Carter, *White House Diary*, 112.

83. NSA diary, October 5, 1977.

84. NSC Weekly Report 31, October 7, 1977, box III: 8.13, Brzezinski Papers, LoC.

85. NSA diary, October 7, 1977.

86. NSC Weekly Report 37, November 18, 1977, box III: 8.13, Brzezinski Papers, LoC.

87. NSA diary, November 3, 1977.

88. NSA diary, November 20, 1977.

89. Bernard Gwertzman, "Carter Enunciated a New, but Somewhat Used, Foreign Policy," *New York Times*, May 29, 1977.

90. NSA diary, June 9, 1977.

91. Dobrynin, *In Confidence*, 397.

92. NSA diary, June 30, 1977.

93. ZB Remarks to Gridiron Club, December 10, 1977 (Brzezinski family private collection, Mark). Speech text confirmed via email with the Gridiron Society, Washington, DC, December 29, 2023.

94. Zbigniew Brzezinski, Gridiron dinner address, Carter administration speeches and remarks by Brzezinski, box III: 9.12, Brzezinski Papers, LoC.

95. NSA diary, October 26, 1977.

96. Russell Watson, Hal Bruno, Scott Sullivan, "Life at Brzezinski U," *Newsweek*, May 9, 1977.

97. Bennett Kovrig, *Of Walls and Bridges: The United States and Eastern Europe* (New York: New York University Press, 1991), 172.

98. NSA diary, July 7, 1977.

99. Helmut Schmidt, *Men and Powers: A Political Retrospective* (New York: Random House, 1989), 54.

100. Schmidt, *Men and Powers*, 58.

101. NSA diary, April 3, 1977.

102. Joseph Nye, interview with author, January 2022.

103. Joseph Nye, interview with author, January 2022.

104. NSA diary, March 23, 1977.

105. Hal Brands, *The Twilight Struggle: What the Cold War Teaches Us About Great Power Rivalry Today* (New Haven, CT: Yale University Press, January 25, 2022), ebook, 63.

106. NSA diary, December 3, 1977.

107. NSA diary, May 8, 1977.

108. NSA diary, September 13, 1977.

109. NSA diary, May 8, 1977.

110. Jimmy Carter, *Keeping Faith: Memoirs of a President* (Fayetteville: University of Arkansas Press, 1995), 56.

111. NSA diary, May 11, 1977.

112. Brzezinski, *Power and Principle*, 293.

113. NSA diary, May 10, 1977.

114. Schmidt, *Men and Powers*, 186.

115. Brzezinski, *Power and Principle*, 26.

116. Carter, *White House Diary*, 172.

117. NSA diary, May 10, 1977.

118. NSC Weekly Report 20, July 8, 1977, box III: 8.12, Brzezinski Papers, LoC.

119. Betty Glad, *An Outsider in the White House: Jimmy Carter, His Advisors, And the Making of American Foreign Policy* (Ithaca, NY: Cornell University Press, 2009), 53.

120. Schmidt, *Men and Powers*, 176.

121. Walter Pincus, "Neutron Killer Warhead Buried in ERDA Budget," *Washington Post*, June 5, 1977.

122. Walter Pincus, interview with author, March 2022.

123. NSA diary, April 12, 1978.

124. NSA diary, April 5, 1978.

125. NSA diary, April 20, 1978.

126. Letters between Carter and Brzezinski (Brzezinski family private collection, Mark).

127. Jessica Matthews (neé Tuchman), interview with author, February 2021.

128. NSA diary, December 15, 1977.

129. Zbigniew Brzezinski, "Remarks, The Trilateral Commission, October 1977, Bonn (Brzezinski family private collection, Mark).

130. NSA diary, November 16, 1977.

131. Craig S. Karpel, "Cartergate: The Death of Democracy," *Penthouse*, November 1977.

132. William Greider, "Trilateral Commission—Web Enough for the Plot-Minded," *Washington Post*, January 15, 1977.

133. Karpel, "Cartergate."

134. Craig S. Karpel, "Cartergate II: The Real President," *Penthouse*, December 1978.

135. Craig S. Karpel, "Cartergate III: Chairman Brzezinski's Thoughts," *Penthouse*, January 1978.

136. "Background Briefing by an Administration Official, Room 450, Old Executive Office Building," December 20, 1977, Office of the Press Secretary, transcript in Brzezinski family collection, Mark.

137. Bernard Gwertzman, "Vance Asks Realism in U.S. Rights Policy," *New York Times*, May 1, 1977.

138. NSA diary, August 29, 1977.

139. Patrick G. Vaughan, "Zbigniew Brzezinski: The Political and Academic Life of a Cold War Visionary" (PhD dissertation, West Virginia University, 2003), 306.

140. Bernard Gwertzman, "Interpreter's Gaffes Embarrass State Department," *New York Times*, December 31, 1977.

141. Zbigniew Brzezinski, *Power and Principle*, 298.

142. Jordan, *Crisis*, 25.

143. NSA diary, December 31, 1977.

144. Jimmy Carter, "Toasts of the President and the Shah at a State Dinner in Tehran, Iran," December 31, 1977, The American Presidency Project https://www.presidency.ucsb.edu/documents/toasts-the-president-and-the-shah-state-dinner-tehran-iran.

7: THE SANDS OF OGADEN

1. NSA diary, May 2, 1978.

2. NSA diary, May 2, 1978.

3. NSC Weekly Report 42, November 18, 1977, box III: 8.13, Brzezinski Papers, LoC.

4. SCC meeting, March 2, 1978, box 28, Jimmy Carter Library, Atlanta, Georgia.

5. Betty Glad, *An Outsider in the White House: Jimmy Carter, His Advisors, and the Making of American Foreign Policy* (Ithaca, NY: Cornell University Press, 2009), 79.

6. Tony Lake, interview with author, January 2021.

7. Jimmy Carter, *White House Diary* (New York: Farrar, Straus and Giroux, 2010), 196.

8. Sergey Radchenko, *To Run the World: The Kremlin's Cold War Bid for Global Power* (Cambridge, UK: Cambridge University Press, 2024), 449–50.

9. Fidel Castro, "Fort Lauderdale Conference," Carter-Brezhnev Project, Fort Lauderdale, Fla., March 23–26, 1995, 71.

10. Transcript of the Musgrove Conference of the "Carter-Brezhnev Project," Saint Simons Island, Georgia, May 6–9, 1994, 160.

11. Anatoly Dobrynin, *In Confidence: Moscow's Ambassador to Six Cold War Presidents* (Seattle: University of Washington Press, 1995), 408.

12. NSA diary, March 2, 1978.

13. NSC Weekly Report 46, February 9, 1978, box III: 8.14, Brzezinski Papers, LoC.

14. NSC Weekly Report 46, February 9, 1978.

15. NSC Weekly Report 55, April 21, 1978, box III: 8.14, Brzezinski Papers, LoC.

16. NSA diary, April 5, 1978.

17. NSA diary, March 15, 1978.

18. NSA diary, March 16, 1978.

19. Patrick Tyler, *A Great Wall: Six Presidents and China, An Investigative History* (New York: PublicAffairs, 1999), 248.

20. Tyler, *A Great Wall*, 249.

21. NSA diary, November 3, 1977.

22. Hamilton Jordan, *Crisis: The Last Year of the Carter Presidency* (New York: Berkley, 1983), 25.

23. Peter Jay, interview with author, March 2021.

24. Ronald Reagan, "To Restore America," March 31, 1976, Ronald Reagan Presidential Library and Museum, https://www.reaganlibrary.gov/archives/speech/restore-america.

25. Carter, *White House Diary*, 86.

26. NSA diary, September 1, 1977.

27. Carter, *White House Diary*, 189.

28. James Mann, *About Face: A History of America's Curious Relationship with China, from Nixon to Clinton* (New York: Vintage Books, 2000), 72–73.

29. Mann, *About Face*, 70.

30. Mann, *About Face*, 71.

31. NSA diary, May 23, 1978.

32. NSA diary, March 27, 1978.

33. George Packer, *Our Man: Richard Holbrooke and the End of the American Century* (New York: Knopf, 2019), 184.

34. President Jimmy Carter, email interview with author, March 2021.

35. Meeting with Deng Xiaoping, memorandum of conversation, May 25, 1978, Peking, China, box III: 8.5, Brzezinski Papers, LoC.

36. Packer, *Our Man*, 184.

37. "Making Friends in Peking," *Time*, June 5, 1978.

38. NSA diary, May 23, 1978.

39. NSA diary, May 23, 1978.

40. Tyler, *A Great Wall*, 255.

41. NSA diary, May 27, 1978.

42. William Safire, "Reading Arbatov's Mind," *New York Times*, April 13, 1978.

43. NSA diary, April 12, 1978.

44. NSA diary, May 27, 1978.

45. NSA diary, May 5, 1978.

46. *Newsweek*, "A New Cold War?," June 12, 1978.

47. NSA diary, April 12, 1978.

48. Elizabeth Drew, "Brzezinski," *New Yorker*, April 23, 1978.

49. NSA diary, May 31, 1978.

50. George McGovern, "Cool Heads Needed, Not Foreign Policy of Confrontation," *Boston Globe*, June 1, 1978.

51. James Fallows, interview with author, March 2022. (Fallows was a speechwriter for President Jimmy Carter.)

52. Anatoly Dobrynin, *In Confidence: Moscow's Ambassador to Six Cold War Presidents* (Seattle: University of Washington Press, 1995), 410.

53. Address at the Commencement Exercises at the United States Naval Academy, June 7, 1978, USNA, Class of 1978, https://www.usna1978.org/president-carters-speech-at-graduation/.

54. Dobrynin, *In Confidence*, 411.

55. Carter, *White House Diary*, 199.

56. Strobe Talbott, *Endgame: The Inside Story of SALT II* (New York: Harper Torchbooks, 1980), 151.

57. NSA diary, August 4, 1978.

58. NSA diary, July 11, 1978.

59. NSA diary, July 11, 1978.

60. NSA diary, July 23, 1978.

61. Stu Eizenstat, interview with author, March 2021.

62. "Weicker Says Brzezinski Views Jews as Impediment to U.S. Policy," *New York Times*, May 9, 1978.

63. Jonathan Alter, *His Very Best: Jimmy Carter, A Life* (New York: Simon & Schuster, 2020), 394.

64. Alter, *His Very Best*, 401.

65. Alter, *His Very Best*, 411.

66. NSA diary, September 14, 1978.

67. NSA diary, September 16, 1978.

68. NSA diary, September 5, 1978.

69. NSA diary, September 9, 1978.

70. NSA diary, September 11, 1978.

71. NSA diary, September 9, 1978.

72. NSA diary, September 11, 1978.

73. NSA diary, September 12, 1978.

74. Alter, *His Very Best*, 399.

75. Carter, *Keeping the Faith*, 401.

76. Carter, *White House Diary*, 238.

77. Carter, *White House Diary*, 242.

78. NSA diary, September 18, 1978.

79. Carter, *White House Diary*, 256.

80. NSA diary, September 19, 1978.

81. NSA diary, September 20, 1978.

82. NSA diary, September 21, 1978.

83. Michael Crawford, "Zbigniew Brzezinski's Tips for Teens," *New Yorker*, May 10, 1993 (Brzezinski family private collection, Mark).

84. Ian, Mark, and Mika Brzezinski, interviews with author, 2020–2024.

85. Blythe Babyak, "A Marriage of Politics and Art," *Newsweek*, October 4, 1978.

86. Joy Billington, "Emilie Benes's Art Debut," *Washington Star*, April 11, 1979.

87. Alter, *His Very Best*, 393.

88. Ian, Mark, and Mika Brzezinski, interviews with author, 2020–2024.

89. Gary Sick, *All Fall Down: America's Tragic Encounter with Iran* (New York: Random House, 1986), 60.

90. James A. Bill, *The Eagle and the Lion: The Tragedy of American-Iranian Relations* (New Haven, CT: Yale University Press, 1988), 248.

91. Gary Sick, interview with author, March 2023.

92. Bill, *The Eagle and the Lion*, 258.

93. Sick, *All Fall Down*, 108.

94. Harrison Smith, "Ardeshir Zahedi, Flamboyant Iranian Ambassador Who Advised the Shah, Dies at 93," *Washington Post*, November 20, 2021; Sally Quinn, interviews with author, March 2023; Jane Mayer, interview with author, June 2023; Gary Sick, interview with author, March 2023.

95. Bill, *The Eagle and the Lion*, 185–88.

96. "Iran: Oil, Grandeur and a Challenge to the West," *Time*, November 4, 1974.

97. Bill, *The Eagle and the Lion*, 201.

98. Bill, *The Eagle and the Lion*, 201–11, provides a clear overview of the US-Iran defense relationship in the mid-1970s.

99. Robert B. Semple, Jr., "Bomb Rocks Site in Iran Just Before Visit by Nixon," *New York Times*, June 1, 1972.

100. Sick, *All Fall Down*, 71–72; Gary Sick, interview with author, 2023.

101. William H. Sullivan, *Mission to Iran: The Last U.S. Ambassador* (New York: W. W. Norton, 1981), 171.

102. NSA diary, November 2, 1978.

103. NSC Weekly Report 78, November 3, 1978, box III: 9.2, Brzezinski Collection, LoC.

104. NSA diary, November 7, 1978.

105. Sick, *All Fall Down*, 83.

106. NSA diary, November 2, 1978.

107. NSA diary, December 19, 1978.

108. Arthur M. Schlesinger, Jr., *Journals, 1952–2000* (New York: Penguin Press, 2007), 457–59.

109. Schlesinger, *Journals*, 459–60.

110. NSA diary, December 21, 1978.

111. Cyrus Vance, *Hard Choices: Critical Years in America's Foreign Policy* (New York: Simon & Schuster, 1983), 118.

112. NSA diary, December 16, 1978.

113. Henry Kissinger, *Years of Upheaval* (New York: Little, Brown, 1982), ebook, location 36005.

114. Tyler, *A Great Wall*, 265. (Holbrooke had already divorced the reporter, Blythe Babyrak. They had gotten married the previous year).

115. NSA diary, December 13, 1978.

116. NSA diary, December 16, 1978.

117. NSA diary, December 17, 1978.

118. Carter, email interview with author, March 2021.

119. Warren Christopher, *Chances of a Lifetime: A Memoir* (New York: Scribner, 2001), 91.

120. Tyler, *A Great Wall*, 273.

121. Mann, *About Face*, 93.

122. Talbott, *Endgame*, 93.

123. NSA diary, December 11, 1978.

124. Talbott, *Endgame*, 179.

125. NSA diary, December 19, 1978; Carter, *White House Diary*, 267.

126. Talbott, *Endgame*, 241.

127. Marshall Shulman, quoted in "Fort Lauderdale Conference," Carter-Brezhnev Project (National Security Archive, George Washington University), 149.

128. Talbott, *Endgame*, 241.

129. NSA diary, December 23, 1978.

130. Talbott, *Endgame*, 243.

131. NSA diary, December 21, 1978.

132. NSA diary, January 29, 1979.

133. NSA diary, January 29, 1979.

134. NSA diary, January 13, 1979.

135. NSA diary, January 15, 1979.

136. Tyler, *A Great Wall*, 273.

137. Tyler, *A Great Wall*, 273.

138. NSA diary, January 29, 1979.

139. Hedrick Smith, "In Teng Visit, a Natural Hit," *New York Times*, February 1, 1979.

140. Tyler, *A Great Wall*, 275.

141. Adam Taylor, "How a 10-Gallon Hat Helped Heal Relations Between China and America," *Washington Post*, September 25, 2015.

142. NSA diary, January 29, 1979.

143. NSA diary, February 3, 1979.

144. NSA diary, February 3, 1979.

145. NSA diary, February 20, 1979.

146. NSA diary, February 28, 1979.

147. Tyler, *A Great Wall*, 281.

148. NSA diary, March 2, 1979.

149. Mann, *About Face*, 97.

150. Mann, *About Face*, 111.

151. Tyler, *A Great Wall*, 284.

8: TWILIGHT OF THE DOVES

1. NSA diary, February 9, 1979.

2. NSC Diary, May 10, 1977.

3. Tony Lake, interview with author, March 2021.

4. Jimmy Carter, *White House Diary* (New York: Farrar, Straus and Giroux, 2010), 288.

5. NSA diary, February 7, 1979.

6. Jimmy Carter to Zbigniew Brzezinski (Brzezinski family private collection, Mark).

7. NSA diary, February 5, 1979.

8. NSA diary, January 30, 1979.

9. William H. Sullivan, *Mission to Iran: The Last U.S. Ambassador* (New York: W. W. Norton, 1981), 220.

10. NSA diary, January 10, 1979.

11. NSA diary, January 3, 1979.

12. Robert E. Huyser, *Mission to Tehran: The Fall of the Shah and the Rise of Khomeini—Recounted by the U.S. General Who Was Secretly Sent at the Last Minute to Prevent It* (New York: Harper & Row, 1986), 121.

13. Sullivan, *Mission to Iran*, 253.

14. NSC Weekly Report 84, January 12, 1979, box III: 9.3, Brzezinski Papers, LoC.

15. NSA diary, January 13, 1979.

16. NSA diary, February 5, 1979.

17. Carter, *White House Diary*, 288.

18. Gary Sick, *All Fall Down: America's Tragic Encounter with Iran* (New York: Random House, 1986), 183.

19. Huyser, *Mission to Tehran*, 273.

20. NSA diary, January 23, 1979.

21. NSA diary, February 20, 1979.

22. NSA diary, March 4, 1979.

23. NSA diary, March 2, 1979.

24. NSA diary, March 6, 1979.

25. NSA diary, March 21, 1979.

26. Bob Gates, interview with author, February 2021.

27. NSA diary, March 12, 1979.

28. NSA diary, March 27, 1979.

29. NSA diary, April 26, 1979.

30. NSA diary, April 26, 1979.

31. NSA diary, August 4, 1979.

32. Cyrus Vance, *Hard Choices: Critical Years in America's Foreign Policy* (New York: Simon & Schuster, 1983), 135.

33. Dobrynin, *In Confidence*, 420.

34. NSA diary, June 4, 1979.

35. NSA diary, June 4, 1979.

36. Sam Nunn, interview with author, April 2021.

37. "Jackson Calls Approval of Pact 'Appeasement,'" *New York Times*, June 13, 1979.

38. Strobe Talbott, *Endgame: The Inside Story of SALT II* (New York: Harper Torchbooks, 1980), 7.

39. Talbott, *Endgame*, 6.

40. NSC Weekly Report 72, September 22, 1978, box III: 9.2, Brzezinski Papers, LoC.

41. NSA diary, June 17, 1979. All references to the evening at the opera and from the Vienna summit are from the same lengthy diary entry.

42. NSA diary, June 17, 1979.

43. NSA diary, June 17, 1979.

44. Dobrynin, *In Confidence*, 426.

45. Rudy Abramson, *Spanning the Century: The Life of W. Averell Harriman, 1891–1986* (New York: William Morrow, 1992), 691.

46. Andrei Gromyko, *Memories: From Stalin to Gorbachev* (London: Hutchinson, 1989), 379–80. Students of British politics will be interested to learn that the Labour left-winger Tony Benn wrote a glowing preface to Gromyko's memoir.

47. NSA diary, February 9, 1979.

48. NSA diary, August 10, 1978.

49. "Senator Church Charges Moscow Has a Brigade of Troops in Cuba," *New York Times*, August 31, 1979.

50. Bernard Gwertzman, "Vance Tells Soviets That Its Troops in Cuba Could Imperil Ties," *New York Times*, September 6, 1979.

51. NSA diary, September 11, 1979.

52. Zbigniew Brzezinski, *Power and Principle: Memoirs of the National Security Adviser, 1977–1981* (New York: Farrar, Straus and Giroux, 1983), 351.

53. NSA diary, July 20, 1979.

54. George Weigel, *Witness to Hope: The Biography of Pope John Paul II* (Harper Perennial, 2004), 225.

55. Weigel, *Witness to Hope,* 279.

56. Weigel, *Witness to Hope,* 279.

57. Bob Pastor, quoted in "Fort Lauderdale Conference," Carter-Brezhnev Project, 40–41 (Pastor was an NSC official under Brzezinski)."The Carter-Brezhnev Project" (National Security Archive, The George Washington University).

58. NSA diary, October 6, 1979.

59. "Homily of His Holiness, John Paul II, Victory Square Warsaw, June 2, 1979 (Vatican Homilies, https://www.vatican.va/content/john-paul-ii/en/homilies/1979/documents/hf_jp-ii_hom_19790602_polonia-varsavia.html.)

60. NSA diary, March 21, 1979.

61. David Rockefeller, *Memoirs* (New York: Random House Trade Paperbacks, 2003), 368.

62. Rockefeller, *Memoirs,* 368.

63. Bernard Gwertzman, "Carter Emissary Dissuaded Shah from U.S. Exile," *New York Times,* April 20, 1979.

64. NSA diary, July 20, 1979.

65. Glad, *An Outsider in the White House,* 177.

66. Glad, *An Outsider in the White House,* 176–77.

67. David W. Kirkpatrick, "How a Chase Bank Chairman helped the Shah of Iran Enter the U.S.," *New York Times,* December 29, 2019.

68. Robert Gates, *In the Shadows,* 129.

69. NSA diary, November 1, 1971.

70. NSA diary, November 1, 1971.

71. NSA diary, November 10, 1979.

72. Rockefeller, *Memoirs,* 372.

73. Anthony Lewis, "Mr. Kissinger's Role," *New York Times,* November 25, 1979.

74. NSC Weekly Report 108, September 6, 1979, box III: 9.5, Brzezinski Papers, LoC.

75. Carter, *White House Diary,* 372.

76. NSA diary, November 27, 1979.

77. NSA diary, December 2, 1979.

78. "Memorandum from the President's Assistant for National Security Affairs (Brzezinski) to President Carter," November 27, 1979, in *Foreign Relations of the United States, 1977–1980,* vol. 11, part 1: *Iran: Hostage Crisis, November 1979–September 1980,* edited by Linda Qaimmaqami (Washington, DC: US Government Publishing Office, 2020), document 61, https://history.state.gov/historicaldocuments/frus1977-80v11p1/d61.

79. "Summary of Conclusions of a Special Coordination Committee Meeting," November 13, 1979, in *Foreign Relations of the United States,* vol. 11, part 1: *Iran: Hostage*

Crisis, November 1979–September 1980, edited by Linda Qaimmaqami (Washington. DC: US Government Publishing Office, 2020), document 70, https://history.state .gov/historicaldocuments/frus1977-80v11p1/d25.

80. "Memorandum from the President's Assistant for National Security Affairs (Brzezinski) to President Carter," December 3, 1979, in *Foreign Relations of the United States, 1977–1980*, vol. 11, part 1: *Iran: Hostage Crisis, November 1979–September 1980*, edited by Linda Qaimmaqami (Washington, DC: US Government Publishing Office, 2020), document 80, https://history.state.gov/historicaldocuments/frus1977-80v11p1/d80.

81. "Contractual-litigational" was Brzezinski's recurring description in memos and his diary of Vance's approach to diplomacy.

82. "Memorandum from the White House Chief of Staff (Jordan) to President Carter," n.d., in *Foreign Relations of the United States, 1977–1980*, vol. 11, part 1: *Iran: Hostage Crisis, November 1979–September 1980*, edited by Linda Qaimmaqami (Washington, DC: US Government Publishing Office, 2020), document 56, https://history.state.gov /historicaldocuments/frus1977-80v11p1/d56.

83. NSA diary, September 25, 1979.

84. T. R. Reid and David S. Broder, "Kennedy Attack on Shah Brings Critical Barrage," *Washington Post*, December 4, 1979.

85. NSA diary, December 6, 1979.

86. NSA diary, January 3, 1980.

87. Jimmy Carter, "Address to the Nation on Energy and National Goals: 'The Malaise Speech,'" July 15, 1979, The American Presidency Project, https://www.presidency .ucsb.edu/node/249458.

88. Rafshoon, interview with author, February 2021.

89. Brzezinski, NSC Weekly Report 122, December 21, 1979, box III: 9.6, Brzezinski Papers, LoC.

90. NSA diary, November 22, 1979.

91. NSA diary, November 16, 1979.

92. NSA diary, November 22, 1979.

93. NSA diary, December 21, 1979.

94. NSA diary, October 30, 1979.

95. Sally Quinn, "The Politics of the Power Grab: Nine Rules of Notoriety," *Washington Post*, December 19, 1979.

96. NSA diary, December 19, 1979.

97. Quinn, "The Politics of the Power Grab."

98. Quinn, interview with author, March 2023.

99. James Reston, "The New Cult of Personality," *New York Times*, December 21, 1979.

100. NSA diary, December 26, 1979.

101. Jonathan Haslam, *Russia's Cold War: From the October Revolution to the Fall of the Wall* (New Haven, CT: Yale University Press, 2012), 326.

102. Meeting with Deng Xiaoping, memorandum of conversation, May 25, 1978, Peking, China, box III: 8.5, Brzezinski Papers, LoC.

103. NSA diary, February 12, 1979.

104. Dick Camp, *Boots on the Ground: The Fight to Liberate Afghanistan from Al-Qaeda and the Taliban, 2001–2002* (Minneapolis: Zenith Press, 2012), 8–9.

105. NSA diary, March 31, 1979.

106. "Memorandum from Marshall Brement of the National Security Council Staff to the President's Assistant for National Security Affairs (Brzezinski) and the President's Deputy Assistant for National Security Affairs (Aaron)," December 28, 1979, in *Foreign Relations of the United States, 1977–1980*, vol. 12: *Afghanistan*, edited by David Zierler (Washington, DC: US Government Publishing Office, 2018), document 112, https://history.state.gov/historicaldocuments/frus1977-80v12/d112.

107. *Foreign Relations of the United States, 1977–1980*, vol. 12: *Afghanistan*, "Summary of the Conclusions of a Special Coordination Committee Meeting," Document 76, October 23, 1980 (Office of the Historian).

108. NSA diary, July 14, 1979.

109. Sergey Radchenko, *To Run the World: The Kremlin's Cold War Bid for Global Power* (Cambridge, UK: Cambridge University Press, 2024), 490–91.

110. Yuri Andropov to Leonid Brezhnev, early December 1979. See "The Soviet Invasion of Afghanistan, 1979: Not Trump's Terrorists, not Zbig's Warm Water Ports: Declassified Documents Show Moscow's Fears of an Afghan Flip," January 28, 2019, National Security Archive, January 28, 2019, https://nsarchive.gwu.edu/briefing-book/afghanistan-russia-programs/2019-01-29/soviet-invasion-afghanistan-1979-not-trumps-terrorists-nor-zbigs-warm-water-ports.

111. Alexander Cockburn and Jeffrey St. Clair, *Whiteout: The CIA, Drugs and the Press* (London: Verso Books, 2014), 175.

112. Radchenko, *To Run the World*, 492–93.

113. Robert M. Gates, *From the Shadows: The Ultimate Insider's Story of Five Presidents and How They Won the Cold War* (New York: Simon & Schuster, 2006), 149.

114. Quoted in Haslam, *Russia's Cold War*, 325.

115. NSA diary, July 24, 1979.

116. Quoted in Haslam, *Russia's Cold War*, 324.

117. Jimmy Carter, interview by Frank Reynolds, *World News Tonight*, ABC, from the Oval Office, December 31, 1979, Jimmy Carter positions and record (2 of 4) folder, box 221, Ronald Reagan: 1980 Campaign Papers, 1965–80, Ronald Reagan Presidential Library Digital Library Collections, 74, https://www.reaganlibrary.gov/public/2022-04/40-656-7386362-221-018-2022.pdf.

118. *Foreign Relations of the United States, 1977–1980*, volume 12: *Afghanistan*, "Hotline Message from General Secretary Brezhnev to President Carter," Moscow, December 29, 1979 (Office of the Historian).

119. Dobrynin, *In Confidence*, 440–43.

120. Brzezinski used this phrase often, but it is not clear when he coined it. He gave a background to the thinking that produced the phrase in *Power and Principle*, 178–90.

121. NSA diary, December 14, 1979.

122. NSA diary, January 2, 1980.

123. NSA diary, January 4, 1980.

124. NSA diary, January 9, 1980.

125. "Article in the National Intelligence Daily," January 14, 1980, in *Foreign Relations of the United States, 1977–1980*, vol. 12: *Afghanistan*, edited by David Zierler (Washington, DC: US Government Publishing Office, 2018), document 166, https://history.state.gov/historicaldocuments/frus1977-80v12/d166.

126. "Editorial Note," January 21, 1980, in *Foreign Relations of the United States, 1977–1980*, vol. 12: *Afghanistan*, edited by David Zierler (Washington, DC: US Government Publishing Office, 2018), document 176, https://history.state.gov/historicaldocuments/frus1977-80v12/d176.

127. NSA diary, January 23, 1980.

128. NSA diary, January 25, 1980.

129. NSA diary, January 28, 1980.

130. "Transcript of Kennedy's Speech at Georgetown University on Campaign Issues," *New York Times*, January 29, 1980.

131. Hamilton Jordan, *Crisis: The Last Year of the Carter Presidency* (New York: Berkley, 1983), 110.

132. "Memorandum from Marshall Brement of the National Security Council Staff to the President's Assistant for National Security Affairs (Brzezinski)," January 26, 1980, in *Foreign Relations of the United States, 1977–1980*, vol. 12: *Afghanistan*, edited by David Zierler (Washington, DC: US Government Publishing Office, 2018), document 180, https://history.state.gov/historicaldocuments/frus1977-80v12/d180.

133. NSC Weekly Report 125, January 11, 1980, box III: 9.6, Brzezinski Papers, LoC.

134. NSC Weekly Report 125, January 2, 1980, box III: 9.6, Brzezinski Papers, LoC.

135. William Borders, "Pakistani Dismisses $400 million in aid Offered by U.S. as 'Peanuts,'" *New York Times*, January 18, 1980.

136. NSA diary, February 4, 1980.

137. "Brzezinski at the Pass: Bonhomie, Bullets," *New York Times*, February 4, 1980.

138. Prince Turki Al-Faisal, interview with author, July 2023.

139. NSA diary, February 9, 1980.

140. NSA diary, February 9, 1980.

9: THE AYATOLLAH AND THE POPE

1. Charles Gati, "The World According to Zbig," *Politico*, November 27, 2013, https://www.politico.com/magazine/story/2013/11/the-world-according-to-zbigniew-brzezinski-100354/.

2. Gati, "World According to Zbig."

3. "False Warnings of Soviet Missile Attacks," National Security Archives.

4. NSA diary, June 3, 1980.

5. "Memorandum from William Odom of the National Security Council Staff to the President's Assistant for National Security Affairs (Brzezinski)," January 18, 1980, in *Foreign Relations of the United States, 1977–1980*, vol. 6: *Soviet Union*, edited by Melissa

Jane Taylor (Washington, DC: US Government Printing Office, 2013), document 258, https://history.state.gov/historicaldocuments/frus1977-80v06/d258.

6. "Memorandum from the White House Chief of Staff (Jordan) to President Carter," in *Foreign Relations of the United States, 1977–1980*, vol. 11, part 1, *Iran: Hostage Crisis, November 1979–September 1980*, edited by Linda Qaimmaqami (Washington, DC: US Government Publishing Office, 2020), document 165, https://history.state.gov/historicaldocuments/frus1977-80v11p1/d165.

7. NSA diary, March 5, 1980.

8. NSA diary, April 13, 1980.

9. Gary Sick, *All Fall Down: America's Tragic Encounter with Iran* (New York: Random House, 1986), 317.

10. NSA diary, March 22, 1980.

11. "Minutes of a National Security Council Meeting," in *Foreign Relations of the United States, 1977–1980*, vol. 11, part 1: *Iran: Hostage Crisis, November 1979–September 1980*, edited by Linda Qaimmaqami (Washington, DC: US Government Publishing Office, 2020), document 217, https://history.state.gov/historicaldocuments/frus1977-80v11p1/d217.

12. NSA diary, March 22, 1980.

13. NSA diary, April 11, 1980.

14. NSA diary, April 22, 1980.

15. NSA diary, April 18, 1980.

16. Marshall Shulman, quoted in "Fort Lauderdale Conference," Carter-Brezhnev Project (National Security Archive, George Washington University),122.

17. NSA diary, April 21, 1980.

18. Warren Christopher, *Chances of a Lifetime: A Memoir* (New York: Scribner, 2001), 102.

19. NSA diary, April 26, 1980. Brzezinski recorded his full account of the "longest day of my service in the White House" two days after it had happened. Most of the account is pieced together from that entry, as well as Jimmy Carter, *White House Diary* (New York: Farrar, Straus and Giroux, 2010); Sick, *All Fall Down*; and the State Department, Office of the Diplomatic Historian's collection of declassified documents in *Foreign Relations of the United States, 1977–1980*, vol. 11.

20. NSA diary, April 26, 1980.

21. NSA diary, April 26, 1980. Brzezinski's direct recollection differs from other accounts that have Carter saying "Darn it, darn it."

22. NSA diary, April 26, 1980.

23. Ian Brzezinski, interview with author, June 2022.

24. NSA diary, April 26, 1980.

25. Bernard Gwertzman, "Vance Urges Senate to Back Arms Pact," *New York Times*, June 6, 1980.

26. Carter, *White House Diary*, 425.

27. Madeleine Albright, interview with author, 2021.

28. Michael Dobbs, *Madeleine Albright: A Twentieth-Century Odyssey* (New York: Henry Holt, 2000), 158.

29. Madeleine Albright, interview with author, 2021.

30. NSA diary, May 8, 1980.

31. NSA diary, May 21, 1980.

32. NSA diary, May 20, 1980.

33. "Zbigniew Brzezinski Oral History," UVA Miller Center, https://millercenter.org/the -presidency/presidential-oral-histories/zbigniew-brzezinski-oral-history.

34. Leslie H. Gelb, "Vance—Torn by Ideals and by Loyalty to Carter," *New York Times*, April 29, 1980.

35. Strobe Talbott, "Almost Everyone vs. Zbig," *Time*, September 22, 1980.

36. Anthony Lewis, "The Brzezinski Puzzle," *New York Times*, August 18, 1980.

37. NSA diary, August 15, 1980.

38. Robert Gates, interview with author, March 2021.

39. NSA diary, June 4, 1980.

40. Ed Magnuson, "Madison Square Garden of Briars," *Time*, August 25, 1980.

41. NSA diary, August 15, 1980.

42. Ian Brzezinski, interview with author, March 2023.

43. NSA diary, August 15, 1980.

44. NSA diary, July 23, 1980.

45. NSA diary, July 23, 1980.

46. Robert Kimmitt, interview with author, November 2022. (Kimmitt was a Brzezinski NSC staffer and lawyer.)

47. "The President's News Conference," August 4, 1980, The American Presidency Project, https://www.presidency.ucsb.edu/node/251538.

48. NSA diary, July 23, 1980.

49. Memorandum from Samuel Huntington of the National Security Council Staff to the President's Assistant for National Security Affairs (Brzezinski), Washington, July 6, 1977, Office of the Historian, https://history.state.gov/historicaldocu ments/frus1977-80v04/d24.

50. Sergey Radchenko, *To Run the World: The Kremlin's Cold War Bid for Global Power* (Cambridge, UK: Cambridge University Press, 2024), 432.

51. NSA diary, January 28, 1977.

52. One of the most succinct accounts of PD-59 appears in William Odom, *The Collapse of the Soviet Military* (New Haven, CT: Yale University Press, 1998).

53. "Jimmy Carter's Controversial Nuclear Targeting Directive PD59 Declassified," The National Security Archive, September 14, 2012, https://nsarchive2.gwu.edu/nuke vault/ebb390/.

54. NSA diary, August 9, 1980.

55. NSA diary, September 4, 1980.

56. Carter, *White House Diary*, 275.

57. NSA diary, January 5, 1979.

58. NSA diary, June 21, 1980.

59. Helmut Schmidt, *Men and Powers: A Political Retrospective* (New York: Random House, 1989), 210.

60. Schmidt, *Men and Powers*, 216.

61. NSA diary, June 21, 1980.

62. NSA diary, July 19, 1980.

63. NSA diary, June 21, 1980.

64. NSA diary, September 25, 1980.

65. Zbigniew Brzezinski to Pope John Paul II, May 5, 1980, trans. Andrzej Grządkowski, folder "John Paul II, 1978–1980," box II: R.250-252, Brzezinski Papers, LoC.

66. Pope John Paul II to Zbigniew Brzezinski, February 8, 1980, trans. Andrzej Grządkowski, folder "John Paul II, 1978–1980," box II: R.250-252, Brzezinski Papers, LoC.

67. Pope John Paul II to Zbigniew Brzezinski, November 11, 1979, trans. Andrzej Grządkowski, folder "John Paul II, 1978–1980," box II: R.250-252, Brzezinski Papers, LoC.

68. Zbigniew Brzezinski to Pope John Paul II, May 5, 1980, trans. Andrzej Grządkowski, folder "John Paul II, 1978–1980," box II: R.250-252, Brzezinski Papers, LoC.

69. Pope John Paul II to Zbigniew Brzezinski, April 22, 1980, trans. Andrzej Grządkowski, folder "John Paul II, 1978–1980," box II: R.250-252, Brzezinski Papers, LoC.

70. This account is drawn from Les Denend, interview with author, May 2022, and NSA diary, June 21, 1980.

71. Denend interview, May 2022.

72. Zbigniew Brzezinski, memorandum of conversation with Pope John Paul II, June 21, 1980, folder "John Paul II, 1978–1980," box II: R.250-252, Brzezinski Papers, LoC.

73. John Paul II to Zbigniew Brzezinski, April 22, 1980, trans. Andrzej Grządkowski, folder "John Paul II, 1978–1980," box II: R.250-252, Brzezinski Papers, LoC.

74. Madeleine Albright, interview with author, February 2021.

75. NSC Weekly Report 149, August 7, 1980, box III: 9.7, Brzezinski Papers, LoC.

76. NSA diary, July 19, 1980.

77. NSA diary, August 24, 1980.

78. NSA diary, August 24, 1980.

79. NSA diary, September 10, 1980.

80. Gary Sick, interviews with author, March 2021 and June 2023.

81. Peter Baker, "A Four-Decade Secret: One Man's Story of Sabotaging Carter's Re-election," *New York Times*, March 18, 2023.

82. Gary Sick, *October Surprise: America's Hostages in Iran and the Election of Ronald Reagan* (New York: Times Books, 1991), 81–88.

83. Baker, "A Four-Decade Secret."

84. Sick, *October Surprise*, 143–54.

85. NSA diary, October 8, 1980.

86. NSA diary, October 22, 1980.

87. Hamilton Jordan, *Crisis: The Last Year of the Carter Presidency* (New York: Berkley, 1983), 336.

88. NSA diary, November 3, 1980.

89. Jordan, *Crisis*, 335–36.

90. NSA diary, November 5, 1980.

91. NSA diary, November 5, 1980.

92. NSA diary, March 4, 1980.

93. Michael J. Berlin, "N.Y. Mayor Koch Calls UN Envoy McHenry 'Anti-Israel,'" *Washington Post*, March 11, 1980.

94. NSA diary, July 25, 1980.

95. NSA diary, July 19, 1980.

96. NSA diary, August 24, 1980.

97. NSA diary, September 3, 1980.

98. NSA diary, September 3, 1980.

99. Patrick G. Vaughan, "Zbigniew Brzezinski: The Political and Academic Life of a Cold War Visionary" (PhD dissertation, West Virginia University, 2003), 357.

100. Ari L. Goldman, "In Jersey City, Polish Father Savors Son's Victory," *New York Times*, September 1, 1980.

101. Benjamin Weiser, *A Secret Life: The Polish Officer, His Covert Mission, and the Price He Paid to Save His Country* (New York: PublicAffairs, 2004), 141.

102. Weiser, *A Secret Life*, 121.

103. Weiser, *A Secret Life*, 104.

104. NSA diary, October 29, 1980.

105. Wolfgang Ischinger, interview with author, April 2021.

106. NSA diary, November 21, 1980.

107. Wolfgang Ischinger, interview with author, April 2021.

108. John Vinocur, "Germany's Reasons for Immobility on Poland," *New York Times*, January 3, 1982.

109. Wieser, *A Secret Life*, 217.

110. NSA diary, December 3, 1980.

111. Weiser, *A Secret Life*, 158.

112. Weiser, *A Secret Life*, 290.

113. NSA diary, November 24, 1980.

114. Radchenko, *To Run the World*, 501.

115. NSA diary, January 9, 1981.

116. Richard Allen, interview with author, June 2023.

117. NSA diary, January 6, 1981.

118. NSA diary, January 6, 1981.

119. NSA diary, December 17, 1980.

120. NSA diary, January 17, 1981.

121. Richard Burt, "Brzezinski Calls Democrats Soft Toward Moscow," *New York Times*, November 30, 1980.

122. Hodding Carter III, "Life Inside the Carter State Department," *Playboy*, February 1981.

123. NSA diary, January 6, 1980.

124. Arthur M. Schlesinger, Jr, *Journals: 1952–2000* (New York: Penguin Press, 2007) 448.

125. Anatoly Dobrynin, *In Confidence: Moscow's Ambassador to Six Cold War Presidents* (Seattle: University of Washington Press, 1995), 457.

126. Schlesinger, *Journals*, 505.

127. Robert Blackwill, interview with author, January 2022.

128. Robert Blackwill, interview with author, January 2022.

129. NSA diary, January 9, 1981.

130. NSA diary, January 20, 1981.

131. Mondale's summary is prominently displayed on the wall of the Jimmy Carter Library in Atlanta.

10: THE CONSERVATIVE YEARS

1. Dierdre Carmody, "Brzezinski Renews His Columbia Ties," *New York Times*, April 2, 1981.

2. Occasionally one would slip through. For example, Michael Perkinson, a naval intelligence officer who joined Brzezinski's School of Advanced International Studies (Johns Hopkins University) class in the early 1990s, did not mention his military career on his application. Letter to author from Perkinson, March 2021.

3. Madeleine Albright, interview with author, 2021.

4. Diana McLellan, "From the Archives: And Then She Said . . . ," *Washingtonian*, June 26, 2014. Corroborated by interviews with all three Brzezinski children.

5. Ian, Mark, and Mika Brzezinski, interviews with author, 2020–2024.

6. Blaine Harden and Lee Lescaze, "Romance Cited in Diet Author's Death," *Washington Post*, March 12, 1980.

7. Brzezinski family, interview with author.

8. Matthew Brzezinski, interview with author, April 2021.

9. Lech Brzezinski, their youngest son, and Zbigniew's sibling, shared all the boxes with me.

10. Richard Allen, interview with author, June 2023.

11. Zbigniew Brzezinski, interview with Justin Vaïsse, 2011.

12. Myra MacPherson, "The First Salvos," *Washington Post*, June 4, 1980.

13. Robert Blackwill, interview with author, 2022.

14. Joseph E. Persico, *Casey: The Lives and Secrets of William J. Casey: From the OSS to the CIA* (New York: Viking, 1990), 207.

15. Ronald Reagan to Zbigniew Brzezinski, April 10, 1989, box II: 220.6, Brzezinski Papers, LoC.

16. Brzezinski interview with the author, March 2011.

17. Trudy Werner, interviews with author, 2021–2024; Brzezinski children, interviews with author, 2021–2024.

18. Trudy Werner, interviews with author, 2021–2024; Brzezinski children, interviews with author, 2021–2024.

19. Confirmed by various interviewees, including David Ignatius, Rick Inderfurth, Charles Gati, and others.

20. Gary Sick, interview with author, March 2022.

21. Inderfurth, interview with the author, May 2023.

22. Kathy Kemper, interview with author, January 2023.

23. Barbara Gamarekian, "Handicapping the Brzezinski Way," *New York Times*, August 25, 1983.

24. Trudy Werner, interviews with author, 2021–2024.
25. Leslie H. Gelb, "Kissinger Means Business," *New York Times*, April 20, 1986.
26. Jeff Gerth with Sarah Bartlett, "Kissinger and Friends and Revolving Doors," *New York Times*, April 30, 1989.
27. Trudy Werner, interviews with author, 2021–2024.
28. Walter Isaacson, *Kissinger: A Biography* (New York: Simon & Schuster Paperbacks, 2005), 76.
29. Zbigniew Brzezinski to Henry Kissinger, February 11, 1982, box II: 3.12, Brzezinski Papers, LoC.
30. Robert Kimmitt, interview with author, November 2022.
31. George Urban, "The Perils of Foreign Policy: A Conversation in Washington," *Encounter*, May 1981, 12–29.
32. In Zbigniew Brzezinski, *Power and Principle: Memoirs of the National Security Advisor, 1977–1981* (New York: Farrar, Straus and Giroux, 1983), 35–47; Brzezinski gave a detailed account of his relationship with Vance.
33. Madeleine Albright, interview with author, March 2021.
34. Walter Goodman, "Books of the Times," *New York Times*, March 21, 1983.
35. Strobe Talbott, "Zbig-Think," *Time*, May 2, 1983.
36. Elisabeth Bumiller, "The Principals of Power," *Washington Post*, March 31, 1983.
37. Bumiller, "The Principals of Power."
38. Bob Woodward, interview with author, April 2023.
39. Benjamin Weiser, *A Secret Life: The Polish Officer, His Covert Mission, and the Price He Paid to Save His Country* (New York: PublicAffairs, 2004), 268.
40. Alexander Haig, *Caveat: Realism, Reagan, and Foreign Policy* (New York: Scribner, 1984), 240.
41. Zbigniew Brzezinski, "What's Wrong with Reagan's Foreign Policy?," *New York Times*, December 6, 1981.
42. Quoted in Patrick G. Vaughan, "Zbigniew Brzezinski: The Political and Academic Life of a Cold War Visionary" (PhD dissertation, West Virginia University, 2003), 330–31.
43. Robert Gates, interview with author, February 2021.
44. "Susan Sontag Provokes Debate on Communism," *New York Times*, February 27, 1982.
45. Patrick G. Vaughan provides the best account of the Hough-Conquest dispute in "Zbigniew Brzezinski," 280–81.
46. Stanislaw Dziwisz to Zbigniew Brzezinski, December 22, 1983, trans. Andrzej Grządkowski, folder "John Paul II, 1981–1983," box II: R.250-252, Brzezinski Papers, LoC.
47. Zbigniew Brzezinski to John Paul II, May 5, 1981, trans. Andrzej Grządkowski, folder "John Paul II, 1981–1983," box II: R.250-252, Brzezinski Papers, LoC.
48. John Paul II to Zbigniew Brzezinski, June 15, 1981, trans. Andrzej Grządkowski, folder "John Paul II, 1981–1983," box II: R.250-252, Brzezinski Papers, LoC.
49. As recounted in Neal B. Freeman, "The Remarkable Frank Shakespeare," *National Review*, February 7, 2024.
50. Interview with Ian Brzezinski, March 2022.

51. Zbigniew Brzezinski, memcon of lunch with Wojciech Jaruzelski, September 25, 1985, Jerzy Kozminski collection, Polish-American Freedom Foundation, Warsaw.

52. David Hoffman, "Chanting Polish Crowds Provide Bush with Footage for '88 Campaign," *Washington Post*, October 3, 1987.

53. Zbigniew Brzezinski, *Power and Principle*, 35.

54. Bumiller, "The Principals of Power."

55. Michael Getler, "Britain Questions 'Star Wars' Impact," *Washington Post*, March 16, 1985.

56. Hedrick Smith, "Democrats' Foreign Policies Veer Away from Past Line," *New York Times*, August 5, 1984.

57. Bush announces national security advisory task force, September 12, 1988, box II: 220.9, Brzezinski Papers, LoC.

58. Madeleine Albright, interview with author, February 2021.

59. Quoted in interview in Vaughan, "Zbigniew Brzezinski," 343.

60. Michael Dobbs, *Madeleine Albright: A Twentieth-Century Odyssey* (New York: Henry Holt, 2000), 332.

61. Zbigniew Brzezinski to Jimmy Carter, September 14, 1988, box II: 220.9, Brzezinski Papers, LoC.

62. James McCartney, "Top Carter Adviser Goes to Bush," *Detroit Free Press*, September 13, 1988, p. 9.

63. Andy Borowitz, *Profiles in Ignorance: How America's Politicians Got Dumb and Dumber* (New York: Avid Reader Press, 2022), 80.

64. "Jimmy Carter Confidant Brzezinski Tells Why He Jumped Ship For Bush," *Defense Week*, October 3, 1988.

65. Ralph Z. Hallow, "Brzezinski, 2 Other Advisers to Presidents, Endorse Bush," *Washington Times*, September 13, 1988, box II: 220.9, Brzezinski Papers, LoC.

66. Maureen Dowd, "Advisor to Bush Quits G.O.P. Post amid Anti-Semitism Allegations," *New York Times*, September 12, 1988.

67. Memorandum of Conversation between Brzezinski and the Pope, April 5, 1989, 7:30–9:10 p.m., box II: R.252, Brzezinski Papers, LoC.

68. Zbigniew Brzezinski, "From Eastern Europe Back to Central Europe," in *A Year in the Life of Glasnost: The Hugh Seton-Watson Memorial Lecture and Other Essays*, Centre for Policy Studies, London, 1988, https://cps.org.uk/wp-content/uploads/2021/07/141105124331-zb2.pdf, 12.

69. Zbigniew Brzezinski, *The Grand Failure: The Birth and Death of Communism in the Twentieth Century* (New York: Scribner, 1989), 225–28.

70. Zbigniew Brzezinski, interview with Justin Vaïsse, June 2011.

71. Brzezinski, *The Grand Failure*, 78–84.

72. Brzezinski, *The Grand Failure*, 190.

73. Margaret Thatcher to Zbigniew Brzezinski, January 4, 1985, box II: 219.10, Brzezinski Papers, LoC.

74. Brzezinski, *The Grand Failure*, 176–78.

75. Zbigniew Brzezinski, "Trip to Poland, March 25–30, 1989" (Brzezinski family private collection, Mark).

76. Jerzy Kozminski, interview with author. (Kozminski was Balcerowicz's aide.)

77. Jeffrey Sachs, email correspondence with author, February 2024.

78. Leszek Balcerowicz, interview with author in Warsaw, June 2022.

79. Zbigniew Brzezinski, "Trip to the Soviet Union, October 26–November 2, 1989: Chronology and Summary of Principal [sic] Events" (Brzezinski family private collection, Mark).

80. Rick Inderfurth, interview with author, June 2023.

81. "Interviews with Zbigniew Brzezinski," Pravda, November 9, 1989, p. 4.

82. Zbigniew Brzezinski, "Brzezinski-Yakovlev Meeting," CPSU Headquarters, Moscow, 10 a.m.–12 p.m. October 31, 1989 (memcon from Brzezinski family private collection, Mark).

83. Bill Keller, "Moscow Says Afghan Role Was Illegal and Immoral," New York Times, October 24, 1989.

84. Vladislav M. Zubok, Collapse: The Fall of the Soviet Union (New Haven, CT: Yale University Press, 2021), 21.

85. Zbigniew Brzezinski, "Trip to the Soviet Union." Most of the account comes from Brzezinski's memo, corroborated by multiple author interviews with Charles Gati (2021–2024) and Angela Stent (February 2022).

86. Jimmy Carter to Zbigniew Brzezinski, November 14, 1989, box II: 219.6, Brzezinski Papers, LoC.

87. Brzezinski, "Trip to the Soviet Union."

88. Brzezinski, "Trip to the Soviet Union."

89. Francis Fukayama, "An Appreciation," in Zbig: The Strategy and Statecraft of Zbigniew Brzezinski, edited by Charles Gati (Baltimore: Johns Hopkins University Press, 2013), 216.

90. Western Union "mailgram" from Richard Nixon to Zbigniew Brzezinski, November 21, 1989, box II: 220.5, Brzezinski Papers, LoC.

91. Zbigniew Brzezinski to Richard Nixon, November 1, 1983, box II: 220.5, Brzezinski Papers, LoC.

92. Zbigniew Brzezinski to Richard Nixon, November 1, 1983.

93. Ian Brzezinski, interview with author, March 2023.

94. Zbigniew Brzezinski to Richard Nixon, July 21, 1989, box III: 220.5, Brzezinski Papers, LoC.

95. Brzezinski family private family collection, Ian.

96. Zubok, Collapse, 60.

97. Memorandum of Conversation between Brzezinski and the Pope, April 5, 1989, box II: R.252, Brzezinski Papers, LoC.

98. Zbigniew Brzezinski to Deng Xiaoping, enclosed to George H. W. Bush, June 14, 1989, box II: 219.1, Brzezinski Papers, LoC.

99. Memorandum for the record of Zbigniew Brzezinski, conversation with George H. W. Bush, June 20, 1989, box II: 219.1, Brzezinski Papers, LoC.

100. Zbigniew Brzezinski to Deng Xiaoping, June 14, 1989, box II: 219.1, Brzezinski Papers, LoC.

101. Memorandum for the record of Zbigniew Brzezinski, conversation with George H. W. Bush, June 20, 1989, box II: 219.1, Brzezinski Papers, LoC.

102. Maureen Dowd, "2 US Officials Went to Beijing Secretly in July," *New York Times*, December 19, 1989.

103. Dowd, "2 US Officials Went to Beijing Secretly in July."

104. "Latest Excuse for Moving Toward War," *Los Angeles Times*, December 6, 1990.

105. George H. W. Bush, "Remarks to the Supreme Soviet of the Republic of the Ukraine in Kiev, Soviet Union," August 1, 1991, George H. W. Bush, Presidential Library and Museum.

106. William Safire, "Ukraine Marches Out," *New York Times*, November 18, 1991.

107. Rowland Evans and Robert Novak, "Bush's Slap in Kiev Talk Enrages Rebel Republics," *Chicago Sun-Times*, August 14, 1991.

108. Zbigniew Brzezinski, "Toward a Modern, Non-Imperial State," *Washington Post*, August 22, 1991.

109. Zbigniew Brzezinski, statement endorsing Bill Clinton, October 16, 1992, box II: 220.10, Brzezinski Papers, LoC.

110. Jimmy Carter to Zbigniew Brzezinski, April 10, 1993, box II: 219.6, Brzezinski Papers, LoC.

111. Zbigniew Brzezinski, *Out of Control: Global Turmoil on the Eve of the 21st Century* (New York: Macmillan, 1993), ix.

112. Brzezinski, *Out of Control*, 217.

113. Brzezinski, *Out of Control*, 158.

114. Brzezinski, *Out of Control*, 181–82.

115. Brzezinski, *Out of Control*, 198–99.

116. Michael Howard, "The World According to Henry: From Metternich to Me," review of *Diplomacy* by Henry Kissinger, *Foreign Affairs* 3, no. 73 (May–June 1994), 132–40.

117. Trudy Werner to Zbigniew Brzezinski, telephone messages, 1983–4, box II: 239.8, Brzezinski Papers, LoC.

118. Weister, *A Secret Life*, 307.

119. Zbigniew Brzezinski, Gerald Ford, Margaret Thatcher, Ronald Reagan, and others to Bill Clinton, November 18, 1992, box II: 219.8, Brzezinski Papers, LoC.

120. Alan Ferguson, "Bosnia's Serbs Vote to Accept UN Peace Plan," *Toronto Star*, January 21, 1993, quoted in Vaughan, "Zbigniew Brzezinski," 351.

121. Zbigniew Brzezinski, Frank Carlucci, and Lane Kirkland, public letter to Bill Clinton, July 27, 1993, box II: 219.8, Brzezinski Papers, LoC.

122. Bill Clinton to Zbigniew Brzezinski, August 2, 1993, box II: 219.8, Brzezinski Papers, LoC.

123. Brzezinski family private collection, Ian.

124. Koźmiński, interviews with author, January 2021.

125. Koźmiński, interviews with author, January 2021.

126. Madeleine Albright, interview with author, February 2021.

127. Bill Clinton to Zbigniew Brzezinski, July 30, 1997, box II: 219.8, Brzezinski Papers, LoC.

128. Weiser, *A Secret Life*, 321.

129. Weiser, *A Secret Life*, 319; Jerzy Koźmiński, interviews with author, 2021–2024.

130. Memorandum of Conversation between Brzezinski and the Pope, folder "John Paul II, 1988–1996," box II: R.250-252, Brzezinski Papers, LoC.
131. Weiser, *A Secret Life*, 321.
132. Weiser, *A Secret Life*, 333.
133. Madeleine Albright, interview with author, February 2021.

11: AUTUMNAL BATTLES

1. Mika Brzezinski, interview with author, June 2022.
2. The moniker never faded. On Brzezinski's death in 2017, the headline by one blogger, Brian P. McGlinchey, was "Zbigniew Brzezinski, Godfather of Al Qaeda and the Taliban, Dead at 89," 28pages.org, May 28, 2017, https://28pages.org/2017/05/28/zbigniew-brzezinski-godfather-of-al-qaeda-and-taliban-dead-at-89/.
3. Charles Gati, ed., *Zbig: The Strategy and Statecraft of Zbigniew Brzezinski* (Baltimore: Johns Hopkins University Press, 2013), 232.
4. Zbigniew Brzezinski, "A Plan for Political Warfare," *Wall Street Journal*, September 25, 2001.
5. Zbigniew Brzezinski, "Confronting Anti-American Grievances," *New York Times*, September 1, 2002.
6. Zbigniew Brzezinski, "A Troubling Paradox," speech delivered at New American Strategies for Security and Peace conference, Washington, DC, October 28, 2003, https://prospect.org/article/must-read-speech/.
7. Zbigniew Brzezinski, "As Clinton Courts Russia's Autocrats, Russians Suffer," *Wall Street Journal*, August 29, 2000.
8. William J. Clinton, "Statement on the Election of Vladimir Putin as President of Russia," March 27, 2000, The American Presidency Project, https://www.presidency.ucsb.edu/documents/statement-the-election-vladimir-putin-president-russia).
9. Zbigniew Brzezinski and Brent Scowcroft, *America and the World: Conversations on the Future of American Foreign Policy, Moderated by David Ignatius* (New York: Basic Books, 2009), 166.
10. "Press Conference by President Bush and Russian Federation President Putin," The White House, June 16, 2001, https://georgewbush-whitehouse.archives.gov/news/releases/2001/06/20010618.html.
11. Brzezinski, "A Troubling Paradox."
12. Brzezinski, "A Troubling Paradox."
13. Maureen Dowd, "Poppy Bush Finally Gives Junior a Spanking," *New York Times*, November 7, 2015.
14. Brent Scowcroft, "Don't Attack Saddam," *Wall Street Journal*, August 15, 2002.
15. Zbigniew Brzezinski, "If We Must Fight . . . ," *Washington Post*, August 17, 2002.
16. Steve Clemons, "Streaming Live—Zbigniew Brzezinski and Brent Scowcroft on 'America and the World,'" HuffPost, September 19, 2008, https://www.huffpost.com/entry/streaming-live-zbignie_b_127820.
17. David Firestone, "Threats and Responses: The Investigation," *New York Times*, December 14, 2002.

18. James Mann, "Brzezinski and Iraq: The Makings of a Dove," in *Zbig: The Strategy and Statecraft of Zbigniew Brzezinski*, edited by Charles Gati (Baltimore: Johns Hopkins University Press, 2013), 175.

19. Zbigniew Brzezinski, interview with Justin Vaïsse, June 2011.

20. Ian, Mark, and Mika Brzezinski, interviews with author, 2020–2024.

21. Mark Brzezinski and Mario Nicolini, "Iraq: Broken Promises: U.S. Lets Down 'New Europe,'" *New York Times*, November 19, 2003.

22. James Mann, "Brzezinski and Iraq," 173.

23. "CNN Late Edition with Wolf Blitzer," transcript, July 13, 2003, https://transcripts .cnn.com/show/le/date/2003-07-13/segment/00.

24. Barbara Salvin, "Candidates Share Common Ground on Foreign Policy," *USA Today*, February 14, 2000, box II: 220.12, Brzezinski Papers, LoC.

25. Undated handwritten Post-it note, presidential campaigns, 2000, box II: 220.13, Brzezinski Papers, LoC.

26. Statement by Zbigniew Brzezinski, October 14, 2000, presidential campaigns, 2000, box II: 220.13, Brzezinski Papers, LoC.

27. Inge Hoffmann, interview with Justin Vaïsse, December 2009.

28. Reuel Marc Gerecht, "On Democracy in Iraq," *Weekly Standard*, April 30, 2007.

29. Unsigned editorial, *Wall Street Journal*, January 31, 2005.

30. Memcon of Zbigniew Brzezinski meeting with John Kerry, May 23, 2004, presidential campaigns, 2004, box II: 220.14, Brzezinski Papers, LoC.

31. Zbigniew Brzezinski to Rand Beers, note, presidential campaigns, 2004, box II: 220.14, Brzezinski Papers, LoC.

32. Zbigniew Brzezinski to Randy Kerry, memo, September 24, 2004, presidential campaigns, 2004, box II: 220.14, Brzezinski Papers, LoC.

33. Michael Tomasky, "Against the Neocons," *The American Prospect*, March 2005.

34. Aleksander Kwaśniewski, interview with author, February 2021.

35. Zbigniew Brzezinski and Joe Scarborough, *Morning Joe*, MSNBC, December 30, 2008.

36. Bob Gates, author interview, February 2021.

37. Mark and Ian Brzezinski, interviews with author, 2020–2024.

38. Zbigniew Brzezinski to Bill Clinton, March 11, 1993, box II: 219.8, Brzezinski Papers, LoC.

39. Memcon between Zbigniew Brzezinski and Tony Lake, December 21, 1993, box II: 219.8, Brzezinski Papers, LoC.

40. Brzezinski notes on trip, 1993, box I: 106.4, Brzezinski Papers, LoC.

41. Brzezinski family private collection, Ian.

42. Zbigniew Brzezinski to Mark Brzezinski, undated but from mid-1990s (Brzezinski family private collection, Mark).

43. Jerzy Koźmiński, interview with author, June 2022.

44. Radek Sikorski, interview with author, April 2023.

45. Alexander Kwaśniewski, interview with author, February 2021.

46. Wolfgang Ischinger, interview with author, March 2021.

47. Zbigniew Brzezinski, *The Grand Chessboard: American Primacy and Its Geostrategic Imperatives* (New York: Basic Books, 1997), 54.

48. Paul Golob, interview with author, January 2021.

49. Walter Russell Mead, review of *The Choice: Global Domination or Global Leadership* by Zbigniew Brzezinski, *Foreign Affairs* 83, no. 2, (March/April 2004): 162–63, https://www.foreignaffairs.com/reviews/capsule-review/2004-03-01/choice-global-domination-or-global-leadership.

50. Mead, review of *The Choice*.

51. Zbigniew Brzezinski, "Moral Duty, National Interest," *New York Times*, April 7, 2002.

52. George H. W. Bush to Zbigniew Brzezinski, September 24, 1991, box II: 21.1, Brzezinski Papers, LoC.

53. Zbigniew Brzezinski to George H. W. Bush, September 19, 1991, box II: 219.1, Brzezinski Papers, LoC.

54. Stephen Walt, interview with author, February 2024.

55. John Mearsheimer and Stephen Walt, "The Israel Lobby," *London Review of Books*, March 23, 2006.

56. "The War over Israel's Influence," *Foreign Policy* 85, no. 4 (July–August 2006): 57–66.

57. Zbigniew Brzezinski, *Second Chance: Three Presidents and the Crisis of American Superpower* (New York: Basic Books, 2007), 157.

58. Zbigniew Brzezinski to Barack Obama, email, June 3, 2007; Notes for lunch with Obama, May 16, 2007, box IV: 49.11, Brzezinski Papers, LoC.

59. Zbigniew Brzezinski to Barack Obama, email August 4, 2007, box IV: 49.11, Brzezinski Papers, LoC.

60. Barack Obama to Zbigniew Brzezinski, email, August 2, 2007, box IV: 49.11, Brzezinski Papers, LoC.

61. Barack Obama to Zbigniew Brzezinski, email, November 13, 2007, box IV: 49.11, Brzezinski Papers, LoC.

62. Al Hunt, "Brzezinski Embraces Obama over Rival Clinton," Bloomberg, August 24, 2007 (https://www.youtube.com/watch?v=caeP33025UY).

63. Speaking notes, "Zbigniew Brzezinski introduces Barack Obama in Iowa," September 12, 2007, box IV: 49.12, Brzezinski Papers, LoC.

64. Ben Rhodes, interview with author, February 2022.

65. Michael Hirsch, "Obama: Good for the Jews?," *Newsweek*, February 23, 2008.

66. Lynn Sweet, "Before Jewish Group, Obama Distances Himself from Brzezinski, Says Farrakhan Fan Rev. Wright like an 'Old Uncle,'" *Chicago Sun-Times*, February 25, 2008.

67. Barack Obama to Zbigniew Brzezinski, email, February 25, 2008, box IV: 49.11, Brzezinski Papers, LoC.

68. Barack Obama to Zbigniew Brzezinski, email, May 10, 2008, box IV: 49.11, Brzezinski Papers, LoC.

69. Alex Spillius, "Barack Obama Supporter Accuses Jewish Lobby Members of McCarthyism," *Daily Telegraph*, May 27, 2008; Ben Smith, "A Brzezinski Headline Obama Could Do Without," *Politico*, May 28, 2008, https://www.politico.com/blogs/ben-smith/2008/05/a-brzezinski-headline-obama-could-do-without-009108.

70. Zbigniew Brzezinski to Barack Obama, email, July 19, 2008, box IV: 49.11, Brzezinski Papers, LoC.

71. Mark Brzezinski, interview with author, May 2023.

72. Ben Rhodes, interview with author, February 2022.

73. Charlie Rose, "The Future of American Foreign Policy," PBS, June 15, 2007.

74. Henry Kissinger to Zbigniew Brzezinski (Brzezinski family private collection, Mark).

75. Kissinger inscribed copy (Brzezinski family private collection, Mark).

76. Rick Inderfurth, interview with author, March 2022.

77. Mika Brzezinski and Joe Scarborough, interview with author, May 2023.

78. Lech and Wanda Brzezinski, interview with author, April 2022.

79. Brzezinski, handwritten memo, Berlin, November 10, 2009, box IV: 49.10, Brzezinski Papers, LoC; Brzezinski handwritten memo, Adlon Hotel, November 9, 2009, Berlin box IV: 49.10, Brzezinski Papers, LoC.

80. Andrjez Lubowski, *Zbig: The Man Who Cracked the Kremlin* (New York: Open Road Distribution, New York, 2011), 6.

81. Zbigniew Brzezinski, "From Poland's Tragedy, Hopes for Better Ties with Russia," *Time*, April 26, 2010.

82. Piotr Zalewski, "Dispatch from Warsaw: The Conspiracy Theory Roiling Poland," *Time*, November 19, 2012.

83. Zbigniew Brzezinski, speech given at the opening of the Emigration Museum in Gdynia, Poland, May 2015, Jerzy Koźmiński collection, Polish-American Freedom Foundation, Warsaw.

84. Strobe Talbott, "Zbigniew Brzezinski: Vindication of a Hard-Liner," *Time*, December 18, 1989.

85. Zbigniew Brzezinski and Brent Scowcroft, *Second Chance*, 171.

86. Zbigniew Brzezinski, "Russia Needs to Be Offered a 'Finland Option' for Ukraine," *Financial Times*, February 22, 2014.

87. Zbigniew Brzezinski, "Transcript: The Eastern Edge of a Europe Whole and Free," in conversation with Edward Luce, Atlantic Council, April 29, 2014, Washington, DC, https://www.atlanticcouncil.org/commentary/transcript/transcript-the-eastern-edge-of-a-europe-whole-and-free/.

88. Brzezinski, "Transcript: The Eastern Edge of a Europe Whole and Free."

89. Edward Luce, "Lunch with the FT: Zbigniew Brzezinski," *Financial Times*, January 13, 2012.

90. Zbigniew Brzezinski, *Strategic Vision: America and the Crisis of Global Power* (New York: Basic Books, 2012), 50.

91. Interview with the author, 2012. It was a line he often repeated.

92. Luce, "Lunch with the FT: Zbigniew Brzezinski."

93. Luce, "Lunch with the FT: Zbigniew Brzezinski."

94. Jacob Bernstein, "Night Out with Emilie and Mika Brzezinski," *New York Times*, May 16, 2014.

95. Muska's annotated copy, supplied to author by Mika Brzezinski.

96. Joe Scarborough, interview with author, May 2023.

97. Joe Scarborough, interview with author, May 2023.

98. Emilie Brzezinski, *The Lure of the Forest*, sculpture exhibit, Kreeger Museum, Washington, DC, September 16–December 27, 2014.

99. Medical details supplied by Trudy Werner and Brzezinski children.

100. Ian Brzezinski, interview with author, March 2023.

101. Zbigniew Brzezinski to Jimmy Carter, email, September 3, 2017, box IV: 3.9, Brzezinski Papers, LoC.

102. Jimmy Carter to Zbigniew Brzezinski, email, September 7, 2015, box IV: 3.9, Brzezinski Papers, LoC.

103. John Hamre, interview with author, January 2021.

104. Trudy Werner, email correspondence with author, March 2024.

105. Zbigniew Brzezinski (@zbig), "In our new age of cyber attacks, for my first tweet, some thoughts on how to prevent 'Anonymous Wars.' #anonymouswars http://on.ft.com/14IJ8lD," Twitter (now X), April 4, 2013, https://x.com/zbig/status/319841062665457664.

106. Ashton Carter, remarks given at Washington, DC, Jerzy Koźmiński collection, Polish-American Freedom Foundation, Warsaw.

107. David Ignatius, email correspondence with author, February 2024.

108. The Nobel Peace Prize Forum, *Nobel Peace Prize Forum Oslo Promotional Video*, March 12, 2017, YouTube, https://www.youtube.com/watch?v=vbVX4JKw2X4&t=1s.

109. Rick Inderfurth, interview with author, March 2022.

110. Brzezinski children, interviews with author.

111. Copy of the letter supplied to author by Henry Kissinger, May 2023.

112. Henry Kissinger, interview with author, February 2021.

113. Mark Brzezinski, interview with author, April 2022.

114. Joe Biden, "Remarks by President Biden and by President Andrzej Duda of Poland in Briefing on the Humanitarian Efforts for Ukraine," March 25, 2022, Rzeszów-Jasionka Airport, Rzeszów, Poland, The White House, https://www.whitehouse.gov/briefing-room/speeches-remarks/2022/03/25/remarks-by-president-biden-and-president-andrzej-duda-of-poland-in-briefing-on-the-humanitarian-efforts-for-ukraine/.

115. Frances Stead Sellers, "Emilie Brzezinski, Artist Who Socialized Among the Political Elites, Dies at 90," *Washington Post*, July 22, 2022.

116. April Austin, "Family Tree: Emilie Benes Brzezinski '53," *Wellesley Magazine*, Fall 2014.

117. Karen De Witt, "Brzezinski, the Power and the Glory," *Washington Post*, February 4, 1977.

118. Lech Brzezinski, interview with author, April 2022.

Index

Luther, Martin, 17
Lviv (Ukraine), 11, 21, 435
Lvov, Battle of (1919), 12

Machiavelli, Niccolò
  The Prince, 285
Madeira School, 378–79
Mahan, Alfred Thayer, 437
Mailer, Norman, 138
Malek, Fred, 396
Malenkov, Georgy, 71, 81, 398
Malley, Robert, 445
Mandelbaum, Michael, 402
Mann, James, 430
Manning, Bayless, 165–66
Mao Zedong, 77, 96, 175, 203, 250, 253, 408
Marcos, Imelda, 270
Marshall, George C., Jr., 52, 178
Marshall Plan, 52
Martin, Jurek, 174
Marxism, 3, 57
  vs. nationalism, 53
Marxist-Leninism, 77, 127, 361, 398, 404, 408, 413
Masaryk, Jan, 52
Masaryk, Tomáš, 52
Matlock, Jack, Jr., 404
Mazowiecki, Tadeusz, 401
McCain, John, 429, 434, 436
McCarthy, Eugene, 132–33, 135, 137–38, 141, 144, 168
McCarthy, Joseph, 76, 389
McClellan, David, 117
McCloy, John, 105–6, 303–4, 478n12
McGill University
  Polish Club, 45
  Progressive Conservative Party (Tory Club), 46–47
  Soviet apologists at, 46
  student activism at, 45–46
  Student Labour Club, 47
  see also Brzezinski, Zbigniew—MCGILL
McGovern, George, 172, 314
  foreign policy of, 169–70
  presidential campaign of, 6, 168–71, 211, 484n66
  on ZB, 257
McHenry, Donald F., 359
McNamara, Robert, 106, 128, 134
McPherson, Harry, 122, 124, 128
Mead, Walter Russell, 438
Mearsheimer, John
  "The Israel Lobby," 440–42
Medvedev, Dmitry, 449
Meese, Edwin, III, 380
Meir, Golda, 176, 224
Menand, Louis, 82

Mengistu Haile Mariam, 243
Metternich, Klemens von, 98, 116, 150
Meyer, Cord, 169
Mickiewicz, Adam, 11
Miller, Leszek, 419
Ministry of the Interior (Poland), 153–54
Miracle on the Vistula, 9–10
Mitchell, George, 409
Mitchell, John, 142
Miyazawa Kiichi, 166
Mohr, Charles, 206
Molotov, Vyacheslav, 10, 87
Molotov-Ribbentrop Pact (Nazi-Soviet Pact), 10, 20, 33, 37
MoMA (Museum of Modern Art), 120
Mondale, Walter, 7, 192, 219
  on the Carter years, 374
  China trip, 283
  as Humphrey's campaign cochair, 137
  as JC's running mate, 186
  nuclear freeze supported by, 393
  presidential campaign of, 172, 174
  size of staff, 424
  as vice president, 195
  and ZB, 220
  ZB's endorsement of, 392–93
  in ZB's memoir, 385
  on ZB's memoir, 393
Monnet, Jean, 166
Monroe Doctrine, 237–38
Monte Cassino, Battle of (1944), 41
Montreal
  beauty of, 28
  as French speaking, 29, 34
  George VI and Elizabeth's visit to, 29–30
  Polish immigrants in, 28
Montreal Gazette, 41, 47
moon landing, 156
Moore, Barrington, Jr., 62, 463
  Terror and Progress USSR, 113
Morgenthau, Hans, 117–18, 120, 150
Morning Joe, 432
Mosley, Philip, 86
Mossadegh, Mohammed, 269
Mount Desert Island (Maine), 120
Moyers, Bill, 122, 138
Munich Agreement (1938), 24, 52, 140, 169, 250, 294, 300
Muskie, Ed, 186
  on the AFL-CIO's pro-Solidarity declaration, 362–63
  and Gromyko, 338
  as Humphrey's running mate, 137, 167–68
  on Iran, 354
  on PD-59, 345

About the Author

EDWARD LUCE is the *Financial Times'* chief US commentator and columnist. He was also the *FT's* bureau chief in Washington and New Delhi. He is the author of *The Retreat of Western Liberalism, Time to Start Thinking: America in the Age of Descent,* and *In Spite of the Gods: The Strange Rise of Modern India.* He appears regularly on CNN, NPR, MSNBC's *Morning Joe,* and the BBC. He lives in Washington, DC, with his wife and daughter.